WHAT DID JESUS MEAN?

WHAT DID JESUS MEAN?

Explaining the Sermon on the Mount and the Parables in Simple and Universal Human Concepts

Anna Wierzbicka

OXFORD
UNIVERSITY PRESS

2001

OXFORD

UNIVERSITY PRESS

Oxford   New York
Athens   Auckland   Bangkok   Bogotá   Buenos Aires   Calcutta
Cape Town   Chennai   Dar es Salaam   Delhi   Florence   Hong Kong   Istanbul
Karachi   Kuala Lumpur   Madrid   Melbourne   Mexico City   Mumbai
Nairobi   Paris   São Paulo   Shanghai   Singapore   Taipei   Tokyo   Toronto   Warsaw

and associated companies in
Berlin   Ibadan

Published by Oxford University Press, Inc.
198 Madison Avenue, New York, New York 10016

Oxford is a registered trademark of Oxford University Press

Library of Congress Cataloging-in-Publication Data
Wierzbicka, Anna.
What did Jesus mean? : explaining the Sermon on the mount and the parables in simple
and universal human concepts / by Anna Wierzbicka.
p. cm.
Includes bibliographical references (p.) and index.
ISBN 0-19-513732-9 (cloth); ISBN 0-19-513733-7 (pbk.)
1. Sermon on the mount—Criticism, interpretation, etc.   2. Jesus Christ—Parables.
3. Bible. N.T. Gospels—Language, style.   4. Semantics.   I. Title.
BT380.2 .W54   2000
226.8'06—dc21   00-021159

9 8 7 6 5 4 3 2 1

Printed in the United States of America
on acid-free paper

For John, Mary, and Clare

When you read Holy Scripture,
perceive its hidden meanings.

St Mark the Ascetic,
early fifth century

Acknowledgments

This book owes a great deal to many people, to some indirectly and to some directly. I am particularly grateful to those who have read and commented on parts of the manuscript: Prof. Andrzej Bogusławski of Warsaw University, Prof. René Dirven of Duisburg University, Rev. Dr. James Francis of the University of Sunderland, Prof. Cliff Goddard and Dr. Jean Harkins of the University of New England (Australia), Prof. Elżbieta Janus of the Polish Academy of Science and Vilnius University, Prof. Francis Moloney SDB of the Catholic University of America, and Prof. Douglas Porpora of Drexel University.

I also want to thank the students and colleagues who have participated over the years in my seminars on the semantics of the Gospels at the Australian National University and who provided invaluable feedback throughout the work on this project. I am grateful to my editor at Oxford University Press, Peter Ohlin, whose enthusiasm for this project, support, and wise advice have meant a great deal to me; I also appreciate the care and expertise with which Nancy Hoagland at OUP saw the manuscript through the process of production.

I also want to thank my research assistants at the ANU: Lea Brown, Helen O'Loghlin, and Ellalene Seymour, whose expert and dedicated help at every stage of the preparation of this book was indispensable. In the final stages I received the same expert and dedicated assistance from Jennie Elliott and Brigid Maher.

Last but not least I want to thank my husband John and my daughters Mary and Clare who all read the entire manuscript and discussed it with me, critically and searchingly, page by page and paragraph by paragraph, and whose interest and involvement was a gift of great price.

Contents

1. Introduction   3
    1. "What did Jesus mean"—Is it worth asking?   3
    2. Different questions about Jesus   4
    3. Conceptual primes and universal human concepts—new tools for the study of Jesus' sayings   6
    4. An illustration   7
    5. Is it possible to separate the universal aspect of Jesus' teaching from its cultural context?   9
    6. Paradoxes of inculturation   11
    7. Universal words: Unfamiliar but not unintelligible   13
    8. The importance of Jesus' Jewish context for the understanding of his teaching   14
    9. Jesus, the teacher of timeless truths?   15
    10. An illustration: The "kingdom of God" explained in universal human concepts   17
    11. The meaning of the word *God*   20
    12. The search for a coherent picture   22

PART I: THE SERMON ON THE MOUNT

2. The Beatitudes   27
    1. Introduction: The importance of the Beatitudes   28

2. Basic facts about the Beatitudes   30
3. Who are the "weeping" ones?   32
4. Who are the "hungry"?   34
5. Who are the "poor"?   36
6. Who are the "meek" (Matthew's *praeis*)?   40
7. Exploring the image of the lamb and some related New Testament images   42
8. Who are the "persecuted"?   46
9. What does it mean to be "blessed"?   47
10. Conclusion   55

3. You Have Heard . . . But I Say to You . . .   57
1. Jesus fulfils the Law   57
2. Whoever is angry with his brother . . .   61
3. Whoever divorces his wife . . .   71
4. Whoever looks at a woman to lust for her . . .   81
5. If your right eye causes you to sin, pluck it out   88
6. Let your 'Yes' be 'Yes' and your 'No', 'No'   93
7. Turn the other cheek   102
8. Love your enemies   111
9. "The righteousness of the scribes and the Pharisees"   122

4. Other Key Sayings   126
1. You are the salt of the earth   126
2. When you do a charitable deed do not sound a trumpet   131
3. Do not let your left hand know . . .   140
4. When you pray, go into your room   144
5. When you fast, anoint your head   149
6. Lay up for yourselves treasures in heaven   155
7. The eye is the lamp of the body   161
8. You cannot serve God and mammon   169
9. Consider the lilies of the field   174
10. Do not judge   179
11. Ask, and it will be given to you   186
12. The golden rule   191
13. Enter by the narrow gate   203
14. Do people gather grapes from thornbushes or figs from thistles?   206
15. The will of my Father   215
16. Building on the rock   219

5. The Lord's Prayer   226
1. Introduction   226
2. The meaning and significance of the word *abba*   228
3. "Father" as a metaphor   232

4. God as someone   234

5 What does God's fatherhood mean (in Jesus' teaching)?   236

6. Hallowed be thy name   237

7. Thy kingdom come   241

8. Give us this day our daily bread   244

9. And forgive us our sins   247

10. For we also forgive everyone who is indebted to us   250

11. And do not lead us into temptation   251

12. Conclusion   254

PART II: THE PARABLES

6. The Sower   257

7. The Hidden Treasure and the Pearl of Great Price   266

8. The Leaven and The Mustard Seed   274

9. The Lost Sheep and The Lost Coin   292

10. The Prodigal Son   300

11. The Unforgiving Servant   310

12. The Laborers in the Vineyard   320

13. The Servant's Reward   332

14. The Great Feast   341

15. The Last Judgment   356

16. The Good Samaritan   373

17. The Rich Man and Lazarus   380

18. The Rich Fool   388

19. The Doorkeeper   397

20. The Talents   404

21. The Dishonest Steward   414

22. The Unjust Judge and the Friend at Midnight   422

23. The Pharisee and the Tax Collector   429

PART III: CONCLUSIONS AND FURTHER PERSPECTIVES

24. An Overall Picture of Jesus' Teaching   441

25. Implications for Theology; Christianity in a Nutshell   444

26. Language: A Key Issue in Understanding Jesus and Christianity   455

Notes   465

References   481

Index   497

WHAT DID JESUS MEAN?

ONE

Introduction

1. "What did Jesus mean"—Is it worth asking?

One current fashion in scholarly circles suggests that it is pointless to ask what Jesus meant since we can't possibly know and we will never find out. Another maintains that it doesn't really matter what he meant: what matters is what his sayings mean to the readers, or "to me." In any case, in the view of some it is no longer acceptable to ask about the authorial intention of any text: a text is a text. To ask what the author meant is naive and irrelevant.

Millions of ordinary readers have not caught up with these fashions, however, and for them the biblical text is of interest, above all, as a means of reaching "the real Jesus"—in the words of distinguished biblical scholar Raymond Brown (1997:828), "a Jesus who really means something to people, one on whom they can base their lives." And for the majority, who do not want to base their lives on Jesus but who do have an interest in Christianity, it is rather more interesting to hear what Jesus may have meant than to hear that it is no longer acceptable to enquire. In fact, "ordinary people's" interest in the authorial intention is shared by numerous biblical scholars who are well aware of the fashions in question but do not feel obliged to bow to them.

The authors of the chapter "Hermeneutics" in *The New Jerome Biblical Commentary*, Raymond Brown and Sandra Schneiders (1990:1148), state that "those who produced the biblical books had in their times a message to convey to their readers and . . . it is important for us to have this message in mind when we read the texts and ask what they now mean for us." Not surprisingly, the authors "reject the systematic scepticism of literary critics about ever knowing the intention of a nonpresent author" and refer with approval to E. D. Hirsch (1967), "who argues that a charge of 'intentional fallacy' is itself a fallacy."

I do not mean to suggest that the meaning of a text (and, in particular, biblical text) can be reduced in any straightforward way to the hypothetical authorial intention. As Schneiders (1991:145) points out, the meaning of the biblical text "could exceed . . . what was consciously intended by the author." Schneiders talks in this connection about a possible "surplus of meaning," which can be established "within the text as text," that is, a meaning that may go "beyond authorial intent." But to say this is very different from saying that any concern with what the author meant is naive or irrelevant.

The question "What did Jesus mean?" sounds rather more venturesome than the more cautious one, "What did the biblical authors mean?" Logically, however, it is not a radically different kind of question. If there is some scholarly consensus for at least some of the sayings attributed to Jesus, the question of what was meant is no less appropriate or valid for him than it is for the evangelists.

In his recent synthesis, *An Introduction to the New Testament*, Raymond Brown (1997:viii) remarks, "Many readers of the NT [New Testament] want to know what Jesus was like, what he thought of himself, and what he said precisely." I think it goes without saying that they also want to know what he meant. Although this book does not presume to conclusively resolve the question posed in the title, it will at least be seriously addressed and not dismissed as naive and outdated; and for a large number of key parables and sayings, explicit and definite interpretations will in fact be proposed.

2. Different questions about Jesus

Many books about Jesus focus on the question "What did Jesus really do?" (see, e.g., the recent volume, *The Acts of Jesus: The Search for the Authentic Deeds of Jesus*, by Robert Funk and the Jesus Seminar 1998.) Others ask, "Who *was* Jesus?" (see, e.g., the book under this title by N. T. Wright, 1992). Still others concentrate on the question "What did Jesus really say?" (see, e.g., Funk, Hoover, and the Jesus Seminar 1993, *The Five Gospels: What Did Jesus Really Say?*). There is also a substantial literature that is trying to decide which among these questions about Jesus is the most important.

All these questions are legitimate, important, and interesting. But they are not the subject of this book. My question is this: "What did Jesus really *mean*?"; I do not raise this question about *all* sayings attributed to Jesus but rather about his "wisdom sayings," that is, parables and ethical aphorisms. The book does assume that some answers are available to those questions, however. Thus, I assume, that there was indeed a historical Jesus; that this Jesus did say some things of general interest; and that to some extent at least, we know—or have good reasons to think we know—what it was that he said.

The question "What did Jesus really mean?" cannot be studied independently of the question "Which of the sayings attributed to Jesus are most likely to be authentic?" But, clearly, it makes sense to start from a core of sayings widely held to be, indeed, authentic.[1] Although I strongly disagree with the scholars of the Jesus Seminar on many points, one must agree with them that some of the sayings attributed to Jesus do evoke the response "That's Jesus!"—with a strong and immediate conviction that a particular saying conforms to the overall Jesus persona (cf. Funk et al., 1993:37). It is these sayings primarily that I want to explore.

Many criteria for determining which sayings are most likely to be authentic (along with other questions about the historical Jesus) have been proposed in recent literature. They include the criteria of multiple attestation, dissimilarity (which asks whether a saying or story seem distinct from both the Jewish background and the developing Christian tradition), embarrassment (to the early church), shock value, memorability (giving a saying or a story a good chance of surviving in oral transmission), and so on. (For discussion see, e.g., Johnson 1996, Meier 1991–1994, N. T. Wright 1992.)

From my viewpoint, however, the most important criterion is coherence, and this is a criterion whose application presupposes semantic analysis. I believe that the bulk of the sayings widely regarded by reputable scholars as preserving Jesus' *ipsissima vox* and *ipsissima verba* do in fact yield a coherent overall picture; and this coherent picture increases, in its turn, the likelihood of the authenticity of many of the disputed sayings, as well as helping us to peel off layers of editorial interventions by the evangelists. But a coherent overall picture cannot be just a matter of "what Jesus really *said*"; it can only be one of "what Jesus really *meant* in what he (presumably) said." (I will return to this question in the last section of this chapter.)

Of course this overall picture will have to be, ultimately, a matter of conjecture: the reconstruction of the intended meaning can no more be a matter of empirical proof than the determination of the *ipsissima verba* themselves. As Witherington (1995:12) says about Jesus' words and deeds, "New Testament scholars can no more *prove* [that] Jesus did or did not do or say something than Roman historians can prove that Nero did or did not have some responsibility for the great fire of Rome in the 60s of the first century. They can only show good probability one way or another."

However, this book proposes new criteria against which the probability of certain interpretations can be tested—criteria arising from the methodological experience of contemporary linguistic semantics. If the book focuses on the meaning of Jesus sayings, this is not because I believe that his sayings are more important than his deeds (or than the story of his life and death). That is, this is not yet another attempted portrait, or interpretation, of Jesus; it is only a study of the *meaning* of (some of) Jesus' utterances and stories. More broadly, it is also a study in the semantics of religious language and in the interpretation of religious metaphors.

In attempting to define the meaning of Jesus' parables and related sayings, I will take into account, as far as possible, the results of contemporary New Testament criticism, including the works of widely respected, "centrist" scholars such as Raymond Brown, Joseph Fitzmyer, L. T. Johnson, John P. Meier, Ben Witherington III, N. T. Wright, and many others. I will also take into account the writings of more controversial authors such as John Dominic Crossan and Marcus Borg, as well as the long tradition of writings on the parables, including, for example, such classic authors as Dodd (1965), Donahue (1990), Jeremias (1972), Lambrecht (1991), Linnemann (1966), Perrin (1976), Via (1974), and many others. Naturally, I will also take account of the very substantial and constantly growing literature on the methodological aspects of the interpretation of the New Testament, including, for example, works such as Blount (1995), R. E. Brown (1985), Fee (1993), Fitzmyer (1994), J. B. Green (1995), McKenzie and Haynes (1993), Moloney (1993), Pregeant (1995), Ricoeur (1975), Schneiders (1991), Schüssler-Fiorenza (1994), Stenger (1993), and Thiselton (1992).

I will not attempt, however, a systematic survey of the huge literature on the subject and in fact will call on that literature explicitly only when the discussion of a particular question justifies it. My primary focus in this book is to launch a new type of exegesis, which can be called *semantic exegesis*. In doing so, I will be drawing on the results and methodology of linguistic semantics and, in particular, on two key analytical tools: conceptual primes and universal human concepts. The use of these tools can open an entirely new perspective on the study of the Gospels, especially on the meaning of Jesus' sayings.

3. Conceptual primes and universal human concepts— new tools for the study of Jesus' sayings

The idea of conceptual primes goes back to Leibniz and to his observation that all explanations of meaning require a core of concepts that are self-explanatory: to be truly explanatory, an explanation must lead from what is complex and obscure to what is at least relatively simple and clear. Ultimately, only explanations based on concepts that are intuitively comprehensible have true explanatory power. Without such a bedrock of self-explanatory concepts, so-called explanations may be no more than exercises in translating unknowns into unknowns. By "explaining" an obscure and incomprehensible saying in terms of an obscure and incomprehensible explanation, an impression of progress may be created with little or no gain in real understanding. As Leibniz (1903) liked to say, all explanations must come to an end. An increase in understanding requires this end to be more intelligible than the beginning.

Semantic research over the last three decades suggests that concepts like GOOD and BAD, SOMEONE and SOMETHING, YOU and I, DO and HAPPEN, KNOW and THINK, or THIS and OTHER (= ELSE) are among those that cannot be made any clearer by further explanations, although volumes can, of course, be written—and have been written—about so-called values, norms, actions, events, objects, self, mind, cognition, intentionality, and so on. When all is said and done, however, the meaning of sentences like

I did something bad.
Someone wants to do something good for someone else.

cannot be further *explained* (although they can, of course, be commented on in various ways). There are no words intuitively simpler and clearer than those in the sentences above that could be used to *explain* their meaning.[2] (For extended discussion of these points, see Goddard 1998; Goddard and Wierzbicka 1994; Wierzbicka 1992, 1996, 1997, 1999a.)

4. An illustration

In accordance with the principle of conceptual primes, we can propose, for example, the following initial explanation or explication of the saying "love your enemies" (for fuller discussion, see Chapter 3, section 8):

> love your enemies =
> if someone wants to do bad things to you
> it will be good if you don't want to do bad things to this person
>   because of this
> it will be good if you want to do good things for this person

All the words used in this explication are taken from a set of independently established conceptual primes (i.e., intuitively understandable, "simple" concepts). This applies not only to the elements GOOD and BAD, SOMEONE (= PERSON) and SOMETHING (= THING), THIS and WANT, and YOU and I, which were listed earlier, but also to the logical concepts IF, BECAUSE, and NOT.[3]

This explication is based not just on the bare text of the utterance but also on its broader context. The sayings attributed to Jesus throw light on one another and jointly contribute to a coherent overall understanding of his teaching (cf. Sevin 1997; N. T. Wright 1996). In fact, by reading the injunction "love your enemies" in the light of the Gospels as a whole, we will see good reasons to add another dimension to the explication and introduce the notion of God and of God's will (thus acknowledging the God-centered character of Jesus' ethics):

> if someone wants to do bad things to you
> it will be good if you don't want to do bad things to this person
>   because of this
> it will be good if you want to do good things for this person
> God wants this

(The concept of God itself is not simple and can be explicated; but it underlies the Gospels as a whole and will be explicated in section 11 of this chapter, not within the explications of the individual sayings and parables.)

Turning now to the notion of universal human concepts, I should point out that most words in any one language are language-specific and do not have exact semantic equivalents in other languages. For example, a sentence like "Love your enemies" cannot be readily translated into many languages of the world because they may lack words that correspond in meaning to either "love" or "enemies"

(cf. Wierzbicka 1992, 1997, 1999a). On the other hand, cross-linguistic semantic investigations suggest that conceptual primes such as those mentioned earlier
(e.g., GOOD and BAD or IF and NOT) do have lexical exponents (i.e., corresponding words) in all human languages. These words may be polysemous (i.e., have
more than one meaning), but on one meaning at least they match. For example,
in all languages one can say the exact equivalent of

if someone wants to do bad things to you . . .

even if the word for BAD in a particular language may also have a second and
even a third meaning, such as "crooked," "angry," or whatever, or if the word
for WANT may have a second and even a third meaning, such as "lack," "seek,"
or "love." It is in this sense that we can speak of universal human concepts (e.g.,
BAD and WANT but not "love," "enemy," or "revenge").

The correspondence between conceptual primes and universal words may seem
surprising at first: why should the two sets coincide, as empirical investigations
suggest? But when one thinks about it, this correspondence makes a great deal
of sense. If all human understanding rests on the basic set of concepts that are
intuitively self-explanatory and thus require no further explanation, this set cannot be acquired by any explanations or even be contingent on the vagaries of
individual experience. As Pascal ([1667]1954) eloquently argued, it must be innate and must in fact underlie our interpretation of all our experience. If it is
innate, however, it does not depend on the language and culture of the community into which an individual is born but is the same for all human beings. It is
hardly surprising, therefore, that we find the same set of basic concepts, on which
all human understanding rests, present in all languages in the form of universal
words: universal words stand for universal human concepts, that is, the universal building blocks of human thoughts.

In fact, it is not only certain words—such as words for GOOD and BAD or SOME-
ONE and SOMETHING or KNOW and WANT—that are universally present but also certain grammatical (syntactic) patterns. Although the syntax of each language is to a
considerable extent language-specific, cross-linguistic investigations suggest that some
syntactic patterns are universal. For example, it emerges that in all languages there
are IF-clauses, so that in any language one can say the equivalent of "if someone
wants to do bad things to you. . . ." Similarly, all languages have malefactive and
benefactive constructions, and in all languages one can speak about "wanting to
do bad things to someone" or about "wanting to do good things for other people";
in all languages one can combine words for GOOD, BAD, and OTHER with the words
for THING and PEOPLE and speak of "good things," "bad things," or "other people."
In other words, what is universally present is not only individual building blocks
like GOOD and BAD or DO and WANT but also ways for putting these building blocks
together into larger configurations, capable of conveying such meanings as "if someone wants to do bad things to you . . ."; "I did something bad"; "other people are
like me"; "if you want to do good things for other people. . . ."

It does not seem to be the case, however, that all languages have semantically
matching imperative constructions, and so the meaning of an imperative in a

particular language cannot be taken for granted but rather needs to be explicated. For this reason (among others), Jesus' words "love your enemies" cannot be translated into the language of universal human concepts as "do good things for those who want to do bad things to you"; the imperative *do*, whose meaning may seem to be crystal clear to us, will not necessarily be crystal clear to the speakers of languages that do not have a semantically matching imperative construction. In other words, despite the simplicity and universality of its vocabulary, a formula like "do good things for those who want to do bad things to you" is still to some extent language-specific and—unlike the explanatory formula proposed earlier—cannot be seen as a truly universal representation of meaning.

In "translating" many of the sayings attributed to Jesus in the Gospels into the language of universal human concepts, I am not suggesting that the proposed translations articulate what was consciously intended by the author *in that very form*. This is not how semantic analysis works. Rather, it seeks to establish—on the basis of publicly stateable criteria—what Schneiders (1991:146) calls "the ideal meaning of a given text." But one can doubt whether a reconstructed ideal meaning would have much interest or relevance if it had no relation to "what the author meant."

5. Is it possible to separate the universal aspect of Jesus' teaching from its cultural context?

As the explication of the injunction "love your enemies" illustrates, this book seeks to demonstrate that some aspects of the meaning of Jesus' sayings can be explicated in sentences that rely exclusively on universal words and universal grammar.

"So what?" the skeptic might say: whatever the historical Jesus said and meant, he didn't speak and think in universal human words and did not use universal grammar. He spoke in Aramaic, using Aramaic words and Aramaic grammatical constructions, and his thinking was heavily embedded in the Jewish culture of first-century Palestine, its norms, its traditions, and its expectations. Whatever Jesus' intended meaning was, it cannot be separated from its cultural context.

The skeptic's position is partially right. Certainly, when Jesus spoke he didn't restrict himself to universal human words (nobody does). He used a particular natural language with all its culture-specific richness, and certainly his thinking *was* heavily embedded in the culture of the time and place to which he belonged. This does not mean, however, that no aspect of Jesus' teaching can be separated from its Jewish context.

The very idea that the Gospel was to be taken beyond the boundaries of the Jewish world and taught to the Gentiles—in Greece, in Rome, and elsewhere—presupposed a view that the core of the intended Gospel message was universal rather than culture-specific. If the early Christians thought that, in Mark's (16:15) words, Jesus had enjoined them to "Go into all the world and preach the gospel to every creature," they must have believed that this Gospel included some universal message.

What is clearer to us today than it could have been to the early Christians is that the content of a message is colored by its medium: if the Gospel does include a universal message, it cannot be fully and accurately articulated and explained—in normal idiomatic prose—in a particular natural language: because of its culture-specific richness, each language creates its own universe of meaning. Thus, although it is undoubtedly true that "even the most competent English translation cannot render all the nuances of the original Greek" (R. E. Brown 1997:36), it is also true that even the most competent English translation cannot help introducing nuances of its own. For example, by saying that in the Matthean Sermon on the Mount Jesus' warnings "are not against pious practices but against ostentation" (R. E. Brown 1997:179), one adds an element of obvious display to what seems to be really essential here. If when I do good things I want other people to know about it and to think good things about me, I may or may not do those things *ostentatiously*, but Jesus' warning "not to do your charitable deeds before people to be seen by them" (Matt. 6:1) would still apply to me. Clearly, then, the word *ostentation* (which does not have an exact equivalent in many other languages) is not of the essence here. What *is* of the essence can be accurately expressed in universal concepts such as DO, WANT, PEOPLE, and KNOW.

The example of *ostentation* may seem harmless enough, but many others could be adduced that introduce into Jesus' teaching tones and shades that, I argue, are alien to it. This applies in particular to the words "obedience" and "obey" (in German, *Gehorsam* and *gehorchen*), which have come to occupy a prominent place in modern exegetical tradition and indeed have found their way into some modern translations of the Gospels, without any basis in the original. For example, *Die Bibel in heutigem Deutsch* (1982) translates Jesus' words in John 4:34, rendered in English (by the New King James Version) as "My food is to do the will of him who sent me" as follows:

Meine Nahrung ist, daß ich dem gehorche, der mich gesandt hat.
"My food is to obey him who sent me."

The word "obey" (*gehorchen*) implies subordination to authority, but this implication is absent from the Greek original, which says "to do the will" (*poiēsō to thelēma*), not "to obey."

The tradition of replacing biblical notions of "hearing (hearkening, heeding) God's voice" and "doing God's will" with "obedience" and "obey" appears to go back to Luther. For example, in Psalm 81, in the Vulgate, God wants his people to "hear his voice" and "hear him," whereas in Luther's translation God wants his people to "obey" (*gehorchen*) and to be "obedient" (*gehorsam*):

12. et non audivit populus meus vocem meam (Vulgate)
    aber mein Volk gehorchet nicht meiner Stimme (Luther)

13. si populus meus audisset me . . . (Vulgate)
    wollte mein Volk mir gehorsam sein . . . (Luther)

Die Bibel in heutigem Deutsch (1982) follows suit:

> 14. Wenn Israel doch meinen Geboten gehorchte. . .
>   "If only Israel had obeyed my commandments . . ."

Examples could be multiplied. An emphasis on obedience is certainly consistent with Luther's theology (see in particular his *Bondage of the Will* 1931). For further discussion of obedience see chapter 4, sections 15 and 16.

Thus, the application of linguistic semantics to the study of the Gospels opens new possibilities for biblical hermeneutics: by translating the key Gospel passages into a semiartificial and yet intuitively intelligible language of universal human concepts, we can separate the two otherwise inseparable strata of the Gospel teaching, the local and the universal. (One could say that in this method of analysis a certain surplus of meaning is removed rather than added—that which is linked to the use of a particular natural language.)

In fact, it could be said that in the Gospels (read in translation) there are not two but three different strata: the Jewish, the universal, and the European. During the first two millennia, the development of Christianity and the dissemination of the Gospels has been dominated first by Greek, then by Latin, and then by the major languages of modern Europe. Concepts such as love, mercy, forgiveness, or humility translate easily across European languages, which have been shaped largely by a common cultural heritage. The way in which the Gospels are usually read at the end of the second millennium is heavily influenced by this common heritage; and not everyone is aware of the fact that such Christian concepts may not readily translate into the native languages of, say, Australia, Africa, or Oceania.

This, then, is the challenge to the student of the Gospels at the threshold of the third millennium: "extracting" the universal message of the Gospels from its cultural and historical crust, that is, from the original Jewish context, and from the legacy of European cultural tradition that is reflected in European languages.

This does not mean that—as the second-century gnostic Marcion affirmed—the New Testament can be separated from the Old. The Old Testament is part of the Christian Holy Scripture, and Jesus' story can only be fully understood in the context of a larger story, including Abraham, Moses, the prophets, and the history of Israel as a whole. But Jesus' teaching—"Do not judge," "Love your enemies," "Do good to those who hate you," "Do not worry about your life," or "Enter by the narrow gate"—can be explained to any human group, anywhere in the world, in any language; and this can be done apart from the teaching's original historical and cultural context. In fact, the biblical metaphor of "a light to the nations" (Is. 42:1–13; cf. John 8:12; Rev. 21:23) implies as much: if a Jewish Messiah is to bring a light to the nations, this Messiah's message must be intelligible to all those nations, and to be intelligible, it must be—to some extent—"outculturated."

6. Paradoxes of inculturation

The project of extracting—and, so to speak, liberating—the universal core of Jesus' teaching from its cultural embedding will no doubt strike many as impossible, if not absurd or offensive. At the end of the second Christian millennium, "inculturation," not "outculturation," is the order of the day (e.g., drawing on African traditions in presenting Christ's teaching in Africa). Increasingly, commentators stress the need for cultural diversity within Christianity, arguing that faith must "take flesh" in particular cultures (see, e.g., Shorter 1997).

In fact, much of the contemporary literature on Jesus' teaching confronts us with a curious paradox: on the one hand, many authors emphasize that his teaching cannot be cut loose from its Jewish moorings, and on the other, many (sometimes the same) authors stress the need for inculturation (in Africa, in Latin America, etc.), regarding it as indispensable in conveying the message effectively. But whereas it is understandable that "incarnating" the faith in particular cultures is now increasingly seen as very important, it should be remembered that there can be no inculturation without outculturation. Because the Gospel message is so heavily embedded in the culture of first-century Palestine and so heavily influenced by the centuries of predominantly European reading, it cannot be adequately transferred to other cultures without first being extracted from its own cultural context. For this message to be clothed in new garments, it has first to be stripped of its old ones.

This stripping of old garments has to be applied, inter alia, to familiar metaphors. Their heuristic and aesthetic value notwithstanding, metaphors can be dangerous. Nothing illustrates this better than the metaphor of fatherhood, which many contemporary writers find deeply problematic. For example, Hans Küng (1980:673) writes, "God . . . is not masculine and must not be seen through the screen of the masculine-paternal, as an all-too-masculine theology did. The feminine-maternal element must also be recognized in him." But the less conventional image of the feminine-maternal, although useful as a corrective to the one-sidedness of the masculine-paternal, is a metaphor, too. In fact Küng recognizes this himself when he writes, "The designation of 'father' for God is misunderstood if it is taken as the opposite of 'mother' instead of symbolically (analogically). 'Father' is a patriarchal trait—for a transhuman, transsexual, absolutely last/absolutely first reality" (p. 673). These explanations, however, also pose problems. For whereas "father" is indeed a symbol (a metaphor), which needs to be explained in nonmetaphorical language, expressions like "absolutely last/absolutely first reality" are also metaphorical (what Küng really means has nothing to do with any temporal sequence).

Thus, regardless of whether one prefers to replace the father symbol with other human symbols like mother and maternal—or with transhuman and transsexual symbols like first/last reality—none of these images or symbols are really integral to the message of the Gospels. Behind and underneath all such images and symbols there is a timeless and universal message that can be articulated in universal human concepts (such as GOOD and BAD, DO and HAPPEN, and KNOW, WANT, or THINK), without recourse to culture-specific metaphors.

The metaphor of fatherhood, so pervasive in the Gospels, reflects, of course, the fact that Jesus' teaching was deeply embedded in the patriarchal culture of first-century Palestine. But the fact that this metaphor can be translated into the nonmetaphorical language of universal human concepts shows that the view that the essence of Jesus' teaching cannot be separated from its cultural context is fallacious.

There is no conflict between the idea of inculturation and the idea of a universal core of Jesus' teaching. In the apostolic exhortation *Evangelii Nuntiandi* (1989), Pope Paul VI wrote of "the task of assimilating the essence of the Gospel message and of transporting it, without the slightest betrayal of the essential truth, into the language that these particular people understand" (p. 67). The same document emphasizes that "the Gospels, and therefore evangelization, are independent of all cultures" (p. 25). Although "the presentation [of the Gospel message] depends greatly on changing circumstances . . . there is the essential content, the living substance, which cannot be modified or ignored without seriously diluting the nature of evangelization itself" (p. 31).

As mentioned earlier, however, the universality of the message requires (on some level) the universality of the medium. Whereas the same universal message can—and for the purposes of evangelization must—be inculturated into different languages and cultures, by the same token for the purposes of exegesis it must be outculturated from its original medium and elucidated in universal human concepts.

7. Universal words: Unfamiliar but not unintelligible

Explanations of Gospel passages couched in universal human concepts will necessarily sound unfamiliar and strange to scholars accustomed to more conventional commentaries on the New Testament. They will also sound strange to the layperson, used to the richness of a natural language and unaccustomed to communicating in a rudimentary minilanguage based on a few dozen universal words. Nonetheless, explications formulated in this rudimentary minilanguage are, in principle, intelligible to the general reader—more so, probably, than some more conventional theological treatises and commentaries. For example, consider again the proposed paraphrase of the injunction "Love your enemies":

> if someone does something bad to you
> it will be good if you don't want to do bad things to this person
>   because of this
> it will be good if you want to do good things for this person

This formula will no doubt strike readers as somewhat stilted because of its lexical austerity and schematic structure, but it is comprehensible to a nonspecialist (unlike many passages in hermeneutic theological literature).

Most important, explicatory formulas of this kind can also be directly intelligible and illuminating to total cultural outsiders in areas of the world relatively little influenced by Christianity and Western culture. For example, such formulas can be readily translated, without any modification of meaning, into the Papuan language Arapesh; and although it will sound unfamiliar and perhaps odd in Arapesh (as it does in English), it will be intelligible and meaningful to the native speaker. Otto Nekitel, of the University of Papua New Guinea, a linguist and a native speaker of Arapesh, has provided (personal communication) the following Arapesh translation—literal and yet readily intelligible:

uba	enen		ni'i	nida	numehelesi-ma		ina'
IF	SOMEONE		WANTS	TO.DO	BAD.THINGS.TO		YOU

bala		suis	uba	ina'	kwe'isi	ni'i	nida
(IT) WILL.BE		GOOD	IF	YOU	DON'T	WANT	TO.DO

numehelisi-ma		enen	alifen	uma		esai'
BAD.THINGS.TO		THIS	PERSON	BECAUSE.OF		THIS

bala		suis	uba'	ina'	ni'i	nida'
(IT) WILL.BE		GOOD	IF	YOU	WANT	TO.DO

sueisi-ma			enei'	alifen
GOOD.THINGS.FOR			THIS	PERSON

Any attempt to explicate the meaning of Jesus' utterances in simple, clear and universally accessible words may be resented (consciously or subconsciously) as an attempt to rob these things of their eloquence and mystery:

> People reject intelligible content since the aura of mystery, so typical of religious experience, seems to be lost. In fact, one Guatemalan Indian translator of the New Testament objected to detailed explanations of the meaning of the biblical text, because, as he insisted, if the meaning becomes too clear, it will no longer be religious. (Nida 1994:195)

But, as Nida also points out "The mystery of faith should not be equated with the unintelligibility of words"; nor, one might add, should it be equated with the unintelligibility of images. Both Old Testament phrases, such as "an eye for an eye and a tooth for a tooth," and New Testament ones, such as "turn the other cheek," do require explanation; and to be truly intelligible to cultural outsiders, these explanations must be phrased (sometimes at least) in simple, clear, and universally available words.

8. The importance of Jesus' Jewish context for the understanding of his teaching

N. T. Wright (1996:5) states that twentieth-century scholarship "has at least one advantage over its predecessors: it has been realized that Jesus must be understood in his Jewish context." Other leading biblical scholars also emphasize that a non-Jewish Jesus is a nonsequitur (see, e.g., Casey 1991; Charlesworth 1991; Chilton and Neusner 1995; Frymer-Kensky et al. 2000; Greeley and Neusner 1991; Klausner 1949; Lapide and Luz 1985; Neusner 1993; E. P. Sanders 1993; Vermes 1973, 1993; for detailed discussion, see, e.g., Witherington 1995). This is true and important. It does not mean, however, that we cannot or should not try to distinguish between the universal and the "Jewish" aspects in Jesus' teaching. Understanding Jesus in his Jewish context is a necessary prerequisite, or at least a necessary corollary, of understanding the universal aspects of his teaching. We must understand the Jewish aspect to be able to distinguish it, in our overall interpretation, from the universal one.

This view may seem to be dangerously close to the target of N. T. Wright's (1996:6) sardonic criticisms of the nineteenth-century "Questers" (for the "real Jesus" in the "Jesus jigsaw puzzle"): "the game was to cut off all those bits of the 'Jesus' piece that appeared too Jewish, too ethnically restricted, leaving the hero as the founder of a great, universal, 'spiritual' religion, so nobly recaptured now by Protestantism, at least since Kant and Hegel."

But my question is not "Who was Jesus?" but "What did Jesus mean (in his parables and other 'wisdom sayings')?" I do not dispute N. T. Wright's (1996) claim that for the question "Who was Jesus?" history cannot and must not be separated from theology. But in a sense, the two *can* be separated, up to a point, for the question "What did Jesus mean?" This book is, in fact, an attempt to separate history (and geography) from theology (and ethics) in Jesus' parables and related sayings and to find out how far one can go in this direction. To achieve this, however, we cannot ignore Jesus' Jewishness. On the contrary, only by learning to understand the Jewish background of Jesus' ways of speaking—his rhetoric, his hyperbole, his imagery and his speech genres—can we hope to unlock the universal aspect of his teaching and to present it in a form in which it could be directly intelligible to cultural outsiders. (See chapter 26).

My approach may also seem dangerously close to N. T. Wright's (1996:5) ironic representation of Rudolf Bultmann's ([1926]1958) "demythologisation" program: "the historical crust of the 'real' message must be identified *and then thrown away*" (author's emphasis). I believe that Wright is using the word "message" here in a figurative sense, referring to Jesus' overall purpose, embodied in his life (and death), as well as in his teaching. But what I am interested in is the meaning of Jesus' sayings (or the sayings attributed to Jesus in contemporary scholarship)—a meaning that I see as universally relevant and which I want to articulate by means of (independently established) universal human concepts.

The other aspects of Jesus' sayings—the images, hyperboles, references to culture-specific artefacts, symbols, assumptions, and values—are for me not a "historical crust of the 'real' message" that "must be identified *and then thrown away*" but a precious historical embodiment of the universal message—an embodiment that must be studied and cherished for its unique and irreplaceable value but which *can* be conceptually distinguished from the universal message inherent in it.

9. Jesus, the teacher of timeless truths?

Thus, in the study of Jesus' wisdom sayings (if not in the study of his life and death) theology (and ethics) can, up to a point, be separated from history and geography. To bring this discussion from an abstract to a concrete level, let us remind ourselves again of at least one example—the explanatory formula cited earlier:

> if someone wants to do something bad to you
> it will be good if you don't want to do something bad to this person
>   because of this
> it will be good if you want to do something good for this person

I believe this message, stated here in universal human concepts, can in principle be understood through any human language, regardless of time and place, and in this sense it is independent of history and geography. In the Gospels as we know them, this message was of course expressed differently: in English as "love your enemies," in the Greek version as *agapate tous ekhthrous humon*, and as whatever it was in Aramaic. As the proposed explication illustrates, however, it is possible to extract a universal grain from the historical linguistic husk of such sayings and to express it in timeless universal concepts.

N. T. Wright (1996) writes with irony about attempts to present Jesus as "the timeless teacher" (p. 657), to seek in his teaching "an eternally valid core of meaning" (p. 658), or to "de-Judaize" him in one way or another. The irony is justified from the point of view of his own project of seeking an answer to the question "Who was Jesus?" From a semantic point of view, however, such an irony would be misplaced. For example, Jesus' saying "If your right eye causes you to sin, pluck it out" can be seen as a counsel applicable to any human being, anywhere, and at any time. But to be made intelligible to anyone anywhere, its core meaning needs to be extracted from its very Jewish hyperbolical form; otherwise, the saying is indeed likely to be misunderstood and lead to the practice of self-mutilation—if not literally, by plucking out one's eyes, then at least by self-castration (as happened by the Russian sect of *skopcy* 'the castrates').

I agree with the criticisms aimed at the view (e.g., Crossan 1991; Mack 1988) of Jesus as a wandering Cynic teacher of timeless wisdom (see, e.g., Witherington 1995; N. T. Wright 1992), and with the protests that "despite numerous attempts in this century to turn Christianity into a philosophy of life it is and has always been a historical religion" (Witherington 1995:10). Nonetheless, for lay people (in contrast to scholars qua scholars) there is also the question of the relevance of Jesus' teaching to their own lives; from this point of view, what, for example, Bockmuehl (1994:5–6) calls Jesus' (and Christianity's) "inalienable religious and historical moorings in Galilee and Judaea" may be less relevant than the "timeless" aspect of his teaching, which may apply to them, too. As argued by L. T. Johnson (1996:66), "The majority of Christians still expect a proclamation of the word of God that somehow is grounded in the gospel and pertains to the ultimate realities of their own lives."

N. T. Wright (1992:97) remarks, ironically, that "first-century Jews knew that they ought to be nice to each other" and so didn't need "to hear someone tell them [that]"; but quite apart from the fact that "being nice to each other" is hardly the same as loving one's enemies, not everyone everywhere is as aware of such ethical principles as first-century Jews may have been.

What applies to the Jewish background of Jesus' teaching applies also to other aspects of its historical context. For example, we may agree with Norman Perrin

(1976:100) that it is possible to read the parable of the lost sheep as a story "of a sudden crisis that changes all values and of a new situation of joy and gladness" (in the context of Jesus' proclamation of the Good News, in first-century Palestine). At the same time, however, it would be hard not to agree with Joseph Fitzmyer (1985b:1075) that to reduce the meaning of the story to one particular time and place "is to miss the point of the parable, which is not a description of the change in situation of a first-century Palestine, but rather of the joy (of God) at the finding of a 'lost' sinner."

According to a random telephone poll taken in 1992 and reported in *Time* magazine, 65 percent of Americans between the ages of 27 and 45 affirm that "religion is very important to me," and 43 percent "read the Bible in the past week" (Price 1997:76). This suggests that millions of Americans probably read the Gospels frequently. Presumably, the majority of these readers are less interested in Jesus' message to Israel than in his message to themselves; they feel included in the random crowds that Jesus taught, and they want to know what he meant—not for academic reasons but hoping to find in his words "the bread of life." For all such people, the insistence of some modern scholars that Jesus' message was addressed specifically to Israel, and only to Israel, is likely to be baffling and frustrating. The biblical claim that "salvation comes from the Jews" (John 4:22) is fully compatible with the hope, and sense, of modern readers that they are included among those addressed.

The content of many of Jesus' sayings can be read on different levels: one intended, presumably, for his disciples; another for "Israel" as a whole; and yet another that is applicable to anybody, anywhere, at any time. Jesus was not just "a teacher of timeless truths." Surely, though, whatever else he was he was that as well. From the perspective of the more general interest in Jesus—a Jesus who, as Raymond Brown (1997:828) put it, "really means something to people, one on whom they can base their lives"—the timeless aspect of Jesus' teaching is surely valid, too. By explaining his sayings in universal human concepts, we can articulate the universal, timeless aspect of his teaching more clearly and accurately than could be done in "normal" prose, whether in English or in any other language, with its own baggage of history, culture, and tradition.

10. An illustration: The "kingdom of God" explained in universal human concepts

The concept of the kingdom of God plays a central role in Jesus' teaching. Debates about the meaning of his teaching are often couched in terms of different interpretations of this key phrase. The range of proposed interpretations is very wide, but they fall into two broad categories: eschatological and noneschatological or eschatological and ethical. The term *eschatological* is understood differently by different scholars, but it is generally agreed that the key distinction is that between this world and the world to come, between a this-worldly and an otherworldly perspective. There is also an ongoing debate about how Jesus saw his own role in the kingdom of God, and whether and in what sense this kingdom was made present in *this* world through Jesus' own life, ministry, and death.

In the approach taken here, the core idea behind the metaphor of the kingdom of God is that of people living with God. But in this world or in the world to come? In my view, Jesus' answer is clear: in both. As Jesus' parables and sayings clearly suggest, one can live with God before one dies and after one dies; death is not a crucial divide in this respect, although after one's death, it will become apparent to a person how one lived before one died and to what extent one did or did not live with God. (Hence the images of the "Last Judgment.")

Since the kingdom of God embraces all people who live with God—the living and the dead—this kingdom is indeed an eschatological reality, otherworldly and not only this worldly. At the same time, for the *living*, ethics and eschatology are inseparable because they both involve living with God.

The kingdom of God is a dynamic concept because it refers to people's living with God, in accordance with God's will (rather than being in some kind of "state"). According to Jesus (as interpreted here), all people can live with God, and God wants this; accordingly, when people live with God (in love), God's will is being fulfilled: God (who loves all people) *wants* all people to live with God. In this sense, the kingdom of God is indeed a God-centred, as well as an eschatological reality; at the same time, however, it is an existential and ethical reality of people on earth (in their earthly lives) living with God (in love).

The notion of people living with God allows us to interpret the kingdom of God as having both an individual and a collective social dimension. On the one hand, every person can live with God; every person can find the "hidden treasure," the "pearl of great price." On the other hand, all people together can live with God, and images such as that of the leaven fermenting "the whole dough" suggest a global view of the whole of humanity as having a final destiny in living with God. (In more traditional language, this is the vision of universal salvation, implicit in the collective prayer addressed to Our Father: "Thy Kingdom come.")

The image of all people living with God in one kingdom suggests a horizontal, social dimension, as well as a vertical, individual one: in the kingdom of God people can live with all other people (just as a person can live with another person). One could say that the second-century Apostles' Creed conveys this idea in the phrase *communio sanctorum* ("the communion of saints"). In universal human concepts, this means, I suggest, that when people live with God they can live with all other people (living with God).

As for Jesus' own role in bringing about the kingdom of God, I would propose the following interpretation. According to Jesus, "all people can live with God" and "God wants this." But the reason why "all people can live with God" is crucially linked with what is happening "here now," that is, in first-century Galilee and Judea. When Jesus says that the kingdom of God has "come near" or "is in your midst," he is clearly alluding to his own mission. In this sense, one can say that history and geography are indeed inseparable from Jesus' proclamation of the kingdom: whereas all people can live with God, this is possible because something is happening here now.

Thus, the kingdom can be seen as already present in the sense that in Jesus' times it has already become possible for all people (i.e., for the whole of humankind) to live with God forever. It can also be seen as yet to come because it is not yet the case that all people live with God according to God's great plan for the whole of humanity. (For further discussion, see in particular chapter 5, section 7; chapter 8, section 3; chapter 25.)

The minilanguage of 60 or so simple and universal concepts has proved to be an adequate tool for dealing with complex and controversial aspects of New Testament theology. In fact, since the explanations formulated in this simple minilanguage are nontechnical and are free from the accumulated deposits of centuries of religious and academic debates, they offer the reader a fresh perspective on Jesus' teaching, bypassing many problems that may have been partly the product of the specialist and technical language used in the past.

The simple and universally accessible phrase "people living with God" is in fact well grounded in biblical language. For example, Revelation 21:3 describes the eschatological destiny of humankind as follows: "And I heard a loud voice from heaven saying, 'Behold the tabernacle of God is with people, and he will dwell with them, and they shall be his people, and God himself will be with them and be their God.'" The image of a (portable) tabernacle of God always having its place among the people's dwellings, so that they can always live with God, has its origin in God's instructions to Moses in the book of Exodus: "And let them make me a sanctuary, that I may dwell among them" (25:8); "And I will meet with the children of Israel, and the tabernacle shall be sanctified by my glory" (29:43).

The use of the expression "to live with God" (in French, *vivre avec Dieu*; in German, *mit Gott leben*)[4] allows us to account for the apparent gradability of "life" that we find in the language of the New Testament. In this language, in which "life" often stands for God, it is implied that people can not only live with God but also live *more* with God. Thus, in John 10:10, Jesus says, "I have come that they may have life, and that they may have it abundantly." The universal concept MORE does not mean comparison but increase (as in "I want more"; "I want to see more"; "I want to know more"; "I want to say more"), and so it seems particularly suitable for explicating this aspect of Jesus' teaching: Jesus does not compare people with one another, and in fact he refuses to promise anyone exalted positions in the kingdom of God (see Mark 10:35-45); rather, he invites everyone to a "more abundant life." (For further discussion, see chapter 1, section 10, and chapter 4, sections 5 and 6.)

Finally, some readers will probably insist that for them, the expression "to live with God" is also metaphorical. Whether it is or is not depends, of course, on our definition of the word *metaphorical*. But if someone insist on using this word in a sense that would make the expression "to live with God" metaphorical, then it should be noted that this is a universal metaphor, intelligible in all languages and cultures, and that it is radically different, therefore, from culture-specific metaphors such as "kingdom," "father," or "bread." The use of expressions such as "to live with God" does not aim at eliminating the mysteries of faith but at stating them in a way that can be as intelligible as possible—to all people in all societies.

11. *The meaning of the word* God

Throughout this book, I will try to explain the meaning of Jesus' parables and sayings in simple words that, evidence suggests, have equivalents in all languages. The reader, however, will quickly notice one exception to this central methodological principle: most, if not all, explications proposed here include the word God, which neither stands for a simple, indefinable concept nor has semantic equivalents in all languages. This exception is deliberate and, I believe, justifiable. God is a key concept in Jesus' teaching, and it recurs constantly in different contexts and in different configurations. If we tried to explicate this concept every time it were mentioned, our explications would be overblown and hard to read. It makes far more sense to explicate it once, at the outset, and then treat it as a unitary semantic molecule.

In explaining what the word God meant in Jesus' speech, we must try to separate what Jesus was saying *about* God from what he meant by the word God as such. It seems reasonable to assume that he used the word God in a sense that could be understood by his first listeners, that is, in a sense derived from and consistent with the Hebrew Bible. First, the God of the Hebrew Bible—like the God of the New Testament—is a personal God, that is, "someone" rather than "something"; someone who "knows," "wants," "speaks," that is, "says things," even "hears," and arguably "feels" (see, e.g., Heschel 1962).[5] Thus:

(a) God is someone

Second, the biblical God is "someone good." Theissen and Merz (1998:274) say that "the God of Jesus is the God of Israel: a blazing fire of ethical energy which seeks to change people in order to kindle the love of neighbour in them," and also that "it is characteristic of Jesus' understanding of God that God will soon . . . come to power as the unconditional will for the good." Leaving aside metaphors like "blazing fire" or "ethical energy" and trying to separate Jesus' teaching *about* God from his understanding of the very concept of God, we could say that the references to both ethics ("changing people") and eschatology ("coming to power") belong to what Jesus teaches *about* God. But the reference to God's "unconditional will for the good" touches on this God's very identity: if Jesus were not teaching about *someone* (someone who has a will) and someone inherently good, we would not know whom he was talking about.

(b) this someone is someone good

Crucially, this "someone good" who is the subject of Jesus' teaching and preaching is not someone human; it is someone radically different from people, and in fact someone unique: there is no one else like this someone (this someone is not "a god"; this someone is the one and only God).

(c) this someone is not someone like people
(b) there isn't anyone else like this someone

Theologians often say that the biblical God is "the ultimate reality," "the first and last reality," and so on (see, e.g., Küng 1980). Phrases of this kind are metaphorical and, of course, are not couched in simple and universal concepts, but what they hint at can be expressed in a nonmetaphorical way by drawing, in particular, on the simple and universal concept EXIST (THERE IS). Thus, to begin with, Jesus' God is eternal, that is, exists always (has always existed and will always exist):

(d) this someone exists always

Furthermore, in contrast to everyone and everything else, this someone exists as a creator, not as a creature. In simple concepts, this contrast can be formulated as follows:

(e) everything exists because this someone wants it to exist
(f) people exist because this someone wants them to exist
(g) this someone exists because this someone exists, not because of anything else

Although (g) is paradoxical and does not sound exactly like simple everyday language, its phrasing is nonetheless simpler and clearer than that of philosophical phrases like "the ultimate reality." In support of component (g) I would also note that it is anchored in the biblical language itself, notably in God's self-revelation to Moses (Ex. 3:14): "I AM WHO I AM"—a statement that also sounds paradoxical and mysterious.

Finally, I suggest that the biblical God is "the living God"—and that the phrase (e.g., John 6:69) is as at home in the language of the Bible as "the eternal God" (e.g., Deut. 33:27; Matt. 16:16). This brings us to the following overall explication of the biblical concept of God, in which Jesus' teaching *about* God is anchored:

God

(a) God is someone (not something)
(b) this someone is someone good
(c) this someone is not someone like people
(d) there isn't anyone else like this someone

(e) this someone exists always
(f) everything exists because this someone wants it to exist
(g) people exist because this someone wants them to exist
(h) this someone exists because this someone exists, not because of anything else
(i) this someone lives

Whether or not some further components should be added to this "definition minimum" (see Wierzbicka 1985:214–218) is debatable. Arguably, however, those listed above are necessary to explicate the biblical concept of God.

12. The search for a coherent picture

As mentioned earlier, to discuss the question "What did Jesus mean?" we have to decide, at least initially, on *some* set of Jesus' sayings. I do not want to pick and choose from the body of sayings attributed to Jesus to suit my personal convictions or hunches; I would want to remain within the domain of public discourse, that is, "to make the nature of my inquiry public" (see N. T. Wright 1996:55). To this end, let me make the following points about the choice of the material, the methodology, and the principles of interpretation.

1. To minimize areas of unnecessary controversy, I will not include in this book any of the sayings found in the Fourth Gospel, which in any case requires a separate study; and neither will I include any from sources outside the traditional canon. This leaves me with the synoptic Gospels. Here, my focus will be on the Sermon on the Mount (including the Beatitudes and the Lord's Prayer) and on the parables; special attention will be paid to the sayings and parables widely regarded as most likely to be authentic.

2. I will argue that the meanings emerging from a semantic analysis of the hard core of relatively undisputed Jesus' sayings are interrelated and that once formulated, they allow us to build a reasonably coherent overall picture. I will also try to show that many sayings whose authenticity has been disputed in fact fit this overall picture as well. I will argue that some of the sayings that have been disputed as allegedly inconsistent with the unquestionably authentic ones are in fact fully consistent with them—provided that they are properly explicated.

3. Although I have no "objective" arguments on my side comparable, for example, to the number of votes cast in the Jesus Seminar, I can claim a methodological advantage that is entirely public and intersubjective. The methodology of semantic interpretation used in this book is severely constrained by public rules, including the exclusive use of (independently established) universal human concepts, the exclusive use of independently established universal syntactic patterns, and the avoidance of metaphors in explanatory formulas.

4. Although the restrictions on the language of the explications stated in point 3 do not force a unique interpretation on any given saying, they do nonetheless severely restrict the range of possible interpretations and help to localize any disagreements in quite specific parts of the explications. As a result, two or three alternative interpretations, divergent but easy to compare, can often be proposed. If one of these interpretations, but not the others, is consistent with the account that is emerging from the analysis of the other sayings, I see this interpretation as more justified and to be preferred over the others.

5. The dependence between judgments of authenticity and judgments of interpretation goes both ways: whereas we cannot establish what Jesus meant without having some knowledge of what he said, we cannot always establish what he did or did not say without having some insight into what the disputed sayings might have meant.

For example, Funk et al. (1993:4, 5) regard "the liberation of the non-eschatological Jesus of the aphorisms and parables from [Albert] Schweitzer's eschatological Jesus" as a "pillar of contemporary scholarship." Since the Fellows of the Jesus Seminar have rejected "the tyranny of . . . an eschatological Jesus," they have also decided that, in Powell's (1998:79) words, Jesus "did not speak in apocalyptic language about the end of the world or a final judgment." Accordingly, some of the key words attributed to Jesus in the New Testament were rejected by the Jesus Seminar as inauthentic. This includes, for example, Jesus' words in Matthew 25:31–46, which are embedded in an apocalyptic judgment scene: "for I was hungry and you gave me food; I was thirsty and you gave me drink; I was a stranger and you took me in," and his reply to the uncomprehending (v. 40): "Assuredly, I say to you, inasmuch as you did it to one of the least of these my brethren, you did it to me."

What is at issue here, however, is above all the meaning of Jesus' words. As I will argue in detail in chapter 15, one can perfectly well accept the authenticity of the core of Matthew 25:31–46 without accepting at the same time that Jesus saw people as divided, for all eternity, into sheep and goats or that he was an advocate of an impending cataclysm in the sense of an imminent end of the world. Generally speaking, the issue of authenticity cannot be separated from the issue of meaning.

As any historical figure whose words have been transmitted to us through intermediaries, Jesus deserves the benefit of the doubt. Granted, there can be many ways of reading and interpreting the sayings attributed to him by the first-century Christian writers, and some of these ways would present his message as being full of contradictions. There is also, however, a way of reading most of these sayings that presents an intelligible and coherent overall picture—one that can be teased out by paraphrasing them in terms of simple, intuitively intelligible, and universal human concepts. This book attempts to show just such a way of reading Jesus' sayings. While presenting a radically new approach to the interpretation of the Bible, in its content it is consistent with mainstream Christian belief.

Finally, should the reader be interested in where I personally stand, I am a believing and "practicing" Roman Catholic. At the same time, my perspective on the Gospels has been strongly influenced by the writings of Jewish, as well as Christian, scholars, and it is broadly ecumenical, which for me includes not only the Catholic and Protestant approaches but also the Eastern Christian tradition. In fact, in my attempts to understand what Jesus meant, I feel I learned most from a saint of the Eastern Church, the seventh-century scholar and mystic Isaac of Niniveh, known also as Isaac the Syrian (see, e.g., 1981, 1995). Isaac's distinction between "interior" meanings of the Scriptures' "discourse about God"— as opposed to the "outer meanings" and the "bodily exterior of the narratives"— and his insight into the symbolic meaning of apocalyptic images, warnings, and threats are, I find, more illuminating than many hermeneutical theories of the late twentieth century. I believe they point the way to a better understanding of Jesus' words and images in the third millennium.

Part I

THE SERMON ON THE MOUNT

The Beatitudes

Matthew's version (5:3-12)

3. Blessed are the poor in spirit,
      For theirs is the kingdom of heaven.
4. Blessed are those who mourn,
      For they shall be comforted.
5. Blessed are the meek,
      For they shall inherit the earth.
6. Blessed are those who hunger and thirst for righteousness,
      For they shall be filled.
7. Blessed are the merciful,
      For they shall obtain mercy.
8. Blessed are the pure in heart,
      For they shall see God.
9. Blessed are the peacemakers,
      For they shall be called sons of God.
10. Blessed are those who are persecuted for righteousness' sake,
      For theirs is the kingdom of heaven.
11. Blessed are you when they revile and persecute you,
      and say all kinds of evil against you falsely for my sake.
12. Rejoice and be exceedingly glad, for great is your reward
      in heaven, for they persecuted the prophets who were before
      you.

Luke's version (6:20-26)

20. Blessed are you poor,
    For yours is the kingdom of God.
21. Blessed are you who hunger now,
    For you shall be filled.
    Blessed are you who weep now,
    For you shall laugh.
22. Blessed are you when people hate you,
    And when they exclude you,
    And revile you, and cast out your name as evil,
    For the Son of Man's sake.
23. Rejoice in that day and leap for joy!
    For indeed your reward is great in heaven,
    For in the like manner their fathers did to the prophets.
24. But woe to you who are rich
    For you have received your consolation.
25. Woe to you who are full,
    For you shall hunger.
    Woe to you who laugh now,
    For you shall mourn and weep.
26. Woe to you when all people speak well of you,
    For so did their fathers to the false prophets.

1. The importance of the Beatitudes

According to the *Catechism of the Catholic Church* (1994:426), "The Beatitudes are at the heart of Jesus' preaching"; numerous works on Jesus' teaching—scholarly and popular, Catholic, Orthodox, and Protestant—express a similar view.

Perhaps the Beatitudes are widely felt to be so crucially important because they address what many people see as the key problem of human existence: suffering. Some, like Jürgen Moltmann, refuse even to call suffering a problem, preferring to use different language altogether, not abstract but existential and experiential:

> God and suffering belong together, just as in this life the cry for God and the suffering experienced in pain belong together. The question about God and the question about suffering are a joint, common question. . . . No one can answer the theodicy question [i.e., the question about the relation between suffering and God] in this world, and no one can get rid of it. Life in this world means living with this open question; it is a critical one. It is an all-embracing *eschatological question*. It is not purely theoretical, for it cannot be answered with any new theory about the existing world. It is a practical question which will only be answered through experience of the new world in which "God will wipe away every tear from their eyes."

It is not really a question at all. . . . It is *the open wound of life* in this world.
It is the real task of faith and theology to make it possible for us to survive, to go on living, with this open wound. (1981:49)

The questions most frequently raised in connection with human suffering are
indeed the theodicy questions: why do people suffer? and how can a good God
permit human suffering? But the Beatitudes address a different question, much
closer to Moltmann's eschatological question: what is God going to do about
it?[1] Moltmann's answer, quoted from Revelation ("God will wipe away every tear
from their eyes") is, in effect, the answer of the Beatitudes.

The key promise of the Beatitudes is that those who weep will laugh, and
those who mourn will be comforted. Everything else can be seen as an amplification of this theme. There are other themes: poverty, hunger, persecution, dependence on God, nonaggression, and nonretaliation. But poverty, hunger, and
persecution can be seen as different modes and different examples of suffering,
whereas dependence on God, nonaggression, and nonretaliation can be seen as
responses to suffering. Although these themes are present elsewhere in Jesus'
teaching as well (e.g., in the Lord's Prayer, in the injunction to love one's enemies, and in such parables as the rich man and Lazarus), nowhere else are they
addressed so directly and emphatically. Above all, this applies to the central theme
of suffering.

Many modern commentators see poverty rather than suffering as the main
concern of the Beatitudes, and undoubtedly poverty *is* a key theme: it is not treated
as just one example of suffering among many but as a particularly salient one.
Ultimately, however, suffering is broader than poverty; and on reflection, most
readers of the Gospels will agree, I think, that for Jesus the suffering of the lepers, the paralytics, or the parents who lost their children did not mean any less
than that of the hungry and the needy. By extrapolation, what applies to the lepers
and others of Jesus' times applies also to the victims of the Holocaust, the Gulag,
"ethnic cleansing," all "plagues," and so on. In the Beatitudes, as in Revelation,
no sharp distinctions are made between different kinds of tears.

But to establish what the main themes of the Beatitudes are we must discuss
their redactional history, decide what exactly derives from Jesus, and explore the
meaning behind the words and the images. One key fact that must be mentioned
at the outset is that the Beatitudes as we know them do not all go back to Jesus'
preaching. Whereas there is a great deal of controversy about the origin and history
of the individual Beatitudes, scholars agree that neither Matthew's (5:3–12) nor
Luke's (6:20–26) version can be fully traced to the historical Jesus. The most
impressive and comprehensive study of the subject, Dupont's (1969–1973) three-
volume *Les Béatitudes*, acknowledges, in agreement with other works of the last
few decades, that both Matthew's and Luke's versions had their source partly in
the teaching of the early church and were molded to some extent by the needs
of the communities to which they were addressed. The evangelists did not aim
at reproducing Jesus' words in their original form but rather at explaining his
teaching as appropriate to the situation in which they were writing and the audi-
ences at which they were aiming. Given the extensive redactional input in both

Matthew's and Luke's version, the question naturally suggests itself: what exactly was "Jesus' version"?

Remarkably, after two millennia of extensive discussions, there is still no consensus on this point and the vast literature on the subject covers an extremely broad spectrum of opinion. But although commentators still do not agree on what the Beatitudes *mean*, there has been in the last three decades or so a growing convergence on the question of what Jesus actually *said* and, in particular, on what he did *not* say. Since the issues involved in these debates are complex and the literature vast, I will start with a simple summary of facts, in seven points, and only later turn to a more comprehensive discussion of the key issues.

2. Basic facts about the Beatitudes

The number of beatitudes

Matthew's version has eight beatitudes (or nine, depending on how one counts, since verse 11 can be regarded either as a restatement of verse 10 or as an additional, ninth, beatitude). Luke's version has four beatitudes and four corresponding "woes."

Shared beatitudes (Matthew's and Luke's)

Strictly speaking, there are no shared beatitudes, but four of Matthew's have partially matching ones in Luke. The key terms in these partially matching beatitudes are poor, *weeping/grieving*, hungry, and *persecuted*.

The source of the shared beatitudes

It is widely held that the shared beatitudes were taken over by Matthew and Luke from a hypothetical shared source known as Q or *Quelle*, (German for "source") and reworked by each evangelist in his own way. The other beatitudes, as well as the Lucan woes, are widely held to have been added to the shared core by the evangelists.

Do all the shared beatitudes go back to Jesus?

Some recent commentators hold that of the four partially shared beatitudes only three go back to the historical Jesus: in their view, that of the persecuted derives from the situation of the early church rather than from Jesus' own ministry. Others, however, (including Dupont 1969–1973) regard it as very likely that this last beatitude, too, is authentic and represents an expanded and reworked version of a saying that does go back to the historical Jesus. On this point, even the Fellows of the Jesus Seminar concur: "There were probably at least four beatitudes in Jesus' repertoire (poor, hungry, weeping, persecuted: Luke 6:20–22)" (Funk et al. 1993:512).

Whose version is closer to Jesus' own, Matthew's or Luke's?

Despite the continuing controversy, there is a growing consensus that on the whole Luke's version of the partially shared beatitudes is closer to Jesus'. Luke's innovations include (probably) the introduction of the word *now* and the substitution of the second-person plural *you* for the third-person plural *they*. As argued by Dupont (1969:II, 21–27; cf. also Gourgues 1995:84), it is likely that Luke projected the *you* of his fourth beatitude, addressed (in his version) to persecuted Christians, onto the earlier ones, treating them all as addressed to the suffering followers of Jesus.

The reconstructed version of Jesus' beatitudes

According to the growing scholarly consensus, therefore, Jesus' own beatitudes are likely to have looked as follows (see, e.g., Gourgues 1995:84):

Blessed are the poor, for theirs is the kingdom of God.
Blessed are those who hunger, for they shall be filled.
Blessed are those who weep/grieve, for they shall laugh.

Reconstructing Jesus' words

Jesus probably did not speak Greek, and in any case he didn't formulate his teaching in Greek; nonetheless, if we want to reconstruct and to understand Jesus' own words, our path must lead through the Greek words in Luke's and Matthew's reworked accounts of his teaching. In the beatitude of the poor, Luke has the word *ptōchoi* "poor" and Matthew has the phrase *ptōchoi tō pneumati*, traditionally translated into English as "poor in spirit." In the beatitude of the hungry, both Luke and Matthew have the word *peinōntes* "hungering" (from *peinaō* "be hungry, hunger"), to which Matthew has added, however, the phrase *kai dipsōontes* "and thirsting" and the complement *tēn dikaiosunen* "righteousness" (in the accusative case). In the beatitude of the weeping/grieving, Luke uses the word *klaiontes* "weeping, crying," whereas Matthew uses *penthountes* "mourning, grieving." Since the Lucan version is generally accepted as being closer to Jesus' own than the Matthean one, it is widely (though not universally) assumed that the key Greek words pointing the way to Jesus' original beatitudes are *ptōchoi* "poor," *peinōntes* "hungry," and *klaiontes* "weeping."

Scholars generally agree that behind the Greek *klaiontes* and *penthountes* we should see the Hebrew (and also Aramaic) *abelim* "grieving/lamenting"; behind the Greek *peinōntes*, the Hebrew *raeb* "hungry," "suffering hunger" (regularly translated into biblical Greek by the verb *peinaō*); and behind the Greek *ptōchoi* "poor," the Hebrew *anawim* and the Aramaic '*inwetân* (Dupont 1969:II, 24–34), whose meaning will be discussed in some detail later.

In what follows, I will discuss the likely meaning of Jesus' beatitudes in some detail, starting from the weeping, proceeding to the hungry before discussing the more difficult problem of the poor, and briefly touching on the controversial question of the persecuted. Having explored the meaning of the categories hinted at by the words "weeping" (*abelim*), "hungry" (*raeb*), and "poor" (*anawim*), I will turn to "blessed" (Greek *makarios*) itself (see Dupont 1969:II, 324–338) and address the question of what Jesus is likely to have had in mind when he pronounced certain categories of people to be "blessed."

3. Who are the weeping ones?

The Greek words *klaiontes* (roughly, "weeping"/"crying") and *penthountes* (roughly, "mourning"/"grieving") are both renderings of the Hebrew and Aramaic word *abelim*, referring to physical manifestations of great suffering, such as (among the Israelites) loud crying and lamenting, tearing of one's clothes, covering of one's head with ashes, and so on (see Dupont 1969:II, 36). Prototypically, behavior of this kind was associated in Jewish culture with the death of a beloved person. Whom could Jesus have had in mind when he said that people who cry and lament like this are blessed?

English doesn't have a word corresponding exactly to *abelim* because there is no corresponding cultural practice in Anglo culture. One should surely assume, however, that Jesus wasn't speaking about any culture-specific ways of expressing suffering but about suffering as such: the image of loud lament was for him a metaphor for all the suffering that people have to endure in their lives. Accordingly, I would identify the target of the beatitude of the weeping/grieving as follows:

> sometimes very bad things happen to people
> because these things happen, these people feel something very bad
> like a person feels something very bad when someone dies

This very general interpretation differs from more specific interpretations that restrict the blessing to people who are suffering for a specific reason—in particular, to those who suffer at the thought of their own sins, at the thought of the sins of other people, or at the thought of *other* people's sufferings (but not their own).

For example, the well-known commentator of the New Testament William Barclay ([1975]1993:93) sums up the second beatitude in the phrase "the bliss of the broken heart," which is more paradoxical than Jesus' utterance itself, and he concludes the relevant section with the following summary (given in capital letters, p. 95): "The real meaning of the second beatitude is: O the bliss of the man whose heart is broken for the world's suffering and for his own sin, for out of his sorrow he will find the joy of God!" Although the word "sorrow" and the phrase "broken heart" are quite apposite here (as a free paraphrase of Jesus' message), the phrase "the bliss of the broken heart," which seems to suggest a masochistic enjoyment of sorrow and grief, is unfortunate, and the references to the world's suffering and to one's own sin seem to be gratuitous additions.

It is widely accepted in the literature on the subject that the beatitude of the weeping invokes the passage from the book of the prophet Isaiah (61:1-2), which the Lucan Jesus quotes at the beginning of his ministry (4:18-19):

> The Spirit of the Lord is upon me,
> Because he has anointed me to preach the gospel to the poor [*anawim*].
> He has sent me to heal the broken-hearted,
> To preach deliverance to the captives,
> And recovery of sight to the blind,
> To set at liberty those who are oppressed,
> To preach the acceptable year of the Lord.

The images and phrases used by Isaiah make it quite clear that the people referred to are those to whom very bad things have happened and who feel something very bad because of this. It is to such people that the Messiah promised by the prophet brings the "good tidings." In the light of Isaiah's prophecy, commentaries such as the following (Strecker 1988:35) seem wide of the mark:

> it is uncertain what the expression *penthountes* ("mourning, grieving") refers to concretely: to grief over the present eon, which at the same time evokes a distance between the mourner and the world? Or is it a question of penitent grief, say, in the sense of the apocalyptic tradition of the Testaments of the Twelve Patriarchs? The latter would include the idea that those grieving over sin are at the same time supposed to stand away from the sin and overcome it. It is also conceivable, however, that Matthew understands *mourn* in the sense of abasing oneself. Thus, James 4:9 attests the imperative "Mourn!" beside "Be wretched!", in addressing sinners, who are thereby called to penitence and humility before God.

It is hard to believe that the author is speaking here about Jesus' good news, promising consolation (in the first instance) to those who grieve over the death of their beloved. The overspecific interpretations (Strecker's "penitent grief," as well as Barclay's "vicarious penitent grief," and "sympathetic grief") can be portrayed as follows:

(a) some people feel something very bad
   because they think that they did something very bad

(b) some people feel something very bad
   because they think that other people did very bad things

(c) some people feel something very bad
   because they think that many bad things happened to other people

Although it can be argued that these three scenarios [(a), (b), and (c)] are compatible with the teachings of Jesus, there is no basis for reading them into the meaning of the beatitude itself. It is the commentators rather than Jesus who restrict the blessing to some specific categories of sufferers and to the kind of suffering that they regard as particularly noble and edifying: suffering for one's sins, suffering for the sins of the world, and suffering for the sufferings of other people. There is no reason to assume that Jesus meant to exclude people who suffer because terrible things have happened to them (e.g., painful illness or death of their children). On the contrary, it is to such people first of all that Jesus (as we know him from the Gospels) shows his compassion. The idea that he meant to exclude them from the hope offered to "those who cry" is arbitrary and groundless, nor are there any compelling reasons to think that that is how Matthew wanted to interpret Jesus' teaching.

According to the *Catechism of the Catholic Church* (1994:427), "The Beatitudes . . . are paradoxical promises which sustain hope in the midst of tribulations" and which "respond to the natural desire for happiness" that "God has placed in the human heart in order to draw people to the One who alone can fulfil it." The reference to "tribulations" points in the direction of "bad things that happen to us" rather than toward "bad things that happen to other people" or "bad things that we do." This is in keeping with the reference to the "natural desire for happiness." Thus the *Catechism* interprets the blessing broadly, as directed at the unhappy; the broken-hearted; those who mourn, grieve, and cry in sorrow—whose unhappiness is contrasted with people's "natural desire for happiness" and to whom it promises an ultimate fulfilment of that desire.

In endorsing such a broad interpretation of the beatitude of the weeping, the *Catechism* recognizes the universalism of Jesus' teaching, evident also in his parables, in his great scene of the Last Judgment (Matt. 25:31-46), in his teaching about the love of enemies, and in the universal application of the concept of neighbour. Jesus' image of the Father in Heaven who "makes his sun rise on the evil and the good, and sends rain on the just and the unjust" (Matt. 5:45) epitomizes his universalism. The Beatitudes, with their sweeping blessing for all those "who weep," epitomize it, too. The blessing is not even focused in any special way on the suffering of the "righteous" and the innocent, as the book of Job was. It is simply extended to everyone who suffers, in Meier's (1980:39) words, "with the full authority of the apocalyptic prophet he [Jesus] assures them of vindication on the last day."

4. Who are the hungry?

Who are the "hungry"—the *peinōntes* of Luke's second beatitude and the *raeb* of Jesus' original beatitude, translated by Luke with this word? The literal meaning of the word presumably used by Jesus is not in question. To quote Dupont,

It is not necessary to insist at length on the fact that the *peinōntes*, about whom the beatitude speaks, are those "hungry" not in the Greek (or the French) sense but in the biblical sense; these people "are hungry" because they do not have the necessities, they are lacking indispensable food. Not only are they hungry, but they have no means to obtain the bread which would appease their hunger. They are the poor, who do not possess the essential minimum. Their real name would be "those suffering hunger" ("les fameliques"). (1969:II, 39)

But it is not enough to understand the literal sense of the word that Jesus is likely to have used because Jesus often used words metaphorically. For example (as discussed above), it seems indubitable that when he spoke of the *abelim* (the "lamenting/grieving" ones), he meant this word figuratively, as a metaphor for, broadly, the unhappy (the sorrowful, the suffering, the afflicted)—that is, in universal terms, all those to whom "very bad things have happened" and who "feel something very bad because of this." Similarly, it seems clear that his word *raeb*, underlying the Greek *peinōntes*, symbolized not only those who suffered hunger, in the literal sense of the word, but also those who suffered thirst, cold, homelessness, and so on, that is, those who were deprived of the necessities of life. As Dupont (1969:II, 39) put it, "they are the poor who do not possess the essential minimum."

There is an ongoing controversy about the meaning of Jesus' first beatitude: who are the "poor" (Luke's *ptōchoi*)? Did this beatitude refer (for Jesus) to a certain spiritual attitude or to a socioeconomic condition? I will discuss this controversy more thoroughly in the next section. But whoever the "poor" (*ptōchoi*) are, the "hungry" must be, above all, those needy in a material, physical sense.

As for Matthew's beatitude that is devoted to those who "hunger and thirst for righteousness," Guelich (1982) and others have noted that is not inconsistent with Jesus' teaching as a whole. But most commentators agree that the phrasing of this beatitude is in all probability Matthew's own and that Jesus' original version corresponded to Luke's "hungry" (*peinōntes*, i.e., *raeb*) rather than to Matthew's "those who hunger and thirst for righteousness." It can be added that here, as elsewhere, the best clue to Jesus' intended meaning lies in his parables.

As pointed out by Dupont (1969:II, 48), the meaning of the beatitude of the hungry is best explained by the parable of the rich man and Lazarus (Luke 16:19–31; see chapter 17). The poor man, Lazarus, is described in this parable as "a certain beggar named Lazarus, full of sores, who was at his [the rich man's] gate, desiring to be fed with the crumbs which fell from the rich man's table. Moreover the dogs came and licked his sores." Lazarus is both hungry and poor, and the two attributes are inextricably linked: he is hungry because he is poor, and his poverty is manifested in his constant desire to feed on the crumbs that fall from the rich man's table. He is a beggar and no doubt lacks life's other necessities in addition to food. And he is "blessed": after he dies, the angels carry him to "Abraham's bosom." The character of Lazarus, then, is our best guide to the intended meaning of Jesus' second beatitude, and it suggests the following formula:

(a) some people don't have anything
(b) because of this many bad things happen to these people

This formula overlaps with that assigned to the beatitude of the weeping since both share the component "many bad things happen to these people." But there is also a difference: the beatitude of the weeping focuses on the *suffering* due to misfortunes ("these people feel something very bad"), whereas the beatitude of the hungry focuses on the *destitution* that causes misfortunes ("these people don't have anything").

5. Who are the poor?

According to the account developed here so far, Jesus did focus in one of his beatitudes on the poor—the destitute, the have-nots, the beggars. Symbolically, he designated this category of people as the hungry. But if "hungry" stands for something like "poor," what does "poor" itself stand for?

The categories of people described by Jesus as blessed are not mutually exclusive, and in fact the "hungry" (*raeb*) and the *anawim* could largely overlap. It was not Jesus but Luke who used the word *ptōchoi* "poor, destitute" (Jesus taught in Aramaic, not in Greek). As mentioned earlier, Jesus used, in all probability, the Aramaic word ʿinwetân, that is, the Aramaic counterpart of the Hebrew word *anawim* (originally, "bowed down"), which was one of the key words of the Old Testament and which also played an important role in the Palestinian Judaism of Jesus' times (cf. Broer 1986; Dupont 1969:II; Gelin 1964; Guelich 1982). Although biblical scholars describe the meaning of *anawim* in many different ways, they generally agree that it was not the same as the Greek *ptōchoi* but covered a broader range (roughly, "needy/lowly/oppressed/depending on God's mercy"). Since there is no exact equivalent of *anawim* in English either, it cannot be elucidated by any one English word (such as "poor") or by a series of nonequivalent English words. It can, however, be elucidated if it is presented as a unique configuration of universal human concepts.[2]

Guelich (1982:68) describes the meaning of *anawim* as follows: "In summary, the poor [i.e., *anawim*] in Judaism referred to those in desperate need (socioeconomic element) whose helplessness drove them to a dependent relationship with God (religious element) for the supplying of their needs and vindication. Both elements are consistently present. . . ."

The literature on the Beatitudes is dominated by heated debates about the intended identity of the "poor" (*ptōchoi*, *anawim*), and the issue is often presented in the form of an alternative: does it refer to those who are materially poor (destitute) or to those who are poor in spirit, that is, have the "right" attitude toward material possessions and seek their existential security in God? In other words, does it refer to a condition or to an attitude?

All those commentators who have looked beyond Luke's Greek word *ptōchoi* agree that the Semitic concept behind it (*anawim*) refers both to a condition and to an attitude, that is, that it has a socioeconomic dimension as well as a religious one (roughly, economically poor, socially oppressed, and religiously dependent on God). To quote Guelich (1982:97) again, "The Old Testament concept of the poor included a dual reference to the socioeconomic condition of the individual as well as the religious dimension of resultant dependency upon God and vindication." This suggests the following explication:

anawim

(a) many bad things happen to some people
(b) because other people do bad things to these people
(c) these people know that they can't do anything because of this
(d) [because they don't have anything]
(e) at the same time these people know that God can do good things for them
(f) they know that they can live because God wants to do good things for them, not because of anything else

Component (a) shows that the *anawim* suffer many misfortunes, (b) adds that they are oppressed by some other people, (c) presents them as powerless, (d) (which appears to be optional rather than essential) links their powerlessness with their poverty, and (e) and (f) show that they know that they depend on God.

In the literature on the Beatitudes there is much discussion of how Matthew, with his phrase "poor in spirit," has "spiritualized," "ethicized," or "interiorized" Luke's simple concept of poor, allegedly more faithful to Jesus' original intention. But much of this discussion appears to be missing two crucial points: first, that Jesus' *anawim* (or its Aramaic equivalent) didn't mean "destitute" but stood for a more complex concept that included a religious dimension; and second, that acknowledging the religious ("spiritual," or "interior") aspect of Jesus' first beatitude is not tantamount to ignoring or downplaying his interest in the poor (the destitute, the hungry, and the dispossessed) because in any case there was also the second beatitude, the beatitude of the hungry, which focused specifically on the poor in the socioeconomic sense of the word. By translating *anawim* as "poor in spirit" (*ptōchoi to pneumati*) rather than simply "poor" (*ptōchoi*), Matthew was evidently trying to explain this concept, for which Greek simply had no ready-made word. As C. Brown (1979:824) puts it, "The enlarged form in Matt. 'the poor in spirit . . .' brings out the OT and Jewish background of those who in affliction have confidence only in God." Gourgues (1995:32) remarks in this connection that in Psalms we often hear

the cry of someone who presents himself as "poor and suffering" (Ps. 69:30), "poor and lonely" (Ps. 25:16), or, most frequently, "poor and unhappy" (Ps. 40; 18; 70; 6; 86:1; 108:22). In the majority of cases, the context clearly indicates that it is not a matter of material poverty. . . . To be poor involves being conscious of one's misery, whatever its face. . . . But what is the most important is the fact that the consciousness of one's misery turns the poor towards God.

Having explicated the Old Testament concept of *anawim* in universal concepts, I have by no means elucidated it fully. To understand the meaning of the *words* used by Jesus is not the same thing as to understand what *Jesus* meant by them. Some aspects of Jesus' teaching were so new that they couldn't be fully expressed in existing words, and much of this teaching could be conveyed only by images and symbolic actions. For example, the new Christian concept of "humility" (*tapeinophrosunē*; see Turner 1980:216–217) was forged not only by specific sayings but also by symbolic actions such as Jesus' washing of his disciples' feet.[3]

Similarly, the full meaning of Jesus' first beatitude was bursting the seams not only of the Greek word *ptōchoi* "poor" but even of the culturally loaded Hebrew word *anawim*. Jesus (as the evangelists understood him) wanted to identify himself with the prophet announced in Isaiah's 61:1–2 (cf. Luke 4:18–20):

> The Spirit of the Lord is upon me
> Because he has anointed me to preach the gospel to the poor [*anawim*].

At the same time, however, he was developing his own idea of the *anawim*, the "poor in spirit," on whom God's special favor rests; and he was developing this idea not only through words but also through images, parables, and occasional symbolic actions. As noted by Dupont (1969:II), one such crucial image was that of a small child, linked with the episode of Jesus' blessing of little children (Mark 10:13–16; Matt. 19:13–14; Luke 18:15–17). To quote from Mark's (10:13–14) version of the story,

13. Then they brought young children to him that he might touch them; but the disciples rebuked those who brought them.
14. But when Jesus saw it, he was greatly displeased and said to them, 'Let the little children come to me, and do not forbid them; for of such is the kingdom of God.'

Since this image throws an important light on the concept of *anawim*, it deserves some discussion in the present context.

The details of Jesus' sayings that involve little children are disputed, but in essence these sayings are generally regarded as authentic and, moreover, as indicating an attitude that was a startling departure from the standards of the ancient world. Funk et al. (1993:89) commented on this as follows: "In support of the authenticity of Mark 10:14, some Fellows pointed to Jesus' dramatic reversal of the child's traditional status in ancient societies as a silent non-participant. This perspective agrees with Jesus' sympathy for those who were marginal to society or outcasts (compare the beatitudes recorded in Luke 6:20–21)."

The question of why the kingdom of God belongs to the likes of little children is debated in the literature. Some say, "because they are innocent" (e.g., Pirot 1935:520); others, "because they are humble" (e.g., Filson 1960:208); still others, "because they are marginal to society or outcasts" (e.g., Funk et al. 1993:89). Dupont (1969:II, 160) rejects what he sees as idealization of children as the basis for an explanation, and he offers the following answer: if the kingdom belongs to little children it is not because of their alleged innocence or humility but "because of God's predilection for those who are little, weak, despised. To share this privilege of little children, adults have to make themselves little, lower themselves, to count for nothing. Not exactly because humility is particularly meritorious but because of what is known about God's dispositions: God resists the proud but gives his grace to the lowly (*tapeinos*)." Dupont adds (p. 181) that the poor are "blessed" because, being like little children, they are the object of God's special love for "those who are little" (literally, "what is little," *ce qui est petit*).

What exactly does it mean, however, that both the poor and little children are "little"? In what sense are little children "little"? And how can adults "make themselves little"? Dupont's (1969:vol. 2) commentary on the links between these sayings and the Beatitudes is engaging, but ultimately it remains metaphorical. Furthermore, his conclusion that it is not the attitude that matters but the condition is unhelpful: in the children's case, it is apparently their condition that makes them especially dear to God, whereas in the case of adults who are supposed to "make themselves little," it would seem to be their attitude. What the two cases have in common is not articulated.

I wish to propose the following interpretation, formulated without metaphors and by and large in universal concepts: little children know that they cannot live if someone (some "big person," i.e., a grownup) doesn't do good things for them; and they trust that some people (prototypically, their mother and father) want to and can do good things for them. And this is, I suggest, the meaning of Jesus' image of the "poor," the "little ones," the *anawim*, on whom God's special favor rests: they are people who know that they cannot live if God doesn't do good things for them and who think at the same time that God can and wants to do good things for them. Thus, the explication that follows can apply both to Jesus' *anawim* ("poor in spirit") and to his model of a "childlike" attitude to God:

Jesus' conception of the anawim *and the childlike*

   (a) some people know that they cannot live
         if God doesn't do good things for them
   (b) at the same time these people think:
   (c)   "God can do good things for me
   (d)   God wants to do good things for me"

The word *know* in (a) transcends, I believe, the need to choose between a condition and a religious attitude: if the people in question *know* that they cannot live without God's help and support, this implies something significant about their objective condition; at the same time, the fact that they are aware of this condition implies something significant about their state of mind as well.

The explication taken as a whole expresses a "God-dependence" and a trust in God, consonant with Jesus' teaching elsewhere in the Gospels, including the

Lord's Prayer and the injunction to ask, to seek, and to knock (Luke 11:9; Matt. 7:7; see chapter 4, section 11).

6. Who are the meek (Matthew's praeis)?

The English word *meek* here is misleading: it is no longer used in English in a way that could make clear what either Jesus' or Matthew's intended meaning might have been. Moreover, in modern English, it has become a somewhat pejorative word, suggesting something like weakness or spinelessness.

Many commentators seem to believe that the beatitude of the meek is of little relevance to Jesus' teaching because it does not go back to the historical Jesus; in fact, they argue, it doesn't even go as far back as the *Quelle*, and so it must be a Matthean creation. But even if we accept that the beatitude of the *praeis* was added by Matthew, the question must still be asked: did Matthew add this beatitude for a good reason? In fact, it seems that Matthew added it to convey more fully what he thought Jesus had meant by his original beatitude of the *anawim*. Steeped as he was in the Jewish religious tradition, Matthew was keenly aware of the inadequacy of the Greek word *ptōchoi* 'poor' as a would be equivalent of the Hebrew *anawim*, so as we have seen, he used instead the phrase *ptochoi to pneumati* 'poor in spirit'. Apparently, however, he wasn't fully satisfied with this translation either because he felt that it didn't adequately express the full meaning of Jesus' *anawim*; and this, it seems, is why he added another beatitude, that of the *praeis*, which the King James Version later translated into English as "meek."

Commenting on Matthew's third beatitude (that of the meek) in relation to the first (that of the poor in spirit) Guelich observed:

> The first, with its reference to Isa. 61:1, and the third, with its reference to Ps. 37:11, ultimately go back to the same Hebrew term for "the poor" ('nwm) [i.e., *anawim*]. . . . This Beatitude most probably arose as a parallel to the first in order to maintain the dual Old Testament force of the socioeconomic and religious connotations of the concept "the poor." The "meek" offered a balance in Greek for the strictly socioeconomic understanding of the "poor" at a time in the Church's mission when the first beatitude was in danger of being misconstrued in an exclusively materialistic sense. (1982:101)

Guelich continues here, essentially, an approach initiated and given a more nuanced form by Dupont (1973:III, 486–545). Dupont, too, argued that Matthew had introduced the beatitude of the "meek" (in Greek *praus*, plural *praeis*) to better capture the full sense of the underlying concept of *anawim*. Dupont noted that Matthew's phrase "poor in spirit" represented his attempt to partially explicate this concept (going beyond what he saw as the inadequate rendering of *anawim* by the Greek *ptōchoi*), and that by introducing the additional beatitude of the meek, he was trying to capture another aspect of the meaning of *anawim*, which was not sufficiently reflected in his phrase "poor in spirit" (*ptōchoi tō pneumati*).

In Dupont's (1973:III) discussion, however, both Matthean beatitudes that descend from *anawim* (the poor in spirit and the meek) preserve some religious and/or ethical aspects of this key concept, focusing, respectively, on people's relation to God (in the poor in spirit) and on their relation to other people (in the meek). Dupont also presents a more complex account of the meaning of *anawim*, pointing to its semantic evolution in Hebrew. In particular, he presents evidence from the Dead Sea scrolls that suggests that in Jesus' times this word was used in Palestine in a new sense, focusing on a person's relations with other people rather than with God. For example, the Rule from Qumran gives an important place to *anawah* (the noun that corresponds to the adjective *anawim*) in the relations among the members of the community. In the context of the Rule, *anawah* appears to suggest something like a patient, sweet, and gentle attitude to others, including those who treat one badly.

It would appear, then, that Matthew added his beatitude of the *praeis* "meek" because he wanted to convey fully not only what *anawim* meant in Hebrew (and in the Jewish religious tradition) but also what Jesus meant when he used this word (or its Aramaic counterpart). And apparently Matthew—and the earlier Christian tradition on which he was relying—thought that Jesus wanted to convey more than the older meaning of the biblical *anawim*.

As emphasized by Jeremias (1971:114), Jesus expressed the bulk of his teaching in images and parables (more than other Jewish teachers), as if he was aware that the old words, with their old meanings, could not adequately express what he really wanted to say. The metaphor of old wineskins, unsuitable for new wine (Matt. 9:16–17), can be understood as applying, inter alia, to Jesus' "picture-language":

16. No one puts a piece of unshrunk cloth on to an old garment; for the patch pulls away from the garment, and the tear is made worse.

17. Nor do people put new wine into old wineskins, or else the wineskins break, the wine is spilled, and the wineskins are ruined. But they put new wine into new wineskins, and both are preserved.

The key biblical word *anawim*, serviceable and important as it was, was such an old garment or old wineskin, and it is remarkable that Matthew saw this fact so clearly.

If we follow Matthew, then, we will assume that Jesus wanted to declare as blessed yet another category of people, in addition to the weeping, the hungry (i.e., poor, needy), and the lowly and poor in spirit. In trying to understand what he may have meant and what the early Christian tradition understood him as having meant, we should look for clues not only in the use of *anawim* (and *anawah*) in Palestine in Jesus' times but also—and in fact, especially—in the New Testament itself. In particular, we should examine the evidence from the use of the word *praus* "meek" elsewhere in Matthew's Gospel and throughout the New

Testament. We should also examine the evidence from the images in which Jesus' teaching was frequently expressed.

Discussions of the meaning of the Greek word *praus* as such can also be misleading; the question is not how this word was used, for example, by Aristotle nor even how it was used in first-century secular Greek, where it was contrasted with *hupsēlokardia*, roughly, "pride, arrogance" (cf. Barclay [1975]1993:97), but what it was intended to mean in New Testament Greek. As I will show below, the gloss "humble, gentle," offered for this word, for example, in the *Concise Greek-English Dictionary of the New Testament* (Newman 1971), cannot be taken as an adequate representation of its meaning.

The best clue to the intended message of the beatitude of the *praeis* "meek" can be found in the pervasive New Testament image of a lamb. If Matthew's phrase *ptōchoi tō pneumati* "poor in spirit" was intended to convey, in part at least, something along the lines of "childlike," his word *praus* "meek" was intended to convey something like "lamblike." Translating this latter image into words (taking into account all the contextual clues), I would propose the following formula:

> some people don't want to do anything bad to anyone
> when other people do bad things to these people
> these people don't want to do anything bad to these other people
>   because of this

In support of this interpretation, I will point to the passage where Matthew's Jesus describes himself as "meek" (*praus*): "Take my yoke upon you and learn from me, for I am gentle [i.e., *praus* "meek"] and lowly of heart [*tapeinos* "humble"], and you will find rest for your souls" (11:29). The fact that the Matthean Jesus uses here (in Matthew's Greek version) the same word, *praus*, that is also used in the beatitude under discussion provides a vital clue to its interpretation. In particular, it suggests that *praus* cannot mean (for Matthew) "humble" because if it did there would be little point in conjoining *praus* with *tapeinos* "humble" (i.e., saying in effect, "humble and humble").

7. Exploring the image of the lamb and some related New Testament images

To explain what he means by *praus* "meek," Matthew offers Jesus as a model. He does not say explicitly what feature or features of Jesus' person he has in mind. Instead, he identifies him with the Servant of the Lord described by Isaiah (42:1–4), in a passage that he quotes in the very next chapter (12:18–21) and to which I will turn shortly.

As noted earlier, the identification of Jesus with Isaiah's Servant of the Lord is very prominent in both Matthew and Luke. In Matthew's Gospel, it is evident in the way Jesus replies to John the Baptist's question: "Are you the Coming One, or do we look for another?" (11:3–5). Jesus' reply echoes Isaiah (42:7, 61:1, and 35:5–6):

4. Jesus answered and said to them: 'Go and tell John the things
   which you hear and see:

5. The blind receive their sight and the lame walk; the lepers are
   cleansed and the deaf hear; the dead are raised up and the poor
   [i.e., the *anawim*] have the gospel preached to them.'

The identification with Isaiah's Servant of the Lord is presented even more explicitly in Luke's gospel (4:18-19), according to which Jesus started his ministry by reading aloud a long passage from Isaiah (42:61:1) in the synagogue in Nazareth:

18. 'The Spirit of the Lord is upon me, because he has anointed me to
    preach the gospel to the poor. . . .'

20. Then he closed the book, and gave it back to the attendant, and
    sat down.
    And the eyes of all who were in the synagogue were fixed on him.

21. And he began to say to them: 'Today this scripture is fulfilled in
    your hearing'.

Clearly, this key passage is echoed in the Beatitudes themselves. Thus, Matthew guides his readers' understanding of the new concept of "meekness" (*praotēs*) as follows: to be "meek" (*praus*) means to be like Jesus, and Jesus was like the figure described by Isaiah (42:1-4). Isaiah's description of this figure (adduced in Matt. 12:18-21) reads as follows:

1. Behold my servant, whom I uphold.
   My Elect One in whom my soul delights!
   I have put my Spirit upon him
   He will bring forth justice to the Gentiles.

2. He will not cry out, nor raise his voice.
   Nor cause his voice to be heard in the streets.

3. A bruised reed he will not break,
   And smoking flax he will not quench.

In essence, what these images add up to is the idea of "not wanting to do anything bad to anyone" and, in particular, "not wanting to do anything bad to other people when these other people do bad things to us." This is of course consistent with Isaiah's key image of the lamb, which is quite crucial here, given the fact that this image is used throughout the New Testament as a synonym for Jesus, summarizing in the most concise way possible Jesus' attitude to both God and people. Here is Isaiah's (53:7-9) lamb image:

7. He was oppressed and he was afflicted,
   Yet he opened not his mouth,
   He was led as a lamb to the slaughter,
   And as a sheep before its shearers is silent,
   So he opened not his mouth. . . .

9. . . . he had done no violence.

The images of the weak reed that the Servant of the Lord will not break and of the smoldering flax that he will not extinguish refute a possible mis-interpretation of the lamb image, that is, the idea that the Servant of the Lord doesn't want to do anything bad to anyone because he is weak and help-less like a lamb. In the light of these images, the Servant of the Lord doesn't want to do anything bad to anyone even if it would be extremely easy to do so.

Thus, the Servant of the Lord is someone who simply "doesn't want to do anything bad to anyone." The reference to not crying out and not raising his voice ("he will not cry out, nor raise his voice") is equally instructive. The Greek word *krauge*, translated in the King James Bible as "cry out," is actually glossed in the *Concise Greek-English Dictionary of the New Testament* as "clamour, angry shouting." This, too, suggests that the Servant of the Lord, identified in the Gospels with Jesus, unmistakably shows by his manner that he does not want to do anything bad to anyone. Since all the evangelists identify Jesus with Isaiah's "Servant of the Lord," who "had done no violence" (cf. Mark 15:28; Matt. 8:17, 12:18-21; Luke 4:18-19; John 12:38-41), they all suggest a message that can be formulated as follows:

> you know:
> a long time ago, someone (prophet Isaiah) said about someone:
>> "this person doesn't want to do anything bad to anyone
>> (this person is like a lamb)
>> everyone can see (know) this"
> Jesus is like this
> you can know because of this that Jesus is this person

Another important context in which the word *praus* "meek" is used in Matthew's Gospel (21:5) is a quotation from the prophet Zechariah (9:9), de-scribing the triumphant entry of the Messiah into Jerusalem:

> Rejoice greatly, O daughter of Zion!
> Shout, daughter of Jerusalem,
> Behold, your King is coming to you . . .
> Lowly [*praus*], and riding on a donkey,
> A colt, the foal of a donkey.

Here, the Greek *praus* is translated by the English "lowly." Sometimes the word *praus* in this passage is translated into English as "poor" or even as "afflicted," presumably because the use of a donkey rather than something grander could be seen as a symbol of poverty. But Matthew's use of *praus* reflects a different interpretation of the prophecy. For him, the King-Messiah, sitting on a donkey, is not coming as a conqueror supported by military power. Although the don-key could lend itself to several different interpretations, it is also consistent with the interpretation of manifestly not wanting to do anything bad to anyone. Dupont states that the donkey is a mount associated with the time of peace, in contrast to the horse, a mount associated with the time of war. This is precisely its meaning in the prophecy in Zachariah 9:9, which is continued in verse 10:

I will cut off the chariot from Ephraim,
And the horses from Jerusalem;
The battle-bow shall be cut off.
He shall speak peace to the nations.

The king who comes on a donkey is the opposite of a warrior king, and this is precisely what the adjective *praus* is meant to indicate here. (1973:III, 544)

The use of the word *praus* in the description of Jesus' entry into Jerusalem shows that the word doesn't really mean "gentle": entering the city on a donkey rather than at the head of an army doesn't show that the Messiah is gentle (has a gentle manner) but rather that he clearly does not rely on violence and military power ("he doesn't want to do anything bad to anyone").

Thus, we have made a number of connections that help us to understand who the "meek" (*praus*) in Matthew's beatitude are: a connection with the Matthean Jesus' self-description as "meek/gentle and lowly in heart"; with the prophet Isaiah's descriptions of the "meek," nonviolent, and lamblike Servant of the Lord; and with Matthew's version of the prophet Zachariah's description of the Messiah's nonthreatening entry into Jerusalem. Another crucial connection links the idea of "meekness" (*praotēs*) with Jesus' image of "turning the other cheek," which will be discussed in detail in chapter 3, section 7.

In explicating Jesus' use of *anawim* by means of *praeis* "meek," as well as *ptōchoi tō pneumati* "poor in spirit", Matthew was following in the footsteps of the translators of the Septuagint (a Greek rendering of the Hebrew Scriptures, undertaken in the third century B.C. for the benefit of hellenized Jews). Thus, in Psalm 37 (11) we find the celebrated line "the meek [*praeis*] shall inherit the earth," on which Matthew's beatitude of the meek is evidently modeled. This doesn't mean, however, that the intended sense of this beatitude can be simply assumed to be identical with the meaning of *praeis* in the Septuagint.

According to Gourgues (1995:53), in the Septuagint "the *praus* is the opposite of the aggressor and the violent. *Praotēs* (*douceur*) can be defined as an attitude of good will (*bienveillance*) and non-violence towards other people." Gourgues goes on to observe that in the New Testament epistles, in which this term occurs 11 times, it also refers to an attitude toward other people, and he concludes that this accords with the distinction that Matthew drew by apparently splitting Jesus' beatitude of the *anawim* into two, that of the "poor in spirit" (*ptōchoi tō pneumati*) and that of the "meek" (*praeis*): "The first one refers to a disposition of openness towards God, and the second, to an attitude of goodness (*bonté*) and respect towards other people" (p. 53).

Gourgues' (1995) observations are very helpful; I do not think, however, that the intended sense of the beatitude of the meek can be adequately articulated by complex and language-specific words like "goodness" (*bonté*), "respect" (*respect*), "gentleness" (*douceur*), or "good will" (*bienveillance*). I suggest the following:

The "meek" (*Matthew's* praeis)

  (a) some people don't want to do anything bad to anyone
  (b) when other people do bad things to these people
  (c) these people don't want to do anything bad to these other people
       because of this

Matthew clearly had in mind a further component: "(d) Jesus was like this."

8. Who are the persecuted?

As mentioned earlier, Luke's fourth beatitude, which corresponds to Matthew's ninth, is widely regarded as due, in its present form, to the evangelists. As Funk et al. (1993:290) remark, "It reflects conditions of the Christian community after persecution had set in." But they acknowledge that "some form of the fourth beatitude in Luke may go back to Jesus." It is also interesting to note that the beatitude of the hated and persecuted was reported, independently of Luke and Matthew, in the gospel of Thomas (Saying 68).

As noted by Dupont (1969:II, 284), the second part of the saying in Thomas' version is unintelligible and its phrasing is likely to be due to a textual error (a displacement of the negation in the Greek text). A clearer variant of Thomas' version of the saying can be found in the *Stromata* of the second-century Christian writer Clement of Alexandria (1962): "Blessed are those who are persecuted because of me, for they will have a place where they will not be persecuted."

Dupont (1969:II, 381) emphasizes the differences between, on the one hand, the first three beatitudes, which in his view form an indissoluble whole and proclaim "the royal justice exercised by God in favour of the disinherited," and on the other hand, the beatitude of the persecuted, which is focused on the person of Jesus and on the sufferings, as well as the happiness, of those who have chosen to follow him. He also notes the second-person phrasing of this beatitude in Matthew, contrasting with the third-person phrasing of the first three beatitudes. At the same time, however, Dupont makes a case for the authenticity of this beatitude in its original (not fully recoverable) form and draws attention to its numerous apparent echoes in other New Testament writings. For example (I Peter 4:12–14),

  12. Beloved, do not think it strange concerning the fiery trial which is
       to try you, as though some strange thing happened to you.
  13. but rejoice to the extent that you partake of Christ's sufferings, that
       when his glory is revealed, you may also be glad with exceeding joy.
  14. If you are reproached for the name of Christ, blessed are you, for
       the Spirit of glory and of God rests upon you.

Dupont (1969:II) notes that "the last beatitude has only a very superficial link with the preceding ones; by its content and the situation which it envisages, it relates to a life context very different and manifestly more recent. It can be fully explained only with reference to the experiences lived through by the primitive church" (pp. 283–284); and he comments:

It is only one step from this to saying that it is a literary creation of persecuted Christians, and many exegetes have gladly taken this step. Too quickly perhaps. Without denying the influence that the experience of the persecution probably exercised on the formulation of the beatitude it should be noted that the beatitude of the persecuted is closely related to a whole complex of utterances in the gospels whose later date of origin is not always clear. Thus, for example, Luke (12:8–9): "Also I say to you, whoever confesses me before people, him the Son of Man also will confess before the angels of God. But he who denies me before people will be denied before the angels of God." It is legitimate, therefore, to ask oneself whether, considered in the context of such sayings, the last beatitude does not have certain connections with the ministry of Jesus and whether one should not recognize in it an aspect of his message. (pp. 283–284)

Without going further into the issue of authenticity, I will sketch a (partial) explication of the beatitude of the persecuted. In doing so, I will take the phrasing that seems most likely to go back to the historical Jesus (i.e., "blessed are those who are persecuted because of me"):

(a) I know:
(b)   some people will want to hear my words
(c)   these people will say that my words are true
(d) I say to every one of these people:
(e)   other people will say bad things about you because of this
(f)   they will want to do bad things to you because of this

I have phrased this explication as a warning of coming persecutions, on the assumption that the present tense in the phrasing of the evangelists reflects the context in which they were writing their Gospels. As for the promise and the exhortation to joy, directed at those who are persecuted, I will come to it in the next section.

9. What does it mean to be blessed?

We have identified several categories of people whom Jesus appears to have singled out as blessed: the poor (*anawim*), the hungry, the weeping, the meek, and (possibly) the persecuted, without yet discussing the question of why and in what way they were blessed. Since the categories singled out in the Beatitudes overlap, many commentators believe that the variation in the phrasing has no deeper significance but rather provides clues to the interpretation of the Beatitudes as a whole. The following discussion makes the same assumption.

In the literature, the Beatitudes are often discussed in terms of "reversal" (see, e.g., Crosby 1995:60). This metaphor (not always recognized as such) is useful, but it needs to be interpreted: what exactly is being "reversed" here and in what way? When we leave metaphorical language aside, the idea that suggests itself is that the key notions involved are those of bad and good.

Meier (1980:39) speaks of "the eschatological paradox and reversal of values," stating that "the very people this world considers most miserable are the ones Jesus proclaims to be supremely happy." This is more helpful than a totally unspecified reference to reversal because the mention of "values" directs our attention to the key notions of good and bad. But even if we assume that the reversal should be understood in terms of these two key notions, there are still many interpretive options to choose from. For example, it could be proposed that the pair "weep" and "laugh" (or "mourn/grieve" and "be comforted") should be understood as (a), (b), or (c):

(a) to those to whom very bad things happen now
    many very good things will happen

(b) those who feel very bad things now
    will feel very good things

(c) for those to whom very bad things happen now
    God will do very good things

There are also other interpretive possibilities, including various combinations of the above.

The requirement that complex and metaphorical terms like *reversal* should be replaced with simple, clear, and nonmetaphorical words like *good* and *bad* forces us to choose between these different options; and if the scholars who agree on the term *reversal* try to explain in simple terms what they mean, they may find that in fact they understand it differently.

There is a Chinese parable whose meaning could also be loosely described in terms of a "reversal." In this parable (reproduced below) the idea is that after bad things have happened to a person, good things can (or will) happen to this person because of this. When we read this parable we can see that this is not the message of the Beatitudes:

Long, long ago, there was an old gentleman who bred the finest horses. One day his prize stallion was lost, leaving no trace. When news of this travelled round, in neighbourly fashion many of his friends called to sympathize with his grievous loss. To their great amazement, the old man appeared apparently unconcerned. On being asked the reason for his indifference, he said equivocally, "The loss of my stallion does not mean that some recompense shall not follow." Strangely, a few months later the stallion reappeared suddenly, accompanied by a beautiful mare, a worthy addition to the handsome stables. His friends now came to congratulate the old man on his good fortune. Again they found him less moved than might be expected. "This does not mean that it will not bring calamity in its wake," were his words. Meanwhile, his only son soon made the beautiful mare his favourite mount. One day, while riding it, he was thrown, and his leg was broken. He would never walk perfectly again. The old man took this quite cheerfully. "The accident, itself unfortunate, was at least not fatal. Perhaps some good will come out of it after all," were his words at this time. Another year passed, and his country was attacked by a neighbouring one. War was declared. In the general conscription, the old man's son was exempted because of his lame leg. Many were killed in the war. (Quoted in Bond 1992:4)

The message of the Chinese parable can be explicated as follows:

when something bad happens to me, it is good to think:
    "something good can happen to me because of this"
if I think like this, I will not feel something very bad
this will be good for me

when something good happens to me, it is good to think:
    "something bad can happen to me because of this"
if I think like this, I will not feel something very good at that time
this will be good for me
if I don't feel something very good at that time,
I will not feel something very bad afterwards

Comparing this parable with the Beatitudes can help us to recognize the religious and eschatological character of the latter. The Chinese parable is clearly about earthly reversals of fortune and offers a recipe for coping with them in this life. The Beatitudes, on the other hand, are concerned with what God will do for people—quite possibly after they have died (as in the case of the poor beggar in the parable of the rich man and Lazarus).

The idea that God's recompense for human suffering may come after a person's death is sometimes rejected by commentators who want to interpret Jesus' teaching as a sociopolitical manifesto and who focus on social justice as an urgent task for the here and now. But in fact one perspective need not exclude the other, and in the light of the Gospels as a whole there is no reason to think that Jesus' "good news" was meant to apply exclusively to *future* sufferers rather than to *all* sufferers, without restrictions.

In the parable of the rich man and Lazarus, the beggar had already died before he was comforted. Even if structural changes effected in all societies at some future stage were to radically improve the lot of all the Lazaruses of that time, from the point of view of the Gospels the Lazaruses of the past are hardly less important. Those who mock the idea of a "recompense" after death would seem to forget the victims of the Holocaust or the Gulag Archipelago, for whom the only conceivable compensation would have to come after death. For the survivors who have lost their families in such catastrophes, the "good news" must include a "recompense" for the dead, as well as for the living and the generations to come.

Moltmann (1996:107) has commented on this question as follows: "It is profoundly inhumane to push away the question about the life of the dead. . . . Nor is there any present happiness or any social progress towards a better future for humanity which could compensate for the injustice suffered by the dead." Moltmann refers in this context, in particular, to theological discussions in postwar Germany: "We perceived the long shadows of Auschwitz, and heard the cries of those who had been silenced." The question that dominated these discussions was this: "Are the murderers to triumph irrevocably over their victims? Can their death be their end?" Moltmann quotes in this connection a fellow theologian, Max Horkheimer: "Theology . . . is the hope . . . that injustice will not be the last word. . . . [It is] the expression of a longing, a longing that the murderer may not triumph over the innocent victim."

But the question of God's justice arises not only in connection with the evil perpetrated by other people but also with all kinds of "natural" disasters: "Think of the life of those who were not permitted to live, and were unable to live: the beloved child, dying at birth; the little boy run over by a car when he was four; the disabled brother who never lived consciously, and never knew his parents; . . . the throngs of children who die prematurely of hunger in Africa . . ." (Moltmann 1996:117). Noting that the lives of all such people "can take on considerable meaning for others," Moltmann asks, "But where will their own lives be completed, and how? Can they somewhere be healed, complemented, lived to the full and completed after they have died?" And he concludes,

> The idea that for these people their death is "the finish" would plunge the whole world into absurdity; for if their life has no meaning, has ours? . . . So I would think that eternal life gives the broken and the impaired and those whose lives have been destroyed space and time and strength to live the life which they were intended for and for which they were born. I think this . . . for the sake of justice which I believe is God's concern and his first option. (p. 118)

This conclusion (which carries an echo of Isaiah 65:17-26), is, I believe, entirely in the spirit of the Beatitudes. Those who "weep now" will be comforted, and this is a matter not only of God's mercy and compassion but also of God's justice. The promises of the Beatitudes are emphatic and categorical.

Another motif in Moltmann's thinking that helps illuminate the meaning of the Beatitudes is the concept of theopathy, that is, God's feelings and especially God's compassion for and involvement in human suffering (a notion with some antecedents in the writings of the early Fathers of the Church, especially Origen). Drawing on the ideas of the Spanish writer and philosopher Miguel Unamuno, Moltmann (1981:38) writes, "A God who cannot suffer cannot love either. A God who cannot love is a dead God. . . . The living God is the loving God. The loving God shows that he is a living God through his suffering." At this point Moltmann quotes Unamuno ([1912]1972:223) directly: "For to us in our suf-

them the highest respect as persons (Matt. 5.28). Women belonged to the inner circle of the disciples (Luke 8.1–3), and they are attested as the first witnesses of the resurrection (Luke 24.1–11; John 20:18). The fourth Gospel begins and ends with the testimony of a woman to the Christ (John 4.29, 20:18). (1993:807)

Achtemeier's (1993) point that Matthew 5:28 reflects the highest respect for women as persons is in my view well taken, and it is curious to see how often this verse has been misunderstood and its radicalism overlooked or denied. A particularly striking example of misinterpretation is provided by Haacker's (1977; quoted in Betz 1995:234) assertion that it is the woman's, not the man's, adultery that is in question. Haacker translates Matthew 5:28 as follows: "Whoever looks at a married woman in such a way that she becomes [or is meant to become] lustful has already seduced her to commit adultery." As Betz notes, while such a translation may be grammatically possible, it loses sight of the context, that is, of the deliberate antithesis presented by verses 27 and 28 ("you have heard . . . but I say to you . . ."), the first of which refers to a man's, not a woman's, adultery. But while Haacker's translation is highly implausible, its very bizarreness is instructive: Haacker, too, takes note of the fact that in Jesus' saying the woman is in focus. She is not in focus, however, as someone sinning but as someone sinned against.

But even apart from commentaries that believe verse 28 refers to a woman's, rather than a man's, adultery, the range of interpretations is still very broad. In fact, this verse belongs to one of the most controversial sayings attributed to Jesus by the evangelists. As Betz (1995:231) remarks, "Not surprisingly, this statement is one of the most thoroughly discussed in the entire SM [Sermon on the Mount]. . . . The question is: What does it mean?" Betz himself articulates the main point of Jesus' teaching as follows: "Clearly, the statement as a whole redefines the term 'adultery', shifting the emphasis from the breaking of the taboo to the psychological predisposition of the heart" (p. 231). And he elaborates, "Adultery is thus committed prior to the physical act, 'already', 'in the heart' (*en tē kardia*). The shift also suggests that if one is to prevent adultery, the course of action must begin in the heart, the center of human personality, where all decisions on moral and ethical behavior are made." But the claim that Jesus is shifting the emphasis from the physical act to the "psychological predisposition of the heart" does not do full justice to the novelty of Jesus' perspective. The Ten Commandments say not only "You shall not commit adultery" but also "You shall not covet your neighbor's wife . . . nor anything that is your neighbor's" (Exod. 20:14, 17; Deut. 5:18, 21); yet Jesus goes beyond that, too.

The Ten Commandments do not *equate* "coveting" thoughts with adultery, as they do not equate hatred with murder (and in fact neither hatred nor anger is included in the Decalogue). Jesus' greater emphasis on the psychological (in contrast to the physical) is therefore undeniable. In the case of "adultery in the heart," however, the shift is not only from the physical act to the heart but also from a perspective in which a woman is a man's possession to a perspective in which a woman is a person—a human being in her own right. In the perspective reflected in Exodus and Deuteronomy, coveting another man's wife is a wrong against that other man. In Jesus' perspective, on the other hand, coveting a woman may be a wrong against that woman. This last statement, however, requires clarification.

First of all, we must clarify what Jesus means by "woman" (in verse 28). Haacker (1977) translates the Greek word *gynē*, used here by Matthew, as "married woman," and on this point Betz (1995:233) concurs. But this cannot be right, given that both Mary Magdalene (Luke 8:2) and Martha (Luke 10:38)—both clearly unmarried women—are also referred to in the Gospels as *gynē*. Evidently, *gynē* means "woman" in general rather than "a married woman." Jesus was not speaking, therefore, about other men's wives but simply about women, and he was using the word *adultery* here, I would argue, as a metaphor, referring to a view that everybody agreed on: that adultery was something very bad. There is a way of looking at (and thinking about) a woman, he was saying, that is degrading to the woman; it is bad to look at (and think about) a woman in this way—as bad as to commit adultery. Meier (1980:52) rightly refers in this context to "the dignity of a woman," which can be violated in many different ways; clearly, according to Jesus, it can be violated by a degrading way of looking at her (or thinking about her).

If Jesus' use of *adultery* is taken literally rather than figuratively, confusion is bound to follow, as it does, I believe, in Guelich's (1982:193) commentary on Matthew 5:28. Guelich translates this verse as follows: "Every man who looks at another's wife as the object of his lust has already committed adultery personally with her in his heart." At the same time, he comments, "The Greek word *woman* (*gynē*) can refer to a married or single woman. Since adultery in Jesus' day and in the Old Testament always involved a married woman, *woman* (*gynē*) more precisely should read *another's wife*." But to translate Jesus' *gynē* (which by Guelich's own admission means "woman," not "married woman") as "another's wife" is to miss the radical novelty of Jesus' point of view.

The meaning of *gynē* is related to the question of whether Betz (1995) was right when he said that in Matthew 5:27-28 Jesus was redefining the concept of adultery. Jesus did challenge the traditional concept of adultery, but this is not what 5:27-28 is about: here, *adultery* is used not literally but figuratively. As we have seen earlier (section 3), in Israelite law, adultery was indeed restricted to actions that involved a married woman—that is (from the male lover's point of view), somebody else's wife. In 5:27-28, however, Jesus was not talking about men's attitude to other men's wives; rather, he was talking about men's attitudes to *women*. He didn't say, "Whoever looks at another man's wife to covet her . . ."; rather, he said, "whoever looks at a *woman* to covet her . . ." (As noted by Guelich 1982:198, the Greek word *epithymeō*, translated in the King James Version and New King James Version as "lust for," is the same word that the Septuagint uses in its rendering of the tenth commandment: "You shall not covet. . . .") This transition from "other men's wives" to "women" represents a fundamental shift in perspective. Thus, Jesus was not only putting a special emphasis on "the psychological predisposition of the heart" but also shifting the emphasis from a man's acts that involved *the wife of another man* to a man's acts (including mental acts) that involved *a woman*. Looking at a woman as if she were an object was wrong, not because this "object" (if married) belonged to another man but because a woman was not to be treated in this way in any case.

For Jesus, then, if a man is looking at a woman with the purpose of desiring her, this is not an infringement of another man's "rights" over this woman nor the potential first step toward such an infringement. I do not agree, therefore, with the commentator who says, with reference to Matthew 5:27–30, that "adultery, even mental adultery, is a kind of theft" (Carson 1994:49). The lust referred to by Jesus in verse 5:28 does not involve a man, a woman, and another man (this woman's husband) but a man and a woman's body (and by extension, a person and another person's body). Jesus objected to men thinking about women as "bodies" and (as discussed in section 3) put forward an ideal of marriage as a lifelong union between two persons—two persons who live together and become "like one person" (Mark 19:8).

On this point I find myself at odds with Pinchas Lapide when he comments on Matthew 5:27–28 as follows:

> Actually there is nothing new in this "reinforcement" of the Torah, for the sayings of Solomon, in the spirit of the tenth commandment, already warn "Let your heart not long for the beauty of your neighbour's wife, nor let her captivate you with her glance" (Prov. 6:24f). Here desire is denounced as mother of the deed and eye as gateway to sin. (1986:55)

I also think that the Fellows of the Jesus Seminar missed an important point when they decided that Matthew 5:27–28 was not sufficiently original to be credited to Jesus: "The injunction against lust occurs commonly in Israelite tradition ('You must not covet your neighbor's wife' appears as one of the ten commandments) and so this admonition did not originate with Jesus" (Funk et al. 1993:142). There is a difference between the Old Testament injunction not to covet another man's wife and Jesus' injunction not to look at any woman as (we would say now) a "sex object." Obviously, the idea of a "sex object" is a modern one, and it would be foolish and anachronistic to suggest that Jesus thought in such terms. But the distinction between a "person" and a "body" clearly did belong to his conceptual universe, as the next passage in the Sermon on the Mount (Matt. 5:29–30) makes clear (see section 5).

For these reasons, I think that Strecker partly misses the point of Jesus' saying when he notes that the Old Testament (Deut. 21:15ff) teaching against adultery "presupposes the patriarchal structure of society":

> This position is not challenged by Jesus: it is presupposed in the counter thesis when not just the deed, but also the longing look is considered as destructive of marriage. Even the man, says Jesus, who looks lustfully at the wife of another destroys her marriage. The man is thus addressed as the responsible perpetrator, even if the legal offence of adultery relates only to the wife. (1988:71)

It is to Strecker's credit, I think, that in his commentary he tries to preserve Jesus' focus on the wrong done by the male to the woman rather than to the woman's (hypothetical) husband. Unfortunately, he, too, takes the word *adultery* literally and is forced, therefore, to restrict Jesus's "woman" to "married woman." Jesus, however, was not speaking about a coveting look at another man's wife; rather, he was speaking about a degrading, "coveting" look at a woman *tout court*.

Other commentators cloud the picture by focusing on the contrast between action and intention instead of on the contrast between wronging another man (the injured husband) and wronging the woman (by a degrading attitude to her). For example, Viviano (1990:642), comparing Jesus' statement on "adultery in the heart" with the Old Testament pronouncement "whoever commits adultery shall be liable to judgement" (Deut. 5:18), comments, "Jesus will correct and deepen this view now. . . . [he] moves from the level of action to the level of lustful intention. . . . This teaches the truth of experience that where a person has seriously decided to commit a moral wrong the moral evil is already present, even though it can be increased by further action."

Few would disagree with the statement that if somebody has "seriously decided to commit a moral wrong, moral evil is already present," but Jesus is not talking here about somebody who has seriously decided to commit adultery. Rather, he is talking about someone who is "looking at a woman with the purpose of desiring her," that is, about a man, roughly speaking, who is reducing a woman to an object of his sexual desire. More precisely, then, and less metaphorically, the situation that Jesus is talking about is that of a man who is thinking about a woman along the following lines: "I want to do some things to this woman's body." Thinking about a woman like this (i.e., in terms of what one wants to do with her body) may or may not be combined with a serious decision to engage in sexual relations with her, but from Jesus' point of view such an attitude is wrong regardless.

The phrasing of the saying "Whoever looks at a woman to lust for her . . ." reflects a man's perspective, not a woman's. This perspective, which reflects the historical context of Jesus' teaching, will be preserved in the phrasing of the explication below. Jesus' key idea, however, is easily generalizable to all persons: not only is it bad if a man thinks, "I want to do something to this woman's body" but also, more generally, it is bad if a person thinks, "I want to do something to this person's body." In essence, then, a "coveting" sexual look, which is a metaphor for a "coveting" sexual thought, can be explicated along the following lines:

> (a) sometimes a man thinks about a woman like this:
>   "I want to do some things to this woman's body"
> (b) it is very bad if a man thinks about a woman like this
> (c) when a man thinks about a woman like this
>   this man is doing something bad to this woman

If the explication proposed here is essentially right, it can apply to any woman, not only another man's wife—and it can even apply to a man's own wife, if he thinks about her as a body "to do things to" rather than as a person. On this point, the following comment by F. F. Bruce is worth quoting:

> Pope John Paul II excited some comments in 1981 by saying that a man could commit adultery in this sense with his own wife. Emil Brunner, in fact, had said something to very much the same effect over forty years before. But there is nothing outrageous about such a suggestion. To treat any woman as a sex object, and not as a person in her own right, is sinful; all the more so, when that woman is one's own wife. (1995:53)

So far, I have focused mainly on the difference between Jesus' teaching about the "degrading look" (and degrading way of thinking about women) and the commandment not to covet one's neighbor's wife. But there is another motif in the Old Testament that is often confused in the literature with Jesus' teaching: a woman as a potential danger to man and to his purity. For example, Betz remarks that "the psychology of sin presented in SM/Matt. 5:27–28 was well-known in first-century Judaism," and to illustrate he quotes passages like the following:

> Sir. 26:9: A wife's harlotry shows in her lustful eyes, and she is known by her eyelids.
>
> Ps. Sol. 4.4–5: His eyes are on every woman indiscriminately . . . with his eyes he speaks to every woman of illicit affairs.
>
> T. Iss. 4.4: For he does not welcome the beauty of a woman lest he would pollute his mind with perversion. (Betz 1995:234)

But even if the "psychology of sin" that is reflected in such passages were indeed the same as Jesus', it seems hardly necessary to point out that Jesus' teaching goes beyond such folk psychology. The first two passages imply that a person can communicate sexual thoughts with one's eyes, and the third, that looking at a beautiful woman may lead to sexual desire. Surely, these are different ideas from those attributed to Jesus in verses 27 and 28 and articulated in the explication.

To suggest that Jesus' teaching about "adultery in the heart" is not really about adultery as such but rather about reducing women to sex objects is not to deny the close link between his teaching on "lust" and his teaching on marriage: obviously, the two are closely related. It is important to emphasize, however, just how radical and how novel Jesus' teaching on men's attitudes toward women was—especially given the widespread belief that his ideas on these matters were commonplace in his society.

Eduard Schweizer (1975:121) cites a number of Old Testament and "intertestamental" passages that can be compared with Matthew 5:27–28, noting that they say, "that even a look can be adulterous, and rabbis say the same thing. But it is always the woman who is considered a danger to the man—such a danger that the devout man will shut his eyes when a woman approaches, preferring to stumble rather than sin."

Even Job's (31:1-2) decision to make a pact with his eyes not to look at young women, which is sometimes cited as a parallel to Jesus' injunction on lust (see, e.g., Stott [1978]1992:78), does not really reflect the same point. Job, like the virtuous man in Betz's (1995) third quote, thought that looking at women (especially young and beautiful ones) could lead to sexual desire, and so he decided not to do so. Job's concern was not that he should not look at a woman lustfully (i.e., "with the purpose of desiring her"). Rather, he decided to avoid looking at young women altogether in order to preserve his own purity. He is not concerned with the question of how a man should or should not think about women. Jesus, on the other hand, did not suggest that men should avoid looking at women and was quite unusually free in his interaction with them. Rather, he suggested that men should not look at women in a way that is degrading to them as people.

Pinchas Lapide equates Jesus' teaching in Matthew 5:27-28 with that of his predecessors, for example, Ben Sirach:

> The Book of Wisdom of Jesus son of Sirach warns of the road to adultery: "Do not go wine-drinking with a married woman . . . lest your heart tend toward her and in your passion you sink into ruin (Sir. 9:9). This earlier Jesus [i.e., Ben Sirach] seems to go even a step further when he warns against all extramarital attraction: "Veil your eyes before a charming woman; look at no beauty that does not belong to you" (Sir. 9:8). . . . A goodly number of further examples could be cited. . . . One practical consequence is that in the orthodox sections of Jerusalem, New York, London and Paris, men and women study, work, and pray apart. . . . (1986:56)

In a way, Lapide is, of course, right: Jesus [of Nazareth] did not avoid being with women, talking with women, or looking at women; in this regard he was more "lax" than Ben Sirach. Clearly, his focus lay elsewhere: not on the possible dangers to his own purity but on fellowship with women as individual human beings, no less worthy of his attention and his love than men. He wanted to talk to them, and he was not afraid of them. Indeed, he showed them that special love and attention that he showed all second-class citizens—the outcasts, the disabled, the children, the "impure," the "sinners." And he wanted them to be treated with respect—as equals of men and as children of God.

5. If your right eye causes you to sin, pluck it out

Matthew 5:29-30

29. And if your right eye causes you to sin pluck it out and cast it from you; for it is more profitable for you that one of your members perish, than for your whole body to be cast into hell.
30. And if your right hand causes you to sin, cut it off and cast it from you; for it is more profitable for you that one of your members perish, than for your whole body to be cast into hell.

Matthew 18:8–9

8. And if your hand or foot causes you to sin, cut it off and cast it from you. It is better for you to enter into life lame or maimed, rather than having two hands or two feet, to be cast into the everlasting fire.
9. And if your eye causes you to sin, pluck it out and cast it from you. It is better for you to enter into life with one eye, rather than having two eyes, to be cast into hell fire.

Since Matthew placed these two parallel sayings immediately after those on adultery and lust (5:27–28) they are often interpreted as an elaboration of the same theme. For example, Carson (1994:48) discusses the eye and hand sayings in a section entitled "Adultery and Purity, 5:27–30," treating the four verses from 27 to 30 as one whole. Other commentators, however, note that these sayings also occur elsewhere (Matt. 18:8–9; Mark 9:43–47) and that there they are not combined with the sayings on lust and adultery but with those on a different topic—giving offence (cf., e.g., Strecker 1988:72).

Funk et al. (1993:142) have raised some doubts about the authenticity of the eye and hand sayings, suggesting that they may be due to the early church rather than to Jesus himself: "It is possible that these sayings are to be understood metaphorically to refer to the 'body' of the Christian community, which later had to develop regulations for excluding members who did not conform to patterns of accepted behavior. To lop off members appeared to be preferable to having a contaminated body."

Such an interpretation may have been used by some in the early church, but most commentators agree that the original sense was different and referred to an individual life. The shocking image of a person mutilating his or her own body and the "absurd" nature of the advice (if taken literally) bear the stamp of Jesus' own style (as even many scholars of the Jesus Seminar have recognised; cf. Funk et al. 1993:142, 215, 86), and the underlying message can be seen as being closely related to that conveyed elsewhere in Jesus' teaching. In particular, there is a close link between the injunction to chop off a part of one's body (so that the body as a whole can be saved) and the injunction to lose one's life (so that it can be saved) instead of trying to save it (in which case it can be lost) (cf. Matt. 16:25; Luke 17:33). Furthermore, Jesus' image of an eye or a hand that is making a person want to do bad things, which this person as a whole doesn't want to do, has a close corollary in Paul's (Rom. 7:13–25) image of his body parts, which are warring against his mind and making him sin against his will:

22. For I delight in the law of God according to the inward man.
23. But I see another law in my members, warring against the law of my mind, and bringing me into captivity to the law of sin which is in my members.

Similarly, in his letter to the Galatians (Gal. 5:15-26) Paul contrasts the "lust of the Spirit" with the "lust of the flesh" (vs. 16-17) and speaks of the need to "crucify the flesh with its passions and desires" (v. 24) to "live in the spirit" and to "inherit the Kingdom of God" (v. 21).

Jesus' dramatic metaphors (plucking out one's eye; cutting off one's right hand) suggest the need for a heroic struggle with one's own sinful impulses and desires, as does also Paul's image of "crucifying one's flesh." The need for such a heroic struggle implies that the desires that a person recognizes as sinful and contrary to his or her moral will can be extremely strong and, subjectively, overwhelming. I suggest that the psychological situation described by Paul and presupposed in Jesus's eye and hand sayings can be portrayed as follows:

The inner conflict

(a) sometimes a person thinks: "I don't want to do bad things"
(b) at the same time this person thinks about something:
(c)   "I want to do this
(d)   I know that if I do it it will be bad
(e)   I cannot not do it
(f)   because I very much want to do it"

Component (a) portrays a person's general desire not to sin. Components (c) and (d) portray a conflicting desire to do something that one recognizes as bad. Components (e) and (f) show that the "bad" desire in question is overwhelmingly strong.

As a way of dealing with such an inner conflict, Jesus offers the images of plucking out one's right eye and cutting off one's right hand. What do these images mean?

Many commentators believe that what is meant is that one should avoid occasions to sin. For example, Albright and Mann (1971:63) have commented: "This verse [29] is an application of the statement on adultery. Sights which are known to stimulate passion must be avoided—i.e., to quote the moral theologians, 'known occasions of sin are to be avoided'." Such an interpretation (which I followed in my earlier explication of this passage in Wierzbicka 1998) seems insufficient, however, because it does not fully account for the dramatic character of the images. On the face of it, there is no reason to assume that avoiding known occasions of sin has to be as painful and as traumatic as plucking out one's eye or cutting off one's hand.

To account for the dramatic character of these images we have to assume, I think, that Jesus was talking about strong desires that are already present in a person's heart, and which seem overwhelming and irresistible, and about external occasions of sin insofar as they are known to stimulate such desires. Accordingly, the first part of the explication [(a)-(f)] has been phrased in terms of an inner conflict, involving, on the one hand, a person's determination not to sin and, on the other hand, some seemingly overwhelming desire to do something that one recognizes as sinful. How (in the light of the eye and hand sayings) can such a conflict be resolved?

Barclay ([1975]1993:149) claims that "the outstanding example in history of the wrong way to deal with such thoughts and desires was that of the hermits and monks in the desert in the time of the early Church," and he asserts that there are only two ways to defeat forbidden thoughts and desires: "The first way is by Christian actions. . . . The second one is to fill the mind with good thoughts." Given the widely recognized spiritual fruits of the lives of the Desert Fathers and their significance as a fountain of spirituality for Western culture as a whole, one can't help being somewhat surprised at the tone in which Barclay dismisses their particular way of trying to live out Jesus' teaching. Undoubtedly, the Desert Fathers would have agreed that their way of life cannot be recommended as a general model. They would also have agreed on this: "The only way to defeat evil thoughts is to begin to think of something else" (p. 150); but this is precisely what they were doing: trying to think of something else. In contrast to Barclay's recommendation, however ("to fill the mind with good thoughts"), they were trying to think about God and the kingdom of God (in the spirit of Matt. 18:8).

In the light of Jesus' teaching as a whole, it seems clear that for Jesus "life" ("It is better for you to enter into life . . .") stands for God and, more precisely, for living with God, and that, correspondingly, "fire," or "everlasting fire," stands for its opposite, that is, for not being able to live with God. Accordingly, in his eye and hand sayings Jesus was urging people to defeat evil thoughts and desires by thinking about God and about the possibility of their own living with God. He recognized that giving up those evil thoughts and desires can be extremely painful and may require a heroic resolve (like cutting off one's hand), but he reminded his hearers that the pain of such an operation would be temporary, whereas life with God would be everlasting.

Needless to say, what Jesus was urging his addressees to do was not just to turn their thoughts toward God and living with God but also to follow these thoughts with actions (in my terms, "to do something because of this"). This brings us to the second part of the explication:

Resolution of the inner conflict

(g) when you think like this it will be good if you think about God
(h) it will be good if you think:
(i)   "if I do this I cannot live with God
(j)   I want to live with God
(k)   because of this I will not do it
(l)   I know: if I don't do it I can feel something very bad for
        some time
(m)   I will not feel like this for ever
(n)   if I can't live with God this will always be bad for me"
(o) it will be good if you do something because of this

As Stott ([1978]1992) put it, Jesus used the image of self-mutilation to convey the idea of voluntary and merciless mortification (comparable to Paul's "crucifixion of the flesh"), and as Stott recognizes, the injunctions in question apply to temptation in general and not exclusively to sexual temptation.

Strecker (1988:72) sees in the eye and hand sayings (especially in the Marcan version) "an unconditional demand for a decision" and "a radical either-or." The explication proposed here is consistent with such an interpretation, insofar as (i) and (j) jointly do represent a radical "either-or," whereas (k), (in its open contrast with (c), does present an unqualified decision. It is important, however, to be quite clear about what exactly the either-or in question consists in. In particular, I do not think that it is the either-or in Funk et al.'s (1993) statements "A crippled body would be preferred to the repeated ravages of temptation" (p. 142) and "A marred, incomplete body—abhorrent in society in Jesus' day—was to be preferred to the wanton submission to temptation" (p. 86). For why exactly should a crippled body be preferred to the "wanton submission to temptation"?

Funk et al. (1993:86) note that the eye and hand cluster of sayings "concerns the final judgment and eschatological salvation beyond the end of history" and see this as a reason to question its authenticity: "It is Mark's habit, but not Jesus', to speak of God's domain in apocalyptic terms." (Funk et al. claim that the apocalyptic motifs in the Gospel of Matthew must be due to Matthew (see, e.g., p. 157, and that the apocalyptic motifs in the gospel of Luke must be due to Luke (see, e.g., p. 332). Without some reference to salvation, however, it is hard to see why anyone should choose a crippled body, and the unpleasantness of temptation as such seems hardly a convincing reason for doing so. Funk et al.'s point that "Jesus . . . characteristically spoke of God's domain as something already present" is a valid one, but the idea of the kingdom of God as living with God can apply to both "now" and "forever"; moreover, giving in to a temptation that one recognizes as sinful can be understood as incompatible with "living with God *now*."

The ultimate either-or, then, with which Jesus confronted his hearers referred to either living with God or not living with God; and the specific either-or behind the eye and hand sayings is between, on the one hand, living with God, and, on the other hand, doing everything that one wants to do and can do (including things that one recognizes as bad). What it means for a person to live with God, in particular, what it means in terms of his or her attitude to other people, is spelled out in other sayings. But if we tried to edit out of Jesus' sayings the idea of "salvation" and of being able to live with God (in the kingdom of God), it would be hard to find cohesion in what remains. Funk et al. remark, "The possibility of a mutilated, incomplete body, which was abhorrent in Near Eastern cultures, is a radical thought and perhaps suits Jesus' posture towards the halt, lame and blind" (p. 215). But whereas the image of self-mutilation is shocking, what is radical is not the image but the idea: the idea that one has to choose between living with God and unconditionally following one's desires. Jesus' ideas about the halt, lame, and blind are, of course, also radical, but they are expressed elsewhere (e.g., in the Beatitudes). The either-or of the eye and hand sayings is related to Jesus' sayings that present a radical choice: a choice between the wide road (which leads to destruction) and the narrow road (which leads to life), between losing one's life and saving one's life, between heavenly treasures and earthly treasures, and between God and mammon. Each of these reflects a particular perspective on one and the same ultimate choice: to enter or not to enter the kingdom of God, to live with God or not to live with God.

6. Let your 'Yes' be 'Yes', and your 'No', 'No'

Matthew 5:33–37

33. (a) Again you have heard that it was said to those of old, 'You shall not swear falsely, (b) but shall perform your oaths to the Lord.'
34. (a) But I say to you, do not swear at all: (b) neither by heaven, for it is God's throne,
35. nor by the earth, for it is his footstool; nor by Jerusalem, for it is the City of the great King.
36. Nor shall you swear by your head, because you cannot make one hair white or black.
37. (a) But let your 'Yes' be 'Yes', and your 'No', 'No'.
    (b) For whatever is more than these is from the evil one.

The complex of sayings about oaths and swearing is one of the most controversial in the Sermon on the Mount. Commentators agree that Jesus did say something about these matters, but there is relatively little consensus about what exactly he said and even less about what he meant. Whatever consensus there is derives largely from the parallel in James' letter (5:12): "But above all, my brethren, do not swear, either by heaven or by earth or with any other oath. But let your 'Yes' be 'Yes', and your 'No', 'No', lest you should fall into judgement."

The references to swearing by heaven, earth, or Jerusalem correspond to casuistic debates among Jesus' contemporaries (some of whom argued that only swearing by God was truly binding); and the reference to swearing by one's own head may have its origin in Greek and Roman swearing practices (cf., e.g., Strecker 1988:79). Accordingly, many commentators regard verses 34b–36 "as an expansion from the Christian community" (Banks 1975:195). Furthermore, 33b can be seen as a mistranslation from Aramaic into Greek (see, e.g., Guelich 1982:212). Since the antithetical phrasing of all the sayings in Matthew 5:21–48 is a subject of controversy, it is not surprising that the authenticity of verse 33a has also been disputed by some commentators (e.g., by the scholars of the Jesus Seminar; see Funk et al. 1993:143). Thus, apart from the contrastive opening, it is undoubtedly verses 34a ("Do not swear at all") and 37a ("Let your 'Yes' be 'Yes', and your 'No', 'No'") that have the strongest claim to authenticity as Jesus' *ipsissima verba*, that is, in effect, those verses that correspond quite closely to the exhortation in James' letter (cf. Luz 1989:312). The ethical radicalism, absolute character, and trenchant simplicity of these verses are also widely recognized as characteristic of the historical Jesus. The fact that such an apparently radical and absolute prohibition of swearing was unique in the ancient world lends support to the view that it originates with Jesus rather than with the Christian community:

> The uniqueness of Jesus' prohibition of swearing becomes visible against its religious-historical background. In ancient Judaism as well as in Greece and in Hellenism, the oath is a largely uncontroversially practiced custom. On the other hand, the ancient literature advises against swearing irresponsibly. The Hellenistic Jew Philo in particular recommends discretion in appealing to God as witness to oaths. Yet an absolute prohibition against oaths is attested only for Jesus . . . it is in harmony with the other ethical radicalisms of Jesus. (Strecker 1988:78)

Similarly, Luz (1989:313–314) says, "Jesus in v. 34 articulates a fundamental and unrestricted . . . prohibition of oaths. Probably he was the first person to draw from the critical attitude toward oaths which are widespread in antiquity the consequence of a fundamental prohibition." Furthermore, "By prohibiting oaths in principle, he [Jesus] is more radical than his Jewish contemporaries" (p. 316). Luz refutes the claims that in another chapter (Matt. 23:16ff) the radical demand "do not swear at all" is weakened, and he rejects the suggestion that the repetitions "Yes, Yes" and "No, No" in Matthew 5:37 can be regarded as a new, "substitute" oath for those excluded in the preceding verses. Banks (1975:195), too, strongly emphasizes the uniqueness of Jesus' stand: "Warnings against the taking of oaths and vows lightly already occur throughout the OT [Old Testament] . . . and Apocrypha . . . and also the Rabbis . . . but these never lead to a prohibition of all oaths as we find in this saying of Jesus."

Such assessments are not inconsistent with citations like the following from the first-century Jewish philosopher Philo (Downing 1988:93): "Not swearing any oath is best, most life-enhancing, most in accord with our rational nature (Philo, de decalogo 84)" because, as Downing notes, there are also other passages "where oaths are permissible if still best avoided . . . and where they seem to be accepted without criticism." Downing also notes Epictetus' milder and qualified formulation: "If at all possible, refuse to take any oath at all. If you have to, make it as minimal as circumstances allow (Epictetus, Encheiridion 33.5)."

The apparent radicalism of the Matthean Jesus' words about oaths strongly contributes to the conviction of many readers of the Gospels, scholars and nonscholars alike, that they can hear in these words Jesus' own voice, his *ipsissima vox*. This widely shared conviction about who is speaking, however, does not carry over to the question of what the passage in question means. Yes, we hear an echo of Jesus' own voice here—but what exactly did he mean?

The paradox is that on the face of it, the meaning of the words attributed to Jesus seems crystal clear; and yet the early church appears to have ignored that seemingly clear meaning and didn't even make excuses for ignoring it, behaving as if it knew that in fact Jesus' words meant something different from what they seem to mean.

In what follows, I will discuss three different approaches to the interpretation of the passage about oaths—one that takes Jesus' words quite literally, one that focuses on various difficulties presented by the literal interpretation and seeks to restrict it in some ways, and one that takes a different tack altogether.

Tolstoy was convinced that Jesus' words "Do not swear at all" (i.e., never take an oath) mean just what they say (or seem to say) and forbid oaths altogether, including oaths of allegiance required by the state, the army, or the courts of law. Referring in particular to oaths of allegiance sworn on the Gospel, Tolstoy ([1884]1958:390) wrote indignantly that "he who takes the oath perhaps kisses the very passage which so clearly and definitely says, 'swear not at all'." In taking such a position, Tolstoy was following in the footsteps of the medieval Cathars and the modern Quakers, to whom oaths of any kind are unacceptable, without exception. In Russia, many adherents of this position, some no doubt influenced by Tolstoy, paid for their strict adherence to it with jail terms, having refused to take a military oath of allegiance.

Luz (1989:321) calls the followers of this approach "nonconformists," remarking that "it does not take much power of persuasion to demonstrate that the interpretation of the nonconformists comes closest to the text." At the same time, however, he notes that "the simple obedience of nonconformism does not solve all the hermeneutical problems of the text." In particular, Luz points out the problem of coherence across the Gospels and the New Testament as a whole. Thus, the same Matthew who in chapter 5 attributes to Jesus the categorical words "Do not swear at all" has Jesus in chapter 23 (16–22) discussing swearing in a way that appears to take the practice for granted and to imply that Jesus has no objections to it in principle. In this chapter, Jesus addresses the Pharisees in the following words:

16. Woe to you, blind guides, who say, 'Whoever swears by the temple, it is nothing; but whoever swears by the gold of the temple, he is obliged to perform it.'
17. Fools and blinds! For which is greater, the gold or the temple that sanctifies the gold?
18. And, 'Whoever swears by the altar, it is nothing: but whoever swears by the gift that is on it, he is obliged to perform it.'
19. Fools and blind! For which is greater, the gift or the altar that sanctifies the gift?
20. Therefore he who swears by the altar, swears by it and by all things on it.
21. He who swears by the temple swears by it and by him who dwells in it.
22. And he who swears by heaven, swears by the throne of God and by him who sits on it.

Later on in the same passage Jesus tells his opponents that they "strain out a gnat and swallow a camel":

23. Woe to you, scribes and Pharisees, hypocrites!
For you pay tithe of mint and anise and cummin, and have

> neglected the weightier matters of the law: justice and mercy and
> faith. . . .
> 24. Blind guides, who strain out a gnat and swallow a camel!

If verse 24 applies to the verses on swearing (16–22) and not only to the immediately preceding verse 23 (about paying the tithe and neglecting justice, mercy,
and faith), the question arises: where *is*, in Jesus' view, the "camel" (that is, the
central issue overlooked by the Pharisees) in the whole matter of oaths? Before
turning to this question, however, and consequently to the third approach to the
interpretation of the passage under discussion (Matt. 5:33–37), let us first note,
with Luz and others, that Paul in his letters repeatedly takes God as a witness
and guarantor of the truth of his words (cf. Rom. 1:9; 2 Cor. 1:23; Gal. 1:20;
Phil. 1:8; Thess. 2:4); for example, "I call God as witness against my soul, that
to spare you I came no more to Corinth" (2 Cor. 1:23). Luz (1989:321) comments on such a practice (calling on God as a witness) as follows: "Jesus' prohibition of oaths was already in early Christianity obeyed only in a limited way. . . .
In contrast to fasting (Mark 2:29), and the renunciation of force (Luke 22:35f),
the distinction from Jesus is never reflected upon."

This brings us to the third approach to the interpretation of Matthew 5:33–
37—one that shifts attention away from God as a witness to a different matter altogether, namely, to the question of truth. As Luz (1989:315) puts it (with reference
to the passage under discussion), "Jesus demands unrestricted truthfulness of the
human word." Jesus' whole apparent attack on oaths is (according to this approach)
a way of saying that one should always try to tell the truth and that it is generally
bad and contrary to God's will to willingly tell people things that are not true: "He
eliminates the distinction between words which have to be true and those which
do not have to be true. . . . The human being in the whole of everyday life is bound
to God without any limitation" (Schlatter 1933:181).

In a similar vein, Banks (1975:195) comments that "the prohibition against
swearing assert[s] the binding character of all words." Limbeck (1995:89) states
that the commandment not to swear "obliges people, in the name of God, to
truthfulness." Lambrecht (1985:104) sees in Matthew 5:33–37 "the appeal for
truthfulness, which is also clearly present in the letter of James"; and Strecker
(1988:80) offers a similar comment: "The closing verse [i.e., 5:37] is attested in
James 5:12 by a parallel that calls for unqualified, truthful speech. . . . Jesus'
prohibition of oaths is thus interpreted as the ethical demand for truthfulness."

But perhaps the clearest statement of this truth-oriented approach to the exegesis of 5:33–37 can be found in Jeremias's discussion of this passage, which
deserves to be quoted here at some length.

> Jesus issues a warning against the danger of untrue words. Matthew 5:33–
> 37 deals with this question. This passage has often been regarded in the
> past as giving instructions against swearing. People have asked whether it
> prohibits even an oath in a court of judgment. In fact, however, the sec-
> tion does not deal with the oath as a legal institution, but, as Matt. 5:37
> shows, with truthfulness. The examples Jesus gives here are therefore not

forms of oath used in court, but the oaths with which the oriental constantly underlines the truthfulness of his remarks in everyday speech (cf. 23:16–22). Jesus' disciples have no need of this expedient, because Jesus expects unconditional truth of them. . . . Each word is to be unconditionally reliable, without needing any confirmation through an appeal to God. For Jesus' disciples know that they will soon have to give account to God for every word that does not accord with truth (*rēma argon*, Matt. 12:36). God is the God of truth, and therefore the truth is a characteristic of his reign. (1971:220)

In support of this third approach I would note that Jesus (as we know him from his most indubitable sayings and deeds) was not interested in social practices per se; he was not interested in what Betz (1995) calls "cultic matters," that is, in questions of ritual, social and religious conventions, behavioral norms, and so on. For example, fasting and almsgiving were of interest to him only in their relation to the love of God and love of other people (see chapter 4, sections 2 and 5). Arguably, swearing as a social practice was also of little interest to Jesus; it was only of interest to him in its relation to a larger (moral and religious) issue of truth.

Jeremias (1971) says that the truth is characteristic of God's reign. The numerous passages in the New Testament that link God with truth warrant, I think, an even stronger statement: truth is, in some way, an aspect of God. It is common for Christian writers to say that "God is love," but in the light of the New Testament it would seem equally justified to say, in addition, that "God is truth." To live with God, one needs to love one's neighbor but also "to walk in truth" (a phrase I will return to shortly):

For I rejoiced greatly when brethren came and testified of the truth that is in you, just as you walk in the truth. (3 John 1:3-4)

And it is the Spirit who bears witness, because the Spirit is truth. (1 John 5:6)

In well-known passages in the Fourth Gospel, Jesus calls himself "the truth" ("I am the way, the truth, and the life"; John 14:6); he also speaks of "the Spirit of truth" and of truth that will make people free:

When he, the Spirit of truth, has come, he will guide you into all truth . . . and he will tell you things to come. (John 16:13)

If you abide in my word, you are my disciples indeed, and you shall know the truth, and the truth shall make you free. (John 8:31–32)

If truth is linked with God, untruth is, according to the Fourth Gospel, linked with the devil:

He [the devil] was a murderer from the beginning and does not stand in the truth, because there is no truth in him. When he speaks a lie, he speaks from his own resources, for he is a liar and the father of it [i.e., the father of lies]. (John 8:44)

Furthermore, throughout the Fourth Gospel, but also elsewhere in the New Testament, there are numerous references to God as light, and arguably, this light is a metaphor for truth:

> . . . God is light and in him is no darkness at all. If we say that we have fellowship with him, and walk in darkness, we lie and do not practise the truth. But if we walk in the light as he is in the light, we have fellowship with one another, and the blood of Jesus Christ his Son cleanses us from all sin. (1 John 1:5-7)

> . . . the light has come into the world, and people loved darkness rather than light, because their deeds were evil. For everyone practising evil hates the light and does not come to the light, lest his deeds should be exposed. But he who does the truth comes to the light, that his deeds may be clearly seen, that they have been done in God. (John 3:19-21)

> I am the light of the world. He who follows me shall not walk in darkness, but have the light of life. (John 8:12).

Obviously, the full meaning of the references to light and truth in the Fourth Gospel goes far beyond the injunction "let your 'Yes' be 'Yes', and your 'No', 'No'" in Matthew's Gospel (see, e.g., La Potterie 1977). There is, however, a common theme, too, which links truth with God and "living with God" with "living in truth," a common link hinted at by Paul. Paul refers to God, emphatically, as "God who cannot lie" (Ti. 1:2), and he urges his brethren to "stand . . . having girded your waist with truth" (Eph. 6:14), and "putting away lying, each one speak truth with his neighbour, for we are members of one another" (Eph. 4:25).

If God cannot lie, God's words are always true and cannot be not true. To live with God, one must "walk in the truth," that is, endeavor to say things that are true and not want to say things that are not true. This brings us to the following partial explication [components (b), (c), and (e) will be added below]:

(a) if God says something about something it is always something true

(d) it will be good if when you say something to other people about something you always want to say something true

The topic phrase "about something" is necessary to restrict the range of sayings described as true to those that *can* be either true or not true and to exclude, for example, commands and questions. The phrase "to other people" in (d) shows that what matters is not so much the truth of a person's statements (e.g., in a monologue) as truthfulness between people. From this point of view, Jesus' choice of examples is very revealing: "Yes" and "No" (in verse 37a) imply exchanges between people (questions and answers), and it is in such exchanges that, Jesus urges, one should try to be truthful.

I say "try to be truthful" rather than simply "be truthful" advisedly. I didn't phrase (d) as "it will be good if . . . you always say something true" because such a formulation would be unrealistic. Obviously, what Jesus' disciples can aim at is at best truthfulness in the sense of *wanting* to say the truth. It would also be misguided to say that it would be good if the disciples wanted all their words to be true: an emphasis on "all words" would obliterate any need for discernment and would introduce a new formalism. Jesus' own conduct showed clearly that he didn't mean that all words should always be true, in some literal sense, and that one's statements should never be formulated in a hyperbolic or paradoxical way, amplified with images, intensified with words like *truly* (cf. his own "amen, amen, I say to you . . ."), and so on. Rather, he meant that his disciples should want to speak the truth and revere truth as something sacred, and he didn't attempt to lay down any detailed instructions on how this general principle should be applied in practice.

In addition, Jesus seemed to be conveying two further messages: one concerning general human untruthfulness [(b) and (c) below] and one counseling his disciples to be so truthful (not in letter but in spirit) that no special assurances of truthfulness on their part would ever be needed (e). These two messages can be represented as follows:

(a) if God says something about something he always says something true

(b) people are not like this

(c) when people say something to other people about something they don't always say something true

(d) it will be good if when you say something to other people about something you always want to say something true

(e) it will be good if other people can know this about you

(f) it will be good if when you say something to other people about something other people can always know that you want to say something true

Thus, it is truth, anchored in God, that can be seen as the "camel" in the sayings on oaths and swearing, to be distinguished from the "gnat" of linguistic, sociocultural, and even religious conventions.

Pilate's question "What is truth?" resonates through the ages; and at the dawn of the second millennium it is asked with increasing frequency, vigor and self-confidence. The word "truth" is written, increasingly, in quotation marks, and the "craving for truth" is mocked as naive, sometimes even infantile. Books with titles like *Dismantling the Truth* (cf., e.g., Lawson and Appignanesi 1989) are multiplying, and it is increasingly held that, as philosopher Richard Rorty (1989:3) put it, "truth is made rather than found." To quote one recent writer,

To those who look at the rich material provided by history, and who are not intent on impoverishing it in order to please their lower instincts, their craving for intellectual security in the form of clarity, precision, "objectivity," "truth," it will become clear that there is only *one* principle that can be defended under *all* circumstances and in *all* stages of human development. It is the principle: *anything goes*. (Feyerabend 1995:199–200)

According to modern intellectual guru Jacques Derrida (1977), there is nothing outside of the text, *il n'y a pas de hors-texte*, a saying that is widely seen as the motto of his intellectual movement (cf. H. Smith [1958]1995:207). Another influential writer, Michel Foucault (1995:45), asks, "Why, in fact, are we attached to the truth? Why the truth rather than lies? Why the truth rather than myth? Why the truth rather than illusion?" Foucault's own answer to this question reflects his profound loss of faith in, and commitment to, truth: "And I think that, instead of trying to find out what truth, as opposed to error, is, it might be more interesting to take up the problem posed by Nietzsche: how is it that, in our societies, 'the truth' has been given this value, thus placing us absolutely under its thrall?" (p. 45).

But it is not just the postmodernists and their sympathisers who seem to have lost their belief in truth. Many others have also absorbed the modern (especially Anglo) ideology of respecting other people's opinions to the extent of giving up (or losing) the very distinction between opinion and truth. ("Since different people hold different opinions, there is no reason why my opinions should be better or more valid than anybody else's.") The position summed up in this (composite) quote often seems to those who hold it to be exceptionally liberal, broad-minded, and enlightened. They cherish "openness" so much that they lose sight of its value as "the initial attitude in the search for truth" (Kane 1994:18) and start to treat it as an absolute value in itself. People who hold this position are "the nihilists of the postmodern era . . . who see that there are many conflicting beliefs in the world, and conclude that, since these can't possibly *all* be true, they must all be phoney" (Anderson 1995:112). The concept of truth appears from this perspective as intellectually and morally suspect. Indeed, the rejection of truth as a meaningful concept and as a value is often celebrated as a sign of an intellectual and moral progress.

Foucault's (1995) question is worth pondering: why indeed should we be attached to the truth? The New Testament's answer to this question is that there is an inextricable link between truth and God. From this point of view, to abandon truth means to abandon God, and to abandon God means to abandon truth.[3] To live with God, one has to, according to the New Testament writers, "walk in the truth." There seems to be a growing consensus that this is what the sayings about swearing and oaths are, ultimately, all about.

Decades ago, Montefiore ([1930]1970:48) commented, "The section about oaths and swearing is not of any great interest to us today," adding that "it is clear from the Rabbinic literature that constant swearing, even in such lesser forms as 'by thy life', was a fault to which the Jewish people, right through the Rab-

binic period, were very liable. . . . The Rabbis are often reported to use oaths."
In a literal interpretation of the passage on oaths and swearing, one can probably agree with this comment today. If, however, we go beyond such a surface
reading and focus on the "camel," that is, on the nature and value of truth, we
must come, rather, to an opposite conclusion: at the end of the second millennium, the question of truth is extremely topical. Perhaps never before has the
value of truth been questioned to the extent to which it is being questioned now,
and perhaps never has there been a greater need to reflect on Pilate's question.

The meaning of Jesus' words about swearing may seem to be crystal clear and
any attempts to go beyond the obvious literal interpretation have often been met
with derision. To quote Tolstoy ([1884]1958) again, "He said: 'Swear not at all'.
That expression is as simple, clear, and indubitable as the words 'Judge not and
condemn not' and as little susceptible of misinterpretation, especially as it is added
in conclusion that anything demanded of you beyond *yes* or *no* comes from the
source of evil" (p. 389). According to Tolstoy, it is quite impossible to misinterpret these words, and yet "pseudo-Christian teachers with extraordinary affrontery
oblige people, on the Gospels themselves, to swear by the Gospels—that is to
say, oblige them to do what is contrary to the Gospels" (p. 390). Yet the same
Tolstoy who defended the literal interpretation so confidently (not to say aggres-
sively) freely admitted that in such an interpretation Jesus' words meant little to
him and perplexed him by their "insignificance":

> Side by side with rules the profundity and importance of which terrified
> and touched me, one suddenly found such an unnecessary, empty, easy
> rule, which was of no consequence to me or others. As it was, I swore
> neither by Jerusalem, nor by God, nor by anything else, and it cost me no
> effort to abstain: besides which it seemed to me that whether I swore or
> not could have no importance to anyone. (p. 387)

But the very "insignificance" of the sayings on swearing, so jarring in the
context of injunctions of "terrifying and touching profundity and importance,"
suggests that their literal interpretation misses their real point. Counsels such as
"If your right eye causes you to sin pluck it out" may also seem utterly clear and
impossible to misinterpret, and yet their real point lies not in the obvious surface meaning but in the hidden, deeper one, which can be reconstructed on the
basis of the New Testament as a whole. Similarly, for the sayings about swearing, the larger context of the Gospels and the early tradition allow us to articulate a more profound meaning—more consistent in depth and transcultural significance with the other sayings of the Sermon on the Mount.[4]

From this perspective, the intransigence of the apparent absolute prohibition
of swearing can be seen as a dramatic way of emphasizing the unconditional
demand for truthful speech. It is not the strict adherence to some arbitrary and
yet mysteriously binding prohibition of swearing that is an absolute value; rather,
truth is an absolute value that people should seek and should endeavour to live
by if they want to live with God.

The two totalitarian movements that cast their shadow on the twentieth century—nazism and communism—were both based on lies and on mendacious propaganda machines of gigantic proportions, yet even nazism and communism paid at least some lip service to the notion of truth. In the postmodern world, however, the notion itself has come increasingly under attack. To those who wish truth well in the third millennium, Jesus' teaching on this subject must remain an important intellectual and moral resource.

7. Turn the other cheek

Matthew 5:38–42

38. You have heard that it was said, 'An eye for an eye and a tooth for a tooth'.
39. (a) But I tell you not to resist an evil person. (b) But whoever slaps you on your right cheek, turn the other to him also.
40. If anyone wants to sue you and take away your tunic, let him have your cloak also.
41. And whoever compels you to go one mile, go with him two.
42. Give to him who asks you, and from him who wants to borrow from you do not turn away.

Nobody doubts that Jesus did say that one should "turn the other cheek." In fact, there is a strong consensus among scholars that at least three of these sayings—39b, 40, 41—if not all of them, go back to the historical Jesus. The scholars of the Jesus Seminar have color-coded four (39b, 40, 41, and 42a) as red (i.e., undoubtedly authentic) and one (42b) as pink (i.e., very probably authentic):

> Among the things Jesus almost certainly said is the trio of "case parodies" in Matt. 5:39–41, with parallels in Luke 6:29. . . . These cleverly worded aphorisms provide essential clues to what Jesus really said. And the consensus among Fellows of the Seminar was exceptionally high. . . . The aphorisms in 5:38–41 are case parodies with a very narrow range of application. In contrast, the aphorisms in 5:42 are universal injunctions: give to everyone who begs and lend to all who want to borrow—everywhere, at all times. These sayings are short and pithy, they cut against the social grain and they indulge in humour and paradox. The person who followed them literally would soon be destitute. It is inconceivable that the primitive Christian community would have made them up, and they appear not to have been part of the common lore of the time. (Funk et al. 1993:144–145)

The reason that the scholars of the Jesus Seminar have excluded the initial two sayings (38 and 39a) from their extremely strong support for the passage as a whole seems to lie in the lack of a close parallel for these sayings in Luke. Many other commentators, however, see no good reason to doubt that 38 and

39a also go back to the historical Jesus (see, e.g., Hübner 1973:231; Manson 1961:159; Percy 1953:148; Piper 1979), and here it will be useful to take these opening lines as a starting point. Whether or not the historical Jesus said the words in 38 and 39a as a prelude to 39b–42, those ideas did constitute his point of departure. His listeners were certainly aware of the doctrine of "an eye for an eye and a tooth for a tooth" (Exod. 21:24; Lev. 24:20; Deut. 19:21), so Jesus' own teaching on retaliation must have been perceived—and was intended to be perceived—against this background.

Furthermore, as pointed out by Piper (1979:204), "Should it be the case that the fifth antithesis [i.e., Matt. 5:38] is Mt's [Matthew's] construction . . . the following treatment should nevertheless show that it coincides essentially with Jesus' intention." In my framework, the same conclusion is reached by explicating the underlying meaning of verses 39b–42: the inner logic of their explication points to the meaning of 38 (the eye and tooth saying) as a presupposed starting point.

It should be noted, however, that verse 38 telescopes, as it were, two different, though related ideas: one is the idea of a law of retribution (to be carried out by the representatives of the "people"); the other, a private desire for retaliation and revenge. Since Jesus is addressing an individual person, enjoining him or her to implicitly "turn the other cheek," he is contrasting this injunction with a person's private desire to "pay the other person back." At the same time, however, he is pointing to the social law of "an eye for an eye" as the background of the ethic of retaliation and revenge. We could shape our explication, then, as follows (on the basis of verse 38):

(a) you have heard that a long time ago someone said to people:
(b) 　　"if someone does something bad to some people
(c) 　　it will not be bad if people do the same thing to this person
　　　　　because of this
(d) 　　it will be bad if they do more
(e) 　　God wants people not to do it"

Components (b), (c), and (d) jointly stand for what is usually referred to as *ius talionis* (or *lex talionis*), 'law of retribution'. The intention behind this law was to promote justice while preventing boundless revenge and violence. Thus, in sayings like "an eye for an eye" the Old Testament did not *encourage* retaliation but *allowed* it as a concession. This is why the phrasing of (c) is, so to speak, concessive: "it will not be bad if people do the same to this person because of this" rather than encouraging: "it will be good if you do the same to this person because of this," whereas the phrasing of (d) and (e) is categorical and proscriptive: "it will be bad if you do more," and "God wants people not to do it."

The reason for such a concession—which goes against the grain of the unconditional commandment "you shall not kill" and of the injunction "love your neighbor as yourself"—can only be understood as the same as that stated by Jesus in the context of his teaching on divorce: "because of the hardness of your hearts" (Matt. 19:8; Mark 10:5). To quote Piper (1979:90), "The *lex talionis* stipulates 'life for life' (Ex. 21:23; Dt. 19–21), but God's will is 'You shall not kill' (Ex. 20:13). . . . Due to man's hardness of heart he injures and kills his fellow man. God therefore gives by concession a legal regulation as a dam against the river of violence which flows from man's evil heart."

In contrast to this Old Testament teaching, the Matthean Jesus categorically rejects the *ius talionis*, the law of retribution, as being inconsistent with God's will, and he proclaims, once again, that "God wants something else." Here as elsewhere, however, his attention is on the individual (not "people" in general but "you"); and he focuses on private retaliation and revenge, illustrating his teaching on this matter with a series of examples, implying a whole series of escalating demands and expectations.

To begin with, the principle of retaliation is unconditionally rejected: "If someone does something bad to you, it will be bad if you think: "this person did something bad to me, I want to do something bad to this person because of this." This is followed by an exhortation to give up a desire to do bad things to one's offender or attacker altogether: "It will be bad if you think: I want to do something bad to this person because of this." On the contrary, "it will be good if you think: I don't want to do anything bad to this person because of this." Furthermore, the image of turning the other cheek suggests that one is determined not to retaliate in any way and that one's firm resolve not to do so is communicated to the other person: "It will be good if this person knows that you don't want to do anything bad to this person because of this."

This last component is extremely important for the proper understanding of the meaning of Jesus' image, which is often obscured by summary generalizations like *nonretaliation* or *rejection of revenge*. *Nonretaliation* is a term that can also be applied to the teachings of the Stoics and the Cynics, the sense of which was in fact quite different from that of Jesus. The difference can be appreciated if one compares Jesus' saying about a slap on the cheek with Epictetus' use of a similar image (cited in Downing 1988:24 as an apparent parallel to Jesus): "If you're inclined to be quick-tempered, practice putting up with being abused, refusing to get cross at insults. You'll be able to go on from that to taking a slap and saying to yourself, I seem to have got entangled with a statue" (Epictetus III:xii, 10).

Epictetus, too, recommends giving up revenge or even anger against one's attacker; he does not recommend, however, "turning the other cheek." He suggests that we can rise above the persons who have insulted us by refusing to take any notice of them (and the slap that they have given us) and by treating them like an object. Jesus' image, on the other hand, suggests that one should (wordlessly) address the attacker and enter into an I-thou relationship with him or her, conveying the message "I want you to know that I don't want to do anything bad to you because of this." The image of turning the other cheek implies not only the absence of any retaliation or revenge but also an active *message* of nonretaliation—a message that sets the scene for subsequent images, which take us further still. It is not enough not to repay the attacker in kind, it is not enough to give up retaliation altogether, and it is not enough to convey one's complete lack of bad intentions; one should go so far as to repay evil with good, that is, to do (or want to do) something good for the "evil person." For example, one should give this person one's coat in addition to the shirt taken by force or go with this person another mile (possibly carrying a burden for him or her as well): "(l) it will be good if you do (or want to do) something good for this person."

Having reached this point, one would have thought that the escalation must stop, but in fact it goes one step further—it expands from the offender to anyone at all (m): "it will be good if you want to do good things for all people" (see section 8). And this is what the sequence was leading to: God's will, as announced by Jesus, is that one should want to do good things for everyone as far as one can (n): "God wants you to do this."

This brings us to the theme of universal love, epitomized in the love of one's enemies, which is the subject of Matthew's next, and last, antithesis (Matt. 43-48). Before turning to this next great theme, however, we have to retrace our steps and look again at the individual sayings in Matthew 5:38-42 in the light of the wide-ranging controversy of which they are the subject. Our discussion can now be based on a full explication of 5:38-42:

Turn the other cheek

(a) you have heard that a long time ago someone said to people:
(b)   "if someone does something bad to some people
(c)   it will not be bad if people do the same to this person because of this
(d)   it will be bad if they do more
(e)   God wants people not to do this"
(f) I want to say something else to you now

(g) I say: God wants something else
(h)   if someone does something bad to you
(i)   it will be bad if you think:
(j)   "this person did something bad to me
(k)   I want to do something bad to this person because of this"
(l)   it will be good if you think:
(m)   "I don't want to do something bad to this person because of this"
(n)   I want this person to know this"
(o)   it will be good if you do (or want to do) something good for this person
(p)   it will be good if you want to do good things for all people
(q)   God wants you to want to do this

Piper (1979:150) states, "The command to love your enemy entails not defending yourself against physical attack (5:39) and giving away your clothing (5:40) and your money (5:42)." I don't think, however, that this is true. Jesus uses images like turning the other cheek or giving away one's shirt and cloak to convey a message that is not spelled out on the surface of his utterances. Elsewhere Piper himself makes the point that we need to "penetrate beneath the surface of Jesus' teaching" (p. 85), and I think that this applies also to the images of the "other cheek" and the "shirt and coat." Piper reconstructs the underlying message as "don't defend yourself against physical attack." But Jesus didn't say that, and I argue, didn't mean that.

The notion that one should never defend oneself and, by extension, never defend one's children (or other people) against a physical attack is so counter-intuitive (as ethical advice) that few commentators are prepared to embrace it wholeheartedly. Some, including Piper (1979), attribute this difficulty to some "tension" in Jesus' teaching. Piper asks, "Can or should a disciple of Jesus . . . ever render an eye for an eye or a tooth for a tooth?" and he answers, "We *cannot* say that a disciple of Jesus, who has come under the powers of the new age, cannot or should not at times act according to the lex talionis . . ." (pp. 96–97). Piper notes that many other commentators are similarly reluctant to rule out the principle of *lex talionis*, and that "because the Kingdom of God is now hidden, there are no ethical manifestos that everyone can consult to determine when to denounce retaliation and when to execute it (p. 98); . . . even at the most personal level the commands of non-resistance and acquiescence are not absolute prescriptions with no exceptions" (p. 99). The ambiguity and equivocality of these conclusions are in striking contrast to the clarity and decisiveness of the interpretations offered in the New Testament itself, notably in Paul's epistles: "repay no evil for evil" (Rom. 12:17); "see that no one renders evil for evil to anyone" (1 Thess. 5:15); "be tender-hearted . . . not returning evil for evil or reviling for reviling" (1 Pt. 3:9); "do not be overcome by evil, but overcome evil with good" (Rom. 12:21).

The Jewish scholar Pinchas Lapide (1986:134) remarks in this connection, "Versed in Hebrew, Paul, the apostle to the gentiles . . . presented the sense of Jesus' ethic better than did Matthew, and certainly earlier than any of the four evangelists." Lapide also draws attention to verse 18 in Paul's letter to the Romans, which directly follows his "Repay no evil for evil": "If possible, to the extent that it depends on you, live in peace with everyone" (Rom. 12:18), and he points out that "the first two phrases are unambiguously intended as much against passive surrender as against keeping oneself out of unavoidable conflict."

If Jesus' teaching on turning the other cheek is rethought in universal human concepts and restated in simple and universal words, the simplicity and clarity of Paul's interpretation can be maintained, and perfectly clear and universally valid ethical advice can be articulated, with no need for exceptions, reservations, and equivocations. The answer to the question of whether the follower of Jesus can or should ever render an eye for an eye or a tooth for tooth can be a simple and clear no, without any implication that they should never defend themselves, their children, or others against a physical attack.

What applies to Piper (1979) applies also to others. For example, Schottroff (1975) writes, "If one takes his starting point from Matt. 5:44f and an interpretation of enemy love as an active love, then the demand to put up with injustice becomes a riddle. Abstaining from resistance, i.e. a total submission to unjust demands of one's enemy, cannot be called 'love'" (p. 219); "Why is resistance forbidden and next to it active enemy love is commanded? What is the act of love supposed to be when one simply offers the enemy the other cheek?" (p. 203). Schottroff tries to solve the dilemma by giving Jesus' injunction a sociopolitical interpretation because in her view, "on the level of a timelessly valid ethic the riddle is unsolvable" (p. 19).

But Jesus did not urge a total submission to the unjust demands of one's enemy. What he did urge is that "one should not do bad things to other people because these people have done something bad to me." Consider again a hypothetical attack on one's children. What Jesus says is that one should not deliberately do bad things to the attackers because they have done something bad to one's children, but not that one should submit to the attack and refrain from resisting the attackers. There is a world of difference between "wanting to do something *so that* these people can't do bad things to my children" and "wanting to do something bad to the attackers *because* they have done something bad to my children"; between wanting to stop the attackers and wanting to pay them back. If the alternative cognitive scenarios are represented in this way, there is no need to restrict Jesus' teaching to the sociopolitical arena and to declare it irrelevant to private life. Contrary to Schottroff (1975), the riddle *is* solvable "on the level of a timelessly valid ethic"—an ethic that can be understood to apply both to the public and private spheres.

The doctrine of nonresistance is one of the most misunderstood in the entire New Testament. These misunderstandings are, to a considerable extent, related to the language used in presenting it, in particular, to the use of complex words like *revenge, retaliation, compliance, submission,* or *nonviolence.* Given how far-reaching, even disastrous, the consequences of these misunderstandings can be, I believe that the matter merits some further discussion and illustrations. Consider, for example, the following passage:

> Against the legal commandment of the Torah, the Preacher on the mount places his own law: not retaliation but renunciation of revenge, not struggle with evil but submission to hostile power! . . . The admonition to renounce resistance may thus not be restricted to "resistance to judgment." The Christian community is, rather, to take its Lord's demand seriously by not confronting a hostile neighbour with violence. . . . The one struck is supposed to offer the other cheek also, as proof of unreserved compliance that seeks neither to preserve one's own honour nor to maintain one's own position of power. (Strecker 1988:82–83)

In this passage, the author uses—as if for elegant variation—a number of phrases that are all supposed to paraphrase Jesus' teaching but which in fact differ vastly in meaning: "renunciation of revenge," "submission to hostile power," "unreserved compliance," "to renounce resistance," "not confronting . . . with violence," and "not retaliation but. . . ." But since these phrases do not mean the same thing, they cannot all accurately represent the meaning of Jesus' image. Some of them are, in fact, so wide of the mark as to appear fanciful; for example, nothing in Jesus' words about turning the other cheek gives any basis whatsoever for an interpretation in terms of "submission" or "unreserved compliance." The expression "unreserved compliance" implies willingness to do what someone wants us to do. One could say that Jesus preached and taught by his own example unreserved compliance with God's will, but not with the will of any human individual or group. He also preached and taught by his own example submission to God's will, but certainly not "submission to hostile power."

To take another example, consider J. J. Bruce's ([1983]1995:71) question: "Can the Christian magistrate practise non-retaliation towards the criminal who comes up before him for judgement? Could the Christian king practise non-retaliation towards a neighboring king who declared war against him?" Bruce answers rather sheepishly: "No single answer can claim to be the truly Christian one," puzzling at the same time at the fact that St. Paul, "who repeats and underlines Jesus' teaching of non-retaliation, regards retaliation as part of the duty of the civil ruler." But, in fact, the Christian magistrate does fit in the conceptual scenario implied by Jesus' image: "if someone does something bad to you, it will be good if you don't want to do something bad to this person because of this." It would be totally inappropriate for a magistrate to think, "This criminal did something bad to me; because of this, I want to do something bad to this criminal" or even to think, "This criminal did something bad to some people; because of this I want to do something bad to this criminal."

It could be argued, of course, that the magistrate represents the society and that it is the society that, so to speak, says to the criminal, through the magistrate's mouth, "You did something bad to me; because of this, I want to do something bad to you." But clearly, this would be inappropriate, too: it would be wrong for the society to be guided by something like a spirit of revenge and retaliation toward the criminal. Rather, the presumed conceptual scenario for criminal justice reads,

> very many people live in this place
> this person did something bad to one (some) of these people
>
> these people don't want things like this to happen in this place
> because of this when someone does something like this
> they want some people to do something to this person
>
> they think that it is good if this happens
> because they don't want anyone to do things like this to anyone

By sentencing a criminal, the society is not retaliating against the criminal but rather is seeking to protect its citizens against crime.

Similar arguments apply to cases of personal or collective self-defense, which some commentators see as the theme of Jesus' sayings under discussion. For example, Schottroff (1978:25) states, "In Matt. 5:39–42 . . . we have several illustrations of the acceptance of injustice without resorting to self-defense." As I see it, however, such a summary of Jesus' teaching is misleading and very dangerous. Jesus did not teach "not resorting to self-defense." For example, if a criminal tries to kill somebody's child, and the child's mother strikes back to protect the child, she is enacting a mental scenario quite different from that envisaged, and discouraged, in Jesus' saying about turning the other cheek. This mother's mental scenario can be represented as follows:

this person did something
because of this I know that this person wants to do something bad to
    me (or: to my child)
if this person does this, something very bad will happen to me (or: to
    my child)
I don't want this to happen
because of this I have to do something to this person
I want to do it

This is quite different from the non-Christian mental scenario discouraged by the "other cheek": "this person did something bad to me; because of this I want to do something bad to this person."

First, in self-defense, the intention is to do something to the other person, not necessarily something bad (e.g., to knock a weapon out of the attacker's hands), whereas in retaliation the intention is to do something bad to this person. Second, in self-defense, the intention is to prevent this person from doing something bad to me, whereas in retaliation, the intention is to pay back (i.e., to do something bad to this person). Third, in retaliation, the hypothetical triggering thought is "this person did something bad to me," whereas in self-defense, it is, rather, "I know that this person wants to do something bad to me." Fourth, in self-defense, there is an assumption that something bad may happen to me because of this, whereas in retaliation this assumption is lacking. Fifth, in self-defense—in contrast to retaliation—there is a sense that one has to do something: one wants to do it only because one thinks that one has to do it.

All in all, the two scenarios are quite different, and it is a tragic mistake to confuse them, to assume that by using the "other cheek" image Jesus condemned not only revenge but also self-defense, defense of other people, defense of one's country, resistance to occupying forces, or protection of one's society from criminals. When all the different conceptual scenarios are sorted out, it becomes clear that this is not what the fifth antithesis is all about.

To quote again the Jewish scholar Pinchas Lapide,

> On July 20, 1944, Dietrich Bonhoeffer was among those men and women who attempted to contain violence and defend countless "neighbours" from certain mass murder by forcibly removing Hitler. In their case nonviolence would have been an act of cowardice, of selfishness, of an indifferent abandonment of innocent fellow humans—in crass contradiction to the spirit of the entire Instruction on the Mount. (1986:133)

What applies to the defense of people on a large scale in war, terror, genocide, and so on, applies also, according to Lapide, in the personal sphere as he notes, "a total repudiation of resistance means that a husband whose wife is raped before

his eyes or whose children are killed in his presence should look on idly without even lifting a finger."

I agree entirely with the spirit of Lapide's (1986) remark. Jesus did not say
that "if someone kills one of your children, offer them another"; he only said
that "if someone slaps you on your right cheek, turn the other to him also." The
image of turning the other cheek is a metaphor, and the misunderstandings that
discussions of it have occasioned underscore the need for a methodological framework within which the meaning of metaphors can be fruitfully explored and
elucidated. The use of complex and unanalyzed labels such as *nonresistance, submission, compliance,* and *nonviolence* obscures the meaning of the injunction to
turn the other cheek and makes it impossible to distinguish it from a hypothetical (inhuman and ungodly) injunction to offer to the attacker another child.
Within the framework proposed here, such seemingly analogous injunctions can
be distinguished and the meaning of Jesus' injunction clearly identified, and explained, in essence, as follows:

Jesus did NOT teach:

if someone wants to do something bad to you
it will be bad if you think: "I want to do something because of this"
it will be good if you think: "I don't want to do anything because of
    this"

Jesus DID teach:

if someone does something bad to you
it will be bad if you think:
    "this person did something bad to me
    I want to do something bad to this person because of this"
it will be good if you think:
    I don't want to do anything bad to this person
    I want this person to know this"
it will be good if you do something because of this

In Robert Frost's poem "A Masque of Mercy," one of the characters, Keeper,
characterizes the Sermon on the Mount as follows:

> A beautiful impossibility . . .
> An irresistible impossibility.
> A lofty beauty no one can live up to.
> Yet no one turn from trying to live up to.

Arguably, the seeming "impossibility" of the Sermon on the Mount comes from
the difficulties that face both ordinary readers and commentators in trying to grasp
its meaning. The blurring of the distinction between defense and revenge, magnified in modern times by the use of well-meaning but potentially misleading
terms like *nonresistance* and *nonviolence,* is a good case in point. The fact that in

Frost's words, "no one [can] turn from trying to live up to [the Sermon on the Mount]" reflects the readers' intuition that Jesus' sayings collected in this text were not *meant* to be impossible to live up to. This intuition demands a continued search for interpretations that allow the Sermon on the Mount to be seen as relevant on earth and not only in heaven.

8. *Love your enemies*

Matthew 5:43–48 (Luke 6:27–36)

43. You have heard that it was said, 'You shall love your neighbor and hate your enemy'.
44. But I say to you, love your enemies, bless those who curse you, do good to those who hate you, and pray for those who spitefully use you and persecute you,
45. that you may be sons of your Father in heaven; for he makes his sun rise on the evil and on the good, and sends rain on the just and the unjust.
46. For if you love those who love you, what reward have you? Do not even the tax collectors do the same?
47. And if you greet your brethren only, what do you do more than others? Do not even the tax collectors do so?
48. Therefore you shall be perfect, just as your Father in heaven is perfect.

The injunction to "love your enemies" is generally regarded as the heart of Jesus' teaching, and nobody doubts either its authenticity or its centrality. To quote Piper's (1979:1) book, which has these words as its title, "'Love your enemies!' is one of the few sayings of Jesus the authenticity of which is not seriously questioned by anyone. Nor is it disputed that this command is crucial in understanding what the earthly Jesus wanted to accomplish." In this case, even the scholars of the ultra-cautious Jesus Seminar concur:

> The Jesus Seminar ranked the admonition to love enemies the third highest among sayings that almost certainly originated with Jesus (the other two included the complex about turning the other cheek, Matt. 5:39–42, and the cluster of beatitudes, Luke 6:20–22). The injunction to love enemies is a memorable aphorism because it cuts against the social grain and constitutes a paradox: those who love their enemies have no enemies. (Funk et al. 1993:147)

Given the consensus about the authenticity and importance of the saying itself, it is interesting that the verse that introduces it has generated an enormous amount of controversy. Unlike the injunction to love one's enemies, the introductory verse 43 does not have its counterpart in Luke's version of the same cluster of sayings. Mainly on this basis, the scholars of the Jesus Seminar have voted verse 43 to be black (as Matthew's addition), in contrast to the core of 44, which they have voted red (as indisputably Jesus' own).

Many other scholars, however, believe the bulk of verse 43 to be authentic, with only the words "and hate your enemy" being a Matthean interpolation. Their reason for questioning this last phrase is that whereas "You shall love your neighbor" is an obvious (if shortened) quotation ("Love your neighbor as yourself"; Lev. 19:18), the phrase "and hate your enemy" does not occur anywhere in the Old Testament. The Jewish scholar Montefiore ([1927]1968:80) says, "It is not only possible but even probable that Jesus never declared that it had been said that 'thou shalt hate thine enemy'. The words may be an interpolation . . . whether all the antitheses, or this particular antithesis, or the mere addition of the 'hate' clause, be unauthentic, one may feel fairly sure that Jesus never said these unfortunate words."

Without entering into the controversy about verse 43, I will try to explicate its underlying meaning, if only to show how Matthew saw Jesus' intentions. Regardless of how much of verse 43 was actually said by Jesus, it seems clear that the commandment to love one's neighbor in Leviticus 19:18 (and its subsequent interpretations) was assumed by Jesus as background to his own teaching. As the Jewish scholar Samuel Tobias Lachs (1987:107) put it (in accordance with the prevailing view), the verse "You shall love your neighbor" (Lev. 19:18) "does not have a universal meaning. Note that it is parallel to *the sons of your people*. ["You shall not take vengeance . . . against the children of your people, but you shall love your neighbour as yourself."] Furthermore, the same chapter has the command that you shall love the stranger ["who dwells among you"; v. 34]."

Some Jewish commentators, including Montefiore ([1927]1968), have argued that an interpretation that the love commandment in Leviticus limits it in such a way may be less than fair to the spirit of the Old Testament, to which the theme of universalism is not entirely alien. Montefiore (p. 85) notes in this connection that there is "a measure of *implicit* universalism in many sayings of Hillel and of other rabbis," and he quotes Hillel's saying, "Love peace and pursue peace; love thy fellow-creatures and draw them near to the Torah," commenting, "This is quite as universalist a saying as anything in the Synoptics." Without disputing these observations, I would note that the Matthean Jesus was, of course, not opposing Hillel or rejecting the love commandment in Leviticus. As the explication below suggests, he was rather opposing a certain interpretation of God's will ("some people say"). That such an interpretation was current in exegetic practice in Jesus' times can hardly be doubted (cf., e.g., Lachs 1987:107). I will start, therefore, with the following (partial) explication:

Matthew 5:43

    (a) you have all heard that some people say:
    (b)   "some people are people like you
    (c)   it will be good if you want to do good things for these people
    (d)   God wants this
    (e)   some other people are not people like you

(f)   you don't have to want to do good things for these people
(g)   if some of these people want to do bad things to you
(h)   it will not be bad if you want to do the same to these people"

Components (b), (c), (e), and (f) limit the commandment to love one's neighbor to fellow Israelites (in a broad sense, including "fellow members of Israel's cultic community,"; cf. Meier 1980:54), whereas (g) and (h) correspond to the phrase "hate your enemy," interpreting it in the sense that "you can hate your enemies if these enemies are not fellow Israelites." The position outlined in (g) and (h)—you may hate your enemies if they are not fellow Israelites—does not correspond to any one quote from the Old Testament, and it may well have been conjured up either by Matthew or by Jesus for rhetorical and expository purposes.

Verse 43 telescopes two contrasts—neighbors versus aliens and friends versus enemies—into one: neighbor versus enemy. This suggests that verse 43 was indeed intended to present a simplified position with which to contrast one's own rather than to "quote" anyone in particular. The fact that the love commandment from Leviticus has not been adduced in full (not "as yourself") supports this interpretation.

The explication of the "hate" phrase proposed here has been worded in a concessive rather than imperative fashion: "you don't have to want to do good things" rather than "you should want to do bad things" in (f) and "it will not be bad" rather than "it will be good in (h) (see the discussion in section 2). Both Jesus and Matthew were no doubt well aware that the Old Testament did not urge Israelites to hate their enemies and that no such recommendation was even implicit in Leviticus. Klassen (1984:43) notes that "the love commandment as Jesus understood it was in fact widely held in Judaism and that understanding was firmly rooted in the Hebrew scriptures." But the formulation of the love commandment in Leviticus was open to the interpretation that one doesn't have to love everyone and that it may be acceptable to hate *some* people (the non-neighbors; cf. Meier 1980:54a). Even the Psalms include passages that express hate for one's enemies or for "the wicked." For example,

> Do not take me away with the wicked
> And with the workers of iniquity,
> Who speak peace to their neighbours,
> But evil is in their heart,
> Give to them according to the wickedness of their endeavours
> Give to them according to the work of their hands.
> Render to them what they deserve. (Ps. 28:3–4)

> But those who seek my life
> Shall go into the lower parts of the earth.
> They shall fall by the sword.
> They shall be a portion for jackals. (Ps. 63:9–10)

In the deuterocanonical/apocryphal books, such a hatred for at least some people was sometimes explicitly allowed in the case of the "ungodly," as in the

Wisdom of Sirach (12:1–7): "Do good to godly man, and you will be repaid—if not by him, certainly by the Most High. . . . Give to the godly man, but do not help the sinner. . . . For the Most High also hates the ungodly." Similarly, the Dead Sea Scrolls show that hatred for some people ("all the sons of darkness," that is, enemies of the Essenes' community) was commanded by the "Manual of Discipline" from Qumran (see Piper 1979).

Lachs' (1987:108) remarks that "the only passage which condones hatred of enemies in Rabbinic literature" is the following: "What is meant by 'and the hatred of mankind'? . . . This teaches that no man should think of saying, 'Love the Sages but hate the disciples', or 'Love the disciples but hate the amha-arez [poor people]'. On the contrary, love all these, but hate the sectarians, apostates, and the informers." Lachs goes on to raise the following interesting question: "Is it possible that 'and hate your enemies' was added by a Judeo-Christian aware of this attitude and some similar teaching directed against the new sect?" Be that as it may, clearly some voices in Jesus' world (however marginal) were saying that it was compatible with God's will to hate *some* people; and these voices Jesus was at pains to rebut. Matthew seems justified, therefore, in interpreting Jesus' words in a contrastive way.

As Funk et al. (1993:147) rightly suggest, Jesus was not only urging his disciples to love their enemies but also, in fact, abolishing the very concept of "enemy": "those who love their enemies have no enemies." Banks (1975:200) has expressed a similar idea, arguing that the sense of Matthew 5:43 "is not 'love your neighbor' and 'love your enemy also', for in the command 'love your enemies' the distinction between enemy and neighbor is completely annulled." In this interpretation, one is not to divide people into "neighbors" and "not-neighbors" but to treat them all, essentially, in the same way (as "neighbors")—just as God treats all people in the same way (as his "children").

In accordance with this interpretation, I will formulate the second part of the explication as follows:

> (i) I want to say something else to you all now
> (j) I say:
> (k)   God wants more
> (l)   God wants you to think about all people:
>   "these people are people like me"
> (m)   because of this it will be good if you want to do good things
>   for all other people
> (n)   God wants this

As the last component suggests, the idea is not to want to do good things for all people, "neighbors" and enemies alike, but rather to see all people as "neighbors"—in the original Levitican sense of "people like me" but with the *scope* of this concept extended from fellow Jews to fellow human beings. Such an analysis can be justified, I think, on several grounds.

First, there is the Leviticus passage in the background, as well as other familiar Old Testament passages, implying a division between Israelites and non-

Israelites. Even though Jesus was not quoting this passage fully or identifying it by name, he was speaking in dialogue with this passage and with its interpretation in the oral tradition.

Second, there is the story of the Good Samaritan, told, according to Luke, with the specific purpose of expanding the concept of neighbor as popularly understood from fellow Israelites to all human beings, including enemies, "schismatics," and "impure" untouchables like the Samaritans. Although the comment that links the story with the meaning of the word *neighbor* is widely regarded as coming from Luke rather than Jesus himself (see, e.g., Fitzmyer 1985b:882), there is a general consensus that the story itself originates with Jesus and that the story makes the same point in images.

Third, the call to perfection, imitating the perfection of God (in vv. 45-48), is focused specifically on extending the circle of those treated with love to *all* people. The analogy with God should be interpreted judiciously, *mutatis mutandis*. The point is not to be perfect like God (presumably an impossible ambition) but to have the same loving attitude to all people (acknowledging them as "people like me"), just as God has the same loving attitude to all people (acknowledging them as his children).

Piper (1979:62) says that "there is nothing specifically Christian in the command to imitate God," and in support of this statement he quotes a Stoic saying recorded by Seneca: "If you are imitating the gods then bestow benefits also upon the ungrateful; for the sun rises also upon the wicked and the sea lies open to pirates." But although there is a similarity, there is also a difference here, highlighted in another dictum of Seneca: "Nature has given you abilities which allow you to rise to be like God; that is, if you don't neglect them" (Downing 1988:29).

Jesus didn't urge people to be like God (let alone to think that they in fact *were* like God), and in consistently using the metaphor "Father" he emphasized that people were *not* like God. But he did encourage them to be, as Merton ([1963]1996:26) put it, "perfect in love," that is, to want to do good things for all people, just as God wants to do good things for all people. In other words, he encouraged people to aim at an *analogy* between their own attitude to other people and God's attitude to people, that is, to learn from God.

Jesus' way of speaking about these matters was in fact much closer to some voices in rabbinic Judaism than to the Stoics. Piper (1979:193) notes the following second-century rabbinic debate: "'You are sons of the Lord your God (Deut. 14:1). When you behave like children, you will be called children. Those are the words of R. [Rabbi] Jehuda (around A.D. 150). R. [Rabbi] Meier (around A.D. 150) said: 'in either case you will be called children'" (quoted in Strack and Billerbeck [1922-1928]1965:I, 371-376). This is how Jesus, too, spoke about people: they *are* all God's children, and *would* be "sons of your Father in heaven" if they wanted to do good things for all people, just as God does. They *are* all God's children in the sense that God was their Father and wanted to do good things for them all; they *would* be God's children ("sons") in the sense that they would be living with God if they wanted to do good things for all other people. This leads us to the following partial explication [components (o), (p), and (q), which are missing here, will be discussed later]:

(r) at the same time I say:
(s)   God wants to do good things for all people
(t)   if you want to live with God
           you have to want to do good things for all other people
           like God wants to do good things for all people
(u)   God wants you to want to do good things for all other people
(v)   when someone wants to do good things for all other people
           this person lives with God

I have formulated the last component of this partial explication in terms of *when* rather than *if* because I don't think that loving one's neighbor (in the broadest, unrestricted sense of the word) is presented by Jesus as a *condition* of living with God (i.e., living in the kingdom of God). Rather, the two appear to be seen as two aspects of the same thing. Piper (1979:77) says, with many qualifications, that "the fulfilment of Jesus' love command is in some sense a condition for entering into the Kingdom of God." I think, however, that he is more on target when he says the following: "To become a son of God and to enter into the Kingdom of God are closely related events. One cannot be a son of God and be excluded from the Kingdom, nor can one be included in the Kingdom of God and be denied sonship." If we wish to speak without metaphors and restrict ourselves to universal human concepts, we can say that these remarks are tantamount to saying that "when someone wants to do good things for all other people, this person lives with God."

It is against this background, I think, that Jesus' teaching on loving one's enemies should be explicated: everyone, and, consequently, even one's enemies, are to be seen as one's neighbors, and so one's enemies, too, are to be treated just as the Old Testament taught that one's neighbors were to be treated. In one word, they are to be treated with *agape*, that is, roughly speaking, "love." What this word is supposed to mean is illustrated by the Matthean Jesus not only with "doing good things for them" (vv. 40, 41, and 42), but also with "praying for them" and, according to some manuscripts, "blessing those who curse you" (cf. the passage from the Psalms quoted earlier). The underlying meaning of these last two manifestations of *agape* (which occur also in Luke 6:27–28) can be represented by "wanting good things to happen to them" and "wanting God to do good things for them." This leads us to the following part of the explication (the components previously omitted):

(o) if someone wants to do bad things to you
         it will be good if you want to do good things for this person
(p) if someone wants bad things to happen to you
         it will be good if you want good things to happen to this
         person
(q) if someone does bad things to you
         it will be good if you want God to do good things for this
         person

In some passages in the Old Testament, "revenge" was left to God ("'Vengeance is mine, I will repay' says the Lord"; Deut. 32–35, quoted by Paul in his letter to the Romans 12:19). According to Jesus, however, even this is not enough. Since one is to identify with one's neighbor and since neighbor means everybody, one can no longer wish for anyone to be punished by God; one has to pray that God should do good things for one's enemy, who is no longer thought of as an enemy.

Also found in the Old Testament are injunctions to help one's enemy in misfortune; for example, "If you meet your enemy's ox or his donkey going astray, you shall surely bring it back to him again. If you see the donkey of one who hates you lying under its burden, and you would refrain from helping it, you shall surely help him with it." (Exod. 23:4–5). According to Jesus, however, even this is not enough: one must also wish good things for one's enemy. The famous passage from the Proverbs (25:21–22), quoted by Paul in his letter to the Romans (12:20), says,

> If your enemy is hungry give him bread to eat,
> If he is thirsty, give him water to drink,
> For so you will heap coals of fire on his head,
> And the Lord will reward you.

The intention with which Paul quoted this passage is disputed, but Jesus' teaching in Matthew 5:43–48 and Luke 6:27–36 leaves no doubt that one was required to wish one's "enemies" well and to pray for them, as well as to help them in need and, generally, to seek to "do good for them."

Commenting on examples like Proverbs 25:21–22 and Exodus 23:4–5 (adduced above) Lachs (1987:108) has remarked, "Nowhere in biblical or Rabbinic Judaism is one called upon to transcend human nature and to love one's enemies. This does not, however, preclude positive moral actions towards those who are your enemies." The "positive moral actions" mentioned by Lachs appear to refer to examples of helping one's enemy in misfortune, such as those cited earlier. What Lachs implies is absent is the injunction to strive for a constant and disinterested desire to do good things for one's "enemies" and to see good things happen to them, in particular, the desire that God should do good things for them, rather than punish them.

As noted earlier, the general commandment to "love one's neighbour as oneself" (Lev. 19:18) was sometimes interpreted in the Old Testament as excluding "bad people," "the ungodly," that is, people seen as enemies of God. See, for example, Psalm 139:19–22:

> Oh, that you would slay the wicked, O God! . . .
> Do I not hate them, O Lord, who hate you?
> And do I not loathe those who rise up against you?
> I hate them with perfect hatred;
> I count them my enemies.

According to Jesus, however, there can be no exceptions to the love commandment. In his teaching, nobody is allowed to judge other people and divide them
into "good people" and "bad people" (see chapter 4 section 10); and in such
parables as the prodigal son and the Pharisee and the tax collector, the "sinners"
are seen not as God's enemies but rather as objects of God's special love.

Thus, whereas it is true that Jesus' teaching of universal love has its roots in
the Old Testament, his interpretation of this theme had some strikingly new
features. Montefiore sets Jesus' injunctions against the background of rabbinic
sayings such as Hillel's "Love thy fellow creatures and draw them near to the
Torah" (cf. also Klausner):

> Jesus unites himself with the *very* best Rabbinic teaching of his own and
> of later times. It is, perhaps, only in trenchantness and eager insistency
> that he goes beyond it. There is a fire, a passion, an intensity, a broad
> and deep positiveness, about these verses, which is new. Jesus suffers no
> exceptions: the Jew may not say, "Isaac is not only my enemy, but he is a
> bad Jew; therefore I legitimately hate him," or "I keep silent before Joseph's
> curses; God will avenge me," or "I keep silent, but I do not forget"; his
> heart must be pure and purged of all hatred and ill-will; he must wish only
> good to the evil-doer; he must seek his welfare, and do him good when
> he can; he must pray for him unto God. I do not deny that there are
> parallels to these injunctions scattered about in the vast Rabbinical litera-
> ture, but they are nowhere collected together in so pregnant, comprehen-
> sive or vivid a form as in Matthew and Luke, and sometimes there are
> qualifications and reservations of them which cannot be wholly ignored.
> Why may we not give to Jesus—himself a Jew—his own glory, and to his
> teaching its own praise? ([1930]1970:85–86)

Montefiore's comments cover almost all the points in the explication proposed
here: wanting to do good things for those who either do or want to do bad things
to us; wanting good things to happen to them; wanting God to do good things
for them; and wanting to do good things for *all* people, without exception. The
ironic statement "Isaac is not only my enemy, but he is a bad Jew; therefore I
legitimately hate him" may even be understood as corresponding to the component "God wants you to think about all people: these people are people like me"
(from Jesus' point of view, it is illegitimate not only to hate Isaac but also to
judge him as a bad person or, indeed a bad Jew).

Similarly, the Jewish scholar Pinchas Lapide (1986:91) states that "it must be
stressed that despite the numerous parallels and analogues in Jewish scripture
which extend love of neighbour even to the most distant and declare all God's
creation worthy of love, the body of Jewish teaching knows no explicit demand
of love of one's enemy. To be precise, 'love your enemy' is an innovation introduced by Jesus." (Understandably and justifiably, Lapide then closes this passage with a rhetorical question: "has it [the love of one's enemy] become a Christian characteristic in practice, as is suggested in so many sermons and lectures?")

In addition to helping us to clarify the relationship between Jesus' love command and its Old Testament background, the explication proposed here can, I hope, help us to better see the differences between Jesus' teaching and its closest parallels in other religious and philosophical traditions (outside Judaism).

Some commentators have suggested that Jesus' teaching on love of one's enemy has close parallels in the writings of Stoics like Seneca and Cynics like Epictetus. In particular, Crossan has recently adduced an oft-quoted passage from Epictetus' *Discourses* 3.54, which at first sight does seem similar to Jesus' teaching: "For this is a pretty strand woven into the Cynic's destiny, that he must be beaten like an ass, and, when he is beaten, must love [*philein*] those who beat him as though he were the father or the brother of them all."

> It is fascinating to watch the Christian nervousness of some earlier translators in handling this passage. Does Epictetus sound too much like Jesus? In the 1910 edition of "The Moral Discourses of Epictetus," for example, Elizabeth Carter compares that passage with Matthew 5-39:44, which speaks of turning the other cheek, giving up your garment, and going the second mile under constraint. She notes that "Christ specifies higher injuries and provocations than Epictetus does; and requires of *all* his followers what Epictetus describes only as the duty of one or two extraordinary persons as such." Not really. (Crossan 1995:120)

In an earlier volume by Crossan (1991:79), of which this one is an abbreviated and toned-down version, this passage ends with the comment "Not true." Crossan's (1995:122) overall conclusion reads, "Maybe Jesus is what peasant Jewish Cynicism looked like." Crossan didn't quite say that Epictetus taught love of one's enemy, just like Jesus, but this is how he has been generally understood. For example, Shorto (1997:151) repeats the quote from Epictetus about the Cynic being "flogged like an ass," together with Jesus' sayings, and he comments, "So the classic aphorisms of Jesus read like a Cynic primer, or seem to. . . . Crossan believes that Jesus' genius was in fitting the Cynic code—the code of the down-and-out—to a Jewish context."

However, as pointed out by earlier commentators (see, e.g., A. Bonhoeffer 1911; Piper 1979), the similarity between Epictetus and Jesus on this point is more apparent than real. Epictetus is primarily concerned about the "moral greatness" of the person who will not be compelled to anger by the greatest provocations; such a concern is alien to Jesus' teaching. Epictetus uses the same images as Jesus but with different messages. The image of a slap on the cheek and Epictetus' (1995) advice that one should treat the attacker "like a statue" was mentioned in section 2. Another example is Jesus' image of letting someone take one's shirt and coat, which has a parallel in Epictetus' Discourse 1.18:5: "Do not admire your clothes, and you will not be angry with the man who steals them. . . . If you give up these things, and look upon them as nothing, with whom will you still be angry? But as long as you admit them, be angry with yourself rather than with others. . . . For a man can only lose what he has. 'I have lost my cloak'. Yes, because you had a cloak." Epictetus concludes that if one practices being indifferent to one's possessions, one will not be angry at those who snatch them away, and in this way one will become "invincible" (p. 45). There is no question here of relating to the robbers as one's neighbors and showing that one wants to do good things for them. Rather—as with the slap on the cheek— the recommended response is to ignore the assault and to maintain perfect self-control and calm (thus preserving one's "moral greatness").

Another interesting parallel is that between Jesus' response to the woman caught in adultery (as related in the Fourth Gospel) and Epictetus' (1995) account of his own response to a man caught in adultery. Epictetus, who strongly disapproved of adultery, describes himself as addressing the adulterer as follows: "How am I to treat you, Sir? . . . How shall I trust you? Indeed, if you were a pot that was so cracked that no use could be made of you, you would be thrown out on the dunghill and nobody would trouble to pick you up. . . . Do you not agree, then, that you too should be thrown on a dunghill, as a useless pot, as mere excrement?" The difference between this exchange and that between Jesus and the adulteress (John 8:2–11; see chapter 4, section 10) is striking.

In the same chapter, "On the Cynic Calling," in which the passage about being beaten like an ass is found, there is also the following (Epictetus 1995:3.62):

> The same young man asked him whether, when he felt sick and a friend invited him to his house so that he could be nursed, it would be right to comply. And where, replied Epictetus, will you find for me the friend of a Cynic? For to be worthy of being numbered amongst his friends, a person must be another Cynic like himself. . . . Or do you think that if a person merely comes up to him and salutes him he will be the Cynic's friend, and the Cynic will think the man worthy to receive him into his house?

Again, the contrast with Jesus' attitude to other people (e.g., the tax collectors Zacchaeus and Levi) could hardly be more striking: Jesus didn't see anyone as unworthy of his friendship and companionship.

To be properly understood, Epictetus' (1995) reference to loving those who beat us must be seen in the context of the overall search for "moral greatness" and "invincibility," combined with a sense of superiority and unwillingness to engage with other, "lesser" people. The man "beaten like an ass and loving those who beat him" is another example of an "invincible man," conscious of his own moral superiority. There is no question in the *Discourses* of wanting to do good things for others, wanting good things to happen to them, and wanting God to do good things for them. The focus is decidedly on one's own moral perfection and invincibility, as it is in Seneca's maxim "It is a pitiably small-minded person who gives bite for bite" (Downing 1988:25) or in his characteristic comment on nonretaliation (also quoted by Downing):

You ask, if a man of sense and understanding happens to get his ears boxed, what is he to do? Just what Cato did when someone boxed his ears. He stayed cool, he didn't retaliate, he didn't even offer to forgive. He refused even to admit that anything had happened. His denial was more high-minded even than forgiveness would have been. (p. 25)

Thomas Merton ([1963]1996:20) did not actually mention either Epictetus or Seneca by name when he wrote of the risk "of wishing to contemplate himself as a superior being, complete and adorned with every virtue, in isolation from all others and in pleasing contrast to them." It seems clear, however, that he did have the Stoics and Cynics in mind. In contrast to Crossan (1995) and others, it also seems clear to me that Jesus' teaching on loving one's enemies meant something very different from that of a Seneca or an Epictetus. Here is the full explication of this teaching:

Love your enemies (Matt. 5:43–48)

(a) you have all heard that some people say:
(b)   "some people are people like you
(c)   it will be good if you want to do good things for these people
(d)   God wants this
(e)   some other people are not people like you
(f)   you don't have to want to do good things for these people
(g)   if some of these people want to do bad things to you
(h)   it will not be bad if you want to do the same to these people"

(i) I want to say something else to you all now
(j) I say:
(k)   God wants more
(l)   God wants you to think about all people:
            "these people are people like me"
(m)   because of this it will be good if you want to do good things
            for all other people
(n)   God wants this

(o)   if someone wants to do bad things to you
            it will be good if you want to do good things for this
            person
(p)   if someone wants bad things to happen to you
            it will be good if you want good things to happen to this
            person
(q)   if someone does bad things to you
            it will be good if you want God to do good things for
            this person

(r) at the same time I say:
(s)   God wants to do good things for all people

(t)   if you want to live with God
                 you have to want to do good things for all other people
                 like God wants to do good things for all people
(u)   God wants you to want to do good things for all other people
(v)   when someone wants to do good things for all other people
                 this person lives with God

9. The righteousness of the scribes and the Pharisees

Matthew 5:20

20. For I say to you, that unless your righteousness exceeds the
     righteousness of the Scribes and the Pharisees, you will by no
     means enter the kingdom of heaven.

Most scholars agree that verse 5:20 as such originates with Matthew, not with
Jesus ("righteousness," in Greek, *dikaiosunē*, was in fact one of Matthew's favorite and distinctive words; see, e.g., Dunn 1991:152). There is less agreement,
however, on the question behind this verse: how did Jesus see the relationship
between his own ethics and that of "the scribes and the Pharisees"? In what
follows, I will summarize my own conclusions on this matter in the form of a
response to the views expressed in one major, recent book about Jesus—E. P.
Sanders's *The Historical Figure of Jesus*:

> Jesus cites the law and then says, in effect, that it is not good enough. The
> section [Matthew's chapter 5] is usually, but not accurately, called "the anti-
> theses". . . . In addition to the statement on divorce, the section contains
> other admonitions to live by a higher standard than the law requires. Not
> only should people not kill, they should not be angry. . . . Not only should
> they avoid adultery, they should not look at others with lust in their
> hearts. . . . Far from retaliating when injured, they should 'turn the other
> cheek'. . . . (1993:201)

Sanders speaks in this context of the "perfectionism" and the "rigorous ethics"
of the Sermon on the Mount. Although accepting that the sayings in question
do originate with Jesus, Sanders nonetheless plays down their importance:

> We note . . . that the reader of Mark and Luke would not know that Jesus
> prohibited anger and lustful thoughts. Admonitions to eliminate feelings
> that are common to humanity is not a characteristic of Jesus' teaching
> generally, but occurs only in this section of Matthew. Otherwise, Jesus was
> concerned with how people treated others, not with what thoughts lurked
> in their hearts.

I disagree. In my reading of the Gospels—and not only Matthew's chapter 5—
Jesus was very much concerned with what thoughts lurked in people's hearts.

In fact, in the very next chapter, Matthew records sayings whose authenticity is not disputed and which affirm that, for example, the value that charitable acts such as almsgiving have in God's eyes depends entirely on the "thoughts in people's hearts."

It is true that "Jesus was not given to censure but to encouragement" (E. P. Sanders 1993:204), and for that reason I have represented Jesus' teaching in the mode "it will be good if you . . ." rather than "it is bad when a person. . . ." I also agree that Jesus "was not judgmental but compassionate" (p. 204), and in this respect I go further than Sanders when he says that Jesus "seems not to have gone around condemning people for their minor lapses" (p. 202). In fact, Jesus did not condemn anyone for anything, not only for minor lapses but also for acts that according to the Law deserved to be punished by stoning (see John 8:10–11). Nor did he condemn his own executioners: "Father, forgive them, for they do not know what they do" (Luke 23:34).

None of this means, however, that Jesus was only "concerned with how people treated others, not with what thoughts lurked in their hearts." On the contrary, he attached extraordinary importance to such thoughts, as recorded not only by Matthew but also by Mark and Luke. Thus Mark (7:20–23) says,

20. What comes out of a man is what defiles a man.
21. For from within, out of the hearts of man, come evil thoughts, fornication, theft, murder, adultery,
22. coveting, wickedness, deceit, licentiousness, envy, slander, pride, foolishness.
23. All these evil things come from within, and they defile a man.

It is particularly interesting to note that purely spiritual sins like coveting, envy and pride are put here on a par with murder. Luke's references to pride (9:46–48) and hypocrisy (12:1–2) are equally eloquent. Above all else, however, his parable of the Pharisee and the tax collector (see chapter 6) makes it very clear that the Lucan Jesus, too, was particularly concerned about the thoughts in people's hearts. It is not a matter of perfectionism or of a particularly rigorous ethics but of attitudes that stand in the way of a person's living with God (in the kingdom of God). This was where Jesus' major emphasis lay, and this was a major focus of his dialogue with those whom he perceived as putting the emphasis elsewhere.

As I will discuss in more detail in chapter 4 (see in particular section 2 and 14), in emphasizing the importance of the heart Jesus did not de-emphasize the importance of doing. As pointed out by the Jewish scholar Pinchas Lapide in his dialogue with the Catholic theologian Karl Rahner (Rahner and Lapide 1987:14), "The most frequently used verb in the preaching of Jesus of Nazareth is the verb *do*. The most frequently used phrase is the kingdom of heaven. That must be more than a simple accident."

Clearly, Jesus did not teach that it doesn't matter what you do. But he very often sought to convey a message focused on ways of thinking. In universal concepts, this message can be articulated along the following lines:

sometimes people think: . . .
it will not be good if you think like this
it will be good if you think: . . .

In particular, Jesus discouraged thinking about God primarily in terms of "What do I have to do?" (which is not the same as "What does God want me to do?"). Instead, he placed the main emphasis on love—universal and unconditional; embracing outcasts, enemies, and aliens; not restricted to "people like us"; and not limited to actions but abiding in a person's heart, as well as in their deeds.[5] As Theissen and Merz (1998:364) put it, in this perspective "one can fulfil God's will only if one does not just fulfil his commandments by one's behaviour but also lets one's own will, down to the innermost emotions, be governed by them." One presumes that this is what St. Augustine had in mind when he tried to sum up Jesus' teaching in the aphorism *Dilige et quod vis fac* 'Love and do whatever you want'.

Finally, it should be noted that Matthew's verse 5:20 appears to have played a considerable role in the modern tendency to pit the Jesus of history against the Christ of faith and the Gospel of Jesus against the Gospel about Jesus. The saying about the "higher righteousness" has been taken to mean that the Sermon on the Mount "proclaims a religion of achievement" (McArthur 1961:69), which seems incompatible with the emphasis on grace in Paul's epistles and elsewhere in the New Testament: "On the surface, at least, the Sermon on the Mount emphasizes the achievement motif. Matt. 5:20 warns the reader that his righteousness must exceed that of the scribes and the Pharisees" (p. 58). McArthur himself finds in the New Testament both an emphasis on grace and an emphasis on achievement:

> There are notes within the Sermon which prevent its being interpreted as proposing exclusively a religion of achievement. The total teaching of Jesus as recorded in the Synoptics heightens the paradox in which achievement and grace are in apparent conflict. The Jesus who heightened the demand made by God on our mortal lives was also the Jesus who proclaimed the divine love and forgiveness even to those who had not fulfilled a portion of that demand. (pp. 72–73).

But to describe Christianity as even partly a religion of achievement seems to me to be inaccurate and misleading. The Matthean Jesus was not urging his disciples to compete with the scribes and the Pharisees in righteousness. Rather, he was urging them to focus on something greater. (If this something were to be summed up in one word, Matthew and Paul would no doubt agree that the word should be *love*.) Injunctions such as "love your enemies," "do not worry about your life," and "do not judge" do not urge the hearers to "achieve" and to "compete" but to change their way of thinking (and, consequently, their way of living). The point of the parable of the Pharisee and the tax collector was not that the Pharisee did not achieve enough and that he should strive to achieve more but rather that he should not think about himself and other people in terms of righteousness and achievement. The idea of comparing oneself favorably with other people was specifically targeted by this parable. It is not possible to understand the reference to a "righteousness which should exceed that of the scribes and the Pharisees" until we recognize that the word "righteousness" is used here as a quote and that it is another instance of New Testament heteroglossia. (For further discussion, see sections 2, 3, and 4.)

FOUR

Other Key Sayings

1. You are the salt of the earth

Matthew 5:13–16

13. (a) You are the salt of the earth, (b) but if the salt loses its taste, how shall it be seasoned? (c) It is then good for nothing but to be thrown out and trampled under feet by men.
14. (a) You are the light of the world. (b) A city that is set on a hill cannot be hidden.
15. Nor do they light a lamp and put it under a basket, but on a lampstand, and it gives light to all who are in the house.
16. Let your light so shine before people that they may see your good works and glorify your Father in heaven.

The "salt of the earth" saying is so well known that in many languages it has become part of everyday speech. Its meaning, however, continues to puzzle commentators. The editors of the Anchor Bible (Albright and Mann 1971:54) go so far as to say, "The saying as it stands in our English versions makes virtually no sense at all, despite all the effort of the commentators. . . . There is no conceivable manner in which salt can be re-salted once it has been diluted." Having said this, the authors offer a new translation of the passage, referring to "low grade salt": "it is the earth itself which is in need of attention. But if salt is of poor quality, of low grade, then the earth itself will suffer loss." Most other commentators, however, understand the metaphor differently, linking "salt" with food (which salt can preserve) and interpreting "the earth" as a parallel to "the world" in verse 14, that is, as referring to people. The explicit reference to "all who are in the house" in verse 15 and the implicit reference to people in 14b ("hidden from people") give additional support to the interpretation that links "the earth" with "people": if "the salt," "the light," "a city . . . set on a hill," and "a lamp put . . . on a lampstand" all refer to Jesus' followers, it makes sense to assume that "the earth," "the world," and "all who are in the house," as well as the implied "people in the countryside around the city," refer to other people. This, then, is the interpretation of the sayings that I will assume in my discussion of their meaning.

But, first, there is the question of authenticity. The bulk of verse 13 (parts b and c) occurs in both Matthew and Luke and so can be seen as derived from their presumed shared source, Q (*Quelle*). There are no reasons not to regard this shared saying as stemming from Jesus. The first clause, however (13a, i.e., "You are the salt of the earth"), occurs only in Matthew, and the scholars of the Jesus Seminar, for example, regard it as Matthew's own creation. Except for this clause, they see verse 13b and 13c as stemming from Jesus himself, but they think that its meaning is unclear and its intended message irrevocably lost: "The second salt saying, however, is an aphorism and is short and memorable. It may also have occasioned surprise. . . . We can no longer determine the precise wording of the original saying and since the original context has been lost, we do not know how Jesus applied it to his situation" (Funk et al. 1993:139).

But even if we don't know for sure in what context Jesus uttered the second salt saying (13b and 13c) we can still try to establish what he could have meant by it, as well as whether we should reject Matthew's interpretation of it (expressed in 13a). One thing seems obvious: Jesus was talking about salt not in a literal sense but in a metaphorical sense, and he was applying this metaphor to people. And what other people could he have had in mind if not his addressees—that is, his actual or potential disciples and followers? Clearly, Jesus was not describing what happens to salt because he was interested in salt as such; rather he was urging his addressees to be like salt in some positive sense, a sense that in first-century Palestine did not have to be specified because it seemed obvious.

Funk et al. (1993:139) say that Matthew "remodelled a simple saying about salt that has lost its saltiness . . . into a saying about Christian presence in the world." They do explain why they think this interpretation stems from Matthew, not Jesus, but their explanation seems to be based on a misunderstanding: "The saying as it now stands commends Christians as the salt of the earth and thus reflects the social outlook of the later community. . . . Jesus himself rejected insider/outsider discriminations of this sort: he included outsiders such as sinners and toll collectors, along with other 'undesirables', among his companions. As a consequence, the Fellows of the Jesus Seminar designated Matt 5:130 black." One can agree that Jesus didn't *commend* his disciples as being the salt of the earth, but this doesn't mean that he didn't *urge* them to be so. The image of the worthless salt being thrown out and trampled under foot shows clearly that on Jesus' lips the comparison with salt was not a commendation but an appeal and a warning (another instance of the biblical *Drohrede*; see chapter 7).

As the commentators of the Anchor Bible (among others) have rightly pointed out, what is at issue here is "the responsibility vested in the disciples" and "the *demands* of the discipleship" (emphasis added), not any putative set of privileges or status distinctions (see Albright and Mann 1971:55). Since Jesus was indeed calling sinners and tax collectors, along with other undesirables, to the discipleship, there can be no question here of excluding such undesirables from the call to become the salt of the earth.

It should also be noted that whereas the sentence "You are the salt of the earth" is not included in Luke's gospel, Luke also linked the saying about salt to the idea of discipleship, placing it in the context of a discourse on what Fitzmyer (1985b:1059) calls the "conditions of discipleship." The preceding verse in Luke (14:33) is this: "So likewise, whoever of you does not forsake all that he has cannot be my disciple." Fitzmyer says, "At this point in the travel account Luke abruptly adds a parable about salt to Jesus' sayings about the conditions of discipleship (14:34–35). It is only loosely connected with the preceding, but is obviously intended as a further comment on those conditions" (p. 1067).

Thus, pace Funk et al. (1993), the link between salt and discipleship cannot simply be written off as Matthew's creation. On the contrary, it seems likely that a call to be the salt of the earth was indeed part of Jesus' intended message. But what exactly does this call mean? Some commentators have equated the physical rotting of food (which can be prevented by salt) with moral corruption (which, they suggest, can be prevented by the Christian presence in the world). For example, Morgan (1960; quoted in Lockyer 1963:146) has observed, "Salt . . . prevents the spread of corruption. If meat is tainted and corrupt, salt will not make it untainted and pure. But salt in its neighbourhood will prevent the spread of corruption to that which otherwise would become tainted." Having quoted these observations with approval, Lockyer adds, "The meaning of the parable is evident. The Lord expects His own to function as a moral, spiritual influence, preventing the spread of sin's corruptive forces" (p. 146).

But this literal-minded interpretation ignores the relationship with Jesus' other metaphors, in particular those set out by Matthew in the adjacent verses, 5:14, 5:15, and 5:16. Again, even if the sentence "You are the light of the world" was Matthew's invention (as claimed by Funk et al. 1993:139), it is hard to see whom, other than his followers, Jesus could have had in mind. Again, Funk et al. reject Matthew's interpretation of this saying on the basis of what looks like a misunderstanding. They claim that it "reflects Christian self-evaluation about its insider role in society, which runs counter to Jesus' admonition to his followers to be self-effacing." But clearly, Matthew wasn't congratulating believers, on Jesus' behalf, on being "the light of the world"; rather, he was articulating what he understood as a call and a task—the same call and task as were also expressed in the salt image.

I disagree here with those commentators who basically accept the Matthean interpretation of the salt and light sayings but who attribute different meanings to the two images. For example, Lockyer (1963:147) links these two images with "the dual function of Christians, namely, their sanctifying and enlightening influences on others." He speculates that "salt operates *internally* in the mass with which it comes into contact," and that when Christians are called to be "the salt of the earth," this refers to "the masses of mankind with whom they are expected to mix," whereas "the sunlight operates *externally*, irradiating all that it reaches." Accordingly, he argues, "the light of the world" refers to something else (an "enlightening" rather than "sanctifying" influence). As I see it, this is an excessively allegorizing interpretation. It is more plausible to assume that the two images (salt and light) are meant to convey, jointly, a single meaning—one that I have articulated in the following explication.

I assume that Jesus was speaking about and to those who "know about God." If so, in what way could they either sanctify or enlighten those who don't? Presumably, not just by talking about God but, as Matthew suggests, by "letting God's light shine through their own lives," so that through them other people will come to know about God and will want to live with God because of that. More precisely, these ideas can be represented as follows:

You are the salt of the earth; you are the light of the world.

- (a) all people can live with God
- (b) God wants this
- (c) some people do not live with God because they don't know about God
- (d) this is very bad for these people
- (e) some other people know about God because they hear my words
- (f) these people know that my words are true
- (g) I say to every one of these people:
- (h)   if you live with God you will do many good things because of this
- (i)   other people will see this
- (j)   other people can know about God because of this
- (k)   other people can want to live with God because of this
- (l)   if you don't live with God maybe many other people will not live with God because of this

The heading given to this explication is not meant to imply that these words, "You are the salt of the earth; you are the light of the world," are taken as Jesus' *ipsissima verba*. Even if these words were added to the original sayings by Matthew, however, they are likely to have represented a rendering of Jesus' original intent. The explication attempts to go to a more abstract and unmetaphorical level of meaning.

This explication makes clear that the addressees are not being treated as privileged but rather as people with a heavy responsibility ("if you, who know about God, don't live with God, maybe many other people will not live with God because of this; this will be very bad for these people"). It does not present Jesus as urging the believers "to do good things, so that other people can come to know about God." Rather, the idea is that if those who know about God live with God, God will become visible in their lives. They will do "good things" (the *kala erga*, 'good works', specifically mentioned by Matthew in verse 16), but these good things will simply follow from their living with God, and God will be their ultimate source.

This interpretation is consistent with that of numerous commentators, for example, the Swiss theologian Leonhard Ragaz (1945:37; quoted in Bauman):

> Therefore we must return to Christ. The good works which he intends derive not from the law but from the true source, from God. We can and shall do such things. He says so and demands it. We are able to do them in the light of the Kingdom and shall do so. . . . Deeds are the true word of God. God speaks through deeds, and we are to speak of him through deeds. (1985: 59)

Jeremias (1961:25) observes that Matthew's light sayings presuppose "a previous, unexpressed sentence, 'I am the light of the world' (John 8:12)." In his view, the sentence "You are the light of the world" (Matt. 5:14), which compares the disciples to the sun, "makes no sense when taken by itself" because, as Bauman (1985:293) puts it, "their weaknesses and failures are not very illuminating." It might be added that in the passage of the Fourth Gospel to which Jeremias is referring here, the sentence "I am the light of the world" is followed by another one, which makes the connection explicit: "He who follows me shall not walk in darkness, but have the light of life."

Emmet Fox (1938:52; also quoted in Bauman), emphasizes in this context the special role of prayer, and allegorizes "city" (in verse 14) as "consciousness" and "mountain" as "prayer or spiritual activity":

> A "city" always stands for consciousness, and the "hill" or "mountain" always means prayer or spiritual activity. . . . The soul that is built upon prayer cannot be hidden; it shines out brightly through the life that it lives. It speaks for itself but in utter silence and does much of its best work unconsciously. Its mere presence heals and blesses all around it without special effort. (1985: 313)

Most commentators accept that the saying about a city built on a hill goes back to the historical Jesus. Funk et al. (1993:140) agree but maintain nonetheless that "since the original context has been lost, we cannot determine what it meant on the lips of Jesus." But the interpretation of the salt and light sayings proposed here is applicable, *mutatis mutandis*, to the city on the hill as well. It is also compatible with the spirit, if not the letter, of Emmet Fox's interpretation. The essential point is, roughly speaking, that if a person lives with God, this is visible in this person's life, including in their deeds:

> if a person lives with God this person does many good things because
>   of this
> other people can see this

other people can know about God because of this
other people can want to live with God because of this

The inherent link between, on the one hand, living with God, and on the other, doing good things, is spelled out by the following words, attributed to Jesus in the Fourth Gospel (John 15:1–8):

1. I am the true vine, and my Father is the vine-dresser. . . .
4. Abide in me, and I in you. As the branch cannot bear fruit of itself, unless it abides in the vine, neither can you, unless you abide in me.
5. I am the vine, you are the branches. He who abides in me, and I in him, bears much fruit; for without me you can do nothing. . . .
8. By this my Father is glorified, that you bear much fruit; so shall you be my disciples.

This echoes Matthew's final verse in the salt and light passage (verse 16): "Let your light so shine before people that they may see your good works and glorify your Father in heaven."

Thus, people who are the salt of the earth are not necessarily those who say that Jesus' words are true or who endeavour to "do good things"; rather they are those who live in such a way that, metaphorically speaking, God's light shines through their life and is visible to other people. To live like this, people must be living with God. If they do live with God, "good works" follow anyway; other people see them, realize that they are the fruit of living with God, and give glory to God because of this.

2. When you do a charitable deed do not sound a trumpet

Matthew 6:1–4

1. Take heed that you do not do your charitable deeds before people, to be seen by them. Otherwise you have no reward from your Father in heaven.
2. Therefore, when you do a charitable deed, do not sound a trumpet before you, as the hypocrites do in the synagogues, and in the streets, that they may have glory from men. Assuredly, I say to you, they have their reward.
3. But when you do a charitable deed do not let your left hand know what your right is doing.
4. (a) that your charitable deed may be in secret; (b) and your Father who sees in secret will himself reward you openly.

Are these authentic sayings of Jesus? The consensus appears to be that verse 1 definitely did not originate with Jesus (and was created by Matthew), whereas verse 3 probably did; as for verses 2 and 4, opinions are divided. In my view, verses 2, 3, and 4 form a coherent whole, which is consistent in both content and form with other sayings attributed to Jesus (such as, for example, the logion about the widow's two mites or the sayings about not seeking glory from other people). It is particularly important to note the hyperbolic and striking style of verse 2 (as well as 3) and the extreme form of the injunctions in all three verses (2, 3, and 4), which are highly characteristic of Jesus. Tannehill (1975:81), in particular, states that "in vss. 2–4 we see immediately that the commands are formulated in extreme language . . . the language is chosen because it is striking and extreme"; and the metaphor "sound no trumpet" "is the strongest image for advertising one's generosity that could readily be imagined in the first century." These features support the view that not only verse 3 but also 2 and 4 (and, as we will see later, 5–6 and 16–18) all go back to the historical Jesus.

As commentators have noted, some Old Testament books also denounce religious hypocrisy (see e.g., Sir. 1:28: "Do not act a part in public, keep watch over your lips") and praised "a secret gift" (Prov. 21:14). Similarly, some first-century rabbis warned "against making the Torah into a crown with which one can boast" (Luz 1989:358). But it is one thing to note the parallels and another to discount Jesus' sayings, such as Matthew 6:2 and 6:4 (in contrast to 6:3), as Matthean creations, as Funk et al. (1993:148) do.[1] Furthermore, the real relationship between the sayings of Jesus and their putative parallels can only be established after careful semantic analysis, and as we have seen again and again, these parallels are sometimes less close than they seem to be at first sight.

What is, then, the message of the sayings attributed to Jesus in Matthew 6:2–4? The phrase "a charitable deed" (which renders in the NKJV the Greek word *eleēmosyne*, more literally "alms") suggests that someone wants to do good things for other people (and especially for those to whom bad things have happened), "to sound a trumpet," that this person wants other people to know about it, and "that they may have glory from men," that this person wants other people to think or to say good things about him or her because of this. As a first approximation, the attitude against which Jesus is warning can therefore be represented as follows:

(a) sometimes a person does something good for other people
(b) because this person thinks:
(c)   "if I do this, something good will happen to me because of
         this
(d)   other people will know that I did this
(e)   because of this they will think something good about me
(f)   I want this"
(g) when this person thinks this this person feels something good

What sort of thoughts, then, does God want to see behind the charitable deeds? The phrase "in secret" may seem to suggest that when one does good things for other people, one should think, "I don't want anybody to know about it" (and act accordingly), but I think it would be wrong to include such a component in the explication. The phrase "in secret" may have been used by the Matthean Jesus partly for rhetorical purposes, as an opposite of deliberate publicity. Presumably, if someone were so intent on helping others that he or she did not give a thought to secrecy, this would not have met with Jesus' disapproval. The real question is not whether one is doing something openly or in secret but *why* one is doing it; and the basic contrast drawn by the Matthean Jesus appears to be between, on the one hand, thinking about one's own gain ("if I do this something good will happen to me because of this") and, on the other hand, not thinking about one's own gain.[2]

Since this passage refers specifically to alms (and, in a broader interpretation, charitable deeds), the "other-oriented" attitude alluded to in verse 4 and contrasted with the "self-seeking" attitude of verse 2 can be understood to be motivated by something like compassion or mercy, that is, by an awareness of other people's misfortunes and a desire to respond to them:

some bad things have happened to these people
because of this I want to do something good for these people

This is, of course, just a special case of the more general (loving) attitude of "wanting to do good things for other people." Thus, whereas people may admire a person for his or her charitable deeds, God wants more: a nonselfish motive. This can be represented as follows:

when you do something good for other people
it will be good if you to do it because you want to do something good
  for other people,
not because you think that something good will happen to you because
  of this

The focus on wanting to do good things for other people rather than on a desire for secrecy resolves the apparent conflict between Jesus' sayings in Matthew 6:2–4 and in 5:16: "Let your light so shine before people that they may see your good works and glorify your Father in heaven" (see e.g., Betz 1995:163). In fact, there is no conflict between these two passages. In 5:16, Jesus does not suggest that his disciples should want their good works to be seen. Rather, he suggests that "if you live with God you will do many good things because of this; other people will see this (know about it); they will say good things about God because of this." In 6:2–4, he suggests that "God wants you to want to do good things for other people not because you think that something good will happen to you because of this." When the two messages are presented like this, it is clear that there is no conflict between them.[3]

As mentioned, in Old Testament and rabbinic Judaism, too, some voices could be heard denouncing religious hypocrisy and extolling "secret alms." Jesus seems to be going further in this direction, apparently implying that a charitable deed done out of a selfish motive has no value in God's eyes at all. The Matthean Jesus uses the metaphor of "reward," which, as I will discuss below (and also in the following section), is often mistaken for "reward" in the literal sense of the word. In Matthew 6:2–4, the whole question is whether in giving alms one is doing something for oneself or for other people, and the thought "if I do this something good will happen to me (because of this)" is implicitly contrasted with a thought about some other people ("I want to do something good for these people"). Doing something for a reward (in a literal sense of the word) means doing it for oneself and thinking of one's own gain.

The Jewish theologian Abraham Heschel has written:

> In the world of Jewish piety two voices may be heard. One voice is severe, uncompromising: good deeds done out of impure motives are entirely inadequate. The other voice is one of moderation: good deeds are precious even if their motivation is not pure. . . . Judaism insists upon the deed and hopes for the intention. . . . Perhaps this is the deeper meaning of the rabbis' counsel: one should always do the good, even though it is not done for its own sake. It is the act that teaches us the meaning of the act. (1959:189)

It seems clear that the Matthean Jesus speaks with the first of these two voices rather than the second.

In his appreciation of good deeds Heschel (1959) goes so far as to speak of "the divinity of deeds" (p. 85) and of "the immanence of God in deeds" (p. 79). Jesus would have agreed with Heschel (p. 82) that "the heart is revealed in the deeds," but he probably wouldn't have said that "the way to pure intention is paved with good deeds" (p. 189). In fact, in Jesus' teaching there seems to be no place at all for the notion of a good deed independent of a pure intention. The sayings under discussion (Matt. 6:1–4; also 6:5–6 and 6:16–18, to be discussed later) suggest (in a hyperbolic form) that for Jesus a pure intention was particularly important and that he was redefining the notion of a good deed in a way that included the intention.

Many Christian scholars who have written about Jesus' emphasis on motive have exaggerated the contrast between Jesus' teaching and that of the Pharisaic Judaism of his times: "For centuries it had been assumed, particularly in Protestant circles, that Judaism, or Pharisaic Judaism in particular, was a narrow, legalistic religion. Pharisees taught a religion of 'works-righteousness', of salvation earned by merit . . ." (Dunn 1991:13). In recent decades, however, a major reappraisal of Pharisaic Judaism has taken place, largely under the influence of E. P. Sanders's (1977) book *Paul and Palestinian Judaism*. "In the light of Sanders' contribution the scales have fallen from many eyes, and we can see, as never before . . . the degree to which early Judaism was in fact a religion of grace and forgiveness" (Dunn 1991:13).

While accepting the validity of this reappraisal, we still need to understand the differences, as well as the similarities, between the teaching of Jesus and that of his contemporaries and his interlocutors; and it seems undeniable that Jesus' perspective on good deeds, merits, and reward—as expressed in the Sermon on the Mount and the parables—was different from that outlined, for example, in the following passage from Solomon Schechter's book *Aspects of Rabbinic Theology*:

> Believing fully in the justice of God, the Rabbis could not but assume that the actions of man form an important factor in the scheme of salvation, whether for good or for evil. Hence the statement that man is judged in accordance with the majority of his deeds, and the world in general, in accordance with the number of the righteous or wicked men it contains. In accordance with this is the notion of the scale of merit (or Zachuth) and the scale of guilt. ([1909] 1961:189)

The Sermon on the Mount emphasizes, on the other hand, that whereas deeds are vitally important, people are judged on the basis of what is in their hearts rather than their deeds as such. The notion of a good deed as a merit seems to be explicitly rejected by Jesus in the parable of unprofitable servants (Luke 17:7–10) in the concluding line: "So likewise you, when you have done all those things which you are commanded, say 'We are unprofitable servants. We have done what was our duty to do.'" (See chapter 13.)

An "unprofitable servant" who has done his or her duty cannot expect any "reward." I agree, therefore, with Jeremias that when the Matthean Jesus speaks of a "reward" (*mistos*), he is using this word in, as it were, quotation marks:

> Religious language is conservative, and in polemical contexts, above all, one has to begin from one's opponents' language. This is especially obvious in Matt. 6.1.ff, a clearly polemical context. . . . That is, when you give, forget it again; your Father, who sees what is hidden, will reward you. Here it is clear that while Jesus takes up the word "reward," he in fact presupposes that the disciples have completely detached themselves from striving for a reward, they are to forget the good deeds they have done. . . . (1971:216)

At this point Jeremias refers, rightly, I think, to the scene of the last judgment in Matthew 25:37–40, where "those who are acquitted at the last judgment are completely surprised by the acts of love as a result of which their acquittal comes. They protest against the recognition that is accorded to them, it is incomprehensible to them." Jeremias remarks, "There are no parallels to this feature in contemporary pictures of the last judgment"; he adds, "And no wonder, for this is the abolition of the idea of reward" (p. 216). The scene of the last judgment shows also, of course, that deeds—what Jeremias calls "acts of love"—are crucially important for Jesus. But in the context of the Gospels as a whole, it is clear that Jesus' emphasis is on acts of love rather than on "acts of righteousness" (for which one could take credit or expect a reward).

As I will argue in the next section, Jeremias's (1971) idea that Jesus is using the word "reward" in quotation marks is strongly supported by the paradoxical image of the left hand not knowing what the right hand is doing: the disciples do not think of themselves as "doers of good deeds," and so they cannot possibly expect a reward for those deeds.

Jeremias's (1971) interpretation is persuasive and it is surprising to see that some contemporary commentators still attribute to the Matthean Jesus the idea of "reward" in the literal sense. For example, Betz (1995:360) writes that: "the reason for the secrecy is to protect one's eschatological reward: 'and your Father who sees in the hidden will compensate you'. . . . A good deed done in this way has been done according to God's will and as the Torah requires, but its reward is still outstanding. Consequently, God, who is righteous, will provide the reward due at the last judgement." And again, "The doctrine of reward (*mistos*) contained in [Matthew] 6:1–6, 16–18, conforms to Jewish theology generally, but the idea that one must avoid all reward in this world so as to ensure reward by God in the world to come is a specialty of the SM" (p. 346).

In saying this, Betz (1995) implies that the Sermon on the Mount places *more* rather than *less* emphasis on reward than rabbinic theology did and that the Matthean Jesus is telling his disciples not only to *expect* a reward but also to act in such a way as to *ensure* reward. As strongly emphasized by E. P. Sanders (1977), among others, rabbinic theology disapproved of reward as a motive, although it encouraged it as an expectation: "Although the Rabbis emphasize repeatedly that the commandments carry rewards (or punishment for nonfulfilment), they also warn against fulfilling the commandments *in order* to earn payment. Rather, one should perform the required commandments without ulterior motive and because they are in themselves good ('for their own sake') or from love of God ('for the sake of heaven')" (p. 120). By contrast, Betz implies that Jesus *encouraged* his disciples to act "so as to ensure reward," and he calls this "a specialty of the SM [Sermon on the Mount]."

Similarly, Strecker (1988:101) writes that "the hypocritical behaviour is realized in concrete deeds that are aimed at the approval of the spectators. But, says Matthew, the meaning of good works is thereby distorted, for they are done with an audience in mind for the sake of earthly advantage." As for doing good works for the sake of *heavenly* advantage, however, Strecker thinks that from the Matthean Jesus' point of view there is nothing wrong with that: "Matthew presupposes the profit motive and takes for granted its validity. The hypocrites are not denied the reward that is due to them for their good works. Nevertheless, through the approbation that they seek from the spectators, they have already received their reward; there is nothing left for them to expect." In conclusion, Strecker states that "Matthew wants to emphasize the necessity of doing good deeds with a view toward God and not in view of people" (p. 101; see also Limbeck et al. 1987:66).

Thus, whereas rabbinic theology warned against the profit motive (although it insisted that God, being just, would reward good deeds), Matthew (according to Strecker 1988) "presupposes the profit motive and takes for granted its validity." This seems to me to be a reductio ad absurdum of Jesus' whole dramatic attack on impure motives in Matthew 6:1–18 and his equally dramatic plea for a pure motive. To say that the Matthean Jesus takes for granted the validity of the profit motive is to miss the irony of the passage, and—to use Bakhtin's (1981) term—its "heteroglossia," that is, the fact that Jesus is using here not his own language but that of his interlocutors (see section 14).[4] A "pure motive" must be a selfless motive, that is, doing something either out of love for other people or out of love for God (or both). The apparent conflict between Jesus' insistence on a pure motive and his use of the concept of reward can only be resolved if we accept that, as Jeremias (1971) suggested, Jesus was using the word "reward" in quotation marks, and that he really meant something other than its literal meaning.

On the face of it, there seems to be a curious paradox in the verse "Your father who sees in secret will himself reward you openly," because Jesus seems to be promising here a heavenly reward to those who do charitable deeds with a pure motive—and who do not expect any reward. Jeremias (1971:217) tries to resolve this paradox by contrasting the notion of reward with that of recompense: "If Jesus nevertheless speaks of *mistos*, he is not concerned with the claim to a reward but with something quite different: the reality of divine recompense. . . . There is no question of merit here. Merit has an eye to human achievement; recompense looks to God's faithfulness. That God is trustworthy and offers recompense stands ensured." I do not think, however, that this strategy of substituting "recompense" for "reward" solves the problem of Matthew 6:4, for what would be the point in promising a recompense to those who are not supposed to expect one? Surely, an expectation of recompense would be just as incompatible with the "forgetting" of one's own good deeds, which as Jeremias has argued is the whole point of Jesus' injunction.

My solution to this dilemma draws on the distinction between "thinking that something good will happen to me" and "knowing that something is good for a person." To expect a reward or a recompense implies the expectation that something good will happen to me because of what I have done. If I try to do good things for other people with an expectation that something good will happen to me because of this, this very expectation robs my act of its value; such an act does nothing good for my soul. If, however, I try to do good things for other people, knowing that it is good for a person to want to do good things for other people, this general knowledge does not necessarily turn my thoughts toward myself and detract from the value of my act. This is, I think, what Jesus meant by "reward." Jesus implied that if one does good things for other people "with a pure motive" and without expecting a reward or a recompense, this is good for this person; something good happens to this person right then and there—something that, metaphorically speaking, brings the person closer to God.

As Jesus' other sayings suggest, ultimately there is only one thing that is always good for everyone (the hidden treasure, the pearl of great price): living with God. In the sayings under discussion, the idea is not that a person doing a charitable deed out of love will be either rewarded or recompensed by God but rather that doing so is inherently good for this person because in doing so this person is already, as it were, living with God; and living with God is the one thing that—according to Jesus—is truly good for all people and is not like anything else. This brings us to the following overall explication:

Do not do your charitable deeds before people

(a) sometimes a person does good things for other people
(b) because this person thinks:
(c)   "if I do this, something good will happen to me because of this
(d)   other people will know that I did it
(e)   because of this they will think something good about me
(f)   I want this"
(g) when this person thinks this, this person feels something good
     because of this

(h) it will not be good if you do good things for other people because
     you think like this
(i) it will be good if you do good things for other people because you
     think:
(j)   "bad things have happened to these people
(k)   I want to do something good for these people because of this"
(l) if a person does something good for other people because this
     person thinks like this
(m) this is good for this person
(n) something good happens to this person because of this

Montefiore ([1927]1968:97) writes, commenting on Matthew 6:1–4, "Jesus uses simple eudemonistic [i.e., happiness-seeking] motives quite naively and comfortably . . . any simple religionist, whether Christian or Jew . . . expects and hopes for a reward; but he does not love God, and he does not act righteously, for the sake of a reward." The difficulty with such an interpretation is that if we take Jesus' "simple eudemonistic motives" at face value, he does seem to be recommending doing good for the sake of a reward. If, on the other hand, we interpret him as undermining the concept of reward, rather than using it "naively," we cannot believe that he was encouraging his followers to expect and hope for a reward. As I will argue in the next section, verse 3 makes it clear that in fact the notion of expecting and hoping for a reward was *not* part of Jesus' teaching. (If a person's left hand doesn't know that this person's right hand is doing a charitable deed, this person can hardly expect and hope for a reward.)

Jesus did encourage people to pursue what, according to his own teaching, was uniquely and supremely good for them: that is, living with God. At the same time, however, he did not encourage his disciples to expect a reward and, in fact, warned them against thinking about themselves and about God in such terms. Living with God is to be achieved not through good deeds as such but through love (active and fruitful love, but love). To live with God, one needs to think about other people and to want to do good things for other people. One can expect a reward if one thinks of oneself as a doer of good deeds; but if one doesn't think about oneself at all and simply feels compassion for some other people and wants to do something good for them, one is already, as it were, living with God. This was the ideal put forward, for example, in the parable of the Good Samaritan (see chapter 16).

Jesus' criticisms of charity done ostentatiously referred to the practice that he observed among some of his contemporaries and to the motive (gaining glory for oneself) that he attributed to it. No doubt, the Pharisees would have agreed that giving alms in secret is better than giving alms ostentatiously (they were themselves saying that it is better if alms are given for the love of God than for one's own glory). What was distinct in Jesus' teaching was precisely his idea that a reward was *not* to be hoped for and expected, first, because an expectation of reward implies that one sees oneself as someone deserving of it, that is, as a doer of good deeds (a view of oneself that Jesus was at pains to discourage, for example, in the parable of the Pharisee and the tax collector) and second, because in his vision charitable deeds ought to be done out of compassion, with one's thoughts focused on the other person rather than on one's own actions. When a charitable deed is done out of compassion, without an eye on any future reward, something happens to the disinterested doer then and there (something that brings this person closer to God), and this is, I think, what Jesus meant by his use, in quotation marks, of the word "reward."

Jesus' paradoxical use of this word was discussed, in a particularly interesting way, by Bultmann ([1926]1958): ". . . love with the secondary motive of reward, love with a backward look on one's own achievement, would not be love. Jesus' attitude is indeed paradoxical; he promises reward to those who are obedient without thought of reward." Unlike Jeremias (1971), Bultmann did not draw the conclusion that Jesus was using the word "reward" in quotation marks, insisting that Jesus held firmly to the idea of reward. In saying this, Bultmann was trying to differentiate Jesus' ethics from what he calls "the idealistic ethic": "He knows nothing of *doing good for good's sake*; the idea that every good deed is its own reward is foreign to him" ([1926]1958:62). I agree with Bultmann on this point, and despite appearances, the interpretation that I am suggesting here does not involve such an idealistic ethic. I agree that something good *happens* to the disinterested giver because of his or her act, but it is confusing and misleading to insist that this good thing is a reward in the literal sense of the word "reward." It is clear from Bultmann's discussion that in fact he, like Jesus, is using the word "reward" metaphorically:

> According to Jesus' view man does not win value for himself, but if he is obedient God rewards him, gives him more than he has. This can be made clear from the fact that in the relation between man and man the actual reward for kindness shown is not the kindness itself, but the joy and gratitude which are awakened by it and enrich the giver. This reward can evidently never become the motive of the act, and nevertheless we should misunderstand and fail to appreciate what happens between man and man, if we did not see that for the kindness of man this reward is promised. So also the man who is obedient is enriched by God. (pp. 62–63)

In Bultmann's ([1926]1958) example, an act of kindness "enriches the giver." Clearly, such an enrichment is not a "reward" in the literal sense of the word because a reward in a literal sense means something good done to a person, after the act, by another person (in recognition of the merit inherent in the act). The same applies to what Bultmann calls God's reward: it is not a question of God's doing something good for a person after this person has done something good, in recognition of this person's merit, but rather of something good happening to this person, as it were, there and then. When Jesus said that "it is more blessed to give than to receive" (Acts 20:35), presumably he did not mean that giving, in contrast to receiving, will be rewarded but rather that a (disinterested) act of giving is in itself a blessing (a happy thing). It enriches the giver because, I suggest, it brings that person closer to God. The view that "good deeds done out of impure motives are entirely inadequate" (Heschel 1959:189) may indeed sound severe, even harsh. If we ask, however, whether self-seeking deeds can enrich people's souls, make their heart more loving and bring them closer to God, a negative answer does not sound severe or harsh but rather realistic.

Discussing the authorship of the passage under discussion, Betz (1995: 347–348) writes, "The possibility also remains that Jesus himself composed 6:1–6, 16–18. If one assumes this possibility, however, the question arises why elsewhere the Jesus-tradition has no trace of these doctrines." What Betz appears chiefly to have in mind is the doctrine of reward. I believe, however, that Betz was mistaken in attributing to Jesus (as the source of Matt. 6:1–6 and 6:16–18) the doctrine of reward (in a literal sense). There is no trace of such a doctrine anywhere else in Jesus' teaching, and there is no trace of such a doctrine here either: as Jeremias (1971: 216) put it, Jesus "abolished" the very idea of reward.

3. Do not let your left hand know . . .

Matthew 6:3

But when you do a charitable deed, do not let your left hand know
   what your right hand is doing.

This sentence about the left and right hand has puzzled many commentators. Betz (1995:358) has observed, "The proverb 'Let your left hand not know what your right hand is doing' is as famous as its meaning is disputed." By calling this saying a "proverb," Betz seems to be inviting the inference that it is not one of Jesus' original and unique sayings, carrying an original and unique message. In fact, however, there are good reasons to think that this saying became a proverb later (see Luz 1989:357), and Betz himself notes, "Surprisingly, there do not seem to be parallels to this proverb in biblical, contemporary Greco-Roman, or Jewish sources" (p. 358). Parallels in later Arabic and Mandean literature, noted by Betz, could well depend on Matthew (as Luz believes they do). It is quite probable, therefore, that Jesus' saying was original. (As Funk et al. 1993:148 note, its paradoxical character is certainly consistent with Jesus' style.)

What could Jesus have meant by this saying? Betz (1995) compares it with the Latin proverb *Manus manum lavat* 'one hand washes the other': "It is worth mentioning that both the Latin saying and the one in 6:3 have a slightly immoral tinge in that they describe daily dealings of some dubious nature. If one hand does not know what the other is doing, can this be anything but a sign of disorganization or dishonesty?" (p. 359). But the implication of disorganization, which is now linked with this saying when used as a proverb in both German and English, was clearly not part of the original meaning; and the same applies to dishonesty. The Latin proverb does indeed suggest illicit dealings beneficial for the parties involved, but the context makes it clear that there was no implication of dishonesty in Jesus' injunction. In fact, the context of this saying suggests, at least prima facie, an interpretation along the lines suggested by (among others) John P. Meier (1980:58): "Disciples must give alms in complete secrecy, which is expressed by the hyperbole of the ignorant left hand."

The trouble with this interpretation, however, is that it is hard to reconcile with the logic of the image: the left hand is a part of the same person who is doing a deed (with the right hand), so how can it stand for other people? From this point of view, the idea put forward centuries ago by Clement of Alexandria (1962) seems far more convincing, namely, that the two hands stand for aspects of the same person, his or her deeds and self-image (in my terms, doing and thinking): "If thou doest alms, it is said, let no one know it; and if thou fastest, anoint thyself, that God alone may know, and not a single human being. Not even he himself who shows mercy ought to know that he does show mercy" (*Stromata* 4.138.2).

In modern times, this interpretation was passionately championed by Dietrich Bonhoeffer. Commenting on the apparent contradiction between Jesus' injunction that the good deeds of his disciples should be visible to other people (Matt. 5:16) and the injunction that they should also be hidden, Bonhoeffer ([1937]1959: 142) says, "There is a pointed contrast between chapters 5 and 6. That which is visible must also be hidden. . . . We have to take heed that we do not take heed of our own righteousness." Bonhoeffer asks, "How is this paradox to be resolved?" And he replies, "The first question to ask is: From whom are we to hide the visibility of our discipleship? Certainly not from other people, for we are told to let them see our light. No. We are to hide it from ourselves" (p. 142). And this is what the metaphor of the left hand means:

All that the follower of Jesus has to do is to make sure that his obedience, following and love are entirely spontaneous and unpremeditated. If you do good, you must not let your left hand know what your right hand is doing, you must be quite unconscious of it. . . . If the left hand knows what the right hand is doing, if we become conscious of our hidden virtue, we are forging our own reward. (p. 143)

I believe that Bonhoeffer's interpretation is insightful and essentially right. Unfortunately, however, it was phrased in a way that alienated other commentators instead of convincing them. To some, it sounded as if Jesus was urging some new kind of hypocrisy and self-deception: pretending to oneself that one doesn't know what one is doing while, of course, knowing it perfectly well. For example, Luz (1989:357) insists that the saying "must not be pressed. It does not mean that 'even the person who practices the mercy may not know that he or she practises mercy'. The ideal conception of doing 'entirely spontaneous and unpremeditated good' (see D. Bonhoeffer [1937]1959:138) is alien to the text. The image only means: Nobody, not even the closest confidant, needs to know about your almsgiving."

Strecker comments as follows (also with reference to D. Bonhoeffer):

> According to a wide-spread interpretation it means that proper doers of good deeds are not conscious of them. . . . Yet the Preacher on the Mount aims his demand of righteousness at the doings of people who are conscious of their own selves. What is required is not a renunciation of the knowledge of one's own actions; rather, the proverbial expression makes clear the required action, which—because it occurs in secret—is set against the externally focussed behavior of the hypocrites. The doing of good is supposed to remain hidden, not from the doer, but from the people, in order to escape public honor as the substitute for heavenly reward. (1988: 100–101)

Betz (1995:358), too, rejects Bonhoeffer's interpretation: "The point in SM/Matt. 6:3 is not that almsgiving should be done in such a way that the donor is not aware of the act. Rather, the donor's knowledge of the gift should not be used to let others know of it, but to keep it secret."

As I mentioned earlier, however, the problem with Bonhoeffer's ([1937]1959) interpretation may lie more in its slightly unfortunate phrasing than in the basic idea. It would indeed be hard to accept that the donor should not be aware of the act (Betz 1995) or that what is required is "a renunciation of the knowledge of one's own actions" (Strecker 1988). I think, however, that Bonhoeffer's and Clement of Alexandria's (1962) main idea would be less vulnerable to criticism if it were rephrased as follows:

(a) sometimes when a person is doing something good for other
     people
(b) this person thinks: "I am doing something good for other people"
(c) (because of this, this person feels something good)
(d) it will not be good if you think like this
(e) when you are doing something good for other people

As I see it, the question is not what the doer of a good deed *knows* but what he or she *thinks*; and if the person thinks, "I am doing something good for other people," this does smack of the kind of self-congratulatory smugness and self-righteousness that Jesus denounced in his teaching (e.g., in the parable of the Pharisee and the tax collector). Whether or not a component that makes the smug feeling explicit ("because of this, this person feels something good") is justified is a question that I will leave open.

To insist that Jesus' saying about the ignorant left hand suggests nothing more than doing good deeds in secret is to deny that this saying adds anything to the message of verses 2 and 4. If, however, it is interpreted along the lines suggested here, that is, in accordance with Clement of Alexandria's (1962) and Dietrich Bonhoeffer's ([1937]1959) approach, it adds a great deal.

In addition to repudiating smug, self-congratulatory attitudes, verse 3 throws important light on the meaning of "reward" in Jesus' speech, notably, on the question of whether it is meant literally, as, for example, Betz (1995), Limbeck (1995), and Strecker (1988) believe, or metaphorically, as, for example, Jeremias (1971) insists.

I have quoted Strecker (1988:101) as saying that "the doing of good is supposed to remain hidden, not from the doer, but from the people, in order to escape public honor as the substitute for heavenly reward." This means that the doer of good deeds is conscious of his or her good deed and does expect a heavenly reward. Betz (1995:360) puts this view even more bluntly when he says (commenting on Matt. 6:4) that "the reason for secrecy is to protect one's eschatological reward: 'and your Father who sees in the hidden will compensate you'. . . . A good deed done in this way has been done according to God's will and as the Torah requires, but its reward is still outstanding." But the desire to "protect one's eschatological reward" presupposes the thought that "I am doing something good (for other people)" or "I have done something good (for other people)." I have tried to show, however, that such a thought would be inconsistent with the image of the ignorant left hand. If such a thought is absent, there can be no thought of protecting one's eschatological reward either.

The question of what the doer of good deeds is *thinking* is crucial from Jesus' point of view, as the parable of the Pharisee and the tax collector clearly illustrates. Strecker (1988:101) says that in 6:1–18 "Matthew wants to emphasize the necessity of doing good deeds with a view toward God and not in the view of people." Simone Weil ([1951]1973), on the other hand, has suggested that any thought about God (let alone about a heavenly reward) would detract from the value of a charitable deed in God's eyes. In her interpretation, when one is doing a charitable deed, it is not the time to turn one's thoughts toward God: "There are times when thinking of God separates us from him. . . . He who gives bread to the famished sufferer for the love of God will not be thanked by Christ. He has already had his reward in this thought itself. Christ thanks those who do not know to whom they are giving food" (p. 151).

Simone Weil's ([1951]1973) interpretation suggests that the doer should focus on the person for whom he or she is doing the charitable deed rather than on God (let alone on oneself or on one's heavenly reward); that is, that the doer should think along the following lines:

something bad has happened to this person (these people)
I want to do something good for this person (these people) because of
   this

Such an other-centered thought appears to be quite consistent with the attitude of the good Samaritan, who, when he saw the wounded man, "had compassion on him" (Luke 10:33). If, however, the good Samaritan had started to think while bandaging the man's wounds, "I am now doing something good for another person" (and to feel something good because of this), this would mean that the left hand did know what the right hand was doing, and the Samaritan would be having his reward there and then. In Simone Weil's interpretation, even the thought that "I'm now doing something good for God" could be seen as the left hand knowing what the right hand is doing.

Strecker (1988:102), who strongly emphasizes the motive of reward in Matthew 6:1–4, 5–8, and 16–18, feels compelled, as a result, to question the authenticity of these sayings. Having quoted Braun's (1969: 2, 56) statement that "the naive expectation of reward was de facto overcome by the core of Jesus' message," Strecker adds, "This compels the conclusion that the inferred pre-Matthean form of the three catechetical pieces presumably does not go back to Jesus" (p. 102). But this conclusion is quite unnecessary if the references to "reward" in Jesus' sayings are interpreted as metaphorical and ironic, as Jeremias (1971:216) has urged they should be and as Jesus' teaching about the left hand not knowing what the right hand is doing clearly encourages us to do. In the interpretation proposed here, Jesus' use of the word "reward" can be seen as entirely consistent with "the core of Jesus' message," in which "the naive expectation of reward was de facto overcome." In fact, the saying about the left hand not knowing what the right hand is doing epitomizes one of the central themes in Jesus' teaching: his condemnation of self-righteousness, of seeing oneself as a "good person" and a "doer of good things"; in his teaching, people are certainly expected to do "good things," but with a different mindset.

4. When you pray, go into your room

Matthew 6:5–6

5. And when you pray, you shall not be like the hypocrites. For they love to pray standing in the synagogues and on the corners of the streets, that they may be seen by men. Assuredly, I say to you, they have their reward.
6. But you, when you pray, go into your room, and when you have shut your door, pray to your Father who is in the secret place; and your Father who sees in secret will reward you openly.
7. But when you pray, do not use vain repetitions as the heathen do. For they think that they will be heard for their many words.
8. Therefore do not be like them. For your Father knows the things you have need of before you ask him.

Strecker (1988:103) calls the example of the "hypocrites," standing and praying on the street corners, "caricaturing": "The polemical reproach suggests the purpose ascribed to the hypocrites: their prayer is an exhibition. They are displaying themselves before the people instead of addressing God while alone. Since they satisfy their egotistic desires under the pretext of prayer, they have received their reward." Proper prayer, according to Strecker, "must not satisfy a passion for public recognition but should be an act of obedience. It must concentrate exclusively on the God who is addressed in prayer" (p. 104).

The contrast that Strecker draws between displaying oneself before people and concentrating exclusively on God seems to identify the main point of Jesus' message in this passage. (The only point that may seem questionable is the mention of obedience, to which I will return later.) Strecker's reference to egotistic desires is, I think, right insofar as it can be represented in the following components (in the attitude of the "exhibitionist"):

if I do this something good will happen to me because of this
(people will think good things about me)
I want this

Whether the person who is praying ostentatiously is in fact satisfying his or her desire for a personal advantage is not really discussed by Jesus. Here as elsewhere, his reference to "reward" should, I think, be taken as quotational and figurative: the real point is that whereas seeing oneself, in one's imagination, through the eyes of an admiring audience can make one feel good, it is not good for a person to pray like the hypocrites do; however, praying in the way recommended by Jesus is always good for a person, not because God will do something good for this person *because* of his or her prayer, but because the act of genuine (God-oriented, not people-oriented) prayer is in itself good for the person who prays.

When the reference to "reward" is interpreted in this way (see the discussion in sections 2 and 3), it removes the apparent contradiction between an exclusive focus on God and a simultaneous thought of reward, which has troubled some commentators. For example, Luz (1989:359); writes: "Prayer has to be oriented alone on God, who again is designated as Father and so as the God of Jesus. The statement that he will reward right prayers, which is due to the symmetry of the strophes, is very troublesome." Luz adds in a footnote: "It is not a question of the promise of answering prayers in the quiet little room but of the reward for such praying in the last judgement." One can agree with the first of these sentiments but scarcely the second: there would be an inherent contradiction in encouraging a person to focus one's full and undivided attention on God and to keep an eye on the final reward at the same time.

What Jesus really means here, I think, is that genuine prayer is always good for the person who does it; just as disinterested giving is good for the giver, disinterested worship of God is good for the worshiper. The "reward," the "treasure," is not extrinsic to the act but lies in the act itself because the act itself brings a person closer to God, and this is the good thing that happens to the praying person there and then.

Basing ourselves on this interpretation of "reward," let us examine more closely the two kinds of prayer depicted by Jesus: the "wrong," self-interested and people-oriented, and the "right," God-oriented. Prayer, of course, is not a universal human concept. Trying to explain this concept to cultural outsiders we can say, above all, that what is involved is speaking to God, that is, saying things to God. A full explication of the concept of prayer would need to include some other components as well (for discussion, see Wierzbicka 1993b), but it is not necessary to undertake such a full explication here. What matters in the present context is the difference between two kinds of speaking to God. Using the language of the ancient commentators (see Luz 1989:359), we can say that the essential difference between the two lies not in the place (*topos*) where this speaking to God should be done, and not even in the manner (*tropos*), but in the aim (*skopos*). The *skopos* of the hypocrites as depicted by Jesus can be represented as follows:

(a) sometimes a person says many things to God because this person
       thinks:
(b)   "if I do this something good will happen to me because of this
(c)   other people will know that I did it
(d)   they will think that I did it because I wanted to say some
              things to God
(e)   they will think good things about me because of this
(f)   I want this"
(g) when this person thinks this, this person feels something good

I have used the phrase "many things" rather than "some things" or "something" in component (a) because this seems to be implied by the image of someone standing for some time on street corners to be seen by other people (and "loving it"). Verse 7, with its reference to "vain repetitions, as the heathens do," seems similarly to support the phrase "many things."[5]

Component (a) shows also that what matters is the thinking behind the act, (b) and (f) jointly show a self-interested motive (Strecker's 1988 "egotistical desires"), (c) portrays an expectation of publicity, and (e) shows an expectation of human glory. Component (d) needs further consideration: does the hypocrite think that other people's expected admiration will depend on the attribution of a pious motive? For the time being, I would like to leave this question open. In any case, it is clear that with or without component (e), Jesus' judgment about the hypocritical attitude is negative and that he wants to discourage his disciples from adopting a similar attitude:

(h) it will not be good if you say things to God because you think like
       this

Turning now to the kind of prayer suggested by Jesus as an alternative, I would represent it as follows:

(i) it will be good if you say things to God because you think:
(j)   "I want to say some things to God
(k)   I know that when I say something to God, God can hear my
              words

(l)   at the same time I know that God wants to say some things
        to me
(m)   I want to hear God's words"

Here again, (i) shows that what matters is the motive, and (j) identifies the right
motive as wanting to say some things to God (Strecker's 1988 "concentrating exclusively on the God who is addressed in prayer" and Luz's 1989 "orientation on
God alone"). Components (k), (l), and (m) may all seem superfluous at first glance.
But the conviction that God can hear one's words seems to be a necessary assumption behind the notion of prayer (otherwise, why say things to God at all?). In fact,
verse 7 confirms this assumption (almost) explicitly: the heathens think that they
will be heard for their many words, and what is wrong with that is the emphasis
on "many," not the conviction that their words will be heard. Furthermore, Jesus
says that "your Father knows the things you have need of before you ask him." If
he knows, why does he want to be prayed to at all? The implication seems to be
that he wants to hear people "say things to him": they can't impart to him any
information, and yet he wants to hear their words addressed to him all the same.
"Why?" one may ask; and in modern language, the answer can only be: for the
sake of the relationship (the I-Thou relationship). Although public (collective) prayer
no doubt had a place in Jesus' conception of worship, he clearly thought that an
intimate I-Thou relationship could not be sustained by community prayer alone—
let alone by individual prayer done in public for public display.

As many commentators have pointed out, Jesus' emphasis on private prayer
and his own practice of it (when he would leave his disciples and go to a de-
serted place to pray) are both distinctive. Montefiore ([1927] 1968: 98) notes,
"He [Jesus] is not thinking here of synagogal worship, and certainly not depreci-
ating it. But he is anxious that his disciples should practise what he himself
cherished and practiced: the habit of private prayer." Montefiore, in whose view
the original portions of the Sermon on the Mount are not very numerous
(p. 127), believes that Jesus' teaching on private prayer (Matt. 6:6) is one of its
most original and novel aspects.

What mattered to Jesus, then, was not just an absence of ostentation and public
display but also the need for private prayer, for speaking to God on an I-Thou
basis, "having shut the door of the storeroom" (the Greek word *tameion* refers
to an inner, windowless room). Jesus' use of the intimate, familiar word *Abba*
for addressing God is highly relevant in this regard. Jeremias (1971:67) says that
"it expresses the heart of Jesus' relationship to God." (For further discussion,
see chapter 5, section 2.)

Private prayer, recommended by Jesus to his disciples, was to be based on an
attitude reflected in the word *Abba* as a form of address. It was not just a matter
of secrecy but one of intimacy. It was important to talk to God to maintain and
nourish a relationship with God thought of as Abba; and for this relationship
to thrive, it was just as important to hear God's words as to speak to God oneself. I have included components (l) and (m) in the explication, although they
are difficult to justify on a strictly textual basis, because I think they represent

an important aspect of Jesus' conception of private prayer as reflected in the Gospels as a whole. It is only in solitude, in a windowless room with the door shut, that one can speak to God in secret and *also* hear God's words addressed to oneself. Consider, for example, such Gospel references to Jesus' praying as this (Luke 6:12–13): "Now it came to pass in those days that he went out to the mountains to pray, and continued all night in prayer to God. And when it was day, he called his disciples to him; and from them he chose twelve whom he also named apostles. . . ." Presumably, in spending all night in prayer, Jesus was not only *speaking* to his Father but also *listening* to him; and his actions the following morning seem to suggest a resolve reached not only through talking to his Father but also through listening to him and seeking to know his will.

This brings us back to the question of obedience. As mentioned earlier, Strecker (1988:104) believes that "proper prayer should be [according to Jesus] an act of obedience." In my view, however, for Jesus, proper prayer (like "proper fast"; see the next section) should be an act of love rather than an act of obedience. But love for God is expressed, in Jesus' teaching, by wanting to do God's will; and to want to do God's will, one has to seek to know what God's will for one is. Presumably, this is what Jesus was doing in his private prayer in solitude, and this is what he was encouraging his disciples to do. Jesus cautioned against exclusive reliance on understanding God's will as expressed through detailed commandments of the Law and instead encouraged a more personal relationship between a human being and his or her Abba. So he was also implying a greater need for a person to listen to God's voice in private prayer, "in secret" and in the privacy of a personal I-Thou relationship with God.

Here, then, is my proposed explication of the message in Matthew 6:5–6:

But you, when you pray, go into your room . . .

  (a) sometimes a person says many things to God because this person thinks:

  (b)   "if I do this something good will happen to me because of this

  (c)   other people will know that I did it

  (d)   they will think that I did it because I wanted to say some things to God

  (e)   they will think good things about me because of this

  (f)   I want this"

  (g) when this person thinks this, this person feels something good

  (h) it will not be good if you say things to God because you think like this

  (i) it will be good if you say things to God because you think:

  (j)   "I want to say some things to God

  (k)   I know that when I say something to God, God can hear my words

  (l)   at the same time I know that God wants to say some things to me

(m)   I want to hear God's words"

(n) it will be good for you if you say things to God because you think like this

5. When you fast, anoint your head

Matthew 6:16–18

16. Moreover, when you fast, do not be like the hypocrites, with a sad countenance. For they disfigure their faces that they may appear to men to be fasting. Assuredly, I say to you, they have their reward.
17. But you, when you fast, anoint your head and wash your face,
18. so that you do not appear to men to be fasting, but to your Father, who is in the secret place; and your Father who sees in secret will reward you openly.

The question of whether the Matthean Jesus' sayings about fasting go back to the historical Jesus is disputed, mainly because elsewhere in the Gospels (Matt. 9:14–15; Mark 2:18–20) one hears Jesus defending his disciples for not fasting—in contrast to the Pharisees and the disciples of John the Baptist, who did fast:

14. Then the disciples of John came to him, saying: 'Why do we and the Pharisees fast often, but your disciples do not fast?'
15. And Jesus said to them, 'Can the friends of the bridegroom mourn as long as the bridegroom is with them? But the days will come when the bridegroom will be taken away from them, and then they will fast.' (Matt. 9:14–15; cf. Mark 2:18–20)

Meier (1980:63) states that, according to Jesus, "a genuine fast in the sight of God can never take place in the sight of men," adding, "Since the historical Jesus forbade his disciples to fast because the joyful time of salvation had come (Mt. 9:14–15a), some think that the early church created this teaching on a proper fast when it took up the practice of fasting (as reflected in Mt. 9:15b)." Many other commentators, however, do not think that Jesus forbade fasting. For example, Carson (1994:80) views the sayings on fasting attributed to Jesus in Matthew 6:16–18 differently: "Just as Jesus did not demean almsgiving and prayer, so likewise does he refrain from speaking against fasting *per se*: he assumes his disciples will fast. On the other hand, in another context he is found defending his disciples for *not* fasting (Matt. 8:14–17). In any case, here in the Sermon on the Mount Jesus is interested in condemning the abuses of the practice, and in exposing its dangers."

Thus, whereas Meier thinks that Jesus forbade his disciples to fast, Carson thinks that he assumed that his disciples would fast; and Betz (1995:418) comments, "One should admit that we are inadequately informed about the historical Jesus' attitude toward fasting."

Since elsewhere in his Gospel Matthew (4:1-2) has Jesus fasting in the desert, it seems unlikely that he thought that Jesus had forbidden fasting. Luke (4:1-2), too, attributes to Jesus a long fast; and as pointed out by Fitzmyer (1981), Jeremias (1954:123), and other commentators, there is no reason to think that this didn't have a real basis in the life of Jesus, although Jesus may have, of course, translated his experience into figurative language. It is also interesting to note that the early Christian community described in Acts (13:2-3) did fast: "As they ministered to the Lord and fasted, the Holy Spirit said, 'Now separate for me Barnabas and Saul for the work to which I have called them.' Then, having fasted and prayed, and laid hands on them, they sent them away."

It is possible, of course, that both Meier (1980) and Carson (1994) are right and that although Jesus did not encourage his closest disciples to fast when he was with them, he did assume that they would fast later on. It is also possible that his counsel on fasting was aimed, more generally, at all those who did fast at the time of his teaching. As Funk et al. (1993:150) remark, refering to verse 6:17, "The saying enjoins those who do fast to obscure their practice rather than advertise it." Similarly, Strecker (1988:129) says that "the Jewish custom of fasting is indisputably presupposed yet defined in a new way." The question addressed here is not whether or not it is good to fast but how to fast—and how not to fast—if one is fasting at all.

On balance, I think that there are no strong reasons for thinking that the sayings in Matthew 6:16-18 do not go back to Jesus, and it is interesting to note that even the scholars of the Jesus Seminar are willing to accept that at least verse 17, which they regard as the core verse of the cluster 6:16-18, may well do so (see. Funk et al. 1993:150). As noted by Montefiore ([1927]1968:106), however, the satirical vignette in 6:16 is also consistent with Jesus' style. Having quoted a rabbinic parallel to it in the saying of a Shulchan Aruch that "he who fasts and makes a display of himself to others, to boast of his fasting, is punished for this," Montefiore adds that "the teaching of Jesus would be on such lines, and is, as usual, put in a hyperbolic and picturesque form." (For further discussion of this point, see Tannehill 1975:82-83.)

Furthermore, although Jesus' picturesque and hyperbolic style is in evidence in verses 16 and 17 rather than in 18, it is verse 18 that Montefiore identifies as most unlike anything in rabbinic teaching. As mentioned earlier, Montefiore believes that only a very few passages in the Sermon on the Mount "do not harmonize with, or are not easily paralleled by, Rabbinic teaching and passages." It is particularly interesting to note, therefore, that he singles out Matthew 6:18 as one of those strikingly original (nonrabbinic) verses. Montefiore's reason appears to lie in Jesus' emphasis on private, hidden fasting in contrast to ritual, public fasting ("public" not in the sense of display but in the sense of a shared observance of collective ritual). To quote: "the Rabbis were, upon the whole, not very anxious to stimulate the practice of self-imposed fasting over and above the public fasts enjoined upon the whole community. . . . The occasional ascetic touches in the Gospels are, speaking generally, off the Rabbinic line" ([1930]1970:138).

Among more recent commentators, Luz, in particular, emphasizes the private and hidden nature of the fast recommended by the Matthean Jesus and sees both the content and the form of the sayings in Matthew 6:16–18 as a whole as characteristic of Jesus. Luz points out that

> washing is not only an expression of everyday life but also a figurative illustration of hiddenness, exactly like the "quiet room" and the saying of the left and the right hand. The listener himself or herself has to determine what "washing and anointing" means tangibly. Again, such stirring "focal-point formulations" appeal to creative fantasy and to the liberty of the listener. As such, they fit not only formally but also in terms of content with Jesus. (1989:361).

Luz concludes that the passage on fasting "presupposes it [fasting] as an expression of piety in order to inculcate the right orientation of the fasting person to God alone. The subject is the human being and not the religious custom" (p. 362).

Luz's (1989) conclusion is at odds with Betz's (1995) analysis of 6:16–18 in terms of cultic instruction and ritual (consistent with Betz's approach to Matt. 6:1–18 as a whole). For example, Betz (1995:418) remarks, "SM/Matt. 6:16–18 does not recommend non-observance . . . but modifies the reason of, as well as the performance of, the ritual." Betz's phrase "the reason of" seems right, but it is difficult to agree with his words "performance" and "ritual." It is true that on the surface of the text the Matthean Jesus is speaking about how to fast (the answer: secretly) rather than why to fast. We have seen, however, that in the case of alms and prayer, too, Jesus appears to be talking about the how rather than the why and that nonetheless there are reasons to think that the language of the how conveys in those passages a message about the why. I argue that the same applies to the passage about fasting: as Luz says, the subject is not the religious custom but "the human being" and "the right orientation of the fasting person to God alone." The manner of fasting (secretly) is relevant only to the extent to which it bears on the motive: what matters is that fasting should not be done for public display. Presumably, Jesus' image of washing one's face and anointing one's head did not mean to suggest deception of a new kind (e.g., pretending that one is going to a banquet when one is actually fasting) but rather a total absence of a desire to be seen and admired by other people.

I assume, then, that the passage about fasting is indeed, like the passages about almsgiving and prayer, essentially about the motive rather than about the right performance of a ritual (the *skopos* rather than the *tropos*). In fact, I suggest that, in a sense, this passage is even more about the motive than are the passages about almsgiving and prayer. Almsgiving and prayer may at least *seem* to have some meaning even apart from the motive: the person who gives alms is, even apart from the motive, "doing something good for other people"; and a person who is praying is, even apart from the motive, speaking to God, and thus performing a religious act of sorts. But a person who is refraining from eating can only give his or her act some meaning by a motive; a person who is giving a lot of money

to the poor can expect to be admired for the act itself, but a person who is refraining from eating can expect to be admired only for the act combined with
an apparent religious motive.

Before attempting even a partial explication of Matthew 6:16–18, therefore,
we must determine what the ostensible motive of the ostentatious fasting might
be and, ipso facto, what the pure motive of fasting, as seen by the Matthean Jesus,
must be, too. Once the question has been asked, the answer seems clear—it has
to be done for the sake of God: "For fasting is not supposed to count on the
people's approbation but to happen for God's sake. Hence, the summons to fast
in such a way that the orientation towards God is ensured" (Strecker 1988:129).
As noted by Betz a precedent for such fasting can be found in the story of Joseph in the so-called "Testaments of the Twelve Patriarchs" (The Old Testament
Pseudepigrapha (1983), from the second century B.C., where Joseph says about
himself, "For those seven years I fasted, and yet seemed to the Egyptians like
someone who was living luxuriously, for those who fast for the sake of God receive
graciousness of countenance" (1995:421).

What exactly does it mean, to fast for the sake of God? Three different explications phrased in universal human concepts suggest themselves here as possibilities to explore. First, it might be suggested that people fast because they think that
God wants them to do it. This would be consistent with the suggestion made by
some commentators that here as elsewhere, what matters is obedience. I think,
however, that in the case of private and hidden fasts, which go well beyond any
prescribed ritual fasting, this word is particularly unhelpful. But even if we discard
the word "obedience," which suggests thinking in terms of what one has to do
rather than of what one wants to do, the suggestion that private fasting should be
explained simply in terms of doing God's will seems unconvincing. It is the prescribed, required fasting that can be explained in these terms; private fasting, although not inconsistent with it, seems nonetheless to involve something extra.

A second possibility is that of wanting to do something good for God—a kind
of voluntary gift to God, expressing that love that was the theme of the first, and
greatest, commandment: "to love [God] with all the heart, with all the understanding, with all the soul, and with all the strength" (Matt. 9:13). But whatever
the merits of such an idea in other contexts, it does not seem to provide the
right solution here, if only because it doesn't seem to apply to Jesus' own fasting. Assuming that Jesus did go into the desert for some time, as the evangelists
tell us he did, and that he fasted there, why did he do it? The answer that "he
did it because he wanted to do something good for God" (give sacrifice to God)
would seem odd.

A third possibility is that of "wanting to be close to God"; a person under-
taking a private and hidden fast may do so out of a desire to be closer to God.
Here, the main problem is the seemingly metaphorical character of the expression "close to God," although it can be argued that a metaphor may be a fitting
way of expressing something that does not seem to be expressible in any other
way—as long as it is not culture-specific and therefore in need of further explanations. Can one say "close to God" in any language and be understood? The matter
requires empirical investigation.

Furthermore, "close to God" is metaphorical only on the assumption that "close" as such is a purely spatial concept. But this must not be taken for granted. Just as BIG and SMALL may not be restricted to physical objects but may also be usable with reference to, say, requests or favours, so NEAR (CLOSE) and FAR need not be inherently spatial but may be also applicable to relationships. Finally, even if we decided that the universal concepts CLOSE and FAR are best conceived of as purely spatial, we might still be able to use CLOSE in an explication as a basis for a universal simile: not "to be close to God" but "to be as it were close to God," "as if close to God," "like close to God."

The matter requires further investigation. For the time being, however, I suggest (very tentatively), that the underlying purpose of a religious fast undertaken "for the sake of God" can perhaps be represented as "wanting to be close to God." Arguably, the "hypocrites" in the satirical vignette in Matthew 6:16 pretend that this is precisely what they are doing: refraining from eating out of a desire to be close to God. This leads us to the following partial explication ("eat" is not universal, but I will not try to explicate it here):

> sometimes a person is doing something
> [not eating anything for some time]
> because this person thinks:
>> "if I do this something good will happen to me because of this
>> other people will know that I did it
>> they will think that I did it because I wanted to be close to God
>> they will think something good about me because of this
>> I want this"
> when this person thinks this this person feels something good

From Jesus' point of view, there doesn't seem to be much value in a religious fast of this kind. Betz (1995:418) has remarked, "One must conclude that the recommendation is critical of the common view that fasting as such is religiously and ethically valuable, no matter how it is done"; and in this case I can only agree with Betz's conclusion.

In Matthew 6:1–18, ostentatious fasting is presented, of course, in a way that is fully symmetrical to ostentatious almsgiving and ostentatious prayer, but one wonders whether this symmetry doesn't to some extent come from Matthew's presentation. The explications proposed here are not entirely symmetrical because the explication of fasting, in contrast to that of almsgiving at least, does imply a pious motive. What is wrong with ostentatious fasting as interpreted here, then, is not only that people do it to seek admiration but also that they do it, as it were, under false pretenses: they want to be admired for a pious motive, whereas in fact their motive is not pious but self-seeking. Thus I propose the following overall explication:

When you fast . . .

(a) sometimes a person is doing something [e.g., not eating anything for some time] because this person thinks:

(b)   "if I do this something good will happen to me because of this
(c)   other people will know that I did it
(d)   they will think that I did it because I wanted to be close to God
(e)   they will think something good about me because of this
(f)   I want this"
(g) when this person thinks this, this person feels something good

(h) it will not be good if you do something [e.g., not eat anything for
       some time]
          because you think like this
(i) it will be good if you do the same thing because you think:
       "I want to be close to God"

(j) if a person does something [e.g., doesn't eat anything for some time]
       because this person thinks like this
(k) this is good for this person
(l) something good happens to this person because of this

In this explication, I have prefaced the reference to "not eating anything for some time" with an "e.g.," treating it as just an example of a religious action. The same explication could in fact also stand for almsgiving that is aimed at one's own glory and at the same time pretends to a pious motive. But ostentatious fasting is a particularly clear example of a falsely pious action because, unlike charitable deeds, it seems to have no justification at all other than a God-oriented motive: as mentioned earlier, a self-seeking charitable deed may be good for the receiver even if it is not good for the giver, but a self-seeking fast seems to do no good to anybody.

Perhaps this is why early Christian communities apparently remembered Jesus as someone who was generally opposed to fasting. For example, Betz (1995:419) says that "the earlier Christian references to fasting are critical of the Jewish practice. . . . This situation seems to be the result of Jesus' own critical attitude toward the ritual. The passage SM/Matt. 6:16–18 suggests that ostentatiousness was the reason for this attitude." As noted earlier, however, there are good reasons to think that what Jesus was really opposed to was the deception and pursuit of one's own glory behind ostentatious fasting rather than the idea of a religious fast as such. It is interesting to note in this connection Barclay's ([1975]1993: 237–238) comments on fasting in his commentary on Matthew 6:16: "There are many reasons why a wise fasting is an excellent thing. (i) Fasting is good for health. . . . (ii) Fasting is good for self-discipline. . . . (iii) Fasting preserves us from becoming the slaves of a habit. . . . (iv) Fasting makes us appreciate things all the more."

These may all be excellent reasons for fasting, but they are hardly relevant to what Jesus was talking about. Jesus did not suggest that it is good for a person to fast, although he didn't deny it either. What he did say (or at least convey) is, I think, compatible with the interpretation that it is good for a person to do *anything* (assuming it is nothing inherently bad!) if one does it because one thinks, "I want to be close to God." For when a person does something because he or she wants to be close to God, something good happens to this person, and perhaps this person can be said to be, as it were, closer to God. The last phrase echoes, in fact, Jesus' reply to the scribe who said to him that "to love [God] with all the heart, with all the understanding, with all the soul, and with all the strength, and to love one's neighbour as oneself, is more than all the whole burnt offering and sacrifices" (Matt. 9:13): "You are not far from the Kingdom of God."[6]

6. *Lay up for yourselves treasures in heaven*

Matthew 6:19–21

19. Do not lay up for yourselves treasures on earth, where moth and rust destroy and where thieves break in and steal.
20. but lay up for yourselves treasures in heaven, where neither moth nor rust destroys, and where thieves do not break in and steal.
21. For where your treasure is there your heart will be also.

Luke 12:33–34

33. [Sell what you have and give alms;] provide yourselves money bags which do not grow old, a treasure in the heavens that does not fail, where no thief approaches nor moth destroys.
34. For where your treasure is, there your heart will be also.

What is the treasure that Matthew and Luke are talking about? Luke makes his interpretation clear by appending to the passage the sentence "Sell what you have and give alms": obviously, he identifies the treasure in question as material possessions which can be sold and turned into alms. Matthew, on the other hand, gives no indication that treasure is to be understood here in the sense of possessions and wealth, and so it is rather surprising that many commentators and even translators do not hesitate to equate the Matthean treasure with wealth. For example, Funk et al. (1993:150) render the passage as "Don't acquire possessions here on earth, where moth or insect eats away. . . ." In accordance with this translation, they sum up the passage in question as "injunctions against wealth."

But is such an interpretation justified? Isn't Matthew talking here about treasures in a more general sense, as everything that people are attached to? As both Matthew and Luke have it, "where your treasure is, there your heart will be also," and surely people's hearts can be attached to other earthly treasures, not only to wealth.

Funk et al. (1993:151) refer to the sentence "For where your treasure is your heart will be also" as a proverb, remarking that "the proverb may have been a piece of common lore that was attributed to Jesus in oral tradition or by the author of Q." On the other hand, Betz says,

At first sight, this sentence looks like a proverb, but it appears to be more than simply commonplace. It has no parallel, to my knowledge, in any of the collections of proverbs from all antiquity. This uniqueness may be accidental, since we do not possess all the proverbs that existed in antiquity, but the absence of parallels in the Old Testament and subsequent Jewish literature almost rules out a proverbial origin. Many scholars have therefore taken the sentence to be an original creation of Jesus. (1993:151)

Whether or not it originated with Jesus, the saying does seem to suggest that Jesus was indeed talking about treasures in the sense of things that are *treasured*, rather than in the sense of material possessions as such. Viviano (1990:645) comments on the word "treasure" in Matthew 6:19 as follows: "A Matthean interest; cf. 13:44," where "13:44" refers to the parable of the hidden treasure. But after all, the word *thesauros* "treasure" is used not only in Matthew's verses 19, 20, and 21 but also in Luke's verses 33 and 34, and so it probably comes in this context from their shared source (*Quelle*), rather than solely from Matthew. Furthermore, both Matthew and Luke distinguish between *thesauros* "treasure" (Matt. 6:19–21; Luke 12:33–34) and *mamōnas* "mammon" (Matt. 6:24; Luke 16:13). If *mamōnas* stands for money, wealth, and possessions, there are good reasons to think that *thesauros* stands for treasure in the more general sense of good things to which one is attached and on which one has set one's heart.

The contrast between God and mammon is more absolute than that between treasures on earth and treasures in heaven; in the latter case there is a common denominator (treasure), whereas in the former case there is none. According to Jesus (as reported in Matt. 6:24; Luke 16:13), one cannot serve God and mammon at the same time. But the same categorical either-or does not necessarily apply to desiring earthly treasures and heavenly treasures. Jesus did not condemn the desire for earthly treasures in the sense of good things that happen to people on earth. Rather, he encouraged a certain detachment from such desires: one may want good things and one may even pray for them (see. Matt. 7:7–11); but it is good to remember that one will die and that good things that may happen to one before one dies will not be good for one forever. This means that Jesus did not oppose an other-worldly perspective on life to a this-worldly one but rather encouraged a perspective that embraces both sides of the divide. In the explication that I will propose here, therefore, the emphasis will be on "things that will always be good for you," rather than on "things that will be good for you after you have died."

Good things that cannot continue to be valuable for eternity include not only wealth but also social status, prestige, comfort, good looks, intelligence, health, independence, and so on. Jesus' teaching is certainly radical when it presents the stark alternative God or mammon, but it is also radical when it opposes good things that can be permanent to good things that can only be transient." For many people, it may be easier to rise in their minds above a love of mammon than to rise above respect for intelligence, prestige, good looks, or personal independence. Unlike many other teachers of wisdom, Jesus was not denying the value of earthly good things; rather, he kept drawing people's attention to a larger picture, including not only earth but also heaven.

The fact that the Gospel teaching about transient and permanent treasures is not without parallels in other religious traditions does not make Jesus' teaching on this point any less radical, and it is difficult to agree that it "does not echo his distinctive voice" (Funk et al. 1993:341; cf. also p. 151). There are certainly parallels elsewhere, but their existence is not inconsistent with a view that the sentences about treasure, moth, and rust do in fact echo Jesus' own distinctive voice. And even when one compares the sayings attributed to Jesus by Matthew and Luke with their alleged parallels, Jesus' sayings do strike one as distinct. For example, Betz cites the following parallels to Matthew 6:19-21 from the Greek and Jewish literature (not a complete list but a representative selection):

> Happiness does not dwell in herds nor in gold; the soul is the dwelling place of the daemon. (Democritus).

> Blessed he who has earned wealth from divine thoughts. Wretched he who cherishes a dark delusion concerning the gods. (Empedokles).

> Because, sirs, I conceive that people's wealth and poverty are to be found not in their real estate but in their hearts. (Xenophon).

> For the ways of men are known before him always, and the storerooms of the heart are understood before they happen [*sic*]. (Philo) (1995:429)

> For as I have said, the treasures of evil things are in ourselves; with God are those of good things only. (Philo)

These are all very interesting quotations, but to my mind they highlight rather than undermine the originality and distinctiveness of Jesus' treasure sayings. They do not present life on earth *sub specie aeternitatis* and do not relate either life before death or life after death to God (Jesus' "heaven").

The same applies to putative parallels in the Old Testament and in the Jewish wisdom and apocalyptic literature like the following:

> Measure your alms by what you have; if you have much give more; if you have little do not be afraid to give less in alms. So doing you will lay up for yourself a great treasure for the day of necessity. For almsgiving delivers from death and saves people from passing down to darkness. Almsgiving in the most effective offering for all those who do it in the presence of the Most High. (Tobit, 4:4-11 Jerusalem Bible).

This is a fine text, and there are clearly some echoes of it in the Lucan version of the treasure sayings. But the sayings attributed to Jesus are not a simple repetition of Tobit 4:4-11. In particular, it seems clear that the injunction in Tobit applies specifically to alms, as a source of value that transcends death, and that it is not contrasting heavenly treasures with earthly treasures in general (in the sense of any good things to which one is strongly attached).

According to Betz, in Judaism the notion of treasures in heaven was more than a metaphor. Rather, it points to a metaphysical concept, according to which there is a location above the earth, where the good works of the faithful are either kept in storage, or where they are registered in "the book of life". . . . The idea of justice requires that there be . . . a record somewhere where human deeds, good and bad, are kept available for inspection at the last judgement. This memory bank of good deeds is what is meant by "treasures in heaven". These treasures consist of accumulated "merits," which must not be spent but must continuously be increased through more good deeds. (1995:434)

Betz's presentation of the rabbinic idea of treasures in heaven can be disputed (see, e.g., E. P. Sanders 1977:146). But even if one accepted Betz's presentation as part of the background of Jesus' use of the image, the question remains: what could this image have meant on Jesus' lips? The notion of good works as accumulated merits is foreign to the Gospels. In the Sermon on the Mount itself, good deeds are presented as the natural fruit of a good tree and not as something that a tree can take any credit for (see section 14). The notion of good works as accumulated merits for which one can take credit is also explicitly rejected in parables such as the Pharisee and the tax collector. To quote Stott,[7]

Jesus was certainly not teaching a doctrine of merit or a "treasury of merits" . . . as if we could accumulate by good deeds done on earth a kind of credit account in heaven on which we and others might draw, for . . . [this] contradicts the gospel of grace which Jesus and his apostles consistently taught. . . . It seems rather to refer to such things as these: the development of Christlike character (since all we can take to heaven is ourselves); the increase of faith, hope and charity, all of which (Paul said) "abide". . . . ([1978]1992:156)

I think four interrelated ideas lie behind Jesus' metaphor of treasures in heaven. First, "heaven" stands here for God, so "treasure in heaven" refers in some way to living with God. Second, since Jesus' God is defined essentially by love (he is a Father, who wants to do good things for people), living with God cannot be a selfish goal but must be understood as intimately linked with wanting to do good things for other people (not because one thinks that something good will happen to one because of this). Third, living with God is closely related, in Jesus' teaching, to wanting to do God's will; and since God's will is that one should want to do good things for other people, points three and two are closely related and jointly elucidate the meaning of point one. Fourth, living with God is a person's supreme good (the hidden treasure, the pearl of great price); so striving to live with God is not opposed to a desire for lasting happiness but, on the contrary, is a sure path to it.

In Luke's Gospel, the link between this lasting happiness (to be found in living with God) and wanting to do good things for other people is symbolized by almsgiving; it is also symbolized by almsgiving in Jesus' reference to treasure in heaven in his advice to a rich young ruler (Mark 10:21; Matthew 19:21; Luke 18:22): "One thing you lack: Go your way, sell whatever you have and give to the poor, and you will have treasure in heaven."

Doing good things for other people is often associated in the synoptic Gospels with the image of "reward" (cf., e.g., Matt. 5:12, 6:2, 10:42; Luke 6:35). But there is no reason to regard this image as anything more than just an image. Other images used by Jesus, such as the "pearl of great price" and "the hidden treasure," present living with God as in itself a source of lasting happiness rather than a reward, and the references to "treasure in heaven" in Matthew 6:19–21 and Luke 12:33–34 are consistent with such an interpretation. Wanting to do good things for other people is presented by Jesus as sharing in God's life and therefore as an aspect of living with God rather than as a means to an end.

In Salinger's (1962:147) novel *Franny and Zooey*, the heroine, Franny, a college student, talks about her revelation that "college was just one more *dopey, inane* place in the world dedicated to piling up treasure on earth and everything. I mean treasure is *treasure*, for heaven's sake. What's the difference whether the treasure is money, or property, or even *culture*, or even just plain knowledge?" (emphasis in the original). Franny's brother Zooey meets her attack on all earthly treasure with a counterattack: he observes that there is little difference between piling up earthly treasures and piling up heavenly, that is, spiritual, treasures. "Is there all the difference in the world, for you, in which side somebody lays up his treasure—this side, or the other? The one where thieves can't break in, et cetera? Is that what makes the difference?" Zooey concludes; "As a matter of simple logic, there's no difference at all, that I can see, between the man who's greedy for material treasure—or even intellectual treasure—and the man who's greedy for spiritual treasure." Against his expectations, Franny agrees: "That's exactly what's *bothering* me so. Just because I'm choosy about what I want—in this case, *enlightenment*, or *peace*, instead of money or *prestige* or *fame* or any of those things— doesn't mean I'm not as egotistical and self-seeking as everybody else. If anything, I'm more so!"

But, of course, Jesus wasn't suggesting that one should pile up spiritual treasures instead of material, intellectual, or any other earthly treasures. Rather, he was urging a change of attitude—and a shift of one's main focus in life from "I want many good things to happen to me" to, essentially, "I want to live with God" (and, accordingly, to "I want to do good things for other people"). He wasn't trying to persuade people not to seek what is good for them, but he was pointing out that seeking what is good for one can be distinguished from a fixation on the thought "I want many good things to happen to me." The I-want-good-things-to-happen-to-me attitude is natural, but it is good if it is accompanied by some detachment; and such a detachment can be provided by remembering the "moth," "rust," "thieves," and death. Without a detached attitude to transient good things, it may be impossible to focus on the one nontransient thing: living with God, manifested in wanting to do good things for other people.

Do not lay up for yourselves treasures on earth

(a) many people think all the time:
(b)   "I want many good things to happen to me
(c)   if these things happen I will feel something very good

(d)   I want to do many things because of this"

(e) if you think like this, it will be good if you think something else at
    the same time

(f) it will be good if you think:

(g)   "at one time I will die
(h)   these things can be good for me before I die
(i)   they will not be good for me after I have died"

(j) if you want to do good things for other people
(k) not because you think something good will happen to you because
    of this
(l) this will always be good for you
(m) God wants you to want to do good things for other people
(n) like God wants to do good things for all people
(o) if you want to do good things for other people you can live with
    God
(p) if you live with God this will always be good for you

Components (a)–(d) portray the attitude of people who are constantly preoccupied with chasing earthly treasures (good things that they want to happen to
them). Components (e)–(i) do not discourage a desire for good things or an effort to secure them but suggest some detachment, by reminding the addressees
that they are mortal and that those good things will not serve them after their
death. Components (j)–(p) contrast the transient good things referred to earlier
(good things that may happen to a person) with the good things that will always
be good for this person, identifying them as good things that one wants to do
for other people—provided that one is not motivated by a desire for personal gain.
It also spells out the link between wanting to do good things for other people,
living with God, and finding what is truly and enduringly good for us.

The explication proposed here seeks to capture the paradox of the relation
between self-interest and selfishness. It assumes that people want what is good
for them, but it distinguishes this from a self-centred pursuit of good fortune
and suggests that one sure way to attain what is truly and enduringly good for
us is to love, that is, to want to do good things for other people. The catch is
that if one wants to do good things for other people because one thinks that
something good will happen to one because of this, this defeats the purpose of
any other-oriented activity and robs it of its potential eternal value. As (j)–(p) try
to convey, ultimately the only thing that is *always* good for *anyone* is living with
God (the treasure in heaven). Wanting to do good things for other people cannot be used as a means to an end (not even to *that* end). Rather, if one *disinter-
estedly* wants to do good things for other people, one can in doing so live with
God, who wants to do good things for all people, and unlike physical life, this
living with God can continue forever. A further paradoxical aspect of the complex of ideas under discussion (not referred to in the treasure sayings but elsewhere in the Gospels, including in other parts of the Sermon on the Mount) is

that it is through living with God that one can most effectively do good things for other people.

It could be objected that (apart from Luke's reference to alms) wanting to do good things for other people is not explicitly invoked in the treasure sayings; and in fact as we saw earlier, the exhortation to seek treasures in heaven is sometimes understood as an exhortation to a rather selfish and self-centred pursuit. Such an interpretation, however, can only be arrived at if one reads the passages in question in isolation, not if one reads them in context. As noted by Lambrecht (1985:178), "In 6:19-24, Jesus, with his prohibitions and commands, intends that Christians do not become closed and imprisoned in themselves. To serve God alone, to seek first his Kingdom and his righteousness, what does this imply? . . . But although helping one's neighbour is not explicitly mentioned in these two pericopes, the reader knows from Mt 5 and 6 that Matthew has it clearly in mind." What Matthew clearly has in mind is the link between wanting to live with God, wanting to do God's will, wanting to do good things for other people, and seeking what is always good for one. This is the linchpin that holds together all of Jesus' teaching about the kingdom of God.

One final question to ask in the present context is that of "quantification". I have suggested earlier that if a person lives with God, he or she can (in the light of the Gospels) live *more* with God. The image of "treasures in heaven" seems to support this notion. "More" not in the sense of "more than other people" but in the sense of a possible increase of life with God (as in "I want to live more with God"). The revered Franciscan nun from the well-known monastery of Laski in Poland, Zofia Sokołowska, has writtten, "One gives to other people not as much as one wants to give but as much as one has God in oneself." Translated into universal human concepts, this means that "when a person lives more with God this person can do more good things for other people." Although I have not incorporated this idea in the proposed explication of the treasure sayings, I think it is useful to consider it when trying to understand what Jesus meant by them.

7. The eye is the lamp of the body

Matthew 6:22-23

22. The lamp of the body is the eye. If therefore your eye is good, your whole body will be full of light.
23. But if your eye is bad, your whole body will be full of darkness. If therefore the light that is in you is darkness, how great is that darkness!

Luke 11:34-36

34. The lamp of the body is the eye. Therefore, when your eye is good, your whole body also is full of light. But when your eye is bad, your body also is full of darkness.

35. Therefore take heed that the light which is in you is not darkness.
36. If then your whole body is full of light, having no part dark, the
    whole body will be full of light, as when the bright shining of a
    lamp gives you light.

Meier (1980:65) calls the sayings about the eye and the light a "mysterious parable," and most commentators agree that it is not at all clear what they originally meant. On the basis of the context in which Matthew has placed these verses (immediately after the sayings about the heavenly and earthly treasures), Meier hypothesizes that "the mysterious parable in vv.22–23 probably signifies for Matthew the need for man to be illumined by Jesus' teaching on the transitory nature of earthly wealth, lest he fall into darkness and illusion." But Meier himself doesn't seem to be entirely convinced by this interpretation because he adds, "The problem is that this parable of the healthy and diseased eyes carries no interpretation, and may originally have referred to a kindly and generous spirit versus a mean and envious one" (p. 65).

This last suggestion corresponds to the view held by some commentators that the eye that is "not sound" should be linked with the notion of the evil eye. For example, Lachs (1987:127) suggests that the key to understanding this section "is the meaning of the 'sound eye' and its opposite, 'the unsound eye'. One who gives with or possesses a 'good eye' is generous in his acts and thoughts." Lachs quotes in this connection Old Testament and rabbinic sayings like the following: "An evil eye is grudging of bread and he is miserly at his table" (Sira 14:10). "R. Joshua said: 'The evil eye and the evil nature and the hatred of mankind puts a man out of the world' (M. Avot. 5:19)." At the same time, however, Lachs notes that "there is by no means unanimity among scholars as to the meaning of this passage. Manson [1937/1961], for example, rejects the idea of the eye representing generosity" (p. 127).

Lambrecht (1985:176–177) interprets the sayings in verses 22–23 as "a warning against greed." Strecker (1988:133–134), too, links verse 23 with "greed" but verse 22 with "faith" and "obedience to the law." Luz (1989:397) suggests that "our text is not concerned with the *nature* of human beings but with their *actions* which make them full of light or darkness. . . . If everything is not right with your acting, your obedience, your generosity, then the darkness is total." Lockyer (1963: 149) states that "the teaching of the parable before us is that of singleness of aim, looking right at an object, as opposed to tracing two aims in view."

In what follows I will not discuss the numerous interpretations that have been proposed for the eye and light sayings, but I will simply follow the line of interpretation that I regard as the most convincing and most illuminating, developing it within my own framework and supporting it with additional arguments. I will invoke in support of this interpretation two general criteria: depth and coherence.

By the criterion of depth I mean the one that was suggested by Tolstoy ([1884]1958) in his discussion of the passage on oaths and swearing (Matt. 5:33–37): one does not expect to find "side by side with rules of terrifying and deeply moving profundity and importance" sayings of banal content or of limited scope and significance (such as, for example, warnings against envy, greed, or mean-ness). And why should something so banal (in the Jewish context) need to be rendered in a particularly subtle, complex, or mysterious way? An interpretation that shows a given passage from the Sermon on the Mount to be no less pro-found and far-reaching in its implications than the others is therefore, to my mind, more plausible.

The second criterion, the criterion of coherence, requires that the sayings about the eye and the light be read against the backdrop of the New Testa-ment as a whole. This will remind us that the metaphor of light is gen-erally associated in the New Testament not with generosity, kindliness, single-mindedness, or obedience but with truth; and this fact alone must strengthen any interpretation of the eye and light sayings that links them with the notion of truth. For the moment, I will limit myself to citing only two examples of this use, one from the first letter of John and one from Paul's second letter to the Corinthians:

> This is the message which we have heard from him and declare to you, that God is light and in him is no darkness at all. If we say that we have fellowship with him, and walk in darkness, we lie and do not practise the truth (1 John 1:5-6).

Paul applies the image of light specifically to the truth of the Gospel, which he calls "the light of the gospel of the glory of Christ" (2 Cor. 4:4). It is this truth that Paul sees as his mission to preach:

> For we do not preach ourselves, but Christ Jesus the Lord, and ourselves your servants for Jesus' sake. For it is the God who commanded light to shine out of darkness who has shone in our hearts to give the light of the knowledge of the glory of God in the face of Jesus Christ (2 Cor. 4:5-6).

An interpretation of the eye and light sayings that links them directly to the notion of truth can be found in John Paul II's (1993) encyclical letter "Veritatis Splendor." This is the interpretation that I find the most persuasive. The letter opens with the following sentence (here as elsewhere, I have replaced the generic "man" with "people"): "The splendour of truth shines forth in all the works of the Creator and, in a special way, in people created in the image and likeness of God (cf. Gen. 1:26). Truth enlightens people's intelligence and shapes their free-dom, leading them to know and love the Lord. Hence the Psalmist prays: 'Let the light of your face shine on us, O Lord' (Ps. 4:6)." The encyclical recalls in this context other biblical passages that refer to light, seeing, and blindness and, in particular, Jesus' exchange with the blind man to whom he had restored sight (John 9:35-41):

> 35. Jesus heard that they [the Pharisees] had cast him out; and when
> he had found him, he said to him, 'Do you believe in the Son
> of God?'

36. He answered and said, 'Who is he, Lord, that I may believe in him?'
37. And Jesus said to him, 'You have both seen him and it is he who is talking with you.'
38. Then he said, 'Lord, I believe!' And he worshipped him.
39. And Jesus said, 'For judgment I have come into this world, that those who do not see may see, and that those who see may be made blind.'
40. Then some of the Pharisees who were with him heard these words, and said to him, 'Are we blind also?'
41. Jesus said to them, 'If you were blind, you would have no sin; but now you say, We see. Therefore your sin remains.'

Whereas this passage is clearly related to the sayings on eye and light, its meaning is not altogether transparent. In particular, the statement that Jesus has "come into this world that those who do not see may see and that those who see may be made blind" is bound to puzzle many modern readers. But presumably the phrase "those who see" is an ironic reference to those who *think* they see and who in fact do not see, and the stated goal of making those people "blind" is a figure of speech for the goal of shaking them out of the complacency that makes them unable to see the truth.

As used in the New Testament, "light" appears to refer to truth—truth revealed to people, first of all, in their hearts and, more particularly, through Jesus. Both these paths to truth are referred to, jointly, in the Prologue to the Fourth Gospel (John 1:6–9):

6. There was a man sent from God, whose name was John.
7. This man came for a witness, to bear witness of the Light, that all through him might believe.
8. He was not that Light, but was sent to bear witness of that Light.
9. That was the true Light which gives light to every human being who comes into the world.

The Light to which John the Baptist bore witness (in verses 7 and 8) stands for Jesus, but the light that enlightens "every human being who comes into the world" (in verse 9) must be assumed to refer to the moral law that, according to Paul (Rom. 2:15), all people, Gentiles as well as Jews, have "written in their heart"; thus, "Gentiles, who do not have the law, by nature do things contained in the law."

Referring to the same passage in Paul's letter to the Romans, which speaks of the law written in people's hearts, another Catholic document, "Gaudium et Spes," comments,

In the depth of their conscience people detect a law which they do not impose on themselves, but which holds them to obedience. Always summoning them to love good and avoid evil, the voice of conscience can when necessary speak to their hearts more specifically: "do this, shun that." For people have in their hearts a law written by God. To obey it is the very dignity of human beings; according to it they will be judged (cf. Rom. 2:14–16). (1966:16)

It seems likely, then, that it is this innate inner knowledge about good and evil that is symbolized by Jesus' image of a human body full of light (a human body or a human person: according to Lachs 1987:128, in this passage "body is a translation of an Aramaic expression meaning 'you yourself'.") It also seems likely that a person's "eye" which makes this knowledge accessible, symbolizes the same reality as "the voice of conscience." To quote again the encyclical "Veritatis Splendor,"

> Conscience . . . compromises its dignity when it is culpably erroneous, that is to say, "when people show little concern for seeking what is true and good, and conscience gradually becomes almost blind from being accustomed to sin" ("Gaudium et Spes" p. 16). Jesus alludes to the danger of the conscience being deformed when he warns: "The eye is the lamp of the body. So if your eye is sound, your whole body will be full of light; but if your eye is not sound, your whole body will be full of darkness. If then the light in you is darkness, how great is the darkness!" (Mt. 6:22–23).(John Paul II 1993:99)

According to the interpretation developed in both "Veritatis Splendor" (John Paul II 1993:97) and "Gaudium et Spes" (1966:16), a person's inner light may sometimes be insufficient to guide one to the truth about moral good because of invincible ignorance. If this is the case, the conscience "does not on that account forfeit its dignity"; this cannot be said, however, when a person's moral blindness is due to their own failure to seek what is true and good. The first principle of natural law, which constitutes its very foundation, is (according to "Veritatis Splendor," p. 94) "the rational conviction that one must love and do good and avoid evil." This principle "expresses the primordial insights about good and evil, that reflection of God's creative wisdom which, like an imperishable spark (*scintilla animae*), shines in the heart of every person." The natural law so understood is not the same as conscience: "whereas the natural law discloses the objective and universal demands of the moral good, conscience is the application of the law to a particular case."

Adapting this interpretation of Jesus' eye and light sayings to my own framework, I propose the following explication:

(a) all people can know some things

(b) they can know that some things are true
(c) they can know that some things are good
(d) they can know that some things are bad

(e) they can know that a person can want to do bad things
(f) they can know that a person can want to do good things

(g) they can know that it is bad if a person wants to do bad things to
      other people
(h) they can know that it is good if a person wants to do good things
      for other people

(i) they can know these things not because other people say these
      things
(j) they can know these things because God wants them to know
      these things
(k) they can know that these things are true

(l) sometimes a person doesn't know these things
      because this person doesn't want to know these things
(m) it is very bad for a person if this person doesn't want to know
      these things
(n) it will be good if you always want to know these things

This explication is very general and doesn't attempt to define the notion of conscience but rather focuses on the "primordial insights about good and evil" symbolized, as "Veritatis Splendor" (John Paul II 1993) suggests, by the image of natural, inner light. The concepts that it does take for granted are TRUE, GOOD, and BAD; and it assumes that these three are indeed essential to Jesus' conception of the innate light ("the lamp of the body"), which people are born with, as they are born with two eyes. I will note in passing that Jesus' metaphor of the eye curiously echoes Plato's metaphor of the eye of the soul, through which we have "nonsensuous, preconceptual, prelinguistic, metaphysical intuitions into the nature of reality" (Griffin and Smith 1989:22); for an extensive discussion of other parallels, see Betz (1995:442–449).

But although these three concepts (TRUE, GOOD, and BAD) form the basis of Jesus' teaching about the natural light, the tenets of this teaching can be articulated only in the form of a series of sentences. The image of natural light implies that there are some things that all people can know ("by nature," as Paul says in his letter to the Romans); and given the use of "light" and "darkness" in the language of the New Testament, it is clear that this universally accessible knowledge concerns truth and moral good. (The words attributed to Jesus in John 3:19–21, linking light with truth and darkness with evil, are also relevant here.)

Accordingly, (a)–(d) of the explication refer to what "all human beings can know": that "some things are true," "some things are good," and "some things are bad." An alternative phrasing that is worth considering would replace the phrase "all people" with "at all times in all places," used in the following carefully phrased statement by theologians David Griffin and Huston Smith (Griffin and Smith 1989:62), who say that "these are primordial truths that are in principle available to human beings in all times and places." Although from a philosophical and anthropological point of view, such a phrasing may be more appropriate, as an explication of Jesus' intended meaning "all people" seems preferable: Jesus was not a philosopher or a scholar interested in broad generalizations about all times and all places but a teacher interested in people (in "everyone").

The nature of moral norms accessible to all people through their innate "inner light" is not specified in the passage under discussion, and the metaphors of light and darkness suggest little beyond the rudimentary notion that (f) "a person can want to do good things" and (e) "a person can want to do bad things." I have, nonetheless, included two more specific moral norms, which in the light of the Bible as a whole can be seen as the core of the universal moral law: (g) "it is bad if a person wants to do bad things to other people" and (h) "it is good if a person wants to do good things for other people".

Components (i) and (j) convey the idea that the source of knowledge presented in (a) to (e) is potentially accessible to everyone, and they identify it as not human but divine. In the context of the New Testament as a whole, the metaphors of light and darkness imply also that these absolute and universally accessible moral truths have their source in God. Component (k) links this knowledge with truth. Finally, (l), (m), and (n) attempt to explain Jesus' reference to darkness, linking it with ill will: people can "extinguish" the light within them. Jesus does not overtly distinguish darkness due to ill will from darkness due to ignorance, but delivered as a warning ("take heed") his words are unlikely to refer to something that the addressee couldn't do anything about.

It could be said that (e) and (f) refer to a person's basic religious orientation, in the broad sense of the term *religious*, that is, an orientation toward good rather than evil (for those who believe in God, this means an orientation toward God). Components (g) and (h), on the other hand, refer to a person's basic orientation toward other people.

At the end of the second Christian millennium absolute and universal moral truths have come increasingly under attack, especially in academic circles influenced by the philosophy of postmodernism in its relativist and nihilist version. As the philosopher Walter Truett Anderson (1995:240) put it, according to "the postmodern verdict . . . our eternal truths now appear to be inseparable from the cultures that created them and languages in which they are stated."

By contrast, Jesus evidently assumed that there *were* eternal truths—truths about good and evil—and that these truths were accessible to all people, or at least to all people whose inner eye was sound; he warned that people may allow the "light which is in them" to become "darkness." I have attempted to portray these warnings in components (l) and (m): "sometimes a person doesn't know these things because this person doesn't want to know these things" and "it is very bad for a person if this person doesn't want to know these things."

Jesus' sentence "If therefore the light that is in you is darkness . . ." can be read as a warning against intellectual and moral ills of many different kinds. It can also be seen as applicable to the intellectual temptation of moral relativism and moral nihilism, which seek to undermine the possibility of truth, the validity of the distinction between good and evil, and the notion of any "larger picture" that might include God as a ground in which moral norms could be anchored.[8]

Huston Smith (1995:214) refers to "a minimally articulated meta-narrative of faith" as escapsulating what all the great religions of the world have in common. Arguably, the core of the explication of Jesus' eye and light sayings could serve as the starting point for such a meta-narrative. It is dismaying that at the close of a century that brought us both the Holocaust and the Gulag Archipelago, many thinking people still seem prepared to deny the absolute, transcultural, and transpersonal validity of such statements as "people can do bad things" and "it is bad if people want to do bad things to other people."[9]

Some would say, no doubt, that it is not that they *want* to deny the absolute validity of such statements but rather that they feel *compelled* to do so, simply because those statements are expressed in English and therefore depend in their meaning on the historically shaped and culture-specific semantic system of the English language. Thus philosopher Richard Rorty (1989:4-5) makes a distinction between "the claim that the world is out there" and "the claim that truth is out there," arguing that the first one is defensible but the second is not: "To say that truth is not out there is simply to say that where there are no sentences there is no truth, that sentences are elements of human languages, and that human languages are human creations."

But whereas human languages are indeed largely human creations, shaped by different cultures and different history, they also share a common core, evidently independent of all such differences and presumably shaped by a basic pan-human, innate conceptual system, of which the distinction between GOOD and BAD appears to be part. Thus, although words like *good* and *bad* in English, *bonus* and *malus* in Latin, or *ii* and *warui* in Japanese are indeed human creations, the fact that we find such words—with exactly the same meaning—in all languages suggests that the concepts they express are innate, or to use Rorty's (1989) terms, "found" rather than "made."

Sentences like "it is bad if a person wants to do bad things to other people" also match across languages and cultures, in the sense that we can construct their counterparts, with exactly the same meaning, in any language. In each language their form will be dictated by local linguistic conventions, which are indeed human (cultural) creations. Their meaning, however, need not be affected by the features of any particular language. Thus, Rorty's (1989) syllogism about truth, sentences, and languages cannot defeat the idea that some sentences, matching in meaning across languages and cultures, express truths accessible to all people with the help of their "natural inner light."[10]

The existence of language universals, increasingly confirmed by empirical linguistic investigations, shows that the postmodernist argument—that any universal, natural moral law is impossible because of the diversity of languages and cultures—is fallacious. The existence of such universals doesn't *prove* that propositions such as "it is bad if a person wants to do bad things to some other people" or "it is good if a person wants to do good things for some other people" are eternally true. But it removes one obstacle to their being acknowledged as such, an obstacle erected on the basis of a mistaken belief that there are no universals and that diversity is endless.

Empirical investigations in comparative religion and anthropology also suggest the existence of certain universals: universals of human belief (cf., e.g., A. Huxley [1947]1961; Rost 1986; H. Smith 1992). Griffin (Griffin and Smith 1989:92) include among these "universal constants" (as he calls them) the "distinction between good and evil": "Every human society has moral and legal codes which are based on the presupposition that a distinction between good and evil exists." The recognition of this distinction is linked with a recognition that evil exists in people's hearts: "There is, after all, surely a deep truth in the testimony of the world's religions to the presence of a transcultural proclivity to evil deep within the human heart." In universal concepts, this means that all religions hold that people can do bad things; that, moreover, sometimes people want to do bad things; and, in particular, that sometimes people want to do bad things to other people. More generally, there is the testimony of the world's religions concerning the possibility of choice that all people have in matters of good and evil. Griffin and Smith speak in this connection of "the direct experience of values" (p. 43). In my terms, this consists of knowing—without being told by other people—that a person can want to do bad things and that a person can want to do good things.

By way of postscript to this discussion of Jesus' sayings about the inner light, I will briefly consider the relationship between that inner light and inductive generalizations about transcultural human values. In addition to universal beliefs about the distinction between wanting to do good things and wanting to do bad things, and also between wanting to do good things for other people and wanting to do bad things to other people, empirical investigations in comparative religion and anthropology suggest the existence of certain universal assumptions about what is *good for people* (see, e.g., Finnis 1980:83). These latter universals can also be formulated in universal human concepts, along the following lines (this time, with a reference to "all times" and "all places"):

at all times in all places people think that:
1. it is good for people to live
2. it is good for people to live with other people
3. it is good for people to know many things
4. it is good for people to be able to do some things because they want to do these things, not because they have to do these things

Universally recognized human values of this kind correspond to what philosophers of natural law describe as the values of "life," "sociability," "knowledge," "freedom," and so on (see, e.g., Finnis 1980:86-89). Arguably, values of this kind, describable in terms of "it is good for people . . ." should be distinguished from the absolute moral (or religious) values describable in terms of "it is good if . . ." or "it is bad if. . . ." It is latter—absolute—values that Paul had in mind when he wrote about the moral law "written in people's hearts," and Jesus when he spoke of "the light which is in you."

8. You cannot serve God and mammon

Matthew 6:24; cf. Luke 16:13

No one can serve two masters; for either he will hate the one and love the other, or else he will be loyal to the one and despise the other. You cannot serve God and mammon.

Betz (1995:454) notes that the notion of undivided loyalty and devotion to God is nothing new to the Jewish religion, and he asks, "Then what is the point?"; and he replies that "the saying is peculiar in that it sees this undivided loyalty as threatened by the service to another deity, Mammon, that is directly opposed to God." Apparently, then, what is seen as peculiar to Jesus' saying is its identification of money (and perhaps material possessions in general) as being directly inimical to God:

> The choice is a clear-cut one, without allowing compromises; it sets up the alternative terms: service versus enslavement, hatred versus love, devotion versus contempt, external materialism versus internal dedication, slavery of the money lovers versus freedom of "the sons of God". . . . The singling out of materialism as a pseudo-religious alternative to the appropriate conduct of worship makes this passage unique (p. 455).

I think these comments are essentially right. I suggest, however, that the single-minded devotion and service to God urged by Jesus is more accurately described as a constant attention to God's will and willingness or even eagerness to do it rather than as "the appropriate conduct of worship." In my terms, this can be represented as follows:

it will be good if you think at all times:
    "God wants me to do something now
    I want to do it"

Such a constant attention to "what God wants me to do now" is presented by Jesus as incompatible with a constant preoccupation with material possessions, that is, in my terms, with a frame of mind summed up in the thoughts "I want to have many things" and "I have to do many things because of this."

As in the saying about the narrow gate, the saying about two masters appears to refer to people who do care about God and who think that they want to live with God. In my terms, the people referred to do think "I want to live with God" and "if God wants me to do something I want to do it." At the same time, however, these people think "I want to have many things, I have to do many things because of this," and so their minds are divided and they cannot always pay attention to the matter of "what God wants me to do now."

On this point, then, I agree with Betz (1995:457), according to whom "you cannot" (in the sentence "You cannot serve God and mammon") "addresses readers who are engaging precisely in what they should rule out" and that it "addresses the futility of something the addressees are seen as doing." Stott has developed this point in more detail:

> Some people disagree with this saying of Jesus. They refuse to be confronted with such a stark and outright choice, and see no necessity for it. They blandly assure us that it is perfectly possible to serve two masters simultaneously, for they manage it very nicely themselves. Several possible arrange-

ments and adjustments appeal to them. Either they serve God on Sundays and mammon on weekdays, or God with their lips and mammon with their hearts, or God in appearance and mammon in reality, or God with half their being and mammon with the other half. ([1978]1992:158)

I have attempted to account for this aspect of the sayings about the two masters in the first cluster of components (a–f) in the explication proposed below.

I also agree with Betz (1995) and others that Jesus is not attacking here money or ownership of property as such but rather enslavement to money and possessions: "The message is that money and property are not just that, but that they can easily ensnare and possess people. They exercise power that is none other than what we call materialism" (p. 458). Similarly, Strecker writes,

The either-or before which the Preacher on the mount places his follow-ers does not mean that one should fundamentally renounce possessions. . . . A complete separation from money and means is not demanded; rather, the call to decision is defined by the verb *doulenein* ("serve"). Recognition of the dominion of God excludes service under the law of wealth. Enslave-ment to earthly possessions cannot be brought into harmony with service to the community of Jesus Christ. (1988:135)

But words like "service" or "enslavement" are metaphors, as are also refer-ences to "turn[ing] [one's] vision away from earthly possessions and direct[ing] it toward God" (p. 135) and the like. Trying to go beyond such metaphorical language, I suggest that what is really involved is constant preoccupation with money and possessions, that is, above all, perpetual thinking about what one has to do either to acquire them or not to lose them. Enjoying wealth and rely-ing on it as a source of existential security are, of course, not recommended by Jesus either, but this is not the specific topic of the God or mammon saying. Seeking one's ultimate security in wealth is incompatible with seeking it in God, but this is treated elsewhere (cf., e.g., the discussion of the parable of the rich fool in chapter 6, section 13). What the God or mammon saying focuses on is *serving* money and possessions, that is, in my terms, thinking that one *has* to do many things because of them (and doing these things).

I agree with Betz (1995:457–458) that serving mammon cannot be seen as quite analogous to serving God because, as he put it, serving God "describes a relation-ship with God that befits free human beings," whereas serving mammon "results in self-enslavement." Consequently, one must choose: "One can either serve God in freedom or serve Mammon in slavery." In my terms, this difference is repre-sented as a contrast between, on the one hand, *wanting* to do what God wants one to do and, on the other hand, *having* to do many things (because one wants to have many things). Jesus' apparent identification of God and mammon as two masters, in a similar or even the same relationship with the servant, is an instance of paradoxical hyperbole, so characteristic of his way of speaking.

It is interesting to note that the Fellows of the Jesus Seminar have voted the God and mammon saying pink in all its three versions (Luke 16:13, Matt. 6:24,

and Thom. 47:2) and that there were no black votes. One reason for this unanimity is that the saying in question "is terse, pithy, and memorable. It accords
well with the way the disciples remembered Jesus' public speech" (Funk et al.
1993:359). It is also interesting to note the following comment: "The conclusion that sets up an opposition between God and wealth gives the proverb an
unconventional twist: the popular view was that prosperity was a sign of divine
favour. Jesus may have been encouraging the poor while challenging the rich"
(p. 151). In what way, one wonders, may a warning not to be enslaved to money
have been intended to encourage the poor? Were they being encouraged not to
envy the rich, who run the risk of being enslaved to mammon? But presumably
poverty as such does not exclude a desire to have many things and a preoccupation to acquire them. What really seems to matter, then, is not so much one's
actual economic status as one's attitude toward material possessions:

> The saying puts the attitude toward money very radically: God or mam-
> mon! Which is going to govern your life? For no one can serve both of
> them! If one allows oneself to get involved in the servile pursuit of wealth
> and reduces oneself to a slave of it, then one cannot really serve God.
> Mammon thus becomes the god that one serves. So the saying puts the
> question to the Christian reader: Which do you want to serve? (Fitzmyer
> 1985b:1107)

There is one more question that I need to address before attempting an explication of the God or mammon saying: is "mammon" used here in a figurative sense, to stand for any "rival lord" (i.e., any desired "good things"), or is
this "mammon" (in the sense of "wanting to have many things") part of the
intended message itself? Commentators are divided on this point. For example,
Viviano opts for the former interpretation, regarding "mammon" as no more than
an example:

> This is another Q saying (see Luke 16:13). It teaches again the impossibil-
> ity of serving God with a divided heart, or, positively, the need to make a
> basic decision to love God above all things and all other things only inso-
> far as they fit into that basic love. The rival "lord" can be anything or
> anyone, but at the end of the verse one example is given, "mammon," a
> Semitic word for money or wealth. (1990:646)

In a similar vein, Barclay (1994:210) remarks, in broad terms, that "serving God
can never be a part-time or a spare-time job. Once a man chooses to serve God,
every moment of his time and every atom of his energy belongs to God—God is
the most exclusive of masters. We belong to him totally or not at all."

On the other hand, as we have seen earlier, commentators such as Stott
([1978]1992), Fitzmyer (1985b), and Betz (1995) link the message of the God or
mammon saying specifically with material possessions, that is, with having *things*
in the most literal and basic sense of the word *have*. Although both approaches
seem to me to be reasonable in the light of the Gospels as a whole, on balance

I find the latter more convincing. If we allow "having" to stand here for any attachment whatsoever, the saying would lose some of its force and its pungency. It seems more justified to acknowledge that Jesus did have something to say about the right attitude to material possessions, rather than treating material possessions as a figure of speech, on a par with entering through a "narrow gate," "bearing good fruit," and so on.

Strecker (1988:135) says quite explicitly that "in verse 24 [i.e., the God and mammon verse] Matthew means basically the same thing that he said in verses 19–21" (i.e., "Lay up treasure in heaven"). I think, however, that a level of abstraction that would identify the meaning of these two passages would be too reductive and would impoverish them both. In particular, the "call to decision," mentioned by several commentators, appears to be more applicable to the God or mammon saying than to the treasure sayings. It does seem significant that only the former was formulated as an either-or. The treasure sayings do not address specifically the wish to combine two things, God and something else, but rather discourage a single-minded devotion to the pursuit of good things that cannot last; by contrast, the God or mammon saying addresses specifically the illusion that one can pursue both things at the same time.

This brings us to the following explication:

God or mammon

(a) many people think:
(b)   "I want to live with God
(c)   if God wants me to do something I want to do it"
(d) at the same time they think:
(e)   "I want to have many things
(f)   I have to do many things because of this"

(g) I say to you:
(h)   if you want to have many things
(i)   you can't want to live with God at the same time

(j) if you think that you want to live with God
(k) it will be good if you think at all times:
(l)   "God wants me to do something now
(m)   I want to do it"
(n) you can't think this at all times if you think at the same time:
(o)   "I want to have many things
(p)   I have to do many things because of this"

Here the aspiration to serve God is presented in the form of two components: thinking that "I want to live with God" and thinking about what God wants us to do. The interest in material possessions is also represented in the form of two components: thinking that "I want to have many things" and that "I have to do many things because of this." The common assumption is that both these interests can be combined. Jesus, however (as presented in these sayings), rejects this assumption; he points out that while one's thoughts are divided in this way, between God and possessions, one cannot truly want to live with God and that wanting to do God's will requires constant attention, which is incompatible with such a divided mind. Furthermore, his contrast between "love" and "hate" implies that if one focuses one's thoughts on material possessions, one can't even *want* to serve God (one may think that one wants to, but one cannot sustain this desire in the long run).

The explication does not include a categorical assertion that to be able to live with God one has to think about God's will at all times, but it encourages such an attitude [components (j)–(m)]. What it does assert categorically is that one can't want to live with God while one keeps one's mind and one's heart on money and possessions [(g)–(i)]. Components (n)–(p) point out the incompatibility between giving full attention to God's will and devoting it to money and possessions, whereas (a)–(f) portray the divided thinking whose futility is exposed in parts (g)–(l) and (n)–(p).

9. Consider the lilies of the field

Matthew 6:25–33; cf. Luke 12:22–31

25. Therefore I say to you: do not worry about your life, what you will eat or what you will drink; nor about your body, what you will put on. Is not life more than food and the body more than clothing?

26. Look at the birds of the air for they neither sow nor reap nor gather into barns; yet your Heavenly Father feeds them. Are you not of more value than they?

27. Which of you by worrying can add one cubit to his stature?

28. So why do you worry about clothing? Consider the lilies of the field, how they grow: they neither toil nor spin;

29. and yet I say to you that even Solomon in all his glory was not arrayed like one of these.

30. Now if God so clothes the grass of the field, which today is, and tomorrow is thrown into the oven, will he not much more clothe you? O you of little faith.

31. Therefore, do not worry, saying, 'What shall we eat?', or 'What shall we drink?', or 'What shall we wear?'

32. (a) For after all these things the Gentiles seek.
    (b) For your heavenly Father knows that you need all these things.

33. (a) But seek first the Kingdom of God
    (b) and his righteousness,
    (c) and all these things shall be added to you.

There is a general consensus among the commentators that the discourse about the lilies of the field and the birds of the air (Luke uses *ravens*), taken by Matthew and Luke from their presumed shared source (*Quelle*) and repeated by them with minor modifications, is one of the most important and distinctive thing that Jesus said: comment on this point as follows: "Among the most important things Jesus said are a series of pronouncements on anxieties and fretting. It is possible that we have before us here the longest connected discourse that can be directly attributed to Jesus, with the exception of some of the longer narrative parables" (Funk et al. 1993:152).

But although these sayings are widely regarded as both authentic and central to Jesus' teaching, there is no consensus about how they should be interpreted and in fact quite a wide range of interpretations has been proposed. For example, Funk et al. (1993:153) remark, "This string of sayings is addressed to those who are preoccupied with day-to-day existence rather than with political or apocalyptic crises. Jesus believed that God would provide for human needs." In contrast to other commentators, Funk et al. regard Matthew's verses 32 and 33 (in their entirety) as a secondary accretion.

On the other hand, many other commentators believe that verse 33 (in Luke's version, 31) is authentic (with the exception of part b, which has no counterpart in Luke) and is a key to the whole passage. For example, Fitzmyer (1985b:977) comments on Luke's version, "The crucial point of the exhortation occurs in verses 30b–31). . . . Priority of values is proposed again. . . . Direction in life should come from a preoccupation with God and his Kingdom; concern with earthly details may prove to be only an obstacle to the single-minded pursuit of and service to the Kingdom." Viviano (1990: 646) makes a similar comment about Matthew's version: "*seek first the Kingdom [of God] and his justice*. This is the climactic verse of the whole chapter. The ultimate goal of all our activity must be the highest value, the Kingdom of God, which is here defined as justice."

What seems to be uncontroversial is that Jesus is contrasting two attitudes, and he enjoins his (actual and potential) followers to adopt one of them rather than the other. What is not so uncontroversial is, first, what exactly these two attitudes are and, second, whether the injunction in question is restricted to some particular people and situations or whether it can apply to all people at all times.

Funk et al.'s (1993) reference to "political or apocalyptic crises" suggests that they do not attribute to these sayings any universal significance. Some other commentators also hesitate to attribute to them universal applicability, although for other reasons. For example, Viviano (1990: 646) remarks, "This teaching presupposes Galilean prosperity and would be insensitive in places or situations of destitution." I would argue, however, that to restrict the import of Jesus' saying in these (or other) ways is to miss their deeper meaning. When he was contrasting an existential attitude of anxiety and worry with an existential attitude of trust, he wasn't assuring his addressees that nothing bad would ever happen to them. Rather, he was pointing out that they owe their very life to God (in my terms, "You live because God wants you to live"); that having created them God hasn't forgotten them ("God does good things for you all the time"); that God's love for them, manifested in the fact that he created them and has sustained them so far, will continue ("God wants to do good things for you"); that God, who can "clothe the lilies of the field and feed the birds of the air," both can and wants to do good things for people ("God can do good things for you"; "God wants to do good things for you); that God knows people's fundamental need of his sustenance ("God knows that if he didn't do good things for you all the time you couldn't live") and all their specific needs of any given moment ("God knows everything about you").

The whole discourse on "the birds of the air and the lilies of the field" (often referred to as the discourse on anxieties) focuses on bad things that can happen to a person in the future. Some commentaries (e.g., Betz 1995) contrast this discourse with the sayings on earthly treasures (Matt. 6:19–21), in terms of life versus possessions: *thesauros* 'treasure' is believed to refer to a concern for material goods (i.e., wanting to have many things), whereas *psychē* 'life; life/soul' refers to a concern for one's life (i.e., wanting to live and not wanting to die). I think, however, that "treasure" and "life" should be understood here as metaphors, standing, respectively, for "wanting (many) good things to happen to one" and "not wanting bad things to happen to one." A desire for possessions as such is dealt with in the God and mammon passage (Matt. 6:24), whereas the treasure and anxiety sayings are concerned with good fortune and misfortune in general. The common human preoccupation with possible future misfortunes (e.g., hunger, poverty, destitution, as well as illness and anything else) can be represented as follows:

(a) many people think all the time:
(b)   "some bad things can happen to me some time after now
(c)   I don't want these things to happen
(d)   I have to do many things because of this"
(e) because these people think this, they feel something bad
(f) no one can say that something good happens to these people
     because they think like this

One might add to this formula another component: "if these things happen I can die" (before "I don't want these things to happen"), but I think doing so would unnecessarily restrict the applicability and significance of Jesus' discourse on anxieties. If, as Betz (1995:471) put it, most people are "anxiety-ridden" most of the time, it is a matter of common experience that this anxiety doesn't have to be focused on the thought "if these things happen I can die"; rather, it can be focused on many other fearful thoughts. It is true that "the phrase 'what you shall eat [or what you shall drink]' . . . is proverbial and sums up what life is all about, given popular standards." But although anxiety about one's life is no doubt referred to in this passage, it can be taken as a metaphor for all other anxieties about one's necessarily uncertain future.

The reference to the duration of the anxiety ("many people think *all the time*") is, I think, important and is highlighted by the version of these sayings in the Gospel of Thomas (logion 36): "Jesus said: 'Do not worry from dawn to dusk and from dusk to dawn about what you (plur.) will wear'." The reference to the uselessness of such constant preoccupation ("no one can say that something good happens to these people because they think like this") is justified by Matthew's verse 6:27 ("Which of you by worrying can add one cubit to his stature?").

Despite the paradoxical and hyperbolic verse 33c (which may or may not have been added by the redactor), Jesus was not discouraging such useless preoccupation with possible future misfortunes by assuring his addressees that nothing bad would happen to them. Rather, he was suggesting a different direction for their thoughts: seeking the kingdom of God in the present (including perhaps present tribulations) rather than focusing on an imaginary future. On this point I broadly agree with Betz's interpretation:

> If it is wrong to be anxious on account of the future, and particularly on account of tomorrow, then the right way to care for today is not by being anxious (*merimnan*) but by seeking the Kingdom and righteousness of God (verse 33) in the troubles of each day. This conclusion is in fact identical with the ethics of the SM [Sermon on the Mount] as a whole. (1995:486)

I believe, however, that the reference to tomorrow (in contrast to the future in general) is not significant: I think "tomorrow" is to be understood here as a metaphor for the future in general, the really significant contrast being that between now and some time after now. Another questionable point in Betz's commentary is the reference to "righteousness," which does not occur in Luke's version and can be regarded as a Matthean addition. The phrase "the troubles of each day" may also go beyond the discourse on the birds and the lilies, although it is no doubt compatible with the teaching of the Gospels as a whole. What this particular discourse focuses on is the contrast between, on the one hand, a meaningless preoccupation with possible future misfortunes and, on the other hand, a meaningful focus on "what God wants me to do now" (and what I *can* do now):

(g) it will not be good if you think like this
(h) it will be good if you think: . . .

The attitude encouraged by the injunction "seek first the Kingdom of God" can be represented as follows:

(i) "I know that all people can live with God
(j) I know that God wants this
(k) I want to live with God
(l) because of this I want to do something now
(m) I know: God wants me to do something now"

Betz (1995) and others are right to emphasize that the injunction to seek the kingdom of God is not offered as an alternative to work and other practical pursuits necessary for life: "As intended by the SM, the disciple of Jesus is not a quietist who simply sits and waits for what God gives, like an animal. . . . The text is clear that earthly needs and worldly concerns are not to be ignored or covered up by pious preoccupations with the hereafter" (pp. 482-483). Similarly, Stott ([1978]1992:165) has said that "*believers are not exempt from earning their own living*. We cannot sit back in an armchair, twiddle our thumbs, mutter 'my heavenly father will provide' and do nothing. We have to work. As Paul put it later: 'If anyone will not work, let him not eat.'"

I think, however, that we should be careful not to interpret verse 33b ("and all these things shall be added to you") too literally, as some commentators (including Betz 1995) appear to have done. For example, Betz formulates the conclusion of the discourse on the lilies of the field as follows: "If God cares for lesser creatures in this way, he will care even more for his highest creatures, human beings, in the same way. He will provide the clothing for them, and one has no reason to worry even in the face of transitoriness and perishability" (p. 479). In a similar vein, Betz contrasts the pagans, given to "materialism and consumerism," with "faithful Jewish disciples," who "avoid such reprehensible excessiveness" and expect from God no more than "the so-called necessities of life" (pp. 480-481).

But the question of materialism and consumerism is addressed in the sayings on God or mammon and earthly versus heavenly treasures rather than in those about the birds and the lilies. Here, the concern seems to be with the necessities of life rather than with luxuries and, more generally, with the fear of misfortune rather than with greed for good fortune. We still must ask, therefore, when Jesus promised, in verse 30, that God would clothe all people, as he clothes the lilies of the field, was he using the image of clothing as a metaphor for all the necessities of life in a literal sense (food, clothes, and shelter), or was he rather using it as a metaphor for God's providential care in some more abstract sense? And if so, in what sense exactly?

I submit that he was indeed using this image as a metaphor for something other than the necessities of life in a physical sense. He was not promising the end of hunger, homelessness, and poverty in a literal sense, nor was he announcing an end of illness and death, in a literal sense. Rather, he was encouraging trust in God *despite* the observable fact of hunger, poverty, illness, and death. The underlying message can be portrayed as follows:

    (n) you live because God wants you to live
    (o) God does good things for you all the time
    (p) God knows that if he didn't do good things for you you couldn't live
    (q) God knows everything about you
    (r) God wants to do good things for you
    (s) God can do good things for you

This message does not include components like "nothing bad will ever happen to you" or "you will not die," and yet it urges the addressees to believe that God both can and wants to do good things for them, as he can and wants to do good things for the lilies of the field and the birds of the air.

This brings us to the following overall explication:

The birds of the air, the lilies of the field

(a) many people think all the time:
(b)   "bad things can happen to me some time after now
(c)   I don't want these things to happen
(d)   I have to do many things because of this"
(e) because they think this, these people feel something bad
(f) no one can say that something good happens to these people
        because they think like this

(g) it will not be good if you think like this
(h) it will be good if you think:
(i)   "I know that all people can live with God
(j)   I know that God wants this
(k)   I want to live with God
(l)   because of this I want to do something now
(m)   I know: God wants me to do something now"

(n) you live because God wants you to live
(o) God does good things for you all the time
(p) you can live because God does good things for you
(q) God knows everything about you
(r) God wants to do good things for you
(s) God can do good things for you

Components (a)–(f) represent the attitude of people who are constantly worried about and preoccupied with the future. Components (g)–(m) contrast this (futile) anxiety with a focus on seeking the kingdom of God in the present. Components (n)–(s) portray God as someone who has created people, who sustains them in their lives, who knows everything about them, and who can and wants to "do good things for them."

10. Do not judge

Matthew 7:1–5; cf. Luke 6:3–7

1. Judge not, that you be not judged.
2. For with what judgment you judge, you will be judged; and with the same measure you use, it will be measured back to you.
3. And why do you look at the speck in your brother's eye, but do not consider the plank in your own eye?
4. Or how can you say to your brother: 'Let me remove the speck from your eye'; and look, a plank is in your own eye?
5. Hypocrite! First remove the plank from your own eye, and then you will see clearly to remove the speck from your brother's eye.

Here again, the first question must be, did Jesus really say these things? And the prevailing view of the commentators is that he did. Indeed, even the scholars of the Jesus Seminar, who are usually more skeptical than many others, were prepared to attribute to Jesus the mote and beam passage, in which "vivid, exaggerated, and humorous images are used . . . to call attention to the heavy irony of fault-finding" (Funk et al. 1993:154), although the first two verses of the passage in question ("Judge not," down to "it will be measured back to you") were not regarded by them "as sufficiently distinctive to be attributed to Jesus."

There is no reason, however, to assume that only "distinctive" sayings (dissimilar to anything that anyone else had said in Palestine or elsewhere in the ancient world) can be plausibly attributed to Jesus. Furthermore, it is impossible to know whether a saying is distinctive before its meaning has been elucidated; otherwise, a superficial similarity in words and images can conceal the novelty of the message. From a formal point of view, a short and readily remembered saying like "Judge not, that you be not judged" could easily have survived the oral period of transmission, and the fact that it was recorded by both Matthew and Luke lends further support to its authenticity. Above all, however, the idea behind the instruction not to judge plays such an important role in the Gospels as a whole, recurring in a variety of genres, that it can rightly be regarded as one of the key themes of Jesus' teaching.

But to establish the role and significance of this theme, we have to determine the meaning of the key injunction, "Do not judge . . ."—a meaning that, as the history of its exegesis shows, is open to many different interpretations. As Betz notes,

> The history of the interpretation of the passage reveals a great deal of uncertainty regarding the precise meaning. Some determine the content by looking at vss [verses] 1-2, other by focussing on vss 3-5. Tolstoy thought that the social demand of abolishing the entire system of public justice is stated in these words, while Welltonsen, arguing against Tolstoy, thinks of a moral injunction against private judging that was much in vogue among Jews and Christians, an ugly vice to be rooted out from human fellowship. Thus, determining the very content of the passage depends to a large extent on the presuppositions with which one approached it. (1995:487)

Betz, who himself casts his vote for an interpretation based on the idea of prudence, says that "the rule implies that judging others is not such a bad thing, but to do it rightly one must keep the proper procedures in mind. The requirement is indispensable because on it rests justice and fairness . . . it can be recommended as prudence" (p. 493). He adds,

> The kind of judgement one passes on others comes back to the person who started it. Gossipers become targets of gossip; critics must face being criticised, and so forth. The prudent person, so goes the advice, will break the vicious cycle by withholding such judgment because the same mechanism will work in the reverse direction as well. Restraint will motivate others to exercise equal restraint. (p. 490)

The idea that "not judging others" should be justified by prudence is evidently based on a literal, or almost literal, interpretation of verse 2: "For with what judgment you judge, you will be judged; and with the same measure you use, it will be measured back to you." But is this really justified? Doesn't the threat of judgment refer symbolically to the Last Judgment, and isn't it used here to emphasize the seriousness of the exhortation? The symbolic character of the language used in this passage was clearly recognized in St. Augustine's (1948) commentary on the Sermon on the Mount: "Can it be . . . that if we give expression to a judgment that is rash, God will also judge us rashly? Or if we measure with an unjust measure, that in God's case too, there is in store an unjust measure by which it shall be measured to us again?" St. Augustine's questions are, of course, rhetorical, and he replies, "No, not at all. God neither judges rashly nor does He requite with an unjust measure." Nonetheless, Augustine, too, suggested that "the very rashness with which you penalize another must rebound on you"; and Betz's (1995) idea of prudence is consistent with this suggestion.

It is hard to see, however, how the idea of praiseworthy prudence could be reconciled with the vehemence of verse 5: "Hypocrite! first remove the plank from your own eye, and then you will see clearly to remove the speck from your brother's eye." This image and the sharp rebuke that follows suggest that what Jesus is concerned about is not the "imprudence" of judging other people but the presumption of condemning other people (who do bad things) as bad people and setting ourselves above them as their judges—as if we were not like them ourselves and never did bad things.

The image of the plank and the speck (or beam and mote) is of course hyperbolic, and deliberately so. It is hard to see how such a paradoxical metaphor could be used to encourage moderation and restraint in anything, which is why I find comments like the following rather unconvincing:

> The context clearly implies that *krinein* ["pass judgment"] refers to the perpetual human obsession to criticize and correct the behavior of other people. . . . It is true that human conduct inevitably involves taking the measure of each other. . . . What is criticized . . . is the degeneration of this process. This happens when a person denigrates another by harsh and unfair criticism, with a lack of sympathy and understanding, if not a pathological delight. . . . The person who is unable or unwilling to see his or her flaws lacks self-criticism and is, for this reason, declared incompetent to criticize another. (Betz 1995:490–492)

Comments of this kind do not do full justice to the ethical radicalism of Jesus' "absolute prohibition of judging" (Strecker 1988:143)—a radicalism that prohibits thinking of anyone as "a bad person" and of regarding anyone who "does bad things" as radically different from oneself ("I am not someone like this"). Thus Betz is in my view much more on target when he links (in a footnote) the judging attitude with the characters of the Pharisee (Luke 18:9–14) in the parable of the Pharisee and the tax collector and of the older brother in the parable of the prodigal son (Luke 15:25–32). The powerful images of the Pharisee and the older brother are indeed most illuminating in the present context because they involve the notion of dividing people into two categories: good people, for example, "myself," and bad people, who are not "like me" (e.g., the tax collector or the prodigal son).

A division of this kind goes far beyond such vices as "the perpetual human obsession to criticize and correct the behavior of other people, in particular those with whom one is closely associated" (Betz 1995:490). In fact, the Pharisee in the parable was not closely associated with the tax collector and was not obsessed with criticizing or correcting either him personally or other tax collectors. He did, however, regard tax collectors as bad people and "not like me"—and so, according to the parable, he did not go to his house justified.

Above all, however, Jesus' attitude toward judging other people and the meaning of the exhortation "Do not judge" have been made clear in the story of the woman caught in adultery, reported in the Fourth Gospel (see chapter 3, section 3). Since this story provides a vital commentary on this exhortation, I will quote it here again, this time in extenso.

2. But early in the morning he came again into the temple, and all the people came to him; and he sat down and taught them.

3. Then the scribes and Pharisees brought to him a woman caught in adultery. And when they had set her in the midst,

4. they said to him, 'Teacher, this woman was caught in adultery, in the very act.

5. Now, Moses, in the law, commanded us that such should be stoned But what do you say?'

6. This they said, testing him, that they might have something of which to accuse him. But Jesus stooped down and wrote on the ground with his finger, as though he did not hear.

7. So when they continue asking him, he raised himself up and said to them, 'He who is without sin among you, let him throw a stone at her first.'

8. And again he stooped down and wrote on the ground.

9. Then those who heard it, being convicted by their conscience, went out one by one, beginning with the oldest even to the last. And Jesus was left alone, and the woman standing in the midst.

10. When Jesus had raised himself up and saw no one but the woman, he said to her, 'Woman, where are those accusers of yours? Has no one condemned you?'

11. She said, 'No one, Lord.' And Jesus said to her, 'Neither do I condemn you; go and sin no more.'

The story of the adulteress, which is not found in any of the important early Greek manuscripts, is widely regarded as a later insertion in the Fourth Gospel. Nonetheless, it is also widely accepted as a truly ancient story and, in Moloney's (1988:262) words, "an ancient and precious witness to Jesus of Nazareth." As noted by Raymond Brown (1966:335), "Ambrose and Augustine wanted it read as part of the Gospel, and Jerome included it in the Vulgate." Why then, Brown asks, "did it not immediately become part of the accepted Gospels?" And he replies, "Riesenfeld [1952] has given the most plausible explanation for the delay in the acceptance of this story. The ease with which Jesus forgave the adulteress was hard to reconcile with the stern penitential discipline in vogue in the early Church. It was only when a more liberal penitential practice was firmly established that this story received wide acceptance."

The story, which in Raymond Brown's (1966:336) words portrays Jesus "as the serene judge," portrays also with great clarity the "holier than thou" attitude at which Jesus' exhortation in Matthew (7:1–5) is aimed. It also highlights the basic point that "God alone is good" (cf. Matt. 19:17), and therefore God alone can judge people. People can judge *deeds*, but they cannot judge other people (in the sense of condemning them as bad people), because those who set themselves up as judges do bad things themselves. Nobody, therefore, is in a position to say about another person, "This person is a bad person; this person is not someone like me." This is, essentially, what Paul says about judging other people in his letter to the Romans (2:1): "Therefore you are inexcusable, O man, whoever you are who judge, for in whatever you judge another you condemn yourself; for you who judge do the same things."

The story of the adulteress is so unforgettable and so quintessentially Jesus-like that even the Fellows of the Jesus Seminar, who decided that the words attributed to Jesus in the story "did not originate in their present form with Jesus," nevertheless "assigned the words and story to a special category of things they wish Jesus had said and done" (Funk et al. 1993:426). There is a certain irony in this assessment. Both the story and the words bear the unmistakable imprint of Jesus' personality. Obliquely, the Fellows are saying in their commentary that "if this is not Jesus speaking then let's imagine another Jesus, even more Jesus-like than Jesus himself, and let's attribute these words and this story to him." The simplest possibility, however, is that this *is* Jesus speaking. One can also ask, where might the Fellows have found the "higher ideal" in the name of which they wish "Jesus had said and done" such things?

This, then, is my proposed explication of the "Do not judge . . ." passage (Matthew 7:1–5):

Do not judge . . .

   (a) people often think about another person:
   (b)   "this person is someone bad
   (c)   this person is not someone like me"

   (d) I say to you:
   (e)   it will be bad if you think like this about another person
   (f)   if you think that someone did something bad
          it will be good if you think at the same time:
   (g)   "this person is someone like me
   (h)   I do bad things like other people do bad things"
   (i)   it will be good if you think something else at the same time:

(j)   "I don't know everything about this person
(k)   God knows everything about this person
(l)   like God knows everything about me"

The image of removing the speck (or the mote) from one's brother's eye amplifies the teaching of the injunction "do not judge." The contrast in size
between the plank (or the beam) in my own eye and the speck (or the mote)
in my brother's eye is not meant to convey that my sins are necessarily greater
than those of other people; rather, it is meant to convey that my blindness
must be truly colossal if I don't realize that I, too, do bad things. The bad
things that I do should be especially clear to me because I know my thoughts,
whereas in the case of other people I don't know what really happens in their
hearts.

This doesn't mean, however, that according to Jesus one has no right ever to
rebuke or admonish one's brother, or that one can only do so after one has
become holy oneself (that is, in all likelihood, never). Rather, it means that all
attempts to morally help one's brother are bound to be futile if one undertakes
them without an awareness of one's own faults and without an on-going effort
to clean one's own life. But if one recognizes that one does "bad things" oneself, if one repents and wants not to do these things any more, then one may be
able to "see clearly how to" (v.5) speak to one's brother; and one may even be
able to help one's brother, instead of antagonising him and sinning against him
by judging him and putting oneself above him.

This brings us to the following explication of the "speck and plank" image:

(a) maybe you think about another person like this:
(b)   "this person does bad things
(c)   this is bad
(d)   it will be good if this person doesn't do it any more"
(e) maybe you want to say this to this person

(f) at the same time, you don't think:
(g)   "I do bad things
(h)   this is bad
(i)   I don't want to do these things any more"

(j) it will be good if you think like this
(k)   before you say anything to this other person
(l) when you think like this you will know
(m)   how you can say something to this other person

Jesus' injunction "do not judge" and the image of the speck and the plank
should not be confused with the idea reflected in the late-twentieth-century English word *judgmental*.

A criticism sometimes made of moral welfare workers is that they are judgmental in their approach to clients. (*Oxford English Dictionary* 1992)

... and you should treat people fairly and not judge them, and, moralistically ... Diversity. I don't think we should be judgmental of other people. (Porpora, in press, from a set of interviews conducted in the United States in the 1990s.)

Roughly speaking, the word *judgmental* suggests that one has (and tends to express) strongly negative views about other people's personal lives, which do not really concern us. It is related to the modern ideals of tolerance; broad-mindedness; and respect for other people's opinions, values, and private lives. A person who is seen as judgmental is someone who (from the speaker's point of view) fails to understand or to accept that what he or she sees as bad may (legitimately) not be seen as bad by everybody else. There is an assumption here that one must not impose one's own standards on other people; in their private lives (if not more generally), other people have the right to adopt their own values. Usually a line is drawn at actions negatively affecting other people; but as long as someone's actions do not impact on others, it is thought that one has no right to condemn those actions as bad. This modern notion that it is bad to be judgmental can be represented along the following lines:

Being judgmental

   (a) some people want to say about other people:
   (b)   "these people do bad things
   (c)   it is bad if someone lives like this"
   (d) it is not good if someone says things like this about other people
   (e) it is not good if someone thinks like this about other people

The Pharisees who brought to Jesus the woman caught in adultery saw this person as a bad person, who did something very bad. A modern reader of the Gospels might think that they were being judgmental (in the modern sense of the word), but this was not Jesus' point. He was not implying that different people can have different moral standards, and in particular, he was not relativizing the moral status of adultery. At the same time, however, he was pointing out that since all people do bad things, no one is in a position to say about another person, "This person is a bad person; this person is not someone like me." Newbigin (1986:19) describes the modern ideal of nonjudgmentalism as follows: "There are no 'right' or 'wrong' styles of life. Perhaps the only thing which is really wrong is condemning as wrong the lifestyle of another." This is not what Jesus' injunction "Do not judge" means.

The explication proposed here allows us to see why, exactly, Tolstoy was wrong in assuming that Jesus had condemned all human law and judicial systems. Tolstoy claimed that "the human courts were not only contrary to his [Jesus'] commandment but in direct opposition to the whole doctrine of Christ and that therefore he must have forbidden them. . . . Christ says: 'Make no distinction between the just and the unjust.' Courts of law do nothing else. Christ says: 'Forgive all.' . . . 'Love your enemies.' 'Do good to them that hate you.' Courts of law do not forgive, but they punish. . . . So that the true sense of the doctrine is that Christ forbids all courts of law" ([1884]1958:25).

But consider the two key components of the explication: "this person is a bad person, this person is not someone like me." Do the judges in the human courts have to think about the accused in such terms? Clearly not. The judges have to focus on the question of whether the accused person in fact committed the alleged offences, not whether the accused is "a bad person" and a "person not like me." So the injunction "Do not judge (people)" does not mean that Jesus condemned all human law and justice. To see this clearly, however, we need to explicate the real meaning of the injunction rather than look at the words as such. The point is not that Jesus' words were meant to apply to private life and not to public life, as many commentators have alleged (see Bauman 1985:19), but that deeds should be distinguished from people.

Tolstoy refers in this context to the story of the woman caught in adultery: "In the case of the adulteress, he [Jesus] positively rejects human justice and proves that, on account of each man's own sinful nature, he has no right to judge another" ([1884]1958:26). Tolstoy treats here the words "Do not judge . . ." as if they were unambiguous and self-explanatory. In fact, however, they are not self-explanatory, and to really understand them we need to go beyond the surface of the text and explicate its deeper meaning, in the context of the Gospels as a whole.

11. Ask, and it will be given to you

Matthew 7: 7–11; cf. Luke 11: 9–13

7. Ask, and it will be given to you; seek, and you will find; knock, and it will be opened to you.
8. For everyone who asks receives, and he who seeks finds, and to him who knocks it will be opened.
9. Or what man is there among you who, if his son asks for bread, will give him a stone?
10. Or if he asks for a fish, will he give him a serpent?
11. If you then, being evil, know how to give good gifts to your children, who much more will your Father who is in heaven give good things to those who ask him.

The triple exhortation—to ask, to seek, and to knock—recorded in both Matthew and Luke, and so attributed by scholars to their shared source Q, is so memorable and so extraordinary that even the scholars of the Jesus Seminar did not doubt that it stems from Jesus himself: "The trio of sayings in Q makes the assurance to those who ask, seek, knock unconditional. The promise that every request will be met is a gross exaggeration and surprising, to say the least. That aspect led many Fellows to think it stemmed from Jesus; they agreed on a pink designation" (Funk et al. (1993:155).

But did Jesus really promise in this passage that "every request will be met"? Is this really the meaning of the passage? Jesus compares God's attitude to people to the loving attitude of parents toward their children, but does he really say that a loving parent fulfills the child's every request?

He envisages a situation with which all his hearers will have been daily familiar, namely a child coming to his father with a request. If he asks for bread, will he be given something which looks a bit like it but is in fact disastrously different, e.g., a stone instead of a loaf, or a snake instead of a fish? . . . Of course not! Parents, even though they are *evil*, i.e., selfish by nature, still love their children and give them only *good gifts*. Notice that Jesus here assumes, even asserts, the inherent sinfulness of human nature. At the same time, he does not deny that bad men are capable of doing good. On the contrary, *evil* parents give *good gifts* to their children, for "God drops into their hearts a portion of his goodness". . . . So the force of the parable lies rather in a contrast than in a comparison between God and men. It is another *a fortiori* or "how much more" argument: if human parents (although evil) know how to give good gifts to their children, how much more will our heavenly Father (who is not evil but wholly good) *give good things to those who ask him?* (Stott [1978]1992:184–185)

I believe that this is indeed one important aspect of the intended message: if people ask God for good things, God will give them good things. The idea is not that people can manipulate God and make him do what they want by means of prayer. Stott rightly observes that to interpret Jesus' triple exhortation and triple promise as saying that every request will necessarily be fulfilled (by virtue of being uttered) is to replace prayer with magic:

It is absurd to suppose that the promise "Ask, and it shall be given you" is an absolute pledge with no strings attached; that "Knock, and it will be opened to you" is an "Open, Sesame" to every closed door without exception; and that by the waving of a prayer wand any wish will be granted and every dream will come true. The idea is ridiculous. It would turn prayer into magic, the person who prays into a magician like Aladdin, and God into our servant who appears instantly to do our bidding like Aladdin's genie every time we rub our little prayer lamp. ([1978]1992:188)

And yet, although both Stott's points are convincing (that children may ask for things that are bad for them and that no doubt prayer was not meant by Jesus as a magical formula), there is also something slightly disturbing about his interpretation. Stott (pp. 188–189) says that "the promises of the Sermon on the Mount are not unconditional"; they depend on how well founded the request is: "We can thank God that the granting of our needs is conditional—not only on our asking, seeking and knocking, but also on whether what we desire by asking, seeking and knocking is good."

But the idea that God will fulfil a request if it is well founded seems to imply that, within certain limits, one *can* influence God. This implication is one that Stott (1992:186) himself denies, saying that "the reason why God's giving depends on our asking is neither because he is ignorant until we inform him nor because he is reluctant until we persuade him. So in prayer we do not 'prevail on' God, but rather prevail on ourselves to submit to God." However, if God's gifts do not depend on our requests, what exactly did Jesus mean when he said, "Ask and it will be given to you"? And is it really true that Jesus' promises are not unconditional? And if it *is* true that they are not unconditional, does the condition really lie in the fact that the request is well justified? Does it mean that if a request is (as far as anybody can see) well justified, it will definitely be fulfilled by God? But what, then, of all those requests that seem to be well justified beyond any possible doubt and which nonetheless are not fulfilled?

It seems to me that to say that "only those requests that are not justified do not get fulfilled would be a little too glib. To say this is to assume that people can know why some requests are fulfilled and some are not, and thus to rob praying of its mystery. Surely praying for one's daily bread, as recommended by Jesus, is well justified, and yet millions of people have died and are dying of starvation—no doubt many of them still saying the Lord's Prayer.

For many people, of course, the presence of massive evil and suffering in the world is in itself a compelling reason to doubt the efficacy of prayer (or indeed, the existence of any loving God). But consider, for example, the following vignette of the German theologian and anti-Hitler activist Dietrich Bonhoeffer, praying on the night before his execution (recorded by the prison doctor): "Through the half-open door of a room in one of the huts I saw Pastor Bonhoeffer still in his prison clothes, kneeling in fervent prayer to the Lord his God. The devotion and evident conviction of being heard that I saw in the prayer of this intensely captivating man moved me to the depths" (Hefley and Hefley 1988:215). On the following morning, Bonhoeffer and his companions "were marched to the place of execution and told to strip. One last time Bonhoeffer knelt to pray. Then he stood up. Shots pierced the stillness of the woods. The most famous Christian martyr of World War II was dead."

Bonhoeffer knew that he was going to be shot and that any prayers for his deliverance had not been fulfilled. Yet he clearly continued to believe that his and his family's prayers were heard by God and that something good happened because of them; evidently, he felt that such a belief was consistent rather than inconsistent with his own life experience.

Returning to the question of whether and in what sense God's promises to fufil requests are unconditional, we could perhaps say that the Gospels do suggest some necessary conditions, without, however, trying to explain or even intimate what the sufficient conditions might be. Clearly, one condition is that of thinking about God as a Father, that is, as someone who *can* do good things for people and who *wants* to do it. This suggests that the exhortation to ask should be understood against the background of the prior assumption, that it is good to think about God as Father, and that this is indeed how God wants people to think about him. In my terms, this can be represented as follows:

(a) it will be good if you think about God like this:
(b)   "God wants to do good things for all people
(c)   God can do good things for all people"

Another obvious condition is that what one is asking for is something good for someone, as, for example, receiving some food; clearly, Jesus' promise "Ask and it will be given to you" was not meant to apply to the request for some bad things to happen to one's enemy or one's competitor. Furthermore, if we read the injunction and the promise in the light of the Lord's Prayer, it will also be clear to us that the request for some good thing can be made on behalf of other people ("*Our* Father," "Give *us* this day *our* daily bread"). This means that not only can I always say to God (thought of as Our Father); "I want you to do something good for me" but I can also say the same thing about someone else: "I want you to do something good for this person." This second aspect of petitioning God in prayer can be represented as follows:

(d) if you think about God like this, you can always say to God:
(e)   "I want you to do something good for me"
(f) you can always say the same about another person:
(g)   "I want you to do something good for this person"
(h) it will be good if you say things like this to God
(i) God wants to hear this

Beyond the two conditions discussed (thinking about God as Father and asking for something good), Jesus' promise does indeed appear to be unrestricted— but again, not in the sense that God will necessarily do the very thing that one is asking for simply because one has asked for it. What Jesus had in mind seems to be something along the following lines: if you ask God (thought of as being like a loving father) to do something good for you (or for another person), something good *will* happen to you (or to that other person), and it will happen because God wants it to happen. Whether or not the good thing that happens is the very thing that one has asked for is left open; the effect of prayer, then (prayer of request), can be represented as follows:

(j) if you say it to God like this something good will happen to you
(k) if you say it about another person something good will happen to this person
(l) it will happen because God wants it to happen

This explication does not imply that God's gifts *depend* on human petitions; it does not imply that the person praying can influence God's will, and it does not imply that the fulfilment of the request depends on its being "well founded." Furthermore, the explication does not assert that every request will be fulfilled by God. What it does imply is that if one acknowledges God as the people's loving Father and if one asks for something good (whether for oneself or someone else), every request will be responded to: "if you ask for good things, good things will happen to you; and they will happen because God wants them to happen." Whether God will give the praying person precisely what he or she is asking for, or some other good thing, is not specified by Jesus in his exhortation and his promise ("Ask, and you will receive"). The bread and fish are mentioned by name in the simile as examples of things asked for and received by children, but the things given by God to people who pray to him are only referred to in the most general terms, as "good things."

Luke is more specific on this point than Matthew since instead of "good things" he says here, "the holy Spirit," ("how much more surely will the heavenly Father give the Holy Spirit to those who ask him?") Scholars generally agree that the addition of "the Holy Spirit" is due to Luke's redaction (in accordance with his overall emphasis on the Spirit; see e.g., Fitzmyer 1985b:913). Presumably, Luke wanted to prevent misunderstandings of precisely the kind that we can see in Funk et al. (1993): the idea that God will always give the very thing that one is asking for simply because one is asking for it. But the substitution of "the Holy Spirit" for "the good things" does not change the basic message of the passage—that the prayer will have an effect, that good things will indeed happen.

Of course, God (as Jesus presents him) doesn't need people to inform him what their needs are: "For your Father knows the things you have need of before you ask him" (Matt. 6:8). But in his parables and sayings, Jesus affirms that God "needs" (wants) to be acknowledged by people as their loving Father who *wants* to give them good things and who *wants* them to talk to him on an I-Thou basis (see Buber 1970). Urging people to ask God for good things Jesus highlights and reiterates this motif of his overall message.

Betz (1995:506) notes that according to most scholars, the passage in question (Matt. 7:7-11) is "an exhortation concerning trust in the meaningfulness of praying to God. What is recommended is unconditional trust in God's readiness to grant petitions by humans." For his part, Betz finds this common interpretation unsatisfactory: "The position taken by the SM [Sermon on the Mount] . . . is not a naive trust in God that leads to ask him all kinds of things in the belief that he will surely grant them. Even 7:11 does not assume that God will grant just anything he is asked for, but that he will give what is good."

The explication below is consistent with these comments: it does not imply that God will grant anything he is asked for but that he will give what is good. At the same time, however, the explication is also consistent with the general view that the passage in question "is an exhortation concerning trust in the meaningfulness of praying to God." In the light of this explication, praying and asking for specific good things is meaningful not in the sense that God will grant every specific request but that every request will bring some good—not automatically or magically but because God wants this to happen.

Betz who, as we have seen, has questioned the common assumption that Matthew 7:7-11 "is an exhortation concerning trust in the meaningfulness of praying to God," has summed up his own interpretation of this passage as follows:

I conclude . . . that the recommendation pertains first of all to a general approach to life, an approach based on the assumption that one can trust life as good. In spite of the observed fact that humans are evil, life is not. This conclusion makes sense in the face of scepticism. Contrary to what the sceptics would recommend, the SM holds that it is more prudent to encounter life without suspicion. Be one who asks, be a seeker, take courage and knock on doors! Most of the time, these initiatives will find positive responses. Experiences among humans, as well as with God, bear this out. This is the message. (1995:506)

But Betz's worldly wisdom is unconvincing. Although it is generally agreed that on the whole the importance of prayer may be more emphasized by Luke than it is by Matthew, Matthew's verse 7:11 makes it abundantly clear that in his interpretation, too, Jesus' instruction here is about trusting God and not about trusting *people* or trusting *life*; and there is no evidence that anything else was intended by Jesus himself.

Finally, it should be noted that the message of the triple exhortation and the triple promise is also the subject matter of the parable of the unjust judge and the parable of the friend at midnight, and both these parables throw some further light on this message (and vice versa). I will discuss those parables in chapter 22. Here, let me close with a full explication of the Ask passage (Matt. 7:7–11):

Ask, and it will be given to you . . .

(a) it will be good if you think about God like this:
(b)   "God wants to do good things for all people
(c)   God can do good things for all people"

(d) if you think about God like this, you can always say to God:
(e)   "I want you to do something good for me"
(f) you can always say the same about another person:
(g)   "I want you to do something good for this person"
(h) it will be good if you say things like this to God
(i) God wants to hear this

(j) if you say it to God like this something good will happen to you
(k) if you say it about another person something good will happen to this person
(l) it will happen because God wants it to happen

12. The golden rule

Matthew 7:12

Therefore, whatever you want people to do to you,
do also to them, for this is the Law and the Prophets.

Luke 6:31

And just as you want people to do to you,
you also do to them likewise.

The so-called golden rule, known by this name since the eighteenth century, is the subject of extensive literature and heated controversy about its origins, meaning, and significance. The first question to consider is authenticity. Many scholars of the Jesus Seminar have expressed doubts on this point, although even in this skeptical body opinion is divided (resulting in a gray status for to both the Matthean and Lucan version): "It [the golden rule] is a piece of common lore found in ancient sources, Christian, Judean, and pagan. . . . It is not surprising that the same proverb is attributed to Jesus since it fits in a general way with his injunction to love enemies"(Funk et al. 1993:156).

But whether the golden rule in either the Matthean or Lucan version is indeed "a piece of common lore" is disputed, and despite the extensive literature devoted to this question, no genuinely close parallels that predate Jesus have actually been cited. (For the latest survey of putative parallels, see Wattles 1996; among earlier such surveys, see especially Abrahams [1917]1967; Dihle 1962; Lachs 1987; Montefiore [1927]1968; Rost (1986; see also Strack and Billerbeck [1922-1928]1965.) The parallels usually thought to be close take the negative form, like Rabbi Hillel's version, quoted by nearly all the writers on the subject: "What you hate, don't do to someone else" (see e.g., Lachs 1987). Hillel's formulation (which echoes one in the apocryphal Old Testament book of Tobit 4:15) was noteworthy in that he described the injunction as the whole Law in a nutshell: ". . . that is the whole Torah. All the rest is commentary." Later, a similar formula was used by the first-century Jewish philosopher Philo: "A man must not do what he'd hate to have done to him" (quoted in Downing 1988:27). But the very difference between Hillel's and Tobit's negative form and Jesus' positive one means that Jesus' version cannot simply be written off as a piece of common Israelite lore, given that no ancient Judaic or, for that matter, any other close parallels of the positive version are cited in the extensive literature on the subject. (For related but significantly different ancient sayings, see Dihle 1962; see also the concluding section of this chapter.)

In fact, it would be difficult to deny the plausibility of Jeremias's (1971) suggestion that Jesus' version (as reported in Matthew) was formulated with reference to and, so to speak, in dialogue with Hillel's version. The Matthean Jesus echoed Hillel's negative saying and made a similarly sweeping claim for his positive version: "for this is the Law and the Prophets." Jesus' reformulation can be seen as dialogical rather than polemical: one could say that it takes up Hillel's statement and reasserts it in a deliberately rephrased form.

As pointed out by Jeremias, context is very important to understanding Jesus' intent. Whereas the immediate contexts in Matthew and Luke are different, in both Gospels the positive golden rule appears in the broad context of the teaching on the love of one's neighbor; it makes sense, therefore, to see the switch from the familiar negative form to the novel positive one to underscore that teaching: "In Mark 12.28–34 . . . Jesus describes loving one's neighbour as the greatest commandment after loving God, and in Matt. 7.12 he calls the golden rule the sum of the whole of the New Testament. . . . Jesus takes up Hillel, but it is not, of course, a coincidence that he puts the golden rule in a positive way. . . . Jesus' positive version is a summons to a demonstration of love" (Jeremias 1971: 211–212). In a footnote, Jeremias adds that in the parallel Luke 6.31, the sentence "for this is the Law and the Prophets" is missing, and, he says, "It is shown to be original by the way in which it takes up Hillel. In the Lucan version it will have been omitted with an eye to the Gentile-Christian reader."

The vexed (but ultimately irrelevant) question of which of the two versions of the golden rule is more fundamental or superior should not be confused with the question of what place this rule occupies in Jesus' teaching and what it means in that context. The fact that some later Christian documents include the golden rule in the negative version (for references, see Betz 1995:516; Dihle 1962:107; Jeremias 1971:212) does not show that the reversal in Matthew 7:12 was not significant or deliberate. The negative and the positive form can be seen as complementary and it is quite likely that they both had a place in Jesus' teaching. But if the whole Law and Prophets were to be summarized in one sentence, the Matthean Jesus choses the positive, not the negative one, and Jeremias makes a strong case for the hypothesis that the historical Jesus did so also.

In addition to the alleged lack of originality of Jesus' golden rule, many Fellows of the Jesus Seminar were inclined to a gray or black designation because "in its traditional form, the golden rule expresses nothing that cuts against the common ground, or surprises and shocks, or indulges in exaggeration or paradox" (Funk et al. 1993:156). But whereas the saying is in itself non-paradoxical, it is short and readily remembered, and the reversal of the form from negative to positive may well have been surprising and seen to cut against the common ground.

Betz (1995:513) sums up his discussion of what he believes to be different versions and different interpretations of the golden rule as follows: "The SM [Sermon on the Mount] claims that its peculiar understanding of the Golden Rule goes back to Jesus of Nazareth, and one has no reason to doubt that in such an old source as the SM this claim is reliable." He concludes, "One can have no real doubt that the Rule was a constitutive part of his [Jesus'] teaching" (pp. 515–516).

Having established that the golden rule as presented in Matthew 6:12 and Luke 6:31 in all probability does go back to Jesus, the next crucial step is to determine what this rule means. The range of interpretations offered in the literature is wide. Some commentators have questioned the authenticity of the rule on the basis of its alleged banality. Others have suggested that it is incompatible with Jesus' overall teaching. Dihle (1962) has claimed that Jesus didn't *advance* the golden rule but rather *rejected* it in favor of a new ethic, based on the principle of love of one's neighbor. This claim (that Jesus rejected the golden rule) is closely linked with Dihle's interpretation of it as being identical in essence with the ancient *ius talionis* 'law of retribution'. Since Jesus rejected retribution, in Dihle's view he must also have rejected, rather than taught, the golden rule.

But the meaning of the golden rule as presented in Matthew 7:12 is quite different from the law of retribution, as several commentators have persuasively argued (see in particular Ricoeur 1990) and as I will try to show below within my own framework. Dihle's (1962) argument illustrates in a particularly striking fashion that the issue of authenticity is closely related to that of accurate interpretation. If in one interpretation a well-attested saying appears to be inconsistent with Jesus' overall teaching, one should question that interpretation before dismissing the saying itself as nonauthentic.

In what follows, I will attempt an interpretation of Jesus' version of the golden rule, which I believe is fully consistent with his overall teaching. In doing so, I will not try to explicate the words or phrases used in the surface form of the saying but rather to reconstruct the underlying intended message, using all available clues. For the positive version, I propose the following:

> you know: you want other people to do good things for you
> it will be good if you do good things for other people
> like you want other people to do good things for you
> God wants you to do this

Hillel's negative version, sometimes described as the "silver rule" (cf. Bull 1969; Porpora, in press), can be portrayed symmetrically:

> you know: you want other people not to do bad things to you
> it will be good if you don't do bad things to other people
> like you want other people not to do bad things to you
> God wants you not to do this

Admittedly, the word "good" is not used in the surface form of Jesus' saying (just as the word "bad" is not used in the surface forms of Hillel's); but in the context of his teaching, it seems obvious that this is what is meant. In Matthew, it comes at the end of a passage about parents doing good things for their children and God doing good things for people. In Luke, the implicit reference to doing good things for other people is almost equally obvious; some (e.g., Spooner 1937:310) would say even more so since it follows on the heels of the injunction "Love your enemies, do good to those who hate you" (6:27) and "give to everyone who asks of you" (6:30).

The word "good," though not present in the surface form of the sayings as they are generally known, does in fact appear in many of their early (Latin) versions. The entry on the golden rule from the *Encyclopedia of Religion and Ethics* states that

> the train of thought [in Matthew] would seem to be that, as God gives good gifts to those who ask Him, so we as Christians ought to render to others the sort of service, the good things, which we should wish them to render to us. That this is the connexion of thought which the earlier translators recognized in the passage is made probable by the fact that most of

the early Latin versions, though not the Vulgate itself, render: "Whatever *good* things, therefore, you wish that others should do unto you, even such do unto them; for this is the law and the prophets" (Spooner 1937:310)

The difference in phrasing between Matthew's "whatever you want . . ." and Luke's "as you want . . ." should not, I think, be given undue significance; the underlying message in both cases involves an analogy, LIKE (or AS); and the explication proposed here is valid, I think, for both these versions.

The first century C.E. work of hellenistic Judaism known as the "Slavonic Book of Enoch" includes the following quasiparallel to the golden rule (Piper 1979:37):

Just as a man asks (sc. something) for his own soul from God, so let him do to every living soul (61:1)

In universal concepts this can be paraphrased as follows:

it will be good if you do good things for everyone
like you want God to do good things for you

Piper refers to this saying as a "positive love command. . . . expressed in a form of the Golden Rule" (p. 37). Although I wouldn't go so far as to call it a form of the golden rule, it *is* obviously akin to it, and it supports the view that what is involved (in both the golden and the silver rules) is not reciprocity but rather analogy: treat everyone as you want God/other people to treat you.

Some of the criticisms of the golden rule in the literature make one wonder whether the critics are aware of the immediate contexts in Matthew and Luke (not to mention the larger context of the Gospels as a whole). Some are being facetious. Wattles (1996:6) quotes George Bernard Shaw: "Don't do to others as you want them to do unto you. Their tastes may be different." Shaw was deliberately distorting the meaning of the saying. But if Wattles is right, many professional philosophers have ignored the implicit reference to doing good things (obvious in context) without any facetious intent. According to Wattles (1996:6), "Many scholars today regard the rule . . . as embarrassing if taken with philosophical seriousness. Most professional ethicists rely instead on other principles, since the rule seems vulnerable to counterexamples, such as the current favorite, 'What if a sadomasochist goes forth to treat others as he wants to be treated?'"

The meaning of the rule that these professional ethicists apparently have in mind can be stated as follows:

you know: you want other people to do some things to you
it will be good if you do the same things to other people

One glance at this formula and at the formula proposed earlier for Jesus' saying should be sufficient to make anyone realize that the sadomasochist's rule, as well as the rule contemplated by George Bernard Shaw, is quite different in meaning and form from that attributed to Jesus.

It is misleading, I think, to talk about the golden rule in terms of reciprocity, as Bull (1969:154–159) does in comparing the "iron rule" ("an eye for an eye"), the "tinsel rule" ("Treat others as they deserve to be treated"), the "silver rule" (Hillel's), and the "golden rule" (Jesus'): Bull states that "the lowest level of reciprocity is the hard metal of iron retaliation—'eye for eye, tooth for tooth'" (p. 155). On the other hand, "the highest level of reciprocity is enshrined in the universal Golden Rule. . . . : 'As ye would that men should do to you do ye even so to them.'" Such a ranking of "levels of reciprocity" is misleading because it suggests that there is some underlying common principle of reciprocity in all these cases. But what is this reciprocity that the "iron rule" and the "golden rule" are supposed to share? If reciprocity is to mean anything, it must involve interaction between two specific individuals (or two specific groups). The "eye for an eye" principle does involve that; the golden rule, however, does not. If the idea is that we should do good things for other people, just as we want other people to do good things for us (whether or not those others actually do good things for us), reciprocity doesn't come into it at all, any more than it does into Enoch's rule to "treat everyone as you want God to treat you."

Reciprocity doesn't come into Hillel's negative (silver) rule (as explicated here) either. Whether or not it comes into the tinsel rule ("Treat others as they deserve," Bull 1969:155) depends on how this rule is interpreted. In interpretation (a), the tinsel rule does involve reciprocity, whereas in interpretation (b) it does not:

> (a) if someone does bad things to you
>   it will be good if you do bad things to this person
>   if someone does good things for you
>   it will be good if you do good things for this person

> (b) if someone does bad things to other people
>   it will be good if you do bad things to this person
>   if someone does good things for other people
>   it will be good if you do good things for this person

The word "deserve" in the phrasing of the tinsel rule implies that in treating other people in certain ways we can set ourselves up as judges of their conduct, and this is reflected in interpretation (b). As pointed out by Bull, however, and in my formula (a), "in practice the tinsel rule turns out, on closer investigation, to be little more than the Iron Rule dressed up" (p.156). What is important in the present context, however, is that the golden rule—unlike the iron rule or one version of the tinsel rule—is not based on reciprocity.

Paul Tillich (1964:30–32) finds shortcomings in the golden rule from a rather different perspective. To quote Wattles (1996:5), "For him, biblical command-ments of love and the assurance that God is love 'infinitely transcend' the golden rule. The problem with the rule is that it doesn't tell us what we *should* wish." One could agree with Tillich if one were to focus on the letter of Jesus' saying but not if one tries to grasp its spirit. In context it is clear that Jesus' saying presupposes that people want others to do good things for them, and it urges them to do good things for others themselves. It is true that the saying does not specify *what* good things one ought to do for other people, but the commandment to love one's neighbour doesn't specify that either. The story of the Good Samaritan is offered by the Lucan Jesus as an example of what love of one's neighbor means, but it is no more than an example. If the commandment to love one's neighbor "infinitely transcends" the letter of the golden rule, it is not because the golden rule is insufficiently specific but because it refers to *doing* good things for other people (rather than to loving them); and as rightly emphasized by the Jewish scholar Abrahams (1967:22), "Love is greater than doing" (a statement with which Jesus would have agreed).

But it is not justified to contrast the golden rule with the love commandment in this way because, as pointed out by Jeremias, in both the Matthean Sermon on the Mount and the Lucan Sermon on the Plain the golden rule can be seen as a corollary of the love commandment rather than an alternative to it. As we saw earlier, Jeremias' (1971) argument is that Jesus was reversing the negative golden rule (which was likely to be familiar to his audience from Hillel's summing up of the whole Torah) in the light of the love commandment. Whether or not one accepts Jeremias' argument in its entirety, it is hard not to agree that taken in context (whether Matthean or Lucan), Jesus' positive golden rule can be seen as an adjunct to the commandment of love. The difference between *wanting* to do good things for other people (in the love commandment) and *doing* good things for other people (in the golden rule) may be due simply to the dialogical function of the latter: Jesus' golden rule echoes the phrasing of Hillel's rule, substituting at the same time "good" for "bad" and "do" for "not do" (not on the surface but in the underlying message).

Elsewhere in his Gospel, Matthew (22:37–40) uses an almost identical formulation for the "double love" commandment ("You shall love the Lord your God with all your heart" and "You shall love your neighbour as yourself"; "on these two commandments hang all the Law and the Prophets"). Clearly, in the eyes of the Matthean Jesus, the golden rule and the love of one's neighbor (translating the love of God to the human level) stand very close indeed.

Porpora (in press) states that "most Christians believe that the golden rule both goes back to Jesus and epitomizes his ethical teaching." Noting the lack of universal consensus on the first point, Porpora comments, "What is certain is that the golden rule was not the main thrust of Jesus' charismatic ethic, which, rather, was far more radical than the golden rule"; moreover, "it is clear that what Jesus demands radically exceeds the golden rule. . . . For Jesus, God is our moral exemplar. Thus, if Jesus's ethics were to be formulated as a rule, that rule would not be, 'Do unto others as you would have them do unto you', but rather, 'Do unto others as God does unto you.'"

Porpora goes on to observe that "the golden rule itself is banal." This may be so if it is interpreted as many of Porpora's interviewees tend to do, using the language of "conventional reciprocity," "utilitarian calculation," and "self-fulfilment." One interviewee says, "I try to live by the golden rule: Do unto others as I would have them do unto me. Morally, I try not to be judgmental, particularly, to stay out of other people's lives as long as they're not hurting anybody." When asked why she follows the golden rule, she replies, "Why? It pays off. First of all, you have a. . . . It gets you self-satisfaction. It gives me satisfaction to make somebody feel good, to tell you the truth." But Porpora emphasizes that "his [Jesus'] was not an ethic based either on payoff or self-fulfilment." The golden rule was in fact anything but banal in its original meaning, which I have tried to explicate here in simple and universal concepts.

I agree with Porpora (in press) that Jesus' demands in the Sermon on the Mount "radically exceed the golden rule" (even in its original sense). But I also agree with Jeremias (1971) that Jesus' purpose in putting forward the golden rule was not to sum up his teaching but to propose a corrective, or an essential supplement, to Hillel's silver rule: "Yes, God wants you not to do bad things to others (as you want others not to do bad things to you); but in fact God wants more: God wants you to do good things for others, as you want others to do good things for you."

I agree, then, that the "moral exemplar" offered by Jesus was God and that, as Porpora (in press) says, "It is God's excessive goodness, not our own banal goodness, that is to set the moral standard of behavior" (p. 211): "Do unto others as God does unto you" (for a similar argument, see Ricoeur 1990). But as I see it, the original golden rule didn't offer human goodness as the moral standard of behavior either. It didn't say, roughly speaking, "Do good things for others, as good people do good things for others," and it didn't question, or compete with, the injunction (conveyed in Matt. 5:43–48) "Do good things for others, as God does good things for all people." Rather, it said, "Do good things for others, as you want others to do good things for you." The two formulas below are not incompatible; rather, they focus on different themes:

(a) it will be good if you want to do good things for other people
     like God does good things for all people
(b) it will be good if you do good things for other people
     like you want other people to do good things for you

Formula (a) points to God as a model for human goodness; formula (b), on the other hand, encourages people to identify with other people's need for human help and benevolence, taking one's own needs as a measure of and a guide to theirs.

Although the golden rule [roughly, (b) above] doesn't sum up Jesus' teaching and is less central to it than the commandment of love, it does nonetheless constitute an important corrective and/or supplement to the silver rule: "However small the intended difference between the golden rule attributed to Jesus and the silver rule attributed to Hillel and Confucius, there is a great, consequential difference in the lived moral postures epitomized by those two rules" (Porpora in press).

Finally, let us consider Rudolf Bultmann's (1963:103) famous comment on the golden rule, in which he dismisses the difference between the positive and the negative version as fortuitous: "It is a piece of self-deception to suppose that the positive form of the rule is characteristic for Jesus, in distinction from the attested negative form among the Rabbis. The positive form is purely accidental, for whether it be given positive or negative formulation the saying, as an individual utterance, gives moral expression to naive egoism."

Whether Jesus' choice of the positive form was accidental (as alleged by Bultmann 1963), or deliberate (as argued by Jeremias 1971) is ultimately a matter of conjecture, which cannot be conclusively decided one way or another. But the claim that the golden rule in both Jesus' version and Hillel's version "gives moral expression to naive egoism" is, it seems to me, rebutable by semantic analysis. What Bultmann appears to have in mind is a not-so-golden rule such as the one formulated by Seneca (Downing 1980:27): "Take care not to harm others, so others won't harm you." In universal human concepts this can be represented as follows:

> it will be good if you don't do bad things to other people
> if you do bad things to other people other people can do bad things to
> you because of this
> you know: you don't want other people to do bad things to you
> because of this, it will be good for you if you don't do bad things to
> other people

This admonition includes an assumption that it is in one's interest not to do bad things to other people and it seeks to support moral advice ("it will be good if you don't do bad things to other people") with an appeal to this assumption. Bultmann's charge of "naive egoism" does seem justified here. There are no comparable components, however, in the semantic structures assigned either to Jesus' or Hillel's formulations. Since Bultmann doesn't offer any evidence or discussion in support of his assimilation of Jesus and Hillel to Seneca, it is impossible to address his argument any further.

I will close my discussion of the golden rule by briefly considering Abrahams's comments, which Montefiore ([1927]1968:119–120) described as "a model of impartiality":

> One cannot share the opinion of some Jewish scholars . . . that there is *no* difference between the negative and positive formulations. But Bischoff [1905] is equally wrong in asserting that Hillel's maxim differs from that of Jesus just as "*Neminem laede*" ['don't harm anyone'], differs from "*Omnes iuva*" ['help everyone'], or, as Clough puts it in his fine satirical version of the Decalogue: "Thou shall not kill, but needst to not strive officiously to keep alive." ([1917]1967:22)

One can also agree with the Chinese neo-Confucian philosopher Chen Chun (twelfth-thirteenth century), who commented on Confucius' (negative) version of the golden rule as follows: "When the Grand Master said, 'Do not do to others what you do not want them to do to you', he was speaking about one side of the question. Actually one should not only refrain from doing to others what one does not want them to do to him; whatever one wants others to do to him he should do to others" (Wattles 1996:25).

Abrahams ([1917]1967) rightly points out that the satirical tone directed at the "silver rule" is misplaced and that St. Augustine, like other early Christian writers, used the negative version alongside the positive one as if they were quite close to one another. Abrahams suggests that in fact "the negative form is the more fundamental of the two" and that "the negative rule goes deeper into the heart of the problem." It is not clear why Abrahams regards the negative version as more fundamental, but in any case it is worth noting his final conclusion: "This criticism does not dispute, however, that the Gospel form is a splendid working principle which has wrought incalculable good to humanity" (p. 22).

As Porpora's (in press) interviews illustrate, at the end of the first Christian millennium many people in the Western world appear to think that the golden rule can provide a moral compass in life. At the same time, there is a great deal of confusion about what the golden rule actually means, or should mean. One can help to overcome this confusion by clarifying the questions and sharpening the options.

This bring us back to the widespread belief that the golden rule as found in the Gospels is a commonplace of ethical thought throughout the world: "Moralists of all ages and all faiths, attending only to the relations of men towards one another in an ideal society, have agreed upon the 'golden rule', 'Do as you would be done by'" (T. H. Huxley 1894; cited in Rost 1986:15). As the extensive search for parallels undertaken by Dihle (1962), Rost, Wattles (1996), and others shows, the parallels found show have at best a family resemblance. In addition to many different versions of the silver rule, these parallels include partial golden rules that are restricted to friends and relatives, advice to rulers to show benevolence to their subjects, and injunctions of universal well wishing. Since space doesn't permit an extended survey, I will present only one or two examples of each category, together with a semantic formula.

In the *Mahabharata*, Rost (1986:78) says, that "we find this approximation of the Golden Rule":

Do not do to others what ye do not wish
Done to yourself; and wish for others too
What ye desire and long for, for yourself.
This is the whole of Dharma, heed it well.

The first two lines of the text express the silver rule:

it will be good if you don't do bad things to other people
like you don't want other people to do bad things to you

The second two lines express the well-wishing rule:

it will be good if you want good things to happen to other people
like you want good things to happen to you

A version of a universal well-wishing rule is also part of Jesus' teaching ("Bless those who curse you," Luke 6:28), and it is mentioned by the Lucan Jesus in one breath with a do good rule ("Do good to those who hate you," Luke 6:27). But wanting good things to happen to other people is obviously not the same thing as doing good things for them.

From the sacred books of Jainism and Buddhism, Rost (1986) cites versions of the silver rule, and from the Buddhist work *Sutta Pitaka* (*Teaching Basket*, sixth-fifth century B.C.) the following positive rule: "In five ways should a clansman minister to his friends and familiars . . . —by generosity, courtesy and benevolence . . . by treating them as he treats himself, and by being as good as his word." This rule appears to include doing good things for one's "friends and familiars" and wanting good things to happen to them. What exactly is meant by "treating them as [one] treats [oneself]" is not entirely clear, but in any case there is no mention here of doing good things for all other people.

On the basis of these and other examples, Rost (1986:41) concludes, "In Chapters 5, 6, and 7 we have noted the fundamental importance of the Golden Rule in the three great faiths of Indian origins: Hinduism, Jainism, and Buddhism. As one scholar claims, 'It is the common ethical ideal in Indian thought.'" But this generalization could only be valid if the term "the Golden Rule" were being used in some sense different from that applying to the golden rule in the Gospels. It is not clear, however what exactly such an extended, broader sense could be.

What applies to the parallels from Hinduism, Jainism, and Buddhism adduced by Rost (1986) applies also to those from other traditions. Some of these parallels are ethically very impressive, but they are nonetheless different in meaning from the golden rule found in the Gospels. For example, Rost quotes the following statement from Lao-Tse (sixth century B.C.E.): "to those who are good (to me) I am good; and to those who are not good (to me), I am also good" (p. 45). This can be paraphrased as "I am good to everyone"— a statement that, although quite remarkable in itself, is nonetheless different in meaning from the universal injunction to "do good things for all other people, as you want other people to do good things for you." Unlike both the golden and the silver rules, this statement appears to present an ideal rather than a categorical imperative; and it lacks the reversal of perspective that requires one to take another person's point of view and see his or her needs as one's own.

To take one further example, in the chapter on Islam, Rost (1986:103) includes among various "Golden Rule statements attributed to Muhammed" the following: "Whatever you abhor for yourself, abhor it also for others, and whatever you desire for yourself desire also for others." The meaning of this statement can be represented as follows:

> it will be good if you don't want bad things to happen to other people,
> as you don't want bad things to happen to you
> it will be good if you want good things to happen to other people,
> as you want good things to happen to you

But again, although Rost calls this very fine maxim "a Golden Rule statement," wanting good things to happen to other people is not the same thing as doing good things for other people.

From Judaism, in addition to Hillel's silver rule, a passage from the so-called Letter of Aristeas is often mentioned as an example of the golden rule. Rost (1986:70) says that in this letter "the negative and the positive versions of the Golden Rule are combined in some advice to a king: 'As thou desirest that evils not befall thee, but to partake of all that is good, thou shouldst act in this spirit to thy subjects and to offenders, and shouldst very gently admonish such as are virtuous; for God draws all men (to Him) by gentleness.'" Strictly speaking, however, this advice includes neither the silver rule nor the golden rule, although it is related to both. Its message can be represented as follows:

> it will be good if you want good things to happen to people in your
>   country
> like you want good things to happen to you
> it will be good if you do something because of this
> it will be good if you want bad things not to happen to people in your
>   country
> like you want bad things not to happen to you
> it will be good if you do something because of this

As the explication spells out, the advice given to the king includes well-wishing components, as well as a reference to doing things with the intention of causing some good things to happen, and some bad things not to happen, to one's subjects. Apart from other differences, however, setting standards for a king is not the same as requiring such conduct and attitudes from all people.

Examples could be multiplied, but these should be sufficient to show that maxims cited in the literature as parallels to the golden rule in fact differ markedly in meaning from the rule found in the Gospels, and also from one another.

In summary, then, it is a mistake to regard the golden rule as formulated in the Sermon on the Mount as an ethical commonplace or to dismiss it as inauthentic on the basis of its alleged banality. An examination of parallels reveals, rather, its originality. While one can agree with Abrahams ([1917]1967) that "love is greater than doing," in Jesus' teaching loving and doing are closely related. The golden rule is certainly not a summary of his teaching, and it is true that the injunction "Love your enemies" epitomizes his teaching better than his version of the golden rule; but it is obviously not an accident that the love injunction is combined in the same verse with a do injunction ("Do good to those who hate you"). To appreciate the place of the golden rule in Jesus' teaching, we should stop thinking of it as a rule of reciprocity and see it rather as an injunction to do good things for others and to identify with others—as one needs to identify with others to be able to love one's neighbor as oneself.

13. Enter by the narrow gate

Matthew 7:13–14

13. Enter by the narrow gate; for wide is the gate and broad is the way
      that leads to destruction, and there are many who go in by it.
14. Because narrow is the gate and difficult is the way which leads to
      life, and there are few who find it.

Luke 13:24

24. Strive to enter through the narrow gate, for many, I say to you, will
      seek to enter and will not be able.

The metaphor of two roads to represent choice can be found in the Old Testament and also has its parallels in other traditions. For example, in Psalm 1, "the path of sinners" is contrasted with "the way of the righteous"; and in Jeremiah (21:8), the Lord says to the inhabitants of Jerusalem, "Behold, I set before you the way of life and the way of death." In the New Testament, the image of two roads has been amplified by the introduction of references to gates and doors. Commentators have invested a great deal of effort into trying to sort these images out and explain their details (see, e.g., Betz 1995:521–527). Ultimately, however, what matters is not the images but the message associated with them in a particular text, and Jesus' overall message that is conveyed in Luke's and Matthew's texts is clear enough.

Lambrecht (1985:187) explains this message as follows: "In the first pericope, the entry through the narrow gate and the finding of the Lord's way is nothing other than the doing of God's will. Most people choose the wide gate and the easy way, but this leads to destruction and not to life." In essence, I think Lambrecht is right, but his brief summary doesn't fully explain the meaning of the metaphors. For in what way is doing God's will similar to passing through a narrow gate or choosing a narrow and rough road? Why is doing God's will not similar to taking a wide and smooth road? And what *is* the "place" to which the narrow road leads and to which the narrow door gives access?

Other commentators are rather more explicit. For example, Stott explains the images of the two roads in considerable detail:

One way is easy. The word means "broad, spacious, roomy" . . . and some manuscripts combine these images and call this way "wide and easy." There is plenty of room on it for diversity of opinions and laxity of morals. It is the road of tolerance and permissiveness. It has no curbs, no boundaries of either thought or conduct. Travellers on this road follow their own inclinations, that is, the desires of the human heart in its fallenness. Superficiality, self-love, hypocrisy, mechanical religion, false ambition, censoriousness—these things do not have to be learnt or cultivated. Effort is needed to resist them. No effort is required to practise them. That is why the broad road is easy. The *hard* way, on the other hand, is narrow. Its boundaries are clearly marked. Its narrowness is due to something called "divine revelation," which restricts pilgrims to the confines of what God has revealed in Scripture to be true and good. ([1978]1992:194–195)

Stott also explains in detail the image of the gate or the door, and he rightly recalls the saying attributed to Jesus in the Fourth Gospel: "I am the door. If anyone enters by me, he will be saved" (John 10:9):

> Secondly there are two gates. The gate leading to the easy way is *wide*, for it is a simple matter to get on to the easy road. There is evidently no limit to the luggage we can take with us. We need leave nothing behind, not even our sins, self-righteousness or pride. The gate leading to the hard way, on the other hand, is *narrow*. One has to look for it to find it. It is easy to miss. As Jesus said in another connection, it is as narrow as a needle's eye. Further, in order to enter it we must leave everything behind—sin, selfish ambition, covetousness, even if necessary family and friends. (p. 195)

These explanations are helpful, but they are largely metaphorical themselves. Furthermore, references to superficiality, selfishness, hypocrisy, and so on are Stott's own examples of what he thinks Jesus had in mind rather than an exegesis of Jesus' actual words.

In his commentary on the Lucan version of the saying, Fitzmyer links the image of a narrow road with the idea of effort and exertion; he points out that Jesus avoids the question "Lord, are there few who are saved?" (Luke 9:23) when he responds with the exhortation to enter through the "narrow door":

> Jesus is asked how many will share in the salvation promised in the Kingdom: Are only a few to be saved? . . . Jesus does not answer the question directly. He gives rather a practical warning that people should strive or struggle to enter the Kingdom by its "narrow door." This is Jesus' concern; he leaves to God himself the answer about how many will find salvation. He puts emphasis instead on the effort that human beings will have to exert to get in. (1985b:1022)

Thus, Lambrecht (1985) stresses doing God's will; Stott ([1978]1992), restrictions on conduct illuminated by the Scriptures; and Fitzmyer (1985b), effort. Other writers reach for different explanations. Some focus on the uncertainty of outcome, the ever-present possibility of failure, and the poor chances most people seem to have of ever entering the kingdom of God:

> There is thus the possibility of failure even for Jesus' disciples, who may have set out on the road but who end up being unsuccessful. This means that the SM [Sermon on the Mount] is not a fool-proof how-to-do instruction that sets up the conditions that, if met, guarantee success automatically. Rather, following the commendations of the SM means that only those

who persist have a chance, but that chance is tenuous and depends on the arduous process of "seeking and finding." Being a member of the group means nothing, if the individual fails. The chances of failure are greater than the chances of success, a sobering message. (Betz 1995:527–528)

But is this really Jesus' message? As Fitzmyer pointed out, Jesus declined to answer the question about the number of those who will be saved. Betz says that "the 'narrow gate' is unquestionably the entrance to the Kingdom of the heavens" (p. 525), but is he right in implying that according to Jesus only a minority have a chance of ever entering?

I think it is more justified to interpret Jesus' words as a reference to choices that people make on earth (i.e., before they die) and to the obvious failure of the majority to choose the narrow road, which indubitably gives access to "life" (i.e., to living with God)—that is, the narrow road of sainthood. Most people are not saints; in fact very few people are. Most people take (at least part of the time) "the wide and smooth road that leads to destruction"; very few choose, consistently, the narrow way. But this does not mean that Jesus was predicting destruction as the final outcome of most people's lives. To interpret the gate and road sayings in this way is to misunderstand their genre: they are exhortations, not predictions.

Fitzmyer (1985b:1022) calls the sayings in question "minatory": "Form-critically considered, most of the utterances recorded in this passage [Luke 13:22–29] are to be explained as minatory sayings of Jesus. Bultmann (1963:93) was inclined to regard v.24 as a wisdom-saying. . . . It serves, nonetheless, to introduce the minatory sayings that follow." Minatory sayings are instances of what in the German exegetical tradition is called *Drohrede* (see, e.g., Imbach 1995:73–74): a special genre of biblical warnings and admonitions (*Mahnrede*), which are meant to convey an urgent call, an urgent appeal. They are certainly not factual predictions. Their function is monitory (cf. Strecker 1988:157), as well as minatory. They call for conversion, and they call for it in the name of what all addressees want themselves: their own good, their own lasting happiness.

This brings us to the following explication:

The narrow gate

(a) many people think: "I want to live with God"
(b) at the same time, they think:
(c)   "if I want to do something I will do it
(d)   if I don't do it I will feel something bad
(e)   I don't want to feel bad things
(f)   if I don't want to do something I will not do it
(g)   if I do it I will feel something bad
(h)   I don't want to feel bad things"
(i) when someone thinks like this this someone can't live with God

(j) it will be good if you don't think like this
(k) it will be good if you think:
(l)   "I want to live with God

(m)   because of this if I think that God wants me to do something
         I will do it
(n)   if I think that God doesn't want me to do something I will
         not do it"

(o) it will be good for you if you think like this
(p) God wants you to think like this
(q) if you always think like this you can always live with God

Component (a) presents living with God as the goal of life, and so it applies the gate and road sayings, above all, to people who do want to live with God and suggests that the contrast between the two roads should be seen in that perspective. This is consistent with Betz's (1995) point that the sayings apply, first, to believers or disciples.

The two indented sets of components [(c)–(h) and (l)–(n)] present two different attitudes to life: one focused on following one's own inclinations and on avoiding "bad feelings" (suffering) which would follow from doing what one doesn't feel like doing or not doing what one does feel like doing, and the other focused on following God's will (as suggested by Lambrecht 1985).

Component (i) suggests that following all one's inclinations and avoiding suffering at all cost is incompatible with the goal of living with God. This component does not suggest that a person who is following his or her inclinations "cannot be saved" (can never live with God); rather, it suggests that the road followed by such a person—at the time when it is followed—does not lead to living with God. Component (q) suggests that if a person is consistently focused on doing God's will (i.e., on doing what they think God wants them to do and not doing what they think God doesn't want them to do), they can live with God always, before they die as well as after (i.e., for all their lives, as well as for all eternity).

14. Do people gather grapes from thornbushes or figs from thistles?

Matthew 7:15–20

15. Beware of false prophets, who come to you in sheep's clothing, but inwardly they are ravenous wolves.
16. (a) You will know them by their fruits. (b) Do people gather grapes from thornbushes or figs from thistles?
17. Even so, every good tree bears good fruit, but a bad tree bears bad fruit.
18. A good tree cannot bear bad fruit, nor can a bad tree bear good fruit.
19. [Every tree that does not bear good fruit is cut down and thrown into the fire.]

20. Therefore by their fruits you will know them.

Luke 6:43–45; cf. Matthew 12:33–35

43. For a good tree does not bear bad fruit, nor does a bad tree bear good fruit.
44. (a) For every tree is known by its own fruit. (b) For people do not gather figs from thorns, nor do they gather grapes from a bramble bush.
45. A good man out of the good treasure of his heart brings forth good; and an evil man out of the evil treasure of his heart brings forth evil. For out of the abundance of the heart his mouth speaks.

A series of sayings about trees and fruit is reported, with some variation, by both Matthew and Luke. Commentaries often focus largely on Matthew's verse 7:15, warning against false prophets; many biblical scholars, however, hold that there are good reasons to think that this verse originated with Matthew, not with Jesus: "Matthew himself created 7:15 and with this expansion of the text showed how he wanted to have the rest of the pericope understood" (Lambrecht 1985:192). Matthew's verse 19: "Every tree that does not bear good fruit is cut down and thrown into the fire" has no parallel in Luke either, and in fact comes straight from the preaching of John the Baptist as reported in Matthew 3:10. According to Dupont (1969: I, 125), it is generally acknowledged that this verse is a Matthean creation.

By comparing the Matthean and Lucan versions of the tree and fruit sayings, Lambrecht (1985:189) has posited the following hypothetical "Q-text" which underlies both these sets and is therefore closer to the historical Jesus (the numbering corresponds to Luke's text):

43. For no beautiful tree bears sick fruit, nor again does a sick tree bring forth beautiful fruit.
44. (a) For each tree is known by its fruit. (b) Are figs gathered from thorns, and grapes picked from a bramble bush?
45. The good man out of his good treasure produces good, and the bad man out of his bad treasure produces bad things; for out of the abundance of the heart his mouth speaks.

It is on these verses, then, that I will focus my analysis.

As many commentators point out, the tree and fruit sayings have parallels elsewhere, for example, in the Proverbia Aesopi aphorism: "Its fruit will be clear proof for every tree of the nature that it has" (see Betz 1995:536). Fruit as a metaphor for deeds, good or bad, was also used in the Old Testament (see Fitzmyer 1981:643). But despite such parallels, even the scholars of the Jesus Seminar do not doubt that "the quip about thorns and figs ["Do people gather grapes from thornbushes or figs from thistles?"] is traceable to Jesus. Like other genuine Jesus' sayings, it relies on exaggerated concrete images to dramatise a point otherwise left unexplained. The rhetorical question is particularly provocative and almost absurd. It sounds like a retort" (Funk et al. 1993:157). As for the more abstract generalizations, the fact that they may echo some older sayings doesn't mean that Jesus didn't make use of them, adapting them for his own purposes and filling them with new meaning.

What could Jesus have meant, then, by his tree and fruit sayings in general and by the "grapes from thornbushes or figs from thistles" saying in particular? The first interpretation that may come to mind is that there are two kinds of people: good people and bad people. Some, like the second-century Gnostic Marcion, went so far as to conclude "from the opposition of the two trees that there were two gods who created them" (Luz 1989:448). But if one considers these sayings in the context of the Gospels as a whole, it is clear that Jesus did not mean that people can be divided into good people and bad people. On the contrary, Jesus was at pains to emphasize that people must not judge others (see e.g., Matt. 7:1–5; Luke 6:37–42). It is of course true that thornbushes, bramble bushes, and thistles can be taken to symbolize bad plants (which don't bear fruit), but this doesn't mean that Jesus intended that some *people* can be seen as being, by their very nature, bad people or others, by their very nature, good.

Jesus did not teach that people are unchangeable. A sixth-century Christian wrote, "Non dixit: Arbor mala non potest fieri bona ('he [Jesus] did not say: a bad tree cannot become a good tree')" (Luz 1989:44). Clearly, Jesus was calling *all* people to bear good fruit, including sinners, tax collectors, and prostitutes, as well as Pharisees, scribes, and other righteous worthies. He was calling both the sinners and the righteous to a *metanoia*, a transformation, a change of heart. Everyone needed to be born again (see John 3:1–3), and everyone *could* be born again if one wanted to. The theme of choice was developed, in particular, by the third-century theologian Origen, who stressed that since all people have free will, all can choose to become either a good or a bad tree: "bona arbor dicatur, si per arbitrii potestate elegerit bona, aut mala dicatur, si elegerit mala ('a person may be called a good tree if through the power of the will they have chosen good things, or they may be called a bad tree if they have chosen bad things')" (p. 44.).

Some translators and commentators (e.g., Lambrecht 1985) prefer in fact to talk about beautiful trees and sick trees rather than good trees and bad trees, to avoid the impression that the sayings refer to trees of different species, which are good and bad by nature and cannot change. The use of the words *kalos* 'good, beautiful' and *sapros* 'rotten, bad', alongside *agathos* 'good' and *ponēros* 'bad', in the Greek text of the relevant passages supports such a translation.

John the Baptist was remembered to have used the tree and fruit image in calling people to repentance and a change of heart: "Therefore bear fruits worthy of repentance. . . . And even now the axe is laid to the root of the trees. Therefore every tree which does not bear good fruit is cut down and thrown into fire" (Matt. 3:8–10). A similar call to change and fruitfulness lies behind the parable of the barren fig tree (Luke 13:6–9):

6. He also spoke this parable: "A certain man had a fig tree planted in his vineyard, and he came seeking fruit on it and found none.

7. Then he said to the keeper of his vineyard, 'Look, for three years I have come seeking fruit on this fig tree and find none. Cut it down; why does it use up the ground?'

8. But he answered and said to him, 'Sir, let it alone this year also, until I dig around it and fertilize it.

9. And if it bears fruit, well. But if not, after that you can cut it down.'"

This parable implies that the question is not so much whether one is a thornbush or a fig tree but whether one is barren or bears fruit; and if one *is* barren, like the barren fig tree, one is called to a change of heart so that one can start to bear fruit. Fruitless trees, Matthew notes, are useless and are cut down. But Jesus did not make predictions of what would happen to people who lived like fruitless trees. Rather, he was urging people to turn to God and as a consequence become like fruitful trees; and by the same token, he was telling them that they *could* become like good trees and bear fruit—and that God wanted them to do so.

The image of a beautiful tree bearing beautiful fruit and a sick tree bearing sick fruit is quite illuminating here. A tree is not beautiful or sick by its very nature, and given proper care a sick tree can in principle become a beautiful tree. As the parable of the barren fig tree makes clear, given proper care, a barren fig tree *can* start to bear fruit. Figuratively speaking, then, Jesus was telling people, "God wants you to be like a healthy tree" and "God wants you to bear good fruit." He was also warning people that they couldn't start bearing good fruit until they became like healthy trees.

But whereas the image of a sick tree and a healthy tree is illuminating, so is the image of different species because it highlights the *impossibility* of bearing good fruit if one doesn't become the kind of *person* who could bear good fruit. It is impossible to produce grapes if one is a thornbush or figs if one is a thistle. Betz (1995:538) remarks that "the strong emphasis on the 'impossible' appears to point to a radical dualism and a kind of predestination" and that "this point was not lost on later interpreters, especially the Gnostics and the Manichaeans." If one considers these metaphors from the point of view of the Gospels as a whole, however, it becomes clear that this is not what Jesus meant. The parable of the barren fig tree is particularly relevant here. The point is not that it is impossible for a thornbush to turn into a fig tree, or for a bad person to turn into a good person, but rather that it is impossible for a barren fig tree to start to produce figs without some change in the tree itself, just as it is impossible for a thornbush to start to produce figs at all. Similarly, a person whose heart (or spirit or soul) is sick cannot do "good things" without first being transformed. It is not impossible, however, for a barren fig tree to respond to the ministrations of the gardener or for a person whose soul is sick to choose to respond to God's call and God's grace (see Meier 1980:73).

Both in Luke (6:45) and in Matthew (12:35) Jesus refers to a good man and a bad man, linking the distinction with that between "the good treasure of [a person's] heart" and "the evil treasure of [a person's] heart": "A good man out of the good treasure of his heart brings forth good things, and an evil man out of the evil treasure brings forth evil things" (Matt. 12:35). References of this kind do not mean, however, that there are two kinds of people, good and bad, who can be recognized as such by their deeds; rather, they mean that what matters is a person's heart, and a person's good and bad deeds simply follow from what is in this person's heart. In fact it can be argued that references to a good man and a bad man are phrased in language that is not really Jesus' own. In saying, figuratively, that to do good things one needs to be, as it were, a good person, Jesus was not endorsing the idea of a good person and a bad person per se but rather using language that would make the point clear to his addressees. The phraseology of "good treasure of a person's heart" and "bad treasure of a person's heart" seems much more at home in Jesus' overall teaching than that of a "good person" and "bad person." Here as elsewhere, Bakhtin's (1981) notion of heteroglossia helps to make clear what Jesus really meant: the question is not whether Jesus *used* expressions like "a good man" and "an evil man" (or elsewhere, the word "reward") but whether he was speaking in his own voice or was instead echoing some other people's language. (I will return to this point shortly.)

The emphasis on a person's heart as the moral basis and moral criterion of their deeds is one of the leitmotifs of Jesus' teachings. What matters is what is happening in a person's heart, and a heart can always change. The question often raised in other philosophical and religious frameworks, "Why do bad things happen to good people?" (see e.g., Kushner 1981), has no place in Jesus' teaching because he does not accept the assumption that people can be divided into good and bad.

Speaking of Jesus' dictum "I did not come to call the righteous, but sinners" (Mark 2:17b), said in reply to the Pharisees and scribes who reproached him for his relations with sinners, Dupont (1969: II,230) has commented, "In his responses, Jesus doesn't question his interlocutors' idea about so-called 'righteous' and so-called 'sinners'; he adopts the point of view and the language of his adversaries, in order to try to make them see, starting from there, his own point of view. . . ." I think the same applies to the idea of a good person and a bad person, reflected in the phraseology of good and bad trees. Certainly, there are many references to "righteous people bringing forth good fruit" in rabbinic literature, for example, "As the mountains are sown with wheat and bring forth fruit, so the righteous bring fruit [i.e., good works]"; "As the abysses can't be sown and bring no fruits, so the ungodly have no good works and bring no fruits" (Strack and Billerbeck 1965:466); "The fruit of a righteous man is his good conduct" (Lachs 1987:148). It seems likely that Jesus' sayings about good fruit and bad fruit take as their starting point this kind of phraseology, used in Palestine in his time.

I argue, then, that it is a mistake to interpret the Matthean and Lucan Jesus' references to good trees and bad trees in terms of good people and bad people. It is also a mistake to interpret the Matthean and Lucan Jesus' references to good fruit and bad fruit as indications of an emphasis on people's deeds as such (regardless of the thoughts, wants, and feelings associated with them).

Commenting on Matthew's tree and fruit sayings (Matt. 7:15–20) from the point of view of rabbinic literature, Montefiore ([1930]1970:153) has written, "For my purposes it is unnecessary to consider any parallels to these verses. The maxim, 'By their fruits ye shall know them', would be in accordance with Rabbinic teaching. The test is the deed." Matthew's saying "by their fruit ye shall know them," with which he seals his warning against false prophets in verse 15, is indeed consistent with the rabbinic teaching that "the test is the deed." As noted by Albright and Mann (1971:86), however, these Matthean lines (15 and 20) are only loosely related to the sayings about trees and fruit (verses 16b–19); and it is precisely these sayings (16b–19) that have their parallels in Luke (6:43) and can be assumed to go back to Matthew's and Luke's presumed joint source *Quelle* and to the historical Jesus. There is also no counterpart of the saying "By their fruit you shall know them" in Thomas' version of the tree and fruit sayings, which is worth quoting in extenso:

> Jesus said: "Grapes are not harvested from thorn trees, nor are figs gathered from thistles, for they yield no fruit. A good person brings forth good from the storehouse; a bad person brings forth evil things from the corrupt storehouse in the heart and says evil things. For from the abundance of the heart this person brings forth evil things." (*The Gospel of Thomas* 1992: saying 45)

The emphasis on the contrast between good people and bad people reflects, no doubt, Thomas' gnostic leanings, but apart from that, his version of Jesus' teaching is consistent with that of the *Quelle* (i.e., the common core of Matthew and Luke), and it points to the importance of the heart rather than deeds as such: bad deeds come out of "the wickedness stored up in the heart."

Thus, the sentence "by their fruit you will know them," which Montefiore ([1930]1970) treats as a summary of Jesus' sayings on trees and fruit, is in all probability Matthew's own creation, which was meant to strengthen his warning against false prophets. It was Matthew, not Jesus, who put the emphasis on deeds. Dupont (1969: II, 262) refers in this connection to "the importance of the theme of 'fruit' in the first gospel" and speaks of "very significant alterations introduced by the evangelist," alterations that insist (inter alia) "on the necessity of fruits." Jesus' own point seems to have been different: what matters most is the heart; conduct, important as it is, is only an expression of what is in the heart. The rhetorical question "Can people gather figs from thistles?" does not mean that one can tell a fig tree (i.e., a good person) from a thistle (i.e., a bad person) by the presence of figs (i.e., good deeds); rather, it means that deeds follow from what is in the treasure of the heart: good deeds from a good treasure of the heart, and bad deeds from a bad treasure of the heart. The references to the treasure of the heart in Matthew 12:35 and Luke 6:45 would make no sense in these passages if their point were that what really matters is the conduct (i.e., the fruit) and not the state of the tree (i.e., the state of the person's heart).

To say that the apparent emphasis on fruits (i.e., deeds) is due to Matthew's alterations does not mean, of course, that Jesus regarded deeds as dispensable.

Rather, it means that Jesus placed the emphasis on the heart as a source of both good and bad deeds. Nothing illustrates Jesus' emphasis on the heart better than his well-known comments on violations of the ritual purity laws (Matt. 15:11–20):

11. Not what goes into the mouth defiles a person; but what comes out of the mouth, this defiles the person. . . .
17. Do you not understand that whatever enters the mouth goes into the stomach and is eliminated?
18. But those things which proceed out of the mouth come from the heart, and they defile a person.
19. For out of the heart proceed evil thoughts, murders, adulteries, fornications, false witness, blasphemies.
20. These are the things which defile a person, but to eat with unwashed hands does not defile a person.

Arguably, when Luther interpreted "the good tree" as faith, from which "all good works then subsequently originate as fruit, almost by themselves" (Loewenich 1954:180; Luz 1989:449), he was closer to the spirit of Jesus' tree and fruit sayings than those commentators who saw in them a comment on the importance of works. Jesus' original sayings, however, did not refer to faith but to the heart— seen as the real source of both good and bad deeds.

But what exactly did Jesus mean by "heart"? Metaphorically speaking, he obviously meant what is "inside" a person, in contrast to what is outside, as he made clear in his outburst against the Pharisees (Matt. 23:25; cf. Luke 11:39–40): "Woe to you, scribes and Pharisees, hypocrites! For you cleanse the outside of the cup and dish, but inside they are full of extortion and self-indulgence" (Luke says, "of greed and wickedness").[11] Funk et al. (1993:243) note that both Luke's and Matthew's version of this saying is a mixed metaphor: the outside refers to cups but the inside to persons, and they regard Thomas' version as closer to Jesus' original saying. In any case, however, Jesus was obviously referring to people and was pointing out the importance of what is "inside a person," that is, a person's habitual patterns of thoughts and wants and, especially, a person's orientation toward good and evil, the key question is whether a person wants to do good things or bad things.

Thus in emphasizing the importance of the "heart" Jesus was not deemphasizing deeds; rather, he was affirming that the value of the deeds depends on the intention that accompanies them. He was not saying that the inside is more important than the outside but instead was emphasizing the inextricable link between the purity of the inside and the outside (cf. "Blind Pharisee, first cleanse the inside of the cup and dish, that the outside of them may be clean also," Matt. 23:26). In other words, Jesus was suggesting that from God's point of view, no action constitutes a genuinely good deed unless it flows from a good will, that is, that there are no inherently good outer deeds. He was, in effect, redefining the notion of a good deed.

As discussed earlier, a person's inability to produce good fruits is not presented in the Gospels as irreversible. The purpose of the tree and fruit sayings is not to judge people whose hearts are like thornbushes or thistles but to warn everyone and to call everyone to a change of heart, a *metanoia*, a transformation that should occur now and result in a permanent new orientation of the will:

> it will be good if you think now:
> "I don't want to do bad things any more
> I want to live with God"
> it will be good if you always think like this

According to the first-century C.E. Jewish philosopher Philo, "God judges by the fruit of a tree, not by the roots" (Lachs 1987:149). Matthew's verse 7:19, "Every tree that does not bear good fruit is cut down and thrown into the fire," with its transparent allusion to God's judgment (see Betz 1995:538), seems to point in a similar direction. Jesus' own sayings, however, point to a different conclusion: people have to judge the fruits (and cannot judge the trees at all because they cannot see their roots); God, however, sees the roots and judges the trees by the roots.

An epilogue of sorts to the tree and fruit sayings in Matthew and Luke is provided by yet another set of sayings with similar images—that in the "true vine" discourse, attributed to Jesus by the Fourth Gospel (John 15:1–8):

1. I am the true vine, and my Father is the vine-dresser.
2. Every branch in me that does not bear fruit he takes away; and every branch that bears fruit he prunes, that it may bear more fruit. . . .
4. Abide in me, and I in you. As the branch cannot bear fruit of itself, unless it abides in the vine, neither can you, unless you abide in me.
5. I am the vine, you are the branches. He who abides in me, and I in him, bears much fruit; for without me you can do nothing. . . .
8. By this my Father is glorified, that you bear much fruit; so shall you be my disciples.

This, then, is the Fourth Gospel's explanation of the metaphors of fruitlessness and fruitfulness: a branch cannot bear fruit of itself, just as a thornbush cannot produce grapes or a thistle, figs. It can only bear fruit if it abides in the vine. The contrast is not between bad branches and good branches but between branches that abide in the vine and those that don't. *Every* branch can abide in the vine, and indeed every branch (person) is enjoined to do so; and every branch shall be fruitful if it does abide in the vine.

The idea of abiding in Christ belongs to the Fourth Gospel, not to the synoptic Gospels. Yet the idea of living with God (in the kingdom of God) as the ultimate source of people's goodness and love is inherent in the synoptic Gospels, too. If, as Jesus says, "No one is good but one, that is, God" (Matt. 19:17), where could people's goodness come from if not from living with God? If people's good deeds come from a "good heart," where does a "good heart" come from?

The heart may be free to choose between wanting to do good things and wanting to do bad things, but what nourishes and sustains the desire to do good things rather than bad things? The Fourth Gospel suggests that living with God does that: God's goodness affects, or infects, the person who is living with God, wakening and sustaining the desire to shun bad things and to do good. Thus, to push our interpretation of the tree and fruit sayings one step further, in the light of the Fourth Gospel, the following fuller explication can be proposed:

Plants (trees, thistles, thornbushes, vine) and fruit

    (a) if a person doesn't live with God
         this person cannot do good things
    (b) God is someone good
    (c) if a person lives with God
         this person can do many good things because of this
    (d) when a person wants to do bad things
         this person cannot live with God

Component (a) suggests that a human being cannot be the source of goodness and that isolated from God, people cannot do good things. Component (b) notes that God is someone good (and, by implication, a source of goodness). Component (c) links a person's capacity for doing good things with living with God. Component (d) spells out the link between a person's free will and the capacity to live with God; wanting to do bad things is an obstacle to living with God.

To sum up, Jesus' saying "Do people gather grapes from thornbushes or figs from thistles?" does not purport to give advice on how to test other people's moral stature (or the validity of their teaching); and it certainly does not endorse any division of people into good and bad, righteous and sinners, productive and worthless. Rather, it affirms that people can only do good things if in their hearts they live with God. As suggested by Origen, people's free choice of either good or evil is essential insofar as wanting to do bad things and not wanting to do good things prevent people from living with God; and if one doesn't live with God, one cannot be like a healthy tree and bear healthy fruit. At the same time, however, the ability to bear such fruit does not depend simply on a person's decision ("I will do many good deeds today"). If one wants to do many good things, one has to live with God, and this requires a radical orientation of the will toward good.

Thus, a full explanation of the tree and fruit sayings must include not only the tree and the fruit but also the gardener. A person cut off from God, Jesus suggests, is bound to be like a thistle; when living with God, however, the same person can be like a fruitful fig tree. Gourgues (1997:88) sums up the message of the parable of the fig tree (Luke 13:1–9) in the words "Convert and bear fruit!" The same message can be heard also in the other tree (plant) and fruit sayings: it is important for a person to do good things, but to be able to do good things one has to live with God. Jesus doesn't say to people: "Do good!"; nor does he say: "Be a good person!" Rather, he says: "Live with God!"; and also: "If you

live with God, you will do many good things because of this." The use of simple
and universal concepts such as DO, WANT, GOOD, and BAD and intuitively understandable simple sentences such as "Some people think . . ." or "God wants this"
allows us to understand this message more clearly and to see better how it coheres with the meanings of Jesus' other sayings.

15. The will of my Father

Matthew 7:21

21. Not everyone who says to me, 'Lord, Lord' shall enter the
    Kingdom of heaven, but he who does the will of my Father in
    heaven.

Luke 6:46

46. But why do you call me 'Lord, Lord', but do not do the things
    which I say?

Most commentators agree that of the two parallel sayings in the end of Matthew's
Sermon on the Mount and of Luke's Sermon on the Plain (just before the parable of the two builders), Luke's is the more original. As noted by Fitzmyer
(1981:644), the Lucan version is more consistent with the message of the parable of the two builders, which follows this verse in both Luke and Matthew.
But even in its Lucan form, Fitzmyer observes that "it is very difficult to trace
it [this verse] to the historical Jesus . . . because of the use of the title kyrios in
the sense of 'Lord.' . . ." This use "probably stems from the early community"
(p. 644). If Luke's version, which is regarded as more original, cannot be attributed to the historical Jesus, Matthew's version cannot be either. Nonetheless, there
are reasons to think that the main *idea* behind Matthew's verse 7:21 *can* be traced
to the historical Jesus. Speaking metaphorically, that idea is that the way to enter
the kingdom of God is to do God's will.

Betz (1995:542) observes that "Lord, Lord" in Matthew 7:21a "has been created artificially for no other purpose than to be rejected. The intent . . . is satirical. The positive saying follows in v. 21b . . . : 'Whoever does the will of my
Father who is in heaven shall enter into the Kingdom of heaven'."

Whether or not this positive saying (in this form) can be attributed to Jesus,
the insistence on doing God's will is clearly one of the key motifs in Jesus'
teaching, expressed, for example, in such undisputedly authentic sayings as
Matthew 12:50: "For whoever does the will of my Father in heaven is my
brother, and sister, and mother." As discussed earlier (see also section 16), this
motif is sometimes misrepresented in the literature, with its frequent insistence
on the word *obedience*. For example, Barclay ([1975]1993:289–290) in commenting on Matthew 7:21, writes, "Fine words can never be a substitute for fine
deeds. There is only one proof of love, and that proof is obedience. . . . Faith

without practice is a contradiction in terms, and love without obedience is an impossibility."

But Jesus didn't teach blind obedience, and it is a misrepresentation to equate his reference to the will of the Father with obedience. *Obedience* suggests an attitude that can be represented as follows:

> someone (A) thinks about someone else (B):
> "if this person (B) wants me to do something I have to do it"

The attitude to God's will that is urged by Jesus is different: it has to do with *wanting* to do God's will rather than thinking that one *has* to do it.[12] This is reflected, for example, in the parable of the two sons (Matt. 21:28-31):

> 28. But what do you think? A man had two sons, and he came to the
>   first and said, 'Son, go and work today in my vineyard.'
> 29. He answered and said, 'I will not', but afterwards he regretted it
>   and went.
> 30. Then he came to the second and said likewise. And he answered
>   and said: 'I will go, Sir', but he did not go.
> 31. Which of the two did the will of his father? They said to him, 'The
>   first'. Jesus said to them, 'Assuredly, I say to you that tax
>   collectors and prostitutes enter the Kingdom of God before you.'

As the parable implies, the two sons have a choice: to do or not to do their father's will. Neither of them thinks, "I have to do it," and clearly this is not what the father expects. What the father does want and expect is that the sons will think, "I want to do it (because my father wants me to do it)" and will do it because of this.

Several other parables and similes point in the same direction. For example, the image of the two roads (see section 13) suggests that people can choose between a wide road and a narrow road. There can be no doubt about which road God wants them to choose, but the choice is theirs. God wants them to choose the narrow road and the narrow gate, and thus to enter into the kingdom of heaven, but (Jesus implies) he doesn't want them to think, "I have to." Jesus' saying about the treasure is particularly telling in this regard: "For where your treasure is, there your heart will be also." God, as presented by Jesus, wants people to see that doing what he wants them to do is their treasure, something that they *want* to do. In John's Gospel, Jesus calls it his food: "My food is to do the will of him who sent me" (John 4:34). He also appeals directly to people's love: "If you love me, you will keep my commandments" (John 14:15).

This is, then, the first reason that the teaching about doing God's will is not a doctrine about obedience. The second (related but conceptually distinct) reason is that obedience implies doing what somebody else wants us to do regardless of the content of what that person wants us to do. In the case of God's will, however—as presented by Jesus—the overall content of this will is made abundantly clear: God's will is indistinguishable from God's love. In Jesus' teaching,

God wants to do good things for all people, and this is his will and his love; also he wants people to want to do good things for other people, thus participating in his life of love. The idea of *wanting* to do God's will is pervasive in the New Testament. For example, in John's Gospel Jesus says about God, "If anyone wants to do his will, he shall know . . ." (7:17). Elsewhere, this willingness is indicated even more strongly, by the use of the verb "to seek" (*zēteō*): "I do not seek my own will but the will of the Father who sent me" (5:30). The Johannine Jesus also makes it clear that he has voluntarily "come down from heaven" because he wanted to do "the will of him who sent me," and that "the will of him who sent me" is that people should have "everlasting life" (John 6:38–40). Jesus' references to doing the will of the Father need to be seen in the context of these implications of willingness and freedom. The key concept is not obedience but FIAT (as in Mary's response to the Annuntiation).

Thus, although entering the kingdom of God can be seen from three different points of view, they all point to the same reality: wanting to live with God, wanting to do good things for other people, and wanting to do God's will all come to the same thing, the symbolic designation of which in Jesus' teaching is the kingdom of God. The fact (noted by Theissen and Merz 1998:274) that Jesus did not call God "king" but "father" and that for him the "kingdom of God" was not the kingdom of a "king" but the kingdom of a "father," is significant in this respect: for Jesus, God's will did not stand for power (which people have to recognize and bow to) but rather for love (which people can accept and share in).

Lambrecht (1985:193) observes that in verse 7:21, Matthew "replaces 'do what I tell you' by 'do the will of my Father in heaven' (cf. 6:10), because, for Matthew, Jesus' words in the Sermon on the Mount express this will (cf. 7:24)." The phrase "do what I tell you" is the Lucan (6:46) counterpart of Matthew's "do the will of my Father in heaven"; and Lambrecht's point is that in substituting the latter for the former, Matthew sought to spell out what he thought Jesus really had in mind. Meier (1980:74) makes a similar point when he says that "all his [Jesus'] standards simply explain the will of the Father, which is, in one word, love. . . . The wise disciple acts decisively by building his whole life on the firm foundation of Jesus' words—more precisely, *these* words of mine, contained in the sermon on the mount. . . . The wise disciple realizes that these words of Jesus the Son are identical with 'the will of my Father' (v.21)."

Different parts of the Sermon on the Mount seek to illuminate different aspects of Jesus' overall teaching, but they are all closely interrelated: God's love, God's invitation for people to participate in this love, God's desire for people to live with God, and God's intimation that this is how people's own desire for lasting happiness and eternal life can be fulfilled. The interrelatedness of these themes is emphasized with particular clarity in John's first letter (1 John, chaps. 1–4), where fellowship with God and abiding in God (comparable to living with God) are linked directly to sharing in God's love and doing God's will:

5. This is the message which we have heard from him and declare to you, that God is light and in him is no darkness at all.

6. If we say that we have fellowship with him, and walk in darkness, we lie and do not practise the truth. . . . (1:5-6)

5. But whoever keeps his [God's] word, truly the love of God is perfected in him. By this we know that we are in him. . . .
10. He who loves his brother abides in the light. . . .
11. But he who hates his brother is in darkness and walks in darkness. . . .
17. And the world is passing away, and the lust of it; but he who does the will of God abides for ever. . . . (2:5-17)

11. For this is the message that you heard from the beginning, that we should love one another. . . . (3:11)

7. Beloved, let us love one another, for love is of God; and everyone who loves is born of God and knows God. . . .
16. . . . God is love, and he who abides in love, abides in God, and God in him. (4:7-16)

What is particularly striking in this letter is the stress on "everyone" and "whoever": "and everyone who loves is born of God and knows God." What applies to love applies also (in 1 John) to God's will because (for the author of this letter) the two amount to the same thing. There is a similarly universalist implication in Matthew's verse 7:21, which presumably reflects how the disciples remembered Jesus' own teaching. Frequently discussed contrasts such as hearing versus doing, theory versus practice, or faith versus works may obscure this universal dimension of Jesus' teaching, in which doing God's will is given priority over words and ideas. What the Matthean Jesus appears to imply in 7:21 is that doing God's will is more important than anything one might say or think about God. By implication, this applies to non-Christians, as well as to Christians. The Matthean Jesus here implies not only that people cannot live with God if they do not do God's will but also that regardless of their beliefs and ideologies people who do God's will *can* live with God. Even if most words in verse 7:21 are not Jesus' *ipsissima verba*, there is no reason to think that Matthew would have put these words in Jesus' mouth if they had no basis in Jesus' teaching as remembered by his disciples. And indeed, other sayings transmitted through the oral tradition support the general idea behind Matthew 7:21 as Jesus' own. The parable of the two sons is relevant in this respect, too; after all, it didn't matter what the sons said but whether or not they did what their father wanted them to.

Jesus' words in Matthew's scene of the last judgment (25:31-46) point in the same direction. Whereas the authenticity of this passage as a *whole* is disputed (see, e.g., Limbeck 1995:284), its "stunning universalism" (Meier 1980:304) makes it hard to believe that their substance could have been invented by Matthew or anybody else among Jesus' followers. In the grand judgment scene painted by Matthew, nobody is asked about their beliefs; the only criterion by which people's lives are judged is that of love—love shown in doing good things for other people (see chapter 6, section 10).

What all this suggests is that for the Matthean Jesus (and, almost certainly, for the historical Jesus as well) the way toward living with God involved wanting to do good things for other people and thus fulfilling God's will. The prime example was Jesus himself, who willingly accepted the "cup" (of which he was mortally afraid) "for many, for the remission of sins" (Matt. 26:28). In Mark's version (chapter 14), the two references to cup occur almost side by side, one (at the Last Supper, verses 23-24) emphasizing Jesus' free act ("he took the cup") and the other (in Gethsemane, verse 36), his acceptance of God's will:

23. Then he took the cup, and when he had given thanks he gave it to them, and they all drank from it.
24. And he said to them, 'This is my blood of the new covenant, which is shed for many.' . . .
36. And he said 'Abba, Father, all things are possible for you. Take this cup away from me; nevertheless, not what I will, but what you will.'

The commentaries on Matthew's verse 7:21 ("not everyone who says to me, 'Lord, Lord' . . ." that focus on the controversies and divisions in the early church seem to be missing an important point about Jesus' teaching, reflected, however indirectly, in this verse. It is not about practice being more important than theory or fine deeds being more important than fine words, but rather it is about the central importance of living in accordance with God's will (which entails sharing in God's love for all people) and therefore of living with God. This aspect of Jesus' teaching (reflected in Matthew's verse 7:21) can be explicated along the following lines:

(a) it is good if a person always thinks:
(b)   "if God wants me to do some things, I want to do these things because of this"
(c) it is good if a person does these things because of this
(d) when a person lives like this, this person can live with God

In accordance with the earlier discussion, there is no mention here of thinking, "I have to do it because God wants me to do it;" rather, it is a question of thinking, "I want to do it because God wants me to do it."

16. Building on the rock

Matthew 7:24-29; Luke 6:46-51

24. 'Therefore whoever hears these sayings of mine and does them, I will liken him to a wise man who built his house on the rock:
25. and the rain descended, the floods came and the winds blew and beat on that house; and it did not fall, for it was founded on the rock.

26. Now everyone who hears these sayings of mine, and does not do
   them, will be like a foolish man who built his house on the
   sand:
27. and the rain descended, the floods came, and the winds blew, and
   beat on that house; and it fell. And great was its fall.'
28. And so it was, when Jesus had ended these sayings, that the people
   were astonished at his teaching,
29. for he taught them as one having authority, and not as the scribes.

The image of two houses and two foundations has parallels in other traditions,
and on this basis some commentators have questioned the authenticity of
Matthew's parable of the two builders and of its close counterpart in the concluding part of Luke's Sermon on the Plain. For example, Funk et al. (1993:158–
159) have printed both the Matthean and the Lucan version of this parable in
black (as nonauthentic) and have commented on the Matthean version as follows: "The image of the two foundations belongs to common Israelite, Judean
and Rabbinic lore. Several rabbis of the late first and early second centuries are
credited with creating similar parables to stress the need of putting teaching into
practice" (pp. 158–159); and on the Lucan version: "The analogy of two kinds
of foundations for houses was well known in the ancient Near East. If Jesus made
use of such images, he was drawing on the general fund of wisdom sayings. For
this reason, and because the complex provides no additional information about
who Jesus was, the Fellows designated the passage black" (p. 299).

The Fellows' conclusion that the passage is commonplace and doesn't tell us
anything about Jesus contrasts sharply with the reaction of Jesus' listeners as
depicted by Matthew, who says that "the people were astonished at his [Jesus']
teaching, for he taught them as one having authority, and not as the scribes."
Of course, it could be said that the people's alleged astonishment (not mentioned
by Luke) was invented by Matthew, as a narrative device. It could also be said
that the people were astonished at Jesus' magisterial manner rather than at the
content of his teaching. But whereas Jesus' manner was indeed different from
that of other Jewish teachers, in the parable of the two builders the message was
very different, too. Other Jewish teachers spoke and wrote as commentators on
the Torah and as transmitters and interpreters of an ancient tradition. Jesus, on
the other hand, spoke of his own teaching as the rock on which people can build
their lives. As noted by Jeremias (1971:254), "In contemporary Judaism, it was
said, 'The person who hears the words of the *Torah* and does good works builds
on firm ground'; here we have, 'The person who hears *my* words' (Matt. 7.24–
27)." In John 7:46, the men sent to Jesus by the Pharisees are reported as saying: "No man ever spoke like this man!" Thus, although throughout the Sermon on the Mount, the *how* may have been more astonishing to the crowds than
the *what*, in the final passage the difference between the *how* and the *what* virtually evaporates since here the Matthean Jesus claims that his own teaching can
provide people with an unshakeable foundation for their lives.

According to Jesus' own explanation (in verse 24), building a house on the
rock involves not just *hearing* his words but also *doing* them. Commentators agree

that this, in fact, is what the final passage of the Sermon on the Mount is all about: it is about hearing and doing, that is, about doing what one has heard. But what exactly does it mean? Since the phrase "these sayings of mine" refers to a long series of sayings rather than to any single injunction and since these sayings do not refer to actions ("do this" or "don't do that") but rather to attitudes (e.g., "love your enemies" or "do not worry about your life"), the intended meaning may be less obvious than it appears at first sight. I submit that what "doing Jesus' words" means in this context is living according to the Sermon on the Mount, "living like this." As Meier (1980:75) puts it, commenting on this passage, "The wise disciple forms his whole existence according to these words; he *does* them"; and A. M. Hunter (1953) refers to the Sermon on the Mount as a "Design for Life." "Doing" Jesus' words, then, means living in a certain way. In the Sermon on the Mount, Jesus the builder (for that's what *tektōn* meant, rather than specifically "carpenter") tells people how to build the house of their life.

I do not agree, therefore, with interpretations in which "building a house on the rock" means, essentially, obedience:

> Is there any word in which *hearing* and *doing* are summed up? There is such a word, and that word is *obedience*. Jesus demands our implicit obedience. To learn to obey is the most important thing in life. . . . It is Jesus' claim that obedience to him is the only sure foundation for life; and it is his promise that the life which is founded on obedience to him is safe, no matter what storms may come. (Barclay [1975]1993:292).

Similarly, Jeremias comments on the parable of two builders as follows:

> The Scripture said that only the house built on the sure foundation-stone laid in Zion would abide the onset of the flood (Isa. 28.15). . . . Jesus' contemporaries taught that the man who knows and obeys the Torah cannot be moved. Jesus takes them back to the Scriptures, but he gives a new answer, drawn from his own profound consciousness of authority: 'Everyone who hears these words of mine and does them. . . ." Merely knowing about his words leads to perdition; everything depends on obedience. (1966b:153)

This is Bultmann's ([1926]1958) interpretation of Jesus' teaching, with obedience as the central concept. Barclay ([1975]1993) even goes so far as to extol those ready "automatically and unquestioningly to obey orders," whereas Jeremias (1996b) stresses that the "obedience must be complete." In my view, however, this is not what the parable of the two builders is about. The basic message of the Sermon on the Mount is that people can live in the kingdom of God (in accordance with God's will); it is, in effect, a pressing invitation for everyone to do so, and a set of guidelines on how to live if one wants to accept the invitation. These guidelines do not constitute commands: "Do this!" or "Don't do that!, so they cannot be obeyed or disobeyed. Counsels such as "Love your enemies" or "Don't judge other people" cannot be a matter of obedience. It is not a question of *doing* something but of *living* in a certain way (in accordance with God's will); and this way of living, counseled by Jesus, refers to a person's thoughts, intentions, and feelings as much as—or more than—to one's actions.[13] Accordingly, Jesus' summing up in verse 24 (Matt. 7:24) can be represented in universal human concepts as follows:

> (a) I say all these things because I want people to know
> that they can live with God
> (b) if you hear my words you can think:
> "if I live like this I can live with God"
> (c) it will be good for you if you think this
> (d) it will be good for you if you live like this because of this
> (e) it will be very bad for you if you don't live like this

The Sermon on the Mount confronts every individual hearer with the thought "If I live like this I can live with God" and, consequently, with the question "Do I want to live like this because of this?" Jesus assures every individual addressee that it will be good for him or her to live like this (i.e., to try to follow the model of life outlined in the Sermon on the Mount), and warns that it will be very bad for this person if he or she doesn't. The parable of the two builders amplifies this assurance and this warning with symbolic images.

The exact meaning of these images is disputed. Some commentators think that the rain, flood and wind refer to personal catastrophes that may befall a person in one's earthly life (see, e.g., Limbeck 1995:129–130); others think that they refer, rather, to God's judgment and to the absolute value of a person's life as it will be revealed to him or her at the time of that judgment: "As the torrential autumn rains, accompanied by storms, test the foundation of the houses, so the deluge will set in overnight and put your lives to the test. The Sermon on the Mount ends with the last judgment! Who will survive it? The 'wise man', i.e. the man who has recognised the eschatological situation" (Jeremias 1966b: 153). Jeremias implies that flood does constitute, in effect, a global and cosmic image, when he says that according to Isaiah 28:15, "only the house built on the sure foundation-stone laid in Zion would abide the onset of the flood" (see also Strecker 1988:171–172).

The two lines of interpretation are not necessarily incompatible. Images of storms and floods seem to fit life's misfortunes and disasters better than they do the last judgment. Apocalyptic images tend to be global and cosmic, whereas rains, winds, storms, and torrents point to more local and personal disasters. In any case, however, an existential interpretation makes, I think, a great deal of sense. For regardless of God's, and one's own, final judgment about one's life as a whole, from the point of view of a person in the middle of his or her life ("in the midst of earthly life," in the words of one of Luther's well-known hymns) the question of existential security must loom large—often even larger than eschatological security. Since one knows that a misfortune, indeed disaster, can strike at any moment, one needs to know whether one has some rock on which to stand in such an event—something that would not be washed away. And the Matthean (and Lucan) Jesus says that his words can provide such a rock. Tentatively, I would represent this as follows:

(f) if you live like this, you can always live with God
(g) you know that some very bad things can happen to you at some time
(h) if you don't live with God, you can think when these things happen to you:
   "I can't live now"
(i) if you live with God you will not think like this
(j) you will know that you can live if you live with God

Component (f) links living "like this" (i.e., living in accordance with the teaching of the Sermon on the Mount) to living "with God" (not only after one's death but before as well—always). Component (g) refers to possible misfortunes and disasters; (h) refers to the existential despair that could befall a person at such a time, and both (i) and (j) show how living with God would protect a person from such despair and give a sense of unassailable security and of hope. This is contrasted with the sense of existential insecurity and defencelessness of a person who is not living with God (h): "if you don't live with God, you can think . . . 'I can't live now.'"

Limbeck et al. (1987:130) stress that the Sermon on the Mount has a message not only for those who are concerned about their future after death but also for everyone else: "It is significant for all those who don't want to live in vain, who want to build their house not on sand but on rock. . . . The individual decides here . . . whether his or her life in *this* world will become 'a bit of eternity' or whether their earthly past will at one time collapse and disappear as worthless and groundless." This interpretation is somewhat different from that suggested here because it does not refer to existential despair in the face of misfortunes and disasters. But it is not inconsistent with it and could be incorporated into the proposed explication.

This explication has both an existential and an eschatological dimension (i.e., it refers both to life before death and to life after death). In particular, (j) refers both to the moral courage and strength that a person can find in the face of disaster and to the faith that even if one died one lives on, for life doesn't end with death. Since this faith is presented in (j) as knowledge, life after death is here assumed as a fact, and this gives the explication its eschatological dimension.

The full explication of the whole passage (Matt. 7:4–27) reads as follows:

The two builders

(a) I say all these things because I want people to know that they can live with God
(b) if you hear my words you can think: "if I live like this I can live with God"

(c) it will be good for you if you think this

(d) it will be good for you if you live like this because of this

(e) it will be very bad for you if you don't live like this

(f) if you live like this you can always live with God

(g) you know that some very bad things can happen to you at some
      time

(h) if you don't live with God you can think when these things
      happen to you:
           "I can't live now"

(i) if you live with God you will not think like this

(j) you will know that you can live if you live with God

This explication is consistent with the image of rock in the Psalms, where God
is the rock on which a person can build his or her life. For example:

> The Lord is my rock and my fortress and my deliverer (Psalm 18:2)
> For you are my rock and my fortress (Psalm 31:3)
> But the Lord has been my defense
> And my God the rock of my refuge. (Psalm 94:22)

The references to deliverance, defense, and refuge link the image of God as one's
rock with the idea of bad things happening to people. This is spelled out explicitly in Psalm 27:

> For in the time of trouble
> He shall hide me in his pavilion . . .
> He shall set me high upon a rock. (Psalm 27:5)

Although the parable of the two builders has often been compared with later
rabbinic literature, and especially with two parables attributed to Elisha ben
Avuyah (dating from the second century), its closest parallels are in fact in such
Old Testament images of God as a rock.[14] First, it makes sense to link the images of floods and winds in Jesus' parable with the references to the time of trouble
in the Psalms, rather than with any symbolic storms and torrents "in the catas-
trophe of the last judgment" (Luz 1989:452). Second, it seems right to link Jesus'
image of building a house on the rock with the references in the Psalms to God
as the ultimate rock. In this interpretation, it is not human deeds that are presented as a reliable ground to build on, but living with God; and living with
God is defined in the parable of the two builders as trying to live according to
the Sermon on the Mount.

It is particularly interesting to note what the important rabbinic commentary
on the book of Deuteronomy, Sifre (1986), has to say about the passage (32.4)
that calls God "the Rock": "The Rock, his work is perfect; for all his ways are
justice. A God of faithfulness and without iniquity, just and right is he." Sifre
links this passage with God's reward for a *mitsvah* (i.e., a right deed). Commenting
on the phrase "A God of faithfulness," he says, "Just as he pays the completely

righteous the reward of a *mitsvah* which is fulfilled in this world [after he is] in the world to come, so he pays the completely wicked the reward of a minor commandment which he fulfilled [while he is] in this world." And on the phrase "and without iniquity," Sifre comments, "When a man departs from the world, all his deeds come before him one by one and say to him: 'Thus and so you did on such a day and thus and so you did on another day. Do you declare these things to be accurate?' And he says 'Yes'. They say to him, 'Place your seal' and it is said: '*By the hand of every man he will seal, so that every man may know his work*' (Job 3.7)."

E. P. Sanders (1977:128) stresses, "The theme of reward and punishment in the world to come is not a statement of justification by works, but an extension of the theory of the justice of God." Although I accept Sanders's point, it is nonetheless interesting to note that the image of God as a rock is linked here with the notion of reward for a right deed: God is a rock who can be counted on to reward the right deeds. A person is saved by God's mercy and by the covenant between God and Israel and not by his or her own deeds; yet the notion of a right deed plays an important role here and it is linked with the image of a rock.[15]

Jeremias (1971:116) emphasizes the fact that "Jesus said again and again that salvation was for sinners, not for the righteous" and that this message was without parallel at the time. "It is unique. The literature of Qumran has confirmed this uniqueness" (p. 12). In view of this key feature of Jesus' teaching, it is important to bear in mind that his "house built on the rock" does not stand for the practice of righteousness (i.e., for right deeds). Rather, it represents the possibility of living with God, which is open to all sinners (i.e., to all people).

In summary, then, there are three semantic ideas which provide the keys to the interpretation of the parable of the two builders: first, that a person can "live like this" (referring to the model of life developed in the Sermon on the Mount); second, that very bad things can happen to people; and third, that a person can always live with God.

FIVE

The Lord's Prayer

*Luke 11:2–4; cf. Matt. 6:8–13*1

1. He [Jesus] was praying in a certain place, and when he ceased, one
   of his disciples said to him: 'Lord, teach us to pray, as John
   taught his disciples'.
2. So he said to them, 'When you pray, say: [Our] Father, hallowed be
   thy name. Thy kingdom come.
3. Give us day by day our daily bread;
4. and forgive us our sins, for we also forgive everyone who is indebted
   to us; and do not lead us into temptation.'

1. Introduction

There are two different versions of the "Lord's Prayer": a Lucan and a Matthean
one. The Matthean version is more familiar to most people, and in fact it is part
and parcel of European "cultural literacy": it is the version which from very early
on was accepted by the Church and which, inter alia, has been incorporated into
the Christian liturgy. Nonetheless many scholars believe that (apart from some
details in wording) it is the Lucan rather than the Matthean version which goes
back to the historical Jesus, although some hold that the two versions may continue two independent traditions and may both derive from Jesus (see, e.g.,
Charlesworth 1994).

Be that as it may, in this chapter I will focus on Luke's version, which is shorter, and which—apart from minor differences in wording—represents the shared core of the two. I will not discuss here the meaning of the second and seventh Matthean petitions: "your will be done" and "deliver us from evil,"[1] which many scholars regard as having been added to an earlier, shorter version by Matthew. As for the difference between Luke's "Father" (pater) and Matthew's "Our Father who art in heaven," it is also widely (though not universally) believed that Matthew expanded the shorter version and that in fact both versions constitute Greek renderings of the Aramaic word *abba*. Jeremias (1967) has argued that *abba* as a way of addressing God was (alongside with *amen*) one of Jesus' two most distinctive ways of speaking, and given that this claim is still at the center of the scholarly debate about the Lord's Prayer (e.g., Barr 1988a and 1988b; Betz 1995; Charlesworth 1994; Fitzmyer 1985a; Meier 1994), the meaning and significance of this word requires some discussion in the present context. But regardless of the relationship between Jesus' presumed *Abba* and Luke's Greek *pater*, most commentators agree that the "stark simplicity" (see Bultmann 1952:22–24) of a one-word way of addressing God ("Father") was highly unusual at the time.

Fitzmyer (1985:903) says that "The simplicity of the address, 'Father', stands in contrast with the elaborate modes of addressing God used in many Jewish prayers." Some, for example, Schweizer (1975:149), put it even more strongly, saying that "to address God simply as 'Father', without further additions, as is done in Luke 11:2, is without parallel in Palestinian Judaism at the time of Jesus" (see also Harrington 1991:97).

Although very strong claims of this kind have recently been disputed, there is still a general agreement that this one-word form of address was unusual and that Matthew's more elaborate formula, "Our Father who art in heaven," was more in line with Jewish usage in Jesus' times. The point is important because the one-word apostrophe, "Father"—in contrast to an elaborate reverential formula—highlights the meaning of the metaphor of God's fatherhood as a key to understanding the relationship between people and God.

As pointed out by many commentators, this metaphor plays a central role in the New Testament as a whole. According to Hamerton-Kelly (1981:98), in the New Testament "God is designated 'father' 170 times by Jesus, and is never invoked by another name in Jesus' prayers," whereas in the entire Old Testament (which is, of course, much longer) God is described as "Father" only 11 times. In a similar vein, Ricoeur has written,

> The finding that is most important and at first glance most confusing is that, in the Old Testament . . . the designation of God as father is quantitatively insignificant. Specialists in Old and New Testament scholarship are in agreement in emphasizing—and at first being surprised at—this great reserve limiting the use of the epithet "father" in the writings in the Old Testament (1974:482).

It is against this background that we can understand the Lord's Prayer: Abba, which we could translate as "dear father." . . . Jesus dares to address

himself to God as a child to his father. The reserve to which the whole
Bible testifies is broken at this precise point. The audacity is possible because a new time has begun. (pp. 489–490)

As pointed out by Theissen and Merz, the prominence given by Jesus to the
metaphor of father goes hand in hand with a virtual abandonment of the metaphor of king:

The new thing in the preaching of Jesus is . . . something which is not
obvious at first sight: Jesus never speaks of God as "king". . . . As a rule
Jesus speaks only of the "kingdom" of God. In other Jewish writings we
usually find a juxtaposition of "king" and "kingdom." . . . This juxtaposition is absent from the words of Jesus. This can be interpreted to mean
that for Jesus God's nature is expressed as goodness in his fatherhood.
And as father he will come to power. For Jesus "power" is not a value
in itself but serves to make God's goodness break through universally.
(1998:274)

Theissen and Merz are referring here to such sentences as the following from
the *Old Testament Pseudoepigrapha* (1983–1985): "Lord of all, king on the lofty
throne, you who rule the world" (Testament of Moses I:929); "then indeed the
most great kingdom of the immortal king will become manifest over men"
(Sibilline Oracles I:363); "Lord, you are our king forever" (Psalms of Solomon
II:665).

Given the centrality of the metaphor of father to the New Testament as a whole,
its meaning needs to be carefully considered, a task to which I cannot do justice
in the present chapter; one central clue, however, must be at least briefly discussed: the word *abba*.

2. The meaning and significance of the word abba

Given the complexity of the debate about *abba*, and the necessarily cursory character of the present discussion, I will organize my comments around two basic
concerns: the word's meaning and Jesus' use of it.

The first question then, is this: did Jesus use the word *abba* to address God?
On this point, nearly all scholars agree that he did. Jeremias (1967:111) wrote that
"the address itself is without question an incontestable characteristic of the *ipsissima
vox Jesu*." Although some aspects of Jeremias's discussion of this matter are now
often disputed, on this point even his critics agree: "What can be said about Jesus
and the Lord's Prayer? Jesus customarily avoided the usual Jewish expressions for
God (*elohim, adonai elohenu*) and called God Abba, as we know from Mark 14:36
(*abba, ho patēr*). Fitzmyer [1985a] rightly underscores Jeremias' conclusion that Abba
is an example of *ipsissima vox Jesu*" (Charlesworth et al. 1994:10).

In fact, Fitzmyer also supports Jeremias's view that Jesus' use of Abba to address God was distinctive:

When he writes, "for Jesus to address God as 'my Father' [i.e., *Abba*] is therefore something new," he is right. It would be better formulated, however, thus: There is no evidence in the literature of pre-Christian or first-century Palestinian Judaism that 'abba' was used in any sense as a personal address for God by an individual—and for Jesus to address God as *abba* or 'Father' is therefore something new . . . *abba* . . . was preserved in his [Jesus'] own mother-tongue, even in Greek-speaking communities, precisely as the sign of his use of it. . . . Such preservation is a strong argument for the recollection of a term used by the historical Jesus himself. (1985a:28, 31–32)

A similar view was expressed (also with reference to Jeremias 1967) by Raymond Brown:

Jesus' uses of *abba* (the Aramaic word for "father"), without modifier, in addressing God is distinctive. It was so distinctive that it was remembered in the early Church, so that Paul could write to the Galatians and to the Romans and cite the Aramaic term to these Greek-speaking communities. . . . The use of 'Father' for God was, of course, known both to pagan ('Father Zeus') and Jew. However, the contemporary Jewish prayers tended to use the Hebrew term *ab* and to accompany it by a possessive such as 'our'—thus, 'Our Father', *abînû*. They did not use the Aramaic *abba* without qualification. (1968:284)

Brown also notes that "when the Aramaic is used, it is also in the form 'Our Father', *abûunan*."

Although the uniqueness of Jesus' use of *Abba* is now disputed by some scholars, the argument for its distinctiveness, referring to the preservation of this word in the Greek New Testament, is still widely accepted. For example, Luz (1989:376) states that "it is likely that the thesis of Jeremias is correct in this general form: The Aramaic address of God, which is preserved in Greek New Testament texts as *abba* . . . shows that the Christian communities saw something special in this address of God by Jesus." Luz comments further that the position of the word "Father" (*Pater*) as a separate intonational unit, which demands a pause afterward, "shows what importance rests on this address. It fits into Jesus' proclamation of God, who is close with his love to the poor, sinners, and the underclass; it also fits the parables of the father, so important for Jesus . . . and his certainty that God hears prayer, a certainty that comes strikingly to the forefront." Even Jeremias's critics, Charlesworth et al. (1994:11), acknowledge, "While Jesus' message that God is *Abba* was not unexpectedly new, he does seem to have elevated it to prominence."

The second question is this: what did *Abba* as a form of address mean in Jesus' speech and in the general usage of the time? On this point, opinion varies. Jeremias (1967:59) argued that *abba* originally "derived from the language of small children"; that this fact "was never forgotten"; and that although in Jesus' times it could also be used by a man's grown-up sons and daughters and, by extension, as a courtesy title for respected men, it remained "an everyday word, a homely family-word" (p. 97). Although Jeremias (1966a:66) used in fact the German phrase *lieber Vater*, which in the English text of Jeremias's (1967:95–98) book was quite properly translated as "dear father," nonetheless some scholars thought that he was claiming that *Abba* was comparable to the English "Daddy."[2]

The fact that the vocative *Abba* could also be used by grown-up sons and children shows that comparing *Abba* to *Daddy* is misleading, and suggestions of this kind have been rightly rejected (cf., e.g., Barr 1988b; R. E. Brown 1968; Charlesworth et al. 1994; Fitzmyer 1985a). But the widely recognized "nuance of intimacy" in the vocative *Abba* does require some recognition in the interpretation of Jesus' teaching. Given the likelihood that *Abba* underlies the Greek *Pater* in the Lord's Prayer, it also requires some recognition in the interpretation of this prayer in particular:

> In this mode of prayer Jesus instructs and authorizes his disciples to address God as "Father," using the very title that he himself employed in his prayer of praise (10:21 [twice]) and will employ again (22:42). Gal. 4:6 and Rom. 8:15, which preserve an early tradition about Spirit-inspired prayer, not only include the Aramaic counterpart of the address, '*abbā*', but reflect a recollection about how Jesus himself addressed God—in a way exclusive to himself and otherwise unknown in pre-Christian Palestinian Jewish tradition. The nuance of intimacy that it carries is thus extended to use by the Christian community. "Father" is no longer meant in the corporate or collective, national, or covenantal sense of old . . . but suggests an intimate relationship between the disciples and God that is akin to that of Jesus himself; God is not merely the transcendent lord of the heavens, but is near as a father to his children. Neither Matthew nor Luke explain the fatherhood of God further, but the connotation of the Aramaic '*abbā*', correctly translated by Luke (*páter*), reveals its proper nuance. (1985b:898)

Even if one replaces the phrase "in a way exclusive to himself and otherwise unknown" with "in a way characteristic of himself and otherwise rare," what Fitzmyer (1985b:898) calls the "nuance of intimacy" is not captured in the usual English translation "Father." Compared to "Father," the word *Abba* as a term of address seemed to have an intimate and familiar ring and possibly even suggested an element of feeling. Although it is misleading to compare *Abba* with either "Daddy" (which is childish) or with "dear Father" (which sounds formal rather than familiar and intimate), *Abba* as a term of address may still have had an attitudinal (roughly speaking, affectionate or warm) component in its meaning, along the lines of "when I think about you I feel something good." The precise interpretation of such a component would have depended on the context in which the word was embedded, but in any case it would have been more compatible with an attitude of affection, love, trust or respect than of fear.[3]

Barr (1988b:38) rightly points out that in contrast to Aramaic or Hebrew, "words somewhat similar in nuance and usage to our 'Daddy' did exist in Greek but there is no hint of any of them in the language of the Bible." This does not show, however, that *abba* was fully equivalent to the Greek *pater* 'father': since in Aramaic *abba* was not in contrast to another word and *pater* was, their value was necessarily different.

Barr also rightly points out that Jeremias, "like many exegetes of his time . . . allowed diachronic arguments about origins . . . to interfere with the assessment of the synchronic state of language in the given period" (p. 39). But it still remains to be established what the precise synchronic value of *abba* was; and the fact that it was used as a form of address by small children does suggest that this value was different from that of the English *father*.

Although he has criticized Jeremias's (1967) characterization of *abba* as childlike, Barr (1988b) nonetheless acknowledges the validity of Jeremias's discussion on some important points:

1. "It may . . . be quite true that the use of *abba* was original with Jesus and historically genuine: I have no wish to dispute this" (p. 39).
2. "It is fair to say that *abba* in Jesus' time belonged to a familiar or colloquial register of language . . ." (p. 46).
3. "*Of course abba* had a noticeable connection with children . . . because children are more dependent on parents and more likely to address them frequently. *Abba*, as Jeremias himself insists, is used by all sorts of people of all sorts of ages. But young children are likely to use it more frequently than adults, and more likely to use it in a vocative function, calling for the attention of a father than any other group. Thus it may be quite right that *abba* was specially associated with small children" (pp. 36–37).

Having acknowledged the association of *abba* with small children, however, Barr then says that "the same would be true of any term with the meaning 'father', especially a term used in a vocative function" (p. 37). But this last claim is debatable. If one language offers the speaker a choice between "Father" and "Daddy" and another language has only one word that can be used as a vocative (*Abba*), the only word of this second language (*Abba*) will no doubt have a stronger association with children than the "adult" word of the first ("Father").

Charlesworth et al. (1994:9) say in this connection that "*Abba can* mean 'Daddy', and little children obviously addressed their father this way in ancient Israel. . . . But there is no compelling evidence that Jesus used Abba in that sense." To put it this way, however, is to imply that *abba* was polysemous: one meaning was "daddy," and another was "father." But polysemy should not be postulated without necessity (Occam's razor); it is methodologically preferable to posit only one meaning for *abba* and to say that this word never meant "daddy"; rather, when it was used as a vocative, it included an unspecified feeling component— perhaps weaker than "dear" but quite tangible (such as "when I think about you I feel something good").

In fact, if *abba* (as a vocative) had a strong association with children, it seems unlikely that it would not have an affective (warm) component in its meaning: terms of address used by children for their fathers (e.g., *papá* in French, *pápa* in

Russian, *babbo* in Italian, and *tato* in Polish), normally do include an affective component; it would be strangely cold for a child to address his or her father with a word that does not (e.g., with the word *father* in English). It seems probable, therefore, that *abba*, too, did have a low-level affective component (such as "when I think about you I feel something good"), even though it certainly did not mean "daddy" and—unlike *papá*, *pápa*, *babbo*, and *tato*—was not *specifically* a children's word.

Meier, who agrees that "Joachim Jeremias and scholars dependent on him have overplayed the 'Abba' card in their treatment of Jesus," nonetheless also supports both the view that Jesus' use of *abba* to address God was distinctive and the view that unlike the English "Father," *abba* did include a "feeling component": "Despite the doubts of some recent scholars, Jeremias was probably correct in maintaining that the laconic, almost disconcerting 'Father' (Luke's *pater*) probably reflects Jesus' striking use of the address *abba* ('my own dear father') for God" (1994:358). The use of universal human concepts allows us to preserve many scholars' intuition about a warm feeling component in the meaning of *abba* without equating this component with the meaning of the English word *dear*, for which one could posit a stronger version: "When I think about you I feel something *very* good."

But even if *abba* didn't include a feeling component in its meaning, its "nuance of intimacy" could have contributed to the meaning of the metaphor. If a word meaning "father" suggests, as Betz (1995:387) puts it, an image of God as "creator, sustainer, and protector of his entire creation, the universe," Jesus' choice of *Abba* (as a metaphor for God) can be seen as suggesting some further components along the lines of "You know all people" and "when people say something to You, You hear it." (I will return to these points in section 5.)

Luz (1989:376), who sees Jesus' use of *Abba* as distinctive but not un-Jewish, remarks, "With 'abba' he addresses God, who for Judaism was always Father. The fact that Jesus addresses the God of Israel in everyday language and with great simplicity and directness as 'Father' demonstrates how close and familiar he is with him. . . . One may—one even must—speak of a *special* understanding of God by Jesus, but should not confuse this with an un-Jewish understanding of God." Comments of this kind support, in effect, positing for *Abba* (as a way of addressing God) components such as "You know all people" (familiarity) and "When people say something to You, You hear it" (closeness). As Clement of Alexandria (1962) puts it in his *Stromata* (2.74.4; 7.37.6), "God is all ear and eye."[4]

3. "Father" as a metaphor

The opening invocation *Abba* ("Father") signals the praying person's desire to speak to God ("I want to say some things to You") and shows how this person conceives of God while addressing to him the five petitions that constitute the main body of the prayer ("when I say these things to You, I think about You like this"). Above all, then, the speaker thinks of God as being in his relation to people in some ways comparable to a father in his relation to his children. The notion of father is no more than a metaphor here, an image. To reconstruct the intended meaning of this metaphor, we must interpret it in the context of the prayer, and the Gospels as a whole. The recent *Catechism of the Catholic Church* (1994:666) speaks in this connection of the need to "cleanse our heart of certain false images drawn 'from this world'. . . . The purification of our hearts has to do with paternal or maternal images, stemming from our personal and cultural history, and influencing our relationship with God. God our Father transcends the categories of the created world."

As discussed in chapter 1, because Jesus' teaching is so heavily embedded in the Jewish culture of first-century Palestine, it cannot be adequately transferred to other cultures without first being "extracted" from its own cultural context: to be clothed in new garments (see Shorter 1997:235), it has to be first stripped of its old ones. Some have argued that in the case of the Lord's Prayer this stripping should be done in the very text of the prayer and that, for example, the opening "Father" should be translated as "Mother" or "Parent" or "Mother and Father." I am not suggesting this, and in general I do not think that it would be justifiable to try to rewrite the Gospels by replacing Jesus' metaphors with those from other cultures and historical settings. But the meaning of Jesus' metaphors must be *explained*, and to be effective the explanations themselves must be maximally culture-free—and as far as possible, free of metaphors.

Their heuristic and aesthetic value notwithstanding, without explanations metaphors can be dangerous. Nothing illustrates this better than the metaphor of fatherhood, which many contemporary writers find deeply problematic (see, e.g., Ruether 1981; Sölle 1981). Some, for example, Mary Daly (1973), the author of a book entitled *Beyond God the Father*, find this metaphor so disturbing that, together with the metaphor, they reject the very idea of a personal God as "a not too subtle mask of the divine patriach" (p. 18). Others retain the idea of God but emphasize the need for avoiding one-sex language for God and his or her relationship to people. I quoted earlier the statement by Hans Küng (1980:673) that "God . . . is not masculine and must not be seen through the screen of the masculine-paternal, as an all-too-masculine theology did. The feminine-maternal element must also be recognised in him." As I have noted in chapter 1, however, the less conventional image of the feminine-maternal, although useful as a corrective to the one-sidedness of the masculine-paternal, is a metaphor, too, as is also Küng's translation of "Father" as "transhuman, transexual, absolutely last/absolutely first reality."

Thus, regardless of whether one prefers to replace the "father" symbol with other human symbols like "mother" and "maternal" or with transhuman and transsexual symbols like "first/last reality," none of these images or symbols are really integral to the message of the Gospels. Behind and underneath all such images and symbols is a timeless and universal message that can be articulated in universal human concepts (such as GOOD and BAD, DO and HAPPEN; and KNOW, WANT, and THINK), without recourse to any metaphors whatsoever. (I will attempt to do so in section 5.)[5]

4. God as someone

Separating the Gospel concept of God as a father from its metaphorical and cultural embodiment, one must note that by being presented as a father, Jesus' God—like the God of the Old Testament—is seen quite incontrovertibly as a *personal* God, a someone, not a "something." At the same time, by being presented as a father—a father of all people—this God is being set apart from all people. This apartness or otherness of God can be linked with God's holiness or fundamental goodness, inherent in the very concept of God and extolled in the first petition of the prayer: "hallowed be thy name." Accordingly, we can start our explication of the opening invocation with the following two components: "You are someone not like people";"You are someone good."

The Lucan apostrophe "Father" (*Abba*) is as universalist as Matthew's "Our Father who art in heaven": the very metaphor of God's fatherhood contrasts God with *all* people, not with *some* people. When we combine the meaning of the apostrophe as a speech act ("I want to say some things to You") and the mental frame provided by it ("when I say these things to You I think about You like this") with the contrast between God and people inherent in the metaphor of father, we arrive at the following partial explication:

    (a) I want to say some things to You
    (b) when I say these things to You I think about You like this:
    (c)   You are someone not like people
    (d)   You are someone good

But the contrast between God and people also implies some comparability. The very metaphor of father points to a personal God: it implies that whereas God is not "someone like people," God *is* someone, not something, as a human being is someone, not something.

As many other certainties of the past, the view that God is someone (rather than something) has been questioned in recent times. Some Christians have come to feel uneasy about the fact that Jesus spoke about God, and to God, as someone. For example, James Breech writes this about the Lord's Prayer:

> The prayer opens by addressing someone or something as "Father." . . .
> The prayer addresses the power to which elsewhere Jesus refers as the Kingdom of God, but here he addresses that power personally. Matthew's community understood the Father to be quite literally a person, a personal entity who inhabits a place above the earth (heaven). Whether or not Jesus himself shared this view of God as a mythological being is another matter. . . . The important question is: why did Jesus address this power personally? ([1983]1987:54–55)

Some pages later, the author manages to answer to his own satisfaction the vexing (for him) question of why Jesus addressed "the power usually referred to as 'God' . . . as a person, even though he did not think of God as a mythological entity residing in heaven." But the obvious answer is that Jesus, just like Matthew and his community, did think of God as someone and not as an impersonal power, as Breech himself evidently does. Moreover, there is no justification for assuming that if Matthew and his community thought of God as someone they must have believed that God "inhabits a place above the earth." To assume that Matthew understood all the images that he used literally is to treat him as a simpleton. (For an excellent discussion of this point, see Caird 1980:120.)

Breech ([1983]1987:48) also makes, in passing, the following comment: "I do not think it is necessary to belabour the point that Jesus did not share his contemporaries' mythological conceptions about heaven." But there is no good reason to set up a contrast between Jesus and his contempories in this regard: they all lived in a cultural tradition that thrived on metaphors. Similarly, for Marcus Borg (1994:14), "God does not refer to a supernatural being 'out there' . . . [but] rather . . . the center of existence, the holy mystery that is all around us and within us. God is the non-material ground . . . in which 'we live and move and have our being'." In commenting on this passage in his book *The Jesus Quest*, Ben Witherington III (1995) has written, "One may be forgiven for concluding that this sounds altogether very similar to what we hear from modern advocates of New Age philosophy. . . . If God is an 'it' or a 'force', the possibility for an 'I-Thou' relationship is eliminated. We cannot pray to a ground of being. . . ."

The metaphor of father as a term of address used in prayer provides crucial evidence on this point: one cannot pray (or speak at all) to a "force" or a "ground of being," but according to Jesus one certainly can, and indeed must, pray to God. At the same time, praying to God did not mean for Jesus praying to a male person in the sky. To interpret Jesus' references to "heaven" or "above" in a literalistic way is to misunderstand the cultural world in which he lived. In this world, there was no conflict between thinking of God as a spirit and using spatial metaphors to speak about him (along with other kinds of metaphors, e.g., king, shepherd, or father).

For a proper semantic interpretation of the Gospels it is crucial to have some understanding of different rhetorical tropes, different genres, different literary traditions. In particular, it is crucial to distinguish metaphor and hyperbole, which abound in Jesus' parables and other sayings, from both literal utterances, such as "Do good to those who hate you" (Luke 6:27), and analogical ones, such as those in which psychological predicates like *know, want, love* and *forgive* are ascribed to God. When Jesus was urging people to cut off their right hand or to pluck out their right eye (Matt. 5:29), his way of speaking was clearly both hyperbolic and metaphorical; and when he called God Father or referred to God's kingdom, he was also clearly relying on metaphors. On the other hand, there is no evidence that when he talked about (and to) God as someone, he meant some "superabundant power which can be called 'God'" (Breech [1983]1987:63) rather than really someone—someone who can know, want, love, and hear (as a father or a mother can know, want, love, and hear).

Certainly, when words like *know, want* or *someone* are applied to God, we understand them only by analogy with what they mean in other contexts; but there is a crucial difference between analogical and metaphorical language. Words and expressions like *father*, *in heaven*, or *kingdom* are metaphorical and can be explicated in nonmetaphorical language; but words like *know*, *want*, or *someone* cannot be explicated at all: they are not metaphorical, even though when applied to God they require an analogical mode of understanding.

5. What does God's fatherhood mean (in Jesus' teaching)?

So far, we have focused on two elements of the meaning of Jesus' metaphor of father: its personal aspect ("God is someone") and its transcendent aspect ("God is someone not like people"; "God is someone good"). We will now turn to the other aspects—roughly speaking, those involving God's relation to people, that is, God seen as creator, sustainer of human life, and someone who has a personal relationship with people.

Since the concept of creating someone or something is not universal (there are many languages that do not have a word for it), the word *create* cannot be used in the explication. On the other hand, evidence suggests that the concept of existing (THERE IS . . . is indeed universal, so the relevant aspect of the meaning of 'Father' can be seen to include this concept:

(e) people exist because You want people to exist

According to Gundry (1982:105), the fact that the apostrophe "Father (*Abba*)" is followed by some overtly communal petitions (e.g., "give us each day our daily bread") "makes 'Father' a communal address (even when unaccompanied by 'Our', as in Luke)." I think that in the context of the whole prayer, the initial apostrophe can indeed be so interpreted and, in fact, has to be so interpreted when the prayer is uttered jointly by a group of people. But the partial explication proposed here does not force such a reading: as interpreted here, the prayer also makes sense for an individual speaker, although it always implies and requires thoughts about other people as related to God in the same way as the speaker himself or herself, and therefore as related to the speaker like brothers and sisters.

Another aspect of the metaphor of fatherhood (further highlighted in the petition for daily bread) has to do with seeing God as a sustainer and provider. This can be represented as follows:

(f) people can live because You do good things for people
(g) You can do good things for all people
(h) You want to do good things for all people

The personal character of God's relation to people, highlighted by Jesus' use of the familiar term *Abba*, suggests (as discussed earlier) two further components:

(i) You know all people
(j) when people say something to You You hear it

In the context of such components implying something like intimacy and closeness, the component "You want to do good things for all people," which otherwise might seem to suggest a generalized benevolence, suggests, in fact, something closer to love.[6]

Furthermore, the combination of components (g), "You can do good things for all people," and (h), "You want to do good things for all people," suggests something like trust (on the part of the praying person). This implication is strengthened by the hypothetical "feeling" component, discussed earlier:

(k) "when I think about You like this, I feel something good"

This brings us to the following overall explication of the initial apostrophe:

Father (Abba)

(a) I want to say some things to You
(b) when I say these things to You I think about You like this:
(c)   You are someone not like people
(d)   You are someone good

(e)   people exist because You want people to exist
(f)   people can live because You do good things for people
(g)   You can do good things for all people
(h)   You want to do good things for all people

(i)   You know all people
(j)   when people say something to You You hear it
(k) when I think about You like this, I feel something good

6. Hallowed be thy name

Eugene Nida (1994:194) has observed that "almost no lay person understands the meaning of the first petition in the Lord's prayer." Nida's comment, though surprising, is probably right. What should one, then, tell a believer, or an interested nonbeliever who might ask about the meaning of the first petition ("hallowed be thy name")?

To begin with, one could no doubt say that "name" is also a metaphor, drawn from a particular cultural tradition, and that what really matters in the first petition is how people speak about God. The segment is concerned with the need to praise God (i.e., to say good things about him), to treat God as *sacrum*, and to speak of him with the deepest reverence. The *Catechism of the Catholic Church* (1994:673) says, "The term 'to hallow' is to be understood here ... above all in an evaluative sense: to recognise as holy, to treat in a holy way." But what does recognizing God as holy really mean? How might one explain this idea to speakers of languages that have no words corresponding to "holy" or "hallow"?

I suggest that this first petition builds on some elements introduced in the initial apostrophe: "You are someone not like people" and "You are someone good." Its main theme is something like worship and adoration, but its point of departure can be represented as follows:

(a) I know: You are someone good
(b) no one else is like You

The worship and adoration expressed in the words "hallowed be thy name" sets God apart not only from all beings but also from all things—treating all alternative deities (whether beings or things) as idols. This suggests one further component:

(c) nothing else is like You

These three components are consistent with the explanations offered by many scholars. For example, Johnson (1991:177) remarks, in connection with the first petition, that "the prayer recognizes God's absolute difference from all created things." Kiley (1994:17) comments that "the otherness or sanctity of the Father title is underscored in 23:9: 'call no man on earth Father'." And Barclay ([1975]1993:206) states that "*hagiazesthai*, which is translated to *hallow*, means to *regard as different*, to give a unique and special place to. . . . Therefore, when we pray 'Hallowed be Thy name', it means, 'Enable us to give to thee the unique place which thy nature and character deserve and demand.'"

In addition to recognizing God's inherent goodness, holiness, and uniqueness, the speaker expresses a wish that all other people should recognize it too:

(d) I want all people to know this
(e) I want all people to say this

As pointed out by Fitzmyer (1985b:898) and others, the petition "hallowed be thy name'" evokes the prophecy of Ezekiel 36:23, "in which God says, inter alia, 'And I will sanctify my great name . . .), and the nations shall know that I *am* the Lord . . . when I am hallowed in you before their eyes."

A number of commentators have insisted that both the first and the second petition of the prayer should be understood as eschatological, that is, as referring to the end-time. Consequently, they are sometimes described as virtually identical in meaning:

> For Jesus, the Father reveals his transcendent holiness precisely by bringing in his eschatological kingdom, by assuming his rightful rule over the world. Hence the second petition, which we might almost translate: 'Sanctify your name by bringing in your Kingdom'. The resplendent theophany Jesus thinks of is the appearing of God on the last day; the 'Our Father' is an eschatological prayer, a prayer that God will hasten the end-time. (Meier 1980:60)

Similarly, Schweizer (1975:151) states that "the first two petitions in the Lord's Prayer are in fact the same: God's holy name will be honored ('hallowed') when (and because) his Kingdom comes."

Other commentators, however, dispute this exclusively eschatological interpretation of the first petition. For example, Luz writes,

> If one interprets it eschatologically ... it would pray that God do something for his name in an eschatological self-manifestation. The meaning of the two first petitions would be identical. But ... it is equally possible that God is asked for the hallowing of his name here and now in history, not only in the eschaton. ... The petition would come close to an admonition of oneself: "Let us hallow God's name." This proposed interpretation corresponds to the ... tradition of interpretation which was predominant until the rise of the eschatological explanation of the Lord's Prayer. (1989:378)

Luz concludes his discussion as follows: "All this speaks in favour of an 'open' interpretation. The petition is so general and formulated so briefly that it allows us to think both of human and divine action. However, the majority of parallels [from Judaism] point in the former direction, so that the ethical element must by no means be excluded" (p. 380).

The explication proposed here is consistent with what Luz (1989) calls an open interpretation. Its core lies in the components (d), "I want all people to know this," and (e), "I want all people to say this" (where "this" refers back to "You are someone good," "no one else is like You," and "nothing else is like You"), and both these components can be taken to refer either to all people who live now (including the speaker) or to all people who have ever lived or are going to live. Luz calls the first interpretation "ethical," the second interpretation, "eschatological": people who have already died, perhaps while rejecting God, can only recognize God as holy and good in the "world to come." In the first interpretation (as Luz puts it), "the petition would come close to an admonition ... : Let us hallow God's name"; in the second, it would imply that God "reveals his transcendent holiness ... by bringing in his eschatological kingdom" (Meier 1980:60).

Montefiore ([1930]1970:129) compares the first petition of the Lord's Prayer with the beginning of the Jewish prayer Kaddish, "Magnified and sanctified be his great name": "The meaning of the petition ... is the same to the Rabbis and to Jesus. By establishing his Kingdom God will cause the complete sanctification of his name. ... God's *full* sanctification and his *full* kingship will require that all men [i.e., people] shall acknowledge his Unity and his Rule." I think this reference to "all people" is the crux of the matter for the first petition of the Lord's Prayer: one should pray that all people will recognize who God really is; and perhaps, as a result, come to know God (f). This can be interpreted both eschatologically and ethically, and one interpretation does not exclude the other.

Finally, the ethical dimension of the petition can hardly be reduced to a mere *wish* that all people (including the speaker) should praise God. As has often been pointed out, the petitions of the Lord's Prayer make demands on the person who is praying and are aimed at transforming this person. Simone Weil ([1951]1973:227) says that "it is impossible to say it [the Lord's Prayer] once through, giving the fullest possible attention to each word, without a change, infinitesimal perhaps but real, taking place in the soul"; and Tom Wright (1996:23) remarks that "our task is to grow up into the Our Father." What, then, is the hidden challenge of the petition "hallowed be thy name"?

Jesus' teaching as a whole provides ample clues in this respect. If we really want people to give praise to God, presumably we should be willing to do something because of it and, moreover, we should try to overcome our natural inclination to take credit for anything good that we might do and our desire to have people say good things about us. The key passage is Matthew 5:16: "Let your light so shine before people that they may see your good works and glorify your Father in heaven," as well as John 15:8: "By this my Father is glorified that you bear much fruit." In the light of these passages, we could consider adding to the proposed explication of the first petition two further components:

(a) I know: You are someone good
(b)   no one else is like You
(c)   nothing else is like You

(d) I want all people to know this
(e) I want all people to say this
(f) I want all people to know You
[(f) because I want this to happen I want to do good things]
[(g) when I do good things I want people to say good things about You
        because of this]

Components (f) and (g) do not imply a presumption that the speaker's good deeds could bring about the sanctification of God's name; rather, they imply that the speaker does not see the desire for God's glory as completely divorced from the rest of his or her life. Many commentators emphasize that the Greek word *hagiastheto* should be understood as a *passivum divinum*, referring to God's own action: only God can bring about the fulfilment of the petition (see, e.g., R. E. Brown 1968:290–292). Components (f) and (g), which involve the speaker, are not necessarily incompatible with such an emphasis; I have left them, nonetheless, in brackets because arguably their proper place is in a commentary on the petition rather than in the explication of its meaning.

The notion that God is interested in human worship and adoration has in recent times been ridiculed by writers who interpret it anthropomorphically. For example, Morwood (1998:17) writes, "There is the cosmic bellhop who sits at the end of a cosmic telephone exchange dealing with billions of calls every minute and whom the caller hopes will alter the course of events to suit the caller. There is the God who requires praise." Morwood scorns the very idea that God hears human prayer but praising God seems to him even more laughable than asking God for one's daily bread. If one assumes, however, that God is someone (as both the metaphors of "Father" and of "name" suggest) and that this someone knows and loves all people, the idea that this someone wants people to know and love him in return makes perfectly good sense. Furthermore, if it is true that God is someone good and that no one else and nothing else is like him, then "hallowing" God's name is, above all, a matter of knowing God and acknowledging who and what he really is.

7. Thy kingdom come

The metaphor of kingdom is, needless to say, highly culture-specific. It is also highly ideological, and it has often caused offence among those who are opposed to kings and monarchies. But in the Gospels, including the Lord's Prayer, this metaphor is no more than a means to a goal, and the message apparently intended by Jesus can be stated without any monarchist allusions. As E. P. Sanders (1993:169) notes, scholars generally agree on what the kingdom of God is *not*. However, "It is harder to say positively what Jesus meant by 'kingdom of God'. Intensive efforts over the last hundred years to define the phrase have left the issue more confused."[7]

As discussed in chapter 1, my own proposal is that the kingdom of God should be interpreted, essentially, in terms of people living with God. The notion of living with God allows us to interpret the kingdom of God both in an individual and in a collective sense: a person who is living with God can be described as "entering the kingdom of God" (a phrase repeatedly used in the Gospels; cf., e.g., Mark 9:47, 10:15; Luke 18:17; Matt. 18:3, 7:21, 5:20), wheras the kingdom as a whole can be understood, essentially, as the community of people who are living with God.

Commentators often insist that the Greek word *basileia* would be better translated as "God's reign," "God's rule," or "God's kingly rule" rather than "God's kingdom." It is true that in Jesus' teaching, the *basileia* is a dynamic concept (see, e.g. R. E. Brown 1968:295; Jeremias 1971:98; Schlosser 1980:62) and, of course, does not refer to a state, let alone a place, although in figurative language someone can enter it or have the keys to it (see Matt. 16:19). But "kingdom," too, has its advantages, and not only because of many people's attachment to the traditional rendering. First of all, it implies a social dimension: a kingdom requires many people living together. Furthermore, the kingdom of God can be thought of as a kingdom of love, whereas words like *reign* and *rule* instead evoke power and obedience.

The translation of the Gospels by the Jesus Seminar (the "Scholars Version": Funk et al. 1993) consistently translates *basileia* as "God's imperial rule"; and "your kingdom come" is rendered as "impose your imperial rule." Quite apart from aesthetic considerations, this rendering seems unfortunate in its emphasis on power and submission. The idea that all people can live with God and that God wants this seems to be much more consistent with Jesus' own emphasis on the *basileia* as "good news." It is hard to see why anyone should rejoice at the prospect of some imperial rule being imposed on them.

Meier (1994:II, 298) emphasizing "the God-centered and eschatological orientation" of the second petition, states that its "sense . . . is thus: 'Come, O Father, to rule as King.'" But a "God-centered and eschatological" interpretation can also be preserved without using such metaphors and without necessarily interpreting God's will in terms of rule and power: we can achieve this if we say that all people (i.e., the living and the dead, the whole of humankind) can live with God; that God wants this; and that, roughly speaking, only God can bring this about. Such an interpretation, which deemphasizes power and leaves more room for love, is consistent both with the moorings of this petition in the Old Testament and with Jesus' proclamation that "the Kingdom of God has drawn near" (Mark 1:15) or that "the Kingdom of God has come upon you" (Matt. 12:28). As I will discuss in chapter 8, the component "all people can live with God" is causally linked in Jesus' teaching with the intimations about his own pivotal role in bringing about the kingdom of God: "something is happening here now (i.e., in first-century Galilee); because this is happening, all people can live with God; God wants this."[8]

The idea of people living with God allows us to reconcile not only an individual and a social perspective but also an ethical and an eschatological one. In fact, taken to its logical conclusion, the concern for other people is inseparable from eschatology because other people can include not only the living but also the dead (*vivos et mortuos*, as the Nicene Creed has it). If one wants and prays for *all* people to live with God, one is praying, in effect, for universal salvation.

Cardinal Danielou (1953:340) commented on Christian hope for the coming of the "kingdom" as follows:

> Too often we think about it in an excessively individualist manner as only our personal salvation. And yet hope relates to the great actions of God concerning the whole of creation. It is a waiting for the Parousia, the Return of the Lord, who will come to bring history to its completion. It involves the destiny of the whole humanity. What we are waiting for is the salvation of the world. . . . The hope relates to the salvation of all people— and it is only to the extent that I am part of all of them that it relates to me. (Danielou 1953:340)

Cardinal Danielou notes that "in the course of the centuries there has sometimes been a tendency, in Christianity, to attach exclusive importance to the salvation of the individual soul. . . . We will give back to Christianity its true dimension if we do not reduce it to a preoccupation with personal salvation but see in it an appeal to work at the salvation of the world, to engage in the history of salvation" (p. 341).

The communitarian aspect of the kingdom of God is highlighted more strongly in the Eastern than in the Western tradition of Christianity.[9] As emphasized by Moltmann, however, a communitarian interpretation of the kingdom is inseparable from an *Abba* perspective on God:

> The liberty of the children of God . . . lies in their personal and intimate relationship to the Father and, on the other hand, in their participation

in the Father's kingdom ... the children of God are bound together because they are brothers and sisters. The liberty of the children of God lies not least in the free access to each other which people find in the love that binds them and in the joy they find in one another. (1981:220)

The notion of people living with God allows us to accommodate this communitarian and familial aspect of the kingdom of God in a way that the idea of God's rule or God's imperial rule does not.

To account for both the individual and the social, the present (ethical) and future (eschatological) dimensions of the second petition, I propose the following partial explication:

Thy kingdom come

(a) I know: all people can live with You
(b)   You want this

(c) I say: I want to live with You now
(d)   I want other people to live with You now
(e)   I want all people to live with You forever
(f)   I want all people to live like this with other people

As mentioned earlier, many commentators have suggested that the first and second petitions "are in fact the same: God's holy name will be 'honored' (hallowed) when (and because) the Kingdom comes" (Schweizer 1975:151). The explications proposed here show in what way these two petitions are the same, but also, in what way they are different. When the whole of humankind, the living and the dead, praise and adore God, presumably they will all live with God (as well as in a *communio sanctorum*—with all other people). The two eschatological expectations support and complement each other, but if one of them were deleted part of the overall meaning of the prayer would be lost.

According to Luke (17:20-21), asked when the kingdom of God would come, Jesus replied, "The Kingdom of God does not come with observation; nor will they say, 'See here!' or 'See there!' For indeed, the Kingdom of God is within you." Reflecting on these and related (Luke 12:56) sayings, Bornkam (1966:68) comments that "Jesus fastens upon today and makes of it the present in which the decisions of the *eschaton* are already taking place"; also "he who looks forth to find the Kingdom of God as he would look at the weather or any other event that can be observed ... not only wants to know too much, but is fundamentally in error about God and himself. He is running away from God's call, here and now" (p. 75).

Component (c) of the proposed explication ("I want to live with You now") reflects the speaker's desire to answer God's call in the present; (d) represents an extension of this desire to other people; (e) is an amplification of this extension to eschatological dimensions: *all* people, *forever*. Since the speaker is included among all people, the speaker's hope for personal salvation is encompassed in the more general hope for the salvation of humankind as a whole.

The *Catechism of the Catholic Church* (1994:688) states, "By the second petition, the Church . . . looks first to Christ's return and the final coming of the Reign of God. It also prays for the growth of the Kingdom of God in the 'today' of our own lives." Although the meaning of the second of these sentences is not quite explicit, it could, I think, be linked with the idea that the kingdom of God is a kingdom of love: the kingdom of God will grow in the today of people's lives if they themselves grow in the desire to do good things for other people, as God wants to do good things for all people; and the reign of God will finally come when there is no more hatred and when love reigns supreme—that is, in universal terms, when all people want to do good things for other people. Symbolically speaking, it will also be a time when "the wolf . . . shall dwell with the lamb" and "the leopard shall lie down with the young goat" (Isaiah 11:6), that is, in universal terms, when no one will want to do anything bad to anyone else. The reason for this will be that "the earth shall be full of the knowledge of the Lord, as the waters cover the sea" (Isaiah 11:9), and as I interpret it, the knowledge of the Lord is attained by wanting to do good things for others and not wanting to do bad things to others.

If we wanted explicitly to interpret the "kingdom of God" as the "kingdom of love," we could expand the proposed explication along the following lines (cf. Wierzbicka 1999b):

(g) I know: You want people to want to do good things for other
      people
(h)   as You want to do good things for all people
(i)   You want people not to want to do bad things to other
      people
(j)   when people live like this they can live with You always
(k)   at the same time, they can live with all other people like
      a person can live with another person

Arguably, however, components such as (g)–(k) are best regarded as a legitimate commentary on the second petition rather than as part of this petition's meaning. The meaning of the petition (in its eschatological and God-centered as well as its ethical and social, dimension) can be seen as sufficiently explicated in (a)–(f).

8. Give us day by day our daily bread

Asking for bread in Palestine is like asking for rice in China or Japan; obviously, the metaphor applies to rice and to other basic foods as well. But bread is a metaphor that stands not only for food but also for all the other good and necessary things in life. To ask God for our daily bread means to recognize our constant dependence on God: at all times, I am able to live and to act because God is doing good things for me, and if he stopped doing those good things I would no longer be able to live. The phrase "the bread of life," so characteristic of the Gospels, underscores the meaning of "bread" as a symbol of life and all that is necessary for its continued sustenance:

(a) I know: I can live because You do good things for me
   other people can say the same

As has often been pointed out, "bread" does not symbolize all good things that we might desire (e.g., wealth, fame, popularity, and success); rather, it symbolizes only those good things that are essential to life at any given moment: "So we say to God: Give us bread. Not delicacies or riches, nor magnificent purple robes, golden ornaments, precious stones, or silver dishes. Nor do we ask Him for landed estates, or military commands, or political leadership. . . . We do not say, give us a prominent position in assemblies or monuments and status raised to us . . . no—but only bread!" (St. Gregory of Nyssa 1954:63–64). The daily bread that God gives people can be seen as a continuation of the act of creation, symbolized by the word "Father" in the opening of the prayer. If "father" symbolizes someone without whose creative act people could not exist at all, "bread" symbolizes everything without which their life could not continue.[10]

Many modern commentators rightly emphasize the need not to overspiritualize or over-eschatologize this meaning of "bread" (as some exegetes, ancient and modern, tend to do). For example, Schweizer (1975:153) writes, "The prayer is not overconcerned with spirituality; the bread we need each day is taken seriously, as it is throughout Jesus' life." Similarly Luz (1989:383) says, "'Bread' as the most important food in Semitic idiom can stand as *pars pro toto* for 'nourishment.'" Luz's apparent restriction of "bread" to food in a strict sense ("but [it] should not be extended beyond this to any sort of necessities for life") is understandable if it is read as a reaction to Luther's excessively broad interpretation of Jesus' "daily bread" as "food and clothing, home and property, work and income, a devoted family, orderly community, good government, favorable weather, peace and health, a good name and true friends and neighbors" (quoted in Luz, 1989:383). Luz rightly insists that such a broad interpretation "does not agree with the intention of the text." I hope that the explication proposed here strikes the right balance between the two extremes and implicitly excludes, for example, "favorable weather" without excluding, say, shelter and clothes. At the same time, it is consistent with the view that, "the primary reference here is certainly to physical bread, bread a man can put his teeth into" (Hunter 1953:71) and not just an eschatological banquet in heaven, as some commentators seem to believe.

Having set forth this basic assumption concerning one's constant dependence on God for the necessities of life, the speaker proceeds to ask for the continuation of this life-giving sustenance:

(b) I say: I want You to do these good things for me now
   as You always did before

The dependence on daily bread is not seen in the prayer as restricted to the speaker ("me") but as a shared human condition: "*our* daily bread." In asking for bread for oneself, therefore, one must remember one's fellow human beings:

(c) at the same time I say:
      I want You to do good things for other people
      as I want You to do good things for me

In fact, this formula echoes and, so to speak, explicates the second of the two great commandments (Matt. 22, 39): "Love your neighbor as yourself" ("I want You to do good things for other people as I want You to do good things for me").

The request addressed to God on behalf of other people could sound presumptuous (as if one thought that one cared for other people more than God himself does) were it not for the presupposition that stems from the earlier parts of the prayer:

(d) I know: I can say this to You always
      because You want to do good things for all people
      all people can say this to You always

The metaphor of day and dailiness deserves some discussion, too. If one feels that one always depends on God's life-giving actions, on the "bread of life" given to one by God alone, why does one have to ask for this bread on a daily basis? Why cannot one rather ask God that he should ensure once and for all that one will always have the bread necessary for one's survival? There is, of course, a good reason for this limitation: it is the eternal insecurity of the human condition that helps one remember one's constant dependence on God and which encourages people to turn to God continually with their needs. In this way, one remembers the nature of one's relationship with God as someone who can, and who wants to, do good things for people, to nurture them as a parent does. Thus, instead of asking for *constant help*, one is encouraged to *ask constantly* for the help necessary at any given moment. This can be portrayed in the form of the following semantic components:

I don't say: "I want You to do these good things for me always"
I say: "I want You to do these good things for me now"
I know: I can say this to You always

I have refrained, however, from including these further components in the semantic formula because they seem more justified as an explanatory comment than as an integral part of the meaning. The meaning as such can be adequately summed up in (a)–(d):

(a) I know: I can live because You do good things for me
          other people can say the same
(b) I say: I want You to do these good things for me now
          as You always did before
(c) at the same time I say:

> I want You to do good things for other people
> as I want You to do good things for me

(d) I know: I can say this to You always
> because You want to do good things for all people
> all people can say this to You always

9. And forgive us our sins

The notion of forgiveness is, as many commentators have observed, at the heart of Jesus' teaching. At the same time, however, it is not an easy notion to understand; and if it is difficult to explain what it means in human relations, it is even more difficult to grasp its sense in the relation between people and God. Some recent commentators seem, in fact, to have stopped trying to come to grips with this notion altogether. For example, Morwood, the author of a book entitled *Tomorrow's Catholic*, writes,

> This image of a God who takes offense at human wrongdoing and reacts, who listens and responds, permeates the general Christian attitude to prayer. Take, for example, a prayer such as, "O my God, I am heartily sorry for having offended you. . . ." What does it mean to suggest that God is "offended" by our sin? Does God somewhere-out-there react and want to punish our sin? (1998:13)

The tone of these questions is satirical, but the questions themselves do need to be considered by anyone interested in Jesus' teaching. After all, this *is* how Jesus told his disciples to pray.

As usual, our focus must not be on the English word ("forgive") or even on its Greek model (*afiēmi* 'forgive, cancel, remit, let go') but on Jesus' conception, which he explained in images, in particular, in the image of the father in the parable of the prodigal son. Although the younger son in the story did not say to his father, "Forgive me," and the father did not say to the son, "I forgive you," we can assume that the story best shows what Jesus had in mind.

The son's initial assumptions, suggested by both his words and his behavior, can be represented as follows:

(a) I know: I did bad things to you
(b) I know: you could feel something bad because of this
(c) I know: you could want to do something bad to me because of this
(d) I know: you can now feel something bad when you think about me
(e) I know: I can't live with you now as I could before
> if you don't say something good to me

If the prodigal son had had the time and courage to ask explicitly for forgiveness (and if he had been able to speak in the language of universal human concepts), he could have added some utterances along the following lines:

    (f) when I think about this I feel something bad
    (g) I don't want you to feel something bad when you think about me
    (h) I want you to feel something good when you think about me
    (i) I want to live with you now as I could live with you before I did
        these things

The father's response to that unspoken plea (running to meet the son, kissing him, reinstating him through the ring to his previous position in the household, and giving a party) suggests a message along the following lines:

    (j) when I think about you I don't feel anything bad any more
    (k) I feel something good
    (l) I don't want to do anything bad to you
    (m) I want to do good things for you
    (n) you can live with me now as you could before you did these things
    (o) I want this

I am not suggesting that these formulas provide full answers to questions such as those raised by Morwood (1998), but I think that they do give us a good idea of what Jesus understood by forgiveness—both in human relations and, *mutatis mutandis*, in the relation between people and God.

    The request "forgive me my sins" does not imply that "I did bad things to You (God)" but rather that I did "bad things." (A human being can hardly do something bad to God.) So this is the first difference between the situation of asking for human forgiveness (a) and that of asking for God's forgiveness (b):

    (a) I know: I did bad things to you
    (b) I know: I did bad things

In human interaction, the wronged person "could feel something bad because of what I did." Could God, too, feel something bad because of what a human being did? Parables such as the great feast and the lost coin suggest that Jesus's God, unlike the "unmovable mover" of the Greek philosophers, can indeed feel something because of what people do: when they refuse to live with him (in the parable of the great feast, to come to his banquet) or are cruel to other people (as in the unforgiving servant), he feels something bad; when they show that they do want to live with him (in the parable of the lost coin, when they are found), he feels something good.

    The reason that Jesus' God "feels something bad" when people do bad things is not that he is angered by their disobedience but, in universal terms, that when people do bad things they cannot live with God, who is inherently someone good. God wants all people (including me, the speaker) to live with him, and so he *can* feel something bad when I make this impossible by doing bad things.

    In the case of human forgiveness, the main purpose of asking for it is to try to restore the former good relations with the other person, damaged by their bad feelings, caused by the offender's bad deeds. In the case of asking for forgiveness from God, the purpose is similar: one needs to ask for forgiveness to be able again to live with God as one could before one did those bad things. This interpretation of Jesus' teaching is consistent with the traditional biblical metaphors of distance and separation (cf., e.g., Isaiah 59:2: "But your iniquities have separated you from God"). It is also consistent with the traditional Christian interpretation as expressed, for example, by Vorländer:

> Just as the fact that man is a sinner has destroyed his relationship with God . . . forgiveness takes the central place in Christian proclamation as the means whereby this relationship is restored. . . . forgiveness is not merely a remission of past guilt, but also includes total deliverance from the power of sin and restoration to fellowship with God. (1975:701–702)

As in the case of human forgiveness, the "restoration of the fellowship" with God cannot be achieved by the human being alone but requires an act of God, which can be interpreted as a speech act: this restoration cannot happen unless God "says something good" to the sinner.

In the case of human forgiveness there is also the question of a possible desire on the part of the wronged or offended parties to do something bad to the other people because of what they have done (to "pay them back," to retaliate, or to punish). There can, however, be no question of God's wanting to do something bad to anyone, no matter what he or she has done.[11] If I ask God for forgiveness, therefore, this cannot mean that I ask God not to do anything bad to me because of what I have done. Rather, it can only mean asking him to enable me to live with him again; I want to live with him, I recognize that it is very bad for me not to live with him, and I realize that I can't achieve this by my own efforts.

Once again, however, it is not only one's own sins that one is to ask God to forgive: sinning—like needing bread—is a universal human condition, and according to Jesus, in asking forgiveness we must remember our fellow human beings, who are also sinners and who also need God's forgiveness (and "forgive *us our* sins"). Therefore,

I know: other people are like me
        other people do bad things, as I do bad things
I say: I want You to say the same to other people

Thus, the overall formula for the fourth petition can read as follows:

Forgive us our sins

(a) I know:
(b)   all people can live with You
(c)   You want this
(d) at the same time I know:
(e)   You are someone good

(f)   when someone does bad things this person can't live with
        You
(g)   because of this, when people do bad things
        You feel something bad
(h) I know: I did some bad things
(i) I know:
        because I did these things I can't live with You now
        if You don't say something good to me
(j) I say:
        I want You to say it
        I want to live with You
(k) I know:
        other people are like me
        other people do bad things, as I do bad things
(l) I want You to say the same to all other people
(m) I want all people to live with You

10. For we also forgive everyone who is indebted to us

The thought of other human beings raises the question of the parallel between
the bad things that I have done (thus alienating myself from God) and the bad
things that other people may have done to me. Although Luke's phrasing of the
parallel between divine and human forgiveness differs from Matthew's ("as we
forgive those who trespass against us"), the meaning behind both that was intended by Jesus is hardly in doubt. The *Catechism of the Catholic Church*
(1994:682) phrases it as follows: ". . . this outpouring of mercy cannot penetrate our hearts as long as we have not forgiven those who have trespassed
against us." Similarly, Tom Wright comments,

> . . . the Lord's Prayer contains, at this point, a most unusual thing: a clause
> which commits the pray-er to actions which back up the petition just of-
> fered. The pray-er realises that failure to forgive others . . . like God is always
> willing to forgive all people would be like "cutting the branch you were
> sitting on"; and so he or she has to find in their own heart a willingness
> to forgive others, too. (1996:54–55)

Some commentators have interpreted the relation between our forgiveness for
others and God's forgiveness for us in terms of a condition. For example, Hunter
(1953:72) writes, "But there is a condition attached to God's forgiveness—a condition which made Augustine call this 'the terrible petition'—that we must have
forgiven our erring brethren." This sounds like an overtly literalist interpretation of the parable of the unforgiving servant: if the servant does not forgive his
fellow servant, the king will not forgive him either but will "deliver him to the
torturers until he should pay all that was due to him" (Matt. 18:34).

It is true that Matthew (6:14) has followed his version of the Lord's Prayer with a formula that does sound like a condition: "For if you forgive people their trespasses, your heavenly Father will also forgive you. But if you do not forgive people their trespasses, neither will your Father forgive your trespasses." As with the parable of the unforgiving servant, however, Matthew's words should not be interpreted as setting limits to God's mercy. It is instructive to consider the comment of the Jewish scholar Abrahams ([1917]1967:II, i.97): "Liturgically, the Synagogue did not make man's repentance a precise *condition* of God's pardon. Still less did it make man's forgiveness a condition. The unforgiving man does not deserve pardon, but who does?" Commenting on this quote, Montefiore ([1927]1968:103) suggests that "Matthew means no more than: 'Forgive us, even as we, following Thy commands, seek to forgive those who have wronged us'"; and, as noted by Montefiore, this is consistent with Luke's formulation, too.

Here, as elsewhere, Jesus' meaning is clearly not that God will imitate people but rather that "God's behavior . . . [is] the norm for humans" (Johnson 1991:178): we must do unto others as we want God to do unto us, and as in fact God does unto us. This could be called Jesus' "platinum rule," more radical and demanding than the golden rule ("Do unto others as you want others to do unto you"). When applied to forgiveness, this platinum rule can be formulated along the following lines:

(a) I know:
(b)   when I say these things to You You want me to say
            something else at the same time
(c) I want to say it

(d) I say:
(e)   sometimes someone else does something bad to me
(f)   sometimes I feel something bad because of this
(g)   I don't want to feel something bad when I think about this
            person
(h)   I don't want to want to do something bad to this person
(i)   I want to feel something good when I think about this person
(j)   if I lived with this person before this happened
            I want to live with this person after it happened
        as I lived with this person before

11. And do not lead us into temptation

The interpretation of the sixth petition is a subject of debate. Some say that the speaker is asking to be spared temptations; others, that it is, rather, a request for help in not yielding to temptation; still others, that what is meant here is not temptation but a time of trial, being put to a test. The *Catechism of the Catholic*

Church (1994:684) says that the Greek means here both "do not allow us to enter into temptation" and "do not let us yield to temptation" and that "this petition implores the Spirit of discernment and strength."

All these different interpretations can be rendered, and indeed clarified, in the language of universal human concepts. Without entering into an extensive theological debate on the matter, I will simply focus on explicating what seems to be the most traditional interpretation. The main objective of doing so is to show that this petition can be explained in nonmetaphorical language based exclusively on universal human concepts. If contending alternative interpretations were also explained in these terms, this would clarify the differences and perhaps facilitate resolution of the debate.

Thus, in asking not to be led into temptation, we acknowledge our weakness and capacity for doing bad things; we recognize that under certain circumstances we may do something very bad—even if in principle we don't want to. Recognizing human weakness, Jesus encourages his disciples to, as Matthew's version spells out, "deliver them from evil." I propose, then, an explication along the following lines:

do not lead us into temptation

   (a) I know: sometimes I want to do bad things
   (b)   sometimes I do bad things because of this
   (c)   I am like this
   (d I know: when a person does bad things
          this person cannot live with You
   (e) I know: if some things happen to me
          I can do very bad things because of this
   (f) I want not to do these very bad things
   (g) I want to live with You always
   (h) I know: if You do something I can NOT-do these very bad things
   (i) I say: I want You to do it
   (j) I know: other people are like me
          sometimes they want to do bad things
          as I sometimes want to do bad things
   (k) at the same time I know:
          if You do something they can NOT-do these things
   (l) I say: I want You to do this

Components (a)–(c) reflect the speaker's recognition of his or her weakness and capacity for doing bad things. Component (d) expresses the recognition that, as discussed in section 9, by doing bad things one separates oneself from God. Component (e) suggests an apprehension of what one's weakness might lead one to, at a particularly difficult time. Components (f) and (g) show the speaker's desire not to do bad things—not because one is afraid of transgressing some abstract moral code but because one doesn't want to be separated from God (one wants to live with God). Component (h) recognizes God's capacity to help people in their weakness, without spelling out exactly what form of help is expected; the phrasing is vague and could apply both to someone praying to be spared particularly testing situations and to someone praying for help in withstanding such situations. Component (i), with its direct appeal to God, is the key point of the petition. Components (j)–(l) reflect the fact that, like the other petitions, this one, too, would apply to other people.

Discussions concerning the meaning of the final petition of the Lord's Prayer are often couched in terms of the alternative: eschatology or ethics. The explication proposed here frees us from the necessity of making such choices because it is compatible with both interpretations. In particular, (g)–"I want to live with You always"–can be taken to refer to daily life, to life in times of special crises, or to life after death.

Breech ([1983]1987:52) objects to the Revised Standard Version's (1962) translation of the last petition as "lead us not into temptation" because it interprets the petition "morally, as [referring to] a temptation to transgress ethical or religious prohibitions." He suggests that we should adhere instead to what he regards as the more literal translation: "and put us not to the test." Personally, I have no problems with either translation, but both are metaphorical and thus need a nonmetaphorical explication. I think, however, that we need not be excessively afraid of a moral interpretation; the petition does refer to the possibility that we may do bad things, indeed, very bad things. This, after all, is what sin is all about, and Jesus was not only telling people "your sins are forgiven" (e.g., Luke 5:20, 7:48) but also "sin no more" (cf., e.g., John 5:14, 8:11). Indeed, he urged them to, metaphorically speaking, pluck out their right eye rather than sin (Matt. 6:29) and called them to repentance (e.g., Luke 13:3–5). At the same time, I agree that what is at issue is not the transgression of prohibitions but rather living–or not living–with God.

Many commentators have noted the closeness between the petition concerning temptation and its Jewish parallels, and on the whole those who make this point support an existential rather than a primarily eschatological interpretation. Montefiore ([1927]1968:103) says, "'Lead us not into temptation.' A prayer extremely familiar to Jewish readers. . . . 'Temptation means severe trials, such as the trials of the flesh, or of any special circumstances which are likely to lead to sin. . . . 'Lead us not', i.e. 'Bring us not within the influence of temptation', 'Cause us not to come into circumstances when temptation will befall us.'"

Luz (1989:384) comments, "An eschatological interpretation has been proposed also for . . . the *temptation petition* : *peirasmos* would mean the tribulation of the end time. Almost all evidence speaks against this view: Neither in Jewish apocalyptic nor in the New Testament is *peirasmos* an apocalyptic technical term. . . . The Jewish parallels also speak in favour of thinking of the temptations which occur in everyday life." Fitzmyer (1985ba:901) similarly notes parallels between the petition concerning temptation and Jewish prayers, such as "Bring me not into the power of sin, or into the power of guilt, or into the power of temptation." Parallels of this kind support an existential understanding of the petition, while being fully compatible with an eschatological interpretation as well. The explication proposed here excludes neither.

12. Conclusion

Needless to say, I am not suggesting that Bible translators around the globe should henceforth start translating the Lord's Prayer into universal concepts, avoiding culture-specific images and metaphorical terms such as *father, kingdom,* or *bread.* Images and terms of this kind are part of Jesus' teaching, and some equivalents for them must be found, or forged, in any language into which the Gospels are translated. The intended meaning of these images and terms, however, can be further elucidated in a language so simple that even children could understand it; for behind the imagery and metaphors there lie quite specific messages—messages that can be reconstructed in a plain, entirely nonmetaphorical language and which can be understood literally.

I would not claim that the semantic explications proposed here are easy to understand for everyone. Obviously, their stylized wording, contrary to the usual norms and cadences of English speech, makes them seem strange to the native speaker. A natural language offers us a kind of shorthand for the language of thought, and in everyday life we are so accustomed to this shorthand that any attempt to explicate it fully, down to the elementary building blocks of meaning, must create difficulties for the reader. Nonetheless, explications couched in these terms are possible to understand.

So although, in a sense, the semantic exegesis proposed here can be seen as a running commentary on the Lord's Prayer, in another sense, it can be seen as a new kind of radical translation, reaching beyond the culture-specific metaphors to a nonmetaphorical meaning that can be understood directly and literally.

It is very easy to recite a text such as the Lord's Prayer without fully understanding its meaning; one can simply, so to speak, glide across the surface of the text. Any attempt to fully grasp the meanings of the successive phrases requires an effort. The formulas proposed here can, I think, help the reader to go beyond surface gliding and to elucidate the full meanings hidden in phrases so familiar that their intelligibility is likely to be taken for granted. The use of explications forces us to ask ourselves what these phrases really mean.

As noted earlier, the words used in natural language are for the most part language-specific. Complex concepts such as kingdom, bread, forgiveness, or temptation are by no means universal. But the core message of the Lord's Prayer has always been regarded by Christian tradition as universal. If it is indeed universal, it should be possible to explain it to any group of people regardless of their particular language and culture. This can be achieved through the use of universal human concepts. An exegesis based on such simple and universal human concepts can overcome many widespread misunderstandings about the substance of Jesus' teaching. The metaphor of father is a good case in point.

Part II

THE PARABLES

SIX

The Sower

Mark 4:3–8; cf. Matthew13:3–8; Luke 8:5–8

3. Listen! Behold, a sower went out to sow.
4. And it happened, as he sowed, that some seed fell by the wayside; and the birds of the air came and devoured it.
5. Some fell on stony ground, where it did not have much earth; and immediately it sprang up because it had no depth of earth.
6. But when the sun came up, it was scorched, and because it had no root, it withered away.
7. And some seed fell among thorns; and the thorns grew up and choked it, and it yielded no crop.
8. But other seed fell on good ground and yielded a crop that sprang up, increased and produced: some thirtyfold, some sixty, and some a hundred.

The parable of the sower, preserved in all the synoptic Gospels (as well as in the Gospel of Thomas), is widely regarded as authentic, although it is commonly assumed that all versions reflect some editorial modifications (Matthew's and Luke's more so than Mark's or Thomas'). Whereas it is widely agreed that the interpretation of the parable that we find in Mark 4:14–20, Matthew 13:18–23, and Luke 18:11–15 was added to the original text at a later stage, "few scholars have doubted the authenticity of the parable itself" (Boucher 1981:80).

Since the interpretation appended to the parable by the evangelists (and usually referred to as Markan) plays an important role in all relevant discussions,
including this one, let me quote it here in full before proceeding any further:

13. And he said to them, 'Do you not understand this parable? How
    then will you understand all the parables?
14. The sower sows the word.
15. And these are the ones by the wayside where the word is sown.
    And when they hear, Satan comes immediately and takes away
    the word that was sown in their hearts.
16. These likewise are the ones sown on stony ground who, when they
    hear the word, immediately receive it with gladness;
17. and they have no root in themselves, and so endure only for a
    time. Afterwards, when tribulation or persecution arises for the
    word's sake, immediately they stumble.
18. Now these are the ones sown among thorns; they are the ones who
    heard the word,
19. and the care of this world, the deceitfulness of riches, and the
    desires for other things entering in, choke the word, and it
    becomes unfruitful.
20. But these are the ones sown on good ground, those who hear the
    word, accept it, and bear fruit: some thirtyfold, some sixty, and
    some a hundred.'

Many scholars have commented on the special importance of the sower in the
body of Jesus' parables. Boucher (1977:6) calls it "the most important parable
in the Gospel" and "the key to understanding all the other parables." Similarly,
Lockyer (1963:177) speaks of "the importance of this parable, an importance we
cannot exaggerate." Capon accompanies his list of all the "parables of the Kingdom" and their sources with the following comment:

> The first thing to note about this list is the star billing that the Synoptic
> Gospels give to the parable of the Sower. Not only do all three of them
> make it the introduction to the first deliberate collection of Jesus' parables;
> they also devote a disproportionate amount of space to it and to the com-
> ments Jesus made in connection with it. For the record, Matthew gives
> this material twenty-three verses; Mark, twenty-five; and Luke, fifteen. . . .
> (1985:61)

Capon concludes: "Therefore, the parable of the Sower stands quite easily as
what the Synoptics make it: the great watershed of all Jesus' parables" (p. 64).

But whereas most commentators see the sower as both Jesus' own and particularly important, they do not all agree on what the parable means. Borsch
(1988:125) observes, "What seems in some ways like the simplest of parables
can also be heard as one of the most mysterious." Commenting on how modern scholarship has managed to "separate the parable from its interpretation"

and to establish that the interpretation was added to the parable at a later stage, he remarks that "it has proved far more difficult to know how it [the parable] then would have been heard or, for that matter, to know how it might best be understood today."

Similarly, Hedrick (1994:261) notes, "Modern interpreters differ widely in their understanding of the story." Elaborating on this comment, Hedrick lists the following main interpretations:

> The meaning of the story (1) focusses on responses to the preaching of Jesus ... (Cadoux, Smith, Jones, Perkins); (2) is about the Kingdom of God ... (Dodd, Taylor, Crossan, Lane, Carlston, Mann); (3) is lost (Linnemann); (4) is about the eventual success of Jesus' preaching ... (Jeremias); (5) has an authority of its own and witnesses to Jesus 'in its own way' (Wilder); (6) is substantially preserved in Mark's interpretation (Michaels); (7) presents God's ruling activity under the most unfamiliar guises (Scott).[1] (1994:261)

Other commentators (e.g., Boucher 1977) believe that despite the diversity of opinion, all the interpretations of the sower can be reduced to two main ones: the original, that is, Mark's, and the eschatological, championed in particular by Joachim Jeremias. In essence, Jeremias (1972) argued that the harvest in verse 8 symbolizes an impending world crisis—the coming of the kingdom of God—and that the parable promises the final victory of this kingdom. Mark, on the other hand, saw the parable as speaking about hearing, understanding, and responding to the word of God.

In fact, Michaels (1981) is not the only commentator who believes that the meaning of the parable originally intended by Jesus is substantially preserved in Mark's interpretation. Many commentators see Mark's interpretation as extremely plausible, indeed, as perfectly fitting the parable:

> The view of the present study is that the Markan interpretation gives a very natural rendering of the parable, one which fits it perfectly. The hearer would have to be told that the parable as a whole has to do with hearing the word; but once so informed, he would have little difficulty in apprehending many of its constituent meanings. That the scattering of seed stands for the dissemination of the word; the ground for those among whom the word is broadcast; the poor and rich soil for those respectively who fail and who succeed in receiving and keeping the word; and the final yield of grain for righteousness—these are meanings that are derived quite naturally from the story. There is nothing in the broad lines of the interpretation that strains the sense of the reference in the parable itself. Even a simple, uneducated hearer of the kind that must have largely made up the audiences of Jesus would have been able to supply these constituent meanings, once he had perceived the whole meaning to be about the word. . . . What the author of the interpretation (whoever he may have been) has done with the parable . . . is by no means a falsification of its meaning. (Boucher 1977:49-50)

Like Boucher, Michaels, and many others,[2] I, too, believe that Mark's original interpretation is convincing and fits the parable very well. It also fits Jesus' teaching as a whole. Most important, it is an interpretation that although consistent with Jesus' overall teaching, throws additional light on it and, moreover, gives the parable a universal relevance and significance.

I do not suggest that Mark's interpretation should be accepted in every detail or argue that if we simply translate it, verse by verse, into the language of universal human concepts we will obtain a full and adequate explanation of the parable's meaning. Nonetheless, the main ideas in Mark's explanation, which are expressed in simple and clear—though partially figurative and, of course, not universal—language, make perfect sense in the context of Jesus' overall teaching. To my mind, they have not been superseded by the later approaches (including the latest scholarly hermeneutics, to which I will return at the end of this chapter).

Mark's crucial and incontrovertible idea is that "the sower sows the word" (v. 14) and that people react to this word (obviously, God's word) in different ways, with different results. In my own explication of the parable's message I will build on these Markan ideas. But one proviso should be added here.

The most important modern breakthrough in the understanding of parables was, as most scholars agree, Adolf Jülicher's distinction between parables and allegories: a parable has an overall message, and one should not try to attribute distinct meanings to the individual details of the story. On this point modern interpreters do have an edge over Mark, who sought to assign individual explanations to the images of the wayside, the rocks, and the thorns. As noted, for example, by Dodd (1965:136), "The birds, the thorns, and the rocky ground are objects familiar to every farmer, illustrating the kind of thing with which he has to reckon. They are part of the dramatic machinery of the story, not to be interpreted symbolically" (see Jülicher [1888]1963:514–538). Jülicher's later critics are right, I think, in emphasizing that there is no hard and fast contrast between parables and allegories and, also, that a parable's overall message can be quite complex and by no means reducible to one main point, as Jülicher seems to have thought. Nonetheless his basic insight is extremely important, and it is particularly relevant to the interpretation of the sower, to which Mark assigned an overly allegorical interpretation.

We can start the explication, however, with a cluster of components fully consistent with Mark's explanation:

(a) God says things to people all the time
(b) God wants people to hear God's words
(c) God wants people to know what God is saying with these words
(d) God wants people to want to live with God because of this

Blomberg (1990:228) has summed up the message of the parable in three points, the first of which is that "like the sower, God spreads his word widely among all kinds of people." I think this is essentially right, except that Jesus' emphasis is always on kinds of responses rather than on kinds of people. According to B. T. D. Smith (1937:126), the parable illustrates "the truth that the spoken word can only bear fruit when its hearers are receptive." Such references to God's word, to the hearers' receptiveness, and to the word that bears fruit are consistent with the partial explication proposed above.

Jeremias (1966b:119) insists that the parable refers not only to "doing the word" but also to the kingdom of God. Jeremias calls this the eschatological point of the parable, which he interprets in terms of an impending crisis: "God's hour is coming . . . in spite of every failure and opposition, God brings from hopeless beginnings the glorious end that he has promised" (p. 120). In effect, Jeremias identifies the message of the sower with that of the mustard seed—referring to the final victory of God.

But this misses the point of the different human responses to God's word, clearly suggested by the various images of the parable. As emphasized by Ryken, among others, the parable concentrates not on the harvest (i.e., God's final victory) but on the kinds of soil. Ryken says that

> the whole interest is with the soil, that is, the hearers of the Gospel. . . .
> Jesus delineates three inadequate responses to his message of the kingdom. It is a warning to the listeners to avoid these errors. The fourth response provides the opportunity to choose a better way. . . . To sum up, the parable of the sower stresses human responsiveness to God's message of salvation. It sets up options from which the listener must choose. (1984:336)

Similarly, Carlston (1975:144) notes that "five verses of the parable are devoted to the seeds and the different kinds of soils (vs. 4–8), while only part of the last verse speaks of harvest." In fact, some commentators (e.g., Jülicher [1888]1963; Lockyer 1963; Ryken 1984) insist on calling the parable "the parable of the Soils." An interpretation of the parable that focuses on the harvest and completely ignores the theme of different soils is therefore unconvincing.

In my view, an adequate explication should do justice to both aspects of the parable: the reference to the kingdom of God, implied (as often in the New Testament) by the image of a bountiful harvest, and the reference to a variety of human responses, symbolized in the parable by the wayside, the stony ground, the thorns, and the fertile ground. This is the purpose of component (d), which links the idea of the kingdom of God (i.e., of people living with God) with that of a human response (people *wanting* to live with God). It is also the purpose of a number of other components to be added shortly.[3]

The images of the seed devoured by the birds, scorched by the sun, or choked by the thorns jointly suggest these further components:

(e) sometimes people don't hear God's words
(f) sometimes when people hear God's words they don't know what
      God is saying with these words
(g) sometimes when people know what God is saying they don't want
      to live with God
(h) all these things are very bad for these people

Components (e)–(g), which refer to various kinds of human failure, do not attempt to follow closely the story's triplet of wayside, rocks, and thorns; as pointed out by many commentators, triple images were likely to be used in Jesus' parables for rhetorical and mnemonic reasons rather than for reasons of content. The fact that in my explication the three images are linked with three components [(e)–(g)] has no significance. Nor should (h) be understood as allegorizing people as seeds: the fact that, in the story, bad things happen to the seeds and, in the explication, things happen to some people that are bad for these people does not mean that seeds stand here for people. Rather, the message of the parable is global; and although certain aspects of the message are suggested by certain aspects of the images, no simple parallels should be drawn. (Once again, Jesus' parables are not allegories.)

The next part of the explication refers to people who respond to God's word in the way desired by God, that is, who are like a good soil:

(i)   sometimes people hear God's words
(j)   sometimes people know because of this what God is saying to
      people
(k)   sometimes people want to live with God because of this

Boucher (1981:81), with whose discussion of the parable I largely agree, has observed that in "the Markan interpretation . . . the parable is . . . a lesson on hearing and doing the word." If "doing the word" means, roughly speaking, responding to the word by wanting to live with God, then I agree. I have not, however, included in the explication any components about doing something because I think the emphasis is not on any particular deeds but on living with God. Of course, in Jesus' teaching, living with God always bears fruit in deeds: healthy fig trees bear figs and grapevines, grapes (cf. chapter 4, section 14). But what God wants is that people should live with God, not that people should do good things: doing many good things is a visible result of living with God.

(l)   God wants all people to live with God
(m)   God does many things because of this
(n)   if people live with God this is very good for these people
(o)   these people do many good things because of this

Let us consider how these components can be supported by the text of the parable. God is like a sower, who is doing many things (m) because he wants a bountiful harvest. In the New Testament, as mentioned earlier, a harvest usually stands for the kingdom of God (cf. Dodd 1965:134), that is, in my terms, for "people living with God." God wants this result: just as a sower wants all seeds to grow and flourish, so does God want all people to live with God (l). How do we know (from this parable) that it is very good for people to live with God (n)? Partly, from the logic of the images: it is very bad for the seeds to be devoured by the birds, scorched by the sun, or choked by the thorns, and it is very good for them to find themselves in a fertile soil. Similarly, it is very bad for people not to hear God's words, not to know what God says to people, and not to want to live with God; and it is very good for them to hear God's words, to know what God says to people, and to want to live with God because of this. The image of a bountiful yield ("hundredfold") suggests, of course, not only a healthy plant but also a fruitful one; and as mentioned earlier, in the language of the Gospel, the "fruit" usually refers to deeds, generated by a person who is "like a healthy plant"—not because of the person's own virtue ("without me, you can't do anything," John 15:5) but because he or she lives with God. This is my component (o).

The final part of the proposed explication presents the appeal to the hearer:

- (p) it will be good for you if you hear God's words
- (q) it will be good for you if you know what God is saying with these words
- (r) it will be good for you if you want to live with God because of this

These components correspond, in fact, quite well to statements made by many commentators on the hortatory aspect of the parable of the sower. For example, Ryken (1984:305) calls the parable "a challenge" and "a warning": "it sets up options from which the listeners must choose." Similarly, Linnemann (1966:119) comments, "The realization, 'not all bear fruit', becomes the anxious knowledge that a man can fail in his life, and forces him to ask, 'How does it stand with me?'"

This brings us to the following overall explication:

The sower

- (a) God says things to people all the time
- (b) God wants people to hear God's words
- (c) God wants people to know what God is saying with these words
- (d) God wants people to want to live with God because of this

- (e) sometimes people don't hear God's words
- (f) sometimes when people hear God's words they don't know what God is saying with these words
- (g) sometimes when people know what God is saying they don't want to live with God
- (h) all these things are very bad for these people

- (i) sometimes people hear God's words
- (j) sometimes people know because of this what God is saying to people
- (k) sometimes people want to live with God because of this

- (l) God wants all people to live with God
- (m) God does many things because of this
- (n) if people live with God this is very good for these people
- (o) these people do many good things because of this

(p) it will be good for you if you hear God's words
(q) it will be good for you if you know what God is saying with these
		words
(r) it will be good for you if you want to live with God because of this

This explication draws together many of the threads running through the debate on the parable of the sower: God's activity among people, God's goals and plans for a kingdom of God, people's different responses to God's plans and activities, hearing versus non-hearing, understanding versus nonunderstanding, wanting to live with God versus not wanting to live with God, and the fruits of living with God.

Commentators who see the sower as the key to Jesus' other parables are, I think, correct. By highlighting the importance of hearing and understanding God's words, this parable encourages the hearers and readers of all the parables to hear in them God's message and to try to understand what God says to people with the help of the images. It also introduces the central theme of Jesus' teaching as a whole: the theme of the kingdom of God, of God's desire that all people should live with God (in God's kingdom), of the kingdom being open to all who want to respond to God's words, and of God's call for people to respond.

According to Madeleine Boucher (1977:46), in talking about sowing the seed of God's words, Jesus was referring in particular to his own parables. Since the parables are so central to Jesus' teaching, "the seed stands for the parables. That is a parable on the right hearing of parables. That is why Jesus says to his disciples, 'Do you understand this parable? How then will you understand all the parables? (v. 13)." Of course, there is no way of knowing whether Jesus really said the words attributed to him in Mark's verse 13, and most scholars today would say that these words—unlike the parable itself—originate with Mark, not Jesus. Nonetheless the meaning behind this verse is consistent with the meaning of the parable itself, and so this additional verse can be seen as an apt comment on the parable.

As I have tried to show, it is possible to arrive at a coherent interpretation of the sower, building on the ideas of Mark's original explanation and reading the parable in the context of Jesus' teaching as a whole. I have also tried to show that this interpretation (unlike the one proposed by Jeremias 1972) is well grounded in the images of the story, fits both the parable itself and its place in the synoptic Gospels as an overture to the parables, and allows us to see the parable as rich in content and relevant to the modern reader.

Crossan (1980:25) opens his lengthy study of the sower by quoting a view that "despite numerous exegetical-hermeneutical probings of the Parable of the Sower, the scholarly community is far from reaching consensus on what message Jesus intended to convey through the Parable. Some commentators concede his message is lost to us. Others contend it is yet to be discovered (Weeden:1979)." Crossan's own conclusion is that the parable is "intrinsically polyvalent" (p. 52), that is, that it has many meanings—meanings that reflect the reader's own ideas rather than any ideas of Jesus himself. What the parable teaches us, says Crossan, is that we ought to abandon the very idea of looking for an intersubjectively valid interpretation: "Accepting the parable of the Sower as a parable parabling [sic] the Kingdom, as a metaparable of hermeneutical polyvalence, as a mirror rather than a window parable, I can see certain important connections between the interpretation of interpretation it proposes and specific problems in fields as diverse as politics and education, literature, philosophy and theology" (p. 54).

Crossan (1980) asks whether "too great a thirst for univalence . . . [is] an indication of totalitarian imagination" and concludes: "Within the vocabulary of these contemporary hermeneutical theories, then, Jesus' parable of The Sower is a dialectical rather than a rhetorical text, a writerly text of bliss rather than a readerly text of pleasure, and instead of our interpreting the parable we find its polyvalence has turned on us and forced us to rethink our interpretation of interpretation itself" (p. 64).[4] Crossan quotes with approval the literary theorist Wolfgang Iser (1978:10), who "has indicated very clearly the polyvalent possibility of structural control over the presumably univalent intentionality of authorial control." At the risk of betraying a "totalitarian imagination," in this chapter I attempt to answer the question "What did Jesus mean?"—thus aiming at a "univalent reading" and searching for "authorial intention."

Yet the whole emphasis of Jesus' parables is on hearing the message. As noted by Funk et al. (1993:54), the saying "He who has ears to hear, let him hear!"— appended by Mark to the sower—occurs repeatedly in the Gospels (as well as in Revelation). Funk, Scott, and Butts (1988:52) specify that "it appears 21 times in connection with words ascribed to Jesus." It seems likely, therefore, that this saying was remembered as actually used by Jesus. In fact, Michaels (1981:111) suggests that "Jesus' parabolic teaching as a whole was punctuated by this same invitation [to hear]" with which the Markan version of the sower begins and ends (Mark 4:3, 9). It would seem clear that Jesus wanted his hearers to hear *his* message rather than to weave their own polyvalent interpretations. It is ironic that of all Jesus' parables it is the sower that should have been chosen as a "metaparable" to deconstruct all parables and to attack the very idea of a message intended to be heard and understood.

SEVEN

The Hidden Treasure and
The Pearl of Great Price

Matthew 13: 44-46

44. Again, the kingdom of heaven is like treasure hidden in a field,
which a man found and hid; and for joy over it he goes and
sells all that he has and buys the field.
45. Again, the kingdom of heaven is like a merchant seeking beautiful
pearls,
46. who, when he had found one pearl of great price, went and sold
all that he had and bought it.

John Dominic Crossan (1994:93) writes, aphoristically,

The kingdom of God is like this
   A trader sold all his merchandise to buy a single pearl
(But how is the Kingdom of God like that?)

Exactly the same question must, of course, be asked about the double of the pearl
parable, that is, the parable of the hidden treasure; and one "abstract" formula
provides, I suggest, an answer both to Crossan's question about the pearl and
to an analogous question about the treasure. As Lambrecht (1991:171) puts it,
"In both parables the introductory sentence is the same: 'the Kingdom of heaven
is like . . .' [and] the content, too, amounts to the same thing."
    In a collection of 100 personal testimonies on "Who is Jesus of Nazareth—
for me?" Heinrich Spaemann (1973:27-28) adduces the testimony of one re-

spondent who replies that Jesus of Nazareth "means nothing for him" and who points, in particular, to the parable of the hidden treasure as an "immoral story." Shouldn't the man who found the treasure report it to the owner of the field rather than hide it and buy the field for himself? Such a reading takes too seriously the details of the image instead of concentrating on the central point. But to argue effectively against such a misunderstanding, we must be prepared to state what we see as a more valid reading. It is hardly sufficient to say that the story is "just a metaphor" and that, consequently, its meaning neither can nor needs to be stated in any other way than by rereading the metaphor. (See, e.g., Te Selle 1975.)

The fact that quite a few parables come in pairs (two different images but one message) shows that the message is not inseparable from the images. This is not to say, of course, that the message can be conveyed as effectively and powerfully without images as with them; but a message articulated without images can be helpful in elucidating the intended meaning and in preventing misunderstandings such as the one cited by Spaemann (1973). Pairs of parables are particularly helpful as a guide to the right interpretation of either one; in particular, they can assist us in our attempts to draw a line between the narrative details (which are different in each parable) and the message (which should be articulated in a way that is consistent with both parables). For example, Maillot (1993:65) assumes that the idea of searching is very important to the parable of the pearl: one should look for the kingdom of God as the merchant in the parable searched for beautiful pearls. But although the idea of searching is consistent with Jesus' teaching (cf. "Seek and you will find," Luke 11:9), the twin parable of the hidden treasure helps us to establish that it is not part of the message of either parable (the man who found a hidden treasure was not searching for it).

In fact, other commentators (e.g., Eichholz 1984:116) emphasize the chance aspect of the discovery of the hidden treasure and see this as an important part of the message; some see this happy chance as a part of the message of both parables. For example, Linnemann (1966:117) points out that even for the pearl merchant, "it is a great piece of luck to discover an extremely valuable pearl. Admittedly, he is looking for pearls in the course of his job, but he was not looking for the pearl of great price. It just comes his way." Similarly, Dupont (1967/1968:414) states, "In both cases, it is a case of a lucky chance. The joy experienced by the worker highlights this aspect of the story. We have to do here with two men who have just made a discovery which represents their life's unique chance; the rest is there only to make the story picturesque."

Which point of view should we reflect in the explication, the search or the sheer luck? I think neither—both belong to the narrative fabric. What does matter is that there is this one unique thing which is always good for everyone and is hidden, in the sense that many people don't know about it: this thing is the kingdom of God. The "hiddenness" of the kingdom of God is emphasized by many commentators, and it has been allegorized in various ways. For example, Maillot (1993:58) says of the hidden treasure that "the key word (mot clef) of this parable is 'to hide' (cacher)": "Thus, the Kingdom of God is now hidden in the great field of the world"; he suggests that it is very important that "the man buys the *whole* field." Maillot deduces from this a need for accepting the world, in some sense, and seeing it as "a world which is more than just a world": it is "a world-which-contains-a-treasure." But although this line of thought is attractive, it seems to go beyond the shared message of the two parables. Speaking nonmetaphorically, I think that the "hiddenness" of the kingdom of God suggested by these two parables means that many people don't know about the unique chance and the highest good that living with God represents.

As I see it, the key point of the two parables is that there is something that is good for all people—incomparably good—and that many people don't know about it. Whether or not the knowledge of this great good comes to one as a huge surprise ("the greatest surprise of one's life," Eichholz 1984:124) is not part of the parables' message. As a first approximation, therefore, I would articulate the core message of the two parables as follows:

> there is one thing that is always good for all people
> a person can live with God
> if a person lives with God this is always good for this person
> nothing else is like this
> many people don't know this

The central idea in this explication is that people can live with God and that it is good for a person (read: "you") to do so—in fact, incomparably better than anything else. This is, then, the "pearl of great price" (or the "treasure"), which is so valuable that it is worth selling everything else for and "going for broke" (see Dodd 1965:85) to live with God. Nothing is better for a person than to possess this pearl of great price, and nothing is more worth striving for.

People's lives are often dominated by a desire to have good things happen to them, and their activities often have this end in view. All this can change, the parable suggests, if they find the pearl of great price: instead of thinking all the time, "I want good things to happen to me," they find the center of their life, their treasure, elsewhere (in living with God), and this will bring them joy and peace. But the treasure is hidden; the most beautiful pearl must be sought after. In another pair of twin images, the kingdom of God is likened to a very small seed, the mustard seed, which will grow into a great shrub, and to a tiny bit of leaven, which is hardly visible in three measures of flour but which is going to transform the whole dough. What all these images of smallness and hiddenness suggest is that many people don't know about the one thing that could transform their lives and satisfy their hearts' desires and that it is important for the addressee to become aware of the hidden treasure ("it will be good for you if you know this"; "you will not want anything else").

Closely related to the pearl and treasure parables is the whole family of texts contrasting transitory treasures, unrelated to the kingdom of God, and permanent treasures, pertaining to living with God, especially the following (Matt. 6:19-21; see Chapter 4, section 6):

19. do not lay up for yourselves treasures on earth, where moth and
    rust destroy and where thieves break in and steal;
20. but lay up for yourselves treasures in heaven, where neither moth
    nor rust destroys and where thieves do not break in and steal.
21. For where your treasure is, there your heart will be also.

(In the Gospel of Thomas, the reference to the treasure that "no moth comes to devour" is in fact combined into one saying, saying 76, with the reference to the merchant of pearls.) The emphasis in the treasure in heaven sayings is different from that in the parables of the pearl and the treasure, and each text deserves a full explication of its own. In all these texts, however, there is a chance of possessing a treasure, and nothing else is more worth aiming for.

The incomparable value of the pearl and the treasure suggests that, in fact, some sort of comparison *is* involved—a comparison with all other possible goals of human activity and objects of human desire, which are all discarded as incomparably inferior to the pearl and the treasure. Some of the other goals that people pursue may be like false pearls, like trash rather than treasure. This can be represented in universal human concepts as follows:

many people think something like this all the time:
    "I want good things to happen to me"
because of this, these people do many things
if these things happen to these people they are not always good for
    these people

The realization that there is one thing that is always unfailingly good for all people can free a person who has discovered this one thing from all other, often futile and disappointing pursuits and can make the person focus on that one value that cannot fail. Giving up those other pursuits will not then be seen as a loss and a sacrifice but as something potentially liberating. Knowing that one thing exists that is always good for all people and is not like anything else, and that one can have that thing, can make one want to give up everything else gladly:

if you know this you will not think all the time:
    "I want good things to happen to me"
you will think about God
you will want to live with God
you will know that you can live with God
you will feel something very good because of this
you will not want anything else

In fact, in the literature on the hidden treasure and the pearl, there is an ongoing debate about whether these parables should be seen in terms of sacrifice and cost or of investment. For example, Donahue (1990:68) observes that "traditionally, they (the Hidden Treasure and the Pearl) have been interpreted in terms of the 'cost of discipleship'—that is, like those who sell all they have to secure their discovery, disciples are to sacrifice all to respond to the proclamation of the kingdom." On the other hand, Hedrick (1994:119) speaks of the willingness to "invest all," Capon (1985:176) of "fabulous purchases," and Linnemann (1966:98) of "exceptional profit" (cf. also Derrett 1970:6).

Jeremias has commented on this point:

> These two parables are generally understood as expressing Jesus' demand for complete self-surrender. It is really quite misunderstood if it is regarded as an imperious call to heroic action. The key-words are rather 'in his joy'. . . . When that great joy, beyond all measure, seizes a man, it carries him away, penetrates his inmost being, subjugates his mind. All else seems valueless compared with that surpassing worth; no price is too high, and the unreserved surrender of what is most valuable becomes a matter of course. (1966b:158)

Similarly, according to Boucher,

> The emphasis in both parables is on the joy of discovering a thing of supreme value. These parables are not intended as a call to self-sacrifice; the stress is not on what must be given up in order to buy a valuable object. The point lies in the surpassing worth of the treasure compared to which all else seems worthless. The find is of such value that the discoverer, overjoyed, is glad to pay any price. This is how the true disciple responds to the discovery of the reign of God. (1981:107)

I think that my (partial) explication is consistent with such observations. The metaphor of cost and the notion of sacrifice imply that one does something that one, on one level at least, doesn't want to do and that one feels something bad because of this (even though one is doing these things intentionally and so, on another level, wants to do them). The explication proposed here doesn't include any references to feeling something bad; on the contrary, it includes references to feeling something good (the joy, the gladness). Nonetheless, it doesn't exactly follow the metaphor of investment either. Although the finder of the treasure and the pearl merchant may indeed have been shrewd, resourceful, and calculating, (like the dishonest steward in another parable; see chapter 21), and although they may have done their cost-benefit analysis, this is not part of the message either and has not been included in the explication. There are no references in the explications to thinking about bad things and good things that will happen to one because of one's decision, with no weighing of the consequences. McKenna's (1994:16) phrase "shift of priorities" ("there is some sort of shift of priorities going on in the story") is more apposite here, I think, than either investment or shrewdness: it is a shift from wanting some things to wanting something else more, rather than a process of calculating "what is best for me."

On the other hand, what I think *is* part of the message and *should* be included in the explication is the apparent foolhardiness of throwing everything else to the winds, the foolishness of such an act in the eyes of the world, contrasted with the subjective certainty of the person who found the treasure that this indeed is a treasure and a valid ground for rejoicing. I formulate this as follows:

> when you want to live with God you will do many things because of
>   this
> many other people will say that it is bad for you to do these things
> you will know that this is not true
> because you will know that it is good for you to live with God
> you will know that nothing else is like this

Wanting to live with God will naturally lead one to some actions that other people will see as foolish and not in one's interest (such as selling all one's possessions to buy one pearl or one field); but the person who has discovered the joy of living with God will have a different view of what is really good for him or her. This bring us to the following overall explication:

(a) many people think something like this all the time:
    "I want good things to happen to me"
(b) because of this these people do many things
(c) if these things happen to these people
    they are not always good for these people

(d) there is one thing that is always good for all people
(e) a person can live with God
(f) if a person lives with God this is always good for this person
(g) nothing else is like this
(h) many people don't know this

(i) if you know this you will not think all the time:
    "I want good things to happen to me"
(j) you will think about God
(k) you will want to live with God
(l) you will know that you can live with God
(m) you will feel something very good because of this
(n) you will not want anything else

(o) when you want to live with God you will do many things because
    of this
(p) many other people will say that it is bad for you to do these things
(q) you will know that this is not true
(r) because you will know that it is good for you to live with God
(s) you will know that nothing else is like this

According to Dodd (1965:85), "The only real question which arises in the interpretation of the Hidden Treasure and the Pearl is whether the *tertium comparationis* is the immense value of the thing found, or the sacrifice by which it is acquired." On balance, Dodd believes that the focus is on the latter rather than on the former because for Jesus' addressees, the value of the kingdom of God would have been something that they took for granted. Accordingly, Dodd summarizes Jesus' intention in both the hidden treasure and the pearl as follows: "You agree that the Kingdom of God is the highest good: it is within your power to possess it here and now, if, like the treasure-finder and the pearl-merchant, you will throw caution to the winds: 'Follow me!'" (p. 86)

My explication is not entirely consistent with Dodd's (1965) remarks, and I do not think that it should be. The emphasis on the *Sitz im Leben* (the setting of a particular saying in Jesus' life) can sometimes obscure the universal meaning of Jesus' parables and other sayings. Even if Jesus' first addressees took it for granted that the kingdom of God was the highest good, there is no reason to assume that his message was aimed exclusively at them. Furthermore, the Gospels as a whole show that the metaphor of the kingdom of God didn't mean the same for Jesus as it did for all his contemporaries. I would argue, therefore, that it *was* living with God that Jesus wanted to present as the hidden treasure, the pearl of great price, and that his purpose was not restricted to the injunction "Follow me," aimed at his first listeners. As in his other parables of the kingdom (e.g., the mustard seed and the leaven), here, too, Jesus was *telling* people about the kingdom of God (the possibility of living with God) and not only urging those physically present to avail themselves of this opportunity.

Dodd's (1965) words "here," "now," and "caution" also raise some questions relevant to the optimal phrasing of the explication, and so do the words "risk" and "opportunity," used by many other commentators (see, e.g Linnemann 1966:100–101). As the explication now stands it doesn't include any references to "here" and "now," and I am not convinced that it should. Undoubtedly, the concept of now does play an important role in Jesus' teaching as a whole, especially in the parables that focus on the need for watchfulness, but it is not clear that either the treasure or the pearl parable focuses on the need to do anything *right now*. It is true that in the narrative fabric of the two stories it is important for the protagonist to act decisively and promptly, to sell everything and to buy the pearl or the land without delay. But the message of the two parables seems to concentrate on something else: roughly speaking, on the pricelessness of the pearl or the treasure; on the desirability and wisdom of acquiring them, whatever the price, and on the joy inherent in doing so. If the message were concerned also with the need for a quick decision and for prompt action, as well as with the uniqueness of the opportunity, which may otherwise be lost, it would perhaps be uncharacteristically overloaded and pointing in a number of different directions all at once. On balance, therefore, it seems to me more justified to keep the explication as it is (and it is quite complex as it is), without introducing considerations of urgency and the need to act now, important as they are in other parables.

The same applies to caution and risk taking. It is true that the pearl merchant and the treasure finder do not behave cautiously and take what seem to be enormous risks. But how relevant are these aspects of their behavior to the parables' message? From Jesus' point of view, choosing the pearl of great price is not really a risk but the only safe choice (like building one's house on the rock); so throwing caution to the winds is not really the point.

Hedrick (1994:132) has claimed that the hidden treasure is a "polyvalent" story, with multiple interpretations; and he has noted that different commentators (e.g., Crossan 1979; Derrett 1970;Scott 1981) have come up with different assessments of the man who found the treasure: "Matthew regarded him as a 'wise' man; Scott sees him as a foolish man who sold everything to possess a treasure he could not use; to Crossan he is an immoral shyster; Derrett regards him as a shrewd man who obeyed the letter of the law; and I have described him as a resourceful, decisive man." Hedrick concludes, "One must attribute the multiplicity of interpretation to the universal and nonspecific making of the story. Its imprecision creates a 'polyvalence' that leaves it open to many possible readings, none of which in the final analysis exhausts the story" (p. 132).

However, if we look beyond the narrative details and try to grasp the underlying message and if we interpret this message in the light of the twin parable of the pearl the alleged "polyvalence" of the parable of the hidden treasure will disappear. The character of the man who found the treasure is simply irrelevant to the message: the lack of any definite information on this point makes the parable neither polyvalent nor imprecise. Rather, it shows that the point of the parable must be sought elsewhere.

According to Blomberg (1990:279), the message of the hidden treasure and the pearl can be formulated in one short sentence: "The Kingdom of God is so valuable that it is worth sacrificing anything to gain it." Funk et al. (1993:515) have summed up this message in a similar short formula: "God's imperial rule [i.e., the kingdom of God] is worth a priceless pearl, which one will do well to acquire no matter what the cost." Clearly, formulas of this kind can provide only a very rough summary, but to my mind these particular ones are sounder and more useful than interpretations that attribute to the story polyvalence, imprecision, and an unlimited multiplicity of readings. The explication proposed here aims at a higher level of accuracy and explicitness than such formulas, but it continues the earlier interpretive tradition in searching for the most plausible and best justified reading and in not shying away from the basic question: "What did Jesus mean by that?"

EIGHT

The Leaven and the Mustard Seed

The leaven (Luke 13:20–21)

20. And again he said, 'to what shall I liken the kingdom of God?
21. It is like leaven, which a woman took and hid in three measures of
    meal till it was all leavened.'

The mustard seed (Matthew 13:31–32)

31. Another parable he put forth to them, saying: 'The Kingdom of
    heaven is like a mustard seed, which a man took and sowed in
    his field
32. which indeed is the least of all the seeds; but when it is grown it is
    greater than the herbs and becomes a tree, so that the birds of
    the air come and nest in its branches.'

The mustard seed (Thomas 20)

20. The followers said to Jesus, 'Tell us what heaven's kingdom is
    like.' He said to them, 'It is like a mustard seed. It is the
    smallest of all seeds, but when it falls on prepared soil, it
    produces a large plant and becomes a shelter for birds of
    heaven.'

In their "Red letter edition" of the parables of Jesus, the spokesmen for the Jesus
Seminar, Funk et al. (1988:90), place the parable of the leaven in both Luke's

and Matthew's versions at the very top of all "red vote" parables, one that "transmits the voice of Jesus as clearly as any ancient record can" (Funk et al. 1993:195). The Fellows of the Jesus Seminar also agreed that the mustard seed parable originated with Jesus (p. 346) and give its simplest version (in Thomas' Gospel) a red designation. Explaining the Fellows' extremely high ratings for the mustard seed, Funk et al. write,

> In the original form of this parable, Jesus compares Heaven's imperial rule to the mustard weed [sic]. The mustard seed is proverbial for its smallness. It is actually an annual shrub, yet in Matthew (and in Luke) it becomes the largest of all garden plants, and is then blown up into a tree. . . . As Jesus used it, however, the image of a lowly garden plant, a weed, is a surprising figure for God's domain. The mustard seed is a parody of the mighty cedar of Lebanon and the apocalyptic tree of Daniel. It pokes fun at the arrogance and aspirations connected with that image. (1993:194–195)

Of the parable of the leaven, Funk et al. (1993:195) write, "Jesus employs the image of the leaven in a highly provocative way. In Passover observance, Judeans regarded leaven as a symbol of corruption, while the lack of leaven stood for what was holy. In a surprising reversal of the customary associations, the leaven here represents not what is corrupt and unholy, but God's imperial rule—a strategy the Fellows believe to be typical of Jesus." In addition, the authors point out that the parable of the leaven "exhibits marks of oral tradition," that it "is short and tightly composed and has no superfluous words," and also that its phrasing in Matthew and Luke is virtually identical and thus shows no signs of editing by either of the evangelists.

Thus, the authenticity of the two parables is not in question: although Matthew and Luke may have edited the mustard seed (in contrast to the leaven) in some details, nobody doubts that both these short and rather cryptic parables originated with Jesus. Furthermore, nobody doubts that they occupy an important place in Jesus' teaching and that in fact they contain "one of the central elements of the preaching of Jesus" (Jeremias 1972:89).What *is* very much in question is their meaning; and here, the range of differences among scholars is very wide indeed. Rather than discussing these differing views in any detail, however, I will propose my own reading of the two parables, focusing in particular on the leaven, and referring to the literature only in a very selective way.

Let me start by listing, in a loose form, a number of themes that most commentators agree are evoked by this parable. The most obvious is the theme of transformation: the yeast (or leaven) thoroughly transforms the dough. Another theme is hiddenness: people can't see the yeast in the dough (at first, it is hidden in the flour and, later, it is invisible in the dough). The hiddenness is linked with mysteriousness: most people don't know exactly how the yeast operates. People do see, however, the final result of the yeast's operation: they see the big loaf of bread at the end.

There is also the theme of the limited capacity of human effort: the woman does have to do something (put the yeast in the flour and, no doubt, knead it);

however, it is not really the woman's effort that makes the dough grow but the hidden power of the yeast. While the yeast does its work, people cannot contribute much; they must be patient and let the yeast exercise its power. But exercise its power it will, and there is no doubt about it: the result cannot not happen. Hence the theme of irresistibility, which is closely linked with the theme of certainty: one can be quite certain of the result. In any case, the woman-baker is above all an image of God. Evidently, God, too, has to be patient.

In addition to being irresistible, the action of the yeast is all-embracing: it will not cease until all the whole flour is leavened. The result of the process will be surprising, indeed astonishing, because of the spectacular contrast between the tiny amount of the yeast used at the outset and the huge amount of flour transformed into bread at the end (in the parable, enough to feed a hundred people—obviously, a quantity whose magnitude is symbolic). Finally, the irresistible force of the yeast means that there is a close inner link between the initial and the final stage of the whole process: while the dough is growing gradually, the relationship between the yeast and the bread is not gradual; the power of the yeast is an inherent property of the yeast and is as miraculous as the outcome: it is not so much the process of growth that is astounding as the contrast between the small amount of the yeast and its spectacular final effect (see Crossan 1992:49–50).

All these themes, frequently discussed in the literature, readily lend themselves to interpretation of the parable's central topic, as stated by Jesus: "to what shall I liken the kingdom of God?" Since the parable is not an allegory (as established by Jülicher [1888]1963 a century ago), it would not be illuminating or appropriate to start with such questions as: "What does the flour stand for?" and "Who does the woman stand for?" Rather, we need to delineate the larger picture, treating the references to a woman, flour, and yeast as clues rather than as distinct symbols charged with independent meanings.

The most important clue of all is Jesus' explanation that the parable is meant to tell people about the kingdom of God—not everything there is to tell because there are other parables about the kingdom, with different meanings or a different emphasis, but *some* things. Since a parable, even a short one, usually conveys a complex and richly developed message, the elements of the parable of the leaven can be expected to be interrelated and to constitute a coherent whole, with a linear as well as a stereoscopic structure. I start the explication of this whole as follows:

(a) God wants all people to live with God
(b) some people think: this cannot happen
(c) I say to you: it can happen, God wants it to happen

As argued throughout this book, the kingdom of God refers, essentially, to people living with God. In some parables, this living with God is presented from the *people's* point of view (e.g., as a pearl of great price or a hidden treasure, to be sought and found), and in others it is represented from *God's* point of view. In the parable of the leaven, the latter is the case: God has a goal (to establish a kingdom of God, just as the woman-baker has a goal: to bake a large quantity of bread)—hence the first line of the explication: "God wants all people to live with God."

The insignificant amount of yeast used, and perhaps also the polluted and dirty nature of leaven in Jewish everyday life and in Jewish religious symbolism, make God's goal seem impossible to achieve ("some people think: this cannot happen"). On the level of religious interpretation, the apparent impossibility of God's goal ever being realized is no doubt understood in terms of sin and evil, whose presence in the world must be obvious to everyone: how could all people ever live with God, given what everyone knows about human sinfulness and the human propensity for evil? To this incredulous (implicit) question, Jesus' parable gives a firm and confident answer: "I say to you: it can happen, God wants it to happen."

On what does Jesus base his confidence in the final "victory of God" (see N. T. Wright 1996)? As numerous commentators (in particular, Dodd 1965) have emphasized, Jesus' confidence is based on his assumption that something extraordinary is happening here and now, in first-century Palestine, and that this something creates the conditions for God's victory and, indeed, ensures that this victory will be a fact: Jesus gives people to understand that the Kingdom is breaking in in his own person, in his teaching, and in his life. As Witherington (1992:63) says of the parables of the leaven, mustard seed, and the seed growing secretly, they "suggest a connection between what is happening in the present in Jesus' ministry and what will happen in the future when the whole lump is leavened, or when the mustard seed produces its large bush, or when the seed growing secretly produces a harvest." Moltmann (1981:71) observes that "it is impossible to divide Jesus' proclamation of the kingdom from his person." Raymond Brown (1994:66), who refers to the parables of the leaven and the mustard seed in the context of a broader discussion of Jesus' understanding of who he was and how he saw his own role in the kingdom of God, says that they "show that there is both present activity and future climax in the Kingdom." The best solution to the debate about whether the kingdom of God was, according to Jesus, present or future is "along the lines that the kingly rule of God was already making itself present in Jesus' person, proclamation and actions, but the complete and visible manifestation of the kingdom lay in the future and would also be brought about through Jesus, the Son of Man" (p. 66). The component "something is happening here now" in the explication is an allusion to this inherent link between Jesus' proclamation of the kingdom and his own person. This brings us to the second part of the explication:

(d) something is happening here now
(e) many people don't know about it
(f) after some time all people will know about it
(g) because this is happening here now all people can live with God
(h) God wants this

Capon (1985:119) argues, with reference to the parable of the leaven, that God's "yeast" has been operating in the world since the beginning of creation

and that "there is not, and never has been, any unkingdomed humanity anywhere in the world." No doubt this statement makes good sense, but this doesn't
seem to be the sense in which Jesus likens the kingdom of God to yeast. Rather,
he is linking the act of adding the yeast to the flour with God's special intervention in human history through his own (Jesus') mission in the world; and this
is what the explication seeks to reflect. Component (d) refers to Jesus own life
(and death).

Component (d) is vague, but it would probably be a mistake to try to make it
more specific. The key point is that because of what is happening here now the
possibility of living with God is somehow open to all people: "(g) because this
is happening here now all people can live with God." Thus, Jesus' life and ministry do not mean that the kingdom of God has already come in its fullness,
because it is not yet the case that all people live with God; at the same time,
however, Jesus' life and ministry have created the conditions for this final fullness and have started the process, which is likened to the irresistible operation
of the yeast in the dough: "because this is happening here now all people can
live with God." This way of putting it is consistent with the views of commentators like Boucher (1981), Dodd (1965), and Jeremias (1972). According to
Boucher, "God's reign is thus both 'already and not yet'" (p. 69); and Dodd
says that "the coming of the Kingdom of God is in the teaching of Jesus not a
momentary event, but a complex of interrelated events including His own ministry, His death, and what follows, all conceived as forming a unity" (p. 131).

But what about the people who don't want to live with God? Will they be
forced to do so? Clearly, this is not what Jesus means. Jesus' other parables (e.g.,
the prodigal son) make it clear that nobody will be forced to live with God, indeed, that a person cannot live with God if he or she doesn't want to. The parable of the leaven does not contradict this view and in fact implicitly reaffirms it
with its strong emphasis on a thoroughgoing transformation: there will be no
leavened bread without the transformation of the dough. As his numerous
parables illustrate, Jesus does assume that some people don't want to live with
God: the invitees refuse the invitation to the feast, the sheep wanders off and
gets lost, the younger son decides to leave home and go to a distant country—
and when people don't want to live with God, they can't live with God: their
willingness is a necessary condition of entering the kingdom:

(i) some people don't want to live with God
(j) when a person doesn't want to live with God, this person cannot
        live with God

But, Jesus implies, it is only a matter of time. As Lambrecht (1991:167) says,
commenting on both the mustard seed and the leaven, "God's Kingdom is stronger than human refusal"—not that human refusal will be ignored but that it will
sooner or later melt away, presumably, under the influence of God's love (cf.
Maillot 1993:41).

This, then, is the meaning of the great transformation, suggested by the image of the yeast, which is fermenting a huge quantity of flour: because of God's

mysterious plan of salvation effected through Jesus himself, people will be "leavened" by God's power (presumably, the power of God's love) and will be transformed, so their resistance to God's love will disappear and they will *want* to live with God:

(k) because this is happening here now, something will happen to all people
(l) at some time, all people will want to live with God

How will this seemingly unlikely transformation occur? Jesus does not try to explain this. On the contrary, he hints (especially in the parable of the seed growing secretly) at the mysteriousness of the process: people don't know how it will happen and in fact they *can't* know how it will happen. What he does make clear—both here and in several other parables, including the mustard seed and the seed growing secretly—is that the process is not controlled by human action but by God; also, God's power (presumably, the power of God's love) is irresistible, and despite appearances its final victory is assured:

(m) people can't know how this will happen
(n) God knows this
(o) it will happen not because people will do some things
(p) it will happen because God wants it to happen
(q) it cannot not happen

Perhaps the most far-reaching aspect of the parable's meaning concerns its implicit intimation of universal salvation: "till it was all leavened." This insistence on completeness is not an accidental detail but an intrinsic aspect of the metaphor of leaven as used in Jesus' times. As several commentators have pointed out, this is how Paul, too, speaks (figuratively) about leaven: "A little leaven leavens the whole lump" (Gal. 5:9); "Do you not know that a little leaven leavens the whole lump?" (1 Cor. 5:6).

Thus, just as the image of one lost sheep out of a flock of a hundred emphasizes that every person matters, so does the image of a bit of leaven acting on three measures of flour (enough to feed a hundred people), "till it was all leavened." Although this message of totality was not traditionally emphasized in the commentaries on the parable of the leaven, recent commentators have increasingly turned their attention to this aspect. For example, Capon (1985:118-119) speaks of "the Word, who is the yeast that leaves not one scrap of this lump of a world unleavened," adding, "Take the 'whole' (*holon*) first. When Jesus says the *whole* is leavened, he's not kidding. The lump stands for the whole world. . . . The note of the *catholicity* of the kingdom, therefore, stands as the major emphasis of this parable." Herman Hendrickx, too, emphasizes the importance of the word *holon* in the parable:

The term *holon* ("all," "whole") found in both Pauline texts is also found as qualification of the end-term in Mt. 13:14 and Lk. 13:21, "till it was all leavened." One can be practically sure, therefore, that originally this parable, which was connected with the parable of the mustard seed, also had the adjective "small" qualifying "leaven" (cf. Gospel of Thomas). It expressed the contrast between the small, insignificant beginning of Jesus' ministry which scandalised the disciples, and the great final results, the fulfilment of the Kingdom of God. It is in this sense that the original parable should be explained. (1986:47)

Fitzmyer (1985b:1019), in his commentary on Luke's Gospel, makes a similar comment on Luke's version of the parable: "The Lucan parable compares the Kingdom of God with leaven and alludes to its power to affect the whole lump of dough into which it is mixed (or 'hidden'). The kingdom, once present in human history—even in a hidden way—cannot help but leaven the whole of it because of its characteristic active ingredients." In a similar vein, Kistemaker (1980:50) comments that "in the parable of the yeast, Jesus focuses attention on the internal power of the Kingdom which leaves nothing unaffected . . . the point of the parable is that the yeast, once added to the flour, permeates the entire batch of dough until every particle is affected"; and Hendrickx (1986:47) similarly remarks, "In this parable Jesus tells his disciples: in spite of the contrary appearances, my mission is the real beginning of the divine intervention which is going to transform the world. . . . The Kingdom is like what happens when leaven is put into meal and mysteriously transforms the whole mass from within."

Maillot (1993:40) makes a similar point about the mustard seed, suggesting that the birds, finding shelter in the branches of the great mustard shrub, represent the whole of creation:

This means that all Creation, absolutely all . . . will find refuge there . . . because—and this is what he [Jesus] wants to show—a day will come when the smallest thing will be the greatest, and when indeed it will be the only thing which remains. There will be nothing then but that Kingdom which will shelter all in its shade, even these birds which could have devoured it [in the parable of the sower] at the beginning; the Kingdom which will restore everything. The only thing which will remain then will be the great tree of life: the Cross will project its redemptive shadow upon everything and everyone. The great tree which will shelter the forest of history, finally at peace. (1993:40)

Not all commentators who speak about the message of the leaven or of the mustard seed in terms of "totality" or "allness" (rather than merely "great size") interpret it explicitly as universal salvation. As the quotes above illustrate, the relevant comments are often somewhat vague and metaphorical, and it is not always clear what the authors have in mind when they emphasize the universal scope of the two parables (especially of the leaven). Nonetheless, comments of this kind are illuminating and I think broadly supportive of the interpretation proposed here. As Maillot (1993:184–188) says in connection with the Lost Sheep, God "wouldn't consent to become an owner of ninety nine sheep. Because even if only one of his sheep were missing . . . his happiness as God would be finished, his joy as God would be extinguished, he would only see the one sheep which was missing. . . . A single human being abandoned would mean the net of God's mercy had been torn for ever. A single creature forgotten by God, and the Cross itself (where there hangs in agony a single abandoned human being) would be denied and repudiated." It seems clear that what applies to the lost sheep applies also to the leaven: if a single lump of dough failed to grow, the whole irresistible force of the yeast on which Jesus insists would be called into question; there would no more be any question of God's kingdom being "stronger than human refusal" (Lambrecht 1991:167) or of the final victory of God.

I propose, then, the following overall explication for the parable of the leaven and also for its twin, the parable of the mustard seed:

The leaven and the mustard seed

(a) God wants all people to live with God
(b) many people think: this cannot happen
(c) I say: it can happen, God wants it to happen

(d) something is happening here now
(e) many people don't know about it
(f) after some time all people will know about it
(g) because this is happening here now, all people can live with God
(h) God wants this

(i) sometimes people don't want to live with God
(j) when a person doesn't want to live with God, this person cannot live with God

(k) because this is happening here now something will happen to all people
(l) at some time all people will want to live with God

(m) people can't know how this will happen
(n) God knows this
(o) it will happen not because people will do some things
(p) it will happen because God wants it to happen
(q) it cannot not happen

In phrasing the first part of the explication [(a)–(c)], I have tried to allude to the astonishment that many commentators (e.g., Crossan 1992:38, 50) sense in the message of these parables. At the same time, I have refrained from attributing to Jesus the direct declaration "it will happen," replacing it with a confident but not declaratory statemen, "it can happen, God wants it to happen." I have done so in accordance with the widespread conviction in Christian theology that universal salvation should be treated as a matter of hope rather than as a matter of certain knowledge (cf., e.g., Balthasar 1986; Hryniewicz 1990; Moltmann 1967); and in fact this is the best and the only justifiable reading of Jesus' intimations on the subject. Even if the hope of universal salvation is experienced as "firm and unshakeable" (in the phrase of St. Isaac of Niniveh, 1984:77), it is widely felt not to be a suitable subject for doctrinal assertions. The eminent Protestant theologian Karl Barth expressed this intuition in the following formula: "Whoever doesn't believe in the apokatastasis [i.e., universal salvation] is an ox, and whoever teaches it [as a doctrine] is an ass" (quoted in Hryniewicz 1990:41). According to some commentators, the doctrine of *apokatastasis* as formulated by Origen was officially condemned by the early Church (in 543) precisely because he formulated it as a doctrinal certainty and not as a subject of Christian hope.[1]

The second part of the explication [(d)–(h)] refers to the kingdom of God, "breaking in" in Jesus' own life and ministry. As Dodd (1965:142) says, with special reference to the mustard seed, "We must suppose that in this parable Jesus is asserting that the time has come when the blessings of the Reign of God are available for all people." This breaking in of the kingdom is not yet widely perceived or understood—it is hidden—but its consequences will be visible to everyone. The third part [(i) and (j)] acknowledges people's freedom to reject the kingdom of God. Admittedly, this theme is expressed more explicitly in such parables as the great feast or the prodigal son than in the mustard seed or the leaven. However, the idea of the transformation of human hearts, evoked by the image of the leaven (and also of the metamorphosis of a seed into a shrub) is at least consistent with the assumption that the kingdom will not be imposed on people but that they will really change. The fourth part [(k) and (l)] spells out this transformation that will occur in people's hearts, turning them toward God, and it links it to the onset of the kingdom of God. (See Maillot's 1993:41 comment on the mustard seed: "Christ introduced love into the world, that love which will never perish.") Finally, the fifth part ([(m)–(q)] refers to God's mysterious, hidden, and yet irresistible power (the power of love), which will accomplish this astonishing transformation.

Perhaps the most debatable component is the last one—"it cannot not happen"—which may seem open to the charge of determinism of salvation, denying human freedom. I emphasize, therefore, that this component (posited only very tentatively) refers to the transformation of the human will and not to universal salvation as such. The explication doesn't say, "all people will live with God," and "this cannot not happen"; it says, "at some time all people will want to live with God," "this cannot not happen." As it is phrased here, it reaffirms the doctrine of human freedom and the voluntary nature of salvation: nobody will be forced to live with God; on the contrary, when a person doesn't want to live with God, this person cannot live with God.

And yet the image of the small quantity of leaven, transforming, in an invisible way, a huge quantity of flour, suggests something irresistible about the power it represents (the power of God's love). What the parable intimates is not that people will be pulled into the kingdom of heaven against their will, or regardless of their will, but that they will themselves turn toward God in a mysterious process of inner transformation (whether before a person's death or after, as envisaged in the fourth century by Gregory of Nyssa and increasingly by modern Christian theologians).

As argued by Hryniewicz (1996:173), when the church rejected the doctrine of *apokatastasis*, "it understood it as a kind of determinism of salvation in the form of an obligatory amnesty on the part of God." In doing so, "the Church was defending the faith in people's responsibility for their bad deeds, referring to the warnings and admonitions of the Scriptures." In the process, Hryniewicz suggests, "there occurred some monumental misunderstandings—the real intention of those who professed a hope of salvation for all people was not rightly understood"; and he asks, "how can this hope be rescued?"

As the new theology that is trying to rescue this hope is well aware, one way of pursuing this goal is to explore in greater depth Jesus' parables and other relevant sayings. The parable of the leaven is a good case in point:

> We find in the Gospels a disturbing question addressed by someone to Jesus: "Lord, will only few be saved?" (Luke 13:23). It is noteworthy that the Evangelist placed this question in the chapter which opens with a call for conversion (Luke 13:1–9), and then shows in a parable an astonishing growth of the Kingdom of God, compared to a mustard seed and to the leaven (Luke 13:18–21), which leavens "everything." He doesn't declare universal salvation. He calls to conversion and warns: "Try to enter through the narrow gate" (Luke 13:24). (Hryniewicz 1990:72)

The Lucan Jesus doesn't proclaim universal salvation and evades the question about the number of those to be saved by responding with a warning and a call to conversion. At the same time, the parable of the leaven does suggest an answer to the question, although in an indirect way, as does also the parable of the lost sheep, which in Luke's Gospel comes close on its heels (Luke 15:1–7). It is debatable whether Jesus' implicit answer warrants the explicit component "all people will live with God" in the explication. Arguably, it is significant that Jesus does not state this promise *expressis verbis* and only intimates it through images. But as far as the transformation willed by God is concerned the images seem eloquent enough. In fact, it is striking how often those commenting on the parable of the leaven emphasize its *irresistible* power. For example, Manson ([1937]1961:122) states that "the obvious point" is that "once the beginning has been made, the result is inevitable . . . a process has been started which *must* go on to its inevitable end. . . . Once the leaven has been put into the dough the leavening process goes on inevitably till the whole is leavened." Fitzmyer (1985b:1019) refers to the two parables as "stressing the inevitable growth of the Kingdom and its active power"; Dodd (1965:143) refers to the leaven as "propagating itself . . . by a kind of infection"; Capon (1985:123) remarks that "no matter what you do, the yeast works anyway"; Kistemaker (1980:49) speaks of the leaven's "hidden power"; and so on. Given this widespread perception that the action of the leaven is meant to be seen as irresistible (and the growth of the mustard seed as unstoppable), I am inclined to think that the inclusion of the component "it cannot not happen" in the explication is justified.

Let me quote in this connection the comments on the "omnipotence of God's love" and its relation to the sinner's "freedom of choice" by the Anglican theologian John A. T. Robinson:

> With equal conviction as it declares the awfulness of the decision [against God], the Gospel asserts that the final reality for the subject is not the final description of the universe in God. To all as to each, the impossible, that on which no one can presume, must happen. Hell, so limitless to the man who has chosen it, is still bounded by the "nevertheless" of the Divine love. And that love must win. . . . This love will take no man's choice from him; for it is precisely his choice that he wants. But its will to lordship is inexhaustible and ultimately unendurable: the sinner must yield. (1950:122-123)

Although I haven't spelled this out in the explication, it is hard not to think of the irresistible leaven in Jesus' parable as an image of love. It is also hard not to think that Isaac of Niniveh must have been thinking of this parable when he said that "God's love embraces and transforms everything" and that "a time will come when no part will be missing from the whole" (from an unpublished work, quoted in Bettiolo 1990:339).

Turning to the parable of the mustard seed, we note different images but similar themes: the hiddenness of the seed (proverbially the smallest of all seeds); the inevitability of its growing (once planted); the consequent certainty of the outcome; the mysteriousness of this growth and its lack of dependence on human effort; the amazing transformation of a tiny seed into a large shrub; the shift from something hidden and imperceptible to something visible, tangible, and indeed spectacular. All these themes are emphasized in the literature in connection with the mustard seed as well as the leaven, as I will illustrate with a few representative quotes. Thus, Donahue (1990:67) remarks that both the mustard seed and the leaven "stress the hidden nature of the Kingdom." Fitzmyer (1985b:1019) says of the leaven and the mustard seed that they both stress "the inevitable growth of the Kingdom and its active power"; and he also says of the mustard seed that "the growth and development . . . are implied as taking place through the mysterious operation of divine power in the plant; that power is already operative."

Dodd (1965:134) says of the mustard seed that "the parable lays stress on the fact that growth is a mysterious process independent of the will of man"; and Borsch (1988:122-123) says (also in connection with the mustard seed) that "humans do not have that much to do with the growth that takes place . . . it is first and foremost the activity of God"; moreover, "humans bear responsibility but they are not finally in charge." Imbach observes that both the mustard seed and the leaven (and also the seed growing secretly) emphasize that

> the Kingdom of God is a sheer gift of grace: as the seed rises by itself and grows and develops while the farmer busies himself with his daily occupa-

tions, as the smallest of all seeds (known at the time) develops into a large bush without human assistance, and as the yeast ferments the flour without any further help from the housewife, so will also the Kingdom of God become reality by itself, when only people open their hearts to it. (1995:94)

Boucher (1981:76) speaks in connection with both the leaven and the mustard seed (and also the seed growing secretly) of the paradox that the reign of God is at once present and future. Just as the full-grown harvest or shrub is in some way already contained in the seed but does not yet exist, so God's reign is already breaking in with the words and works of Jesus but has not yet fully come. In the growing seed, the aspect given special emphasis is the mysteriousness and certainty of the event that is now in process; in the mustard seed, it is the contrast between the small beginnings and the great end; and in the Leaven it is the hiddenness of the energy already at work.

The theme of universality does not emerge as clearly in the mustard seed as it does in the leaven, but as illustrated earlier by a quote from Maillot it can be seen as consistent with the message of this parable, too. After all, what would be so astounding about the growth of the kingdom of God if this growth consisted only in an increase of numbers? If it is true that, as Paul says, God wants "all people to be saved and to come to the knowledge of the truth" (1 Tim. 2:4), then, as Hryniewicz (1990), Maillot (1993), and others have pointed out, a mere increase of numbers would represent a defeat rather than a victory of God.[2] But although the world doesn't seem to be heading in the direction of all people living with God, Jesus implies that the unlikely *will* happen in the end and that in fact the crucial process has already been set in train. The attainment of God's goal may seem as unlikely as the turning of a tiny seed (proverbially, the smallest of all) into the largest shrub in the whole garden, but—Jesus proclaims—it will definitely happen.

One is, of course, reminded in this connection of the other context in which Jesus reportedly invoked the proverbial smallness of the mustard seed in a simile: "If you had faith as a mustard seed, you would say to this mulberry tree, 'Be pulled up by the roots and be planted in the sea, and it would have obeyed you" (Luke 17:6). As emphasized by Scott (1981:76), the parable of the Leaven, with its emphasis on the hiddenness of the kingdom, stresses the need for faith: "To see leaven as compatible with three measures [of flour] demands faith on the hearer's part," and the same can be said about the mustard seed. It takes faith to believe in the final and total victory of God, but in his parables of the leaven and the mustard seed Jesus seems to be saying that such a victory is assured. Hendrickx observes about the parable of the leaven,

In its original form the parable drew attention to the contrast between the small amount of leaven and the exceptionally big amount of dough it leavens. . . . To compare the Kingdom of God to the action of leaven in dough is to say that the kingdom will not stop its working in the world 'until it is leavened' (Hosea 7:4), just as the leaven did not cease its activity 'till it was all leavened' (Mt. 13:33). (1986:50)

What else could this possibly mean if not the universal transformation of human hearts?

According to a number of commentators, both the metaphor of leaven and that of the mustard seed can and should be understood as referring to the future spread of the Gospel in the world. For example, Kistemaker remarks (with special reference to the mustard seed):

> By means of the parable, Jesus teaches that God's Kingdom may seem unimportant and insignificant, especially in Galilee of A.D. 28. But the gospel of the Kingdom proclaimed by a carpenter-turned-preacher will have a tremendous impact upon the world at large. Jesus' followers consisted of a few "uneducated" fishermen who were told to make disciples of all nations. These followers set the world on fire with the message of salvation, which today is proclaimed in nearly all the known languages of the world. The tiny seed sown in Galilee at the dawn of the new age of Christianity has become a tree which today provides shelter and rest to people everywhere. And yet the day is not spent. (1980:47)

In this exposition the seed appears to stand for Jesus' word (as it does in the parable of the sower), and the large shrub, or tree, for Christianity. Thus, Kistemaker appears to be talking about the spread of the good news about the kingdom of God rather than about the kingdom of God itself. But was Jesus really interested in making predictions about the future course of history, about the growth and spread of his church and the future numbers of Christians? Wasn't he rather speaking about God and about the great mass of humanity, that is, about the kingdom of God that will transcend all history and geography? A kingdom to be realized in the future, but in *statu nascendi* now? And did he not say "all" ("whole") rather than "many"?

Another commentator, Blomberg (1990:284), identifies the "central point" of both the mustard seed and the leaven as follows: "The kingdom will eventually attain significant proportions despite its entirely inauspicious outset." Blomberg's summary, referring to the kingdom itself rather than to the news about it, is clearly more in line with Jesus' own introductory question ("to what shall I liken the kingdom of God?") than Kistemaker's (1980). On the other hand, if we assume that both the large plant (in whose branches the birds of the air can come and nest) and the leavened dough of eschatological (Meier 1980:149 says, "ridiculously large") proportions stand for the kingdom of God, Blomberg's statement that this kingdom "will eventually attain to significant proportions" seems to be a bit of an understatement. Is this all Jesus says God can achieve—a kingdom of "significant proportions"? But didn't Jesus say "till it was all leavened"? And did he not use an image of a ridiculously large amount of flour? Boucher (1981:75–76) comments on this last point as follows: "The quantity of meal, 'three measures' . . . is enormous: it is approximately 50 pounds or 40 litres of flour, which would produce enough bread to feed a hundred people. This hyperbolic feature demonstrates that we are dealing with divine realities." The hyperbolic character of the image, combined with the parable's insistence on the total scope of the outcome ("till it was all leavened") seems inconsistent with the interpretations suggested by summaries such as Blomberg's.

But it is not only the universal and holistic aspect of the image of the leaven that is transforming the dough that has profound theological implications; it is also its transformational aspect, or rather, the combination of these two aspects. What the parable suggests is that whereas all people will ultimately live with God, "like one thing," before this occurs a profound transformation must take place, presumably in people's hearts. This implication of a profound transformation is important because it frees the prospect of universal salvation from features of an obligatory amnesty, that is, those features that (rightly or wrongly) were attributed to Origen's version of *apokatastasis*:

> If out of pity and humanity we admit the necessity, i.e. the inevitability of universal salvation, we must deny the freedom of the creature. Origen's doctrine of apokatastasis contradicts his own doctrine of freedom. The salvation of the whole world, understood as a reinstatement of all in the condition prior to the Fall, is conceived as the result of an externally determined process independent of human freedom. All creatures will be compelled in the end to enter the Kingdom of God. . . .
>
> When Origen said that Christ will remain on the cross so long as a single creature remains in hell, he expressed an eternal truth. And yet we must admit that to regard salvation as predetermined is to rationalize the eschatological mystery. . . .
>
> The fundamental antinomy which confronts those perplexed by the problem of hell is this: human freedom is irreconcilable with a compulsory, predetermined salvation, but the same freedom rebels against the idea of hell as a predetermined doom. (Berdyaev [1937]1954:273)

The image of the leaven provides a vital clue in any attempt to deal with this antinomy. In the light of Jesus' teaching as presented in the Gospels, the universal scope of God's project cannot be in doubt, nor can Jesus' confidence that this project will ultimately succeed. At the same time, Jesus makes it very clear (e.g., in the parable of the great feast) that any compulsory universal salvation would not be consistent with that project, that it really is a matter of an invitation (as suggested by the image of a great feast). Without presuming to solve what Berdyaev ([1937]1954) refers to as an "eschatological mystery," we can nonetheless note that a transformation of human hearts would remove what looks like a contradiction: if the hearts and minds of people who don't want to live with God, or who don't put him ahead of other priorities, change, nothing will stand in the way of a voluntary and universal acceptance of that invitation. Thus, the image of an all-transforming leaven can be seen as an image of hope.

As mentioned earlier, Lambrecht (1991:167) says in connection with both the leaven and the mustard seed parables that "God's Kingdom is stronger than human refusal." Without the image of hidden and mysterious transformation, a statement like this could suggest that human refusal will simply be ignored by God; with the image, however, it can be understood as a way of highlighting the parable's confidence in that mysterious transformation.

As some commentators (e.g., Capon 1985:119) have pointed out, the image of the all-transforming leaven is also striking in its catholicity, that is, in the way it ignores any putative distinctions between the sinners and the righteous, the good and the bad; the whole mass of humanity, it suggests, is in need of a transformation:

> Human will which sharply divides the world into two parts imagines hell as an eternal prison house in which the "wicked" are isolated, so that they can do no more harm to the good. Such a conception is, of course, not divine but human through and through. It is the culmination of the life of our sinful world on this side of good and evil. The possibility of real victory over evil, i.e. of the regeneration of the wicked, is not even thought of. . . . (Berdyaev [1937]1954:275)

Yet it is precisely such a regeneration of human hearts—and not only of "the wicked" but also of all human hearts—that Jesus foresees in the parable of the leaven; and he does so, as Perrin (1976:158) says, with "supreme confidence." In the vision of the prophet Ezekiel (19:19), God speaks of the future restoration of Israel in terms of a transformation of hearts: "Then I will give them one heart, and I will put a new spirit within them, and take the stony heart out of their flesh, and give them a heart of flesh . . . and they shall be my people, and I will be their God." In his parable of the leaven, Jesus appears to be extending this vision to all people.

According to Gregory of Nyssa (1971:79-80), God "mingled himself" with human nature through Christ's incarnation, "in order that by this mingling with the Divine Being our nature might become divine, being delivered from death and set free from the tyranny of the adversary." This image of God "mingling himself" with humankind (through Jesus) so that all people may become transformed, purified, and saved appears to be a deliberate reference to Jesus' own image of leaven:

> This and the like teaching is contained in the great mystery of Divine Incarnation. For by mingling with humanity, and sharing all the characteristics of our nature, birth, nurture, growth, going even so far as to experience death, He effected all the results that we have previously described, delivering man from vice and healing the very author of vice [Satan]. For the healing of an ailment consists in the purging of the disease, even though the process is painful. (p. 83)

Gregory seems also to be deliberately echoing Jesus' parable of the leaven when he speaks of "the lump of our humanity"—using the same form, *furamatos*, which Paul (1 Cor. 5:6), whom he quotes, had used to say that "a little leaven leavens the whole lump"—and when he stresses this "lump's" inherent unity and Christ's role in it:[3] Thus Gregory says that even He Who through the resurrection was exalted along with His Godhead, just as in the case of our bodies the action of one of the organs of sense communicates a common sensation to the whole organism which is united with the particular part, so, inasmuch as the whole of our human nature forms, as it were, a single living being, the resurrection of the part extends to the whole, and in virtue of the continuity and unity of the nature communicates itself from the part to the whole.

The images of a large amount of leavened flour and an unexpectedly large plant complement the images of the lost sheep and the lost coin in yet another important way, insofar as the latter two highlight the final destiny of every individual, whereas the former two bring to mind the final destiny of humankind as a whole. In both pairs, the message is that all people can live with God and that God wants this; and in both, the implication of the images is that God will bring about the desired result: the sheep will be brought back to the flock, the coin will be found, the seed will grow into a large plant, the flour will be transformed by the leaven, and the dough will grow. But in the case of the lost sheep and the lost coin, the emphasis is on the individual person; in the case of the leaven (and perhaps also the mustard seed), the emphasis is on all people: all people will be transformed, all people will want to live with God, and, arguably, all people will be (in some sense) like one thing, finally united through their common desire to live with God.

It is interesting to note in this connection Perrin's (1976:158) statement that the parable of the mustard seed "looks from the present beginning to the future consummation" and implies that the process will be consummated "in a moment when all people come *together* [my emphasis] into the Kingdom of God." Not only does Perrin not hesitate to let *all* people into the kingdom of God, but also he views this universal salvation from a collective rather than individual point of view: "all people come *together* into the Kingdom of God."

The image of leaven, fermenting the whole mass of dough, is also strikingly consistent with the idea of the essential unity of all humankind, developed by Christian theologians such as, for example, Paul Tillich or Sergius Bulgakov (1976:126–127), who stated that "the soul of Orthodoxy is *sobornost'* . . . in this one word there is contained a whole confession of faith." As Bulgakov comments, the noun *sobornost'* is derived from the verb *sobirat'* 'to gather' and so *sobornost'* is "the state of being gathered together." Writing in the tradition of Eastern Christianity, Bulgakov clearly links the idea of human solidarity and togetherness with the hope of universal salvation. Writing from a different perspective, Tillich (1964:434–435) makes a similar point: "Christianity was indirectly influenced by the strong dualistic tendencies in the later period of Hellenism. . . . The doctrine of unity of everything in divine love and in the Kingdom of God deprives the symbol of hell of its character of 'eternal damnation'."

At this stage, however, I have refrained from adding to the explication of the parable of the leaven a component along the lines of "when this happens all people can be like one thing," first, because I am not sure what the optimal phrasing should be and second, because I am not sure that it really *is* part of this parable's intended message. The unity of all humankind as part of God's purpose is expressed quite explicitly (though still figuratively) in sayings such as those attributed to Jesus in John (10:16): "And other sheep I have which are not of this fold; them also I must bring, and they will hear my voice; and there will be one flock and one shepherd." In the parable of the leaven, the idea of human unity is suggested by the image but perhaps is not part of the parable's intended message. (See, however, Paul's words in 1 Cor.10:17, curiously reminiscent of this parable: "For we, being many, are one bread and one body.")

According to Perrin, the parable of the leaven speaks about

> the activity of God as King. The beginning of the activity in the experience of people confronted by the challenge of Jesus and his ministry will reach its climax in the consummation of it, as the putting of leaven into meal reaches the climax in the batch of leavened dough. . . . The emphasis is upon God, and the parable, like all the parables in this group, is an expression of the supreme confidence of Jesus in God and God's future. (1976:158)

This confidence of Jesus in God and God's future, expressed in the parables of the leaven and the mustard seed, was shared by the Fathers of the church such as Clement of Alexandria (second century), who wrote about Christ and his mission of salvation as follows:

> Wherefore . . . all men are His. . . . He is Saviour not of some, and of others not. . . . And how is He Saviour and Lord, if not Saviour and Lord of all? But He is the Saviour of those who have believed . . . and the Lord of those who have not believed . . . for His exceeding love to human flesh, despising not its susceptibility to suffering, but investing Himself with it, came for the common salvation of men. (1962:524–525)

A hundred years ago, a similar confidence was expressed by the revivalist preacher Christoph Blumhardt, quoted recently with wholehearted approval by Jürgen Moltmann (1996:254): "There can be no question of God's giving up anything or anyone in the whole world, either today or in eternity. . . . The end has to be: Behold, everything is God's!"

How do the intimations of universal salvation implicit in the parables of the leaven and the mustard seed cohere with Jesus' dramatic warnings that one's life on earth is a unique opportunity, that this opportunity can be lost, and that losing one's life in that sense would be a matter of enormous regret and pain? At the threshold of a new millennium, theologians seem increasingly to accept that there is no contradiction here at all. In records of death-bed insights, many people see their earthly lives as wasted, and the world's great literature also provides rich testimony in this regard. On his deathbed, Ivan Ilyich, for example, sees his life was pretty much wasted. And yet how many readers of Tolstoy's immortal story would want to reject the possibility that salvation was still open to Ivan Ilyich?

Jesus' so-called parables of judgment (see, e.g., Capon 1989) do indeed embody a clear message about the possibility of losing one's life, in the way Ivan Ilyich lost his, and an urgent warning to everyone not to allow this to occur. But the unavoidable pain and regret of the realization that one has lost the unique opportunity of one's life on earth does not have to be interpreted as an objective "hell," that is, as an eternal and irrevocable separation from God. To interpret Jesus' symbolic images of that regret and pain as an ultimate defeat of God's plan to save the whole of humankind is to reject the message of parables like the lost sheep, the lost coin, the mustard seed, and the leaven.

NINE

The Lost Sheep and the Lost Coin

Luke 15:1–10; see Matthew 18:10–14

1. Then all the tax collectors and sinners drew near to him to hear him.
2. And the Pharisees and scribes murmured saying, "This man receives sinners and eats with them!"
3. So he spoke this parable to them, saying:
4. "What man of you, having a hundred sheep, if he loses one of them, does not leave the ninety-nine in the wilderness, and go after the one which is lost until he finds it?
5. And when he has found it, he lays it on his shoulders, rejoicing.
6. And when he comes home, he calls together his friends and neighbors, saying to them, 'Rejoice with me, for I have found my sheep which was lost!'
7. I say to you that likewise there will be more joy in heaven over one sinner who repents than over ninety-nine just persons who need no repentance.
8. Or what woman, having ten silver coins, if she loses one coin, does not light a lamp, sweep the house, and seek diligently until she finds it?
9. And when she has found it, she calls her friends and neighbors together, saying, 'Rejoice with me, for I have found the piece which I lost!'

10. Likewise, I say to you, there is joy in the presence of the angels of
     God over one sinner who repents."

The parable of the lost sheep, reported in both Luke's and Matthew's Gospels,
must be considered together with its twin, the parable of the lost coin, reported
only in Luke, because it is only when they are taken together that Jesus' underlying message becomes clear; there is no better commentary on the parable of
the lost sheep than the parable of the lost coin.

Both parables are about God and about God's love for all people. Many
commentators say, "God's love for *sinners*" rather than "God's love for *all people*"
and attribute to God a "special love" for sinners, indeed, a "preference" for sinners. Thus, Borsch (1988:62) that "not only does the story [of the lost sheep]
offer acceptance and inclusion without first requiring something of the lost, but
it once again expresses the divine bias towards those in greatest need." According to Dupont (1969:II, 247), too, sinners share this "bias" with the poor, and
"it is the miserable condition of the poor and sinners, and not any more meritorious moral dispositions, which make them the object of God's predilection
and of the tender solicitude of Jesus."

I think, however, that statements of this kind are misleading: God loves sinners not because they are sinners but because they are people; and God loves
all people. The point of these two parables is not that God loves some people
(sinners) more than he loves some other people (nonsinners) but rather that he
loves every single human being, and the fact that people are sinners does not
mean that God loves them less or is prepared to abandon them when they freely
but disastrously (for themselves) move away from him. God wants all people to
live with God. If 99 out of 100 people were to live with God, God would not
be satisfied because he would be intensely concerned about the one person who
was not living with him.

The images of one stray sheep, separated from the other 99, and of 1 coin,
separated from the other 9, do not mean that according to Jesus people can be
divided into two categories: those who are lost and those who are not lost; nor
do they mean that God values some people more than others. The striking image of the shepherd who leaves 99 sheep to look for the 1 that is lost is meant
to emphasize just how important each one is. The point is not, as is sometimes
said, that the 99 righteous persons are somehow less important to God than the
1 sinner; rather, it is that God knows and cares about every individual human
being.

It is therefore difficult to agree with Hendrickx' (1986:160) suggestion that
the "proportion of ninety-nine to one intends to emphasize the apparent lack of
importance of the one sheep. That it is sought is in the first place due not to its
own individual importance, but to the fact that it belongs to the flock. The flock
should be complete." On the contrary, the proportion of 99 (or 9) to 1 emphasizes the importance of *every* individual. Yes, the flock should be complete, but
this is not the only reason that every individual is important to God. Rather,
God loves every individual and has him or her carved in the palm of his hand
(Isa. 49:16).

Furthermore, Jesus' images suggest that God's love for every person is so great that it defies any attempts to quantify it. It is immeasurable, and so from the point of view of Jesus' teaching it doesn't make sense to say (except as a figure of speech) that God loves some people more than others. If God's love for every human being is immeasurable, it cannot really be graded and all comparisons are pointless. The point is not that God rejoices more over some people than over some others but that he loves and cares about every one among them—including those who by human standards might seem to be the least deserving of God's love. It is therefore a mistake to take literally Luke's rhetorical assertion in verse 15:7, as the following two quotes appear to do: "God rejoices more over one of these moral outcasts who repents than over ninety-nine righteous persons who do not need to repent" (Kistemaker 1980:209). "At the last judgment . . . God's joy over one repentant sinner will be greater than over ninety nine righteous who stayed on the right path" (Hendrickx 1986:149).

Rather than taking Luke's numerical formulations literally, we should see them as hyperbole, as suggested by Linnemann (1966:66): "The strangeness of the similitude is easily solved if it is understood as hyperbole, as an exaggerated representation to bring out what is at issue. The leaving behind of the ninety-nine to look for one lost sheep, this revaluation, '1 = more than 99', makes clear the emotion that is felt over a loss." The emotion is God's emotion over every individual loss, as well as every individual find. Just as the figure 77, given as the number of times that one should forgive one's brother (Luke 17:4), is symbolic and means "always," so the figure 99 is symbolic and means "none": none is more important to God than the one who is in danger of getting lost. As noted by Dupont (1969:II, 248–249), the apparent antithesis between sinners and the righteous is not found in the parable of the coin, which focuses entirely on the lost coin and doesn't concern itself at all with the remaining 9 coins. Thus, the two parables are not "doublets" (saying the same thing twice) but two stories that complement and elucidate one another (cf. p. 248). In particular, the parable of the lost coin provides a crucial commentary on that aspect of the parable of the lost sheep that appears to contrast sinners with the righteous: it makes it clear that the message is about the importance of every single sinner and that any comparisons and divisions between people are external to this message and, in fact, incompatible with it.

The figures (99 out of 100 or 9 out of 10) can also be seen to represent the notion of *majority* (most) rather than the notion of *totality* (all), and the idea that God cares about the majority rather than about the totality is dramatically rejected: God cares about *all* people, and he cares about every single one among them so much that any calculations in terms of majority versus minority are meaningless to him. He loves *all* people and he wants *all* people in his kingdom. He won't be satisfied with anything less than that.

Accordingly, we can start our analysis of the parables of the lost sheep and the lost coin with the following partial explication:

(a) God wants to do good things for all people
(b) God feels something because of this

(c) God wants all people to live with God
(d) if someone doesn't live with God God feels something bad because
    of this
(e) God wants this person to live with God

Not living with God is a great misfortune for a person, just like getting lost is a misfortune for a sheep; living with God is the best thing that can happen to a person, just as living with other sheep under the protection of the shepherd is the best thing that can happen to a sheep. This suggests the following two further components:

(d) if a person lives with God this is very good for this person
(e) if a person doesn't live with God this is very bad for this person

And yet sometimes a sheep goes astray, and a person looks for his or her happiness elsewhere and doesn't want to live with God. When this occurs, according to Jesus, God doesn't say to himself, "Too bad, I have lots of other people who do want to live with me; never mind this one." Rather, he undertakes an extraordinary pursuit of this one person, an extraordinary search—as if this one person were all that mattered.

The emphasis on the importance every individual "sheep" or "coin" in God's eyes has important implications for the question of universal salvation and the meaning of "hell." Jesus doesn't say anywhere explicitly that all stray sheep and lost coins will definitely be found; he doesn't make any predictions or forecasts about the future. Nonetheless, the images that he uses make it clear that God is supremely concerned about every individual sinner. Insofar as Jesus does imply anything about the future fate of the stray sheep, it is inextricably linked with what he intimates to people about God: what will happen to each and every sinner is that God will search for him or her and will not cease to do so until this particular sinner, too, is found—because God is like this.

Maillot states forcefully that

> since the bond between God and his creature is a thousand times stronger than a feeling of possession [which binds a shepherd to the sheep he owns], he will not consent to become 'a man with ninety nine sheep'. Because even if only one sheep were lacking, even if that bond were broken in only one case, God's happiness would be finished, his divine joy would be extinguished, and he would only see his one missing sheep. . . . This is why he will search for his lost sheep until he finds them. Because then he will find himself. Abandoning his lost sheep God himself would be lost. (1993:186)

Maillot's formulations may seem excessively bold, but in fact they do no more than articulate, in vivid and dramatic language, the implications of Luke's phrases "until he finds it" (15:4) and "until she finds it" (15:8). They are also fully consistent with the striking and bold images of the two parables. The image of a shepherd who is abandoning the whole flock to search for a single lost sheep is arresting enough. Even more arresting or indeed shocking is the image of God as a housewife, sweeping the floor (perhaps even getting down on all fours) to search for a single lost coin (i.e., a single sinner). The image of God in such a role is so extraordinary that even today some commentators find it too much to swallow. Even a radical modern writer like John Dominic Crossan feels compelled to reject the image of God as a housewife with a broom, even though this forces him to reject the image of Jesus and/or God as a good shepherd as well. Accordingly, Crossan comments on the lost sheep and the lost coin as follows:

> We have already seen . . . that the seeker of the lost sheep and the lost coin is *not* Jesus and/or God but the one who is open to and seeking the Kingdom's advent. The tradition admitted as much by being ready to accept Jesus as the Good Shepherd but not quite ready to have him as the Good Housewife. (1992:72)

In Crossan's (1992) interpretation God cannot be likened to a housewife, and since the role of a housewife is parallel to that of a shepherd, he cannot be likened to a shepherd either. As a result, it is a human "seeker" who becomes both the shepherd and the housewife, and God, or God's kingdom, becomes the stray sheep and the lost coin. Crossan seems to be forgetting that Jesus also compared himself to a hen when he lamented over Jerusalem: "O Jerusalem, Jerusalem, the one who kills the prophets and stones those who are sent to her! How often I wanted to gather your children together, as a hen gathers her brood under her wings, but you were not willing!" (Luke 13:34). He also seems to be forgetting that Isaiah (66:12) compared God to a woman who is suckling her child and carrying it on her hips and, elsewhere, to a woman in childbirth (42:14) or that Jesus depicts God as a woman-baker in the parable of the leaven.

The interpretation of the image of a shepherd—and, consequently, also a housewife—as referring to God is strongly supported by the use of this image in the Old Testament (see Borsch 1988:61), in particular, by the Prophets (e.g., Isa. 40:11; Jer. 31:10; and especially Ezek. 34:11–16):

11. For thus says the Lord God: 'Indeed I myself will search for my sheep and seek them out.
12. As a shepherd seeks out his flock on the day he is among his scattered sheep, so will I seek out my scattered sheep and deliver them from all the places where they were scattered on a cloudy and dark day. . . .
15. I will feed my flock and I will make them lie down, says the Lord God.
16. I will seek what was lost, and bring back what was driven away . . . and strengthen what was sick.'

Similarly, the psalmist cries out to God: "I have gone astray like a lost sheep, Seek your servant" (Ps.119:176).

I assume, then, contrary to Crossan (1992) and in accordance with the tradition, that both the shepherd's and the housewife's search symbolize God's search for sinners (rather than a human search for God), and I propose the following further components of the explication:

(f) when a person doesn't want to live with God
     God feels something bad because of this
(g) God wants this person to want to live with God
(h) God does many things because of this

Admittedly, the precise phrasing of these components is not without problems, but these have nothing to do with the impropriety of likening God to a housewife. The main problem is that the two parables do not include any overt (or even symbolic) reference to the sinner's not wanting to live with God. The coin simply gets lost, without any volition on its part, and whereas the Matthean sheep goes astray, the Lucan sheep is in fact lost by the shepherd. We could therefore consider an alternative phrasing of component (f) not referring to the person's will:

(f') when a person doesn't live with God God feels something bad
     because of this

I would nonetheless argue that the earlier phrasing is justified, if only by analogy with the parable of the prodigal son. The prodigal son certainly doesn't *want* to live with his father, and the willfulness of his departure is not in question. Arguably, the "lostness" of the person likened to a lost sheep can also be assumed to have something to do with this person's will. The image of a lost sheep is certainly compatible with a sheep that is willfully following its own desire for what seem to be greener pastures and more or less deliberately ignoring the call of the shepherd. As many commentators have emphasized, the focus of the parable is on the shepherd, not on the attitude of the sheep, and the twin parable of the lost coin reinforces this: there can scarcely be any question of the coin's attitude. Nonetheless the metaphor of a person's "lostness" does seem to suggest that the person chose the wrong way.

It can also be argued that the parables of the lost sheep and the lost coin complement, and are in turn complemented by, the parable of the prodigal son. In the first two, God (represented by the shepherd and the housewife) is active, whereas the sinner (represented by the lost sheep and the lost coin) appears to be a passive object of God's search. In the prodigal son, on the other hand, God (represented by the father) "waits at the window" (see Maillot 1993:220), whereas the sinner (represented by the younger son) returns home under his own steam. These differences, however, do not amount to inconsistencies but rather can be explained as differences in emphasis: the lost sheep and the lost coin emphasize that God does many things, whereas the prodigal son (as I will discuss in detail in chapter 10) emphasizes God's respect for the sinner's free will. The phrasing of the sinner's "lostness" in terms of "not wanting to live with God," and of

God's search for the sinner in terms of God's "wanting this person to *want* to live with God," is consistent both with the message of the prodigal son and with that of the lost sheep and the lost coin.

The parables of the lost sheep and the lost coin both complement and are complemented by the parable of the prodigal son in yet another important way. Just as God seems to be active in the two former and passive in the latter, so the sinner also seems to be active in the prodigal son (returning home and repenting) and passive in the lost sheep and lost coin. This apparent passivity highlights an aspect of Jesus' teaching that is justly emphasized by some commentators, that is, that God searches for the sinner before the sinner repents. Fitzmyer (1985b:1075) speaks in this connection of God's "gracious initiative," manifested "in the ministry of Jesus to 'sinners'—who are the 'lost'"; he notes that "the parable expresses what the Lucan Jesus will say of himself in 19:10, 'the Son of Man has come to seek out and to save what was lost'."

Admittedly, the prodigal son does repent first, but this is a narrative detail of that particular story, not a part of the message. As the lost sheep and the lost coin make clear, God's search for the sinner does not depend on the sinner's repentance: it is the knowledge of the lost condition of the sinner (of not wanting to live with God) that inspires God's compassion, and it is because of this compassion that God does many things. God does these things not in recognition of the sinner's repentance but in the hope of the sinner's conversion (or reversion to God); in other words, God hopes that the sinner will turn from not wanting to live with God to wanting to live with God. (As most commentators agree, the reference to "repentance" in Luke's verse 10 comes, in all probability, from Luke, for whom repentance is a favorite theme; cf., e.g., Fitzmyer 1985b:1075.)

Thus we arrive at the last segment of the scenario of God's search for the sinners:

(i) if afterwards this person wants to live with God
    God feels something very good because of this

This is God's great joy, symbolized by the shepherd's, and the housewife's, festive gathering of friends and neighbors—the joy that many commentators see as the main point of the parables of the lost sheep and the lost coin. Finally, as mentioned earlier, these parables are entirely focused on God: their main purpose is to describe and explain God (in his relation to people). I have included this point in the explication as its final and crowning component (j): "God is like this."

The lost sheep, and the lost coin

(a) God wants to do good things for all people
(b) God feels something because of this
(c) God wants all people to live with God
(d) if a person lives with God this is very good for this person

(e) if a person doesn't live with God this is very bad for this person
(f) when a person doesn't want to live with God
    God feels something bad because of this
(g) God wants this person to live with God
(h) God does many things because of this
(i) if afterwards this person wants to live with God
    God feels something very good because of this
(j) God is like this

TEN

The Prodigal Son

Luke 15:11–32

11. Then he said: "A certain man had two sons.
12. And the younger of them said to his father, 'Father, give me the portion of goods that falls to me.' So he divided to them his livelihood.
13. And not many days after, the younger son gathered all together, journeyed to a far country, and there wasted his possessions with prodigal living.
14. But when he had spent all, there arose a severe famine in that land, and he began to be in want.
15. Then he went and joined himself to a citizen of that country, and he sent him into his fields to feed swine.
16. And he would gladly have filled his stomach with the pods that the swine ate, and no one gave him anything.
17. But when he came to himself, he said 'How many of my father's hired servants have bread enough and to spare, and I perish with hunger!
18. I will arise and go to my father, and will say to him, Father, I have sinned against heaven and before you,
19. and I am no longer worthy to be called your son. Make me like one of your hired servants.'
20. And he arose and came to his father. But when he was still a great way off, his father saw him and had compassion, and ran and fell on his neck and kissed him.

21. And the son said to him, 'Father, I have sinned against heaven and in your sight, and am no longer worthy to be called your son.'
22. But the father said to his servants, 'Bring out the best robe and put it on him, and put a ring on his hand and sandals on his feet.
23. And bring the fatted calf here and kill it, and let us eat and be merry;
24. for this my son was dead and is alive again; he was lost and is found.' And they began to be merry.
23. Now his older son was in the field. And as he came and drew near to the house, he heard music and dancing.
26. So he called one of the servants and asked what these things meant.
27. And he said to him, 'Your brother has come, and because he has received him safe and sound, your father has killed the fatted calf.'
28. But he was angry and would not go in. Therefore his father came out and pleaded with him.
29. So he answered and said to his father, 'Lo, these many years I have been serving you; I never transgressed your commandment at any time; and yet you never gave me a young goat, that I might make merry with my friends.
30. But as soon as this son of yours came, who has devoured your livelihood with prostitutes, you killed the fatted calf for him.'
31. And he said to him, 'Son, you are always with me, and all that I have is yours.
32. It was right that we should make merry and be glad, for your brother was dead and is alive again, and was lost and is found.'"

The parable of the prodigal son has been rightly described as a condensed version of the Gospel as a whole: "a gospel in miniature" (Montefiore [1937]1968:525) and "Evangelium in Evangelio" 'Gospel within the Gospel' (Arndt 1956:350; Bailey 1976:206). It has also been described as the greatest of all of Jesus' parables (Compton 1930–1931:287) and, indeed, "the greatest short story ever told" (Sommer 1948). The literature on this parable is enormous, and although some of it is bizarre (see, e.g. Breech [1983]1987), many commentaries are highly insightful, informative, and illuminating. Nonetheless, it is also widely held that the exegesis of this parable is beset with difficulties. Some commentators, for example, Breech, even assert that "it is . . . certainly the most difficult [parable] to interpret" (p. 205).

The idea that a parable has a meaning that can be expounded in words other than the words of the parable itself is controversial; and given the exceptional beauty and perfection of the story of the prodigal son, some find the notion of such an exposition even more foolish in this case than in others. Thus, Te Selle (1975:13) insists that since "a parable is not an allegory, where the meaning is extrinsic to the story . . . [but] rather . . . an extended metaphor, the meaning is found only *within* the story itself, although it is not exhausted *by* that story." Te Selle's conclusion is that the images of the parable of the prodigal son "are not embellishments but *are* the meaning for there is no way to the meaning except through them" [my emphasis]. Accordingly, the idea of stating the meaning of the parable in an explicit form is rejected. "One *could* [author's emphasis] para- phrase this parable in the theological assertion 'God's love knows no bounds', but to do that would be to miss what the parable can do for our insight into such love" (see also Davidson 1984:262).

I agree that the sentence "God's love knows no bounds" would be entirely inadequate as a full representation of the parable's meaning, but this is not the only possible paraphrase. However, even such an inadequate paraphrase would be preferable, in my view, to some of the alternatives that have been proposed in the literature. To scorn, a priori, *all* paraphrases is in effect to put them all on an equal footing and to lose all capacity for discriminating among them. To try to elucidate the meaning of images in paraphrases is not tantamount to treat- ing images as mere embellishments. It goes without saying that paraphrases cannot *replace* images; this doesn't mean, however, that paraphrases are worthless and cannot be a useful heuristic device.

Parables should be seen as literature, acting on the audience by words and images; but they should also be seen as a form of teaching about God. These two ways of viewing them are not mutually exclusive, and to deny the validity of either would be unjustified. Lambrecht (1976:72) says that "it would be false to deny that the parable is a form of *teaching*. The fact that it can also be regarded as a 'language event'—a perfectly valid point of view—is not an obstacle to taking account of this other aspect." In any case, the fact that a parable is a "language event" is not independent of having a meaning; rather, it is an event that chal- lenges addressees to decode a hidden meaning, that is, "at the outset there is a moment of estrangement: what is the point of this story, what does this strange event mean . . . ? Then suddenly, mostly not without a shock, the meaning breaks through the image. The hearer understands the relevance, penetrates the image and sees what is at stake. There is a recognition of the narrator's intention" (Lambrecht 1991:78).

The real question, then, is not *whether* the hidden meaning of the prodigal son can be stated in words but *how* it can best be stated; and since the message of the parable is intended to be universal, we should try to state it in universal terms.

Given the close relationship between the prodigal son and the lost sheep and lost coin, we can start our explication of the former along similar lines:

(a) God wants to do good things for all people
(b) God feels something because of this
(c) all people can live with God
(d) God wants this
(e) when a person wants to live with God this person can live with God

Components (a) and (b) jointly represent God's love for all people and (d) represents God's desire for fellowship with all people, but (c) and (e) emphasize the fact that the possibility of living with God is open to all. This emphasis on the possibility of living with God, which is open to all, distinguishes the prodigal son from the lost sheep and the lost coin, where the focus is on God's desire and search for people. In the prodigal son, God's love for people is also very much in evidence, but there is a greater emphasis on the possibilities open to all sinners: God doesn't refuse entry to his kingdom to anyone (whatever one has done or has not done); *all* people can live with God; everybody can enter (the younger son, as well as the older son), if only they want to.

As in the lost sheep and the lost coin, here, too, not living with God is a great misfortune, whereas living with God (in unity and love) is a person's supreme good—hence (f) and (g):

(f) if a person lives with God this is very good for this person
(g) if a person doesn't live with God this is very bad for this person

But although not living with God is a great misfortune and living with God is a great good, sometimes people—like the younger son—do not want to live with God and prefer to seek their happiness elsewhere. This can be represented by the following component:

(h) sometimes a person doesn't want to live with God

An important aspect of the prodigal son, absent from the lost sheep and the lost coin, is its emphasis on people's freedom to choose a life away from God:

(i) if a person doesn't want to live with God, this person *cannot* live with God
(j) God doesn't want this person to think: "I have to live with God"
(k) God wants this person to think: "I want to live with God"

As many commentators have emphasized, this is what the father is doing in the parable: when the younger son proposes to go away, taking his inheritance with him, the father doesn't try to stop him—he simply lets him go. Similarly, in the second half of the story, when the older brother refuses to enter the house and to take part in the banquet (thus publicly humiliating the father), the father doesn't order him to go in; rather, he goes out to him, addresses him gently as "my child" (*teknon*), and tries to persuade him lovingly to join in the rejoicing. Thus, the parable suggests that whereas God is prepared to go out of his way to bring his children home (and accepts suffering as a price for it), he is not prepared to put pressure on them: he wants them to choose freely, he wants them to decide that they *want* to live with God.

This freedom that the father gives his children does not mean that he doesn't really mind if they separate themselves from him. On the contrary, all his behavior shows that he cares very much and that he suffers greatly when they go

away and rejoices beyond all measure when they come back. His behavior is
extravagant and defies all cultural norms. He waits for his younger son, watching the road every day so that he can spot him when the son is still far away; he
runs to meet him (unheard of for an elderly man in Palestine); he leaves the
banquet and all the guests to entreat his older son not to be angry (again, accepting public humiliation), and so on. All these actions show great love and an
enormous desire to have his sons back (physically and emotionally). The meaning of all this can be represented in the following components:

> (l) when a person doesn't want to live with God
>   God feels something bad because of this
> (m) God wants this person to want to live with God

But the fact that God wants his children freely to turn, and return, to him
does not mean that he waits passively and doesn't get involved. Even though
the parable of the prodigal son doesn't place as much emphasis on God's active
search for sinners as the parables of the lost sheep and the lost coin do, here,
too, God is active—or in my terms, "does many things"—because of his desire
for people's love and for a "home-coming":

> (m) God wants this person to want to live with God
> (n) God does many things because of this

What exactly does the father do in the parable that would justify (n)? First,
he lets his younger son go: he does it precisely because he wants the son to *want*
to live at home as his son, and so he doesn't want to compel the son to remain
at home against the son's will. Second, he seems to wait by the window so that
he can spot his wayward son from afar. Third, he runs to meet him and to es-
cort him through the village in full honor. Fourth, he showers the returning son
with extravagant and highly symbolic gifts (the best robe, the ring, and the sandals)—according to some commentators (e.g., Bailey 1976), to dissuade him from
his (presumed) plan of living on his own in the village and working for his father as a hired hand and to make him want to be restored instead to a full
"sonship" in his father's house. In the case of the older son, too, the father does
many things to make him want to be truly united with his father: as mentioned
earlier, the father leaves the banquet of which he is the host, he goes outside, he
speaks tenderly to his son, he reassures the son of his heritage, and he invites
the son to join the celebration.

What is particularly highlighted in the parable, as nearly all commentators
emphasize, is the father's joy, symbolized by the butchering of the fattened calf
(which had been kept for a very special occasion) and by the great feast, presumably including the whole village. (Eichholz 1984:213 even suggests that the parable could bear the subtitle "The Father's Joy.") Hence there is a need for the
following component:

> (o) if afterward this person wants to live with God
>   God feels something very good because of this

Finally, the main purpose of the whole story is to make people realize that (p) God is like this. Maillot (1993:201), among others, strongly emphasizes that "the parable is not a detailed description, whether critical or complacent, of human perdition and conversion. No! As the preceding ones [i.e., the lost sheep and the lost coin], it remains above all a parable about the Father, about God."

The story of the prodigal son (i.e., the younger son) is, of course, a story of rebellion, perdition, contrition, and repentance, but this is not what the message of the parable is all about. Although the second part, focused on the older brother, has an additional message of its own (to which I will turn shortly), the first part applies, in essence, to both brothers—so much so that as Rudolf Bultmann (1963) suggested, the parable as a whole could be seen as the "parable of the lost sons" (cf. Eichholz 1984:219). The only significant difference lies in the reality of the father's joy in the case of the younger brother. The story of the older brother is open-ended: we don't know whether he will accept the father's invitation; we don't know whether his heart will turn toward his father (and his brother); we don't know whether he will give his father an occasion for rejoicing, as his younger brother has done.

The prodigal son's repentance is the subject of some controversy. Was he really repentant? Or was it just hunger that drove him home? Derrett (1967:58; quoted in Bailey 1976:175) raises some doubts: "Many wonder how repentance preceded that return. Repentance of what? Was he sincere? Was the father as foolish to readmit him as he was to give him the share initially?" As Bailey says, "Derrett tacitly answers his own question with the further statement, 'This might well be the fundamental weakness of the parable'" (pp. 176–177).But what Derrett sees as a weakness, others see as one of the parable's strengths and an important part of its message. As T. W. Manson ([1937]1971:286), quoted in Fitzmyer (1985b:1086), says, "Jesus in this parable lays down the fundamental principle of God's relation to sinful people: that God loves the sinner while he is still a sinner, *before* he repents, and that somehow it is this Divine love that makes the sinner's repentance possible."

Jeremias (1966ba:104) remarks in connection with the prodigal son that "God's love to the returning sinner knows no bounds," but this seems too restrictive. A formulation offered earlier on the same page attributes to Jesus the message to "see the greatness of God's love for his lost children," and this seems more convincing. As the parable of the lost sheep makes clear, it is not just the *returning* and *repentant* sinner whom God loves, but every sinner. The parable of the prodigal son is consistent with this message.

True repentance, which Jesus' listeners may have expected from the prodigal, could be portrayed in the following four components (the repentant sinner's hypothetical thoughts):

(m$_1$) I did many bad things
(m$_2$) this is very bad
(m$_3$) I want to do some good things because of this
(m$_4$) I want to not do bad things any more

Whether or not the younger son has these thoughts in his head (and the story leads one to believe that he does), his father's welcome was not based on the assumption that he did. The only thing that mattered to the father was that the son evidently wanted to come back home. Bailey (1976:184) notes that "the father's welcome is clearly an outpouring of grace" and "any new relationship must be a pure gift from the father"; in other words the welcome is not based on an assumption of reparations. The father loves the son and waits for his return. He rejoices when he sees that the son wants to live with him again. One can expect that after his return the son will want to "not do bad things any more" and will want to "do good things" and also that this new conduct will follow from his desire to live with his father. This is reflected in component (m), proposed earlier: "God wants this person to want to live with God." Repentant thoughts, sketched in the hypothetical components (m_1), (m_2), (m_3) and (m_4), have not been included in the proposed explication, which in its present form captures the essence of the parable's message as applicable to *both* sons.

Turning now to the second half of the parable (which is sometimes called the parable of the older brother), we must note, first, the similarity between the older brother and the Pharisee in the parable of the Pharisee and the tax collector. Like the Pharisee, the older brother thinks of himself as someone who does good things and doesn't do bad things, and he thinks of someone else (his brother) as someone who does bad things and doesn't do good things. In this case, however, the focus is not so much on the comparison between himself and some other person or persons (along the lines of "I am not like this other person") but rather on the main character's attitude to God, as a dutiful servant or hired hand who deserves his pay (in contrast to some other people, who do not deserve any pay). This can be represented as follows (I will use here a new set of letters):

(a) sometimes a person thinks:
(b)   "I don't do bad things
(c)   I do good things
(d)   because of this God will do good things for me
(d')   [because of this God has to do good things for me?]
(e)   I want God to do good things for me"
(f) at the same time this person thinks about someone else:
(g)   "this person does bad things
(h)   this person doesn't do good things
(i)   because of this God will not do good things for this person
(j)   I don't want God to do good things for this person"

The older brother expects his father to do good things for him, but not because he is aware of his father's love and of his desire to do good things for his children. Rather, he thinks that he has deserved good things from his father and expects them as a payment (d). He wants these good things (e) and he regards them as his due (d). At the same time, he thinks of his brother as someone who doesn't deserve anything from their father (i), and he doesn't want the father to do good things for his brother (j).

Thus, the older son's attitude to his brother is loveless (he doesn't want the father to do good things for his brother, whom he refuses to see as his brother, referring to him as "this son of yours"), and his attitude to his father is that of a paid servant, not that of a son. He doesn't realize that his father loves him and wants to do good things for him out of a desire of his own heart; and he almost thinks that his father "has to" do good things for him because the father owes them to him [hypothetical component (d')].

Unlike the first part of the parable (focused on the prodigal son), the second part is not exclusively about God (God is like this). Rather, it appeals directly to the addressees to see themselves in the older brother and to change their minds and hearts. Eichholz (1984:218) says that "in the second half of the parable the listener is addressed and finds himself involved". But this appeal to the addressee is linked implicitly to a new understanding of God (if one doesn't see one's brother as a brother and relate to him as to a brother, one cannot relate to God as one's own and all people's loving father). This appeal can be represented in components (k) to (o), linked to some further components, (p), (q) and (r), focused on God:

(k) it will be bad if you think like this
(l) it will be good if you think about everyone:
(m)   "this person is someone like me
(n)   God wants to do good things for this person
          as God wants to do good things for me
(o)   I want God to do good things for this person,
          as I want God to do good things for me"

(p) God wants to do good things for all people,
(q) it is not true that if a person has done some very bad things
          God doesn't want to do good things for this person
          as God wants to do good things for all other people
(r) when a person doesn't want God to do good things for other
          people this person cannot live with God
(s) when a person wants God to do good things for other people
          this person can live with God

Component (k) warns the addressee against thinking like the older brother, and (l) suggests a different way of thinking,[1] which (m), (n), and (o) spell out: urging the addressee to identify with other people, to recognize God's love for other people, and to rejoice in that love. Components (p) and (q) focus on God and his love for all people, and (r) and (s) link the way of thinking recommended in (m), (n), and (o) with the nature of God as depicted in (p) and (q): since God loves all people, a person cannot live with God without loving other people, too. This inability to live with God is not presented as a *sanction* for not loving other people but as a kind of logical impossibility (in the light of the fact that God wants to do good things for all people).

This brings us to the final explication, rather different in both size and style from the one rejected by Te Selle (1975)—("God's love knows no bounds"), although consistent with its spirit:

Part I

(a) God wants to do good things for all people
(b) God feels something because of this
(c) all people can live with God
(d) God wants this
(e) when a person wants to live with God this person can live with God
(f) if a person lives with God this is very good for this person
(g) if a person doesn't live with God this is very bad for this person
(h) sometimes a person doesn't want to live with God
(i) if a person doesn't want to live with God, this person can not live with God
(j) God doesn't want this person to think:
    "I have to (= cannot not) live with God"
(k) God wants this person to think: "I want to live with God"
(l) when a person doesn't want to live with God
    God feels something bad because of this
(m) God wants this person to want to live with God
(n) God does many things because of this
(o) if afterwards this person wants to live with God
    God feels something very good because of this
(p) God is like this

Part II

(a) sometimes a person thinks:
(b)   "I don't do bad things
(c)   I do good things
(d)   because of this God will do good things for me
(d') [because of this God has to do good things for me?]
(e)   I want God to do good things for me"
(f) at the same time this person thinks about someone else:
(g)   "this person does bad things
(h)   this person doesn't do good things
(i)   because of this God will not do good things for this person
(j)   I don't want God to do good things for this person"
(k) it will be bad if you think like this
(l) it will be good if you think about everyone:
(m)   "this person is someone like me
(n)   God wants to do good things for this person,
        as God wants to do good things for me
(o)   I want God to do good things for this person,
        as I want God to do good things for me"

(p) God wants to do good things for all people

(q) it is not true that if a person has done some very bad things
    God doesn't want to do good things for this person
    as God wants to do good things for all other people

(r) when a person doesn't want God to do good things for other
    people this person cannot live with God

(s) when a person wants God to do good things for all other people
    this person can live with God

This explication, coming in two extended parts, is so long and so complex that it may well test some readers' patience and stamina. It may also not be perfect, and a further careful consideration of all the components might lead to some revisions. In any case, a search for the parable's true meaning, guided above all by the principle of coherence, is legitimate and necessary.

ELEVEN

The Unforgiving Servant

Matthew 18:21–35; cf. Luke 17:4

21. Then Peter came to him and said, "Lord, how often shall my brother sin against me, and I forgive him? Up to seven times?"
22. Jesus said to him, "I do not say to you, up to seven times, but up to seventy times seven.
23. Therefore the kingdom of heaven is like a certain king who wanted to settle accounts with his servants.
24. And when he had begun to settle accounts, one was brought to him who owed him ten thousand talents.
25. But as he was not able to pay, his master commanded that he be sold, with his wife and children and all that he had, and that payment be made.
26. The servant therefore fell down before him, saying, 'Master, have patience with me, and I will pay you all.'
27. Then the master of that servant was moved with compassion, released him, and forgave him the debt.
28. But that servant went out and found one of his fellow servants who owed him a hundred denarii; and he laid hands on him and took him by the throat, saying, 'Pay me what you owe!'
29. So his fellow servant fell down at his feet and begged him, saying, 'Have patience with me, and I will pay you all'.
30. And he would not, but went and threw him into prison till he should pay the debt.

31. So when his fellow servants saw what had been done, they were very grieved, and came and told their master all that had been done.

32. Then his master, after he had called him, said to him 'You wicked servant! I forgave you all that debt because you begged me.

33. Should you not also have had compassion on your fellow servant, just as I had pity on you?'

34. And his master was angry, and delivered him to the torturers until he should pay all that was due to him.

35. [So my heavenly Father also will do to you if each of you, from his heart, does not forgive his brother his trespasses."]

Is the unforgiving servant an authentic parable told by Jesus? Commentators generally agree that the threatening final verse (35) is Matthew's creation, and some argue that verse 34 is also. In addition, there is wide agreement that Matthew created Peter's question at the outset (v. 21) and that it was he who combined the parable *sensu stricto* (vv. 23–34 or 23–33) with the independent logion (v. 22) urging unlimited forgiveness: "not seven times but seventy times seven," that is, always.

In Luke's Gospel, the logion of limitless forgiveness takes a different form (Luke 17:3b–4): "If your brother sins against you, rebuke him; and if he repents, forgive him. And if he sins against you seven times in a day, and seven times in a day returns to you, saying, 'I repent', you shall forgive him." Funk et al. (1993:362) have printed this saying in black (like its counterpart in Matthew), arguing that "these sentences outline the protocol for dealing with those who stray from established norms" and that "the development of such protocols is itself evidence that we are dealing here with a more mature community."[1] This is not fully convincing, however, given that "seven" is a symbolic number in Jewish culture and is unlikely to have been used here in a literal sense, as a part of a rule or protocol. To quote Fitzmyer (1985b:1140), "'Seven times' is used to denote totality (and is not to be taken literally, as 'seven times in a day' makes clear). The willingness to forgive must be boundless."

Meier (1980:280) makes a similar comment about Matthew's version: "Jesus' reply to Peter, which in Greek can mean either 'seventy times seven' or 'seventy seven times', really means an unlimited number of times (the perfect number seven, multiplied by itself and by ten)." Thus, despite editorial changes introduced in this logion by both Luke and Matthew, the essential message is the same: in Fitzmyer's words, the willingness to forgive must be boundless.

It is important that although many scholars regard Luke's "seven" as more likely to go back to Jesus than Matthew's "seventy times seven," Luke's reference to repentance (one of Luke's favourite motifs, cf. Fitzmyer 1981:237; also Schweizer 1975:377) is likely to have been added by Luke.

Turning now to the question of the authenticity of the parable itself (as distinct from its frame), I must note that although its language shows some signs of Matthew's editing (see, e.g., Lambrecht 1991:58–61), apart from superficial linguistic features the whole style of the parable is characteristically Jesus' own.

As Funk et al. (1993:218) observe, "The parable of the unforgiving slave exhibits marks of both oral tradition and exaggeration that are typical of Jesus' stories." Lambrecht (1991:63), who examines in detail the traces of the Matthean editing, concludes by concurring with Rudolf Schnackenburg (1987:176) that the parable has the unmistakable ring of Jesus' own voice: "Rudolf Schnackenburg is right: Hardly any argumentation can separate this moving parable from Jesus ('Die päckende Parabel lässt sich Jesus nicht absprechen')."

Given this evidence, one might wonder why anyone would want to question the parable's authenticity? Apparently, some commentators feel compelled to do so because they fear that the image of God that is conveyed by the story is unedifying. It is true that at first the king, who can be taken to represent God, shows his debtor boundless mercy, but later on the same king withdraws his mercy and acts like a cruel tyrant. Funk et al. 1993:218 say that in the end, the parable "depicts God as a vindictive person whose mercies are dependent on human behavior." Lambrecht says that

> there is a tension in regard to content which has often been commented upon in recent publications. There is real opposition between the mercy of the lord in verse 27 and his angry, implacable reaction in verse 34. Hence the conjecture: Did the original parable perhaps end with the open question of verse 33 (or even already with v.30a)? But those who take offence at verse 34 probably force their own feelings upon the parable teller. There is a danger that modern interpreters adopt an exaggeratedly moral sense and too easily condemn the ancient teller. We do not think that the content of verse 34 reveals that it has been added to a more original parable.

Lambrecht's defense of the "ancient teller" seems to me not quite apt. If we assume that apart from some superficial editing, the parable is authentic, the "ancient teller" is Jesus. The suggestion that Jesus would have been less sensitive to the king's final lack of mercy than the modern reader and that he would have found the modern reader's moral qualms "exaggerated" seems to me to be dubious. Should not the resolution of the tension noted by Lambrecht himself and other commentators be sought elsewhere?

In my view, there is no more point in defending the moral character of the king in this story than in defending the injustice of the unjust judge in that parable, in which he seemingly also represents God (Luke 18:2-7), or in defending the gentleness and compassion of the harsh lord (who said about himself that he was a "hard man") in the story of the talents (Matt. 25:14-21). Rather, we should simply acknowledge Jesus' narrative technique of choosing shocking images to engage his listeners' attention and to challenge them to think for themselves about what it is that the story tells them about God. In the story of the unjust judge, the character who is representing God is explicitly described as "a judge who did not fear God nor regard man" and as "the unjust judge."

As the Fellows of the Jesus' Seminar rightly observe, this is a strategy characteristic of Jesus: to liken the kingdom of God to the Jewish symbol of corruption (the leaven); to illustrate desirable human characteristics approved by God with the character of a dishonest steward (Luke 16:1–8); and to compare some aspects of God's relationship to people with stories about an unjust judge, a harsh master, or a vindictive and implacable king. The Fellows comment on the ending of the unforgiving servant as follows: "The ending sows confusion for listeners, who now do not know how they are to respond. This is the kind of ambiguity Jesus often builds into his parables. As parable, the story prompts the audience finally to review the story to see how it misleads" (Funk et al. 1993:218–219). But the fact that Jesus wants to make his audience think does not mean that he wants them to remain confused. On the contrary, the parable does have a message, but it is left to the audience to figure out what it is. Funk et al. seem to sense this, because in the end they do in fact formulate what they see as Jesus' message: "Jesus intended the parable to show that forgiveness cannot be compromised without undesirable consequences" (p. 219).

This conclusion strikes me, however, as somewhat lame. Is this all that Jesus intended to show? And what kind of undesirable consequences? In what follows, I will set out my own version of Jesus' intended message, trying to validate my analysis step by step. As in the case of the other parables, the reconstructed message will be quite complex. I hope, however, that its meaning will be clear and intelligible. The proposed formula will avoid not only complicated or technical language but even words like *forgive*, which are less universal than they seem to a speaker of English or most other European languages. In fact, it will be useful to start our analysis by adopting the point of view of a speaker of one of the innumerable languages that does not have a word for forgiveness; for example, one of the indigenous languages of Australia.

Adopting such a perspective and therefore restricting myself to universal human concepts for which every indigenous Australian (and, as far as we know, speakers of any other language) would have a word, I will start the exposition with the background assumptions that arise from Jesus' overall teaching:

(a) God wants to do good things for all people
(b) all people can live with God
(c) God wants this

Against the backdrop of these assumptions, which pervade the Gospels as a whole, the story of the unforgiving servant presents the attitude of a person who wants to receive benefits from God but doesn't want to do good things for other people:

(d) sometimes a person thinks:
(e)   "I want God to do good things for me"
(f) at the same time this person thinks about another person:
(g)   "I don't want to do good things for this person
(h)   this person did something bad to me
(i)   because of this I want to do bad things to this person"

As this partial explication shows, the central theme of the story can be presented in terms of good things, which the protagonist wants from God but doesn't want to do for another person, and bad things, which he wants to do to that other person, in retaliation for some other bad things. In the story, the bad things are symbolized by a failure to pay a debt, and the good things by a remission of debts, but these are only narrative details. What really matters is that one wants to do bad things to another person "because this person has done something bad to me," and at the same time one wants to receive favors (good things) from God. (In the story, the favors received by the servant from the king are huge: the debt canceled is of astronomical, fablelike proportions.)

It is this attitude that the parable targets, wanting hearers to recognize it in themselves and reject it. What reason is offered by the parable to motivate the hearers to such a rejection? Funk et al. (1993) mention "undesirable consequences." In simple language, this would mean that "something bad will happen to you because of this." I propose instead a somewhat different component:

(j) it will be bad for you if you think like this

Component (j) relates to the way of thinking portrayed in (d) to (i); instead of threatening bad consequences, it focuses on the harm inherent in such thinking (not "something bad will happen to you because of this" but "it will be bad for you if you think like this"). The nature of this harm must be seen as vitally important to the parable's message. Funk et al.'s "undesirable consequences" is vague, and it is doubtful whether such a nonspecific hint would motivate the hearers to a radical change of attitude. Matthew's image of being thrown into prison "until all is paid" is specific—and terrifying—enough, given that the debt is astronomical and clearly unpayable, so that the prison term would never end. But since verse 34, which contains this image, may well go back to Jesus, the question must still be asked: what does this image mean?

The widespread assumption that an image of this kind must mean an exclusion from the kingdom of heaven is, to my mind, basically sound, but not if it is taken in the sense of an eternal, everlasting hell. Instead, I would propose the following interpretation:

(k) when a person thinks like this this person cannot live with God

Exclusion from the kingdom of God means that a person cannot live with God. The key feature of (k) is that it is phrased in terms of *when*, not in terms of *if*. A hypothetical component—"if a person thinks like this this person cannot live with God"—would imply that "thinking like this" would have as a consequence a permanent exclusion from the kingdom of God (i.e., something like an everlasting hell). This would be incompatible with the parable's background assumptions that all people can live with God and that God wants this. On the other hand, a formulation phrased in terms of *when* is compatible with these assumptions and is fully consistent with Jesus' overall teaching: while a person is full of hate and ill will toward another human being, this person cannot live with God.

In Jesus' teaching, the kingdom of God is already present, as well as future and eternal. One can enter this kingdom at any time—but not if one's heart is full of hate, resentment, and ill will toward anybody, no matter how deserved this hate and ill will may be. To enter the kingdom of God, one must let go of any such feelings and replace them with a loving attitude toward other people, including those who have done something bad to us:

(l) it will be good for you if you think:
(m)   "I don't want to do bad things to this person
(n)   I want to do good things for this person if I can"
(o) when a person thinks like this, this person can live with God

Although in the symbolic language of the parable forgiveness is represented in terms of an act rather than a process and an attitude, Jesus' teaching as a whole makes it clear that what is meant is in fact a long-term disposition, achieved through a *metanoia*, a change in one's thinking. (This point is emphasized, rightly, in Imbach's 1995:114 discussion of the parable; see also Tillich 1964:239.) But if a person's heart is to be free of hate and ill-will then what is needed is not just a changed attitude toward a particular debtor or malefactor but also a changed attitude toward people in general. Hence the need for an additional, universalizing, component:

(p) it will be good for you if you think like this about everyone

But how are people supposed to bring about the required transformation of their own hearts? Addressing this question, many commentators focus on the experience of being forgiven by God, which (they say) enables, as well as obliges, human beings to pass on this forgiveness to other people: "Jesus shows that the forgiven man must reflect God's mercy and compassion" (Kistemaker 1980:69). "Behind the image of the King stands the God of Jesus who summons people to be forgiving because they have experienced forgiveness" (Donahue 1988:77). "According to Jesus, God's mercy should effect in those who have been forgiven a grateful fruitful reaction towards their neighbors . . . as a forgiven person I must also forgive my neighbor. . . . In the parable . . . Jesus underlines that God's forgiveness *precedes* our effort, or more accurately, that divine mercy actually enables our effort" (Lambrecht 1991:65).

Statements of this kind seem persuasive: in the story, the king did forgive the servant before the servant was called on, and failed, to forgive someone else. But is it true that the same applies to Jesus' message about God's forgiveness? The assumption that God's forgiveness *precedes* human forgiveness pushes the commentators who adopt it toward claiming further that God's forgiveness can be *revoked*, like that of the king in the story. Thus, Meier (1980:209) states that "we cannot earn God's forgiveness, but we can lose it—by trying to hoard it, instead of passing it on to others." Boucher (1981:118) asserts that "unless we grant forgiveness to others, God will on the last day revoke the forgiveness he has granted us." Jeremias (1966b:166) sounds even more categorical: "Woe to you if you try to stand on your rights, if you harden your heart and refuse to hand on to others the forgiveness that he offers to you. Everything is at stake, for God will then revoke the forgiveness of your sins and will see to it that his sentence is carried out in full."

But is this conceivable, that God will grant forgiveness and then take it back? Is it conceivable that if the day after his return the prodigal son mistreats a servant that the father will withdraw his earlier loving forgiveness altogether? Jeremias (1966b:167) has Jesus saying that "he who abuses God's gift faces the full severity of judgment, as if he had never received forgiveness," and he backs this up with a reference to Matt. 6:14, which reads: "For if you forgive people their trespasses, your heavenly Father will also forgive you. But if you do not forgive people their trespasses, neither will your Father forgive your trespasses." But, the reference to Matthew does not support Jeremias's interpretation: not even Matthew, with all his love for the Jewish *Drohrede* (rhetorical threats and warnings), says that God will revoke his forgiveness. To my mind, an interpretation of the parable in terms of forgiveness being revoked is inconsistent with Matthew's explicit formula in 6:14 and flies in the face of Jesus' injunction—used by Matthew as an introduction to the parable—that forgiveness should be boundless and endless: not 7 times but 70 times 7. If human forgiveness should be boundless and endless how could God's forgiveness be anything less than that? Elsewhere, pointing to God's boundless love for the just and the unjust, the Matthean Jesus tells his listeners, "Therefore you should be perfect as your Father in heaven is perfect" (5:48). Would he now be telling them to be more perfect than their father in heaven?

It is true that in the story the king does retract his forgiveness and shows himself to be harsh and merciless. But as pointed out earlier, the king is no more a portrayal of what God is really like than the judge in the parable of the unjust judge or the "hard man" in the parable of the talents.

Commenting on the doubts raised about the authenticity of the unforgiving servant, Meier (1980:62) has written, "A difficulty against the authenticity is said to be the image of God which more or less coincides with that of the lord of the parable. Could Jesus, it is argued, represent a God who in the first scene is so immensely merciful and immediately afterwards, in the third scene, suddenly so harsh and cruel?" But as discussed earlier, doubts of this kind are based on a misunderstanding of the genre to which these stories belong: the king in the story no more represents God in all his actions than the dishonest steward or the dishonest finder of the hidden treasure represent, in all aspects of their behavior, model followers of Jesus.

Lambrecht (1991:62) rightly rejects the doubts of the parable's authenticity that are based on this kind of excessively allegorical reading. However, he then comments: "It can hardly be doubted that Jesus himself announced a last judgment. The degree to which God's mercy will then still play a role is not always clear." The degree of God's mercy may seem to be unclear if the medium is not distinguished from the message. On the level of the message, however, it is clear that God's mercy is presented by Jesus as boundless.

The idea that God's forgiveness can be revoked provides, I think, a striking illustration of the danger of reading parables in a way that is literalist and allegorizing at the same time. The fact that in the story the king withdrew his forgiveness is taken to mean that God will do the same; and the fact that the servant's debt was so huge as to be unpayable is taken to mean that human sins are infinite, as if the hyperbole of the parable were meant to represent the enormity of human sinfulness rather than the enormity of God's mercy.

Thus, for example, Meier (1980:208) writes, "The hyperbole of the parable is obvious. . . . There is no way to pay the almost infinite amount owed (so too is sin an infinite offense against the infinite God, an offense we cannot possibly undo by ourselves)." Meier seems to imply that the almost infinite amount owed symbolizes the infinite offense of the sin. However, the hyperbole that he rightly emphasizes refers not to human sins but to God's goodness. Christian mystics have often said that human sin is infinitesimally small in relation to God's mercy: "Like a handful of sand flung into the great ocean are the faults of all the creatures in comparison with the providence and the mercy of God" (St. Isaac of Niniveh 1981:313). In the parable of the unforgiving servant also, it is God's mercy that is infinite, not human sin.

St. Isaac of Niniveh(1995:172), who interpreted the language of biblical images as symbolic, went to the heart of all the parables' meaning when he said, "Among all His [God's] actions there is none which is not entirely a matter of mercy, love, and compassion: this constitutes the beginning and the end of His dealings with us." This central message about God is perhaps expressed most clearly in the parable of the prodigal son, which provides a model for human forgiveness, but it is also expressed in many other images, including that of the remission of an infinite debt. But if God's mercy is being presented in the parable as infinite, the parable cannot possibly mean that this forgiveness can be revoked. To repeat, the remission of an infinite debt does not stand for a conditional, revokable, and shaky remission of an infinite sin but rather, for the unconditional, inexhaustible, and infinite love and mercy of God.

Jesus taught his disciples to ask God to "forgive us our trespasses as we forgive those who trespass against us" (Matt. 6:12, Luke 11:4); he did *not* tell them: "forgive other people's trespasses as God has forgiven yours—and if you don't he will take his forgiveness back." To say this is not inconsistent with saying that the experience of being loved enables people to love (and to forgive) others, and that God's love precedes human love and enables people to love (and to forgive) others at all.

In the parable of the unforgiving servant, however, the emphasis is on the need for people to forgive other people, as they themselves need and want to be forgiven by God. Speaking very roughly, the message is not so much "forgive other people, as God has forgiven you" as "forgive other people, as you want God to forgive you." Interpreting the parable along these lines will enable us to avoid the scandalous (to my mind) conclusion that God could revoke his mercy and withdraw his forgiveness, while preserving the seriousness of the parable's message. In the proposed interpretation, the message of the parable is not a threat: "If you don't forgive others, then God, who has already forgiven you, will take away his forgiveness from you"; rather it is an exhortation: "You, too, need forgiveness; you need God's forgiveness; you want God to forgive you; think about that and forgive others yourself." More precisely, the necessary awareness of one's

sinfulness before God, of one's need for God's mercy, and of God's unconditional love and goodness can be represented as follows:

(q) it will be good for you if you think at all times:
(r)   "I did many bad things
(s)   I don't want God to do bad things to me because of this
(t)   I want God to do good things for me
(u)   I know that God wants to do good things for me
(v)   I know that God wants to do good things for all people"

If there is any one statement that can be called, with some validity, the parable's
main point, then in my view it is not that "forgiveness cannot be compromised
without undesirable consequences," as Funk et al. (1993) said, but rather this:
if one thinks continually about God's immeasurable goodness, which one needs
and on which one can count, one may be able to give up one's ill will toward
other people, no matter what they may have done to us, and replace it with good
will; and that without this, one cannot live with God:

(w) when a person thinks like this about God
       this person can think about every other person at the same time:
(x)   "I don't want to do bad things to this person
(y)   I want to do good things for this person"
(z) when a person thinks about other people like this
       this person can live with God

I will close this chapter by quoting again St. Isaac of Niniveh, according to
whom "it is only by mercy that human beings are made to be like the Creator"
(quoted in Bettiolo 1990:345). St. Isaac recalls how Moses, after the people of
Israel had made and worshiped a Golden Calf, pleaded with God to forgive them,
saying that "if you will not forgive their sin, I pray, blot me out of your book
which you have written" (Exod. 32:32). For Isaac, mercy is God's last word, and
it is by contemplating God's mercy that human beings can find mercy in their
own hearts. Of a merciful heart, which reflects God's mercy, he writes,

What is a merciful heart? . . . it is a fire raging in the heart, for *every creature*, people, birds and animals, and for the demons, and for everything
that exists, so much so that at the thought of them and at the sight of them
one's eyes fill with tears because of the vehemence of the mercy which fills
the heart. The heart faints and cannot bear to hear or to know about the
slightest harm done to any creature whatsoever, the slightest suffering to
which it is subjected, and because of this it also offers at every moment,
with tears, a prayer for dumb animals and for the adversaries of Truth,
also for those people who offend us, that they may be protected and forti-
fied; even for the reptiles, because of the abundant mercy which floods the
heart, a mercy without measure, in the likeness of God.[2] (1984:344)

The unforgiving servant

(a) God wants to do good things for all people
(b) all people can live with God
(c) God wants this

(d) sometimes a person thinks:
(e)   "I want God to do good things for me"
(f) at the same time this person thinks about another person:
(g)   "I don't want to do good things for this person
(h)   this person did something bad to me
(i)   because of this I want to do bad things to this person"

(j) it will be bad for you if you think like this
(k) when a person thinks like this this person cannot live with God
(l) it will be good for you if you think:
(m)   "I don't want to do bad things to this person
(n)   I want to do good things for this person if I can"
(o) when a person thinks like this, this person can live with God
(p) it will be good for you if you think like this about everyone

(q) it will be good for you if you think at all times:
(r)   "I did many bad things
(s)   I don't want God to do bad things to me because of this
(t)   I want God to do good things for me
(u)   I know that God wants to do good things for me
(v)   I know that God wants to do good things for all people"

(w) when a person thinks like this about God
     this person can think about every other person at the same time:
(x)   "I don't want to do bad things to this person
(y)   I want to do good things for this person"
(z) when a person thinks about other people like this, this person can
     live with God

TWELVE

The Laborers in the Vineyard

Matthew 20:1–16

1. For the kingdom of heaven is like a landowner who went out early in the morning to hire laborers for his vineyard.
2. Now when he had agreed with the laborers for a denarius a day, he sent them into his vineyard.
3. And he went out about the third hour and saw others standing idle in the marketplace.
4. and said to them, 'You also go into the vineyard, and whatever is right I will give you.' And they went.
5. Again he went out about the sixth and the ninth hour, and did likewise.
6. And about the eleventh hour he went out and found others standing idle, and said to them, 'Why have you been standing here idle all day?'
7. They said to him, 'Because no one hired us.' He said to them, 'You also go into the vineyard, and whatever is right you will receive.'
8. So when evening had come, the owner of the vineyard said to his steward, 'Call the laborers and give them their wages, beginning with the last to the first.'
9. And when those came who were hired about the eleventh hour, they each received a denarius.
10. But when the first came, they supposed that they would receive more; and they likewise each received a denarius.

11. And when they had received it, they murmured against the landowner,

12. saying, 'These last men have worked only one hour, and you made them equal to us who have borne the burden and the heat of the day.'

13. But he answered one of them and said, 'Friend, I am doing you no wrong. Did you not agree with me for a denarius?

14. Take what is yours and go your way. I wish to give to this last man the same as to you.'

15. 'Is it not lawful for me to do what I wish with my own things? Or is your eye evil because I am good?'

16. [So the last will be first, and the first last. For many are called, but few chosen.]

Maillot (1993:84) says that "the parable of the Laborers in the Vineyard is one of astonishing richness [*d'une étonnante richesse*]." It is also a parable that as Lambrecht (1991:69) put it, "irritates the modern listener because it goes against sound human logic and against the universally accepted rule 'the same pay for the same work'." To say that this rule is universally accepted is an exaggeration, but the parable does seem to clash with the modern, Western (especially Anglo) value of fairness. Lambrecht attributes to the parable the message of "God's infinite goodness" and remarks that in this respect, "the parable of 'The Workers in the Vineyard' hardly differs from that of 'The Prodigal Son'" (p. 81). Other scholars similarly compare the message of the laborers in the vineyard with that of the Pharisee and the tax collector. Yet despite the close resemblance among these three parables, it is the "laborers in the vineyard" more than any other that is likely to offend the modern reader's sense of equity.

Whereas most of Jesus' parables contradict the listeners' expectations this one does so more spectacularly. Crossan (1992:114) notes that in the laborers "it is reversal of expectation which is central: '*they thought*'"; he asks, rhetorically, "Can one imagine a perfectly reasonable situation in which perfectly reasonable expectations are rudely overthrown?" According to Crossan, then, it is not just that the listeners' expectations are violated in this parable but that they are "perfectly reasonable" expectations. Donahue (1990:81) remarks, in a similar vein, that "hardly any parable in the Gospels seems to upset the basic structure of the orderly society as does this one."

Funk et al. (1993:225) observe that "the behavior of the vineyard owner cuts across the social grain." It is essentially for this reason that the Fellows of the Jesus Seminar "awarded this parable a red designation," despite the fact that it is attested to only by Matthew. If one recalls that even such core parables as the prodigal son and the lost sheep—which would seem to be, beyond any reasonable doubt, Jesus' own—were awarded by the Fellows no more than a pink designation, the red of the laborers, assigned to it on the basis of its shock value, is very eloquent indeed.

What exactly was Jesus trying to say through of this parable? As noted earlier, Lambrecht (1991:81) says that it focuses on "God's immense goodness," as does the prodigal son. But there seems to be a difference of emphasis between the two parables. Jeremias (1966b:104) recapitulates the message of the prodigal son in terms of "God's boundless love," and this difference in the choice of words is symptomatic: while the father in the prodigal son is undeniably the epitome of love, the householder (*oikodespotēs*), or owner (*kyrios* 'lord', 'master') of the vineyard, epitomizes goodness rather than love; and this is what the concluding verse emphasizes: "is your eye evil because I am good (*ego agathos eimi*)?" Accordingly, we could start our explication of the laborers in the vineyard as follows:

(a) God is good
(b) God wants to do good things for all people
(c) all people can live with God
(d) God wants this

This would differ from the initial segment of the explication of the prodigal son in two ways: by including the component "God is good" and by excluding the component "God feels something because of this." Components (c) and (d)—"all people can live with God" and "God wants this" (present also in the explication of the prodigal son)—correspond here to the owner's multiple trips to the market-place and his repeated calls for the people he finds there to come to his vineyard.

As many scholars have emphasized, the parable is clearly aimed at people who, like the laborers hired in the first hour, see themselves as more deserving than some other people—the laborers of the eleventh hour. This time, however, these other people are not sinners, who do very bad things (as the younger brother in the prodigal son or the tax collector in the Pharisee and the tax collector were) but rather people who don't have many good deeds to their credit; and the point of the comparison lies not so much in the division of people into two catego-ries—the righteous and the sinners (the good ones and the bad ones)—as in the expectation of a greater reward for oneself than for these other people. This can be represented as follows:

(e) some people think:
(f)   "I have done many good things
(g)   because of this God will do many good things for me
(h)   this is good
(i)   some other people haven't done many good things
(j)   because of this God will not do many good things for these
         people
(k)   this is good"

Thus, the workers of the first hour are highly conscious of their own good works (component (f)); fully expect a reward from God (g); and see this forth-coming reward as well deserved, as well as pleasing to contemplate (h). They are also highly conscious of the advantage they have in this regard over other people (the laborers of the eleventh hour): those other people haven't done many good things (component (i)), consequently, they can't expect a reward from God (j), and this is also well deserved and quite pleasing to contemplate (k). In the story, this last component is not explicit but implicit in the workers' grumbling and in the reference to their evil eye. The shock they experienced when they saw the generous treatment of the "undeserving" shows what their previous expectations and wishes were.

This is, then, the way of thinking that the parable targets and warns against:

(l) it will be bad if you think like this

The way of thinking depicted in (f) to (k) is bad because it is based on a false idea about God:

(m) God is not like this

The idea of God implied by the image of the grumbling workers of the first hour ignores God's desire to do good things for all people (component (n) below) and God's grace—the free gift of good things—extended by God to all people, regardless of their ethical achievements and performances or their lack. Component (o) indicates that God's grace is available to the workers of the eleventh hour just as much as to anybody else:

(n) God wants to do good things for all people
(o) if some people don't do many good things
      God wants to do good things for these people
      as God wants to do good things for all other people

Component (o) spells out the equal treatment granted by the owner to the first and last workers, thus echoing in a sense the first ones' complaint: "These last men have worked only one hour; and you made them equal to us who have borne the burden and the heat of the day."

In fact many commentators see equality as a key issue in the parable, although its exact meaning is disputed. Some see in the parable an assurance of a democracy in heaven. Thus, commenting on Jesus' words about eternal life, addressed to Peter, which Matthew placed just before the parable of the laborers, Kistemaker (1980:80) states that "the parable shows the saying to mean that in the kingdom of heaven equality is the rule. The work performed by the disciples, and for that matter by any one of Jesus' followers, is transcended by a reward equal for all, even though the work itself may vary." Manson ([1937]1961:719), quoted by Via (1974:154), affirms that "there are no distinctions in the kingdom," and Blomberg (1990:224) deduces from the parable "the precious truth that all true disciples are equal in God's eyes," asserting that Jesus "makes plain that there are no degrees of reward in heaven." Blomberg argues that the Matthean conclusion about the last being the first and the first last (v.16) does not have to be interpreted in terms of reversal but can "just as easily apply to a situation of equality." Comparing the laborers in the vineyard with the prodigal son, Blomberg remarks that "just as the father loved and wooed both of them [the sons] with equal tenderness, so the landowner pays his laborers the same amount" (p. 224).

This emphasis on equality and the same amount seems to me mistaken. It is true that the laborers in the story did receive equal pay (one denarius each), but surely this is just a narrative detail. What really matters is that the kingdom of heaven is open to everyone alike, not that in the Kingdom of heaven equality is the rule. What Jesus meant was not that the reward will be equal for all but that God's benefices are not a matter of reward for any works done but a free gift that God wants to bestow on everyone. This is what (n) and (o) seek to express; the emphasis is not on equality and lack of distinctions but on everyone being included.

There is of course nothing wrong with the words *equal, equally,* and *equality* when they are used to indicate this all-inclusiveness of God's grace, as, for example, in the following sentence (Donahue 1990:84): "God's generosity is equally present to those called last"; but this is different from saying that in the kingdom of heaven equality is the rule or that all true disciples are equal in God's eyes. Whether or not the disciples (or any other people) are equal in God's eyes and whether or not there are distinctions in heaven are points that Jesus does not discuss. What he does make clear, however, is that God loves both the "achievers" and the "nonachievers," the "performers" and the "nonperformers" alike. He also makes it clear that if the achievers and performers can live with God it is not because of their achievements and performances but because of God's grace. I propose, therefore, the following additional components referring to the workers of the first hour:

(p) if some people have done many good things
    God wants to do good things for these people
    because God wants to do good things for all people,
    not because these people have done many good things

The idea behind this component is the subject of some controversy in the literature. In particular, Jeremias (1966b:27) explicitly rejects the suggestion that the parable of the laborers "is intended to teach that all reward is wholly of grace," arguing that "this is erroneous, for the first received their pay, as Paul would say, 'not . . . as a gift but as his due' (Rom. 4.4)." Thus Jeremias rejects the interpretation that God's grace is given freely to all people (including those hired first) and restricts this grace to the workers of the eleventh hour. He concludes that in fact the whole point of the parable lies in God's generosity toward the less deserving, that "the point of the story, surprising to the hearers, is certainly not 'Equal pay for all', but 'Such high pay for the last!'" (p. 27).

But whereas in the parable the laborers of the first hour did indeed receive no more than their due, this is quite compatible with the view that the "lord of the vineyard" wanted to do good things for all the hired men, regardless of how much they had or had not done and that, in any case, this was one of the main points that Jesus wanted to make about God. I agree entirely that the point of the parable is not "Equal pay for all," but I am not convinced that it is simply: "Such high pay for the last!" either, and I find the criticisms of Jeremias's (1966b) position, raised, for example, by Via, quite cogent on this point. According to Via (1974:153–155), the real message of the story lies in what happens at the end to the laborers of the first hour, when the owner says to them, "Take what is yours and go your way." Via sees this final event as "the expulsion of the grumbling workers" and calls it "the tragic conclusion of the complaining workers' story." This "expulsion" is, according to Via, wrongly ignored by most commentators (including Jeremias):

> The result of ignoring this matter is a tendency in theological interpretation to say that the parable does not teach that reward is wholly by grace. It is suggested by some scholars that according to the parable God deals with some people on the basis of merit (the full-day workers) and with others according to grace (the one-hour workers). (Cf. Jeremias 1972:36; Manson 1961:218.) The effort is then made by these interpreters to avoid this unwelcome conclusion by falling back on the one-point approach to the parables. It is said that the real point of the parable is not to make a distinction between grace and merit but rather to emphasize how much the one-hour workers received or to affirm that there are no distinctions in the Kingdom.

Via rejects this approach, suggesting instead that the focus should be on the grumbling workers and their final expulsion.

> When this is seen in connection with their complaint about the householder's generosity to the one-hour workers, then the parable does not teach that God deals with some on the basis of merit. That is, it does not teach that while some need grace, others do not, but rather suggests why some do not receive it. Because of their impenetrable legalistic understanding of existence, grounded in the effort to effect their own security, they exclude themselves from the source of grace.

Via's (1974) claim that the parable has a "tragic conclusion" (involving an expulsion of the first hired) is unconvincing, given that the parable is in fact open-ended: we don't know how the grumbling workers will react to the landowner's explanations. But the point about the importance of these workers to any adequate interpretation of the parable is surely valid, and so one must share Via's dissatisfaction with the attempts to reduce its message simply to "God's generosity for the last." According to the parable, God *is* indeed generous to the last; but surely, the parable also includes a message about the first—and, indeed, a message addressed to the first. As Donahue (1988:79), among others, has argued, "the interaction between the householder and those first hired is the key to interpreting the parable." There is indeed a crucial message here addressed to and concerning the first hired. The question is how this message should be understood.

As mentioned earlier, according to Via (1974) the message about the grumbling workers and addressed to them is the grim message of expulsion: they have excluded themselves from God's grace. But the text of the parable does not support such an interpretation. Rather, as noted, for example, by Lambrecht,

> The conclusion of the parable serves as a warning. A definitive condemnation does not issue forth from the parable. It should be noted that Jesus, as the narrator of the parable, does not recount the labourer's answer to the owner's question. Yet, that question is not rhetorical. . . . We have before us, then, an open parable. The most profound reason why Jesus resorts to this parable is his concern to convince and win over his opponents. (1991:80)

What is it, then, that Jesus wants to convince his opponents and his listeners of? Lambrecht's answer is the one quoted earlier: he wants to convince them "of God's immense goodness." We might ask: immense goodness to whom—to "the last" or to all? And the answer seems clear—to all. God's goodness to "the last" alone would not convince "the first," it is only a message of God's immense goodness to *all* people (including themselves) that could have a chance to convince even "the first." But if God's gifts to "the first" represent a merited reward rather than grace, there would be no evidence of God's immense goodness to all people, including "the first." It must be the case, then, that the parable speaks of God's free gifts to *all* people; of God's love for *all* people, and of God's desire that *all* people should live with him (should live with God).

Kistemaker (1980:78) comments that Jesus' parable "showed that God does not deal with all men in accordance with the principles of merit, justice, and economics." It would seem strange, however, if God dealt with some people on the basis of grace and with others on the basis of merit. Surely, Jesus shows in this parable something different—namely, as Keating (1997:71–72) puts it, "Evidently, entry into the kingdom of God is not a question of merit . . . we enter the kingdom not by meriting but by consenting to the invitation."

Maillot (1993:89) makes a similar point when he says that "man speaks of justice; God speaks of grace." The principle of grace, established through the image of the landowner's dealings with the workers of the eleventh hour, must apply to God's dealings with people in general; otherwise, "our Father" would be only *some* people's father and some other people's master and employer. But if God wants to do good things for all people, regardless of their richness or poverty in good deeds, why should anyone work full time in God's vineyard, enduring the tedium and exhaustion of the long hours and the heat of the day? Is Jesus devaluing such service (on God's behalf)?

This question applies not only to the workers of the first hour but also to the Pharisee in the temple and to the older brother in the parable of the prodigal son; and it is this parable that offers the clearest answer, in the words of the father to the older son: "Son [literally "my child"], you are always with me and all that I have is yours." It is a privilege of the older brother to always be with the father, and it is the privilege of the workers of the first hour to be fully employed in the vineyard. What this image means, I suggest, is that God wants people to *want* to live with God. According to Jesus, the older brother was wrong in seeing himself as a paid servant, slaving for his father to obtain a payment; instead, he could have found happiness in voluntarily living with the father as a son, not as a servant. Similarly, if we see the lord's vineyard in the parable as an image of God's kingdom, and working in the vineyard as an image of living with God, the workers of the first hour will appear to be privileged rather than unfairly treated. After all, according to Jesus, living with God and working in God's vineyard is the best thing that can happen to a human being, it is like finding the pearl of great price.

Thus, Jesus doesn't devalue good works on God's behalf but links their value with a person's attitude to God and with his or her desire to live with God. As the parable of the laborers in the vineyard emphasizes, God is good; anyone who wants to live with God can be expected to want to do good things—not to earn something from God but to be close to God (who is good), to live with God. This suggests the following additional components of the explication:

(r) God is someone good
(s) it will be good if you want to do good things because you want
to live with God,
not because you want God to do good things for you

To deduce this message from the parable we must go, to some extent, beyond the narrative details, but a parable is not an allegory in which every detail can be given an independent interpretation and every aspect of the interpretation must be supported by an identifiable narrative detail. I am not arguing that working in the vineyard as such should be equated either with living with God or with doing good things or that the payment of a denarius should be equated with God's doing good things for people. Rather, the parable must be interpreted as a whole— a complex whole, different parts of which can be supported with judicious references to individual details but always in the context of an overall interpretation that is consistent with the message of Jesus' other parables and sayings.

The link between working (doing good things) and living with God is highlighted more clearly in the prodigal son than in the laborers, but since the two parables are closely related and can each be taken as a commentary on the other, we can see it as part of the laborers in the vineyard, too. As Keating (1997:74) observes about the laborers, "Acceptance of the invitation is the key to belonging to the kingdom"—and awareness of one's own work and merit may be a hindrance in accepting God's invitation: "The problem of a faithful and virtuous life . . . is that it creates the sense of having earned something from God and thus misses the invitation." The people who want and expect a reward or a payment for their good deeds can fail to notice that God is inviting them (along with others) to his kingdom—not in payment for those good deeds but simply out of love. They can also fail to notice that what God wants and expects of them is that they should try to love other people (as God loves all people) and that, consequently, they should want God to do good things for other people, as they want God to do good things for themselves.

The commentators who assume that God deals with some people (the workers of the first hour) on the basis of merit appear to be making the same error as the workers of the first hour did themselves: they, too, assumed that God was going to deal with them on the basis of merit; and so they missed the invitation to a different kind of relationship—one based on grace and embracing *all* people. At the end of the day they, too, thought that God was treating them differently from the workers of the eleventh hour. They failed to notice God's gracious invitation, extended to them all, to the first, as well as to the last, to come to his vineyard.

Capon (1989:54) rightly writes in this connection about the catholicity (i.e., universal applicability) of God's scheme of salvation: "Jesus' story of the Laborers in the Vineyard is every bit as much a parable of grace as it is of judgment, and vice versa. It is about a grace that works by raising the dead, not by rewarding the rewardable; and it is about a judgment that falls hard only upon those who object to the indiscriminate catholicity of that arrangement." The only aspect of this passage that I dissent from is the word "judgment": as noted earlier, the parable is open-ended and the message to the first hired is not one of judgment but one of warning and appeal. However, the content of that warning and of that appeal is, as Capon suggests, that they must accept the "indiscriminate catholicity" of God's plan of salvation. Without understanding and accepting this "indiscriminate catholicity" one fails to grasp God's goodness and love for all people, and one also fails to grasp the link between living in God's kingdom and loving other people. As Donahue (1988:84) says, "God's justice is different from human justice. It forgives unpayable debts and summons the disciples to live a life of forgiveness to others as an expression of gratitude. . . . Not to rejoice in the benefits given others is to cut ourselves off from those benefits we ourselves have received. Our eyes too become evil."

Loving other people and rejoicing in their good is not an arbitrary condition imposed on those who would wish to enter God's kingdom. Rather, it is a logical consequence of who God is and what living with God means. To cut oneself off from other people (no matter how undeserving) is to cut oneself off from God as father of all people: one cannot maintain one's "sonship" (or "childship") of God while rejecting brotherhood with other people. This is the ultimate warning and appeal that is directed at the workers of the first hour:

(u) God wants to do good things for all people
(v) when someone doesn't want God to do good things for all people
    this person cannot live with God
(w) it will be good if you want God to do good things for all people
    as you want God to do good things for you

Finally, the most difficult question about the laborers in the vineyard is that of God's justice. Is God—as seen in the light of this parable—just, and if so, in what sense? As could be expected, commentators disagree. Some insist that God *is* just, pointing to the fact that the first hired received a just payment: one denarius for the day's work, as agreed on and as due. For example, Donahue (1988:82) writes, "Any interpretation of the parable of Jesus must respect the fact that in his parable the order of justice is maintained. . . . Justice forms the background against which goodness can appear as true goodness . . . Jesus does not deny . . . that God is just and calls for justice. In the spirit of OT [Old Testament] prophecy, he states that justice must be seen as wedded to love and mercy."

Donahue (1998) does not explain, however, in what way the parable reflects God's justice and what exactly this justice consists of; in fact, as quoted earlier, he remarks himself that "God's justice is different from human justice." Other commentators, too, emphasize that whereas God is just, God's justice is different from human justice. For example, Keating (1997:71–72) writes, "Human standards of judgment are subverted in this parable. Ordinary standards of justice cannot explain how the Kingdom works." But if God's standards of justice are different from human standards, what exactly does God's justice consist in?

Faced with elusive statements about God's justice being *sui generis*, some commentators seem willing to conclude that God cannot be described as just at all—not that he is unjust but that the category of justice does not apply to him. For example, Maillot (1993:89), quoted earlier, declares, "Man speaks of justice; God speaks of grace"; and Capon (1989:55–56) explicitly rejects the idea that God keeps any records of good or bad deeds, suggesting that God—like the householder in the parable—gives everyone "full pay" without making any distinctions: "Bookkeeping is the only punishable offense in the kingdom of heaven. For in that happy state, the *books* are ignored forever, and there is only the Book of life. And in that book, nothing stands against you: . . . The last may be first and first last, but that's only for the fun of making the point: everyone is on the payout queue and everyone gets full pay." According to Capon, God relied on bookkeeping (so to speak) "for a good thousand years or so to see if anyone could pass a test like that. But when nobody did . . . God gave up on salvation by the books. He cancelled everybody's records in the death of Jesus and rewarded us all, equally and fully, with a new creation in the resurrection of the dead" (p. 56).

Capon's (1989) interpretation of the parable is partly convincing, but only partly. It is convincing in the sense that God as depicted by Jesus does indeed not save people by the book: as the opening lines of the proposed explication suggest, "all people can live with God" and "God wants this." But the further claim that God "cancelled everybody's records" is not equally convincing. Whereas the parable of the laborers doesn't say anything about this matter, elsewhere, for example, in his sayings about laying up for oneself treasures in heaven (Matt. 6:20), Jesus implies that some records exist—if not records of good and bad deeds committed on earth, then records of treasures, which stand against a person as one dies.

What exactly this image of treasures in heaven means is a matter discussed elsewhere (see chapter 4, section 6). Perhaps it means that a person wakes up from death with a certain deposit of love accumulated (in his or her heart or soul) from one's life on earth. The parable of the laborers doesn't say anything about that and no such suggestion has been included in the explication, but it doesn't preclude such a possibility either. It would not be justified to conclude from this parable, as Capon (1989) does, that no personal records exist on the other side of death and that, as Keating (1997:72) puts it, "God does not distinguish between persons." In the light of Jesus' parables and sayings, he may well do so. It is even possible, as suggested by Matthew in verse 16, that some of those last hired will arrive in the other world with greater "deposits of love" (in their person) than some of those hired first. Stott ([1978]1992:156) linked the image of a person's heavenly treasures with "the increase of faith, hope and charity, all of which (Paul said) abide," commenting that "all we can take to heaven is ourselves."

But putting aside verse 16, which is generally held to have been created by Matthew, the parable doesn't say anything about the presence or absence of distinctions among people in the kingdom of God. Nor does it discuss any consequences of people's good or bad deeds or good or bad choices. It seems justified, therefore, to conclude that it is, above all, a parable about God's grace being open to all and, as Lambrecht (1991) says, about "God's immense goodness"; also, it is an appeal to people not to begrudge others this goodness but to appreciate it and to rejoice in it. (The Sermon on the Mount adds that they should try to imitate it in their own lives.)

This brings us to the following overall explication—long and complex, in accordance with Maillot's (1993) observation, quoted earlier, that this is a parable of exceptional richness:

(a) God is good
(b) God wants to do good things for all people
(c) all people can live with God
(d) God wants this

(e) some people think:
(f)   "I have done many good things
(g)   because of this God will do many good things for me
(h)   this is good
(i)   some other people haven't done many good things
(j)   because of this God will not do many good things for these
         people
(k)   this is good"

(l)   it will be bad if you think like this
(m) God is not like this
(n) God wants to do good things for all people
(o) if some people don't do many good things
         God wants to do good things for these people
         as God wants to do good things for all other people
(p) if some people do many good things
         God wants to do good things for these people
         because God wants to do good things for all people
         not because these people do many good things

(r) God is someone good
(s) if you want to live with God it will be good if you want to do good
    things
(t) it will be good if you want to do this because you want to live with
    God, not because you want God to do good things for you

(u) God wants to do good things for all people
(v) when someone doesn't want God to do good things for all people
    this person cannot live with God
(w) it will be good if you want God to do good things for all people
    as you want God to do good things for you

Components (a)-(d) present God's goodness, manifesting itself in his desire to do good things for all people and to open his kingdom to all people. Components (e)-(k) present the way of thinking of the workers of the first hour—conscious of their own merits; expecting a reward; and comparing themselves favorably with other people, who they imagine are not similarly meritorious and deserving of a reward. Component (l) warns against such a way of thinking, as based on a false idea of God (m), and (n)-(p) present a different picture of God, focusing on his desire to do good things for all people, regardless of their achievements. Components (r)-(t) encourage a desire to do good things as a way of living close to God, whereas (u)-(w) encourage a loving and well-wishing attitude to other people, presenting it as a necessary concomitant of living with God—a God who wants to do good things for all people.

THIRTEEN

The Servant's Reward

Luke 17:7–10

7. And which of you, having a servant ploughing or tending sheep, will say to him when he has come in from the field, 'Come at once and sit down to eat'?
8. But will he not rather say to him, 'Prepare something for my supper, and gird yourself and serve me till I have eaten and drunk, and afterwards you will eat and drink'?
9. Does he thank that servant because he did the things that were commanded him? I think not.
10. So likewise you, when you have done all those things that were commanded, say, 'We are unprofitable servants. We have done what was our duty to do.'

The parable of the servant's reward can be misleading. The fact that its authenticity is sometimes disputed (see, e.g. Funk et al. 1993:363) is related, I think, to the difficulties involved in its interpretation: on some readings, this parable "doesn't sound like Jesus" and can be seen as inconsistent with the main thrust of his teaching. I believe, however, that the problem lies in misguided interpretations rather than in the parable itself, and that if it is properly interpreted it shows itself to be perfectly consistent with other parables and sayings generally attributed to the historical Jesus.

The key to the right interpretation lies, I think, in the recognition that this is one of Jesus' "corrective" rather than "expository" parables. If the purpose of, say, the lost sheep is to tell people about God ("God is like this"), the purpose of the servant's reward is to correct one particular misconception about God and his relation to people. Thus the parable can be misleading: it is one-sided, and if the particular correction it offers is seen to be presenting the whole picture or the main picture, Jesus' intention in telling the parable is obscured.

Both the language and the imagery of the parable may seem harsh and may offend modern Western sensibilities. A modern reader of the Gospel is not keen to think of himself or herself as an "unprofitable servant." It is important, therefore, to see through such language and such images to the meaning that lies behind. To anyone who has read the Gospels as a whole it must be clear that Jesus didn't see the relationship between God and a human being to that between a master and a servant but rather as analogous to that between a father (or mother) and a child. Anything, therefore, that Jesus wanted to convey with the image of a dutiful servant must be understood against the background of the basic image of God as father, and more particularly, *Abba* (dear Father)—a loving, loved, and trusted father. The importance of seeing the *Abba* image behind that of a master was justly emphasized by Jeremias:

> If you do not learn to say *Abba* you cannot enter the Kingdom of God. . . .
> This, then, is the beginning of conversion of the new life—learning to call God *Abba* with childlike confidence, knowing that one is safe in his protection, and conscious of his boundless love. But we must recognize that becoming again like a child involves (Matt. 18:4) the confession of guilt (cf. Luke 15:18), an attitude of humility, and an acknowledgement of one's poverty and littleness before God. In the same way, the simile of the Servant's Reward (Luke 17:7–10) is a demand for the renunciation of all pharisaic conviction of one's righteousness.[1] (1966b:152)

The validity of these remarks does not depend on the exact semantic value of the word *Abba* (cf. chapter 5, section 2) but is independently supported by Jesus' sayings, such as the one reported in Mark 10:15: "Whoever does not receive the kingdom of God as a little child will by no means enter it." The childlike attitude toward God, to which Jeremias (1966b) is referring, implies the following components (in a person's attitude toward God):

I know:
    God wants to do good things for me
    as God wants to do good things for all people
I know:
    God wants to do good things for me
    not because I have done some good things
I know:
    God wants to do good things for me
    not because I can do some good things

Although I am not going to include these components in my explication, I think they need to be kept in mind as an essential background to this parable's message. As noted by Jeremias, this trust in God's love must, according to Jesus, be free from any reliance on one's supposed righteousness or on one's achievements and merits; whatever I might do in God's service must not be seen as a basis of God's love because this love is unconditional and preexisting, as the love of a parent for a small child: whatever a small child does, these actions are not the basis of the parent's love.

The corrective character of the parable, seeking to dispel a common misconception, is strongly emphasized by Kistemaker:

> Constantly he [Jesus] had to teach his disciples not to work in God's kingdom for the sake of rewards. God does not employ his servants in order to reward them for their services. No servant can ever say, 'God is indebted to me'. God does not buy services like an employer buying the time and skills of an employee. And because God does not enter into an employer-employee relationship, no one can ever put a claim on God for services rendered. . . . No one can claim a word of appreciation from him for doing his duty. If God grants favors and gives rewards, he does so out of grace and not because of merit. (1980:247–8)

I will return to some of the themes touched on in this passage later; for the moment, I will focus on the implicit assumption that whereas those addressed are not to work in God's kingdom for the sake of rewards, they are nonetheless expected to do some things in God's service. This point, which is usually not disputed in the discussions of the parable's meaning but which is seldom spelled out, complements in an important way Jeremias's (1966b) point about the need to become like little children. God's love, as presented by Jesus, is unconditional and doesn't depend on a person's actions; this doesn't mean, however, that a person is free not to do anything. On the contrary, the idea of God's love is combined in Jesus' teaching with the idea of God's will, a will that God's children should want and strive to fulfill.

With the image of the servant, which can be seen as complementary to the image of the child, the parable dispels the notion that God doesn't care at all about what people do or not do. Rather, it suggests that God does want people to do some things and does care whether or not they do them. As a formula, this can be stated as follows:

(a) God wants every person to do some things

If God as depicted by Jesus didn't want and didn't need human effort, presumably he wouldn't assign any specific tasks to people. The image of a servant implies that God does need and count on human effort to achieve his aims and that he does want to use people as the executors of his plans. But, the story suggests, God is not going to buy human effort, paying for it with good things of one kind or another. Rather, he wants human effort, human cooperation, or human service to be given freely, as an expression of human love for God, just as God's gifts for people are given freely and not in payment for meritorious deeds.

In the traditional language of theology, this would be referred to as God's will: every person must find and try to fulfill God's particular will for him or her. The image of the servant and the reference to having "done all those things that were commanded" imply that a person can do the things that God wants him or her to do:

(b) if God wants a person to do some things this person can do these things

These two components [(a) and (b)] can be viewed as the parable's underlying assumptions. Logically, the parable could lead from these two assumptions to the question of whether or not a person does do what God wants them to do, but this is not this particular parable's concern. Rather, it raises the question of how people think about the things God wants one to do. The model evoked (and opposed) by the parable can be presented as follows:

(c) sometimes a person thinks:
(d)   "God wants me to do some things
(e)   if I do these things, God will do good things for me because of this"

In addition to talking about rewards and merits, commentators often talk about the notion of *claim*: a person who has tried, as best one could, to fulfill God's will in his or her life has no claim on God because of this (God doesn't owe this person anything). Thus, according to Müller (1995:141), the parable of the servant's reward "targets boastful reliance on one's religious merits and achievements, and claims to recompense for service to God. The person who has conscientiously fulfilled God's commandments and Jesus' instructions, should not boast before God and fellow human beings, but rather regard himself or herself as an 'unprofitable', poor, unworthy servant." Müller adds that this applies above all to the community leaders . . . who 'guard and plough' in God's field."

This idea of a claim (or, rather, no claim) on God suggests the thought that "God will have to do some good things for me" because of what I have done; and I think the parable does indeed target this thought, too, as well as the more basic expectation of a reward or recompense ("God will" rather than "God has to"):

(f) I want to do these things because of this
(g) if I do these things, God will have to do some good things for me because of this

In the parable, Jesus rejects the model based on an expectation of reward and on a claim on God, as a wrong model to follow—

(h) it will be bad if you think like this

and he urges the adoption of an alternative way of thinking, which can be roughly
described as one of disinterested and, I would say, devoted following of God's
will:

(i) it will be good if you think:
(j)   "I know: God wants me to do some things
(k)   I want to do these things because of this"

But the desire to do God's will for the sake of doing God's will rather than
for a reward is not presented as high-minded indifference to one's own good.
Rather, in the model of the relation between a human being and God presented
by Jesus, one knows that God wants to do good things for one regardless of what
one has or hasn't done. God's wanting to do good things for people can be taken
for granted; one doesn't have to work toward this goal by conscientious service.
Instead, one can relax in the knowledge of God's unconditional love and benevolence, unrelated to anything that one might do, and respond to it by a desire
to do God's will. Accordingly, I will include in the explication the following component, summing up the three more explicit components discussed at the outset
of this chapter:

(m) I know:
          God wants to do good things for me
          not because I have done some good things
          not because I can do some good things

The point of the parable is clearly related to that made by Paul in his letter
to the Romans (4:4): "Now to him who works, the wages are not counted as
grace but as debt"; the metaphor of a servant (as in a different way, that of a
child) is used, so to speak, in opposition to the metaphor of a worker who is
working for wages and to whom a payment is due. One is like a useless servant
only in the sense that one is not like a laborer to whom God owes a payment.
This is the part of the message of the laborers in the vineyard that is reiterated
in the servant's reward:

it will be bad if you think:
          "I have done some good things
          God has to do good things for me because of this"

As Maillot emphasizes, the parable of the servant's reward makes two main
points, not one, and we cannot understand the second without understanding
the first at the same time. The second point is that in relation to God, a human
being is like a useless servant to whom no payment is due, not like a laborer
who has the right to a payment; the first point, however, is that God has tasks
for every human being and wants them to be fulfilled. If one has fulfilled all
those tasks as best one could one is still like a useless servant—but also, like a
beloved child—in the sense that the goods that God wants to shower on one are

not like payment for a hired laborer but constitute a free gift, a gift of love, whose value is out of all proportion to the value of the work performed and not based on it at all:

> The clumsiest and the most incompetent person can enter the vineyard. Because its master is not a master. He has introduced a new relationship between himself and us: one of gratuitousness. One can therefore peacefully put oneself to work. . . . One knows that this master doesn't owe us anything, because he is pure love. . . . One doesn't seek any more to know whether one is useful; one is thankful to know that God wants to use us. . . . What is decisive is that Christ calls us to work, opens to us his vineyard. . . . The important thing is to do what we are given to do, because we owe it to ourselves to do it. Even if it is done badly. (1993:295-296)

This means that although God doesn't have to do anything for me because of the things that I do, nonetheless God does want me to do some things and it is important that I should strive to do them:

God wants me to do some things
I want to do these things because of this

This brings us to the following overall explication:

(a) God wants every person to do some things
(b) if God wants a person to do something this person can do it

(c) sometimes a person thinks:
(d)   "God wants me to do some things
(e)   if I do these things, God will do good things for me because of this
(f)   I want to do these things because of this
(g)   if I do these things, God will have to do good things for me because of this"

(h) it will be bad if you think like this
(i) it will be good if you think:
(j)   "I know: God wants me to do some things
(k)   I want to do these things because of this"

(l) it will be good if you think at the same time:
(m)   "I know:
            God wants to do good things for me
            not because I have done some good things
            not because I can do some good things"

I have not attempted to reflect in this explication the self-deprecating attitude that some scholars see as part of the parable's message because I do not think that this is really part of it. For example, according to Fitzmyer (1985b:1147), the passage "deals with the inadequacy of service of Christian disciples. In this concluding set [of sayings] Jesus inculcates the idea that after all that Christian disciples have done they are still 'unprofitable servants' (17:7–10)." Fitzmyer also quotes another commentator's, Plummer's (1928: 402), remark: "The point is that man can make no just *claim* for having done *more* than was due," and he adds, "No matter how much a person does in God's service, there is a sense in which he/she is still 'unprofitable'" (p. 1147).

But does Jesus' parable really convey a message about the inherent and inescapable inadequacy of people's service? I think not. Surely the reason that one should not think about one's attempts to comply with God's will in terms of rewards and recompense is not that one's efforts are necessarily inadequate, but rather that one should see oneself as God's child instead of God's employee. As Kistemaker (1980:247–248), quoted earlier, says, "God does not buy services like an employer buying the time and skills of an employee"; "God does not enter into an employer-employee relationship" with people, and "no one can put a claim on God for services rendered." Whether or not one's service can be adequate does not seem to be a question that is addressed. Rather, the parable suggests that one should simply strive to do one's best. Can a child's efforts be adequate? Surely, this is the wrong question to ask.

Accordingly, the harsh words, "unprofitable servants," should not be seen as God's (or Jesus') verdict about people, declaring that people's efforts have no value in God's eyes, but rather as a hyperbolic and paradoxical way of expressing the idea that one must not have this thought: "God has to do some good things for me because of what I have done." People are assigned tasks, and they can show their love for God by striving to fulfill these tasks, but they are not God's employees; God's love for them and his desire to do good things for them does not hinge on how well or how poorly they have fulfilled their tasks.

However, had Jesus compared people, in relation to God, only with children, this could have been (wrongly) understood to be denying the seriousness of their efforts and responsibilities in God's eyes. The complementary metaphor of servant helps to prevent such a misunderstanding; as depicted by Jesus, God does have tasks for human beings and he wants these tasks to be taken seriously—not to test their obedience but to carry out his great plan for humanity. It is important to rehabilitate the parable of the servant's reward by reading it as a corrective to a particular misconception rather than as an attempt to rob human efforts—both individual and collective—of their dignity and usefulness. God has tasks for people; and it seems perfectly reasonable to assume that these tasks include, as many modern theologians insist, trying to improve conditions on earth.

Nocke (1995:98) observes that "the idea that all efforts to improve the life conditions on this earth should be superfluous (because the desired, and perfect final shape of things will be brought about by God) is incompatible with Christian hope, as is also the opposite extreme—that one can or must make a concrete earthly future goal (for example a particular social order) the final goal of history." Referring to the biblical image of the city of God, Nocke speaks of Christian hope as follows:

We are called to collaborate in the building of this city. We cannot fore-
see what final form the construction work will lead to. Perhaps much of
what we are building, perhaps even all of it, will collapse. But our efforts
will not be useless. The city will arise. God will ensure that. . . . we will
not know exactly the final building plan. . . . But we will not see the production of our work being simply discarded by God and replaced by his
own works: rather, we will recognize in the city shaped by God the stones
(and perhaps the ground-plans) on which we have worked. And therefore
it will be our city. (p. 98)

It is important to recognize that the parable of the servant's reward is not incompatible with thinking about human effort along such lines.

Finally, it should be noted that the parable has an important place in the body
of Jesus' sayings because of the light it throws on the intended meaning of all
the other sayings that refer to reward (as discussed in chapter 4 sections 2, 3,
and 4). The servant's reward seems to show conclusively that whereas Jesus did
use the word *reward*, he used it, so to speak, in quotation marks, and did not
view the relations between people and God in these terms. On the contrary, he
explicitly rejected such a view of people-God relations. Not surprisingly, commentators who insist on attributing to Jesus a way of thinking based on the notions
of rewards and punishments have problems with this parable.

For example, Crossan (1992:104–106), who discusses this parable at some
length, tries to determine which parts of it are likely to go back to the historical Jesus. Although assuming that in part at least this parable does go back to
Jesus, he nonetheless asserts that "it is a flat contradition of the logic" of the
other "Servant Parables," notably the doorkeeper (Mark: 13:33–37; Luke 12:35–
38), the overseer (Matt. 24:45–51; Luke 12:42–46), the talents (Luke 19:12–
26), and the throne claimant (Matt. 25:14–30). Crossan calls these four parables
"group A" and says that "17:7 undermines the entire logic of those parables
in which good servants are rewarded and bad servants punished. No matter
how much or how little of 17:7–9 comes from Jesus, it is clear that group A
has been contradicted."

But the alleged contradiction arises only in an interpretation of those other
parables in terms of rewards and punishments. Given that such an interpretation is questionable on other grounds (as discussed in chapters 14 and 15), the
fact that it is also flatly contradicted by the message of the servant's reward suggests that the proper conclusion is to abandon it. To insist on it is to be compelled to either attribute a flat contradiction to Jesus (as Crossan 1992:106 does)
or to discount the parable of the servant's reward as one invented by Luke rather
than due to Jesus (as, e.g., Funk et al. 1993:363 do).

When it is read in the way suggested here, the parable of the servant's reward is entirely consistent with Jesus' overall message and reinforces this message in important ways. Not only does it not devalue human efforts as inadequate,
superfluous, or useless; on the contrary, it suggests that God is counting on them.
At the same time, it repudiates, once more, the idea that people should think of
all their good works as a basis for a future reward and as a means of ensuring

their salvation. To think like this is to misunderstand the nature of the relationship between God and people as it was presented by Jesus. To quote the great
Russian Christian philosopher, Nikolaj Berdyaev,

> A false interpretation of "good works" leads to a complete perversion of
> Christianity. "Good works" are regarded not as an expression of love for
> God and man, not as a manifestation of the gracious force which gives
> life to others, but as a means of salvation and justification for oneself,
> as a way of realizing the abstract idea of the good and receiving a reward
> in the future life. This is a betrayal of the Gospel revelation of love.
> ([1937]:1954:107)

FOURTEEN

The Great Feast

Luke 14:16–24

16. A certain man gave a great supper and invited many,
17. and sent his servant at supper time to say to those who were invited, 'Come, for all things are now ready.'
18. But they all with one accord began to make excuses. The first said to him, 'I have bought a piece of ground, and I must go and see it. I ask you to have me excused.'
19. And another said, 'I have bought five yoke of oxen, and I am going to test them. I ask you to have me excused.'
20. Still another said, 'I have married a wife, and therefore I cannot come.'
21. So that servant came and reported these things to his master. Then the master of the house, being angry, said to his servant, 'Go out quickly into the streets and lanes of the city, and bring in here the poor and the maimed and the lame and the blind.'
22. And the servant said, 'Master, it is done as you commanded, and still there is room'
23. Then the master said to the servant, 'Go out into the highways and hedges, and compel them to come in, that my house may be filled.'
24. [For I say to you that none of those men who were invited shall taste my supper.]

The parable of the great feast (or great supper) exists in three different versions: Matthew's, Luke's, and Thomas's, and it is widely believed that all three writers have altered the original parable in some ways. In particular, Matthew is held to have upgraded the great supper to a royal wedding feast and to have expanded it by adding a wedding guest without a proper festive garment. In my discussion of the parable, I will rely on Luke's rather than Matthew's (or Thomas') version, bearing in mind, however, that according to many commentators Luke expanded the original parable and in particular added a second invitation (v. 21), with its special reference to the poor, the maimed, the lame, and the blind;[1] also, verse 24 is believed by many scholars to have been added by Luke (see Fitzmyer 1985b:1052).

Both Matthew and Luke have allegorized the story in various ways, implicitly linking the different invitations with different groups of people: Jews versus Gentiles, the rich versus the poor, and the important people versus the outcasts. Following this tradition, many modern commentators also see the parable as targeting different ethnic, religious, or social groups (cf., e.g., Schottroff 1987; Vögtle 1996). Other commentators, however, see the central point of the parable in its challenge to the addressee ("And *you*, how are you going to respond to the invitation?"); it is this approach that I will follow in this chapter, focusing, as usual, on the existential and universally applicable aspects of Jesus' message.

Dodd (1965:91) summarizes the "common nucleus of the story" (identified on the basis of Luke and Matthew) as a tale of "how the invited guests were left out of the feast by their own act, and their places taken by rag-tag-and-bobtail." He also says that in its basic form, "the parable suggests the rejection of that call by the 'righteous', and its acceptance by 'publicans and sinners.'" Fitzmyer (1985b:1091) sums up the original message in a similar way, referring in particular to Thomas' version: "Those who were invited to the dinner and refused to respond to the servant's summons will find no place at the Father's banquet; their places will be taken by others brought in from outside, and they will be excluded only because they have excluded themselves." Similarly, Lambrecht states that

> in regard to its essential elements the Jesuanic [as opposed to Matthean and Lucan] parable must have gone more or less as follows: Someone, a rather wealthy person, prepares a banquet and sends his servant to say to the invited guests that everything is ready. However, all make excuses, with the result that nobody comes. The initiator (*sic*) becomes furious and orders his servant to go and bring in others, anyone. His house must be full" (1991:130)

Funk et al. (1993:353), who support the authenticity of the core of Luke's version (except for the second invitation and verse 24), stress its characteristic "Jesus features" as follows: "The secondary guests are as surprised to be included as the listeners were surprised that those first invited all rejected the invitation. The parable, thus conceived, has all the earmarks of a genuine Jesus story." Other commentators emphasize another feature characteristic of Jesus' personal style:

the portrayal of the kingdom of God in terms of a wonderful opportunity that God doesn't want anyone to miss. Nocke, who compares the teaching of Jesus with that of John the Baptist, says,

> While in Jesus' proclamations apocalyptic threats also play a certain role—images of fire, darkness, weeping and gnashing of teeth—next to them we find other motives to conversion: a pressing invitation not to miss the feast, not to remain outside when inside a wedding banquet is going on . . . a summons to a wonderful life in which one can feel oneself to be a child of God, to be someone resembling the father. Such words show that the preaching of Jesus—in contrast to that of John the Baptist—is more inviting than threatening. But this invitation, too, creates a situation in which one must decide. He who doesn't come, who doesn't want to enter the new life, the proposed fellowship with God, the joy proclaimed by Jesus, will in the end see himself outside. Thus with the closeness of the Kingdom of God comes also the nearness of judgment. All Jesus' words about the judgment can be understood as wake-up calls, summoning people to this situation of decision. (1982:71–72)

Roughly speaking, then, this is the meaning of the parable of the great feast: an urgent invitation to a fellowship with God. However, like the laborers in the vineyard and the prodigal son, to which it is closely related, this parable, too, is very complex, and we must try to identify both those aspects of its message that link it with the other parables and those that give it its own distinctive emphasis. The starting point of the parable (not of the story but of the message) is clear enough: God wants all people to come to the heavenly banquet; they are all invited, and in fact God is eager to have them all there. This can be represented as follows:

(a) God wants to do good things for all people
(b) all people can live with God
(c) God wants this

What is not spelled out in the parable but is nonetheless implied from the outset is that the feast is a wonderful occasion and that it can't be in anybody's interest to miss it: if people fail to accept, they will miss out on a unique opportunity whose splendor they seem unable to grasp but whose loss they would be bound to regret later. Referring to both God's invitation to all people to live with him in his kingdom and to the immeasurable value of this invitation, Eichholz (1984:130) speaks about "the wonder of the grace of the invitation" (*das Wunder der Gnade der Einladung*) as a key aspect of the parable: one gets to the kingdom of heaven by invitation, and this invitation is a marvelous gift of God:

(d) if a person lives with God this is very good for this person
(e) nothing else is like this
(f) if a person doesn't live with God this is very bad for this person

The possibility of living with God is open to all people. What this means from an individual's point of view is that one definitely *can* live with God if only one wants to—not because salvation, one's living with God, is in one's own hands but because God wants this:

    (g) if a person wants to live with God this person can live with God
    (h) because God wants this

As many commentators have observed, salvation is not in a person's own hands but in God's hands: one comes to the heavenly banquet by invitation, not on one's own initiative; but the invitation is there, extended to everyone, and this is what (g) and (h) seek to capture.

At the same time, however, the master of the house (who obviously stands for God) does not want to *force* the invitees to come to the feast, and angry and hurt as he is, he does give them the opportunity to refuse the invitation (e.g., he doesn't send his servants to kidnap those who have declined the invitation and to bring them to the party by force). As Fitzmyer (1985b:1053) says, "Those who are excluded from the banquet have only themselves to thank; God will not drag the unwilling into it against their will." As in the case of the prodigal son, then, here, too, God gives people the freedom to refuse his invitation:

    (i) if a person doesn't want to live with God this person *cannot* live
        with God
    (j) God doesn't want this person to think: "I have to live with God"

Fitzmyer (p. 1094) quotes in this context, with apparent approval, the comment by Manson ([1937]1961:130), referring to Jesus' teaching in this parable, that "the two essential points in His teaching are that no man can enter the Kingdom without the invitation of God, and that no man can remain outside it but by his own deliberate choice. Man cannot save himself; but he can damn himself."

It seems to me, however, that this formulation is somewhat misleading. True, Jesus does teach in this parable that people can't save themselves but can only consent to being saved by God; but does it really teach that they can effectively damn themselves? "Damn" is of course an ominous word, with implications of eternal separation from God. Jesus' parables teach that people can get lost in this life (like sheep or coins or prodigal sons), but he doesn't make any predictions about eternal and irrevocable separation from God. Rather, he *warns* people not to become separated from God and calls on them to live with God. Admittedly, he also warns that people *can* separate themselves from God and not live with God, as component (i) states, and also that God doesn't want people to think that they *have to* live with God [(j)]. This is different, however, from saying that Jesus teaches that people can effectively damn themselves (i.e., separate themselves from God for all eternity) and that God will simply sit back and watch this happen. There can be no doubt that God is presented in the parable of the great feast (as well as in the lost sheep, the lost coin, and the prodigal son) as emotionally involved: he doesn't merely extend an invitation to people without caring much whether or not they accept. On the contrary, he is very eager that they should want to accept, and when they don't, he is, so to speak, hurt and angry (he feels something bad because of this). Hence the need for the following component (k):

(k) when a person doesn't want to live with God
     God feels something bad because of this
(l) God wants this person to want to live with God

But God's disappointment, hurt, and anger—or however we choose to imagine his bad feelings in human terms—do not make him withdraw and do nothing further. Quite the reverse: as in the story of the lost sheep and the lost coin, God reacts to people's refusal to come to his party in an active way:

(m) God does many things because of this

In the story of the great feast, what God does is to order his servants to go out and look for some other prospective guests, as if his only real concern were to have his dining hall full, with all the places at the table occupied. To interpret these details of the story, however, we must bear in mind the story's minatory character (cf. Eichholz 1984:136; Fitzmyer 1985b:1053). Like the parable of the laborers in the vineyard, the parable of the great feast is directed above all at the first invitees; sending out the servants to fetch other guests suggests not that the first invitees have already been written off as a lost cause but that they are being warned and appealed to. Once again, Jesus is urging those who refuse the invitation to enter God's kingdom to come to their senses, and in doing so he is employing the traditional Jewish rhetorical device of hyperbolic threats. Luke's final line: "For I say to you that none of those men who were invited shall taste my supper," can easily be misunderstood as God's final verdict, categorically rejecting those who have refused his invitation. But in the literary and linguistic world of the Bible (see chapter 26), threats of this kind are typically attributed to God as a ploy in his attempts to bring his people to conversion, to make them turn from their path and return to him. The seventh-century Syrian mystic St. Isaac of Niniveh (1995:172) has commented on this biblical use of rhetorical threats: "How much to be worshippped is our Lord God's gentle compassion and His immeasurable munificence: He makes many threats, but He makes the punishment small out of grace, all in order to increase love for Him in ourselves. May His name be blessed! Amen."

In contrast to the lost sheep, lost coin, and prodigal son, the parable of the great feast focuses specifically on people who decline the invitation to live with God (in the kingdom of God) because they are preoccupied with other things. It is not so much that these people don't want to live with God (e.g., because they want to do bad things) as that they think they have other things to do, more pressing and more important. This can be represented as follows:

(n) sometimes some people don't want to live with God
(o) because they think:
(p) "I can't live with God now because I have to do some other
things"

Eichholz (1984:130) speaks in this connection of the "pressing business of everyday life," (*Vordringlichkeiten des Tages*), which leads to declining the invitation.
Some commentators (e.g., Donahue 1990:141) speak about "the excuses" offered
by the first group, but this appears to suggest that the people in this group had
other reasons for declining the invitation than those stated. This seems to be an
unnecessary hypothesis. Rather, the parable seems to be as addressed to all people
who genuinely believe that they have other things to do, more important or more
urgent than joining God's banquet, and it urges them to rethink their priorities.

The question of priorities is one of the key themes in Jesus' teaching. It is
not developed in the prodigal son, the lost sheep and the lost coin, or the laborers in the vineyard, but it is clearly addressed in the great feast, and in many
nonparabolic sayings of Jesus as well—and nowhere more clearly than in the
sayings that Luke (14:26) placed immediately after the parable of the great feast:
"If anyone comes to me and does not hate his father and mother, wife and children, brothers and sisters, yes, and his own life also, he cannot be my disciple."
As noted by Funk et al. (1993:353), among many others, the very harshness and
provocativeness of this saying, "which must have been offensive to Jesus' audience when he first enunciated it," are a hallmark of its authenticity: except for
minor differences in the phrasing given to it by Luke, Matthew, and Thomas,
"the Fellows [of the Jesus Seminar] were agreed that Jesus was the author"
(p. 504). "The saying concerns the place of family ties in relation to the claims
made by God's imperial rule. Jesus gave absolute priority to the latter. Of course,
he did not advocate that his disciples exhibit animosity or hostility towards parents, but that they accord their highest allegiances to the Kingdom of God."

Clearly, this is also the main theme of the parable: the kingdom of God must
be seen as the highest priority; and anyone who loves his or her own life more
than the chance of living with God is being foolish and self-destructive: "Do not
worry about your life . . . but seek first the Kingdom of God" (Matt. 6:25–33;
cf. Luke 12:22–31); "Whoever desires to save his life will lose it, and whoever
loses his life for my sake will find it" (Matt. 16:25; cf. Luke 17:33; John 12:25).

Both the parable and the related sayings about priorities implicitly acknowledge the validity of seeking what is good for one but warn against the dangers
of losing sight of the greatest good of all: God. It is the people who get their
priorities wrong and don't see the truth about human life and about God who
are targeted by the parable, with the exhortation presented in the form of a threat:
"If you don't want to join the banquet, I will offer your seats to someone else!"
("If you don't want to live with God someone else will!")

The intended function of the parable as warning, admonition and appeal seems
unmistakable. As noted by Fitzmyer (1985b:1053), it is "a minatory parable which
emphasizes the seriousness of the preaching addressed by Jesus to his compatri-

ots and seeks to elicit from them acceptance, not refusal; they are addressed with an insistent invitation." Dupont (1969:II, 276) insists that the parable of the great feast is "a parable of anger," and of course it is, at one level. But this doesn't force us to interpret its message as one of judgment and condemnation, as Dupont appears to do: "Refusing to reply to the appeal, those invited first draw upon themselves a sentence of definitive exclusion; their places at the feast will be occupied by other guests, apparently much less respectable. The presence of these substitute guests illustrates the impossibility of forgiveness for those invited first" (p. 272). Again, all this, too, may seem plausible on a simple reading of the narrative. But as a message about God it would be contrary to the core of Jesus' teaching. Here as elsewhere, Dupont pursues his favorite theme of God's special love for the "nondeserving" (i.e., for him, both the poor and the sinners), apparently disregarding the fact that those who reject God's call for the sake of their own affairs are also sinners and are also people for whom God cares.

Far more convincing is an interpretation that sees in the parable a renewed invitation and challenge to the addressees, as proposed (among others) by Lambrecht (1991):

> The hearers must have realized that they themselves are addressed. One can make a fuss about one's conceited importance while remaining deaf to God's appeal and thus miss the real opportunity in life. . . . No judgment is pronounced, but nevertheless we hear an earnest warning and at the same time an attempt by Jesus to persuade and win over his opponents. (p. 131)
>
> The hearers are confronted with Jesus' appeal. Will they respond positively to the renewed invitation which the parable contains? That answer implies a rejection of the past, a radical conversion, an existential decision. . . . With this parable . . . Jesus, far from condemning his opponents, invites and challenges them once again. (p. 138).

The reference to the need for the dining hall to be full and for all the places at the table to be taken (v. 23) takes on a particular significance in the light of this approach to the interpretation of the parable. If we assume (as we must) that the master of the house stands for God, this question suggests itself: what does it mean for God's dining hall to be full? How many places are there in heaven? In the light of Jesus' parables taken as a whole the answer to this question seems to be that there are as many places as there are people; God's dining hall will be full only if *all* people take their places. Just as 99 sheep do not make the fold full (and the shepherd content), so 97 invitees will not make up for the 3 who have, respectively, bought a piece of ground, acquired five yoke of oxen, and married a wife because, as Paul says, God "desires *all* people to be saved and to come to the knowledge of the truth" (1 Tim. 2:4).[2] Jesus makes it clear that the threats of the master of the house are in fact thinly disguised appeals.

It is certainly not the case, then, that in Jesus' teaching about the kingdom of God some groups of people can be replaced with others. The narrative detail of

replacement in the plot of this particular story must be interpreted in the context of Jesus' parables as a whole and with an understanding of Jewish rhetorical devices and figurative use of language. Accordingly, it would be wrong to
include in the explication of the parable's message anything along the lines of
"if you don't want to live with God someone else will." Rather, what appears
justified is to follow the representation of the way of thinking of the first invitees
("I can't live with God because I have some other things to do") with explicit
discouragement:

> (q) I say to every one of these people:
> (r) it will be bad for you if you think like this

as well as a positive appeal to adopt an alternative way of thinking:

> (s) it will be good for you if you think:
> (t)   "I want to live with God
> (u)   nothing else is like this
> (v)   if I can't do some other things because of this
>   I will not do these other things"

Dupont (1969:II, 276) stresses the host's "determination to have his banquet
succeed despite the defection of the invitees. The project conceived by God will be
realized, if not for the benefit of the recipients of the promise then for others . . .
attention is focused on the host of the banquet, on his will not to let his project
end in defeat." But what *is* God's project, which he is so determined not to let
end in defeat? Isn't it the project of having all his sheep, without exception, on
one green pasture and of having all his flour leavened? What Paul says *expressis
verbis* in his letter to Timothy, quoted earlier (that God wants all people to be saved),
Jesus says as clearly in images, such as those of the found sheep and of the dough
all leavened. If so, God's project can only succeed if—in yet another image—God's
house (prepared for all humankind) is full, that is, if (sooner or later) all the invitees
accept the invitation. Since in his other parables, such as the leaven and the mustard seed, Jesus expresses "supreme confidence" (Perrin 1976:158) that God's project
will indeed succeed, the parable of the great feast cannot mean an irrevocable condemnation of the first invitees but must rather be understood as an appeal to the
hearers to accept God's pressing invitation to the party.

Thus, I propose the following overall explication:

The parable of the great feast

> (a) God wants to do good things for all people
> (b) all people can live with God
> (c) God wants this
>
> (d) if a person lives with God this is very good for this person
> (e) nothing else is like this

(f) if a person doesn't live with God this is very bad for this person

(g) if a person wants to live with God this person can live with God
(h) because God wants this
(i) if a person doesn't want to live with God this person *can* not live
    with God
(j) God doesn't want this person to think: "I have to live with God"

(k) when a person doesn't want to live with God
       God feels something bad because of this
(l) God wants this person to want to live with God
(m) God does many things because of this

(n) sometimes people don't want to live with God
(o) because these people think:
(p) "I can't live with God now because I have to do some other
    things"

(q) I say to every one of these people:
(r)   it will be bad for you if you think like this
(s)   it will be good for you if you think:
(t)   "I want to live with God
(u)   nothing else is like this
(v)   if I can't do some other things because of this
             I will not do these other things"

This explication does attribute feelings to God[3] (k), but they are not presented here as anger or wrath; the anger of the host is interpreted here as no less metaphorical than the banquet, the house, the man, or the servant. Furthermore, God's determination to do "many things" (m) is not presented as the result of those bad feelings but rather of God's great desire to induce all those who have refused the invitation to change their minds (l). The sequence of components (k)–(m) suggests God's love for people and his desire to overcome their refusal with love. Since the component of God's determination (m) follows the component of God's desire to win people over (l) rather than the component of God's bad feelings (k), the explication rejects, in effect, the interpretations in terms of wrath and retribution. In doing so, it seeks to distinguish the logic of the images from the logic of the message.

St. Isaac of Nineveh (1995:171) has written, "Just because (the terms) wrath, anger, hatred, and the rest are used of the Creator, we should not imagine that He (actually) does anything in anger or hatred or zeal. Many figurative terms are employed in the Scriptures of God which are far removed from His true nature." What is striking about St. Isaac's comments is his deep insight into the nature of the figurative language of the Bible, in particular, into the logic of the relationship between the "outer surface" (p. 163) of the biblical text (or "the bodily exterior of the narratives," p. 171) and its inner meaning. He discusses this relationship with both lucidity and passion:

That we should imagine that anger, wrath, jealousy or the like have anything to do with the divine Nature is something utterly abhorrent for us: no one in their right mind, no one who has any understanding (at all) can possibly come to such madness as to think anything of the sort about God. Nor again can we possibly say that He acts thus out of retribution, even though the Scriptures may on the outer surface posit this. Even to think this of God and to suppose that retribution for evil acts is to be found with Him is abominable. (pp. 162–163)

The explication proposed here does not say anything about the long-term consequences of declining God's invitation, and so it treats verse 24 as an instance of the biblical genre of *Drohrede* (rhetorical threats) rather than as a factual prediction. Any attempts to translate such threats into intimations about the ultimate consequences of people's rejection of life with God can only be speculations. And yet speculations of this kind are hard to resist and perhaps are even necessary, if only because of the need to counter the doctrine of eternal damnation, which is evidently contrary to the spirit of Jesus' teaching as a whole.

What will happen, then, to a hypothetical person who has, throughout his or her life, refused God's invitation to the banquet? As suggested by numerous Christian commentators—from the fourth century Father of the church St. Gregory of Nyssa to eminent twentieth-century thinkers like the Orthodox theologian Sergius Bulgakov, the Protestant theologian Paul Tillich, and the Catholic theologian Hans Urs von Balthasar—the apocalyptic images of fire, darkness, and the weeping and gnashing of teeth (see, e.g. Matt. 8:12) suggest suffering and regret, as well as the need for a painful process of transformation and purification. St. Gregory of Nyssa wrote,

For it is not out of hatred or vengeance for an evil life (in my opinion) that God brings painful conditions upon sinners, when He seeks after and draws to Himself whatever has come to birth for his sake; but for a better purpose He draws the soul to Himself, who is the fountain of all blessedness. The painful condition necessarily happens as an incidental consequence to the one who is drawn. When goldsmiths purify gold by fire from the matter which is mixed with it, they do not only melt the adulterant in the fire, but inevitably the pure metal is melted away with the base admixture. When the latter is consumed the former remains. In the same way when evil is consumed by purifying fire, the soul which is united to evil must necessarily also be in the fire until the base adulterant material is removed, consumed by the fire. (1993:83–84)

The model of this (temporary) after-death exclusion, purification, and pain could be represented along the following lines:

when a person wants to do bad things
    something happens to this person because of this
because of this after this a part of this person is bad

because this part of this person is bad,
>   after this person dies for some time this person cannot live with
>   God
something has to happen to this person before this person can live with
>   God
this something will happen to this person

when this is happening to this person
>   this person feels something very bad because of this

because this is happening to this person for some time
>   after some time this person doesn't have a bad part any more
because of this, after this time this person can live with God
God wants this

Although this model was not spelled out in the Gospels in the way it was in St. Gregory's writings, it is entirely consistent with Jesus' own teaching.

According to St. Gregory (1993), then—and to the whole subsequent theology of hope (as opposed to the theology of fear; cf. Hryniewicz 1990)—any exclusion from God's heavenly banquet can only be temporary, as well as self-inflicted. The question cannot be "Who is included and who is excluded?" but only "Who will be included first and who last?" And to this latter question Jesus' answer seems clear and emphatic—it may be the reverse of what people might expect—those who by virtue of their status and position in this world can be expected to enter the kingdom of God first, may in fact enter it last, and those who can be expected to be admitted last, or not at all, may in fact be admitted first: "So the last will be first, and the first last" (Matt. 20:16), or in a less extreme form, "many who are first will be last and the last first" (Matt. 19:30; cf. also Mark 10:31; Luke 13:30; Thom. 4:2–3).

In support of St. Gregory's (1993) interpretation, it can be pointed out that the language of Jesus' most indisputably authentic references to people entering the kingdom is often strikingly temporal (first vs. last, before vs. after), and it is also striking how in many commentaries this temporal language has been replaced by pronouncements of eternal exclusion. For example, the provocative logion about tax collectors and harlots entering the kingdom first, addressed according to Matthew (21:23) to "chief priests and the elders of the people," is generally regarded as unquestionably Jesus' own: "Assuredly, I say to you that tax collectors and prostitutes enter the Kingdom of God before you" (Matt. 21:31). Funk et al. (1993:232), who note that the majority of the Fellows of the Jesus Seminar regard this saying (v. 31b) as authentic, have commented as follows: "The Fellows who voted red or pink are of the opinion that the contrast in the saying in v. 31b is characteristic of Jesus: the tax collectors and prostitutes, with whom Jesus associated, will enter God's domain, whereas the religious authorities will not. This contrast is analogous to the contrast between the rich and the poor: the rich will not get in, the poor will."

But Jesus did not say that the religious authorities would *not* enter the kingdom of God, only that the tax collectors and prostitutes would enter *before* them.

Jesus was not excluding anybody, he was inviting (on God's behalf) everyone without exception. In fact, even Jesus' references to the temporal sequence (the last, the first) should probably be understood as a contrast of the *present* (positive) response of the tax collectors and sinners to the *present* (negative) response of the religious elders; and the purpose of the contrast can best be understood in terms of exhortation and warning rather than as a prediction of the relative order of different people's entry into the kingdom. Thus, as a first approximation I propose the following:

The last will be the first, and the first last

people think about many people like this:
    "these people are bad people
    these people don't live with God"

I say to you:
    many of these people want to live with God now
    when a person wants to live with God this person can live with
        God

people think about many other people like this:
    "these people are good people
    these people live with God"

I say to you:
    many of these people don't want to live with God now
    when a person doesn't want to live with God this person cannot
        live with God

Since St. Augustine's (1984) *City of God* the tendency to read Jesus' "last" as "excluded for ever" and "before" as "only" has become so entrenched in the prevailing Western theological tradition that many commentators seem not to notice Jesus' temporal (i.e., relative) language and subconsciously read it as absolute and referring to all eternity. The Eastern theological tradition stemming from the writings of the Church Fathers St. Clement of Alexandria and St. Gregory of Nyssa is different. To quote St. Gregory again,

[God] has one goal: when the whole fullness of our nature has been perfected in each man, some straight away even in this life purified from evil, others healed hereafter through fire for the appropriate length of time, and others ignorant of the experience equally of good and of evil in the life here, God intends to set before everyone the participation of the good things in Him, which the Scripture says eye has not seen nor ear heard, nor thought attained. . . . But the difference between a life of virtue and a life of wickedness will appear hereafter chiefly in allowing us to participate earlier or later in the blessedness which we hope for. The duration of the healing process will undoubtedly be in proportion to the measure of evil which has entered each person. This process of healing the soul would consist of cleansing it from evil. This cannot be accomplished without pain. (1993:116)

In a similar vein, Issac of Niniveh (1981:415) affirmed that "the torment of hell consists in regret" and that in fact "those who are tormented in hell are tormented by love." Thus, the punishment for excluding oneself from the feast is the awareness of having excluded oneself from the feast. But this punishment must have an end: "The one who punishes in order to restore health, punishes in love. . . . God punishes in love" (p. 369); "it is absurd to think that sinners in hell are deprived of God's love" (p. 415); "the Gehenna . . . is 'the fruit of sin', 'with a beginning and an end, even though it is not known when this end will come'" (Bettiolo 1990:339). The German editor of Isaac's writings, Barbel (1971:219-222) sums up St. Isaac's argument by saying that "the aim of the punishment lies in the end of the punishment. . . . Justice and goodness are both there together. All has to be paid for, often for a long time to the last farthing . . . but at the end there is God waiting."

The parable of the great feast does not address directly the question of evil that results from wanting to do bad things, but it does address the question of not wanting to "attend the banquet" and thus excluding oneself from fellowship with God. The point that is directly relevant here is that in the light of Jesus' teaching as a whole such an exclusion can be regarded only as temporary, or as eternal only in the subjective sense of the word (subjectively experienced as endless). To quote the Russian philosopher Nicolas Berdyaev (who writes in the Eastern Christian tradition),

Eternal hell is a vicious and self-contradictory combination of words. Hell is a denial of eternity. . . . There can be no diabolical eternity—the only eternity is that of the Kingdom of God and there is no other reality on a level with it. . . . But an infinity of torments may exist in the self-contained subjective realm. In his own inner life a man may feel that his pain is endless, and this experience gives rise to the idea of an everlasting hell. In our life on earth it is given us to experience torments that appear to us to go on for ever. . . . It is only such torments that are really terrifying and suggestive of hell. But their infinity has nothing to do with eternity and has no objective reality. . . . Hell is not eternity at all but endless duration in time. ([1937]1954:269).

The parable addresses the aspect of hell that in Berdyaev's opinion presents the greatest theological difficulty: can people be deprived of the option of choosing hell? Can't some invitees refuse to come to the banquet and never change their minds? According to Berdyaev, this is the crux of the matter—it is not a question of God offering the seats of those rejecting the invitation to someone else or of God condemning them forever but of the right of those rejecting the invitation to persevere in their rejection: "Hell is necessary not to ensure the triumph of justice and retribution to the wicked, but to save man from being forced to be good and compulsorily installed in heaven. In a certain sense man has a moral right to hell—the right freely to prefer hell to heaven. This sums up the moral dialectic of hell" ([1937]1954:267). Berdyaev concludes that the problem of hell (understood as a person's free and persistent refusal to join the banquet) "is an ultimate mystery that cannot be rationalized."

Jesus' parables, such as the leaven, the mustard seed, and the seed growing secretly, which exude "supreme confidence" (Perrin 1976:158) that God's project will ultimately succeed, acknowledge this mystery through their images ("people can't know how this will happen"). In the parable of the great feast, Jesus emphasizes his confidence not so much in God's ultimate success as in God's great desire for the project to succeed and in his determination to see that it does:

> God wants all people to live with God
> God feels something because of this
> God does many things because of this

If we understand the parable of the great feast as a warning and an appeal, we can see the parable itself as one of the things that God does to make his project of universal salvation succeed: he appeals to his hearers to join the party. Many recent commentators insist that this is how it should be understood. For example, Weder says that the contrast between those invited first and those invited second

> does not aim at different groups of people but signifies two sides in the hearer him- or herself: their old indifferent attitude to the other-worldly joyful feast and their new insight into what is happening right now. . . . All hearers are to begin with in the position of the first invitees, in so far as they don't recognize that in Jesus the Kingdom of God is breaking in. And the parable seeks to induce *all* hearers to become like those people in the streets so that they all, like those, gladly accept the invitation to the feast. (1978:65)

Similarly, Imbach (1995:74) writes, "It is not a question of a prediction which must come true, but of an urgent admonition to follow the invitation to believe, while there still is time. What Jesus wants to do is not to announce perdition and damnation, but to call on people to turn back and to follow (him)." (For other similar comments see also Harnisch 1985:251–225; Lambrecht 1991; Petzoldt 1984:60–63.)

Thus, the parable of the great feast is not a story about some "other people" (e.g., Jews vs. Gentiles or the rich vs. the poor) but an open invitation to the hearer. The parable does *not* mean what the story, taken literally, might seem to imply:

> some people don't want to live with God
> because of this, these people will never live with God

God wanted these people to live with God
God doesn't want this any more
some other people will live with God
God wants this

To interpret the parable along these lines would be similar to concluding from Jesus' sayings in Matthew 5:29–30 that he urged people to pluck out their right eye and cut off their right hand. If the culture to which Jesus belonged is properly understood and if the language of hyperbolical images and threats characteristic of that culture is not mistaken for the language of factual information, the deeper meaning of the parable comes to light: here as elsewhere, Jesus insists through his images that "all people can live with God, God wants this" and, more specifically, that "*you* can live with God, God wants this."

In his recent book, entitled *The Coming of God—Christian Eschatology*, in which he highlights the "return of the doctrine of universal salvation" at the threshold of the new millennium, Jürgen Moltmann (1996:237) he evokes the image of the great feast as follows: "In the feast of eternal joy all created beings and the whole community of God's creation are destined to sing their hymns and songs of praise. . . . The feast of eternal joy is prepared by the fullness of God and the rejoicing of all created beings" (p. 338). If the symbolic language of the Scriptures is not misunderstood but is interpreted in the light of the New Testament as a whole, Moltmann's gloss on the great feast will be seen as apt and consistent with Jesus' overall teaching.

FIFTEEN

The Last Judgment

Matthew 25:31–46

31. When the Son of Man comes in his glory, and all the holy angels with him, then he will sit on the throne of his glory.
32. All the nations will be gathered before him, and he will separate them one from another, as a shepherd divides his sheep from the goats.
33. And he will set the sheep on his right hand, but the goats on the left.
34. Then the King will say to those on his right hand, 'Come, you blessed of my father, inherit the kingdom prepared for you from the foundation of the world:
35. for I was hungry and you gave me food; I was thirsty and you gave me drink; I was a stranger and you took me in;
36. I was naked and you clothed me; I was sick and you visited me; I was in prison and you came to me.'
37. Then the righteous will answer him, saying, 'Lord, when did we see you hungry and feed you, or thirsty and give you drink?
38. When did we see you a stranger and take you in, or naked and clothe you?
39. Or when did we see you sick, or in prison, and come to you'?
40. And the King will answer and say to them, 'Assuredly, I say to you, inasmuch as you did it to one of the least of these my brethren, you did it to me.'

41. Then he will also say to those on the left hand, 'Depart from me, you cursed, into the everlasting fire prepared for the devil and his angels:

42. for I was hungry and you gave me no food; I was thirsty and you gave me no drink;

43. I was a stranger and you did not take me in, naked and you did not clothe me, sick and in prison and you did not visit me.'

44. Then they also will answer him, saying, 'Lord, when did we see you hungry or thirsty or a stranger or naked or sick or in prison, and did not minister to you?'

45. Then he will answer them, saying, 'Assuredly, I say to you, inasmuch as you did not do it to one of the least of these, you did not do it to me.'

46. And these will go away into everlasting punishment, but the righteous into eternal life.

This is a very striking text, perhaps one of the most striking in the entire New Testament. Is it a parable? Opinion is divided, and whereas some books on Jesus' parables include a discussion of it, others do not. Among the influential books that do include it are, for example, Jeremias's (1972) *The Parables of Jesus*, Lambrecht's (1991) *Out of the Treasure*, and Donahue's (1990) *The Gospel in Parable*. Without entering into that debate, I will focus on the more interesting question of what Jesus meant by this text (which I *will* call a parable, for convenience).

But does this parable really go back to Jesus himself? On this point, too, scholars are divided, and before we proceed the reasons advanced must be at least briefly considered. Let us begin with the skeptical view of the Jesus Seminar:

> The story is not a parable but a portrayal of the last judgment. The only figurative language is the simile of the sheep and the goats in vv. 32 and 33. It is often said that the sheep are customarily white and goats normally black, which makes it easy to tell them apart. The theme here is judgment and the judge is the son of Adam or the King (vv. 34, 40) who will come in his glory and sit on his throne to render judgment (v. 31). This all fits well into Matthew's theological scheme, which became popular in the post-Easter community. Fellows of the Seminar designated the story black by common consent. (Funk et al. 1993:258)

Thus, the Fellows of the Jesus Seminar reject the story's authenticity without qualification. Yet the only argument advanced against it is that it "fits well into Matthew's theological scheme." A more pertinent question may be this: does the story fit into *Jesus'* theological scheme—in other words, does it cohere with Jesus' teaching as a whole, especially with those parts of it that are by common consent the most indubitably authentic (such as, for example, the parable of the good Samaritan and the first three beatitudes)?

At this point, however, the question of authenticity becomes enmeshed with that of the story's meaning: to decide whether the meaning is consistent with Jesus' teaching as a whole, we must establish what it is. If we decide that it is consistent with the core of Jesus' teaching, the fact that it also fits into Matthew's theological scheme will no longer count against its authenticity.

To my mind, the most convincing argument in favor of authenticity is that by Manson: "This word-picture of the Last Judgment [Matt. 25:31–46] has no parallel in the other Gospels. Whether or not it belongs as a whole and in all its details to the authentic teaching of Jesus, it certainly contains features of such startling originality that it is difficult to credit them to anyone but the Master Himself." This is echoed by Jeremias (1966b:162): "Our pericope [Matt. 25:31–46], although it may not be authentic in every detail, contains in fact 'features of such startling originality that it is difficult to credit them to anyone but the Master himself'" (T. W. Manson [1937]1961:249)[1]

According to the Jewish scholar Montefiore ([1927]1968:325), the parable of the Last Judgment "contains one of the noblest passages in the entire Gospel." Referring in particular to what he calls "the glorious verse 40" ("Verily I say unto you: whatever ye have done unto one of these my humblest brethren, ye have done unto me", he says: "A more sublime reply can hardly be conceived. The worth which Christianity assigned to every human soul brought a new feature into the Roman and heathen world. . . . The doctrine had doubtless immense effects upon civilization and morality in various directions." Montefiore nonetheless stresses that the parable "is *in its present form* a product of Christian thought" [my emphasis] (p. 323).

The view that the present form of the parable does not go back to Jesus is now widely shared. In particular, it is widely accepted that in the original parable Jesus was not speaking about himself but about God (see, e.g., Meier 1980:303–305; for a detailed discussion of the probable Matthean interventions, see, e.g., Lambrecht 1991:265–282). What I want to discuss in this chapter, however, is the core of the story, focusing in particular on its strikingly original features, that is, on the identification of the love of God with the love of the suffering neighbour, the blessed ignorance of the "left hand," and what Meier calls "the stunning universalism of the story" (p. 304). It is probably the use of apocalyptic images and phrases that makes the scholars of the Jesus Seminar consider the whole parable to be inauthentic. Funk, and Hoover (1993:197) comment on another apocalyptic parable, Dragnet (Matthew 13:47–50: "The separation of the good from the bad at the end of the age . . . is a typical Matthean theme. . . . These interests are absent from Jesus' authentic parables and sayings"). It seems that the Fellows of the Jesus Seminar find any references to the final separation of the good from the bad unacceptable and wish to attribute them to Matthew rather than to Jesus—although, in fact, Mark and Luke, too, attribute apocalyptic images to Jesus (cf., e.g., the weeping and gnashing of teeth in Luke 13:18 or "the fire that shall never be quenched" in Mark 9:43).

I, too, believe that Jesus did not make any predictions about an ultimate separation of "the good people" from "the bad people." This doesn't mean, however, that he didn't use apocalyptic images, such as that of the separation of the sheep from the goats. In my view, rather than denying the authenticity of all the texts that attribute these images to Jesus, we need to rethink their meaning and to question their traditional interpretation, as indeed many theologians are now doing. Hryniewicz (1990:11) notes that "the field of Christian eschatology has in the last few decades undergone profound transformations." Another Catholic theologian, Franz-Josef Nocke, has characterized these changes as follows:

> Thus an old eschatology describing, in a seemingly objective manner, a distant future has become a theology of hope. . . . In this century theology has learnt to pay more attention to the hermeneutics of biblical and dogmatic utterances. In eschatology, this has led to the recognition that many utterances were meant not as descriptions containing factual information but rather as encouragement, warning and guidance expressed in images. Thus the stress has shifted from information to hope. The purpose of eschatology lies not in establishing the geography of the heavenly regions but in showing in which direction one can look for heaven and in what present experiences heaven is foreshadowed. (1982:14–19)

These changes—which build on a tradition within Christianity going back to its beginnings—open new possibilities for the interpretation of all the so-called parables of judgment. They enable us to acknowledge the authenticity, or possible authenticity, of the texts that attribute to Jesus the use of apocalyptic images, without attributing to him a teaching about an everlasting heaven for some people and an everlasting hell for others.

More than sixty years ago the Russian philosopher Nicolas Berdyaev ([1937] 1954:272) wrote, "The conception of hell created by the good for the 'wicked' . . . is based upon Gospel texts which are taken literally, without any consideration for the metaphorical language of the Gospel or any understanding of its symbolism. It is only the new Christian consciousness that is worried by the Gospel words about hell; the old rejoiced in them." More recently, the Protestant theologian Paul Tillich (1964:435) observed, "The qualitative contrast between the good and evil ones, as it appears in the symbolic language of both Testaments, means the contrasting quality of good and evil as such (for example, truth and lie, compassion and cruelty, union with God and separation from God). But this qualitative contrast does not describe the thoroughly good and thoroughly evil character of individual persons."

The fact that the majority of the Fellows of the Jesus Seminar have voted the apocalyptic parable of the Last Judgment black (i.e., inauthentic) reflects, I think, the new Christian consciousness that Berdyaev ([1937]1954) was writing about, but it does not reflect the new (or newly rediscovered) insights into the symbolic character of apocalyptic images, emphasized by Tillich (1964). If we recognize these insights and explore their implications in the light of new developments in biblical hermeneutics, literary theory, and linguistics, we can reclaim strikingly Jesus-like texts such as the parable of the Last Judgment as largely Jesus' own, without ipso facto attributing to Jesus any teaching about an objective and eternal hell, peopled with sinners—a teaching that I argue is incompatible with his key parables of the lost sheep, the lost coin, the prodigal son, and the leaven.

In building an explication of the parable's original meaning, I will try to ignore those aspects of the content that according to detailed textual studies such as Lambrecht's (1991), are probably due to Matthew, and I will try to focus on those features of "startling originality," which in many commentators' view point to the historical Jesus himself. Let us start with a quote from Jeremias arguing for the parable's essential authenticity:

> The commentaries on this parable refer to Egyptian and rabbinic parallels, which also talk of deeds of mercy as the decisive factor in the judgment. But what a difference! Both in the Egyptian Book of the Dead and in the Talmud the dead man boasts self-confidently of his good deeds ('I have given satisfaction to God by doing what he loves: I have given bread to the hungry, water to the thirsty, clothes to the naked' is what we read in the Egyptian Book of the Dead). How different is the surprised question of the righteous in vv. 37–39 of our passage, who are not conscious of having rendered any service, apart altogether from any idea that in the persons of the poor and wretched they had been confronted unawares with the hidden Messiah. This conception is attested as a characteristic of Jesus' preaching, and as belonging to the early tradition, by such sayings as we find in Mark 9.37, 41. (1966b:162)

The saying in Mark's Gospel to which Jeremias is referring here reads, "Whoever receives one of these little children in my name receives me; and whoever receives me, receives not me but him who sent me." Other commentators also emphasize the differences between Jesus' parable and its closest parallels in other traditions. What many find particularly striking is the identification of the love shown to suffering people (one's neighbors) with love shown to God. For example, Meier (1980:303) points out that works of mercy were valued in Judaism and other religions, too: "It is not the commendation of works of mercy that is the surprising element here. The elect know they have performed such works, and know that such works are pleasing to God. . . . What astounds them, however, is that the King claims that they did all this 'to me'. When? How?" Meier is referring here to Jesus' identification with all people (his brethren) and, in particular, with all those who suffer.

In the partial explication of the parable below, I will try to reflect the theme of identification without, however, attributing to Jesus, as the speaker of the parable, a christological interpretation. Rather, I will follow Lambrecht's (1991: 273) view that in this parable "with the metaphor of the king, Jesus—like the Old Testament—refers not to himself but to God." Lambrecht says that "for the evangelist, that king became the Son of God, the risen Christ," and this interpretation by Matthew can of course be regarded as inspired. Montefiore ([1927]1968:325) observes that it was the identification of the needy and suffering people with Jesus that gave the message of the Last Judgment its unique power: "doubtless the peculiar combination in Jesus—as simple Christian believers hold—of the man and the God has given an immense power to this special motive, 'for his sake'." Nonetheless, the explication of what Jesus meant should, I think, refer not to Jesus himself but to God. We can, therefore, start the explication as follows:

(a) God wants people to do good things for other people
(b) like God does good things for all people
(c) when bad things happen to some people
(d) God wants other people to do good things for these people
(e) when a person is doing good things for some other people
    because this person knows that something bad happened to
      these people
    this person is doing something good for God
(f) God wants people to live like this

Component (a) articulates the implicit but obvious assumption of the parable that God wants people to love other people and to express this love in deeds. Component (b) has, admittedly, been imported into this explication from other passages in the Gospels, such as Luke's (6:36) "be merciful, just as your Father also is merciful." Component (c) focuses the hearers' attention more specifically on suffering people: whereas God wants people to do good things for other people in general (a), the parable makes it clear that he takes a special interest in those who suffer—the hungry, the poor, the sick, the prisoners, and so on (a point also highlighted in the Beatitudes, as well as in Jesus' own life). And since God clearly takes this special interest in those who suffer, he also wants people—his children— to do likewise and to do good things for other people whenever they know that something bad has happened to them and whenever they are in a position to do so. In fact, the combination of (c) and (d) suggests that God may want to do good things for those who suffer, using for this purpose other people (those addressed by the parable) as his representatives, his servants, his tools, or (adapting the words of a church hymn) a "channel of his mercy." Simone Weil ([1951]:1973:150–151) has written about this as follows: "The love of our neighbor is the love which comes down from God to people. It precedes that which rises from people to God. God is longing to come down to those in affliction. . . . In true love it is not we who love the afflicted in God; it is God in us who loves them."

Component (e) expresses the idea that God identifies with people who suffer and that by doing good things for those afflicted, one is actually doing good things for God himself. As mentioned earlier, Meier (1980:304) believes that this identification refers to Jesus rather than to God, but I think that in trying to articulate Jesus' own original message we can apply to God what Meier says about Jesus: "It is not that he considers these works 'as though' they were done to him; in virtue of his mysterious presence in all who suffer, they *were* done to him."

This explication envisages a condition: by doing good things for those who suffer, one is doing good things for God—if one is doing this in response to their suffering ("because one knows that something bad has happened to them") and not for any other reason. Thus, the *motive* is important, and although this is not referred to in the parable explicitly, arguably it is one of its background assumptions.

The motive, Jesus implies, must be love and compassion; and if he doesn't imply it with total clarity in this particular parable, he makes it abundantly clear elsewhere. It is not good deeds as such that count but good deeds that come from a loving heart. It is not charitable deeds per se that are identified with doing something good for God; rather, it is the loving response to the misfortune of one's neighbor that is identified with the love of God. Meier (1980:305) observes, with respect to this parable, that "love of the (poor) neighbor is practically identified with love of God"; "love of the poor neighbor" means something like compassion, more precisely, that which in Russian is called *žalost'* (see Solov'ev [1883]1966:v. 7:57; for detailed discussion, see Wierzbicka 1992:167–169).[2]

Arguably, although the parable of the Last Judgment does not raise the question of motives in an overt way, the very surprise that the merciful show at the time of judgment suggests a purity of motive: they were doing good things for other people not because they wanted to obtain a reward from God but because they genuinely wanted to do good things for these other people; and in so doing, they were, unbeknown to themselves, doing something good for God. Alluding to the parable of the Last Judgment, Weil ([1951] 1973:150–151) wrote, "God is not present, even if we invoke him, when the afflicted are merely regarded as an occasion for doing good. . . . He who gives bread to the famished sufferer for the love of God will not be thanked by Christ. He has already had his reward in this thought itself. Christ thanks those who do not know to whom they are giving food" (see chapter 4, section 2). For Weil, the metaphor of "not knowing to whom one is giving food" means that the giver is responding to the misfortune (as the Good Samaritan did, being "moved by compassion") and that the giver's full attention is focused on the suffering human being: "It is not time to turn his thoughts towards God. . . . There are times when thinking of God separates us from him" (pp. 150–151). This is what I referred to earlier as "the blessedness of the left hand" (see chapter 4, section 3). If the left hand doesn't know what the right hand is doing, a person can perform acts of love and compassion without thinking at the same time something like this: "I am doing something good for other people" (and perhaps: "God will do something good for me because of this").

It is this kind of intuition that I have tried to reflect in shaping component (e) of the explication. In formulating this component in this way, I think I have also excluded good works that are intended to gain a reward in heaven from the kind of active love that Jesus is talking about in the parable. Berdyaev has highlighted the difference between the two as follows:

A false interpretation of "good works" leads to a complete perversion of Christianity. "Good works" are regarded not as an expression of love for God and people, not as a manifestation of the gracious force which gives life to others, but as a means of salvation and justification for oneself, as a way of realizing the abstract idea of the good and receiving a reward in the future life. This is a betrayal of the Gospel revelation of love. ([1937]1954:107)

Component (f) links the love of one's neighbor with a way of living one's life. How do we know that the acts of love and mercy referred to in the parable are seen by Jesus not as isolated deeds but as a way of life? As other images evoked elsewhere in the Gospels (e.g., the two roads in Matt. 7:13) and sayings that refer explicitly to life and living (e.g., Luke 17:33), the image of sheep and goats in the parable of the Last Judgment suggests a more global perspective on a person's life: as one will clearly see at the time of the Last Judgment, at times one has lived one's life more like a sheep and at other times more like a goat. It is not just a matter of isolated deeds but of the whole orientation of one's life. Component (f) is also useful in linking love and mercy with God's will. Meier, in his comments on the parable of the Last Judgment, has linked love and mercy toward other people with God's will and the love of God:

> Earlier in the gospel, in an Israel-versus-the-disciples context, Jesus identified his brothers as those disciples "who do the will of my Father" (12:50); and this will was interpreted in terms of mercy (9:13; 12:7). Now, in the broader context of the last judgment, he calls all people in need his brothers. . . . These deeds for others are the criterion of judgment because they define a person's essential behavior and relation to the Judge, not just to other people. (1980:305)

I think my phrase "living like this" corresponds, in essence, to the intended sense of Meier's phrase "a person's essential behavior"; and Meier's references to God's will, interpreted in terms of mercy, are also consistent with the idea reflected in the explication that the love of God (manifested in works of love directed toward people) is in a sense closely related to doing God's will. God wants people to live "like this"—that is, to live doing good things for other people, especially those to whom something bad has happened—and this is, in a sense, indistinguishable from his love. He wants people to do good things for the afflicted because through their actions, he wants to do good things for the afflicted himself (he is "longing to come down to those in affliction," in Weil's [1951]1973 words). At the same time, he wants people to "live like this" because when they do they live with God; and this, too, must be seen as an expression of God's love, given that according to Jesus (as interpreted in this book), living with God is the incomparable treasure and the pearl of great price.

This brings us to the next part of the explication—the appeal to the individual addressee, the gentle call, the urgent invitation:

(g) it will be good for you if you live like this
(h) when you live like this you will live with God

Component (h) has not been formulated in terms of a condition: "if you live like this (now) you will live with God (later)." Rather, it refers also to a person's life on earth: "*when* you live like this, you will live with God."

The scope of the concept of one's neighbor that is evoked in this parable is striking in its universality; according to Jesus, one meets God in *any* suffering person, without any restrictions whatsoever.[3]

> The stunning universalism of this revelation must not be blunted by restricting "the least of my brethren" to Christians, to poor or insignificant Christians, or to Christian missionaries. The phrases used in such passages as 10:42 ("little ones" . . . "because he is a disciple") and 18:6 ("these little ones who believe in me") are different, and the context in such places is clearly ecclesiastical; they lack the sweeping universalism of this scene. (Meier 1980:304)

Some commentators (e.g., Blomberg 1990:209) suggest that the parable of the Last Judgment does make a distinction between Jesus' disciples and heathens: the disciples will be judged by faith, but heathens who have never had a chance to hear about the kingdom and to believe will be judged by love. This seems to me a strange and unconvincing idea. The message of the parable is clear: everyone will be judged by love. As St. John of the Cross (quoted in the *Catechism of the Catholic Church* 1994:267) says in one of his "Dichos," "At the evening of life, we shall be judged on our love." The universalism of this saying echoes that of the parable of the Last Judgment.[4]

Since according to Jesus one meets God in other people, especially in those who suffer, such encounters happen in *this* world, in *this* life, and it is in *this* world that one can start living with God. But the consequences of living with God—or not living with God—extend to the life after death, and this is something that the parable of the Last Judgment focuses on in a special way.

At some point, the parable reminds the hearers, each one of them will die, and after they have died, there will come a judgment. At this judgment, Jesus intimates, people's lives will unfold before them in a new way, and all their acts of love, as well as failures of love, will be revealed to them. At that time, they will see their life in a new light. They will realize that whenever they had been doing something good for other people, especially those afflicted, they had been meeting God in those people and were doing something good for God; and that whenever they had had an opportunity to do something good for someone afflicted but failed to do it, they had ipso facto declined to do something good for the suffering God. Thus, the truth of their life will be revealed to them (not only the truth about their past acts but also the truth about their past motives), and they will judge themselves, rejoicing over all the loving acts they see in their past and feeling painful regret for all the acts of coldness and indifference that they will see there, too. All this can be represented as follows:

(i) at some time you will die
(j) after you die something will happen to you

(k) when this happens you will know how you lived
(l) you will know
(m)   that at some times you did good things for some other people
(n)   because you knew that some bad things had happened to
          these people
(o) you will feel something very good because of this
(p) you will know that at those times you were doing something good
    for God

(q) at the same time you will know
(r)   that at some other times when you knew that something bad
          had happened to some people
(s)   you didn't do anything good for these people
(t)   because you didn't want to do anything good for these people
(u) you will feel something very bad because of this
(v) you will know that at those times you didn't want to do anything
    good for God

The most important aspect of this interpretation is that the judgment is interior and that the line between good and evil, or between the presence and the absence of good, does not divide people but divides aspects of every person's life: sheep and goats do not represent different people but rather the different sides of any one person's life.

Although Jesus did use the imagery of absolute opposites, characteristic of religious symbolism in many traditions (e.g., "losing one's life or preserving one's life," and "perishing or having eternal life"), Tillich's (1964) comments on the dualism of religious symbolism should be borne in mind. As we know from other parables and sayings, Jesus did not divide people into good and bad, righteous and sinners, or sheep and goats. He regarded people as changeable, capable of reorientation, and—regardless of their sins—capable of love. His metaphors of good trees and bad trees, wheat and tares, and sheep and goats did not stand for people. For him, the prodigal son was not a bad person, nor the stay-at-home older brother, a good person; similarly, the tax collector was not a bad person, nor the Pharisee in the temple a good one. Jesus rejected such categorization of people, and it is not true that, as often claimed, he rejected it by reversal, as if the prodigal were unexpectedly shown to be good and the older brother, bad, the Pharisee bad and the tax collector, good. He opposed such dichotomous thinking about people and was at pains to emphasize that God loves *all* people and looks for every single lost sheep.

At the same time, he also emphasized that how one lives one's life does matter, that every encounter with another human being is an encounter with God, that God appears in human life incognito, that after one dies the truth about one's life will be exposed, that one will see this truth and perhaps be boundlessly sorry for all one's missed opportunities to love people and thereby to serve God, and that the regret may be so intense and so painful as to seem endless.

Contemporary theologians increasingly believe that read in the light of the parable of the prodigal son, the parable of the Last Judgment refers not to a judgment by an external judge (God) but to a self-judgment—a revelation of the truth about one's life and the recognition of one's sins and failures (the "left side" of one's life). As for the everlasting punishment of those on the king's left hand, according to many contemporary theologians this, too, is an image, a metaphor. For example, Imbach (1987:36) writes, "In the biblical image of the tribunal the point of comparison lies not in a sentence coming to me from without (that is, from God), but in the fact that my refusal, my false decisions, my guilt will become manifest. I will see myself how it is with me. In the presence of God's love I will be (from within) painfully aware of who I am and what I could have become."

Thus, both the reference to the everlasting fire and to the two categories of people, the righteous and the cursed, can be regarded as metaphorical. The whole image can be taken to mean that after people ("you") have died, God lets them see how they lived, that is, reveals to them the ultimate truth about the good and the bad aspects of their lives; images like that of everlasting fire (or elsewhere, of people wailing and gnashing their teeth) can be taken to mean that when people ("you") finally see their lives in that light, they may experience a profound sense of loss and a profound sense of regret. To quote Hryniewicz,

> The Gospel is not a set of speculations about what is going to happen to people after their death. . . . The image of "hell" points to the seriousness of life, to the great importance of human decisions, and to a person's responsibility for realizing or failing to realize the commandment of loving God and one's neighbour. This image expresses God's appeal to human freedom. . . . (1990:96)

> The Last Judgement consists in the fact that one sees and judges oneself in the truth of eternity, in the light of God's creative purpose. Most importantly, it does not separate some people from others; rather, it takes place within every person. . . . The Last Judgement does not consist in dividing people but in dividing the good and the evil in the same person. . . . The words of the Scriptures about "everlasting damnation" could refer to a memory of one's sins and wrong decisions made during one's earthly life, a memory of a loss which one can no longer make up for. An awareness of one's guilt, which can be seen as a "punishment" and a loss, can also be an element of an all-embracing and dominant sense of eternal happiness. Only good remains. There is no eternal dualism of good and evil. (p. 109)

As Imbach points out, the richest and the most illuminating image of the Last Judgment is provided in the Gospels by the parable of the prodigal son, in which the younger son, having squandered all his money, finally comes to his senses and sees his life in the light in which his father must have seen it.

This means: he recognizes his wrong. It is not the father who judges him, but he himself pronounces the judgment: "Father, I have sinned against

heaven and before you, and I am no longer worthy to be called your son."
Precisely this parable has the power of protecting the image of the 'Last
Judgment' from a false interpretation, which forces God into the role of a
vengeful judge (1987:37).

Hans Urs von Balthasar (1983:293) quotes, with approval, indeed admiration, the "bold statement" by the fourth-century Father of the church Ambrose:
"Idem homo et salvatur ex parte, et condemnatur ex parte," 'the same human
being is both partially saved and partially condemned'. Balthasar says that: "the
same human being stands, so to speak, at the same time on the right and on
the left of the Judge," and he quotes the Swiss mystic Adrienne von Speyr: "Every human being will hear both these utterances: 'Depart from me, you cursed,
into the everlasting fire, prepared for the devil and his angels' and 'Come, you
blessed ones of my Father, inherit the Kingdom prepared for you from the foundation of the world'." The person thus judged can only hope "that . . . all in
them that deserves condemnation will be separated from them and hurled onto
the heap of unusable remains to be burnt before the gate of the holy city."

According to a long tradition in biblical interpretation, starting with Origen
and continuing to the present, this self-judgment will be connected with a radical
illumination by the light of Christ. For example, Basil of Caesarea (4th century) says that "the face of the Judge radiates a divine light, which penetrates
the depths of the hearts, and we will have no other accuser but our own sins,
which through this light will have become present to us" (quoted in Balthasar
1983:265).

The explication in this chapter is consistent with this view. It avoids dividing
people into two categories (those who will be saved and those who will be
damned) and also avoids making predictions about anybody's eternal fate (after
death). Instead, it treats references to two categories of people (the sheep and
the goats) as metaphorical, like the references to the furnace of fire, the outer
darkness, or the wailing and gnashing of teeth. In this, as in other respects, the
explication is consistent with the way of thinking that treats texts like the parable of the Last Judgment as *prophetische Drohrede* (prophetic "warning discourse")
addressed to an individual person and urging this person (always a "you") to
orient his or her life towards God.

To repeat: theological views like these are not a twentieth-century invention
but belong to a long tradition going back to the Fathers of the church and saints
like Gregory of Nyssa (fourth century) or Isaac of Niniveh (seventh century). The
Orthodox theologian Sergius Bulgakov has written about this as follows:

In Christian eschatology the question is always present of the eternity of
the pains of hell and the final reprobation of those sent into "the everlasting fire, prepared for the devil and his angels." From earliest times doubts
have been expressed as to the eternal duration of these torments. . . . From
the earliest times there have been two tendencies in eschatology: the rigorists
affirm that suffering is eternal, final, and without end, the others, whom
Augustine ironically calls . . . *misericordes* ("merciful"), deny the eternity of

punishment and the persistence of evil in creation and acknowledge the
final victory of the Kingdom of God, when "God shall be all in all" [Paul
I Cor. 15:28]. The doctrine of *apokatastasis* is not only that of Origen, whose
orthodoxy has been questioned because of certain of his opinions, but also
of St. Gregory of Nyssa, glorified by the Church as Doctor, and his disciples. It has hitherto been thought that the doctrine of Origen was condemned at the Fifth Ecumenical Council, but recent historical studies do
not permit us to affirm this. As to the doctrines of St. Gregory, more thoroughly worked out and free from Origen's theories on the pre-existence of
souls, they have never been condemned. Consequently, they retain their
standing in the Church, at least as theological opinions. (1976:134–135)

It cannot be denied that in the past more literal interpretations of the parables
have prevailed and that the growing emphasis on the interior nature of the Last
Judgment must be seen as a new stage in the two millennia of reflection and
meditation on the New Testament. The well-known Catholic theologian Karl
Rahner (1980:317) says, "Today we ask if we cannot hope that all people will
be saved. Such a question, and such an attitude, is more Christian than the earlier
ones, and is the fruit of a growing maturity of the Christian consciousness, which
is slowly getting closer to Jesus' fundamental message of the victory of the Kingdom of God." [5] The eminent Protestant theologian Jürgen Moltmann recently
formulated this new-old Christian hope very emphatically:

> The eschatological point of the proclamation of the 'Last Judgment' is the
> redeeming Kingdom of God. Judgment is the side of the eternal kingdom
> that is turned towards history. In that judgment all sins, every wickedness
> and every act of violence, the whole injustice of this murderous and suf-
> fering world, will be condemned and annihilated, because God's verdict
> effects what is pronounces. In the divine Judgment all sinners, the wicked
> and the violent, the murderers and the children of Satan, the Devil and
> the fallen angels will be liberated and saved from their deadly perdition
> through transformation into their true, created being, because God remains
> true to himself, and does not give up what he has once created and af-
> firmed, or allow it to be lost. . . . The eschatological doctrine about the
> restoration of all things has these two sides: *God's Judgment*, which puts
> things to rights, and *God's Kingdom*, which awakens to new life. (1996:255)

The key question for Christian theologians has always been that of how to
interpret New Testament texts such as the Matthean Jesus' parable of the Last
Judgment. Christian mystics have always tended—on the basis of their inner
experience rather than analysis—to be on the side of St. Gregory of Nyssa rather
than St. Augustine. Isaac of Niniveh, who was both a mystic and a biblical scholar,
rejected a literalist reading of an "everlasting damnation" as a deplorable misunderstanding and an insult to God: "It is not (the way of) the compassionate Maker
to create rational beings in order to deliver them over mercilessly to unending
affliction (in punishment) for things of which He knew even before they were

fashioned, (aware) how they would turn out when He created them—and whom (nonetheless) He created" (1995:165). In view of this, Gehenna can only be, according to St. Isaac, temporary and part of God's overall love and mercy; to deny that both the kingdom and Gehenna were foreseen by God for the purpose of our good would be blasphemy:

> That we should further say or think that the matter is not full of love and mingled with compassion would be an opinion full of blasphemy and insult to our Lord God. (By saying) that He will even hand us over to burning for the sake of suffering, torment and all sorts of ills, we are attributing to divine Nature an enmity towards the very rational beings which He created through grace. . . . Among all His actions there is none which is not entirely a matter of mercy, love and compassion: this constitutes the beginning and the end of His dealings with us. (p. 172)

Perhaps the most remarkable aspect of Isaac's confident hope of universal salvation is that he finds it entirely consistent with the underlying meaning of the Scriptures. Indeed, he finds this hope in the Scriptures' "discourse about God," beneath the surface of the "figurative terms" and the "bodily exterior of the narratives" (1995:171); by expressing this hope he seeks to reveal the hidden meaning of the Scriptures:

> No part belonging to any single one of (all) rational beings will be lost, as far as God is concerned, in the preparation of that supernal Kingdom which is prepared for all worlds. Because of that goodness of His nature by which He brought the universe into being (and then) bears, guides and provides for the world's and (all) created things in His immeasurable compassion, he has devised the establishment of the Kingdom of heaven for the entire community of rational beings—even though an intervening time is reserved for the general raising (of all) to the same level. (And we say this) in order that we too may concur with the magisterial teaching of Scripture (p. 176).

I quoted earlier Montefiore's ([1927]1968) praise for the parable of the Last Judgment as "one of the noblest passages in the entire Gospel." Montefiore, however, rejected the traditional Christian belief that the parable was spoken by Jesus, not only because in its present form it shows signs of various editorial interventions but also because "the terrible doctrine of eternal punishment . . . is here emphatically asserted, and solemnly put into the mouth of Jesus." What Montefiore, like many Christian theologians, overlooks is that which St. Isaac of Niniveh (1995) saw with particular clarity, namely, that the apocalyptic images of the parable of the Last Judgment need not be interpreted as a doctrine but as appeals expressed in symbolic language—a language that corresponds also to the subjective experience of hell.

Balthasar (1983:281) quotes, as a comment on this point, St. John of the Cross's description of his own experience of hell. Citing a verse from a psalm, "the torments of hell have . . . seized me," St. John of the Cross says: "The soul feels keenly the shadows of death, mortal anguish and the torments of hell. It feels itself as being without God, punished by God and rejected by God, an object of his displeasure and wrath. The soul feels all this, and more: it seems that this state will last forever."

When St. Augustine (1984) in the *City of God* opposed the hope of universal salvation, devoting no fewer than 10 chapters of the work to an elaborate justi- fication of eternal suffering, he was clearly doing so in a desire to be faithful to "what he took to be clear statements of the Scriptures . . . : 'Scripture, infallible Scripture' makes it clear that all sinners, angelic or human, when they have missed the opportunity for conversion, are to be consigned to a punishment that is lit- erally everlasting" (Daley 1991:149). But "clear statements of the Scriptures" can be misleading, especially if symbolic images are mistaken for factual statements. Over the centuries, mainstream Christian theology has gradually come to a bet- ter understanding of this point and to a greater appreciation of insights such as those of Isaac of Niniveh:

> Many figurative terms are employed in the Scriptures of God, terms which are far removed from his (true) nature. And just as (our) rational nature has (already) become gradually more illumined and wise in a holy under- standing of the mysteries which are hidden in (Scripture's) discourse about God—that we should not understand everything (literally) as it is written, but rather that we should see (concealed) inside the bodily exterior of the narratives, the hidden providence and eternal knowledge which guides all— so too we shall in the future come to know and be aware of many things for which our present understanding will be seen as contrary to what it will be then. (1995:171)

In a chapter entitled "The Dispute About the Bible: Pro and Contra Univer- salism," Moltmann (1996:241) notes that "universal salvation and a double outcome of judgment are . . . both well attested biblically." On the pro side, Moltmann cites, inter alia, numerous passages from Paul's epistles (e.g., Eph. 1:10; Col. 1:20; Phil. 2:10f; I Cor. 15:25; Rom. 11:32) that all emphatically express faith in "the restoration of all things," "the homecoming of the universe," and "God's mercy upon all." But since both "universal salvation *and* a double outcome of judgment" can be supported with quotations from the New Testa- ment, "the decision for the one or the other cannot be made on the ground of 'scripture'. If one presupposes that scripture does not contradict itself, because the word of God to which it testifies is inerrant, one can then try to resolve the contradiction in the direction of the one side or the other" (p. 241).

The full realization of the symbolic character of biblical images such as the sheep and the goats provides a key to resolving the apparent contradiction and to a better understanding of the meaning of "Scripture's discourse about God," hidden "inside the bodily exterior of the narratives" (in Isaac of Niniveh's words).[6] Once we have recognized the purely symbolic character of these refer- ences, we can better focus our attention on the parable's central message and its far-reaching implications for individual and social ethics, to which I will now turn.

As Meier (1980:304) puts it, feeding the hungry "is the criterion by which one enters into or is rejected from eternal life. Therefore we are not dealing with supererogatory works, performed to get 'extra points'. On these works of mercy, which most would not consider their strict duty, hangs their salvation or damnation. . . . Neglect of the poor is the decisive not-doing of the will of God which marks one as fit company for the devil." Meier is using here the language of traditional eschatology, which as I have argued throughout needs to be replaced with a new language, or at least supplemented with suitable explanations. But his main point (that acts of compassion are crucial) is, of course, unassailable, and it rightly draws attention to one of the most important messages that Christianity has to offer to the world at large. To illustrate this, I will quote a Christian missionary in Japan, Jan van Bragt, who wrote about what he sees as the "universal role of representing, embodying, and making influential in society the spirit of Jesus Christ":

> I think here especially of concern for justice and of active and universal love. Do the Japanese not know love? Of course they do, but they tend to be satisfied with benevolent feelings and certainly to restrict their love to people of their in-group, ultimately to their fellow Japanese. The moment when I felt proud of our little Japanese Church was . . . when the Vietnamese boat people started drifting to the Japanese shores and the Catholic Church was absolutely the first (soon followed by Protestant churches) to effectively help them by lodging them in church buildings and offering them all kinds of services. A little later that example was followed by some non-Christian religious organizations. We could then see the leaven at work in the dough, exactly what Japan stood in need of at that moment. (1992:56)

Van Bragt does not see the role of Christianity in Japan in terms of gaining more converts and becoming the whole dough,but rather in becoming "a leaven in the dough of a people and its religiosity"; and he interprets the metaphor of leaven in terms of the universal message of Jesus' parable of the Last Judgment:

> Christianity can and must instigate the religions of Japan to discover in their own religiosity motivation for social and ecological action, or, at least, to open their religiosity toward this kind of concern. The consciousness that social concern is an integral part of a religious attitude may be relatively new in Christianity, but it is certainly absent from Japan's traditional religions. (p. 57)

But whereas the widespread "consciousness that social concern is an integral part of a religious attitude" may indeed be relatively new in Christianity, there can be no doubt that the roots of this consciousness lie in such parables as the Good Samaritan and the Last Judgment.

It is true that after 2000 years we can no longer be sure in what precise form Jesus told the story accessible to us today only through Matthew's Gospel. In particular, one can only think—but not know for sure—that it was Matthew who added the final verse (46), although we do know that Matthew added final verses to other parables, including the threatening final verse in the parable of the unforgiving servant. But whatever the changes, to anyone who has ears to hear, the echo of Jesus' voice is unmistakable; and the authenticity of the core of the story appears to be as incontrovertible as its significance and universal relevance.

SIXTEEN

The Good Samaritan

Luke 10:29–37

25. And behold, a certain lawyer stood up and tested him, saying, "Teacher, what shall I do to inherit eternal life?"
26. He said to him, "What is written in the law? What is your reading of it?"
27. So he answered and said, "You shall love the Lord your God with all your heart, with all your soul, with all your strength, and with all your mind, and your neighbor as yourself."
28. And he said to him, "You have answered rightly; do this and you will live."
29. But he, wanting to justify himself, said to Jesus, "And who is my neighbor?"
30. Then Jesus answered and said: "A certain man went down from Jerusalem to Jericho, and fell among thieves, who stripped him of his clothing, wounded him, and departed, leaving him half dead.
31. Now by chance a certain priest came down that road. And when he saw him, he passed by on the other side.
32. Likewise a Levite, when he arrived at the place, came and looked, and passed by on the other side.
33. But a certain Samaritan, as he journeyed, came where he was. And when he saw him, he had compassion on him

34. and went to him, and bandaged his wounds, pouring on oil and
    wine, and he set him on his own animal, brought him to an
    inn, and took care of him.
35. On the next day, when he departed, he took out two denarii, gave
    them to the innkeeper, and said to him, 'Take care of him; and
    whatever more you spend, when I come again, I will repay you.'
36. So which of these three do you think was neighbor to him who fell
    among the thieves?"
37. And he said, "He who showed mercy on him." Then Jesus said to
    him, "Go and do likewise."

The Good Samaritan is generally regarded as one of the key parables in the
Gospels; it is also one of the best known and most treasured. Boucher writes:
"Surely the exemplary story of the Good Samaritan ranks as one of the most
beautiful and compelling of all the Synoptic parables. It illustrates the teaching
of Jesus on love of God and neighbour; there is nothing more central in Jesus'
preaching" (1981:113). Kistemaker (1980:166) notes that "the parable of the Good
Samaritan has become part of our culture and vocabulary. It is not uncommon
to see hospitals and institutions of mercy bearing that name." Thus, the very
word *Samaritan* has become a symbol of the values and attitudes associated with
this parable and with Jesus' teaching in general. The Jewish scholar Montefiore
says that

> the conception of the Good Samaritan is one which the world will not
> easily let go. For the parable is one of the simplest and noblest among the
> noble gallery of the parables in the Synoptic Gospels. Love, it tells us, must
> know no limits of race and ask no enquiry. Who needs me is my neighbor.
> Whom at the given time and place I can help with my active love, he is
> my neighbour and I am his. ([1927]1968:468)

Remarking on the Old Testament antecedents of the message of Jesus' story,
Montefiore asks, "Why should we not also gladly welcome and use a parable
which can appeal with such power to the heart and imagination of young and
old as the parable of the Good Samaritan?"

However, despite the apparent simplicity and powerful appeal of the parable's
message, in recent times this message has become the subject of controversy. In
addition, the parable has also become the subject of elaborate structuralist and
semiotic analyses that ignore its message altogether and focus entirely on the
formal aspects of its structure (described in technical and abstract terms such as
"initial correlated sequence," "final correlated sequence," "sequence aborts," and
the like). Indeed, the complexity and abstractness of the language in some recent studies of the Good Samaritan seem almost caricatural. Thus the French
research team Entrevernes Group writes:

> "Go": the imperative puts an end to the debate. It suggests a movement
> representing a quest to be realized somewhere else with the competence

that was just acquired. . . . With "do likewise" the action to be realized is no longer in a relationship of similarity with the commandment of the Law but is in a relationship of similarity with the performance of one of the characters in the narrative as over against two others. (1978:41)

As Gourgues (1997:30) has noted, the context of the parable in Luke's Gospel warns against abstract and theoretical discussions about the meaning of *neighbor*, in which first-century scribes liked to engage. "Isn't there a similar risk," Gourgues asks, "of getting lost in abstract and detached speculations about transformations of a structural or 'systemic' order, while individuals suffer quite concrete misery and injustice?"

Whatever one may think about the value of content-free approaches to the study of parables, the question that concerns us here is, what did Jesus mean? To this question, simple and commonsense commentaries like Boucher's (1981) or Montefiore's ([1927]1968) seem to provide a sound if simplified answer. But the traditional approach has also been challenged in recent times.[1] For example, Funk (1982:34) writes, "In the traditional reading of the parable the significance of the Samaritan has been completely effaced: the Samaritan is not a mortal enemy, but a good fellow, the model of virtuous deportment." Funk argues that this traditional reading should be rejected in that "the parable does not suggest that one behave as a good neighbor like the Samaritan but that one become the victim in the ditch who is helped by an enemy." But the traditional reading did not ignore the enmity between Samaritans and Jews. When, for example, Montefiore ([1927]1968) wrote about the parable that "love, it tells us, must know no limits of race and ask no enquiry," he was clearly taking this aspect into account, and in fact saw it as inseparable from the message that "who needs me is my neighbour."

Funk (1982:34) further suggests that "the parable of the Good Samaritan may be reduced to two propositions: (1) In the Kingdom of God mercy comes only to those who have no right to expect it and who cannot resist it when it comes. (2) Mercy always comes from the quarter from which one does not and cannot expect it." Jointly, these two propositions can be reduced, Funk suggests, to one, that is, "in the Kingdom mercy is always a surprise" (see also Funk 1996). It is hard to think that Funk's whimsical interpretations are meant seriously, but insofar as they are, they probably reflect a perception of the more traditional interpretation as an ethical commonplace. But surely, if the message of the parable as traditionally interpreted can seem banal, is it only because Christianity has been repeating it for 2000 years?

Crossan, too, challenges the traditional approach by emphasizing the reversal of expectations as the central focus of the parable:

The focal point must remain, not on the good deed itself, but on the *goodness* of the Samaritan. When the story is read as one told to a Jewish audience by the Jewish Jesus it is impossible to avoid facing the good man not just as good but as Samaritan . . . the literal point of the story challenges the hearer to put together two impossible and contradictory words

for the same person: Samaritan (10:33) and neighbor (10:36). The whole
thrust of the story demands that he say what cannot be said: Good + Samaritan. . . . On the lips of the historical Jesus the literal point demands
that the hearer respond to the story by stating the contradictory, the impossible, the unspeakable. . . . The literal point confronted the hearers with
the necessity of saying the impossible and having their world turned up-
side down and radically questioned in its presuppositions. The metaphorical
point is that *just so* does the kingdom of God break abruptly into a person's
consciousness and demand the overturn of prior values, closed options,
set judgements, and established conclusions. (1974:75-76)

Crossan's point about the overturn of set judgements is valid. It is hard to see,
however, why this should be seen as incompatible with the central message of
compassion and love of one's neighbor, whoever he or she might be. A much
more balanced approach is demonstrated, for example, by Bailey (1980:55), who
sees in the parable several interrelated themes: "[1] The Samaritan, a hated
outsider, demonstrates compassionate love. Thus the parable is a sharp attack
on communal and racial prejudices. [2] For Jesus, love is something you feel
and do. [3] The parable gives us a dynamic concept of the neighbor. The question 'Who is my neighbor?' is reshaped into 'To whom must I become a neighbor?' The answer is—everyone in need, even an enemy!"

However, according to Breech ([1983]1987:179), an interpretation of this kind
"remains at a very superficial level and distracts attention away from the story's
true subject matter." Breech seems so bent on denouncing the traditional approach
to the parable that he rejects what the parable says *expressis verbis*; according to
him, the Samaritan "does not feel sorry for the man, but rather acts in order to
communicate to him the ability to resume *his own* story." Whatever this last cryptic
comment means, the story says quite explicitly that the Samaritan felt sorry for
the man. As noted, for example, by Donahue (1990:132), Luke uses here the
rather dramatic Greek verb *esplagchnisthē* 'he was deeply moved with compassion' (cognate with the noun *splagchna* 'entrails').[2] It is the same verb that describes the emotion of the father of the prodigal son when the son returns home
(Luke 15:20), as well as God's merciful compassion for all sinners in Zachariah's
prophecy of salvation (Luke 1:78). It is also the verb that describes Jesus' deep
compassion for the widow of Nain, who is burying her only son, whom he brings
back to life (Luke 7:13), and for others afflicted, unhappy, and lost: "But when
he saw the multitudes, he was moved with compassion for them, because they
were weary and scattered, like sheep having no shepherd" (Matt. 9:36). Clearly,
the Samaritan's compassion is central to the parable, and only someone determined to be original at any cost would deny it.

Simone Weil ([1951] 1973:150) has written, with obvious reference to the
good Samaritan, "God is not present, even if we invoke him, where the afflicted
are merely regarded as an occasion for doing good. . . . We have to bring to them
in their inert, anonymous condition a personal love." Simone Weil places a special
emphasis on the *attention* given to the afflicted person: the Samaritan, moved by

compassion, concentrates all his attention on "this small inert thing of flesh, lying stripped of clothing by the roadside."

The fact that in Jesus' story the Samaritan is deeply moved with compassion makes it clear that he is not regarding the man beaten up by the robbers as an occasion for doing good. He is not even thinking about his own goodness (his left hand does not know what his right hand is doing) and he is not thinking at that moment about God: he is focusing on the other man, with compassion and with a desire to help.[3] Breech, ([1983]1987) however, states, "The very fact that Jesus says he left the next day shows how little interested Jesus is in representing the third man as primarily someone who cares for or who helps others." Given the details of the story (such as the fact that the Samaritan paid the innkeeper for looking after the injured man), the logic of this argument is hard to grasp, and one can only marvel at the commentator's apparent determination to deny the obvious.

Blomberg (1990:233) has proposed the following summary of the parable's message (which, broadly speaking, is similar to that in Bailey 1976): "(1) From the example of the priest and Levite comes the principle that religious status or legalistic casuistry does not excuse lovelessness. (2) From the Samaritan, one learns that one must show compassion to those in need regardless of the religious or ethnic barriers that divide people. (3) From the man in the ditch emerges the lesson that even one's enemy is one's neighbor." My own explication, formulated in simple and universal human concepts, follows similar lines, linking the different aspects of the message into a coherent whole:

The Good Samaritan

(a) it will be good if you want bad things not to happen to other people,
   as you want bad things not to happen to you
(b) it will be good if you think about all other people:
   "these people are people like me"
(c) it will be good if you want to do good things for all other people

(d) if you know that something bad happened to someone
   it will be good if you feel something because of this
(e) it will be good if you think at the same time:
   "I want to do something good for this person"
(f) it will be good if you do something because of this

(g) if you know that something bad happened to someone
(h) it will be bad if you think:
   "I don't have to do anything good for this person"
(i) it will be bad if you think:
   "I don't want to do anything good for this person"

(j) it will be bad if you think about some people:

"these people are bad people
these people are not people like me"

Component (a) can be linked, loosely, with words like "compassion," as well
as with that identification with other people that underlies the commandment "Love
your neighbor like yourself" (aptly used by Luke as an introduction to the parable).
Component (b) reflects the universalism of this self-identification, symbolized by
Jesus' choice of the most unlikely neighbors: a Samaritan and a Jew. Component
(c) refers to active love for other people, expressing itself in deeds. Components
(d)–(f) reflect the ideal sequence of responses illustrated by the story: to *feel* something, to *want* to do something, to *do* something. Components (g)–(i) denounce
indifference and failure to respond to other people's misfortunes, illustrated in the
story by the priest and the Levite. Finally, (j) articulates Jesus' abolition of divisions
between people: insiders versus outsiders, friends versus enemies, good people versus
bad people, people like me versus people not like me.

In the story, this abolition of all divisions among people is closely linked with
the implied exhortation to treat all people lovingly and to help them whenever
possible. We find the same link between the two in Luke's Sermon on the Plain
and Matthew's Sermon on the Mount: "I say to you, listen, love your enemies,
do good to those who hate you. . . . Be merciful, just as your Father is merciful"
(Luke 6:27, 36); "Love your enemies . . . so that you may be children of your
Father in heaven" (Matt. 6:44–45).

We find the same link between active compassionate love and a human solidarity that transcends all boundaries in the memorable scene of the Last Judgment (Matt. 25:31–46) (already quoted in chapter 15, but partly repeated here),
in which God ("the King") identifies with all suffering people:

35. for I was hungry and you gave me food, I was thirsty and you gave
    me drink, I was a stranger and you took me in;
36. I was naked and you clothed me, I was sick and you visited me; I
    was in prison and you came to me.
37. Then the righteous will answer him, saying, 'Lord, when did we
    see you hungry and feed you, or thirsty and give you drink?
38. When did we see you a stranger and take you in, or naked and
    clothe you? Or when did we see you sick, or in prison, and
    come to you?' . . .
40. And the King will answer and say to them, 'Assuredly, I say to
    you, inasmuch as you did it to one of the least of these my
    brethren, you did it to me.'

The very fact that those who have practiced active, compassionate love are surprised
at the King's revelation ("you did it to me") underscores their universalist "blindness": when they were feeding the hungry or taking care of the sick, they did not
ask who these hungry and these sick were—they did not think they needed to know.

Finally, as noted by many commentators, we find the same link between compassion and absolute inclusiveness in Jesus' own attitude toward social and reli-

gious outcasts, which his contemporaries found particularly shocking and, indeed, offensive. Theissen and Merz (1998:393) note that "this . . . markedly shaped his behavior: his concern for those who were discounted by Jewish society, his friendship with 'toll collectors and sinners', which became proverbial at an early stage." In particular, Jesus saw all outcasts as not only the *objects* of love and compassion but also the *subjects* and, in fact, people who can surpass the "righteous" in love shown to others. The prime example is the prostitute in the house of Simon the Pharisee, of whom the Lucan Jesus says to his host (Luke 7),

44. Do you see this woman? I entered your house; you gave me no
    water for my feet, but she has washed my feet with her tears and
    wiped them with the hair of her head.
45. You gave me no kiss, but this woman has not ceased to kiss my
    feet since the time I came in.
46. You did not anoint my head with oil, but this woman has
    anointed my feet with fragrant oil.

Similarly, as also noted by Theissen and Merz (p. 394), it is the tax collector Zacchaeus "who gives half his possessions to the poor, and not the rich young ruler in Luke 18.18ff., who fulfils the Law perfectly in every respect (Luke 19.8)." Clearly, what applies to the outcast prostitute and the outcast tax collector applies also to the Samaritan: they all surpass the righteous in what from Jesus' point of view counts most, that is, active love and compassion. Jesus' message, then, is not only that one should want to do good things for other people but also that one should not think of some people as good people and of some others as bad people. Rather, one should think of all people that one comes into contact with as "people like me" and treat them accordingly, trying to do good things for them whenever one can, especially when something bad has happened to them. One should also strive never to think of oneself as superior to them, remembering that from God's point of view the most despised people of all—the public "sinners," the outcasts, the Samaritans—may in fact be richer (because richer in love) than ourselves.

Earlier I quoted Crossan's (1974) comment that "the focal point [of the parable] must remain not on the good deed itself, but on the *goodness* of the Samaritan." Although I think that the focus is on both, this second point is certainly very important, too—not for the reason suggested by Funk (1982:34), that "mercy always comes from the quarter from which one does not and cannot expect it", but for the reason repeatedly highlighted by Jesus: that one should not think of some people as bad people but rather of all people as "someone like me." The figure of the Good Samaritan epitomises Jesus' emphasis on the close link between this message of human solidarity and universal brotherhood and the message that one should want to do good things for all people—the same link that is also underscored in the key commandment, "Love your neighbor as yourself." At the same time, the choice of the despised figure of a Samaritan as a symbol of this link puts a new spin on the concept of neighbor, as it does on the concept of "people like me."

SEVENTEEN

The Rich Man and Lazarus

Luke 16:19–31

19. There was a certain rich man who was clothed in purple and fine linen and fared sumptuously every day.
20. But there was a certain beggar named Lazarus, full of sores, who was laid at his gate
21. desiring to be fed with the crumbs which fell from the rich man's table. Moreover the dogs came and licked his sores.
22. So it was that the beggar died, and was carried by the angels to Abraham's bosom. The rich man also died and was buried.
23. And being in torments in Hades, he lifted up his eyes and saw Abraham afar off, and Lazarus in his bosom.
24. Then he cried and said, 'Father Abraham, have mercy on me, and send Lazarus that he may dip the tip of his finger in water and cool my tongue; for I am tormented in this flame.'
25. But Abraham said, 'Son, remember that in your lifetime you received your good things, and likewise Lazarus evil things; but now he is comforted and you are tormented.
26. And besides all this, between us and you there is a great gulf fixed, so that those who want to pass from here to you cannot, nor can those from there pass to us.'
27. Then he said, 'I beg you therefore, father, that you would send him to my father's house,

28. for I have five brothers, that he may testify to them, lest they also
    come to this place of torment.'
29. Abraham said to him, 'They have Moses and the prophets; let
    them hear them.'
30. And he said, 'No, father Abraham; but if one goes to them from
    the dead, they will repent.'
31. But he said to him, 'If they do not hear Moses and the prophets,
    neither will they be persuaded though one rise from the dead'.

The authenticity of the parable of the rich man and Lazarus is the subject of some
debate. Most scholars agree that the first part at least does go back to Jesus, and
the authenticity of the second part, too, has many staunch supporters. Hendrickx
(1986:211) says, "Many contemporary exegetes nevertheless opt for the primitive unity of the parable and its attribution to Jesus. They insist especially on
the complementarity of the two parts of the parable, on the originality of ideas,
and on the support which they find in the message of Jesus." Similarly, Fitzmyer
(1985b:1127) notes that although some motifs of the parable could have been
borrowed from an earlier tradition (Egyptian and Jewish), "there is a certain unity
to the two parts of the Lucan parable, which transcends such distinct motifs."
Fitzmyer concludes that "in the long run, there is no solid reason not to ascribe
it as a unit to Jesus himself," and many other commentators concur (see, e.g.,
Gourgues 1997:189-190). The Fellows of the Jesus Seminar were in this case
more skeptical than most other commentators: they "were divided about whether
the story related in 16:19-26 is traceable to Jesus" (Funk et al. 1993:19-26), and
"unanimously attributed the second part of the parable to Luke" (Funk et al.
1988:64).

The analysis proposed here will be based essentially on the first part of the
parable. I will, however, include in the explication (in brackets) an optional cluster
of four components that derive from the second part. By placing these components in brackets, I will be proposing an analysis that assumes the authenticity
of the first part while leaving open the question of the second.

Most commentators recognize a close link between the rich man and Lazarus
and the Beatitudes. Gourgues (1997:202) quotes Luke's first two beatitudes and
the corresponding woes and describes the parable as "a perfect illustration of
these proclamations: one has, so to speak, the impression of reading the Beatitudes in cartoons, visualizing through the story more abstract theological
affirmations." Gourgues also points out that the parable uses the same key words
as the Lucan Beatitudes: *ptōchoi* 'poor', *plousioi* 'rich', *chortazō* 'fill', and *parakaleō*
'comfort'. But as I will try to show in my explication, whereas there is indeed a
very close link between the parable and the Beatitudes, there are also some differences. In particular, the message of the parable is more complex and has its
own emphases.

Inevitably, many commentaries on the parable are phrased in terms of a "reversal." Unfortunately, here as elsewhere, the word *reversal* is often used as if it
were self-explanatory, and no further thought is given to the question of what
exactly is being reversed and how. In the rare instances in which these ques-

tions are explicitly asked, the answers illustrate the dangers of relying in our analyses on simple mechanical images. For example, Montefiore has written,

> The parable, at any rate the first part of it, up to verse 25, must originally have been intended to show that earthly conditions are often reversed after death and in the future life. . . . For though, at present, the poor man has sorrow and the rich man comfort and prosperity, in the next world these conditions shall be reversed. Then the poor shall be happy; the rich shall be miserable. . . . those now poor shall then enjoy the highest good, while those now rich shall be in the sorest distress. ([1927]1968:537)

This commentary takes it for granted that the reversal of the lot of the two men in the story (from bad to good and from good to bad) informs the reader about what is actually going to happen to people in the future: a kind of anticipatory reporting. On the same page of his commentary, Montefiore says that the story is a warning to the rich; unfortunately, he then slips from the language of warnings to the language of reportage.

Blomberg (1990:206) is even more emphatic, finding in the parable a lesson about people's future fates and "irreversible punishment." Alluding to the literal meaning of the name Lazarus ("the one helped by God"), Blomberg sums up the "main lessons" of the parable as follows: "(1) Like Lazarus, those whom God helps will be borne after their death into God's presence. (2) Like the rich man, the unrepentant will experience irreversible punishment. (3) Through Abraham, Moses, and the prophets, God reveals himself and his will so that none who neglect it can legitimately protest their subsequent fate."

Commentaries like Blomberg's (1990) and, to some extent, Montefiore's ([1927[1968) make the error of misinterpreting the illocutionary force of a particular utterance or text, that is, that aspect of the meaning that represents the speaker's purpose. Thus, for example, the purpose of a promise is different from that of a threat; the purpose of an appeal or a call is different from that of a report, a statement, or a description; and the purpose of a warning is different from that of a prediction, a forecast, or an announcement. In narrative parables like the rich man and Lazarus, the same set of sentences can have one illocutionary force on one level (the level of the story line) and a different one on the level of the intended message (the "lesson"). Thus, the story *reports* what happened to the poor man and the rich man after their deaths. But the message of the parable does not report or predict or inform about what will happen to people after their deaths. Rather, it conveys a promise and assurance of God's love for the poor and a warning, an admonition, and an appeal to the rich. Given this difference in its illocutionary force, the parable's messages to the poor and the rich are not symmetrical and the relation between them is not that of a simple reversal.

The message to the poor echoes that explicated in the chapter on the Beatitudes:

(a) some people don't have anything
(b) many bad things happen to these people because of this
(c) these people feel many bad things because of this

(d) I say:
(e)   God knows about this
(f)   God feels something because of this
(g)   after these people die, God will do very good things for these
         people because they lived like this
(h) these people will feel something very good because of this

Components (a)–(c) of this explication are based on the images of Lazarus' earthly life: he doesn't have anything, his body is covered with ulcers, and he suffers pain and hunger. Components (e)–(h) are based on the images of Lazarus' life after his death: at the heavenly banquet he was given a place of honor next to Abraham, "singled out to be the object of the patriach's fatherly love and care" (B. T. D. Smith 1937:135); so obviously God was aware of his suffering on earth, having for him a special love because of this, and gave him a special recompense. (On this point, see also Boucher 1981:135; Gourgues 1997:205.)

Manson ([1937]1961:301) calls the parable of the rich man and Lazarus "a part of the 'Gospel of the Outcast,'" and the partial explication above is consistent with such an appraisal. But although the poor man in the story has a name and the rich man does not, in contrast to the Beatitudes, here the main emphasis is on the rich.

The parable's message to the rich is not a simple reversal of the message to the poor because it doesn't say that God will do bad things to them (as he will do good things for poor people like Lazarus), and in fact it doesn't even say that bad things will happen to them. Rather, as mentioned earlier, the core message is one of warning: if they have very many things, they can do many good things for other people because of this; if they don't do this, this is very bad for them; after they die, there will come judgment, and these omissions will then be glaringly obvious and cause them great pain:

(i) some other people have very many things
(j) many good things happen to them because of this
(k) they feel many good things because of this
(l) I say:
(m)   it can be very bad for these people to live like this

(n) if some people have very many things
        they can do many good things for other people because of this
(o) God wants these people to do this
(p) if these people don't do this it is very bad for them

(q) after these people die, they will know this
(r) they will feel something very bad because of this

The first three components of this part of the explication (i)–(k) are indeed symmetrical with the first three components of the first part (a)–(c), but the following set [(m)–(p)] has no such counterpart. As this set interprets his teaching, Jesus doesn't condemn wealth but rather speaks of its dangers, as well as of its responsibilities. Component (m) doesn't say that enjoying wealth [(i)-(k)] is always bad for people but warns only that it *can* be very bad for them. The danger involved in a life of wealth stems from its special responsibilities, to which rich people can be blind or which they can be unwilling to fulfill.

In the explication, the responsibility is spelled out in components (n) and (o): "if some people have very many things they can do many good things for other people because of this" and "God wants these people to do these things." The danger of failing in this responsibility is spelled out in component (p): "if these people don't do this it is very bad for them."

Components (q) and (r), which refer to what will happen after a person's death, have their counterparts in (g) and (h) of the first part of the explication, but again, they are not based on a simple reversal: (g) and (h) promise a special recompense from God after a person's death, whereas (q) and (r) warn of a judgment (self-judgment) and unavoidable painful regret.

The last part of the explication (see below) spells out the parable's implicit admonition to the hearers (w), pointing out that if they are rich and prosperous, (x) they have an opportunity to do many good things for other people because of this," (y) they should regard this opportunity as an obligation, and (z) they can embrace and fulfill this obligation willingly and indeed lovingly (see Maillot 1993:258-259):

(w) if you have very many things it will be good for you if you think:
(x)   "I can do many good things for other people because of this
(y)   I have to do this
(z)   I want to do this"
(z') it will be good for you if you do many good things for other people because of this

This leaves us with only one aspect of the parable's message unaccounted for: the references to the Scriptures ("Moses and the prophets") in the second part. If we assume, as do many commentators, that verses 27-31 also go back to Jesus and constitute a part of the same whole as verses 19-26, we can integrate this aspect of the parable's message with the rest by inserting the following four components before the final admonition to the hearer:

(s) God wants people to want to do good things for other people
(t) when a person doesn't want to do good things for other people
          this person cannot live with God
(u) God says this to people all the time
(v) if a person wants to hear God's words this person can know this

As pointed out by Maillot (1993:260), the rich man and Lazarus is rather unusual among Jesus' parables in being "Scripture speaking about Scripture." This very fact suggests that the words "Moses and the prophets" are intended to refer to a central aspect of the Bible's teaching, and (s) and (t) above have been formulated accordingly. At the same time, however, their phrasing coheres quite well with the rest of the explication; in the context of components that refer to those who have very many things and can do many good things for other people because of this, a reference to wanting to do good things for other people is naturally interpreted in terms of giving and sharing. The reference to not being able to live with God if one does not do that can in turn be linked with the images of what happens to the rich man in the story after his death. The reference to time ("all the time") in component (u) interprets the Scriptures as the living voice of God, not as a record of some past occurrences, along the lines of "a long time ago God said to some people. . . ."

The rich man and Lazarus is no doubt one of the most frequently misunderstood of Jesus' parables. For example, it has been claimed that it legitimizes poverty or that it offers the poor an illusory consolation—"the opium of the people." It has also been claimed that it denounces private property, demands a redistribution of goods based on strict equality, and proclaims that all rich people will inevitably go to hell.

The explication proposed here tries to show that there is no basis in the parable for any of these claims. The parable's central message is an appeal to the rich and prosperous. This message neither justifies poverty nor seeks to abolish private property; rather, it urges those who *have* to share with those who have not, and it presents this sharing not as a nice gesture, an optional extra, but as a key issue in people's relation to God: when a person who has very many things doesn't do many good things for other people, this person cannot live with God. On this point, the rich man and Lazarus echoes Jesus' apocalyptic parable of the Last Judgment (Matt. 25:31–46), that "inasmuch as you did not do it to one of the least of these, you did not do it to me."

Jesus' teaching on poverty and wealth was anchored in the Scriptures; in particular, it shared with the Psalms and the Prophets the key idea that God was somehow on the side of the poor. At the same time, however, Jesus' message about the dangers of wealth was radical and provocative at the time (and of course remains so two millennia later). Montefiore offers the following comments on the historical context of Jesus' teaching on this point:

> The Rabbis looked at wealth and poverty from a more realistic and common-sense point of view than Jesus. In this matter they were less paradoxical, or, if you will, less idealistic than he. . . . The well-known passage in Aboth vi.8 (with its parallels) is in general accordance with Rabbinic sentiment: "Beauty, strength, riches, honour, wisdom, old age, children, are comely to the righteous and comely to the world." One cannot imagine Jesus saying this; but it is not exceptional for the Rabbis. . . . The Shechinah [divine inspiration] rests only upon one who is wise, strong, rich, and tall. (Sabbath 82a) [elsewhere: "strong, rich, wise, and humble]. . . . Jesus could not have said this, but it is not to be regarded as off the Rabbinic line. ([1930]1970:276–277)

Montefiore notes that the rabbis valued learning more than wealth and that for them the Torah always came first. But they also "shared with their fellows a very considerable dislike of poverty" (p. 275), "sometimes regarded [poverty] as a punishment for sin" (p. 279), and tended to see wealth as an advantage rather than as a danger.

Component (m) of the explication ("it can be very bad for these people to live like this") seeks to capture the implication of grave danger inherent in wealth and comfort, without going so far as to assert that "if a person has very many things this is very bad for this person." The main point of the parable, however, is not just to warn about the danger ("this can be very bad for this person"), but to point out to those who have very many things and who can do many good things for other people because of this that they have to do it—and to encourage them to *want* to do it—for their own sake, as well as for the sake of their neighbors:

> The story of the rich man and Lazarus does not assert that it is good to have a miserable life here on earth, that it is right for society not to fight poverty, and that it is the Church's task to console people in need by referring to heaven. . . . The parable emphasizes the seriousness of the present. What really matters is what we do right now. The story calls us to a real sense of responsibility for the poor and the oppressed. And all this in reference to God's judgment and criterion. (Hendrickx 1986:212)

Crossan has commented on the rich man and Lazarus as follows:

> It seems best . . . to take 16:19–26 as an actual parable of Jesus. Its literal point was a strikingly *amoral* description of situational reversal between the rich man and Lazarus. Its metaphorical point was the reversal of expectations and situation, of value and judgment, which is the concomitant of the Kingdom's advent. . . . Jesus was not interested in moral admonition on the dangers of riches . . . but in the reversal of human situation in which the Kingdom's disruptive advent could be metaphorically portrayed and linguistically made present. (1992:66)

It is interesting that Crossan acknowledges the rich man and Lazarus (printed in Funk et al. 1993 in a skeptical gray color) as an actual parable of Jesus, but his portrayal of it as an "*amoral* description of situational reversal" seems strange— as if Jesus was a player of literary and linguistic games, a structuralist *avant la lettre*, not interested in how people should live their lives, and as if he had never taught "love your enemies," "do not judge," and "you cannot serve God and Mammon." The following explication adopts a very different point of view:

The rich man and Lazarus

(a) some people don't have anything
(b) many bad things happen to these people because of this
(c) these people feel many bad things because of this

(d) I say:

(e)   God knows about this

(f)   God feels something because of this

(g)   after these people die, God will do very good things for these
         people because they lived like this

(h)   these people will feel something very good because of this

(i) some other people have very many things

(j) many good things happen to them because of this

(k) they feel many good things because of this

(l) I say:

(m)   it can be very bad for these people to live like this

(n) if some people have very many things
         they can do many good things for other people because of this

(o) God wants these people to do this

(p) if these people don't do this it is very bad for them

(q) after these people die they will know this

(r) they will feel something very bad because of this

(s) [God wants people to want to do good things for other people]

(t) [when a person doesn't want to do good things for other people
         this person cannot live with God]

(u) [God says this to people all the time]

(v) [if a person wants to hear God's words this person can know this]

(w) if you have very many things it will be good for you if you think:

(x)   "I can do many good things for other people because of this

(y)   I have to do this

(z)   I want to do this"

(z') it will be good for you if you do many good things for other
         people because of this

EIGHTEEN

The Rich Fool

Luke 12:13–21

16. Then he spoke a parable to them, saying: "The ground of a certain rich man yielded plentifully.
17. And he thought within himself, saying: 'What shall I do, since I have no room to store my crops?'
18. So he said, 'I will do this: I will pull down my barns and build greater, and there I will store all my crops and my goods.
19. And I will say to my soul, Soul, you have many goods laid up for many years; take your ease; eat, drink, and be merry.'
20. But God said to him, 'You fool! This night your soul will be required of you; then whose will those things be which you have provided?'
21. [So is he who lays up treasure for himself, and is not rich towards God."]

The story of the rich farmer is simple and straightforward: because of an exceptionally abundant harvest the man decides that he can secure his possessions by building larger barns and then retire and enjoy life for many years to come; but God intervenes and tells him that this very night he is going to die. To understand why God in the story tells this man that he is a fool we need to reconstruct the pattern of the man's thinking:

(a) sometimes a person thinks:
(b)   "I want to always have many things
(c)   if I have many things this will be good for me
(d)   if I have many things I can always feel something good
(e)   I want to always feel something good
(f)   I don't want to think about anything else"

The man's inability to carry out even the first part of his plans is introduced into the story for a dramatic effect. In fact, his ideas are not meant to be taken as just fleeting thoughts but as firm plans destined to affect the remainder of his life (however brief this remainder might be). To account for this aspect I will add one further component to the partial explication:

(g) because this person thinks this this person does many things

The man is already rich, so he doesn't think, "I want to have many things." Rather, he plans to build new barns to take care of his riches and to ensure his prosperity for years to come. His goal can be represented, therefore, as (b) "I want always to have many things." In taking care of his riches, the man is obviously assuming that having them will always be good for him: (c) "if I have many things this will always be good for me."

In the commentaries on this parable, the rich farmer, planning for an enjoyable and secure future, is often accused of greed. In fact, however, this doesn't seem to be the man's main problem. His riches are obviously important to him, but they are not a goal in themselves; rather, he values them as a means to an enjoyable and carefree life. Thanks to them, he thinks, he will be able to "eat, drink, and be merry." Thus, his main goal is not so much "I want to have more" as (e) "I want always to feel something good." Possessions are seen as a means to this end: (d) "if I have many things I can always feel something good." Crucially for the parable's message, thoughts of this kind occupy the man's whole horizon—there is simply no room left for anything else: (f) "I don't want to think about anything else."

As many commentators have noted, in the short dialogue with his soul, the man uses the word *I* 6 times, and the word *my* 4 times; and the 5 sentences with a second-person subject ("you have," "take your ease," "eat," "drink," and "be merry") in fact refer to the same person as the 6 with an overt first-person subject (*I*). In fact, then, all 11 of the man's sentences have himself as the subject; it is not just a question of "me first" but of "me and only me." Other people are conspicuous in this dialogue by their absence, as is God, whose existence is obviously not taken into account at all and whose intervention is totally unexpected.

In suddenly addressing the protagonist as "You fool" (in Greek, *aphrōn*) the unexpected intruder, God, is dramatically reminding the man of his own existence; the parable makes a clear allusion to the well-known opening lines of Psalm 14: "The fool [in the Septuagint, also *aphrōn*] has said in his heart, 'there is no God'."

God's intervention in the story is unique in the whole body of Jesus' parables. The man, (the fool, the *aphrōn*) lives and thinks as though there were no God. The thought of God doesn't enter his mind at all; but this nonexistent God bursts into the parable, into the dialogue that the *aphrōn* is having with his soul, and says something that is utterly unexpected—both to the protagonist and to the hearer. What the protagonist didn't expect in the least is the announcement of his impending death, and what the hearer didn't expect is God's perspective on the *aphrōn's* life. What the hearers could have expected God to say was something like "you wicked man—don't you realize that your life is immoral—that this is a bad way to live one's life?" But in fact, God doesn't take a moral and religious stand at all, and he doesn't condemn the man's life as immoral. Rather, he points out its foolishness, that is, its counterproductiveness from the point of view of the man's own objectives. Bailey (1980:67) has commented on this point as follows: "There is no accusing question, such as 'What have you done for others?' or 'Why have you failed to help those in need?' . . . Rather, God thunders: 'look at what you have done to yourself! You plan alone, build alone, indulge alone, and now you will die alone!'"

The man wants his own good, and God has no quarrel with this goal; in fact, he implicitly endorses it as natural and legitimate. But, he points out to the man (and to the hearer), you are not going to attain your goal in this way because you are looking in the wrong direction; if you live like this you will not find what you are looking for. Although God doesn't speak explicitly about himself, he is dramatically drawing attention to himself by his sudden deus ex machina appearance on the stage and by his emotionally charged reproof: you are acting like a fool because you have forgotten *me*; I am a part of the equation and in fact an answer to your needs and desires.

The full meaning of God's rebuke will be further explored below, but one aspect of the message conveyed in this way to the hearers of the parable can be represented as follows:

(h) it will be bad for you if you think like this
(i) it will be bad for you if you live like this because you think like
     this

What these two components are meant to account for is the parable's message to the hearers that they should not think like the man in the story and should not base their lives on thoughts similar to his. If the hearers' lives are based on thoughts such as those of the *aphrōn's* [(b)–(f)], they are being doubly foolish—because they think like this (h) and because they live like this (i).

Why was the man in the story foolish to think the way he did? And why would the hearers be foolish to think likewise? Several interrelated answers to this question are implied in the parable. The best way to articulate them is to phrase them as warnings to the hearers, reminding them that they don't know their own future; that they are not masters of their own lives; that they can die in the near future; that their possessions will not ensure their well-being after they have died; that after their death there will come judgment; and that if they orient their lives toward possessions, pleasure, and self-indulgence, they will regret it in the light of that judgment. All these warnings can be stated as follows:

(j) you don't know what will happen to you
(k) you live now because God wants you to live, not because you want
   to live
(l) some time after now you will die
(m) this can happen a short time after now
(n) if you have many things now you will not feel something good
   because of this after you have died
(o) after you die you will know that it was bad for you to live like this
(p) you will feel something very bad then

Component (j)—the unknowability of one's future—is implied in the parable's contrast between the man's planned "many years" of a *dolce vita* and God's "this night" ("This night your soul will be required of you"). Component (k)—the illusion that our life belongs to ourselves and that we can confidently plan it—is suggested by the ironic accumulation of the phrases "I will . . . I will . . . I will . . ." and in the phrase "your soul will be required of you." The word *psychē*, translated here as "soul," stands, roughly speaking, for a person's life or for that (invisible) part of a person because of which the person can live; and the word *apaitousin*, translated here as "required," is the same word that was used for collecting a loan (Bailey 1980:67), with the implication that one's life is, as it were, on loan from God and does not belong to the person who "uses" it. As Lockyer (1963:268) notes, in Ezekiel 18:4 God says explicitly, "Behold, all souls are mine." Hendrickx comments on this aspect of the rich fool as follows:

> Securing his future becomes for him [the *aphron*] a calculable factor and is only a question of rationally exploiting the possibilities at his disposal. In this perspective his possessions become the only relevant reality and his life a circular course around his own "I." The story shows that such existence is both ungodly and inhuman. The 'fool' forgets that he *receives* his life from day to day, from moment to moment. He ignores that he is God's creature, acts as if he were the master of his life and would therefore have complete control over it. (1986:105)

Components (l) and (m) are, of course, based on God's direct announcement in the story; the only difference between the story and the message is that in the story God is saying to the protagonist that he *will* die very shortly, whereas in the underlying message Jesus is reminding the hearers that they will inevitably die some day and that this may happen very shortly.

The uselessness of one's possessions after one's death is underscored in the pointed question "then whose will those things be which you have provided?" The implied message is that even if one can enjoy pleasures that derive from wealth before one dies, one certainly cannot enjoy them after one has died (n).

As many commentators have pointed out, however, that observation belongs to secular wisdom. The fact that in the parable it is God who points this out opens an eschatological perspective on the matter. What is implied is that after a person's death comes judgment, and in the light of that judgment one will realize that one's former values were false and that in fact it was bad for one to live under the banner of private wealth used exclusively for self-indulgence (o). Component (p) spells out the painful regret that can be expected to follow such a realization.

What is the point of the parable then? Clearly, as in Jesus' other parables, the warning is linked with a positive alternative: whereas it is bad for you to think and live like the rich fool, it will be good for you to live in a different way, focusing precisely on those concerns and goals that were so conspicuously absent from the *aphrōn's* life: God, other people, and death:

(q) it will be good for you if you think:
(r)   "some time after now I will die
(s)   this can happen a short time after now
(t)   because of this I want to do some good things now
(u)   I want to live with God
(v)   I want to do good things for other people"
(w) it will be good for you if you do many things because of this

Components (u) and (v), which spell out the goals of living with God and doing good things for other people, may seem to be arbitrarily added to the message of the parable, which does not explicitly refer to either of these goals. As many commentators have noted, however, the glaring lacunae in the protagonist's thoughts and ambitions are as eloquent and significant as his actual words. In particular, the *aphrōn's* isolation from other people is almost palpable, not only in the absence of references to other people in his soliloquy, but also in the fact that all the sentences of this soliloquy have himself as a subject. As noted by Donahue (1990:178), "his wealth has isolated him from all human contact."

Thus, the ultimate foolishness of the rich fool's attitude to life can be seen to lie in his false ideas about his own good and his failure to recognize what his real good was: in living with God and in wanting to do good things for other people. Mutatis mutandis, what applies to the man in the parable applies also to the hearer:

(x) if you live like this you can always live with God
(y) if you live with God this will always be good for you

The lacunae in the *aphrōn's* thoughts, interpreted here as part of the parable's message, are pointed out in the parable itself: first, by God's sudden intervention and his exasperated reproach, "You fool!" and second, by the unexpected question about other people: "then who will get what you have prepared for yourself?" (in the New International Bible's translation). Obviously, in the *aphrōn's* thoughts not only God but also other people have been entirely left out of the picture, and the two omissions are linked.

In addition to the clues in the parable itself, there are also Jesus' other parables and sayings, which elaborate the aspects of the message hinted at but not fully developed here. The subject of how one's wealth must be shared with other people is fully developed in the rich man and Lazarus, whose main point can be represented as follows:

> if you have many things it will be good for you if you think:
>   "I can do many good things for other people because of this
>   I have to do many good things for other people because of this
>   I want to do many good things for other people because of this"
> it will be good for you if you do many good things for other people
>   because you think like this

In fact, it could be argued that this message is also implicitly present in the rich fool—an interpretation implied in the comments by the fourth-century Father of the Church Ambrose that "the barns of superfluity were 'the bosoms of the needy, the houses of the widows, the mouths of orphans and children'" (Lockyer 1963:269). It seems more justified, however, to articulate this message in the explication of the rich man and Lazarus, representing the absence of any thoughts about other people by the rich fool in a more general form: "it will be good for you if you think: I want to do good things for other people."

The theme of where one should find one's true good (in living with God) is developed, above all, in the hidden treasure and the pearl of great price; the subject of enduring treasures is of course developed in the treasure sayings in Matthew (6:19-20) and Luke (12:33); the subject of mammon taking the place of God is developed in the God or mammon sayings in Matthew (6:24) and Luke (16:13); the subject of God's judgment being based on what one has done for other people is dealt with, above all, in the apocalyptic vision of the Last Judgment in Matthew 25:31-46. Thus, to be fully understood, the parable of the rich fool has to be read against the background of Jesus' other sayings and stories. Otherwise it is easy to overlook the internal clues provided in the parable itself and to read it as not much different from secular wisdom, such as that expressed, for example, in one of Seneca's "Letters on Moral Matters" (Epistulae Morales, 17:5-7), described by Fitzmyer as "a Roman philosopher's way of putting the lesson of the episode [the parable of the rich fool]":

> Riches have shut off many a man from the attainment of wisdom; poverty is unburdened and free from care. When the trumpet sounds, the poor man knows that he is not being attacked. . . .
>
> Therefore one should not seek to lay up riches first; one may attain to philosophy, however, even without money for the journey. . . .
>
> Nay, your plan should be this: be a philosopher now, whether you have anything or not. . . . "But," you say, "I shall lack the necessities of life." In the first place, you cannot lack them; because nature demands but little, and the wise man suits his needs to nature. But if the utmost

pinch of need arrives, he will quickly take leave of life and cease being a trouble to himself. (1985b:972)

Seneca's lesson is clearly different from that of the rich fool; any thoughts of God, judgment, and other people are absent from it.

What applies to Seneca's epistle applies also to other putative parallels. For example, B. T. D. Smith (1937:143) says about the rich fool that "the lesson of the parable is not a new one. In fact, the parable itself would seem to be a re-presentation in more graphic form of the teaching of Sirach xi, 18, 19." The relevant passage in Sirach's wisdom reads as follows:

14. Good and bad, life and death, poverty and wealth, all come from the Lord.
17. To the devout the Lord's gift remains constant, and his favour will be there to lead them for ever.
18. Others grow rich by pinching and scraping, and here is the reward they receive for it:
19. although they say, 'Now I can sit back and enjoy the benefit of what I have got,' they do not know how long this will last; they will have to leave their goods to others and die.

Taken in context, Sirach's teaching about the uncertain future of the rich; the foolishness of "pinching and scraping"; and the need to "stick to your job, work hard at it and grow old at your work" is really quite different from Jesus' teaching as explicated here; and Sirach's reflections about "the blessing of the Lord [which] is the reward of the devout"; about how "it is a trifle in the eyes of the Lord in a moment, suddenly to make poor rich"; and also how "it is a trifle for the Lord on the day someone dies to repay him as his conduct deserves" (all in the same passage, 11:14–26) are really a long way away from the message of the rich fool. (For a discussion of the differences between the two texts, see also Bailey 1980:63.) Here as elsewhere, on closer inspection apparent similarities between the teaching of Jesus and that of some of his predecessors and contemporaries turn out to be superficial and deceptive. One can also be left with the impression that the message of the parable is purely negative:

The story raises in a dramatic way the question of life's meaning—and more specifically what is the significance of "my" life—but it offers no leads to answering these questions, except to affirm the sheer absurdity of amassing commodities to secure one's future. . . . "Things" will, inevitably, be surrendered to others, and one never knows when that will happen. What then brings meaning to life . . . ? . . . But the narrator is silent. (1994:161)

The narrator may indeed be silent, but in Jesus' parables the narrator nearly always is silent. However, the fact that the parable's message is not spelled out explicitly by the narrator does not mean that it is not intended to be found there by the reader. On the face of it, the narrator is silent, but he leaves behind a trail for the readers to find their way to the intended message. Fitzmyer (1985b:972) notes that "running through the story is the God-fool contrast; recall Ps.14:1, "The fool (LXX: aphrōn) says in his heart, 'There is no God'." The reference to the Septuagint (the Greek translation of the Hebrew Scriptures) is important, but behind the Greek *aphrōn* lies a Hebrew (and Aramaic) word, which no doubt was also instantly recognizable as an allusion to Psalm 14. This implicit reference to the "fool" of Psalm 14 is the parable's main internal clue, though by no means the only one.

Boucher says,

> The exemplary story is not, as we might think, a lesson against greed. Neither is it teaching about the suddenness of death. Jesus here points to the last judgment. The exemplary story is best understood as a warning to the hearers to open their eyes to the approaching crisis. . . . V.21 is a generalizing conclusion added secondarily. It changes the thrust of the exemplary story from an eschatological warning to a moral teaching on the wrong use of possessions. (1981:127)

One can agree that this parable is not just a lesson against greed or about the suddenness of death and that an implicit reference to judgment is part of the intended meaning. But the contrast drawn between an "eschatological warning" and a "moral teaching" seems unfounded. Moral teaching is about how to live. Jesus' answer to the question "how is one to live?" is always, in essence, that one should strive to live with God. Jesus' eschatological warnings point in exactly the same direction: the purpose of human life is to live with God—before death and after death. Thus, from the point of view of Jesus' teaching the opposition between eschatology and ethics seems spurious.

Fitzmyer (1985b:971) has summed up the message of the Rich Fool as follows: "The amassing of a superabundance of material possessions for the sake of *la dolce vita* becomes the height of folly in the light of the responsibility of life itself and the assessment of it which will take place once it is over." This summary, which doesn't aim at either exhaustiveness or simplicity of language, is consistent with the explication's simple and universal concepts.

The message in question may sound to some like boring old-fashioned wisdom, out of tune with modern times. Yet as Bailey (1980:64) points out, given both the materialistic and consumerist attitudes prevailing in wealthy countries at the end of the second millennium, and the rapidly diminishing natural resources of the planet, the parable of the rich fool "speaks clearly to the crucial questions of our time": "With the natural resources of the world dwindling and the pressure for more possessions intensifying, some wrestling with the message of this text would seem to be imperative if we are to survive" (p. 63).

The rich fool

(a) sometimes a person thinks:
(b)   "I want to always have many things
(c)   if I have many things this will be good for me

(d)   if I have many things I can always feel something good
(e)   I want to always feel something good
(f)   I don't want to think about anything else"
(g) because this person thinks this this person does many things

(h) it will be bad for you if you think like this
(i) it will be bad for you if you live like this because you think like
        this
(j) you don't know what will happen to you
(k) you live now because God wants you to live, not because you want
        to live
(l) some time after now you will die
(m) this can happen a short time after now
(n) if you have many things now you will not feel something good
        because of this after you have died
(o) after you die you will know that it was bad for you to live like this
(p) you will feel something very bad because of this then

(q) it will be good for you if you think:
(r)   "some time after now I will die
(s)   this can happen a short time after now
(t)   because of this I want to do some things now
(u)   I want to live with God
(v)   I want to do good things for other people"
(w) it will be good for you if you do many things because of this
(x) if you live like this you can always live with God
(y) if you live with God this will always be good for you

NINETEEN

The Doorkeeper

Mark 13:33–37

33. Take heed, watch and pray; for you do not know when the time is.
34. It is like a man going to a far country, who left his house and gave
     authority to his servants, and to each his work, and commanded
     the door-keeper to watch.
35. Watch therefore, for you do not know when the master of the
     house is coming—in the evening, at midnight, at the crowing of
     the cock, or in the morning—
36. lest, coming suddenly, he find you sleeping.
37. And what I say to you, I say to all: Watch!

Luke 12:35–37

35. Let your waist be girded and your lamps burning;
36. and you yourselves be like men who wait for their master, when he
     will return from the wedding, that when he comes and knocks
     they may open to him immediately.
37. Blessed are those servants whom the master, when he comes, will
     find watching. Assuredly, I say to you that he will gird himself
     and have them sit down to eat, and will come and serve them.
38. And if he should come in the second watch, or come in the third
     watch, and find them so, blessed are those servants.

The theme of a master's return occurs several times in the Gospels and can be found in all three synoptic Gospels; and even the skeptical Fellows of the Jesus Seminar acknowledged that "the image of the landlord returning unexpectedly could therefore go back to Jesus" (Funk et al. 1993:114). It is generally held, however, that some of the versions of the parables with this theme have undergone extensive redactional changes. Mark's version, quoted above, may also have undergone some changes; in particular, the frame (vv 33 and 37) may have been added by the redactor. On the whole, however, the two versions quoted (from Mark 13 and Luke 12) are widely regarded as probably going back to the historical Jesus: "Despite their independent development in the tradition and despite their final redactional modifications, the narrative lineaments of a coherent story can be discerned behind both versions. . . . The basic story, the debris of a parable of Jesus, is still quite visible behind these changes" (Crossan 1992:96–97). Crossan's summary of Jesus' story, visible behind the changes, reads, "The master departs for a night time feast, maybe even a wedding feast. He enjoins the servant who is the doorkeeper to watch so as to expedite his returning entrance."

What could the parable of the doorkeeper have meant in Jesus' version? As reflected in Luke's verse 12:40, the early church interpreted this parable in terms of Parousia, Christ's (the Son of Man's) second coming. Leaving aside the early church's expectation of the Parousia, we note in these parables, above all, the themes of readiness and watchfulness, and it is reasonable to assume that these are the themes that go back to Jesus himself. For example, Manson ([1937]1961:115) notes, "The girt loins signify readiness and the lighted lamps watchfulness. The time when the servants will be required is uncertain. . . . The point is that the master of the servants is absent and the exact time of his return is unknown to them. They will not even see him coming. The first intimation of his presence will be his knock at the door."

Discussing two other parables that also include the theme of the master's return (Matt. 24:43–51 and Luke 12:39–46), Manson ([1937[1961:115) emphasizes, in addition to watchfulness and readiness, the theme of the fulfillment of God's will: "The task of the disciples is not confined to watchfulness. They have positive duties to perform. . . ." I think this theme applies also to the doorkeeper. After all, in this parable, too, the departing master "gave authority to his servants, and to each his works, and commanded the door-keeper to watch"; in this context, watching the door is itself an appointed task, on a par with the work of the other servants ("to each his works").

Meier (1980:302), discussing what he calls the "parables of vigilance" in Matthew 24 and 25 in the context of the parable of the Last Judgment, comments: "put in the terms of chap. 25, what does it mean to be watchful, and ready, and faithful? The answer is that to be watchful means to be able to recognize the Son of Man in all those in need; to be ready means to be loving towards the Son of Man in these people; and to be faithful means to translate this love into active service, into concrete deeds of mercy." I think that in essence, a similar approach is justified also in the case of the doorkeeper. Every person can be seen as a servant of God, with duties to perform. And since God is not looking over our shoulder and telling us at every moment what he expects of us, a person who wants to serve God and fulfil his expectations and wishes needs to be alert, attentive to the needs of the moment, and ready to act.

The parable of the doorkeeper does not focus primarily on a person's willingness to fulfill God's will because this is taken for granted in the metaphor of the servant. Rather, it focuses on the importance of the present moment and the dangers of postponing and delaying one's response to God's will. The tendency to do so, despite a general willingness to do God's will, can be represented as follows:

(a) sometimes people think:
(b)　　"I want to live with God
(c)　　if God wants me to do some things I want to do these things"
(d) at the same time they think:
(e)　　"if God wants me to do some things I don't have to do these things now
(f)　　I can do it at some other time"

Meier's (1980:302) reference to being "able to recognize the Son of Man in all those in need" and "to be loving towards the Son of Man in these people" is based, as he notes himself, on the parable of the Last Judgment (Matt. 25:31–46); and we would be overinterpreting the parable of the doorkeeper if we were to specify his duties in these terms. The doorkeeper's duties are presented in more general terms: paying attention to the master's will at each moment and trying to fulfill it, without delay. But just as in the parable of the Last Judgment the suffering and needy God presents himself incognito in the suffering and needy people, so, too, according to the parable of the doorkeeper, God's will can present itself to every person incognito at any given moment; and if a person wants to be faithful to God, he or she has to try to recognize God's will (and God's need) at every moment.

The French eighteenth-century religious writer Jean Pierre de Caussade developed a whole doctrine on the basis of this one idea: a spirituality "of the present moment." According to de Caussade (1959:9), "The whole essence of the spiritual life consists in recognizing the designs of God for us at the present moment"; each moment brings with it a duty, or a need, to be recognized and faithfully fulfilled: "In the moral and supernatural order the duties of each moment conceal under their outward appearances the true reality of the divine will which alone is worthy of our attention." De Caussade calls this "the sacrament of the present moment" and he extolls it as "bread of angels, heavenly manna, the pearl of the Gospels" (p. 5). As the reference to the Gospels indicates, de Caussade saw the basis for this idea in the Gospels, and I think with good reason: the idea of the importance of the present moment as the time when one can enter the kingdom of God and encounter God seems to inhere, in particular, in the meaning of the parable of the doorkeeper. Crossan (1994:39) offers a poetic summary of Jesus' teaching on the "When and Where" of the kingdom of God:

> The Kingdom of God comes not at some future time
> You cannot point out the sign of its coming
> The Kingdom of God comes not at some special site
> You cannot point out the place of its coming
> The Kingdom of God is already here, among you, now

Crossan elaborates,

> In apocalyptic eschatology, the Kingdom of God refers to the imminent
> and cataclysmic event by which God will restore justice, peace, and ho-
> liness to a world grown old in evil. God's action will occur in specific
> time (soon) and specific place (here). In Jesus' vision and program, the
> kingdom of God is always available and one enters it by a lifestyle of
> radical egalitarianism. Jesus himself does not announce its imminent
> actuality but its permanent possibility. (p. 149)

The phrase "a lifestyle of radical egalitarianism" seems to reflect Crossan's
own particular focus (rather than Jesus'), but apart from that his comment is, I
think, valid: Jesus does indeed announce the permanent possibility of entering
the kingdom of God, linking it, in a way that is not fully explicit, with his own
ministry here and now. To express the idea of a permanent possibility of entering the kingdom in universal human concepts, we could say that a person can
live with God at any time—not only some time after now but also now. But if
we follow de Caussade's (1959) rather than Crossan's (1994) suggestion, this
encounter with God in the present is linked not necessarily with adopting a
radically egalitarian lifestyle but with the recognition of God's will in the duties,
as well as the opportunities, of the present moment (i.e., in essence, in "what
God wants me to do now").[1]

Dan Otto Via (1974:128) observes in connection with another parable of
watchfulness, the wise and foolish maidens, that "the present is not a time which
is to be exhausted by straining to realize the future. There is time and room to
live *now.* . . . The present . . . as time and room to live, is a gift; but it is also a
demand, for uncertainty about when the expected future event will happen gives
to the present a certain urgency. . . . Gift and demand are held paradoxically together." In Jesus' parables of watchfulness, like the doorkeeper, the present
moment is a gift (an opportunity) and a demand in the sense later developed
and articulated by de Caussade (1959): it is a time when one can meet God,
through finding and fulfilling God's appointed task. The metaphor of the doorkeeper illuminates both the idea of a task (being a watchman, a doorkeeper) and
the idea of urgency (the watchman cannot postpone his watch until later, each
moment counts; a single moment of inattention can ruin the whole watch). Thus
in the explication of the parable's message, the thought of postponing one's
current tasks [(d)–(f), repeated here for convenience] needs to be followed by a
firm rejection [(g)–(i)]:

(d) at the same time they think:
(e)   "if God wants me to do some things I don't have to do these things now
(f)   I can do it at some other time"
(g) it will be bad for you if you think like this
(h) you don't know what will happen to you after now
(i) you don't know what you can do after now

In the parables of watchfulness, the servants who postpone fulfillment of their tasks until later are behaving foolishly because they don't know when the master will return. In the faith of the early church, the image of the master's return was interpreted in terms of Christ's second coming; but the message of Jesus' original parable is applicable to everyone: "you don't know what will happen to you." This is a message expressed explicitly in the parable about the rich fool, who was making plans for a long and pleasurable future and to whom God said: "You fool! This night your soul will be required of you" (Luke 12:20); but it is implicitly conveyed in all the parables of watchfulness. Fitzmyer links the parable of the rich fool and the parable of the doorkeeper (in its Lucan version) as follows:

> The big problem in these sayings (or parables) is the term to which the watchfulness refers. Most modern commentators recognize that we are dealing with the Lucan formulation of a tradition about Jesus' sayings on watchfulness. . . . One may further ask whether, in view of 12:20 [i.e., God's utterance in the parable of the rich fool] and its reference to death, the term might not be considered here to be the death of the individual. Though this question cannot be wholly excluded, the main emphasis seems to be on the parousia, in light of the reference to the coming Son of Man in v.40. (1985b:986-987)

But whereas Luke may have indeed meant the Parousia and not the future of the individual, in the original parable Jesus is likely to have meant the latter—and not necessarily the future of the individual in the sense of the timing of his or her death but, more generally, in the sense of what may happen to him or her in the future. The Matthean Jesus says in a different context (24:43) that "if the master of the house had known at what hour the thief would come, he would have watched and not allowed his house to be broken into." What matters most in the parables of watchfulness is that the opportunity to fulfill God's will that presents itself at a given moment may be simply gone in the next. Thus, the present moment is not only a gift and a demand, as Via (1974) put it, but also a unique opportunity: or rather, it is a gift insofar as it is an opportunity to meet God's demand. This brings us to the following part of the explication:

(j) it will be good for you if you think at all times:
(k)   "maybe God wants me to do something now

(l)   I want to know about it
(m)   I want to do this thing
(n)   I want to do this thing now"

I have quoted Meier's (1980:302) statement that "to be watchful means to be able to recognize the Son of Man in all those in need." Recognizing God in other people, especially in those in need, is a theme that is given a special emphasis in the Gospels, and attentiveness to the needs of others must be seen as a key area of application for the watchfulness enjoined by Jesus. As mentioned earlier, however, in the context of the doorkeeper it seems justified to adopt a broader formula: to be watchful means to recognize God in what appears to be God's will for the present moment.

In Luke's version of the doorkeeper, the act of fulfilling God's will is presented, emphatically, as a blessing for the person who does it. Kistemaker (1980:117) points out that "in this short parable the clause 'it will be good for those servants' (Luke 12:37, 38) occurs twice" (in the New King James Version, this clause reads "blessed are those servants"). Why is it good for them? Why are they blessed?

In answer to this question some commentators invoke the notion of reward," but as argued at some length in chapter 4, sections 2 and 14, *reward* had no place in Jesus' teaching (although he did use the word at times as a quote from the language of others). An interpretation along the lines suggested by de Caussade (1959) seems far more convincing: by recognizing and fulfilling God's will for a given moment, one can meet God in "the sacrament of the present moment"; one can, as it were, enter the kingdom of God in that moment. God appears incognito in the duty (or task) of the present moment. Watchfulness and readiness to recognize him alert one to the opportunity of entering his kingdom. In universal human concepts, this can be represented as follows:

(o) when a person thinks like this this person can live with God
(p) if a person thinks like this at all times
     this person can live with God at all times

This brings us to the following overall explication:

(a) sometimes people think:
(b)   "I want to live with God
(c)   if God wants me to do some things I want to do these
          things"
(d) at the same time they think:
(e)   "if God wants me to do some things I don't have to do these
          things now
(f)   I can do these things at some other time"

(g) it will be bad for you if you think like this
(h) you don't know what will happen to you after now
(i) you don't know what you can do after now

(j) it will be good for you if you think at all times:

(k)   "maybe God wants me to do something now

(l)   I want to know about it

(m)   I want to do this thing

(n)   I want to do this thing now"

(o) when a person thinks like this this person can live with God

(p) if a person thinks like this at all times
        this person can live with God at all times

In his book *Source—The Holy Spirit and the Theology of Life*, Jürgen Moltmann (1997:142) has commented on the importance of the theme of watchfulness in Jesus' teaching: "The New Testament does not simply say 'pray'. We are told again and again to 'watch and pray'. Watching in tense expectation is the strongest form of prayer, because it is a great human answer to God's hiddenness. We watch for God." The first Christians tended to interpret this watching for God as waiting for Christ's second coming. But in the light of Jesus' own images, such as God's incognito appearance in needy and suffering people (Matt. 25:31–46), it can be seen as watching for God in other people and, more generally, in the duties and opportunities of the present moment; and this is the interpretation of the doorkeeper's watchfulness reflected in the explication.

TWENTY

The Talents

Matthew 25:14–28; cf. Luke 19:13–24

14. For the kingdom of heaven is like a man travelling to a far country, who called his own servants and delivered his goods to them.
15. And to one he gave five talents, to another two, and to another one, to each according to his own ability; and immediately he went on a journey.
16. Then he who had received the five talents went and traded with them, and made another five talents.
17. And likewise he who had received two gained two more also.
18. But he who had received one went and dug in the ground, and hid his lord's money.
19. After a long time the lord of those servants came and settled accounts with them.
20. So he who had received five talents came and brought five other talents, saying, 'Lord, you delivered to me five talents; look, I have obtained five more talents besides them.'
21. His lord said to him, 'Well done, good and faithful servant; you were faithful over a few things, I will make you ruler over many things. Enter into the joy of your lord.'
22. He also who had received two talents came and said, 'Lord, you delivered to me two talents; look, I have gained two more talents besides them.'

23. His lord said to him, 'Well done, good and faithful servant; you
    were faithful over a few things. I will make you ruler over many
    things. Enter into the joy of your lord.'
24. Then he who had received the one talent came and said, 'Lord, I
    knew you to be a hard man, reaping where you have not sown,
    and gathering where you have not scattered seed.
25. And I was afraid, and went and hid your talent in the ground.
    Look, there you have what is yours.'
26. But his lord answered and said to him, 'You wicked and lazy
    servant, you knew that I reap where I have not sown, and
    gather where I have not scattered seed.
27. Therefore you ought to have deposited my money with the bankers,
    and at my coming I would have received back my own with
    interest.
28. Therefore take the talent from him, and give it to him who has ten
    talents.'

The basic meaning of the parable of the talents seems clear enough. The Jewish
scholars Montefiore ([1930]1970:331) and Flusser (1989:11) state, respectively,
that "the gifts and favours which God has given are to be used in his service;
they are, as it were, to be given back to God with increase . . ."; "Man is obliged
to fully develop his own self in accordance with Him, whose unworthy servant
he is." Though only rough approximations, these formulations seem to me
eminently sound. Many commentators, however, have rejected statements of this
kind and have sought to restrict the message of the parable to some particular
groups of people rather than to recognize it as universally applicable. For example, Dodd (1965:112) suggests that the parable targets "the type of pious
Jew who . . . seeks personal security in a meticulous observance of the Law."
B. T. D. Smith (1937:168) suggests that "the parable formed part of a warning addressed to the scribes, the appointed teachers of God's Law." Jeremias
(1972:62) concurs that "we may assume that Jesus originally addressed the parable of the Talents to the scribes. Much had been entrusted to them: the Word
of God." Lambrecht also seeks to restrict the target to a particular class of people,
namely, the scribes, adding, however, the Pharisees as well. As an argument
against a more universal application, he invokes Jesus' use of the word "wicked"
to refer to the third servant:

> It is difficult to imagine this servant, so emphatically characterized as
> "wicked," as representing all people who do not recognize God's gift as a
> task and thus fall short in living out that task. Rather, Jesus has a definite
> class of people in view with this figure of the "wicked" servant. Jesus is
> more than a mere teacher here. . . . Who is, in fact, intended by the fig-
> ure of the third servant? We think here of the scribes and Pharisees who
> opposed Jesus' view of God and thereby the way in which God, through
> Jesus, brings his salvation to the world. (1991:234)

Other commentators restrict the target of the parables to Jesus' own disciples. For example, according to Kistemaker (1980:271), "The point of the parable is this—that every follower of Jesus is given gifts and opportunities of service . . . everyone who follows Jesus has been endowed with gifts and is given opportunities to put these gifts to work. Each one is expected to make the most of these avenues of service." Similarly, Fitzmyer (1985b:1232), questioning Dodd's and Jeremias's interpretations of the third servant as the symbol of either a pious Jew or of the scribes, observes, "It seems more likely that Jesus would have been speaking to people in his own entourage to whom he had been entrusting his own message . . . and these disciples or 'servants' of his are precisely the ones who are being admonished to do business with what had been entrusted to them, in view of God's day of reckoning."

It is not clear, however, why Jesus' teaching about the talents has to be restricted to any particular class of people—to the Jewish people, to the scribes, to the scribes and Pharisees, or to Jesus' own disciples. Why can't it be understood as universally applicable, as are his nonparabolic injunctions "Love your enemies" or "Do not judge"? Strangely enough, some commentators seem to think that to attribute a universal scope to the parables would cheapen them somehow. Lambrecht's (1991) use of the word "mere" seems symptomatic in this regard: he seems to be implying that the scope of Jesus' message is, as it were, not "merely universal" (my phrase) but rather aimed at a particular class of people. The tradition of rejecting a "merely universal" interpretation of the parable is an old one. B. T. D. Smith (1937:168), who was in favor of linking the third servant with the scribes, rejected a universalist interpretation: "To find in it only an illustration of the theme that men are required to make use of their God-given opportunities of service is, as Dodd (1935:24ff) rightly insists, to run the danger of representing Jesus as the detached exponent of general religious truths." Again, the use of the word "only" for a universalist interpretation seems odd. Although I agree that Jesus was not "the detached exponent of general religious truths," it is hard to see why having a universal message would make him a "detached exponent" of anything.

The historical question "Who were Jesus' immediate addressees when he first told this parable?" should, in my view, be distinguished from the semantic question "What did Jesus mean by this story?" In the parable of the talents, as in most of his other parables, Jesus seeks to affect, to challenge, and to change the hearer, whoever he or she may be. If at the level of its intended meaning the story engages the addressee ("you"), it is true that it cannot be validly characterized as a "general religious truth" (the parable is not about all people but about "you"). But the scope of that "you" at the center of the parable's meaning can be legitimately seen as universal, just as the scope of "you" in the injunction "Love your enemies" is universal.

The parable of the talents—like many of Jesus' other parables and sayings—presents a certain mindset (that of the third servant) and warns the addressee that "it will be bad for you if you think like this." At the same time, the parable presents to the addressee an infinitely preferable alternative: "it will be good for

you if you think: . . ." This is the basic structure of the parable's meaning: a mindset to be rejected followed by a positive alternative. In addition, there is a frame:
a basic assumption at the outset and a rounding-off conclusion or explanation
at the end. Thus, the basic assumptions of the parable of the talents can be formulated as follows:

    (a) God wants people to do good things
    (b) people can do good things because God does good things for
        people
    (c) if God wants someone to do some things this person can do these
        things

    Jeremias (1966b:13) rejected with scorn the idea that "'A reward is only earned
by performance' is the fundamental idea of the parable of the Talents," and I
think he is right: the notions of reward and performance are foreign and indeed
inimical to Jesus' teaching (cf. chapter 4, sections 2, 3, and 14). This doesn't
mean, however, that Jesus placed no value on human actions and saw no place
for them in God's general scheme of things or that he *opposed* the "heart" to the
"deeds." On the contrary, according to Jesus' teaching, a "healthy heart" was to
bear "healthy fruit" in the form of deeds. The metaphor of servant, recurring
throughout the Gospels, is just as eloquent in this regard as that of fruit: God
wants people to do things—not to get credit or a reward from God (see the parable of the servant's reward) and not to become achievers and performers in their
own eyes (see the parable of the Pharisee and the tax collector) but to serve God
in other people (see the parable of the Last Judgment). As the parable of the
Last Judgment illustrates particularly clearly, according to Jesus, God wants people
to do things, not because he wants to test their obedience, but because he wants
them to be instrumental in carrying out his plans and meeting other people's
needs on his behalf. This (Jesus implies) was the wrong the rich man committed daily, ignoring the starving beggar Lazarus, sitting at his gate, so that God
could not feed Lazarus through this rich man's hand. As Paul writes in his letter to the Romans (12:4-7), "For as we have many members in one body, but
all the members do not have the same function, so we, being many, are one body
in Christ, and individually members of one another. Having then gifts differing
to the grace that is given to us, let us use them: if prophecy, let us prophesy in
proportion to our faith; or ministry, let us use it in our ministering; he who
teaches, in teaching."
    Clearly, Paul's "differing gifts" are Jesus' "talents": different people are given
different gifts or talents, but they can all do some good things according to God's
plan, and in doing as best they can what they can, they serve God in one another. Whatever God wants them to do they *can* do because God gives them
the necessary grace: God does good things for people and thus enables them to
do the good things that he wants them to do. Different people have different
talents, but an opportunity to serve God is open to all, regardless of what their
particular gifts and circumstances are.

The phrasing of the component "God wants people to do good things," chosen in preference to a simpler "God wants people to do some things," reflects the emphasis on human initiative and creativity suggested by the story of the Talents. In the light of this parable, doing God's will is not envisaged by Jesus as something to be done in a spirit of passivity and unthinking execution of God's detailed instructions, but rather as a creative activity, done "in the freedom of the children of God" (Rom. 8:21). Just as in Genesis (1:20–31) God saw that what he had created was good, so in the parable of the talents the lord saw that what his two creative servants had done was good. Only the third servant, who was afraid to take risks, failed to do the good things that he could have done.

These, then, are the basic assumptions of the parable of the talents—that God wants people to do good things and that people can do good things (with God's help). These assumptions provide the background against which the two attitudes contrasted in the parable are set before the hearer.

I suggest that the attitude of the third servant can be portrayed (in universal concepts) as follows:

(d) sometimes a person thinks:
(e)   "some other people can do many good things
(f)   I can't do many good things
(g)   I know that I can do some good things
(h)   I don't want to do these things
(i)   if I do these things something bad can happen to me because of this
(j)   I don't want bad things to happen to me"
(k) because this person thinks like this, this person doesn't do these good things

Obviously, a person who thinks like this is lacking in confidence (f) and is afraid to act (i). Whatever confidence this person might have is undermined by the fact that he or she compares himself or herself with other people [(e) and (f)]. Both the lack of confidence and the paralyzing fear are linked with the absence of any thought about God; the mindset portrayed in the partial explication is not that of a disobedient or rebellious person but rather of one who doesn't think about his or her life in terms of God's will, God's grace, and God's love.

It is true that in the story, the third servant does think about the master (i.e., in some respects, God), but his thoughts about the master are dominated by fear ("I knew you to be a hard man. . . . And I was afraid"). He does not trust the master, he does not even dream of counting on the master's benevolence, and of course he does not expect any help from the master (who is absent, having gone to a distant country). Such is the attitude, Jesus suggests, of people who bury their talents in the ground: if they think about God at all, they think about him as an absentee landlord who can be feared but not trusted or expected to help in an emergency. This is not, Jesus warns, a good way to think about God—and not a good way to live one's life:

(l) it will be bad for you if you think like this

(m) it will be bad for you if you live like this because you think like
this

There is, Jesus urges, another way to think about God and another way to
live:

(n) it will be good for you if you think:

(o)   "I know: I can do some good things

(p)   because God does good things for me

(q)   I know: God wants me to do these things

(r)   I want to do these things because of this

(s)   I know that if God wants me to do these things I can do
them

(t)   because God will do good things for me"

This attitude is consistent with Jesus' teaching in his other parables and sayings.
In particular, it is consistent with the message of the servant's reward: if one
thinks like this, one recognizes that God has some tasks for one to fulfill (i.e.,
that one can serve God) and one is willing to fulfill these tasks. One's motives
are pure (to do God's will and to do it not because one has to or because one is
afraid not to, but because one wants to do what God wants and expects one to
do). There is confidence, not in one's own resources, but in God's: "if I can do
some good things, it is because God does good things for me; but if God wants
me to do some good things, then I can do these things because God will enable
me to do them."

If one thinks like this, Jesus implies, one can live, act, and take risks without
fear, trusting in God and counting on God's support. If one lives like this one
can do many good things (no matter what one's particular talents and circumstances); and it is good for a person to live like this, in freedom, trust, and with
the courage to act:

(u) if you think like this you can do many good things

(v) it will be good for you if you live like this because you think like
this

Dan Otto Via (1974:120), for one, has commented on this freedom to act and
take risks:

The man who retreats from risking his life wants to provide his own security. . . . Such seeking for security is death. . . . To know, on the other hand,
that one is sustained by a transcendent and unprovable ground . . . is to
be able to risk one's security (Matt. 6:25-34). And such risking is life, for
in it one is free from the anxious effort to provide one's own security
through the world, and in such freedom life in the world is good.

The awareness that "one is sustained by a transcendent and unprovable ground" means, effectively, a faith in God—not only a faith in God's existence but a faith that "I can do some good things because God does good things for me." Such a faith doesn't necessarily lead one to the conclusion that "nothing bad can ever happen to me" (we don't know whether the enterprising servants felt that kind of insouciance), but it does liberate one from the paralyzing fear of the third servant ("if I do these things something bad can happen to me" and "I don't want bad things to happen to me"). Accordingly, in the portrayal of the positive mindset, there is no mention of any "bad things that can happen to me"—the attention is elsewhere: on the "good things that I can do (with God's help)."

One last theme that needs to be discussed here is the parable's eschatological implications. When Jeremias (1966b:13) scornfully rejected the view that "the fundamental idea of the parable of the Talents" is that "a reward is only earned by performance," he did it not only because he objected to interpreting Jesus' teaching in terms of rewards and performance but also because he thought that if interpreted along such lines, parables like the talents "are stripped of their eschatological import." I agree with Jeremias about rewards and performances, and no such notions are embodied in my explication. I also agree with Jeremias that parables like the talents do have an eschatological import. This aspect has not been accounted for in the explication so far, but it does need to be accounted for, and I propose to do so in the following final group of components:

(w) if a person lives like this it is good for this person
(x) after this person dies this person will know it
(y) at that time this person will feel something very good because of this
(z) if a person doesn't live like this it is bad for this person
(z') after this person dies this person will know it
(z") at that time this person will feel something very bad because of this

It is generally recognized that Matthew's version of the parable includes some eschatological accents that are added by the redactor: the repeated sentence "Enter into the joy of your Lord" (vv 21 and 23) and the grim final command in verse 30, "And cast the unprofitable servant into the outer darkness. There will be weeping and gnashing of teeth." But even apart from these additions, the core parable (both in Matthew's and in Luke's versions) includes the idea of reckoning, which is a key element of the story. As represented in my explication, this final reckoning can occur after a person's death and consist of self-judgment: when in the light of God's truth one takes stock of all one's past opportunities and talents and when one realizes how much was left unused and unfulfilled, one will (Jesus warns) feel "something very bad because of this" [(w)–(z")].

Before leaving the parable of the talents I will briefly consider Borsch's (1988:109) claim that according to this parable "one cannot save anything without risking it" and that this applies to the eternal life as well: "Maybe being willing to lose one's life means being willing to lose eternal life, too." Borsch also states that "Jesus himself can be regarded as a model for reckless, unsafe living" (p. 109). Comments of this kind can be misleading; it is true that Jesus warned people against subordinating their lives to a search for earthly security, but it is not true that he encouraged them to risk losing eternal life too. On the contrary, he urged them to build the house of their life on the rock. Selling everything to buy the pearl of great price was presented by him as a wonderful opportunity, not as an awesome risk.

What I think Borsch (1988:110) really has in mind, however, is that focusing single-mindedly on one's individual salvation can also be a risk: "Living so as to conserve and trying to keep for oneself and one's own is a way of losing"— and this can also apply to efforts to secure one's personal salvation. If this is what he really means, the question arises not so much in the context of the talents as in that of the pearl of great price and the hidden treasure. In my explication for the talents, the great good of living with God is mentioned (v), but it is not in focus, as it is in the pearl and the treasure.

But surely it would be a mistake to reduce Jesus' teaching to any one parable or cluster of parables. The pearl and the treasure were meant to illuminate one aspect of this teaching, the talents another, the Last Judgment yet another, and so on. It is only when taken together that Jesus' parables and other key sayings give us a coherent and adequate portrayal of his teaching. In particular, the central commandment "Love your neighbor as yourself" must not be lost sight of in any such portrayal; without this commandment, a search for the pearl of great price (only for oneself) could indeed become a form of selfishness and as such would be contrary to the core of Jesus' message. In Jesus' teaching, the kingdom of God clearly stands for *people* living with God (not a *person* living with God), and neither indifference to other people nor attempts to use them as means to one's own ends (including that of one's own salvation) are compatible with entering the kingdom oneself.

Borsch (1988:108) is, of course, right in raising such questions, and I think he is right in applying the image of talents to a person's capacity for love: "A muscle that is spared is lost. A capacity for love that is not used in loving (and surely all loving involves risk) after a while becomes empty. Even what one has is taken away." But he doesn't seem to be faithful to the spirit of the Gospels when he concludes his discussion of the talents with the comment that "risking and investing life beyond oneself could also lose" and that "servants are in a tough spot" (p. 110). Jesus' own words (which appear in the Gospels no fewer than six times, with slight variations)—"Whoever seeks to save his life will lose it, and whoever loses his life will preserve it" (Luke 17:33)—do not imply that "servants are in a tough spot." They contain a warning but also an appeal and a promise. In the background there is the image of God as the rock. Here as elsewhere it is important for the modern reader not to misunderstand the language of the Jewish *Drohrede* (rhetorical threats and warnings) and not to mistake the parable's surface meaning for its intended deeper meaning.

I have quoted Lambrecht (1991:234) as saying that "it is difficult to imagine" the third servant, "so emphatically characterised as 'wicked', as representing all people who do not recognize God's gift as a task." But to assume that the third servant represents particular people, or that the master represents God, would be to read the parable as an allegory. If Jesus could use the image of a dishonest judge to speak about God (Luke 18:1–8), he could also use the image of a hard man, who calls some other people wicked and shows no understanding for human fears and insecurities.

This does not mean, of course, that Jesus wanted to *describe* God as either dishonest or hard and lacking in understanding and mercy. On the contrary, in seemingly comparing God to a dishonest judge, he was in fact urging people to pray and to trust God; and by seemingly comparing him to a harsh and merciless master, he was in fact urging people to trust God—and, consequently, to use God-given gifts with courage and in freedom. It should be impossible to read the Gospels and to miss Jesus' central message about God: that he is merciful and loving and can be trusted. The parable of the talents, like all the other parables, can only be fully understood against the background of this underlying central message.[1]

The talents

  (a) God wants people to do good things
  (b) people can do good things because God does good things for
      people
  (c) if God wants someone to do some things this person can do these
      things

  (d) sometimes a person thinks:
  (e)   "some other people can do many good things
  (f)   I can't do many good things
  (g)   I know that I can do some good things
  (h)   I don't want to do these things
  (i)   if I do these things something bad can happen to me
  (j)   I don't want bad things to happen to me"
  (k) because this person thinks like this, this person doesn't do these
      good things

  (l) it will be bad for you if you think like this
  (m) it will be bad for you if you live like this because you think like
      this

  (n) it will be good for you if you think:
  (o)   "I know: I can do some good things
  (p)   because God does good things for me
  (q)   I know: God wants me to do these things
  (r)   I want to do these things because of this
  (s)   I know that if God wants me to do these things
          I can do these things
  (t)   because God will do good things for me"

(u) if you think like this you can do many good things
(v) it will be good for you if you live like this because you think like this

(w) if a person lives like this it is good for this person
(x) after this person dies this person will know it
(y) at that time this person will feel something very good because of this
(z) if a person doesn't live like this, this is bad for this person
(z') after this person dies this person will know about it
(z") at that time this person will feel something very bad because of this

TWENTY-ONE

The Dishonest Steward

Luke 16:1–8

1. And he also said to his disciples: "There was a certain rich man who had a steward, and an accusation was brought to him that this man was wasting his goods.
2. So he called him and said to him, 'What is this I heard about you? Give an account of your stewardship, for you can no longer be steward.'
3. Then the steward said within himself, 'What shall I do? For my master is taking the stewardship away from me. I cannot dig; I am ashamed to beg.
4. I have resolved what to do, that when I am put out of the stewardship, they may receive me into their houses.'
5. So he called every one of his master's debtors to him, and said to the first, 'How much do you owe my master?'
6. And he said, 'A hundred measures of oil.' So he said to him, 'Take your bill, and sit down quickly and write fifty.'
7. Then he said to another, 'And how much do you owe?' So he said, 'A hundred measures of wheat' And he said to him, 'Take your bill, and write eighty.'
8. (a) So the master commended the unjust steward because he had dealt shrewdly.
   [(b) For the sons of this world are more shrewd in their generation than the sons of light."]

The parable of the dishonest (or unjust) steward is one of the most intensely debated of all the Gospel parables. Johnson (1991:246) comments on the "major problems [which] face the interpreter of this passage. . . . So difficult is the solving of them that the 'parable of the wicked household manager' with its attendant sayings has generated a disproportionate amount of scholarly discussion." Donahue (1990:162) observes that "very few chapters in the NT pose as many exegetical challenges as does Luke 16."

The authenticity of the parable (vv. 1–8a) is not in question, although it is also generally agreed that the attendant sayings (8b–13, which, apart from 8b, I have not included) were added to the parable by Luke. Some commentators, for example, Gourgues (1997: 177–178), still think, however, that verse 8b may in fact go back to Jesus. The generally skeptical Fellows of the Jesus Seminar have included the dishonest steward among their small handful of "red vote" parables (i.e., parables of indubitable authenticity), alongside the leaven, the Good Samaritan, the vineyard laborers, and the mustard seed.

Funk et al. (1988:32) have accompanied their "red letter" edition of the parable with the following comment: "The Dishonest Steward embarrassed Christendom from the beginning. The parable vividly characterizes the steward's dishonesty, and, if verse 8a belongs to the original parable, the master in the story commends him for it. Such shocking elements are typical of Jesus' authentic parables." The point is undoubtedly valid, and in fact it can be generalized to the whole history of the parable's interpretation. As noted by Bailey (1976:86), "Many commentators affirm that this parable is the most difficult of all the synoptic parables." Bailey quotes in this connection the following arresting comments by C. C. Torrey:

> This passage [Luke 16:8f.] brings before us a new Jesus, one who seems inclined to compromise with evil. He approves a program of canny self-interest, recommending to his disciples a standard of life which is generally recognized as inferior: "I say to you, gain friends by means of money." This is not the worst of it; he bases the teaching on the story of a shrewd scoundrel who feathered his own nest at the expense of the man who had trusted him; and then appears to say to his disciples, "Let this be your model!" (1936:59)

In commenting on this passage, Bailey (1976:86) also uses the word "embarrassment": "The seeming incongruity of a story that praises a scoundrel has been an embarrassment to the Church at least since Julian the Apostate used the parable to assert the inferiority of the Christian faith and its founder."

In fact, however, incongruity is not a feature of the story but a feature of the interpretive traditions that seek to present the protagonists of Jesus' parables as allegorical portrayals of God or of model human beings. The conclusion of the story, according to which the master praised the dishonest steward for his shrewdness, is certainly surprising, but there is nothing incongruous or uncharacteristic about the parable as a whole. As Funk et al. (1993:359) note, the much debated verse 8a "provides the unexpected and surprising twist that is characteristic of Jesus' metaphorical stories."

Although there is nothing incongruous about the parable, the economic and legal background of the plot is not wholly clear to the modern reader. As the extensive literature on the subject shows, commentators disagree about the exact nature of the shrewd steward's dealings with his master's debtors. But these details are not crucially important in understanding the parable's main message. Despite widespread disagreement about the exact meaning of the plot, most commentators do agree, in broad terms, on its basic message. Although in what follows I will try to articulate this message in a new and more precise way, I believe that the traditional line of interpretation is essentially correct and that it is rightly based on the assumption that the master was praising the steward not for his dishonesty but for his shrewdness and resourcefulness. To quote Manson ([1937]1961:292), "It is the astuteness of the plan that is praised: and there is all the difference in the world between 'I applaud the dishonest steward because he acted cleverly' and 'I applaud the dishonest steward because he acted dishonestly'."

Generally, commentators present the message in terms of shrewdness, prudence, resourcefulness and resoluteness in a time of crisis, and this interpretation is often linked with Jesus' injunction for his disciples to be "innocent as doves and prudent as serpents." B. T. D. Smith (1937:110) says, "Here, according to Jülicher ([1888]1963) and Johannes Weiss (1901), is the original application of the parable. It was intended to illustrate the quick-wittedness, the ready perception and use of present opportunities with a view to future gain, which the religiously minded should display. The disciples should be prudent as serpents, as well as harmless as doves."

Similarly, Dodd (1965:26) writes, "The story tells of a man suddenly faced with a crisis which may mean utter ruin to him; realizing the seriousness of his position, he does some strenuous thinking, and finds out a drastic means of coping with the situation. The hearers are invited to make the judgment: this man, scoundrel as he was, at least had the merit of taking a realistic and practical view of a crisis." Jeremias (1972:46) makes similar comments: "The parable (vv.1–7) describes a criminal who, threatened with exposure, adopts unscrupulous but resolute measures to ensure his future security"; and Montefiore ([1927]1968:528–529) comments (also with reference to the injunction "Be clever as serpents"), "Jesus, the idealist, lays stress on cleverness or prudence. He wanted his disciples to be alert, wide awake, and able to use their opportunities."

Some commentators follow Luke in linking the injunction behind the parable with a wise and prudent use of money. For example, Blomberg (1990:246) states, "Some take it to teach shrewdness in the use of our money; others, prudence in the time of crisis. It seems unnecessary to choose between these. Each by itself seems somewhat truncated and together they yield good sense. Jesus exhorts the disciples to prepare for the Day of Judgment by wisely using everything God has given them, especially their money."

Before discussing the parable's message in detail or attempting a precise explication, let me consider the question of its special importance. Formulated along the lines of prudence, resoluteness, and resourcefulness, this message may seem to make good sense as part of the general picture of Jesus' teaching but it would be hard to argue that it is as startlingly original and radical as, for example, the message of the lost sheep, the leaven, the prodigal son, the Pharisee and the tax collector, the unforgiving servant, or the laborers in the vineyard. Why, then, should the dishonest steward be seen as a parable of such exceptional importance?

The answer to this question lies not so much in the parable's message as in its being a particularly clear example of one of Jesus' characteristic narrative techniques and therefore an important clue to the interpretation of other parables. This technique consists of using mixed or even predominantly negative models to illustrate positive characteristics, both for people and for God. Among others, Bailey (1976:105) notes that "the parables of Jesus have a surprising list of unsavoury characters. In addition to this steward are the unjust judge, the neighbour who does not want to be bothered in the night, and the man who pockets someone else's treasure by buying his field." Bailey refers to the discussion of this by B. T. D. Smith, who argues that the strategy in question is a unique characteristic of Jesus' teaching:

> Tales of the successful rascal have always been popular, as witness the story of the Master Thief. The fact that we do not expect such a tale to be used to enforce a religious lesson appears to be an almost unanswerable argument in favour of the authenticity of this parable. The statement sometimes met with, that it occupies a unique position among the Gospel parables, is not wholly true. The little parable of the Hid Treasure describes an action which cannot be defended on moral grounds. In the parable of the Widow and the Judge a lesson is drawn from the conduct of one who feared not God nor regarded man, and who is accordingly actuated by purely selfish motives. The parable of the Unjust Steward, whose conduct goes from bad to worse, is only the most outstanding example of a class of parable the use of which appears to be a unique and striking feature of Christ's teaching. (1937:109)

In illustrating his teaching with a gallery of "unsavory characters," Jesus, one might say, deliberately compelled his addressees to work out for themselves what a given story really meant. As Funk et al. (1993:218) observe about another parable, the unforgiving servant, "the ending sows confusion for listeners, who now do not know how they are to respond. This is the kind of ambiguity Jesus often builds into his parables."

In the case of the unforgiving servant, the confusion intended to make the addressees think has proved so effective that to this day some commentators are still confused, attempting to defend all aspects of the behavior of the king in the belief that a figure to whom God is being compared must be morally irreproachable. When in the concluding scene of the story this king acts in a merciless way, some commentators feel obliged to infer from this that according to Jesus, God will ultimately deal with (some) people in a merciless way. Similarly, in the parable of the talents, the master deals mercilessly with the servant who out of fear buried his talent in the ground, and since this master is taken to stand for

God, it is concluded that God, too, will deal mercilessly with anyone afraid to put his or her gifts and opportunities to the best use.

The parable of the dishonest steward should act as the best antidote to such an approach to the interpretation. The steward presented by Jesus as a model to imitate in one respect is not to be emulated in all respects. In the case of the steward, explicitly labeled dishonest, this deliberate selectiveness of focus is quite clear, and the story can only be regarded as incongruous or embarrassing to Christianity if one forgets this characteristic feature of Jesus' storytelling. It is also quite clear in the case of the unjust judge, who is explicitly described as one who "neither feared God nor regarded man" but is nonetheless someone to whom God is compared. But it is less obvious in the case of the man who appropriated a treasure found in somebody else's field, or in the case of the king who first showed his servant boundless mercy and then an equally boundless lack of mercy.

Some commentators remain unconvinced that Jesus could have illustrated a desirable attitude with the unedifying behaviour of a rogue. Donahue (1988:164) goes so far as to dismiss this opinion as "casuistic":

> Since patristic times the major problem of interpretation has been how Jesus could commend the apparent dishonesty and chicanery of the steward. The standard casuistic solution has been to focus on the "prudence" (or shrewdness) of the steward ... Christians are to be equally prudent (16:9) without being equally dishonest. The smiles of the congregation which greet this explanation from the pulpit or podium show that this fine distinction is a bit more than the text or human imagination can bear.

The point, however, is not that the steward's dishonesty should be overlooked but, on the contrary, that it should be emphasized, just as the injustice of the unjust judge should be emphasized rather than played down or excused. Jesus' parabolic similes are often based on a deliberate contrast and sometimes also on a deliberate "how much more" argument: if an unjust judge will finally respond to persistent requests, how much more will a loving God respond to trustful and persevering prayer? If a dishonest steward can respond to failure and crisis with positive thinking, how much more should those so respond who believe in God? Thus, as argued by Gourgues (1997) and many others, Luke's interpretation of the parable in verse 8b seems quite apt and entirely consistent with Jesus' rhetorical technique of combining likenesses with contrasts.[1]

Jesus seemed to avoid thoroughly positive characters as models altogether. Perhaps the only exception is the story of the Good Samaritan, in which the protagonist is presented in an unreservedly positive light—but then, he was an unlikely hero and a suspect character on other grounds (as a Samaritan). Otherwise, those who could be expected to be presented positively—the Pharisee who was praying in the temple, the older brother of the prodigal son, the laborers of the first hour—are in fact presented in a rather ambivalent light, whereas less reputable characters like the prodigal son, the sinful tax collector, and the laborers of the last hour are portrayed more sympathetically. It seems clear that this absence of good people and bad people in Jesus' stories is related to his general refusal to categorize people into good and bad and his scandalous table fellow-ship with the so-called sinners. Even those people in Jesus' parables who in some way represent God are usually either perfectly ordinary people, for example, the woman looking for a lost coin or the one baking bread, or people somewhat mixed in character, like the just but harsh master in the talents and the gener-ous but then pitiless king in the unforgiving servant. They may even be presented in a rather satirical fashion, such as the unjust but yielding judge and the un-generous friend who doesn't want to be bothered but ultimately does get up to open the door. In that gallery of picturesque human figures, the dishonest stew-ard is by no means out of place.

Let us now turn to an explication of the exact meaning of the dishonest stew-ard, starting with the idea of crisis, mentioned by many commentators. It is not just prudence or cleverness in general that is being urged by the story, but also prudence or cleverness in a situation of crisis. But what kind of crisis is being referred to here?

In the story, "There was a certain rich man who had a steward, and an accu-sation was brought to him that this man was wasting his goods"; and so there came for the steward a time of reckoning. In real life, this suggests a situation in which a person is forced to judge himself or herself negatively as someone who is wasting God's goods. I will therefore propose the following partial explication (as a portrayal of such a self-judgment):

(a) sometimes people think:
(b)   "I know:
(c)   God did many good things for me
(d)   God wanted me to do some good things because of this
(e)   I could do these good things because God was doing
           good things for me
(f)   I didn't do these good things
(g)   this is very bad"

As this partial explication shows, the message of the dishonest steward is closely related to that of the talents: people receive gifts ("good things") from God (c) and are expected to "to do some good things because of this" (d), and they can do so because they are given the necessary help from God (e). And yet people often fail to bear the expected fruits (f) and have to pass negative judgment on their failures (g).

In the dishonest steward, however, the focus is on how people react to their failures. The story emphasizes Jesus' call for a positive response, but the inter-nal logic of the parable requires that the listeners think first of a negative response, the one that they may be naturally inclined to come up with themselves:

(h) when people think like this, sometimes they think at the same
    time:
(i)   "I can't do these things now
(j)   I can't do anything now"

It is such a negative, despairing and defeatist attitude that Jesus is implicitly urging his hearers to reject:

(k) it will be bad for you if you think like this

Instead, the hearers are urged to emulate the steward's positive, imaginative attitude, not to abandon hope but to look for solutions. Arguably, they are also being urged to trust that God will not abandon them but will continue to help them with gifts. This can be represented as follows:

(l) it will be good for you if you think:
(m)   "I know:
(n)   I can do some good things now, as I could before now
(o)   because God will do good things for me now, as he did
         before now
(p)   if I don't know what I can do I can think about it now
(q)   I want to think about it now
(r)   I want to do some good things now"
(s) it will be good for you if you do something because of this at the
    same time

Components (m) and (n) express confidence that in the new situation one can still do some good things (though perhaps not the ones that one could have done before), and (o) shows the basis of this confidence (trust in God); (p) shows that although at first one may be lost for ideas, one doesn't need to give up; one can decide instead to think and do something [(q) and (r)]; and this decision can be followed by quick action (s).

Viewed in this way, the story of the dishonest steward turns out to have an affinity with the parables of the unjust judge and the friend at midnight, as well as with the Lucan injunction "never to lose heart." Here, however, the focus is on not giving in to despair in the face of one's failures, and on actively looking for a solution oneself (while trusting God at the same time).

Commentators sometimes suggest that the parable of the dishonest steward is not as relevant, or as appealing, to modern readers as are many others. Hendrickx says,

> There are basically two reasons why this parable is not exactly the most popular one for preachers and teachers. The first is the urgency which Jesus teaches here and which is difficult to translate into modern terms. . . . Secondly, how can a contemporary homilist actualize the example of a criminal who, when uncovered, tries to cover up the embezzlement by tampering with the accounts? (1986:195)

Hendrickx remarks that not a few people in the audience may consider a homily based on this parable "improper and risqué" (p. 195).

It seems to me, however, that when explained with reference to Jesus' general narrative strategy, and to parables like the unjust judge, the dishonest steward need not be seen by a modern audience in this way. As for the themes of personal crisis that needs an urgent solution and a personal sense of failure, it seems to me that once they have been clearly articulated, many modern readers or hearers would not find it difficult to relate to them at all. The parable encourages them not to despair, not to lose heart (see Luke 18:1), and not to give up.

The dishonest steward

(a) sometimes people think:
(b)   "I know:
(c)   God did many good things for me
(d)   God wanted me to do some good things because of this
(c)   I could do these good things, because God was doing good
                things for me
(f)   I didn't do these good things
(g)   this is very bad"
(h) when these people think this, sometimes they think at the same
        time:
(i)   "I can't do these things now
(j)   I can't do anything good now"

(k) it will be bad for you if you think like this
(l) it will be good for you if you think:
(m)   "I know:
(n)   I can do some good things now, as I could before
(o)   because God will do good things for me now, as he did
                before
(p)   if I don't know what I can do I can think about it now
(q)   I want to think about it now
(r)   I want to do some good things now"
(s) it will be good for you if you do something because of this at the
        same time

TWENTY-TWO

The Unjust Judge and
the Friend at Midnight

The unjust judge (Luke 18:1–8)

1. Then he spoke a parable to them to this end, that men always ought to pray and not lose heart,

2. saying: "There was in a certain city a judge who did not fear God nor regard man.

3. Now there was a widow in that city; and she came to him, saying, 'Avenge me of my adversary.'

4. And he would not for a while; but afterwards he said within himself, 'Though I do not fear God nor regard man,

5. yet because this widow troubles me I will avenge her, lest by her continual coming she weary me.'"

6. Then the Lord said, "Hear what the unjust judge said.

7. And shall God not avenge his own elect who cry out day and night to him, though he bears long with them?

8. I tell you that he will avenge them speedily. Nevertheless, when the Son of Man comes, will he really find faith on the earth?"

The friend at midnight (Luke 11:5–8)

5. And he said to them, "Which of you shall have a friend, and go to him at midnight and say to him. 'Friend, lend me three loaves;

6. for a friend of mine has come to me on his journey and I have nothing to set before him';

7. and he will answer from within and say, 'Do not trouble me; the door is now shut, and my children are with me in bed; I cannot rise and give to you?'
8. I say to you, though he will not rise and give to him because he is his friend, yet because of his persistence he will rise and give him as many as he needs."

It is generally agreed that verses 1, 7, and 8 of the unjust judge do not belong to the parable as originally told by Jesus but were introduced by Luke to provide a frame for it and to explain its meaning (as he understood it). What is more controversial is the status of verse 6. Funk et al. (1993:368) report that most of the Fellows of the Jesus Seminar attributed it to Luke and voted it black, in contrast to verses 2–5, which were given a pink rating.

Fitzmyer (1985b:1176), however, argues persuasively that verse 6 should be regarded as part of the parable proper: "From the beginning some comment seems to be called for about the attitude of the judge. If one were to regard the parable as consisting only of vv.2–5, then the parable would not be so much one about a dishonest judge, as about an importunate widow." This doesn't mean, of course, that Jesus said what is attributed to him in verse 6 in precisely that form, but rather that he did want in some way to draw the listeners' attention to the judge.

Obviously, in comparing God to an unjust judge Jesus was using a shocking image, and this seems to be the main reason that the scholars of the Jesus Seminar saw this parable as "similar to one originally told by Jesus" (p. 368). Presumably, the shocking character of the simile was also the reason that Luke found it necessary to supply an explanation, to prevent possible misunderstandings. As Fitzmyer (1985b:1177) rephrased this explanation, "If a dishonest judge would yield to the persistence and prayer of a widow, how much more would the upright God and Father of all!" It should also be noted that whereas the additional explanation in verses 7 and 8 is due to Luke, it corresponds very closely to that given in a different context by Jesus himself: "If you then, evil as you are, know how to give your children good gifts, how much more surely will the heavenly Father give good things to those who ask him?" (Matt. 7:13; Luke 11:7–11). Clearly, this is also part of the message of the unjust judge.

My analysis of Jesus' presumed message can be divided into five parts. First, there is a background assumption here (sustained throughout the Gospels) that God *can* do good things for people (just as the judge can do good things for the widow), that God *wants* to do good things for people (unlike the judge, who doesn't want to do good things for the widow), and that God *will* do good things for people (as the judge ultimately does for the widow).

Second, there is an assumption (partially spelled out by Luke in verses 1 and 8 but inherent in the logic of the story) that people (in particular, "you") are likely to get discouraged at times and that their faith in God as a loving father is likely to weaken, if not evaporate altogether. The hearer is reassured that these doubts are unfounded.

Third, there is the theme of prayer, highlighted by Luke in verse 1. Not only does God want people to know and to think that he can, wants to, and will do good things for them but also he also wants them to know that they can always turn to him in prayer, acknowledging their dependence on his love and their trust in it (i.e., saying, in essence, "I want you to do good things for me, I know you will do good things for me").

Fourth, the parable encourages the addressees ("you") to pray at all times (along the lines described in point 3 above) and assures them that their prayers are heard by God and that God *wants* them to pray to him.

Fifth, the parable implies something about the purpose and meaning of prayer. Above all, it affirms that praying and asking for good things does make sense and that it is good for a person to pray.

What, then, is, ultimately, the point of prayer? Why does God want people to pray? Jesus makes it quite clear that God does want this but has he also made it clear why? (One is reminded of the words of Brother Roger of Taizé (1991:cover): "God does not need our prayer: it is a mystery that he sets such store by it."

I think that in the Gospels as a whole, the point of praying *has* been at least partially revealed; some commentators (e.g., Keating 1997:80–82; McKenna 1994:98–112) have even suggested that it has been revealed in this particular parable. The point is, one can surmise that God speaks (i.e., says things) to people himself, that he wants people to hear his word and respond to it, and that people can hear what God says to them if they accept what Martin Buber (1970) called an I-Thou relationship with God. In other words, if people attempt to say things to God, not only will God hear *them* but also *they* will hear God, who was saying things to them in the first place; and if they hear God, they will know that God can do good things for them, wants to do good things for them, and does do good things for them.

Both Keating (1997) and McKenna (1994) go so far as to suggest that *we* are the unjust judge and the *widow* represents God because it is God who is constantly pursuing people and it is people who are constantly refusing to hear and respond to God. This is a paradoxical way of reading the parable, which clearly subverts its intended interpretation. But this subversion, too, is useful and illuminating because it highlights the message that resonates throughout the Gospels—that God "sows" his words, hoping that people will hear and respond, and that he wants to be recognised by people as a loving father whom they can trust and to whom they can talk.

Before attempting a translation of the parable's deeper meaning into universal concepts, we should address the question of the significance, or otherwise, of one other aspect of the story: the widow's persistence in asking. Is this persistence part of the *message* or only part of the *image*?

Some commentators (e.g., Michaels 1981:275) have suggested that persistence should be seen as part of the message, indeed, as the main theme of the parable. Others, however, take a different view. For example, Barclay (1994:146) writes, "The lesson of the parable is not that we must persist in prayer; it is not that we must batter at God's door until we finally compel him for very weariness to give us what we want, until we coerce an unwilling God to answer."

What such conflicting comments point to is that a global label like *persistence* is not clear enough to allow us to clarify the deeper meaning of the parable. Luke's editorial comment is perhaps more helpful here: The point of the parable is not that if God doesn't immediately grant you what you are asking for, you should go on asking him for the same thing until he relents, like the judge in the story. Rather, what matters is that one should not lose faith and that one should continue to *trust* God even if the petitions remain unfulfilled. A person's faith in God (and, consequently, the desire to pray) could be undermined by one major disaster not prevented by God (despite ardent praying) just as much as by a long period of misfortunes (not prevented by God despite repeated prayers). What matters in both cases is that one should not lose faith (which inspires prayer) and that one should continue to pray, under any circumstances. Accordingly, the idea of persistence in asking for a particular thing after repeated refusals has not been included in my explication, whereas perseverance in faith and in talking to God has:

(a) God can do good things for all people
(b) God wants to do good things for all people

(c) people sometimes think:
(d)   "God doesn't want to do good things for me"
(e) it will be bad for you if you think like this
(f) it will be good for you if you think:
(g)   "God can do good things for me
(h)   God wants to do good things for me"

(i) you can say to God at all times:
(j)   "I can't live if you don't do good things for me
(k)   I know that you can do it
(l)   I know that you want to do it
(m)   I want you to do it"
(n) it will be good for you if you say this to God at all times
(o) God wants you to say it
(p) when you say it to God, God hears this

(q) if you say this to God you will know that God can do good things for you
(r) if you say this to God you will know that God wants to do good things for you
(s) if you say this to God you will know that God does do good things for you

(t) God says some things to people
(u) God wants people to hear these things
(v) people can hear these things when they say things to God

This explication does not imply that if I ask God to do something for me he will do it (i.e., that he will comply with all my specific requests). Nor does it imply that if God doesn't do what I have asked him to do, I should ask again and again and that, if I do so, sooner or later he will do what I have asked him to do. Rather, it encourages the addressee never to waver in the belief that God *wants* to do good things for him or her and can do so; and it also encourages the addressee to talk to God at all times, asking him for good things, and not to cease to do it when feeling discouraged.

This explication doesn't attempt to explain in detail *how* God responds to prayer. It doesn't even say that if you ask God for something he will do good things for you *because of this* (either by doing what you asked for or by doing something else). There is no implication here that prayer will affect God, or change God's will. Needless to say, neither is there any implication here that God will *not* do good things for people who do not pray.

What the sayings attributed to Jesus in the Gospels and explicated here do imply is that God wants people to pray (also in the sense of asking for good things); that these prayers are heard; that if the requests remain unfulfilled, it is not because God either can't or doesn't want to do good things for people; and that, on the contrary, God can and does want to do good things for all people. One way or another, they imply that God wants people to acknowledge their dependence on him and to place their trust in him and to do so throughout their lives, regardless of the circumstances.

Crossan (1992:12) includes the parable of the unjust judge among what he calls "the action parables" and places it in the subcategory of parables that depict a situation "where the protagonist faces the problem and acts adequately to the situation": "Parables in which the situation meets with adequate decisional response would be the Friend at Midnight in Luke 11:5-8 and the Unjust Judge in Luke 18:2-5. In both cases one finally accepts the bothersome inevitability of what must be done."

This interpretation appears to reject the one assigned to this parable by Luke himself and by later exegetical tradition, and it is hard to see any justification for this. There are indeed parables that depict a situation that is calling for a decision, and in some of them—for example, in the pearl of great price (Matt. 13:45)—an "adequate decisional response" is indeed reached (although it doesn't involve any "bothersome inevitability"). But although the situation depicted in the unjust judge does involve "bothersome inevitability" (as does that in the friend at midnight), this idea does not belong to the parable's central message. If an unjust judge is such a shocking simile it is precisely because in some respects this judge is clearly *not* like God; God's attitude is *contrasted* with rather than *likened* to that of the judge (see Barclay 1994:222, 146). The central message of the story is that God *wants* people to pray and that he *wants* to do good things for them, not that people's prayers bother him and that he nonetheless feels he must respond. Presumably, this is not what Crossan 1992 meant; but by emphasizing the "bothersome inevitability of what must be done," he is turning attention away from the real theme of the parable, which is that God wants people to pray and that it is good for them to do so and not to lose heart.

The shocking aspect of the image is clearly intended to convey the idea that *even* an unjust judge who *doesn't* want to respond would finally respond to persistent petitions. Unlike the judge, God would respond not to persistent petitions but to unconditional trust, and this unconditional trust is nurtured by prayer itself—which is why verse 6 is so important. Fitzmyer (1985b:1177) says that it "calls attention to what the Judge said in order to make the argument a *minori ad majus* [from the lesser to the greater]: if a dishonest judge would (finally) respond to persistent pestering how much more would 'the upright God and Father of all' respond to prayers that he *welcomes* and *wants* to respond to" (see also Donahue 1990:184).

Traditionally, the friend at midnight parable was regarded as a twin of the unjust judge (see, e.g., Imbach 1995:216), and as I will discuss below, this view is still entirely defensible. It was somewhat undermined, however, by Jeremias (1972:158), who argued that in the parable of the friend at midnight the focus is not on the persistent friend who is knocking on the door but rather on the "friend who is roused from sleep." In accordance with this hypothesis, Jeremias translated verses 5–7 as a rhetorical question: "Can you imagine that, if one of you had a friend who came to you at midnight and said to you, 'My friend, lend me three loaves . . .', you would call out, 'Don't disturb me . . .'? Can you imagine such a thing?"

But although such an interpretation would indeed deemphasize the theme of persistence in asking (see Donahue 1990:186), it would not necessarily change the parable's major theme or make it substantially different from that of the unjust judge. As we saw earlier, persistence in asking doesn't have to be seen as an essential feature of the unjust judge either—prayer, yes, and trust in God, yes, but not necessarily persistence in asking. But isn't prayer based on trust in God also the main theme of the friend at midnight, even as interpreted by Jeremias (1972)?

Fitzmyer (1985b:911), who seems somewhat skeptical about Jeremias's (1972) hypothesis, sums it up as follows: "Thus God becomes the one who hearkens to the cry of the needy and comes to their help." But is this really so different from the essential message of the unjust judge? As Fitzmyer also notes, the story of the friend at midnight "emphasizes the certainty that the prayer will be heard" (p. 910)—and it does so on Jeremias's, as well as on Luke's, interpretation (even if persistence as such were an added Lucan motif). After all, the certainty that the prayer will be heard is worth emphasizing only if one assumes that some would doubt this at times. Even if the man at the door (in the friend at midnight) were not, and didn't have to be, particularly persistent, the point is that one way or another the man in bed *will* get up, "and that we can count on God to do the same" (Michaels 1981:275).

So, although the friend at midnight may not be, ultimately, about persistence in prayer, it surely is—even in Jeremias's (1972) interpretation—about prayer, its basis in trust, and its efficacy. Even if the friend at the door were not particularly persistent, he does knock on the door, and the parable brings reassurance that any such knock at God's door will certainly be heard and answered, too.

I disagree, therefore, with the scholars of the Jesus Seminar, who imply that for Jesus, this parable was not related to the theme of prayer: "The Fellows decided this anecdote probably originated with Jesus, although Luke has obscured its original meaning by adapting it to the context of prayer. He makes it cohere, in other words, with the Lord's Prayer, which precedes, and with the complex of sayings that follow. The burden of the whole section is that if one is persistent in prayer, God will respond" (1993:327). Funk et al. conclude their discussion of the parable by stating that "the original point of the anecdote and the Lucan context clash" (p. 328). The Lucan context may indeed have been secondary, as they suggest, but it is hard to see any clash here. On the contrary, even in Jeremias's (1972) interpretation the original point of the story is highly consistent with the passage that immediately precedes: the Lord's Prayer (with its petition "give us this day our daily bread") and with the passage that immediately follows (Luke 11:9–13): "Ask, and it will be given to you; search and you will find; knock, and the door will be opened for you."

It seems likely, then, that the original point of the parable was the same as that of the unjust judge and that the two were rightly regarded as twin parables. If there was any difference in the intended meaning of the two, it may have been only one of emphasis, linked with different images rather than with different themes. Imbach (1995:217) says that "in the story of the widow the emphasis is on the indefatigableness and persistence of praying, whereas in the story of the persistent neighbour, it is the *certainty* of being heard."

In the cultural context of first-century Palestine, the friend at midnight may have indeed been certain of being heard and responded to, whereas the widow who was pestering the judge may have had less ground for certainty and more need for persistence. But surely, the main point of both parables is the one highlighted by the words "Ask, and it will be given to you; search, and you will find; knock, and the door will be opened for you." I suggest, then, that behind the different images is a close semantic parallel between the parable of the unjust judge and that of the friend at midnight and that the meaning of both can be portrayed by the same formula.

TWENTY-THREE

The Pharisee and the Tax Collector

Luke 18:9–14

9. [Also he spoke this parable to some who trusted in themselves that they were righteous and despised others:]
10. Two men went up to the temple to pray, one a Pharisee and the other a tax collector.
11. The Pharisee stood and prayed thus with himself, 'God, I thank you that I am not like other people—extortioners, unjust, adulterers, or even as this tax collector.
12. I fast twice a week; I give tithes of all that I possess.
13. And the tax collector, standing afar off, would not so much as raise his eyes to heaven, but beat his breast, saying, 'God be merciful to me a sinner!'
14. (a) I tell you, this man went down to his house justified rather than the other; (b) for everyone who exalts himself will be abased, and he who humbles himself will be exalted.

It is generally believed that the frame of this parable, verses 9 and 14b, was added by Luke (v. 9, probably as Luke's own creation and 14b as a "floating logion," i.e., an independently circulating saying). I will therefore treat these verses as Luke's own commentary rather than as part of the parable as such and focus my attention on verses 10–14a.

To many readers this parable is puzzling, and in Jesus' own times it must have been even more so. Apparently, two people went to the temple, a good (righteous) one and a bad one (a sinner); the good one gave thanks to God (no doubt sincerely) and didn't ask for anything, whereas the bad one neither thanked God for anything nor repented for his own sins but simply asked for God's mercy. As a result, unexpectedly, God was pleased with the bad man (the sinner) and displeased with the good (righteous) one. The question is why?

As noted by Jeremias (1966b:113) and many others, "To its first hearers the parable must have seemed shocking and incomprehensible." In his own cultural context, the Pharisee must have appeared to be "the ideal pious man" (Scott 1989:96; cf. Jülicher [1888]1963:2:603; Linnemann 1966: 59): he did all the right things (in fact much more than was required by the Law) and avoided all the vices displayed by people around him. So why was God displeased with him and apparently preferred a sinner, who did not do the right things and whose vices were not in doubt?

If modern Western readers are likely to be less shocked than those to whom Jesus spoke 2,000 years ago, it is only because they have grown up in a culture influenced by Jesus' teaching, including this very story and Luke's interpretation of it. Yet many modern Christian commentators, too, betray some amazement at Jesus' conclusion. Why, they ask, did this man go to his house justified rather than the other? And they find Luke's explanations inadequate. Clearly, the Pharisee was a good man, who tried very hard, acknowledged God's help, and thanked him for it—so why was God so unfair to him? He didn't really "exalt himself" (as Luke's v. 14b suggests), and he didn't really get "abased"; rather, it seems, God took a dislike to him for no good reason at all. And why did God take a liking to the bad man? The tax collector didn't really "humble himself" either, he merely acknowledged (by his demeanor, as well as his words) that he was indeed a sinner, and unlike one other tax collector, Zacchaeus (Luke 19:1–10), he didn't even undertake to change his life and make reparations. There was certainly no reason for this sinner to be "exalted."

Jeremias (1966b:114) asks, "What fault had the Pharisee committed, and what had the tax-collector done by way of reparation?" and replies as follows: "Jesus does not go into this question; he simply says: That is God's decision. He does, however, hint at the reason in God's apparent injustice." This hint lies, according to Jeremias, in the fact that the tax collector appears to be quoting the opening words of Psalm 51: "Have mercy upon me, o God." Since the same psalm contains the words "The sacrifices of God are a broken spirit, A broken and a contrite heart—These, o God, you will not despise" (v. 17), Jesus is saying here, according to Jeremias, that "God's character . . . is such as described in Psalm 51. He accepts the despairing, hopeless sinner, and rejects the self-righteous. He is the God of the despairing, and for the broken-hearted his mercy is boundless. That is what God is like. . . ."

In a similar vein, Dupont (1969:II, 204–214) speaks (with reference to the Beatitudes) of God's "arbitrary" predilection for the sinners (as well as the poor and the afflicted), of the special love that God has for "the most disinherited" (p. 242), "not because of any better religious dispositions on their part, but simply because they suffer and are miserable" (p. 277).

There is something very appealing in such an emphasis on God's special love for suffering sinners, but explanations along these lines do not seem to do full justice to the parable of the Pharisee and the tax collector. If the tax collector suffered, it can indeed be assumed that he was included in God's special compassionate love for the "weeping," to use the term from Luke's third beatitude (i.e. the afflicted, the sufferers). But this wouldn't explain why God was apparently *pleased* with him, that is, why, according to Jesus, he "went down to his house justified." Clearly, this particular tax collector was not only miserable but also was doing something right. Similarly, the Pharisee's problem was not that he didn't suffer (and thus was ineligible for the special compassionate love that God has for the afflicted) but that he was doing something wrong—otherwise, why wouldn't he, too, go down to his house justified?

In trying to discover what it was that the Pharisee was doing wrong, we have, I think, to read between the lines of his prayer. Commentators often insist that everything the Pharisee said in his prayer was true, but was it really? There is no reason to doubt, of course, that he did fast twice a week and give tithe of all that he possessed and that he was not an extortioner or an adulterer. But this is not all that he was saying. Using universal human concepts, we can articulate his deeper message (or "meta-message"; see Tannen 1992:23) as follows:

> I am not like some other people
> these other people are bad people
> these other people do many bad things
> these other people do not live with God
> I do not do bad things
> I do many good things
> I am someone good
> I live with God
> this is very good

If we read this message in this form and then ask again whether it is true we will, I think, see more clearly what Jesus was trying to get his hearers to see. Could the Pharisee really say truthfully, "I do not do bad things"; "I am someone good"? Evidently, Jesus' point was that only those who don't see "the plank in their own eye" (Matt. 7:5) can think that they do not do bad things and therefore are not like other people; and judging any other people as bad people goes right against the stern injunction of "Do not judge." Furthermore, from Jesus' point of view it is also not true that any human being is someone good; only God is someone good (Matt. 19:17).

Above all, the Pharisee is deluding himself about his relationship to God. He thinks, "I live with God," but it is patently clear to the hearers and readers of the parable that he does not. They can sense that the Pharisee is congratulating himself on the righteousness of his external deeds without examining his heart. In particular, he clearly doesn't ask himself the key question: "Do I love my neighbor, for example, this tax collector?" Like the blind Pharisees in Matthew 23:23, he "pays tithe of mint and anise and cummin, and has neglected the weightier matters of the law: justice and mercy and faith."

Just as the elder brother in the parable of the prodigal son refuses to recognize the prodigal as his brother (and refers to him as "this son of yours"), so the Pharisee refuses, or in any case fails, to recognize the tax collector as his neighbor. Jeremias (1966b:104) says of people like the elder brother that "their self-righteousness and lovelessness separate them from God," and the same could be said about the Pharisee: he doesn't live with God because he is loveless, and moreover, since he doesn't see his own lovelessness, he cannot pray to be healed from it. In addition, since the Pharisee is clearly judging himself (very positively) on the basis of his outer conduct (e.g., fasting and giving tithes) and does not notice his lovelessness, the hearers of the story are led to be skeptical about all the good things done by the Pharisee, and the bad things not done by him, and to assume that they were all defined without reference to their accompanying thoughts, wants, and feelings, that is, to all that matters most before God.

The tax collector's message, on which his cry for mercy was based, can be represented as follows:

> I do many bad things
> I am not someone good
> God is someone good
> I do not live with God
> this is very bad
> I want to live with God

From the point of view of Jesus' teaching, all this must be recognized as true. So this is where the Pharisee was wrong and the tax collector right: the tax collector saw the basic truth about himself, about God, and about his own relationship to God, whereas the Pharisee was blind on all these points. The Pharisee knew, of course, that God was someone good, but he thought that he himself was also someone good, and in doing so he was wrong about himself and about his relation to God.

Furthermore, in assuming that he was not like (some) other people, the Pharisee was also fundamentally wrong about his relation to other people. The image of two people that the parable initially seems to suggest—a good man and a bad man—is overturned by Jesus' unexpected concluding verse: "this man went down to his house justified rather than the other." Many commentators speak in this connection of a reversal, but the metaphor of reversal does not explain what exactly Jesus means here. It may even suggest that the good man turns out in the end to be bad whereas the bad man turns out to be good, a conclusion that would be contrary to Jesus' fundamental tenet that people cannot be divided into good people and bad people, and that if one divides people in this way (placing oneself among the good), one separates oneself not only from other people but also from God.

The metaphor of Our Father, which implies both an essential otherness of God and a brotherhood of all people, is very relevant in this context. The

Pharisee's assumptions that he is not like (some) other people and that he is someone good contradict both the idea of the brotherhood of people and that of the Fatherhood of God.

From this point of view it is hard to see how the idea of a special "prerogative" of sinners (Dupont 1969:II, 277) and of a "true privilege of sinners" could be taken in any other than a figurative sense. As Dupont notes himself (p. 230), the division of people into righteous and sinners, which Jesus sometimes seems to adopt, should, when coming from him, be understood as a quotation from the received usage of the time. This applies, in particular, to the polemical passage in Mark 2:15–17, where the scribes and the Pharisees express their dismay at the fact that Jesus "eats and drinks with tax collectors and sinners"; Jesus replies that "those who are well have no need of a physician, but those who are sick. I did not come to call the righteous, but sinners." In using the terms "righteous" and "sinners," Jesus is echoing here the language of his interlocutors. From his own point of view, he came indeed to call the sinners, not the righteous, but this means *all* people, not *some* people (see Gourgues 1997:230–247.); from his point of view, those who see themselves as righteous and regard tax collectors and others as sinners are themselves also sinners. Of course, God could have a special compassionate love for *public* sinners, treated by their society as outcasts, but this would be a special privilege of *outcasts* (qua outcasts), not *sinners* (qua sinners).

It cannot be the case, therefore, that according to Jesus God prefers the tax collector to the Pharisee (Dupont 1969:II, 230) because of his special predilection for sinners; the Pharisee is a sinner, too. God can love both the tax collector and the Pharisee as sinners but cannot love the tax collector more on the grounds of his being a sinner. God (as depicted in the Beatitudes and shown in Jesus' own life) does have a *special* love for the poor, the hungry, and the afflicted because they can be contrasted with the rich, the privileged, and the fortunate. Sinners, however, cannot be similarly contrasted with the righteous because all people are sinners (whether public sinners or private sinners; cf. Bailey 1976:205; McKenna 1994:134).

From the point of view of Jesus' contemporaries, this was a radical and disturbing thought. The interpretation of the parable in terms of humility and pride, implied by Luke's placement of the floating logion about "exalting oneself" and "humbling oneself" as a conclusion to it, fails to do justice to this radicalism. For example, B. T. D. Smith (1937:179) notes that "there are, of course, many Rabbinic sayings which inculcate the need of humility and the danger of spiritual pride," and Psalms and Proverbs speak of God who "hears the cry of the humble" (Ps. 9:12), who "lifts up the humble" (Ps. 147:6), who "will destroy the house of the proud" (Prov. 15:25), and to whom "everyone who is proud in heart is an abomination" (Prob. 16:5). Yet, as any reader of the Psalms would know, the dichotomy between righteous people and sinners was also widely taken for granted, and the very fact (not questioned by anyone) that the Pharisees were scandalized by Jesus' keeping company with "sinners" highlights the common acceptance of this way of thinking.

Jesus' implicit rejection of the distinction between good people and bad people was indeed a very radical thought, which opened an entirely new perspective on life in general and life with God in particular. The Jewish scholar Montefiore acknowledged this, commenting on the parable of the Pharisee and the tax collector as follows:

> No parable in the Gospels is more characteristic than this. None reflects better an essential feature of the teaching of Jesus. A legal religion has its dangers. However unjust Paul was to its merits, it has the defects of its qualities. A "faith" one-sidedness has its dangers; a "works" one-sidedness has its dangers too. And what they are is inimitably hit off in this admirable story. ([1927]1968:556)

Trying nonetheless to defend the Pharisee in the parable Montefiore (p. 557) asks, "Could one not conceive a saintly person who was frankly sure that he (or she) could not rightly be described as sinful, and who was glad of it and who thanked God for it?" As mentioned earlier, however, the Pharisee is not a saintly person. He may be fasting and paying the tithe, but he doesn't see the tax collector as his neighbor and his heart is not full of love. He is, therefore, a sinner, just as the tax collector is a sinner.

What Jesus was doing in this parable, then, was undermining the very distinction between the righteous and sinners—not to say that all people are bad people but to point out that all people are sinners and God alone is good. At the same time, he was showing that God doesn't reject sinners but responds positively when they turn to him and ask for mercy. This does not mean that the sinners are "justified" by asking for mercy but rather that they are forgiven and accepted. It is important to recognize that the word "justified" (*dedikaiōmenos*) is used here as if it were in quotation marks. According to the normal use of this concept in Pharisaic Judaism, the tax collector could not have gone home "justified," but Jesus is challenging this very notion (as he was challenging the notion of the righteous). This is another instance of the heteroglossia in Jesus' speech (see chapter 3, section 9; chapter 4, sections 2, 3, and 14).

Crossan (1992:67) says that "the literal point of the parable is a startling story of situational reversal in which the virtuous Pharisee is rejected by God and the sinful publican gains approval." But is the Pharisee really rejected by God? Isn't it rather the case that God is rejected by the Pharisee? In his self-sufficiency, the Pharisee doesn't need God. He cares about God's approval, but he believes that this approval is not in question, and he has no great longing for God because he is satisfied. As Gourgues (1997:245) puts it, "this man suffices to himself. . . . In a sense, he has substituted himself for God." According to Gourgues, this is where the most important difference between the Pharisee and the tax collector lies: "What place remains for God in the life of the Pharisee satisfied with himself and with his own spiritual performances? On the other hand, someone who sees his own misery knows that they can't put their trust in themselves: God can then enter this person's life" (p. 247).

Thus, as Gourgues (1997:231) rightly points out, the parable is not concerned with the question of prayer as such but with "a person's fundamental attitude towards God and other people, an attitude which manifests itself in prayer." This difference in attitudes has to do with standing before God in truth. Unlike the Pharisee, the tax collector "stands before God in truth. . . . [He] presents himself such as he is, conscious of his indignity and his sin" (p. 247). Gourgues concludes, "'You want the truth in the depth of your heart': such is the attitude without which there cannot exist an authentic relation to God" (p. 248).

But fundamental as this truth in one's heart is, we can take our questioning one step further: why is it so important that one should see oneself in truth? Is *this* some kind of condition set by God (because this is the way God is; because God has a predilection for truth), or does Jesus' overall teaching suggest some further reason behind this need for truth?

Crossan (1992:67) says that "the metaphorical challenge" of the parable of the Pharisee and the tax collector is clear, that is, "the complete, radical, polar reversal of accepted human judgement, even or especially of religious judgement, whereby the Kingdom forces its way into human awareness. What, in other words, if God does not play the game by our rules?" As argued earlier, however, the metaphor of reversal does not give us an adequate explanation because it needs to be explained itself; and as for the "rules of the game", the question is whether God wants people to know what his "rules" are, and if so, how these rules can be articulated.

It is, of course, true that in his parables Jesus subverts and undermines many widely accepted human rules. Above all, he subverts and undermines the rule that "if a person does good things this person is a good person" and the concomitant rule that "if a person does bad things this person is a bad person." This doesn't mean, however, that he doesn't see it as necessary or desirable for people to know what God's rules are. He usually conveys them in images and encourages his hearers to grasp them in this way; and sometimes he states them in words as well.

The two key rules that are articulated in Jesus' teaching (Matt. 22:38–39) come, of course, from the Old Testament: "You shall love the Lord your God with all your heart, with all your soul, and with all your mind" (Deut. 6:5) and "You shall love your neighbour as yourself" (Lev. 19:18). A full-scale semantic investigation of these two commandments would go beyond the scope of this chapter. Two points, however, can be made that are directly relevant to the present discussion. The first is that the commandment to love God must include the following components:

> God wants you to think: "I want to live with God
>   I want this more than anything else"

The commandment to love one's neighbor (as interpreted by Jesus, that is, with a universal scope) must include the following components (see chapter 2, section 8):

> God wants you to think about all other people like this:
>   "this person is someone like me
>   I want God to do good things for this person
>   as I want God to do good things for me"

If we state these rules in this way, it becomes clear where the Pharisee goes wrong and where the tax collector is right: the Pharisee clearly fails to think about the tax collector that "this person is someone like me," and the tax collector yearns for God (wants to live with God).

In the story, the tax collector is not living with God but clearly *wants* to. The Pharisee thinks that he is living with God, but in fact he is not because not being conscious of anything lacking in his life, he doesn't *want* to live with God (he has no longing for it). If asked, the Pharisee would no doubt say that he does want to live with God, and in saying so he would be sincere. In fact, however, he doesn't need God and he doesn't yearn for God. He is fully satisfied with his life.

If God, as depicted by Jesus, is pointing out to the virtuous that they, too, are sinners and that they, too, do bad things, it is not because those bad things done by them would necessarily separate them from God. Rather, God (as portrayed and represented by Jesus) seems to be pleading for a place in their hearts, pointing to their sinfulness in order to shake them out of their complacency and self-sufficiency so that they see themselves as they really are (needy and *not* self-sufficient) and, consequently, turn to God. Seen in this perspective, even harsh invectives like "Blind Pharisee!" (Matt. 23:26) and "Blind guides, who strain out a gnat and swallow a camel!" (Matt. 23:24) begin to look like an expression of exasperation and an urgent attempt to get through to someone rather than anger or hostility.

There is no polar reversal, then, from a seemingly good Pharisee and a seemingly bad tax collector to a bad Pharisee and a good tax collector. Both are sinners, and neither is someone good. *God* is someone good. According to Jesus' teaching, however, both these sinners (as well as all the other sinners in the world) can live with God. God wants this and wants *them* to want it, too.[1]

We can now propose the full explication of the message of the parable:

The Pharisee and the tax collector

  (a) sometimes people think:
  (b)   "I am not like some other people
  (c)   these other people are bad people
  (d)   they do many bad things
  (e)   they don't live with God
  (f)   I am someone good
  (g)   I don't do bad things
  (h)   I do many good things
  (i)   I live with God
  (j)   this is very good"

  (k) it will be bad for you if you think like this
  (l) when a person thinks like this this person doesn't live with God

  (m) it will be good for you if you think:
  (n) "I am not someone good

(o) I do many bad things
(p) God is someone good
(q) I want to live with God"

This explication does not try to portray the full contents of the two men's prayers (including the Pharisee's thanks and the tax collector's cry for mercy), only their basic mindset and its consequences for each man's relationship with God. The Pharisee, who doesn't love his neighbor, does not live with God, but he thinks he does, and so, being satisfied with his life, he is not going to try to change it. The tax collector, on the other hand, realizes his own misery ("I am not someone good, I do many bad things"), and he yearns for a different life—a life with God.

The parable of the Pharisee and the tax collector tends to evoke a lively and approving response from the modern reader—possibly for the wrong reasons. There is always the temptation to feel superior to the Pharisee and to enjoy it, that is, to unwittingly become a Pharisee oneself. Brown et al. (1990:1366) state, "Parables are often like traps that catch us unawares. Contemporary readers who smugly reject the piety of the Pharisee (Luke 18:11, 'I am not like other people') may themselves be 'pharisaical'." This may apply to those modern readers who approve of the parable because they see in it Jesus' social protest and his admirable preference for outsiders over insiders.

> The Pharisee, who thanks God he is not like the sinner standing at his side, is of course presented in caricature, just as the tax official's piety—he asks for mercy, sinner that he is—is exaggerated. Hyperbole gives the parable bite, makes its trenchant criticism of the social world Jesus inhabited by heightening the contrast between the two figures. There can be no doubt that Jesus preferred self-effacement to exhibitions of moral superiority and plainly said so. (Funk 1996:185)

Funk's comment illustrates, it seems to me, our tendency as readers of the parable to identify the Pharisee with some "other people" (the establishment, social elites, mainline churches, etc.) rather than to read it as a warning to ourselves.

Elsewhere in the book Funk (1996:154) states, "The behavior of the two is caricatured: Pharisees are not that hypocritical, and toll collectors are certainly not that humble." But the story does not *describe* Pharisees and tax collectors; rather it *questions* the addressee ("Aren't you perhaps like the Pharisee in the story?"), and it encourages him or her to think about oneself, and about God, like the tax collector and not like the Pharisee.

Part III

CONCLUSIONS AND
FURTHER PERSPECTIVES

TWENTY-FOUR

An Overall Picture
of Jesus' Teaching

In the recent literature on Jesus, one often comes across remarks implying that from a comparative perspective his ethical teaching, outlined above all in the Sermon on the Mount and in his parables, was more or less banal. Reynolds Price (1997:49), in his otherwise remarkable and deeply original commentary on Mark's Gospel, says of the Marcan Jesus' ethical teaching that "virtually no single injunction or opinion is without its parallel in earlier religious lore—whether Jewish, Greco-Roman, Hindu, Confucian, or Buddhist." Price says this lightly, in passing, as if this were a well-known fact; and indeed, numerous parallels to Jesus' sayings have been cited in recent scholarly literature.

As I have tried to show in this book, however, many of these reported parallels are superficial and depend largely on an inadequate language of analysis. If one glides on the surface of the texts and sums up different ethical traditions in ready-made analytical formulas and terms (such as *nonviolence, nonretaliation, compassion, kindness, tolerance, hypocrisy, anger,* etc.), profound conceptual differences are glossed over and everything starts to look like everything else.

As discussed in chapter 4, section 7, there are indeed common themes in different religious traditions, and it is important to identify them. They cannot be identified, however, without an adequate conceptual framework, and, as I have argued throughout, an adequate framework has to rely on concepts that are simple rather than complex and universal rather than culture-specific. Few would maintain that humankind's religious beliefs can be meaningfully compared through culture-bound concepts like predestination, karma, nirvana, or purgatory (e.g., What does Judaism teach about karma? What does Confucianism teach about

purgatory? What does Buddhism teach about predestination?). It is often imagined, however, that concepts like kindness, tolerance, nonviolence, or anger are
of an entirely different nature and can be safely relied on as analytical tools in
comparing ethical teaching across languages, cultures, and religions. As I have
tried to show, this is an illusion.

If we examine afresh Jesus' teaching as presented in the Sermon on the Mount
and the parables, looking at it through the prism of simple and universal human concepts, we discover dimensions of meaning that are otherwise hidden from
view, and many alleged parallels melt into air. This applies, inter alia, to recent
claims that equate some key aspects of Jesus' teaching with that of the Cynics
(see, in particular, Crossan 1991).

It also applies to the current trend in scholarly opinion that asserts (especially
about the Sermon on the Mount) that everything that Jesus taught can also be
found elsewhere in earlier or contemporary Jewish thought and that it was only
a new configuration of old ideas that was distinctly his. For example, Hans Küng
(1993:75) says that "it is not the individual statements made by Jesus which are
not interchangeable [with other statements made within Judaism], but his message as a whole." In my own analysis of these individual statements, carried out
with the methodological tool of universal human concepts, I have come to a
different conclusion (see in particular chapter 3). I do not believe that the vital
matters of Christian-Jewish dialogue are best served by playing down the distinctive
features of Jesus' teaching, whether to retrospectively compensate for the dismaying
anti-Judaic accents in Christian theology in the past or for any other reason. Rather
we should strive for a sincere exchange of views, in an atmosphere of mutual
respect and good will. (Cf. Neusner 1993; Frymer-Kensky et al. 2000.)

But it is not just the relationship between Jesus' teaching and its alleged parallels in earlier, or contemporary, religious lore and philosophical ideas that can
be clarified in this way. Many voices in recent literature insist that Jesus had little
interest in ethics and didn't have much to say about this subject. Some writers
present Jesus' teaching as having, above all, a social and political agenda. Some
read Jesus' parables as primarily literature and would want to see Jesus more as
a poet and storyteller than as a teacher of wisdom. Some focus almost exclusively
on Jesus' mission to Israel and play down the importance of his ethical teaching
(which can apply to all people).

In my reading of the Gospels, however, Jesus—whatever else he was—was very
much a teacher of wisdom; and in my experience, the in-depth study of every
one of his parables and sayings, no matter how familiar, opens new horizons
and reveals unexpected meanings. (The fourth-century Syrian biblical scholar St.
Efrem has written, "The smallest words of Christ contain immense treasures,"
quoted in Gallo 1984:12).

Some scholars argue that the New Testament writers saw Jesus as the embodiment of God's wisdom, drawing on the traditional Jewish language and imagery
of personified wisdom. For example, Dunn (1991:195–201) compares the way
Paul wrote about Jesus in his epistles to the Corinthians and the Colossians (1
Cor 8:6, Col. 1:15–20) with the language of divine wisdom used in the proverbs and in the apocryphal books of Sirach and the Wisdom of Solomon, and

he discusses different interpretations of "Jesus as divine Wisdom." (See also Schüssler-Fiorenza 1994; Torjesen 1998; Witherington 1990, 1994.) Without wishing to enter into these debates, I will express my conviction that Jesus' parables and sayings embody "divine Wisdom" in a very special way and that those who dismiss his ethical teaching as "moral truisms" (see Price 1997:43) have not studied them deeply enough. I will also express my hope that the language of universal human concepts provides a tool for exploring more effectively the meaning of Jesus' parables and sayings than can be done through ordinary language or the technical language of traditional theology and exegesis.

Jesus' ethics as represented here is, of course, rooted in the idea of God and is closely linked with his theology and eschatology. The goal is for people to live with God, now and forever. The question of how to live is linked for Jesus with the question of what one lives for. The answer to the first question depends on the answer to the second. If the purpose of people's lives is to live with God forever, they need to know how to live to be able to live with God.

One could say that Jesus provided two answers to the "how" question: one in his own life and person and one in his teaching; or rather, one answer in two different media, spoken and lived. For example, his table fellowship with "sinners" matched his teaching on not judging people and not dividing them into good and bad, and his prayer for his own executioners matched his teaching on not wanting bad things to happen to anyone and wanting God to do good things for all people. Thus, if Jesus' teaching can be seen as embodying God's wisdom, so can his person. Presumably, this is what the author of the Fourth Gospel has in mind when he has Jesus say (John 8:12), "I am the light of the world; he who follows me shall not walk in darkness but [shall] have the light of life"; "As long as I am in the world I am the light of the world" (9:5); and, above all, "I am the Way" (14:6).

Jesus' ethical teaching offers signposts: "if you live like this you can always live with God." Jesus' own life offers a model: "if you live like this you can always live with God."

TWENTY-FIVE

Implications for Theology;
Christianity in a Nutshell

As I have tried to show throughout this book, very complex issues and ideas can be formulated and discussed in very simple language (without losing any of their complexity). This applies to ethics, and it applies also to theology.

Theology needs a new language. After twenty centuries of Christianity, the sense is growing among Christians and non-Christians alike that the creeds that congregations recite in churches each week are largely incomprehensible even to the congregations, let alone to the outsider. It would, of course, be an illusion to assume that people who publicly confessed their faith in the past always understood the creeds of their churches. But perhaps the need to understand in order to believe was felt less acutely then than now. As individual reasoning and opinions have become the ultimate arbiters of what can and should be accepted as true, understanding has increasingly become essential to faith.

After the two millennia that separate us from Jesus, the meaning of his words (as we find them in the New Testament) has become for many increasingly difficult to grasp—even in those parts of the globe in whose history and culture his message and subsequent reflections on it have played a key role. Ironically, if the words of the New Testament itself have become less and less comprehensible, the words of the commentaries purporting to explain and elaborate on its meaning often seem even less intelligible. One major reason for this lies in the complexity of the traditional language of theology. Another lies in its largely metaphorical character: images that in the past were accepted on faith, now seem to many baffling and alienating. Consider, for example, the following passage from a recent book entitled *Tomorrow's Catholic* (Morwood 1998:13): "How are we to understand language such as 'Jesus came to save us'? From where did he come? What do we imagine caused him to come?" The ironic formulation of the question "From where did he come?" seems intended to express the skepticism of the modern churchgoer and, perhaps in this case, of the author himself (see also Hick 1993).

Whatever anyone may say about the truth or otherwise of any particular metaphor, metaphors can undoubtedly encapsulate profound truths; and in Christianity and other world religions, some of the deepest and most important truths have been formulated, preserved, and transmitted through the centuries in metaphors. But to be helpful rather than baffling or alienating, metaphors have to be recognized as such and their meaning explained. If, for example, a commentator (Kimel 1990:11–12) insists that "God is not just *like* a father, he is *the* Father. . . . 'Father' is not a metaphor . . . it is a name and filial term of address *revealed* by God himself," this is likely to puzzle many readers rather than to help them grasp the meaning of the scriptural passages in question.

To see "father" as metaphorical is not to undermine its meaningfulness. On the contrary, it is only when expressions like *father, kingdom of God, good shepherd, lamb of God,* or *bread of life* are recognized as metaphorical that their meaning can be systematically investigated and explained in fully intelligible, nonmetaphorical language. Only by engaging in such translation from metaphorical into nonmetaphorical language can it be effectively shown that Christianity does not inherently favor kingdoms over republics, patriarchy over other social systems, or bread over rice or manioc.

The distinction between metaphorical and nonmetaphorical language is of crucial importance to the understanding of Christianity and of the Scriptures that are its foundational documents. This distinction can be fully delineated only within the framework of a coherent theory of meaning, which is explicit about its "semantic primitives," or indefinable basic concepts. As was argued by seventeenth-century thinkers such as Leibniz (1903) and Descartes ([1931]1701), not everything can be explained and not everything can be defined. Ultimately, the only way to truly explain anything is to explain it in terms of concepts that themselves are intuitively clear and do not require further definition. Otherwise, all explanations would lead to an infinite regression and would ultimately explain nothing. This simple and incontrovertible principle—that what is complex and obscure can be explained only in terms that themselves are simple and clear— applies to metaphorical language as much as to anything else.

Consider, for example, the following explanation of the concept of the Trinity in a recent book entitled *Essential Truths of the Christian Faith: 100 Key Doctrines in Plain Language*:

> The historic formulation of the Trinity is that God is one in essence and three in person. Though the formula is mysterious and even paradoxical, it is in no way contradictory. The unity of the Godhead is affirmed in terms of essence or being, while the diversity of the Godhead is expressed in terms of person. . . . The term *person* does not mean a distinction in essence but a different *subsistence* in the Godhead. A subsistence in the Godhead is a

real difference but not an *essential* difference in the sense of a difference
in being. Each person subsists or exists "under" the pure essence of deity.
Subsistence is a difference within the scope of being, not a separate being
or essence. All persons in the Godhead have all the attributes of deity.
(Sproul 1992:35)

Explanations like this—ostensibly formulated in plain language—are in fact incomprehensible to most people. I do not wish to imply that the doctrine that this
passage tries to explain is either meaningless or untrue. It seems clear, however,
that the language used here is anything but plain.

Not everything can be explained; religious faith can legitimately include mysteries or affirm that whereas God can know everything about people, people
cannot know everything about God. Sproul (1992:35) is right when he says that
"human analogies such as one man who is a father, son, and a husband fail to
capture the mystery of the nature of God" or that "the doctrine of Trinity does
not fully explain the mysterious character of God." What one cannot agree with
is the suggestion that words like *subsistence* or *essence* will *explain* the essentials
of Christian faith to ordinary mortals. Not everything can be explained, but if,
as Wittgenstein ([1922]1974:3) says, "what can be said at all can be said clearly,"
whatever can be explained at all can also be explained clearly.

There are, of course, good historical reasons for why the traditional language
of dogmatic formulations and of their traditional explanations should be as complex and as technical as it is. The ancient councils such as those of Nicaea
(325 C.E.) and Chalcedon (450–451 C.E.) tended to proceed by negatives because
they were involved in "an exercise in boundary definitions, which thereby makes
clear what is not orthodox thought" (Witherington 1998a:234). For example, to
respond to Arianism, which claimed that Logos ("God's Word") was a created
being and not fully divine, "the church turned to the word *homoousios* and to
the phrase 'begotten, not made.' This in part amounted to saying that Christ
came from the *ousia*, or essence, or very being, of the Father. The point at issue
was whether or not the preexistent *logos* was of the same stuff or nature as the
Father" (p. 239).

Thus the traditional language of theology—including that of the dogmatic formulations—is historically conditioned and sometimes less accessible for this reason. The essence of Christian faith is not inherently bound by that language,
however, and can also be expressed more directly, in simpler and more universally accessible formulations. To quote Raymond Brown,

The battle of biblical criticism has been to get Christians and the church
to recognize that the books of the Bible contain the word of God phrased
in the words of men and that therefore to discover God's revelation one
must take into account the historical situation, the philosophical worldview,
and the theological limitations of the men who wrote them. The same battle
has to be won in relation to the dogmas of the church where once again
God's revelation has been phrased by men. (1975:116)

The time may be ripe for an attempt to rethink Christian faith in simple and universal human concepts and to explore the possibility of explaining its basic tenets clearly and without metaphors.

To try to explain anything without assuming a prior understanding of the domain in question, one needs to have some conception of what terms are simple and self-explanatory and therefore do not require definition. This is not a matter that can be decided on an ad hoc basis; rather, it is one that needs to be carefully considered and tested across a large number of domains and, above all, a large number of languages.

The wide-ranging empirical investigations undertaken within the "NSM" framework (see, e.g., Goddard 1998; Wierzbicka 1996) suggest that words like *someone*, *something*, *because*, *exist* (i.e., *there is*), *one*, and so on (see the table on p. 465) can indeed be regarded as simple and universally comprehensible. They have also shown that regardless of the domain or language, more complex meanings can be explained through the 60 or so universal semantic primitives and their simple and universal grammar. Terms like *father* and *son* are not included in the list of indefinables and therefore do require explanations, both in their literal and in their metaphorical use. The terms *above* and *below* (in a spatial sense) *are* included in the list and therefore, when used in a spatial sense, neither need to be nor can be explained; when used metaphorically (nonspatially), however, they, too, need an explanation. Thus, in such sentences as "Each person subsists or exists under the pure essence of deity," it is not only the phrase "the pure essence of deity" but also the metaphorical use of the word "under" that calls for an explanation.

The same reservations apply to Küng's (1993:153) equally metaphorical explanation in his book *Credo: The Apostles' Creed Explained for Today*: "God, the invisible Father, *above* us, Jesus, the Son of Man, with God *for* us, Holy Spirit, from God's power and love, *in* us." It is an illusion to think that the English prepositions *under*, *above*, *with*, *for*, *from*, and *in* (or their German equivalents) can really help explain the doctrine of the Trinity (even for speakers of English or German, let alone for speakers of languages that have no corresponding prepositions).

It would go beyond the scope of this book to discuss doctrines like that of the Trinity. I will, however, offer some illustrations, based on the same methodology that underlies all the specific analyses in this book. Although the doctrine of the Trinity took several centuries to develop, scholars often point to its roots in Gospel episodes like that of the baptism of Jesus, which Mark (1:9–11) reports as follows:

9. It came to pass in those days that Jesus came from Nazareth of Galilee, and was baptized by John in the Jordan.
10. And immediately, coming up from the water, he saw the heavens parting and the Spirit descending upon him like a dove.
11. Then a voice came from heaven, 'You are my beloved Son, in whom I am well pleased.'

Whoever heard and whoever reported the voice from heaven, it is obviously important for Mark's story (widely believed to have been based on the recollections of Simon Peter) that what this voice said meant something—something intelligible. Trying to unravel some of this meaning in simple and nonmetaphorical language I would start as follows:

> you are someone not like other people
> when someone sees you this person sees God
> when someone knows you this person knows God

Similarly, in a scene (reported in Mark 5:1–20) in which Jesus casts out the "unclean spirit" (i.e., performs an exorcism) the spirit cries out, "What have I to do with you, Jesus, Son of the Most High God? I implore you by God that you do not torment me." Trying to unravel the meaning of these words, as reported by Mark, I would again start along similar lines:

> I know—you are someone not like other people
> I know—when someone sees you this person sees God
> I know—when someone knows you this person knows God

Every reader of Mark's Gospel is free either to believe or to disbelieve what Mark says, but the words reported by Mark (whether those of God or those of the unclean spirit) and their intended meaning are part of this story. We cannot fully understand Mark's story if we do not understand the words attributed by him to his key protagonists.

Obviously, Mark believes his own story to be true; and if, as many scholars believe, he wrote his Gospel in the 60s in Rome, where Christians were persecuted and his own life was threatened, his sincerity can hardly be doubted. For Mark faith and history were inseparable. Thus, when he writes that on Resurrection Sunday Mary Magdalene and her companions found an empty tomb, and that a young man sitting in the tomb told them that Jesus had risen, the meaning of the words "Jesus is risen"—words that he assumes to be true—is an important part of his story; and so is the meaning of the words pronounced by the voice from heaven at Jesus' baptism. To understand Mark's story we need to understand these words and distinguish what was meant literally from what was meant metaphorically.

The language used about God—for example, "God wants," "God knows," and "God lives"—is often described by various writers as metaphorical, but as pointed out earlier, this is a loose and vague use of the word, which is not anchored in any explicit set of independently postulated indefinables. Without such a set, debates about whether or not some expression is metaphorical cannot be resolved and are, ultimately, pointless. Within the system of primitives used in this book, concepts like KNOW, WANT and FEEL cannot be decomposed into any simpler and more intelligible building blocks. Consequently, such expressions as "God knows" cannot be meaningfully described as metaphorical because they cannot be explained in any simpler, nonmetaphorical language (see chapter 5).

What does it mean, then, to say that "Jesus came to save us" or that he is "the living bread which came down from heaven" (John 6:15)? Again, a comprehensive discussion of such sentences would go far beyond the scope of this book. I will, however, try to sketch—without images and in simple and universal concepts—a larger picture in which sentences of this kind can be better understood.

Christian faith in a nutshell

God's plan for people

1. people exist because God wants people to exist
2. God wants people to exist
     because God wants to do good things for people
3. God wants all people to live with God
4. it is good for people to live with God
5. nothing else is like this
6. it is bad for people not to live with God
7. if people don't want to live with God, they *can* not live with God
8. God wants people to want to live with God
9. God does many things because of this

10. God always knew that people would not always want to live with God
11. because of this God said before anything had existed:
12.   "I want to live with people for some time like people live
13.   if I live with people for some time like people live,
          people will know me
14.   when people know me they will know
          that I want to do good things for all people
15.   they will want to live with me because of this"

The incarnation

16. because God said this something happened at one time in one
      place [Palestine, first century]
17. someone lived at that time in that place [Jesus]
18. this person lived with people like people live
19. this person was one of the people
20. at the same time this person was not like other people
21. when people knew this person they knew God

Jesus' life, death, and Resurrection

22. this person [Jesus] lived with people for some time like people live
23. he told people many things about God
24. he told people that after they die they can live
25. he told people that if they want to do good things for other people
      they can always live with God

26. he told people that after they die they can live with God forever

27. after some time some people did some very bad things to him
28. he felt something very bad because they did these things to him
29. he died because they did these things to him
30. he didn't have to die like this
31. he could have said: "I don't want to die like this"
32. he didn't say this
      because he wanted to do something good for all people

33. he wanted people to know God
34. he wanted people to know that God wants to do good things
      for all people
35. he wanted people to want to live with God

36. a short time after he had died something happened to him
37. before he died he said this would happen
38. because this happened to him, after he died he lived
39. other people knew this
40. other people could see him
41. at the same time they knew that he lived after he died
      not like he lived before he died

The Ascension, the Holy Spirit, the church

42. some time after this people couldn't see him any more
      because he didn't live with people like people live any more
43. he now lives like God
44. people will see him another time

45. before people will see him another time people will not see God
46. at the same time people can know that God lives with people now
      [the Holy Spirit]
47. they can't see God now
48. at the same time they know
      that they can do many things now because God lives with
      them now
49. many people know now that God lives with people
50. they can all now live with God like one person [the church]

The Second Coming and the Last Judgment

51. when people see him [Jesus] another time, all people will see him
52. at that time all people will know how they lived before they died
53. they will know when they did good things
54. they will feel something very good because of this
55. they will know when they did bad things
56. they will feel something very bad because of this

The resurrection of the dead, the forgiveness of sins, eternal life

57.   after this all people will live
58.   they will live not like people live before they die

59.   if they want to live with God they will all live with God
            as God has always wanted all people to live with God
60.   they will know God
61.   they will see God
62.   they will live with God like a person can live with another person
63.   at the same time they will live with all other people
            like a person can live with another person
64.   they will not want anything else
65.   they will live with God with other people forever

This abridged outline of the Christian faith (which can be seen as, in essence, the story of God's love for people; see Loughlin 1997) attempts to articulate the traditional Christian belief that derives from the New Testament and later tradition and is affirmed by Christians around the world in such texts as the Nicene Creed; and to do so in a form that is free (or almost free) of metaphors and not bound to any particular language or culture. For example, in John's Gospel, Jesus says, "I have come down from heaven not to do my own will but the will of the one who sent me, and this is the will of him who sent me, that I lose nothing of all that he has given to me, but raise it up on the last day" (6:38–39). In the story as related here, the metaphor of coming down from heaven is elucidated in simple terms such as "God said . . . 'I want to live with people for some time like people live,'" and in the references to Jesus as someone who "was one of the people" but "was not like other people."

The metaphorical references to "losing nothing" and "raising it up on the last day" are explained in plain statements such as "God wants all people to live with God," "after [people die] they will live," and "they will live with God forever." The use of simple and universal concepts does not rob the doctrines of their ultimate mystery but does, I hope, provide clearer insight into their meaning.

I will not discuss this thumbnail sketch of Christianity in any detail but rather briefly compare some elements of it with a recent account proposed by the well-known scholar and popular writer Marcus Borg (1999). Borg emphasizes, as I do, that expressions like "Son of God" are metaphorical and that the tenet that Jesus is the only begotten Son of God, who is of one substance with the Father, has been formulated in language shaped by its historical context (the fourth-century theological debates, the need to rebut Arianism, etc.). Borg refers in this connection to his encounter with black seminarians in South Africa as an occasion when "the cultural relativity of credal and biblical language hit home": in that particular culture, he discovered, the status of the oldest brother is higher than that of an only son, and so it is seen as a more appropriate way of speaking about Jesus. Borg adds, "To say the obvious, if the creed had been formulated in a different culture, its language would have been very different. This awareness relativizes the creed and the Trinity" (p. 154).

Borg's (1999) observation about the cultural underpinnings of the language of the creed is indisputably true. But his references to the relativity of the creed and to its being a culturally relative product of the ancient church seem somewhat ambiguous: is there or is there not a stable, constant, culture-independent set of beliefs that all Christians who are reciting the creed can share? Borg tells us that when he, as a practicing Christian, recites the creed, he understands himself "to be identifying with the community which says these words together . . . [and] not only with the community in the present, but also with the generations of long-dead Christians who said the same ancient words as they stood in the presence of sacred mystery." He also suggests that "we would understand the purpose of the creed better if we sang it or chanted it" (p. 155).

But the crucial question is this: does one identify with the universal church by reciting the same words or by affirming the same faith? And if it is a matter of shared faith, what is this shared faith and how can it be articulated? Despite the ambiguity of Borg's (1999) formulations, it appears that he does mean a shared set of beliefs and not only a shared string of words; and he summarizes ("as he has thus far been able to understand") "what the creed and the [dogma of the] Trinity affirm about Jesus" (p. 154) in three points: (1) "the living risen Christ is a divine reality," (2) "the risen living Christ is . . . not a second God but is one with God," and (3) "what happened in Jesus was 'of God.'" This summary does sound simpler and clearer than Sproul's (1992) "plain language" explanations, but it does not adequately express the shared faith of Christians across all centuries, languages, and cultures.

First, expressions like "divine reality" could not be translated into most human languages because no counterparts for the words *divine* and *reality* could either be found or easily forged. Expressions of this kind are no less language- and culture-bound than the Nicene phrase *consubstantialem Patri* ("of one substance with the Father"). Second, the expression "one with God" relies on English idiom and could not be readily rendered in many other languages either. Third, the meaning of the sentence "what happened in Jesus was 'of God'" is not fully lucid even in English. The phrase "what happened in Jesus" is metaphorical, and its intended meaning is not clear (the Gospels tell us what Jesus did and what happened *to* Jesus but not what happened *in* Jesus), and the phrase "of God" is enigmatic and obscure. The sentence "what happened in Jesus was of God" could not be readily translated into all languages, as it relies too heavily on the grammatical structure of languages like English.

At the same time, Borg's (1999) summary seems to leave out important credal tenets about Jesus that can be expressed in all languages: that he was one of the people and that at the same time he was not like other people and that when people knew him they knew God. Formulations of this kind preserve the air of mystery inherent in the doctrine of the Trinity while still relying on simple, ordinary language. At the same time, they are consistent with traditional theological statements affirming both "the unity of the Godhead" and "the deity [as well as humanity] of Christ" (Witherington 1998a:240). They are also consistent with the faith of past generations of Christians, extending back to the beginning of the first millennium. To give up the belief that when people knew Jesus they knew God would mean giving up—to quote Witherington's (1998b:139) remark about the Resurrection—"on the possibility of any real continuity between . . . [one's] own faith and that of a Peter, a Paul, a James, a John, a Mary Magdalene, or a Priscilla."

When the black seminarians in South Africa to whom Borg (1999) was speaking (in English) about the Son of God as "a divine reality," as "one with God," and as someone "in whom" things happened that were "of God" went on to talk to their own congregations, it is likely that all these phrases would have failed them, being not transferable into the local languages. On the other hand, once the concept of God had been introduced and explained, sentences like "when people knew this someone they knew God" would not fail them because they could be transferred into any local language. (As for the concept of God itself, it can be explained in any language in the way shown in chapter 1.)

Borg (1999) and other scholars may not accept the interpretation of the credal statements about Jesus "the Son of God" that is proposed here, but since it is rendered in simple and universal human concepts, it can at least serve as an adequate platform for discussion, debate, and clarification of differences.

In his book *The Plain Man Looks at the Apostles' Creed*, William Barclay has written (with special reference to the Apostles' Creed),

> It is close on eighteen hundred years old. The Church has come a long way in experience and in thought since the latter half of the second century. There are unquestionably difficulties in the Apostles' Creed for the modern mind. It is a fact of history that all the great creeds of the Church have what might be called an apologetic basis, and that they were wrought out to face the particular theological dangers of their time. It may well be that a first reaction today is that it is high time that there was a restatement of faith, . . . made in twentieth century terms, and made specifically for twentieth century man. . . . But there are formidable difficulties. . . . It may be natural to long for such a creed stated in modern terms; it will probably prove impossible ever to construct it. ([1967]1990:381)

The twentieth century is now gone, and at the beginning of the new millennium it is natural to long for more—not just for a statement of faith "for twentieth century [European] man" but also for one for all people, that is, one intelligible in a global and universal perspective: in Africa, South America, Asia, Papua New Guinea, and everywhere else. It may be impossible to formulate a tenable creed "in modern terms" because "modern" is constantly becoming dated, and in any case what is modern for some will be culturally alien for others. But although we cannot find terra firma in modernity, we can find it in universality: universal human concepts give us a stable and firm reference point that no localized, transient modernity could ever provide. If Christianity aims to be (in the words of the Nicene Creed) a "una, sancta, catholica et apostolica Ecclesia," that is, one universal church, Christians must strive for a universal rather than a local and culture-specific statement of their faith. Limited as our knowledge of the languages of the world still is, it is now sufficient, nonetheless, to allow us at least to attempt such a statement. The "Christian faith in a nutshell" is offered as a possible first approximation.

If I may be allowed a personal note, several years ago I received a letter from a Christian missionary in Western Australia asking for linguistic advice on how to explain Christian faith to the Australian Aborigines that he was working with. He had heard from some linguists doing fieldwork in the same area that my colleagues and I were working on a semantic theory based on universal human concepts, which could be used for explaining meanings across languages and cultures. Could we offer any practical advice on how to explain Christ's words, which are part of the liturgy: "This is my body . . . which will be given up for you . . . this is the cup of my blood, the blood of the new and everlasting covenant. It will be shed for you and for all so that sins may be forgiven"? In that Aboriginal language there were no words for either "sin" or "forgiveness," not to mention "covenant." In addition to the strictly linguistic task of translation, that of explanation was even more daunting. Could such things be explained simply and intelligibly?

At the time, I was not able to answer the missionary's questions to my own satisfaction. I could explain the principles and illustrate their application with examples drawn from Jesus' ethical teaching, but I was not able to respond directly to the questions about the new covenant, the remission of sins, and the meaning of Jesus' death and Resurrection. Several years later, however, it seems to me that I can now offer some practical answers. In particular, I believe that the version of the Christian Nicene creed proposed here could be readily translated into that Aboriginal language, and, moreover, that this version would also go some way at least toward *explaining* some key elements of the Christian faith.

The task of explaining the Christian faith requires—now more than ever—a global, universal perspective on Jesus' teaching. It also requires an awareness of cross-cultural differences in ways of speaking and of difficulties and misunderstandings that such differences may give rise to, as I will illustrate in the next (and last) chapter.

TWENTY-SIX

Language: A Key Issue in Understanding Jesus and Christianity

Western readers have often found Jesus' way of speaking strange, even absurd. Chesterton (1909:268–270) called it "curiously gigantesque . . . full of camels leaping through needles and mountains hurled into the sea." Jesus, he said, first "called himself a sword of slaughter, and told men to buy swords if they sold their coats for them" and then "used even wilder words on the side of non-resistance."

Ballantine (1925:64–66) called Jesus' way of speaking "extraordinary," pointing out that he encouraged people to enter a life of love by demanding that they should hate the members of their own families—"if any man comes to me and does not *hate* his father and his mother and his wife and his children and his brothers and his sisters, yes, and his own life also, he cannot be a disciple of mine" (Luke 14:26).

Cadoux observed that certain of Jesus' sayings were marked by obvious absurdities, as

> when Jesus bade the critic consider the beam in his own eye before he offered to take the mote from his brother's eye; when he accused the Pharisees of straining out the gnat and swallowing the camel; when he said that it was easier for a camel to go through a needle's eye than for a rich man to enter into the kingdom of God . . . in all these cases his figures are undeniably absurd. (1930:243)

As did many other commentators, Cadoux (p. 251) pointed, in particular, to "the absurdity" of the saying about plucking out one's right eye (Matt. 5:29–30).

What is often striking in such comments (these three are from Ryken 1984) is the absence of any cross-cultural perspective: Jesus' hyperboles and paradoxes are discussed in a cultural vacuum, as if they were simply idiosyncrasies of his individual style. But in fact, "wild" hyperboles and "absurd" metaphors were part and parcel of the cultural tradition to which Jesus belonged. The images used by Old Testament prophets would no doubt also strike a modern Western reader as absurd. For example:

> The mountains and the hills before you shall break forth into singing, and all the trees of the field shall clap their hands. (Isa. 55:12)

> The sword shall devour and be sated, and drink its fill of their blood. (Jer. 46:10)

And here is one extended example from the book of Job (29:2–19), in which Job recalls his own happier days:

> 2. ... when God watched over me
> 3. When his lamp shone upon my head ...
> 6. When my steps were bathed with cream,
>   And the rock poured out rivers of oil for me! ...
>
> 14. I put on righteousness and it clothed me;
>   My justice was like a robe and a turban.
> 15. I was eyes to the blind, and I was feet to the lame. ...
> 17. I broke the fangs of the wicked, and plucked the victim from his teeth.
> 18. Then I said, 'I shall die in my nest, And multiply my days as the sand.
> 19. My root is spread out to the waters, and the dew lies all night on my branch.'

Dunn (1991:198),[1] speaking of the language of personification in Paul's epistles and of the personification of God's Wisdom in particular, comments that "such vigorous metaphorical usage is wholly in line with the vigor of Hebrew poetry and imagery." We see the same metaphorical "vigor" in the Hebrew Scriptures in general, and we also see it in Jesus' speech in the Gospels.

To say this is not to call into question the view (strongly voiced, e.g., by Funk et al. 1993) that Jesus had his own characteristic, personal style. But to understand what he meant, we need to appreciate not only his personal style but also the wider tradition, linguistic and cultural, to which he belonged.[2] I believe this is particularly important in understanding Jesus' eschatology.

In the past, the understanding of Jesus' eschatological parables and sayings has suffered from this lack of cross-cultural awareness. The images he used—for example, those of the loving father and the merciless judge—contradicted one another, and for a reader to whom the cultural, literary, and linguistic traditions that underlay Jesus' speech were alien, this lack of coherence was disturbing. If there was an obvious metaphor (e.g., a "mote" in one's brother's eye and a "beam" in one's own eye), the reader was prepared to accept the hyperbole as an image, but when a literal interpretation seemed possible (as in "everlasting fire") the image tended to be taken literally.

Even now, when most readers have come to realize that images like "the furnace of fire," "outer darkness," and "weeping and gnashing of teeth" should not be taken literally, the hyperbole of words like "everlasting"[3] often continues to be unrecognized. And yet even in colloquial English, phrases like "for ages" or "forever" can be used as a hyperbole for "a long time" (especially when referring to waiting). If this is possible in modern Anglo culture, which values understatement and on the whole is inimical to hyperbole, how much more should it be seen as possible in the context of the Jewish prophetic "Drohrede" (see, e.g., Bella 1926; Gressmann 1929; Gunkel [1927–1932]1969; Hayes 1973; Koch 1969; Wolff 1987), that is, the language of rhetorical threats and warnings. In fact, this is precisely how it was seen by early Fathers of the church such as Clement of Alexandria, Origen, and St. Gregory of Nyssa, who held that all suffering ("punishment") after death has a spiritual, healing, and purifying character and must therefore come to an end.

The traditions of the Jewish *Drohrede* seem to be as unfamiliar to most Western readers as the traditions of the Jewish curse, which was prominent in the Old Testament (e.g., in the Psalms) and which continued (through Yiddish) well into the twentieth century (see Matisoff 1979), for example:

> There are as many types of curses as there are people cursing, but the hardest to explain is the mother cursing her child. The child may be crying because he is hungry. The mother bursts out, "Eat, eat, eat. All you want to do is eat. May the worms eat you. May the earth open up and swallow you alive." This mother loves her child, she is only pouring out the bitterness that's in her heart in the only way she knows. But in translation she sounds like a monster. (Butwin 1958:9)

In recent times, a number of biblical scholars and theologians have pointed out that Jesus' parables cannot be properly interpreted if one is unaware of the "Drohrede" (see, e.g., Hryniewicz 1990; Imbach 1987, 1995; Nocke 1982). The parallels between Jesus' apocalyptic warnings and the warnings of the Old Testament prophets are indeed very striking. For example, in the book of Jeremiah, God urges "his beloved people" Israel to abandon their iniquities and to come back to him, but he tells them that he has abandoned them and "hates" them. He declares that he will not forgive them and, virtually in the same breath, expresses his never-ending love and forgiveness:

> Behold, my anger and my fury will be poured out on this place—on man and on beast, on the bees of the field and on the fruit of the ground. And it will burn and not be quenched. (7:20)

> Behold, I will surely bring calamity on them which they will not be able to escape; and though they cry out to me, I will not listen to them. (11:11)

Apparently, God is so furious with his people (whom he calls, nevertheless, "the dearly beloved of my soul," 12:8) that he forbids Jeremiah to even pray for them (11:14). At the same time, however, God begs his people to return to him:

> If you will return, O Israel, says the Lord,
> Return to me,
> And if you will put your abominations out of my sight. (4:1)
> Then you shall not be moved

> Return, backsliding Israel, says the Lord,
> And I will not cause my anger to fall on you,
> For I am merciful, says the Lord,
> And I will not remain angry for ever.
> Only acknowledge your iniquity. . . . (3:12)

Although God's forgiveness may seem to depend on his people's conversion and return to him, despite the threats one can discern unconditional love and forgiveness:

> I will make a new covenant with the house of Israel and with the house of Judah . . .
> I will forgive their iniquity, and their sin I will remember no more. (31: 31–34)

> I will cleanse them from all their iniquities by which they have sinned against me, and I will pardon all their iniquities by which they have sinned and by which they have transgressed against me. (33:8)

The prophet Isaiah also issues terrible threats on behalf of God—only to disavow them elsewhere. For example, in chapter 65, Isaiah's God complains bitterly about the people who have rejected his love (quotes from the RSV):

> I was ready to be sought by those who did not ask for me,
> I was ready to be found by those who did not seek me.
> I said, "Here am I, here am I" to a nation that did not call on my name.
> I spread out my hands all the day to a rebellious people,
> Who walk in a way that is not good following their own devices. (65:1)

In the same passage God seems to be dividing his own people (the people of Israel) into "the sheep and the goats," and while promising all sorts of blessings and bliss to the former, tells the latter ("you who forsake the Lord") that they will be destroyed:

> I will destine you to the sword,
> and all of you shall bow down to the slaughter;
> because, when I called, you did not answer,
> when I spoke, you did not listen,
> but you did what was evil in my eyes,
> and chose what I did not delight in. (65:12)

Yet terrible as such threats sound, the context makes it clear that their purpose is not to give people factual information about future events but rather to appeal to them again and again to "turn to me [God] and be saved" (49:22); the same God who promises destruction and slaughter to the unfaithful elsewhere reveals that all the bad things of the past will be forgotten:[4]

> For behold, I create new heavens and a new earth;
> and the former things shall not be remembered or come to mind.
> But be glad and rejoice for ever in that which I create;
> for behold, I create Jerusalem a rejoicing, and her people a joy. (65:17–18)

The same applies to several other prophets. For example, as noted by Wolff (1987:20), "Amos announces nothing less than the death of Israel (5:2). . . . Hosea totally negates the old covenant relationship: 'You are not my people and I am not your God! (1:9)." At the same time, however, the same prophets make it clear "that Yahweh's harsh measures still are only his corrective by which to lead his beloved people into an enduring and conclusive connection of love with him."

The Jewish theologian Abraham Heschel writes in *The Prophets* of the "mysterious paradox of Hebrew faith":

> The All-wise and All-mighty may change a word that He proclaims. . . .
> The anger of the Lord is instrumental, hypothetical, conditional, and subject to his will. . . . The message of anger includes a call to return and to be saved. The call of anger is a call to cancel anger. . . . Its purpose and consumation is its own disappearance. (1962:286)

Commenting on the anger expressed by the prophets on God's behalf, Heschel points out that God's love is repeatedly described as everlasting (and is contrasted in this respect with God's anger)—thus, Jeremiah (31:3): "I have loved you with an everlasting love"; and Isaiah (54:8): "In overflowing wrath for a moment I hid My face from you, but with everlasting love I will have compassion on you, says the Lord, your Redeemer." (See also Buber 1960:2.)

One exegete who has paid a good deal of attention to the biblical *Drohrede* (which he calls "prophetic hyperbole") is G. B. Caird:

> Prophecy deals more often than not in absolutes. The prophets do not make carefully qualified predictions that the Israelites will be destroyed unless they repent. They make unqualified warnings of doom, accompanied by unqualified calls to repentance. . . . What appears to be an unconditional verdict turns out to contain an unexpressed conditional clause. (1980:112)

Caird illustrates this "prophetic hyperbole" with Isaiah's announcement of imminent death to the king Hezekiah: "When Hezekiah is dangerously ill, Isaiah says to him, 'This is the word of the Lord: Give your last instructions to your household, for you are a dying man and will not recover' (Isa. 38:1). But once the king has offered a penitential prayer, the prognosis is reversed."

One cannot fully comprehend Jesus' teaching without taking the prophetic tradition into account. The fact that the New Testament includes no fewer than 590 references (explicit ot otherwise) to Isaiah alone (J. A. Sanders 1987:75) underscores the importance of this tradition for understanding Jesus. Modern scholars who speak of "the dark side of God" and take the eschatological threats found in the Gospels at face value seem to be forgetting the Jewish prophets. For example, Theissen and Merz, in their otherwise balanced and judicious account of Jesus' preaching, write,

> Jesus, too, knows the dark side of God. His preaching of judgment brings it out in a threatening way. But in it God's punitive and lethal energy is here concentrated as the power to punish sinners. Thus it has an ethical orientation—and in the last resort is distanced from God, because human sin comes into the centre. . . . (1998:273-275)

The dark side of God? God's punitive and lethal energy? One would like to think that the authors must be talking here about imagery, not about meaning. However, they also build on such images in their theological reflections. For example, they write about "whatever causes the evil—God's dark side, human sin and Satan's activity. . . ." Whereas they write about God ("the God of Jesus") as "the unconditional will for the good," they also appear to interpret literally the threat of an everlasting hell:[5] "The God of Jesus is the God of Israel: a blazing fire of ethical energy which seeks to change people in order to kindle the love of neighbour in them; but which becomes the devasting fire of hell for those who exclude themselves from salvation"(p. 274).

Theissen and Merz (1998:266) themselves emphasize that Jesus "seeks to prevent damnation by announcing it, to save those on whom it announces judgment" and, therefore, that "this announcement of judgment is not final." They note that "Jesus explicitly compares himself with the prophet Jonah (Matt. 12.41f.)—a prophet whose message of judgment led to the conversion of Niniveh." Only in the case of his woes over the Galilean cities (Luke 10:13-15); Matt. 11:21-24) "does Jesus seem to have anticipated God's final verdict ('Capernaum, you will be cast down into hell')" (p. 266). But this is not "God's final verdict," this is the language of the Jewish prophets—the language of appeal and lament, of sorrow and love; the same language that we also hear in Jesus' lament over Jerusalem (Matt. 23:37):

> O Jerusalem, Jerusalem, the one who kills the prophets and stones those who are sent to her! How often I wanted to gather your children together, as a hen gathers her chicks under her wings, but you were not willing!

As for the "dark side of God" and God's "punitive and lethal energy," let me quote once again St. Isaac of Niniveh (the same Niniveh to which the prophet Jonah had, on behalf of God, announced imminent destruction, only to see his announcement invalidated by God's mercy): "Among all his [God's] actions there is none which is not entirely a matter of mercy, love, and compassion: this constitutes the beginning and the end of His dealings with us" (1995:172). Isaac does not deny that some utterances in the Scriptures seem to suggest otherwise, but he firmly rejects a literalist reading: "That we should imagine that anger, wrath, jealousy or such like have anything to do with the divine Nature is something utterly abhorrent to us. . . . Nor again can we possibly say that He acts thus out of retribution, even though the Scriptures may on the outer surface posit this" (p. 162).

The book of Jonah ends with a charming epilogue. The prophet, dispirited and displeased with God for going back on his word and sparing Niniveh after all (contrary to Jonah's announcement of destruction) sits outside the city's gate in the shade of a plant and is very grateful for the plant and the shade it provides. But overnight the plant withers, and when Jonah sees this the following morning, he is upset. Then God says to Jonah (4:10–11),

> You have had pity on the plant for which you have not labored, nor made it grow, which came up in a night and perished in a night.
>
> And should I not pity Niniveh, that great city, in which are more than one hundred and twenty thousand persons who cannot discern between their right hand and the left, and also much livestock?

Heschel (1962:287) comments, in the spirit of Isaac of Niniveh, that "beyond justice and anger lies the mystery of compassion."

The hyperboles and the paradoxes of Jesus' parables and sayings belong to the same tradition. For a contemporary Western reader, accustomed to value and to expect consistency, precision, accuracy, measured speech, rational argument, and so forth, without some explanations Jesus' way of speaking is bound to be misleading, as well as disturbing. The metaphorical character of such phrases as "the furnace of fire" or "weeping and gnashing of teeth" is now readily understood, but the figurative character of the hyperbolic and apocalyptic phrasing of the calls to conversion is still widely unrecognized.

In fact (as Butwin 1958 pointed out), there is no contradiction between a Jewish mother's use of curses and her love for her child. Similarly, there is no contradiction between, on the one hand, the biblical conventions of *Drohrede* and, on the other hand, the message of unconditional love—conveyed by images such as that of a woman who is searching for a lost coin, a shepherd who is leaving everything to search for one lost sheep, or an old father who is running to meet a returning prodigal son.

Reynolds Price (1997:133), in his engaging commentary on the Gospel of John, includes among its striking features "John's near omission of that awful Judge who spreads his terror through the other gospels." But this is not a difference between John's and the synoptics' understanding of God. The God of Luke's prodigal son is the same God as the God of John's good shepherd. The difference lies in language, style, and the type of discourse.

It thus needs to be recognized that a proper understanding of texts that originate in other cultures requires, inter alia, some attention to cross-cultural pragmatics and some awareness of how different the "cultural scripts" (see Wierzbicka

1991) that prevail in different cultures and in different types of discourse can be. It is particularly important to realize that in the Jewish cultural tradition to which Jesus belonged, not only a story narrated in the past tense, but also a vision presented in the future tense could have the illocutionary purpose of an injunction, an appeal, or a call.

The speech genre of the prophetic *Drohrede* can be explained to people from other cultural and linguistic backgrounds along the following lines:

> sometimes a person says something to people [of Israel]
> because this person thinks: "God wants me to say it"
> this person could say something like this to people:
>> "if you live like this you can't live with God
>> if you don't live with God this will be very bad for you
>> something very bad will happen to you because of this"
>
> people think that when this person says something like this
> God wants to say something like this to people:
>> "I don't want you to live like this
>> when you live like this you can't live with me
>> I want you to live with me
>> I want to do good things for you
>> if you live with me you will know that this is good for you
>> you will know that nothing else is like this"

Other culture-specific ways of speaking can be similarly explained in universal concepts. For example, the Yiddish curse can be explained as follows:

> sometimes someone says to another person something like this:
>> "I want something very bad to happen to you"
>
> this person says this because this person feels something very bad,
> not because this person wants something very bad to happen to this
>> other person

Biblical curses, blessings, beatitudes, woes, laments, jeremiads, hyperboles, and so on, all need to be *explained* to cultural outsiders no less than the modern Jewish (Yiddish) "blessings, curses, hopes, and fears" (cf. Matisoff 1979).

The same applies to unfamiliar Jewish conventions of debate, argument, private rebuke, and public polemic. As noted recently by several scholars (both Christian and Jewish), in the past the lack of familiarity with the Jewish rhetorical tradition has often led to a misunderstanding of the polemical style of Jesus and the evangelists (with tragic consequences for the relations between Christians and Jews):

> Despite all the controversies and debates—indeed because of his untiring, often impetuous dialogs with scribes and fellow teachers, a method that is to this day still the best rabbinic way of determining truth and interpret-

ing the Bible–Jesus' faithfulness to Torah in both word and deed remains the best-kept secret in the Synoptics. (Lapide 1985:91)

Lapide says that Jesus, with "his fiery temperament, his vivid use of imagery, and his passionate love for Israel," speaks "exactly like the prophets before him," that "Isaiah also publicly denounced the leaders of Israel," that "Malachi thunders in the name of the Lord against the predecessors of the same Sadducees whom Jesus reprimands," and so on. Lapide asks rhetorically, "Do not the laments of Jesus sound loving and reserved by comparison with the reprimands and threatening curses of the prophets? Yet their common concern is one and the same: a call to repentance issued to the people, a holy anger directed against the wicked shepherds who feed themselves, and above all, a deep longing for the salvation and welfare of Israel" (pp. 97–98).

Jesus' message is universal, but to understand it we need to understand Jesus' Jewishness. In particular, we need to understand that the New Testament world of discourse includes rhetorical conventions that are unfamiliar and even alien to the modern Western reader. This applies also to the prophetic *Drohrede*, which sometimes seems to announce God's final verdict but in fact expresses, to use Lapide's (1985:98) words, "a deep longing for the salvation and welfare of Israel"–Israel and the whole world.

Jesus was a Jew, and doubtless he saw his mission as directed, in the first place, toward Israel. But Israel was to bring, in the prophet Isaiah's words, "a light to the nations" (42:6; cf. Luke 2:32). Christians see Jesus' teaching as embodying this "light." For this teaching to be intelligible to people of all nations, it needs to be seen both in its cultural context and in a universal perspective. As I have tried to show, this can be facilitated through the use of universal human concepts.[6]

Using these concepts, we can make it clear (in any language) that according to Jesus' teaching, "God wants to do good things for all people," that "all people can live with God," and that "God wants it," as well as how people can live if they want to live with God. Furthermore, we can make it clear that Jesus never taught that "God wants to do bad things to some people" (those who "have done very bad things") or that "some people cannot live with God"; any such ideas would be totally incompatible with what he did teach about God. We can also clarify, in simple and yet universal concepts, the meaning of the culture-specific speech genre of prophetic warnings and threats and thus help explain the source of the misunderstandings that surround the notion of hell.

According to the French historian Jean Delumeau (1989), the doctrine of an everlasting hell, which has for centuries dominated European preaching, is one of the main causes of the de-christianization of the West in modern times: "Because the churches of the West did not pay sufficient attention to the arguments of the 'heretics' who refused to believe in an eternity of hell, there emerged since the sixteenth century a movement rejecting Christianity, which was identified by the 'libertines' as a theology of the punishing God" (p. 504). This movement intensified in the post-Enlightenment period. "The refusal of hell led Meslier, Diderot, d'Holbach, Helvétius, and a whole posterity after them to deny at the same time all transcendance" (p. 571). And yet there is no mention of hell in the Christian creed!

It is only recently that historians like Delumeau (1989) have drawn attention to the price Christianity has paid for St. Augustine's (mis)interpretation of the apocalyptic images of the Gospels (the dreadful chapters 17-27 of Book XXI of the *City of God*) and of its influence over the first two Christian millennia. Thankfully, this particular aspect of Augustine's influence appears to be finally coming to an end, and one must hope that it will not persist far into the third millennium.[7]

Notes

1. The word *authentic* is not unproblematic and it is used here only for convenience. As L. T. Johnson (1999:78) notes, "Christians . . . regard the compositions of the New Testament together and separately not as inadequate sources for historical recovery . . . but as invaluable witnesses to a living reality." An interest in Jesus' *ipsissima verba* and *ipsissima vox* (his very own words and voice) does not mean that one does not regard other sections of the New Testament as what Johnson calls "revelatory texts."

2. The full set of universal concepts as they emerged from empirical cross-linguistic investigations can be represented in the form of the following table:

Substantives	I. YOU, SOMEONE(PERSON), SOMETHING(THING), PEOPLE, BODY
Determiners	THIS, THE SAME, OTHER
Quantifiers	ONE, TWO, SOME, MANY/MUCH, ALL,
Attributes	GOOD, BAD, BIG, SMALL
Mental predicates	THINK, KNOW, WANT, FEEL, SEE, HEAR
Speech	SAY, WORD, TRUE
Actions, events, movements	DO, HAPPEN, MOVE
Existence, and possession	THERE IS, HAVE
Life and death	LIVE, DIE
Logical concepts	NOT, MAYBE, CAN, BECAUSE, IF
Time	WHEN(TIME), NOW, AFTER, BEFORE, A LONG TIME, A SHORT TIME, FOR SOME TIME
Space	WHERE(PLACE), HERE, ABOVE, BELOW, FAR, NEAR, SIDE, INSIDE

Intensifier, augmentor	VERY, MORE
Taxonomy, partonomy	KIND OF, PART OF
Similarity	LIKE (HOW, AS)

3. In this book, as in the other books by the author and colleagues, semantic explications follow special graphic conventions. These include not only a "semantically transparent" layout, but also no capital letters at the beginning of sentences and no periods at the end. These conventions reflect the fact that the language of the explications is not ordinary English but a semi-artificial semantic language: NSM or the Natural Semantic Metalanguage.

4. The English verb *to live* is polysemous: one of its meanings is "life" and another is a person's "living quarters." French and German distinguish lexically between the meaning intended here (*vivre, leben*) and the other meaning of the English *live* (*habiter, wohnen*), which is a somewhat distracting connotation in the present context.

5. According to Gerard Loughlin (1999:179), God is not someone but an event: "For Christian faith God is known only as that which happens; not as a being or as a thing, but as an event. . . . God is not a thing—not a being or even Being itself . . ." Whatever the merits of such a perspective on Christian faith, an event cannot know people, love people, want to do good things for people, nor can one pray to an event (not even to a "God event"). For this reason alone, a simple explanation, intelligible and potentially useful to all people, must start with God as someone, not with God as something that happens.

CHAPTER 2

1. Moltmann (1981:51) refuses, in my view rightly, to draw a sharp line between the suffering of the guilty and that of the innocent: "Even the customary phrase about 'innocent suffering' still actually presupposes that we could accept 'guilty suffering'. But in actual fact the experience of suffering goes far beyond the question of guilt and innocence, leaving it behind as totally superficial."

2. One further complication should be mentioned: in the Old Testament there are two variants of the word, *anawim* and (older) *aniim*. Although the relationship between the two is not absolutely clear, scholars usually assume that *aniim* (from the verb root *ny*) and *anawim* (from the verb root *nwm*) bore essentially the same meaning.

3. According to Turner (1980:217), "*Tapeinos* in secular Greek was the physically lowly, like flat ground and low-lying rivers, but, on the personal side, it was 'humbled' or 'abased'. Clearchus reassured Tissaphernes, 'The Mysians who were troublesome to you, with our present troops I think I could render *tapeinos* towards you. It is small, poor, weak or submissive, and sometimes, in low estate or obscurity. 'Your mind is too much *depressed* to persevere in your resolves', Pericles informed the people of Athens at the second Peloponnesian invasion, and often the word indicates what is mean or debased." Turner comments that whereas the new "Christian words" . . . "are often the ordinary vocabulary of ordinary people in the secular world," they belong to a new system of thought and carry new meanings.

4. It could be suggested that the poor, the hungry, and those who weep can live more with God. I think this idea merits further consideration; at this stage, however, I have not incorporated it into my explication of the message of the Beatitudes. (For further discussion of this idea, see chapter 4, sections 5 and 6.)

CHAPTER 3

1. Strictly speaking, "Israel" stands not for all the descendants of Abraham but only for the descendants of his grandson, Jacob. The formula sketched here is, necessarily, a simplified one.

2. Matthew has placed the passage on divorce and adultery (5:31–32) after that on the "adultery in the heart" (5:27–30), but in fact to understand the latter we need to understand the former. Section 5:31–32 explains Jesus' notion of adultery, whereas 5:27–30 builds on this notion and uses it metaphorically. In my discussion of these passages, therefore, I have reversed their order.

3. Rorty (1989:5) states that "the suggestion that truth, as well as the world, is out there is a legacy of an age in which the world was seen as the creation of a being who had a language of his own." Rorty's view that there is a connection between a belief in truth and a belief in God seems curiously consonant with the ideas of St. Augustine and St. Thomas Aquinas about God as the ultimate guarantor of truth. To St. Augustine, God is "the first and subsistent truth. . . . Only God fully verifies the idea. He is truth" (O'Farrell 1967:327). St. Thomas Aquinas (1964) speaks of truth as a transcendental property of being anchored in God (De veritate 1.1).

4. As noted earlier, Tolstoy ([1884]1958) himself found a solution to the paradox in the notion of civil disobedience (cf. Maude 1930:35).

5. Dunn (1991:271) comments, "The real issue between Judaism and Christianity was not about whether 'Love your neighbour as yourself' was a legitimate summary of the law regarding human relationships. There were plenty within Judaism who would have agreed with Jesus and Paul that Lev. 19.18 encapsulated such social obligations and that 'the neighbour' could include a Gentile. The real dispute was whether love of neighbour could only properly be exercised by bringing the neighbour within the law or could be offered to the neighbour without condition."

CHAPTER 4

1. Funk et al. (1993:148) do not explain on what basis they attribute verses 2 and 4, in contrast to 3, to Matthew; they only note that 3 is "a memorable aphorism of a paradoxical nature," of a kind "characteristic of Jesus." One can presume, however, that they see the rabbinic parallels as an argument against verses 2 and 4.

2. Betz (1995:330–331) calls Matthew 6:1–18 "a cultic *didache*, or ritual instruction," whose aim is "to make a distinction between proper and improper performances, and to recommend doing them in the right form." Betz says, "Cultic duties, after all, can fulfil their purpose only if they are rendered in the appropriate way." In my reading, however, Matthew 6:1–18 is not about cultic duties, proper performances, or the right form at all. Rather, it is about the motive: sefish or unselfish. Even the overt contrast between doing things to be seen by people and doing things in secret symbolizes here a deeper contrast between a self-seeking (self-oriented) and un-self-seeking (other-oriented) motive.

3. Discussing "inconspicuous piety," Betz (1995:344) noted the closeness between the Sermon on the Mount's teaching and Paul's idea in his letter to the Romans (2:28–29) that "the true Jew is the hidden Jew": "For he is not a Jew who is one outwardly, nor is that circumcision which is outward in the flesh, but he is a Jew who is one inwardly, and circumcision is one of the heart, in the Spirit, and not in the letter; whose praise is not from men but from God." Betz comments, "Not denying the value of externality, Paul emphasizes that the status of a person before God is decided by what is

in the heart and not by conspicuous performances of external rituals." I think this comparison is apt and the comment right. This means, however, that ultimately the contrast is not one between ostentation and secrecy (the "how" of the act, or its *tropos*) but rather between an impure and a pure motive (in traditional exegetical language, its *skopos*, i.e., aim).

4. The New Testament is shot through with heteroglossia and hidden dialogue. A good example is provided by the passage in St. Paul's letter to the Romans at 12:20, which has baffled many Christians:

> Therefore if your enemy hungers feed him;
> If he thirsts, give him a drink;
> For in so doing you will heap coals of fire on his head.

This passage seems strangely inconsistent with, inter alia, Paul's hymn to love in his letter to the Corinthians (13:1–13). In fact, Paul is quoting and at the same time engaging in dialogue with a passage from the Proverbs (25:21). He concludes, "Do not be overcome by evil but overcome evil with good." (For further discussion, see chapter 7, section 3.)

5. Admittedly, verses 7 and 8 are generally regarded as having been brought from some other context and inserted here by Matthew's editorial decision, but wherever they come from, there seems to be a link between "ostentatious praying" and "long prayers." Even if Jesus referred to these two features on separate occasions, he may nonetheless have thought them linked. An alternative to "saying many things" (also consistent with the image of standing on street corners) would be "sometimes a person says things to God for some time" or even "for a long time." But Jesus himself was remembered as having often prayed for a long time, so it was probably not time as such that he had in mind but rather "many words."

6. As discussed in chapter 1, the image of being closer to God can be linked with the idea of living more with God, which will be discussed again in the next section.

7. Stott ([1998]1992) refers in this context to the terminology of "the medieval Roman Catholic church." It is worth noting, therefore, that whereas the recent *Catechism of the Catholic Church* (1994:487) retains the concept of merit, it subordinates it to the concept of grace and also quotes from the Council of Trent: "Our merits are God's gifts." *The Catechism* comments: "The saints have always had a lively awareness that their merits were pure grace," and, quoting St. Thérèse of Lisieux, "After earth's exile, I hope to go and enjoy you in the fatherland, but I do not want to lay up merits for heaven. I want to work for your *love alone*. . . ." In this perspective, working (for God and for other people) is important, but it is dependent on God's grace and its value is dependent on love.

8. To quote Lesslie Newbigin's *The Gospel in a Pluralist Society*:

> The culture in which this type of thinking has developed is one in which the most typical feature is the supermarket. In a society which has exalted the autonomous individual as the supreme reality, we are accustomed to the rich variety offered on the supermarket shelves and to the freedom we have to choose our favorite brands. It is very natural that this mentality should pervade our view of religion. One may stick to one's favorite brand and acclaim its merits in songs of praise; but to insist that everyone else should choose the same brand is unacceptable. . . . The true statement that none of us can grasp the whole truth is made an excuse for disqualifying any claim to have a valid clue for at least the beginnings of understanding. There is an appearance of humility in the protestation that the

truth is much greater than any one of us can grasp, but if this is used to invalidate all claims to discern the truth it is in fact an arrogant claim to a kind of knowledge which is superior to the knowledge which is available to fallible human beings. (1989:168)

9. The well-known literary scholar Tsvetan Todorov (1998:266) has recently commented, "What can we do with evil in the past, how can we put it to use in the service of our moral education? Nazi crimes are the sort that render it impossible to confuse values: that evil really did exist and is in no way relative. For that reason alone, we must preserve a living memory of it." Although he says that he "was not raised as a believing Christian," Todorov goes on to denounce—as did Jesus—the common tendency to divide *people* (rather than *acts*) into good and bad: "The second step in this education would then consist of rejecting the tendency to identify evil pure and simple with the Other, and good with ourselves, and recognizing . . . that inhumanity is part of being human."

10. As noted by Finnis (1980:32), according to Aquinas (1964:I-II, 94),"some propositions are self-evident to 'everyone', since everyone understands their terms; other propositions are self-evident only to 'the wise', since only the relatively wise (or learned) understand what they mean." The NSM (Natural Semantic Metalanguage) theory of language and thought, on which this discussion is based, is consistent with St. Thomas' tenet that only those propositions of which it can be said that "everyone understands their terms" can be regarded as "self-evident to everyone." The set of empirically established universal human concepts developed in the NSM framework provides a tool for stating any such self-evident propositions whose terms everyone understands.

11. Modern readers of the Gospels often find the violence of the language used in this and other similar outbursts shocking. For example, Luz (1985:165) speaks of "the truly oppressive and unjust speech of the Pharisees in Matthew 23." This perception, however, may be due largely to a cross-cultural misunderstanding. For discussion, see chapter 26.

12. Obedience can, of course, be combined with eagerness and zeal: the obedient person may sincerely *want* to do whatever one's superior requires. Nonetheless, the assumption "if this person wants me to do something I have to do it" still applies. It does not apply, however, to the relationship envisaged by Jesus.

13. As discussed in chapter 4, section 15, responsiveness to God's will is not the same thing as obedience, and yet many modern theologians seem to equate the two. References to obedience are indeed so widespread in modern Christian theology that, as mentioned in chapter 1 and in chapter 4, section 15, they sometimes find their way into translations of the Bible. For example, one modern German translation (*Die Bibel: Die Gute Nachricht in heutigem Deutsch* 1982:515) translates the Psalmist's request for a "pure heart" (in the NKJV, "Create in me a clean heart, O God"; in the Vulgate, "Cor mundum crea in me Deus") as "[Gott], Gib mir ein gehorsames Herz" 'give me [O God] an obedient heart'.

14. Elisha ben Avuyah's parables read as follows:

Elisha ben Avuyah says: One in whom there are good works, who has studied much Torah, to what may he be likened? To a person who builds first with stones and afterwards with brick; even when much water comes and collects by their side, it does not dislodge them. But one in whom there are no good works, though he studied Torah, to what may he be likened? To a person who builds first with bricks and afterwards with stones: even when a little water gathers, it overthrows them immediately.

He used to say: One in whom there are good works, who has studied much Torah, to what may he be likened? To lime poured over stones: even when any number of rains fall on it, it cannot push it out of place. One in whom there are no good works, though he studied much Torah, is like lime poured over bricks: even when a little rain falls on it, it softens immediately and is washed away. (Goldin 1974:103)

Young (1989:255) explains the context of the rabbinic parables that used the imagery of two builders, pointing out that they were related to "what was probably one of the greatest controversies in Judaism of late antiquity. It revolved around the question: What is more important, the study of Torah or its observance in the form of good deeds?" Young comments that "it is difficult for the modern mind to grasp the controversial nature of this question within the framework of ancient Judaism. Nevertheless the sources indicate that this issue was discussed and debated extensively." As Young notes, opinion was divided and, for example, in the Jerusalem Talmud, it is accepted that study should take precedence over practice. Some argued that study is more important because it leads to action. Young comments, "Elisha ben Avuyah's parables in Avot Derabbi Nathan illustrate the importance of having good deeds as well as study. The parables seem to suggest that good deeds are more important than study or at least that they must accompany study. A danger was present that some sages might emphasize study to the neglect of practice" (p. 256).

Clearly, knowing much about God and studying the Torah was of immense importance in ancient Judaism (see, e.g., Feldman [1927]1975:260), and whereas it was held that "the scholar's deeds should exceed his wisdom" (p. 259), the pursuit of knowledge was also regarded as supremely important and supremely valuable in God's eyes. Marmorstein ([1920]1968:50) quotes Rabbi Meir as saying, "He who studies the Law acquires many merits, it makes him worthy in such a degree, as if the whole world were created for his sake." Although the importance of "doing" was always stressed, "some Rabbis thought that study was greater than doing" (Montefiore [1930]1970:157) and that "as the punishment for not studying is greater than for not doing so too the reward for study is greater than the reward for doing" (Sifre 79b). Montefiore emphasizes "the distinctly intellectual element in the Rabbinic religion" and observes, "The ideal is study, learning for its own sake, and there *is* a sense in which the study of the Law transcends its practice." Such a strongly intellectual element is absent from Jesus' teaching; and it is interesting to note Flusser's (1981:103) observation that "Jesus speaks of 'hearing' and 'doing', whereas oddly enough the verb 'to study' (*lernen*) in its characteristic Rabbinic-pedagogical sense does not occur in the Gospels at all."

15. The metaphor of building on the rock has of course a second use in the Gospels, in the famous words addressed by Jesus to Simon (in Matt. 16:18): "I . . . say to you that you are Peter, and on this rock I will build my church, and the gates of Hades shall not prevail against it." The question of whether or not these words originated with Jesus is disputed. Funk et al. (1993:207) seem to have no doubt that it is "a construction of Matthew": "The play on Peter's name (*petra* in Greek means 'rock') makes him the foundation on which the congregation is built: this undoubtedly reflects Peter's position in Matthew's branch of the emerging Christian movement. . . . All of this is Christian language and reflects conditions of the budding institution." It is interesting to note, however, that what Funk et al. call "Christian language" has in fact a close parallel in rabbinic literature (Lachs 1987:256; Schechter [1909]1961:59):

The matter is to be compared to a king who was desiring to build; but when he was digging for the purpose of laying the foundations, he found only swamp and mire. At last he hit on a rock, when he said: "Here will I build." So, too, when God was about to create the world, he foresaw the sinful generation of Enoch . . . and the wicked generations of the deluge . . . and he said, "How shall I create the world whilst these generations are certain to provoke me (by their crimes and sins)?" But when he perceived that Abraham would one day arise, he said 'Behold, I have found the *petra* on which to build and base the world." Therefore he called Abraham Rock, as it is said, look to the rock from which you were hewn . . . (Isa. 51.1–2). (Schechter [1909]1961:51)

All commentators agree that Jesus' words addressed to Simon Peter in Matthew 16:18 point to an Aramaic original (see, e.g., Albright and Mann 1971:195; Meier 1980:181; Montefiore [1927]1968:234). In particular, Meier highlights the fact that "up to this time in ancient Palestine, Peter (*Petros* in Greek, *Kepha* in Aramaic) had not been used as anyone's personal name. . . . Jesus is not changing one first name to another; he is conferring on Simon a new title, 'the Rock.'" Meier suggests that in conferring this title on Simon, Jesus was referring to the passage in Isaiah (51:1–2) where Abraham is called "the rock" (from which the people of Israel were hewn) and that "similarly, Peter will be the human patriarch and foundation-stone of the new people of God."

Another interesting ramification of the rock motif is the polemical exchange between John the Baptist and the Pharisees (Matt. 3:7–10), in which John warns the Pharisees and the Sadducees "not to rely on the principle of *zekhut avot*, 'the merit of the fathers,'" that is, not to assume that they will escape punishment "by virtue of the fact that they are the descendants of the patriarch Abraham" (Lachs 1987:42). When John says, "God is able from these stones to raise children to Abraham," he seems to be invoking Isaiah's reference to Abraham as the rock from which the people of Israel will be hewn and to be contrasting this image of the rock (Abraham) with that of any "stones" anywhere from which God can raise up true (spiritual) children to Abraham.

CHAPTER 5

1. For a tentative exploration of these two petitions see Wierzbicka (1999b).

2. Jeremias's (1966a:161) translation of Luke's version of the Lord's Prayer into German starts with the words *Lieber Vater* ('Dear Father'). As far as I am aware, he never suggested that the invocation should be rendered as *Vati* or *Pappi* ('Daddy').

3. The component "when I think about you I feel something," postulated here as part of the meaning of the vocative *Abba*, does not refer to some "feel-good" experience that many contemporary writers associate with religious and spiritual life. Rather, it articulates the good feeling toward another person that is included in concepts like affection, devotion, and love. (For a detailed discussion of the semantics of emotion concepts, see Wierzbicka 1999a.)

4. Moltmann (1981:163), who emphasizes the difference between Jesus' *Abba* and "the universal patriarch of father religions," writes, "Knowledge of the Father and free access to him are the characteristics which place the freedom of God's children above the freedom of his servants. Children belong to the family. They cannot be dismissed as servants. They are one with the father" (p. 219). If children are "one with the father" and "cannot be dismissed," there cannot be any eternal and irrevocable hell for any of them—an implication of Jesus' teaching that Moltmann (1996) explored most fully in his book *The Coming of God*.

5. The implications of the metaphor of *father* are in fact different from those of *mother*, as they are different from the implications of *King*, *Shepherd*, or *Rock*. By saying that a particular metaphor is not integral to the meaning of the Gospels I mean that it can be

explicated in non-metaphorical language, not that it can be replaced with another metaphor without a change of meaning.

6. Component (h) underscores God's love for *all* people; (i) and (j), God's closeness to *all* people. In the Psalms, too, God is thought of as somene who knows and hears the person praying to him. At the same time, however, in many Psalms he is still a "tribal God"—a "king" who wants to do good things for his own people at the expense of others:

> We have heard with our ears, O God,
> Our fathers have told us
> What deeds you did in their days,
> In days of old:
> How you drove out the nations with your hand,
> But them you planted,
> How you afflicted the people and cast them out . . .
> Because you favored them. (Ps. 44:1-3)

Such ideas are conspicuously absent from the New Testament. In Jesus' teaching, God is both near to the individual and loving to the whole of humankind (see John 3:16). The new covenant (Mark 14:24), in contrast to the old one, embraces all people.

7. The literature on the kingdom of God is enormous and cannot of course be surveyed here. Recent book-length discussions include Carmignac (1979), Chilton (1984), Moltmann (1981), Perrin (1966), Schlosser (1980), and Willis (1987). For a comprehensive discussion, see also Meier (1994:III), E. P. Sanders (1993), and N. T. Wright (1996); for a survey of recent discussions, see Chilton (1994).

8. The explication proposed here is compatible with two ways of interpreting Jesus' references to the future dimension of the kingdom. First, there is an eschatological vision of a time (the end time) when all people will live with God; second, there are sayings that can be interpreted as references to Jesus' own forthcoming death as an event that will be the culmination of all that is happening here now and because of which all people will be able to live with God. Many scholars affirm that Jesus "claimed that God was about to do something momentous through the Son of Man, something that would change the world forever" (Powell 1998:174). Couldn't this "imminent direct intervention of God in history" (E. P. Sanders 1985:153) refer to Jesus' own death on the cross?

If we linked Jesus' future-oriented kingdom sayings with his own forthcoming death, as well as with the end time, we could still accept, with N. T. Wright 1999(a) and others, that Jesus was also "predicting what was to come upon his generation in the near future," that is, that "he predicted that Jerusalem and the temple would be destroyed but that his followers would escape the conflagration, and that these events would be signs that vindicated his (and their) message about the reign of god . . . events [which] did occur, pretty much as Jesus said they would" (Powell 1998:158).

9. Similarly, Berdyaev ([1937]1954) writes, "The morality of personal salvation leads to a distortion of the idea of paradise and of the Divine Kingdom . . . Crucifixion, pain and tragedy will go on in the world until all mankind and the whole world are saved, transfigured and regenerated. (p. 294). "The 'good' must take upon themselves the fate of the 'wicked', share their destiny and thus further their liberation" (p. 282). "Moral consciousness began with God's question, 'Cain, where is thy brother Abel?' It will end with another question on the part of God: 'Abel, where is thy brother Cain?'" (p. 276).

10. The correspondence between God's act of creation (implied by the image of father) and his sustaining of life was noted by Gregory of Nyssa (1954:67) in his com-

mentary on the Lord's Prayer: "My life I have from Thee—from Thee let me also have the needs of life."

11. "That we should imagine that anger, wrath, jealousy or the such like have anything to do with the divine Nature is something utterly abhorrent to us. . . . Nor again can we possibly say that He acts thus out of retribution, even though the Scriptures may on the outer surface posit this. Even to think this of God and to suppose that retribution for evil acts is to be found in Him is abominable" (St. Isaac of Niniveh 1995:162).

CHAPTER 6

1. The sources of Hedrick's references are as follows: Cadoux (1931:155); Carlston (1975:146); Crossan (1992:50-51); Dodd (1965:134); Jeremias (1972:150-151); Jones (1964:101-102); Lane (1974:163); Linnemann (1966:117); Mann (1986:261); Michaels (1981:90); Perkins (1981:80-81); Scott (1989:36-362); B. T. D. Smith (1937:126); V. Taylor (1959:251); Wilder (1982:98-99).

2. Raymond Brown (1968:329, 333) also argues that behind the Gospel explanation as it now exists there may lie "an original and recognizable allegorical explanation of the parable by Jesus Himself. . . . Such a rooting of the explanation of the parable in Jesus' ministry and words is, we believe, far more plausible than the theory of spontaneous introduction of allegory by the Church."

3. An interpretation of the kingdom of God along the lines of "people living with God (now)" and "all people living with God (in the future)" is of course different from Jeremias' "impending crisis" ("God's hour is coming"), but as noted by several commentators, the idea of an impending crisis has no support in the images of the parable of the Sower. Since in Jesus' teaching the kingdom of God is presented as, in a sense, already present (though, in another sense, still to come), the idea that people can live with God now is consistent with his teaching about the kingdom, as is also the idea that all people can live with God and that God wants it. It is also an idea that allows us to combine an ethical and an eschatological perspective in our interpretation of the parables, including the sower.

4. For a critique of Crossan's essay on the sower, see Moore (1989).

CHAPTER 8

1. According to some (e.g., the Russian Orthodox theologian Sergius Bulgakov 1976:135) Origen's doctrine was condemned because it was enmeshed in his theory of the preexistence of souls. Bulgakov emphasizes that, Gregory of Nyssa's teaching on universal salvation has never been condemned and that St. Gregory has continued to be honoured as a "Doctor of the Church." Pope John Paul II (1994:185) has recently mentioned the fact that "the ancient councils rejected the theory of the 'final apokatastasis' . . . a theory which indirectly abolished hell": "But the problem remains. Can God, who has loved people so much, permit the people who reject Him to be condemned to eternal torment?"

2. According to John Robinson (1950:122), "We are asked to believe that perpetually throughout eternity we must envisage the most terrible defeat of the love of God— the prospect, as it were, of the horror of a concentration camp in the midst of a blissful countryside."

3. In another chapter (37) Gregory of Nyssa (1917:108) applies the image of leaven, more specifically, to the body of Christ: "For as a little leaven, according to the saying of the Apostle, assimilates to itself the whole lump, so the Body, which was raised by

God to immortality, by passing into our body transmutes and translates it to itself"
(p. 108). But in Chapter 26, Gregory directly links "the great mystery of Divine Incarnation" with the hope of universal salvation. It is also interesting to note that whereas
Paul follows the Jewish tradition by using the metaphor of leaven in a negative sense,
as a symbol of corruption, Gregory follows Jesus in using it in a positive sense, as a
symbol of what he calls "incorruption" (p. 112).

CHAPTER 10

1. It is striking that some contemporary commentators seem to overlook the second
part of the parable altogether and to adopt the older son's initial, unreconstructed point
of view. For example, Funk (1996:186–187) rejects with disdain the traditional and, one
would have thought, incontrovertible interpretation in terms of God's boundless love
and forgiveness as "the standard, sentimental interpretation." In contrast, Funk expresses
extremely strong disapproval of the father in the story: "The doting father is permissive
and excessive in his relations to the spoiled brat of the family. . . . He certainly has not
given the proper son [sic] the recognition due him." Funk also claims that such an alternative perspective on the father figure was deliberately built into the parable from the
outset (the parable was meant, according to Funk, to be "ambiguous and polyvalent").
He accuses the earlier interpreters of burying this central ambiguity "under an avalanche
of familiar meaning": "From the perspective of the older son, the old man has been
beset by senility or something worse. But crystallized familiarity—the standard, sentimental
interpretation—has fixed prodigal love as the property of the father, who stands for God
the Father, so that the actual details of the story are not allowed to interfere with that
sense. . . . In this traditional reading the father is no longer prodigal and senile . . ."
(pp. 187–188). For a similarly inventive interpretation of the parable—iconoclastic at all
costs—see Breech [1983]1987).

CHAPTER 11

1. Funk et al. (1993:217) confidently dismiss the authenticity of both verses 21 and
22: "Nothing in this relatively long complex can be attributed to Jesus. The Q [*Quelle*]
community's rules of order are being reported and modified by Matthew." Yet in another book co-authored by Funk (Funk et al. 1988:49), it is acknowledged that "verse
22 may go back to Jesus." Whether the hyperbolically phrased commandment of boundless forgiveness in verse 22 goes back to Jesus or was formulated by Matthew, the radical and startlingly original teaching behind it must be seen as Jesus' own. At the same
time, the fact that this hyperbolically phrased saying is included in Matthew's Gospel
casts doubt on Funk et al.'s assertion that "for Matthew, the moral of the story is: God
will not forgive you if you don't forgive your fellow human beings." Undoubtedly,
Matthew used the traditional Jewish *Drohrede* (language of rhetorical threats) more than
any other New Testament writer, but it would be anachronistic to assume that Matthew
took his own *Drohrede* literally. The fact that he either recorded or even formulated the
ideal of boundless mercy (v. 22) suggests that Matthew himself believed in such an ideal;
and the fact that he also preserved for us Jesus' saying "You shall be perfect, just as
your Father in Heaven is perfect" (5:48) suggests that he saw human goodness and mercy
as a reflection of God's goodness and mercy. Given these two facts, his own verse 35
could only be an instance of the *Drohrede*, which was part of the cultural tradition to
which he belonged. (For further discussion, see chapter 26.)

2. The author of the commentary on Matthew's Gospel in the *Expositor's Bible Commentary* (1984:402) does not hesitate to offer the following comment on the unforgiving servant: "Jesus sees no incongruity in the actions of a heavenly Father who forgives so bountifully and punishes so ruthlessly, and neither should we." This is the kind of unfortunate conclusion that an allegorizing reading of parables can lead to. There can be no better response to such a conclusion than Isaac of Niniveh's reflection on human, and divine, mercy.

CHAPTER 13

1. In quoting the published English translation of Jeremias' comment I have replaced the words "humiliation," "self-abasement," and "self-righteousness," which I find inappropriate and inaccurate, with "humility," "poverty before God," and "conviction of one's righteousness." The words used in the German original (Jeremias [1965]1988:128) are *die Beugung, das Armwerden,* and *Selbstgerechtigkeit,* and the word *Verzicht* 'renunciation' is accompanied by the adjective *demütig* 'humble'.

CHAPTER 14

1. Many scholars believe, nonetheless, that Luke's words about inviting the maimed, the lame, and the blind do go back to the historical Jesus, and they see in them a conscious rejection of the earlier tradition, grounded in Leviticus (21:17–21), which excluded such people from the priesthood: "Speak to Aaron, saying: 'No man of your descendants in succeeding generations, who has any defect, may approach to offer the bread of his God. For any man who has a defect shall not approach: a man blind or lame, who has a marred face or any limb too long, a man who has a broken foot or broken hand.'" Dunn points to the continuation of this tradition among the Qumran Essenes, observing that Jesus' words in Luke 14.13 and 21 seem to echo the Qumran regulations: "No man smitten with any human uncleanliness shall enter the assembly of God. . . . No man smitten in his flesh, or paralysed in his feet or hands or lame or blind or deaf or dumb or smitten in his flesh with a visible blemish. . . .":

> The parallel is both positive and antithetical. Positive, because both Jesus and Qumran evidently regarded their table-fellowship as of eschatological significance. . . . But much more striking is the echo of the list of those excluded fom the Qumran table-fellowship—the maimed or crippled, the lame, the blind. *The very ones whom Qumran went out of its way to exclude from its table-fellowship and so from the eschatological banquet, are the very ones Jesus says firmly are to be included.* Those to whom he speaks and of whom he speaks in Luke 14 are urged to make particular point of including in their table-fellowship just those whom Qumran excluded. . . . Almost certainly . . . Jesus said what he is remembered as saying in Luke 14.13 and 21 precisely as a protest against and challenge to the Qumran practice of table-fellowship and [as a] vision of the messianic banquet. (Dunn 1991:112–113)

2. In his book *Crossing the Threshold of Hope*, Pope John Paul II (1994:185) quotes these words of Paul's and comments on them as follows: "This phrase from the letter to Timothy is of fundamental importance for understanding and preaching the Last Things. If God desires this . . . can people be damned, can they be rejected by God? . . . Can God, who has loved people so much, permit the people who reject him to be con-

demned to eternal torment?" (I am replacing here the word "man," used by the English translators, by the word "people.")

3. "The suffering of God with the world, the suffering of God from the world, and the suffering of God for the world are the highest forms of his creative love, which desires free fellowship with the world and free response in the world" (Moltmann 1981:60).

CHAPTER 15

1. Few aspects of the New Testament are more striking than the absence of the point of view reflected, for example, in the following passage (Ps. 44:4–9):

> You are my King, O God;
> Command victories for Jacob.
> Through you we will push down our enemies
> Through your name we will trample those who rise up against us.

In my view, the shift from the image of God that is reflected in this passage to that reflected in Matthew 25:31–46 cannot be due to Matthew; it can only be due to Jesus.

2. The foundress of the Focolari movement, Chiara Lubich, starts her book *To Write the Gospel with One's Life* with the same "glorious verse 40," saying that it "gives a synthesis of the whole message of the Gospel" (Lubich 1995:1).

3. As I wrote in my 1992 book, "when the Russian religious philosoper Vladimir Solov'ev ([1883]1966:v. 7,57) calls *žalost'* 'the root of an ethical attitude towards other human beings and towards living creatures in general', he doesn't mean *pity*. He means something that constitutes, roughly speaking, a kind of cross between *pity* and *love*." Thus, the readers of the English translation of Berdyaev's ([1937]1954:107) *Destiny of Man* may be baffled by the assertion that "pity is one of the loftiest human feelings, a true miracle in the moral life of man" and by the accompanying comment that "the burning, poignant sense of desolation and the readiness to share it embraces the whole of the animal world and all created things." In fact, Berdyaev is, of course, not talking about *pity* but about *žalost'*, which has no exact equivalent in English.

4. The universalism of the parable of the Last Judgment is sometimes disputed in the name of a "missionary" interpretation, according to which the word "brethren" was originally meant to apply to Christian missionaries (see, e.g., Cope 1969; quoted in Donahue 1990:111). To my mind, this interpretation carries little conviction for Matthew and none whatever for Jesus.

5. *The Expositor's Bible Commentary* (1984:8, 519) acknowledges that "the great majority of scholars understand 'the least of these brothers of mine' (vv. 40, 45) to refer to all who are hungry, distressed, needy" and then makes the following astonishing comment: "The weakness of this general position is the identification of the least of Jesus' brothers with *the poor and needy without distinction*" (my emphasis). To remedy this "weakness," the commentary comes up with"two excellent alternatives," both replacing Jesus' universalism with sectarian particularism.

6. In *Crossing the Threshold of Hope*, Pope John Paul II (1994:187), whose published statements about the prospect of universal salvation are, on the whole, very cautious, has commented on the theme of the Last Judgment as follows: "*Before all else, it is Love that judges* [author's original emphasis]. God, who is Love, judges through love. It is Love that demands purification, before people can be made ready for that union with God which is their ultimate vocation and destiny. Perhaps this is enough."

7. The *Expositor's Bible Commentary* (1984:523) notes the possible devastating consequences of the interpretation of the Last Judgment in terms of an everlasting heaven for some and an everlasting hell for others, but it decides to disregard them and to adhere to that interpretation nonetheless: "Some have argued that this doctrine has turned many people into infidels; but so have other Christian doctrines. The question is not how men respond to a doctrine but what Jesus and the NT writers actually teach about it." What these comments fail to take into account is that Jesus' *teaching* cannot simply be identified with Jesus' *images*. To find out what Jesus meant by his images we must take note of his cultural background, including the rhetoric of the *Drohrede*, and we must be guided by the methodological principle of coherence: the Jesus who spoke about the sheep and the goats was the same Jesus who told the parable of the lost sheep.

CHAPTER 17

1. By the traditional approach to the parable's interpretation I mean the prevailing modern approach. Fitzmyer (1985b:885) notes that "over the centuries the history of its exegesis has witnessed many modes of exposition, most of them allegorical and extrinsic. From Marcion and Irenaeus, through the Middle Ages and the Reformation period, until the nineteenth century, it has often been given a christological explanation (Christ is the Good Samaritan). . . ."

2. For further discussion of this verb and its special role in the New Testament, see Barclay (1958:156-160).

3. According to St. Isaac of Niniveh (1984:31), "the merciful man [is] not he that simply shows mercy to his brother by giving him something. . . . Whoever burns within his heart when he sees or hears of something that grieves his brother, such a one is truly merciful."

CHAPTER 18

1. De Caussade (1959:5) distinguishes two kinds of "fidelity to God's plan": active and passive. The active kind consists in the fulfillment of one's duties, as they present themselves at any given moment, and the passive, "in the loving acceptance of all that God sends us at every moment." As far as I can see, however, both kinds can be subsumed under the notion of "doing something." Waiting (including waiting for God) can be construed as doing something, and so can thinking, watching, praying, and "psyching oneself" for what needs to be done or to be endured.

CHAPTER 20

1. Let me close this chapter with a note on the English word *talent*:

[In] its earliest usage in English, in the thirteenth century, 'talent' meant 'inclination', 'disposition', which was the meaning of the Latin *talentum*. . . . In the fourteenth century, 'talent' was adopted (again from Latin *talentum*) as the word to render the sum of money known in Greek as *talanton* (. . .). Wycliff used the word in his Bible translation in 1382 to render the parable of the talents in Matthew 25:14–30 (it is still there in the Authorized Version of 1611), and it is from this usage that the modern meaning 'mental ability', 'intellectual gift' developed in the fifteenth century. (Room 1991:261)

Thus in English, as in many other European languages, the modern concept of talent developed under the influence of the language of the Bible, and concomitantly, the notion that it is bad to "bury one's talents in the ground" became part of European cultural literacy. It is often said, and rightly so, that "Christian concepts, values, and practices . . . pervade European civilization" (Huntington 1996:305). The metaphor of a talent that is given to every individual to develop and to bear fruit can be seen as one of such key concepts, inextricably linked with the Western emphasis on enterprise, initiative, individual freedom of action, and personal responsibility.

The eminent nineteenth-century Russian philosopher Vladimir Solov'ev ([1883]1966:20) states that "from the very beginning of human history there was a clear contrast between two cultures—Eastern and Western. The basis of the Eastern culture lay in the subordination of human beings in everything to a superhuman power, the basis of Western culture—in human independent action." Solov'ev links the Western emphasis on human independence and energy with its historical roots in Greece and Rome; and he suggests that the different development of Christianity in the East and in the West can be explained in part by reference to these differing fundamental orientations of the two traditions. If Solov'ev is right, in the West the parable of the talents found a particularly receptive soil. In Eastern Christianity, other parables and other themes may have had greater appeal and a greater impact.

Chapter 21

1. Breech ([1983]1987:109) calls the traditional approach to the interpretation of the dishonest steward "unacceptable":

> For two thousand years the dominant Christian and scholarly interpretation of this parable has been that its point lies in the example of the steward's decisiveness; he is seen as an example of how the Christian should behave when confronted by "the preaching of the kingdom," in other words the Christian should act in his own best interests, since the kingdom is thought of as a better security than worldly goods. It is no wonder that Nietzsche bridled at this attitude. In his view, the religious person is just as acquisitive and unattractive, basically, as anyone concerned with piling up treasure. The only difference is that moths don't eat and rust does not destroy what he wants. But the same personality configuration is evident in the steward and in this type of Christian.

In fact, however, Breech misrepresents the traditional approach, whose main point was to draw a line between the steward's shady character and actions and his decisive and positive thinking in a situation of crisis. Nietzsche's critique of an acquisitive attitude to spiritual treasure is simply irrelevant to the parable's message, as traditionally interpreted.

Chapter 23

1. According to Flusser (1991:165), in Jesus' time "the division of human beings into just and sinners"—so important in the Old Testament—was beginning to be questioned. "The strict morality of the old Covenant was clearly inadequate for the new sensitivity of the Jews of Jesus' time. Having now recognized that human beings are not sharply divisible into righteous and sinners, it was practically impossible for one to love the good and hate the wicked."

CHAPTER 26

1. In addition to the traditions of Jewish rabbinical discourse and prophetic speech, there are also huge differences between ancient and modern polemical conventions in general. (For an informative discussion, see especially Johnson 1989.) Dunn emphasizes in ancient polemical discourse "a robustness . . . which Enlightenment liberalism finds profoundly disturbing", and he applies this in particular to the language of the New Testament:

> In the more sensitive, sophisticated and mild-mannered present, not only an Inquisition's treatment of "heretics," or a Calvin's burning of Servetus disturbs and offends. But also the bluntness of a prophet's denunciation of unfaithfulness, or Jesus' rebuke of Peter as "'Satan,'" or Paul's similar denunciation of other "apostles of Christ." We should beware of reading such language with pedantic literalism—not least because we hear only one side of the several disputes. We should certainly be slow to let our own sensitivities dictate a verdict of anti-Judaism or anti-semitism on those whose world of discourse was so very different from our own. (1991:161)

2. Speaking of Jesus' saying that "it is easier for a camel to pass through the eye of a needle than for a rich man to enter the Kingdom of God" (Mark 10:25), Caird (1980:133) states that "in this last instance plodding literalists have suggested that the needle's eye was the name for a low gate, like the door into the church of the Nativity at Bethlehem, or that a camel was a kind of rope. But the Semitic bravura of Jesus' speech resists all such pathetic attempts to tame it."

3. The meaning of the Greek *aiōnios* (from *aiōn* 'age') and the underlying Hebrew word *olam* is debated by biblical scholars (see, e.g., Hryniewicz 1990:103). Some argue that both the Greek and the Hebrew words could refer to long duration, as well as eternity. But whatever the literal meaning of these words, there is also the question of the hyperbole—and the *Drohrede*. If we don't take this into account, we are likely to misunderstand Jesus' teaching and to miss its internal coherence.

4. The appeal "Turn to me and be saved" is not restricted to Israel but is addressed to the whole of humankind: "Turn to me and be saved, all the ends of the earth" (Isa. 45:22). And the solemn promise of final reconciliation also embraces all people:

> By myself I have sworn
> from my mouth has gone forth in righteousness
> a word that shall not return:
> 'To me every knee shall bow,
> every tongue shall swear.' (Isa. 45:23)

5. One book—Sproul's *Essential Truths of the Christian Faith*—assures the reader that hell is not only eternal but also consists actually in the *presence* rather than in the *absence* of God:

1. The suffering of hell is beyond any experience of misery found in this world.
2. Hell is clearly included in the teaching of Jesus.
3. If the biblical descriptions of hell are symbols, then the reality will be worse than the symbols.

4. Hell is the *presence* of God in His wrath and judgment.
5. There is no cruelty in hell. Hell will be a place of perfect justice.
6. Hell is eternal. There is no escape through either repentance or
   annihilation. (1992:287)

The tone of grim satisfaction in all this seems unmistakable. The effect of the terrible picture is relieved only by the touch of unintended humour in point 5: "There is no cruelty in hell. Hell will be a place of perfect justice." It is interesting to compare Sproul's words with St. Paul's statement that "where sin abounded, grace abounded much more" (Rom. 5:20) and also with Jesus' words in Luke 19:10: "The Son of Man has come to save that which was lost."

6. The use of universal human concepts can also allow us to better understand the paradoxes and apparent contradictions in Jesus' teaching that arise from his extensive use of heteroglossia. As the hundreds of explicit and implicit quotes from Isaiah illustrate, Jesus' language is inherently dialogical. His use of words like *reward, righteousness, righteous*, and *justified* is also dialogical. If the implicit quotation marks that accompany such words in Jesus' speech are not recognized, some aspects of his teaching are bound to be baffling and to seem internally inconsistent. (For discussion, see chapter 3, section 9; chapter 4, sections 2, 3, and 14.)

7. Delumeau (1989) calls the rejection of the concept of everlasting hell for part of humankind (Augustine's *massa damnata*) the "rehabilitation of God." Quite apart from the doctrine's implications for the image of God, however, its acceptance is incompatible with any sense of human solidarity: it is bound to breed either hatred or indifference for fellow humans (or both). The question is, therefore, far from academic. Those who—impatient with both heaven and hell—dismiss eschatology as irrelevant to life on earth should note that the goal of building the kingdom of God on earth, for the whole of humanity, is incompatible with an attitude that accepts radical divisions among people (the righteous and the wicked; the saved and the damned; the *Übermenschen* and the *Untermenschen*; the people and the enemies of the people; those who deserve to live and those who need to be killed). Human ideas about God are closely related to human attitudes to other people; religion has implications for politics; and ethics is, ultimately, based on eschatology.

References

Abrahams, Israel. 1925. Adultery (Jewish). In James Hastings, ed. *Encyclopedia of Religion and Ethics*, 1:130-131. Edinburgh: T & T. Clark

Abrahams, Israel. [1917]1967. *Studies in Pharisaism and the Gospels*. New York: KTAV Publishing House.

Achtemeier, Elizabeth. 1993. Women. In Bruce Metzger and Michael Coogan, eds. *The Oxford Companion to the Bible*, pp. 806-807. New York: Oxford University Press.

Albright, W. F., and C. S. Mann. 1971. *The Anchor Bible, Matthew: Introduction, Translation and Notes*. New York: Doubleday.

Anderson, Walter Truett. 1995. Four Different Ways to Be Absolutely Right. In Walter Truett Anderson, ed. *The Truth About the Truth*, pp. 110-116. New York: Putnam.

Arndt, William F. 1956. *The Gospel According to St. Luke*. St. Louis, Mo.: Concordia.

Bailey, Kenneth Ewing. 1976. *Poet and Peasant: A Literary Cultural Approach to the Parables in Luke*. Grand Rapids, Mich.: Eerdmans.

Bailey, Kenneth Ewing. 1980. *Through Peasant Eyes*. Grand Rapids, Mich.: Eerdmans.

Bakhtin, M. M. 1981. Discourse in the Novel. In Michael Holquist, ed. *The Dialogic Imagination: Four essays by M. M. Bakhtin*, pp. 259-422. Austin: University of Texas Press.

Ballantine, William. 1925. *Understanding the Bible*. Springfield, Mass.: Johnson's Bookstore.

Balthasar, Hans Urs von. 1983. *Theodramatik*, Band IV. Einsiedeln: Johannes Verlag.

Balthasar, Hans Urs von. 1986. *Was dürfen wir hoffen*. Einsiedeln: Johannes Verlag.

Banks, R. J. 1975. *Jesus and the Law in the Synoptic Tradition*. Cambridge: Cambridge University Press.

Barbel, Joseph. 1971. Commentary to St. Gregory of Nyssa [Gregor von Nyssa]. *Die große katechetische Rede*, pp. 95-212. Stuttgart: Anton Hiersemann.

Barclay, William. 1958. *More New Testament Words*. London: SCM Press.

Barclay, William. [1967]1990. *The Plain Man Looks at the Apostle's Creed*. Glasgow: Collins.

Barclay, William. [1975]1993. *The Gospel of Matthew*, vol. 1. Edinburgh: Saint Andrew Press.

Barclay, William. 1994. *The Gospel of Luke*. Edinburgh: Saint Andrew Press.

Barr, James. 1988a. 'Abba, Father' and the Familiarity of Jesus' Speech. *Theology*, 91:173–179.

Barr, James. 1988b. 'Abba Isn't 'Daddy'. *The Journal of Theological Studies*. New Series 39:28–47.

Bauman, Clarence. 1985. *The Sermon on the Mount: The Modern Quest for Its Meaning*. Macon, Ga.: Mercer University Press.

Bella, Emil. 1926. *Die Droh- und Schelworte Amos*. Leipzig: Alexander Edelmann.

Berdyaev, Nicolas. [1937]1954. *The Destiny of Man*. London: Geoffrey Bles.

Bettiolo, P. 1990. Avec la charité comme but; Dieu et la création dans la meditation de l'Isaac de Ninive. *Irenikon*, 63:323–345.

Betz, H. D. 1995. *The Sermon on the Mount: A Commentary on the Sermon on the Mount, Including the Sermon on the Plain (Matthew 5:3–7:27 and Luke 6:20–49)*. Minneapolis: Fortress Press.

Die Bibel: Die Gute Nachricht in heutigem Deutsch. 1982. Stuttgart: Deutsche Bibelgesellschaft.

Bischoff, E. 1905. *Jesus und die Rabbinen*. Leipzig: Himichs.

Blomberg, Craig. 1990. *Interpreting the Parables*. England: Apollos.

Blount, B. K. 1995. *Cultural Interpretation: Reorienting New Testament Criticism*. Minneapolis: Augsburg/Fortress Press.

Bockmuehl, M. 1994. *The Jesus: Martyr, Lord, Messiah*. Edinburgh: Clark.

Bond, Michael Harris. 1992, June 10–14. Finding the Middle Way: The Role of Emotions in Chinese Life. Paper presented at the International Conference on Emotion and Culture, University of Oregon, Eugene.

Bonhoeffer, Adolf. 1911. *Epiktet und das Neue Testament*. Giessen: Töpelmann.

Bonhoeffer, Dietrich. [1937]1959. *The Cost of Discipleship*. Trans. R. H. Fuller. London: SCM Press.

Borg, M. J. 1994. *Meeting Jesus Again for the First Time*. San Francisco: HarperCollins.

Borg, Marcus. 1999. Was Jesus God? In Marcus Borg and N. T. Wright. *The Meaning of Jesus: Two Visions*, pp. 145–170. San Francisco: HarperSanFrancisco.

Bornkam, Gunther. 1966. *Jesus of Nazareth*. Trans. Irene and Fraser McLuskey, with James M. Robinson. London: Hodder & Stoughton.

Borsch, Frederick Houk. 1988. *Many Things in Parables*. Philadelphia: Fortress Press.

Boucher, Madeleine. 1977. *The Mysterious Parable: A Literary Study*. Washington, D.C.: Catholic Biblical Association of America.

Boucher, Madeleine. 1981. *The Parables*. Wilmington, Del.: Michael Glazier.

Braun, Herbert. 1969. *Spätjüdisch-häretischer und frühchristlicher Radikalismus: Jesus von Nazareth und die essenische Qumransekte*, 2 vols. Tübingen: Mohr [Siebeck].

Breech, James. [1983]1987. *The Silence of Jesus*. Philadelphia: Fortress Press.

Broer, Ingo. 1986. *Die Seligpreisungen der Bergpredigt*. Bonn: Peter Hanstein Verlag.

Brother Roger of Taizé. 1991. *Songs and Prayers from Taizé*. (Ateliers de Taizé). Chicago: GIA Publications.

Brown, C. 1979. Poor. In *Dictionary of New Testament Theology (II)*, p. 824. Grand Rapids, Mich.: Zonderman.

Brown, Raymond E. 1966. *The Gospel According to John*, i–xii. Garden City, N.Y.: Doubleday.

Brown, Raymond E. 1968. *New Testament Essays*. Garden City, N.Y.: Doubleday.

Brown, Raymond E. 1975. *Biblical Reflections on Crises Facing the Church*. London: Darton, Longman & Todd.

Brown, Raymond E. 1985. *Biblical Exegesis and Church Doctrine*. New York: Paulist Press.

Brown, Raymond E. 1994. *An Introduction to New Testament Christology*. London: Geoffrey Chapman.

Brown, Raymond E. 1997. *An Introduction to the New Testament*. New York: Doubleday.

Brown, Raymond E., John R. Donahue, Donald Senior, and Adela Yarbro Collins. 1990. Aspects of New Testament Thought. In Brown et al., eds. pp. 1354–1381.

Brown, Raymond E., and Sandra M. Schneiders. 1990. Hermeneutics. In Raymond E. Brown, Joseph A. Fitzmyer, and Roland E. Murphy, eds. *The New Jerome Biblical Commentary*, pp. 1146–1165. Upper Saddle River, N.J.: Prentice-Hall.

Bruce, F. F. [1983]1995. *The Hard Sayings of Jesus*. London: Hodder & Stoughton.

Buber, Martin. 1960. *The Prophetic Faith*. New York: Harper & Row.

Buber, Martin. 1970. *I and Thou*. Trans. Walter Kaufmann. New York: Scribner.

Bulgakov, Sergius. 1976. *A Bulgakov Anthology*. James Pain and Nicolas Zernov, eds. Philadelphia: Winchester Press.

Bull, Norman J. 1969. *Moral Education*. London: Routledge & Kegan Paul.

Bultmann, Rudolf. [1926]1958. *Jesus Christ and Mythology*. New York: Scribner.

Bultmann, Rudolf. 1958. *Jesus and the Word*. Trans. L. P. Smith and E. H. Lantero. London: Collins.

Bultmann, Rudolf. 1963. *The History of the Synoptic Tradition*. Trans. J. Marsh. Oxford: B. Blackwell.

Butwin, Frances. 1958. Translator's introduction to Sholom Aleichem *The Old Country*, pp. 7–11. London: André Deutsch.

Cadoux, A. T. 1930. *The Parables of Jesus; Their Art and Use*. New York: Macmillan.

Caird, G. B. 1980. *The Language and Imagery of the Bible*. London: Duckworth.

Capon, Robert Farrar. 1985. *The Parables of the Kingdom*. Grand Rapids, Mich. Zondervan.

Capon, Robert Farrar. 1989. *The Parables of Judgment*. Grand Rapids, Mich.: Eerdmans.

Carlston, Charles E. 1975. *The Parables of the Triple Tradition*. Philadelphia: Fortress Press.

Carmignac, Jean. 1979. *Le mirage de l'eschatologie: Royauté, règne et royaume Dieu . . . sans eschatologie*. Paris: Letouzey et Ané.

Carson, D. A. 1994. *The Sermon on the Mount*. Carlisle, Eng.: Paternoster Press.

Casey, Maurice. 1991. *From Jewish Prophet to Gentile God: The Origins and Developments of New Testament Christology*. Louisville, Ky.: Westminster/John Knox.

Catechism of the Catholic Church. 1994. Homebush, NSW: St Paul's Publications.

Charlesworth, James H. 1991. *Jesus' Jewishness: Exploring the Place of Jesus Within Early Judaism*. New York: Crossroad.

Charlesworth, James H. 1994. A Caveat on Textual Transmission and the Meaning of Abba: A Study of the Lord's Prayer. In James. H. Charlesworth, Mark Harding, and Mark Kiley, eds. *The Lord's Prayer and Other Prayer Texts from the Greco-Roman Era*, pp. 1–14. Valley Forge, Pa.: Trinity Press International.

Charlesworth, James H., Mark Harding, and Mark Kiley, eds. 1994. *The Lord's Prayer and Other Prayer Texts from the Greco-Roman Era*. Valley Forge, Pa.: Trinity Press International.

Chesterton, G. K. 1909. *Orthodoxy.* London: Bodley Head.

Chilton, Bruce. 1984. *The Kingdom of God in the Teaching of Jesus.* Philadelphia: Fortress Press.

Chilton, Bruce. 1994. The Kingdom of God in Recent Discussions. In Bruce Chilton and Craig Evans, eds. *Studying the Historical Jesus,* pp. 259–280. Leiden: Brill.

Chilton, Bruce, and Jacob Neusner. 1995. *Judaism in the New Testament.* London: Routledge.

Clement of Alexandria. 1962. *Stromata.* In Alexander Roberts and James Donaldson, eds. *The Ante-Nicene Fathers: The Writings of the Fathers Down to* A.D. *325,* vol. II. Grand Rapids, Mich.: Eerdmans.

Compton, J. E. 1930–1931. The Prodigal's Brother. *Expository Times,* 42:287.

Cope, Lamar. 1969. Matthew XXV:31–46: The Sheep and Goats Reinterpreted. *Novum Testamentum,* II:32–44.

Crosby, Michael. 1995. *Spirituality of the Beatitudes.* Maryknoll, N.Y.: Orbis Books.

Crossan, John Dominic. 1974. Parable and Example in the Teaching of Jesus. *Semeia,* 1: 63–104.

Crossan, John Dominic. 1979. *Finding Is the First Act: Trove Folktales and Jesus' Treasure Parables.* Philadelphia: Fortress Press.

Crossan, John Dominic. 1980. *Cliffs of Fall: Paradox and Polyvalence in the Parables of Jesus.* New York: Seabury.

Crossan, John Dominic. 1991. *The Historical Jesus: The Life of a Mediterranean Jewish Peasant.* San Francisco: HarperCollins.

Crossan, John Dominic. 1992. *In Parables: The Challenge of the Historical Jesus.* Sonoma, Calif.: Polebridge.

Crossan, John Dominic. 1994. *The Essential Jesus: What Jesus Really Taught.* New York: HarperSanFrancisco.

Crossan, John Dominic. 1995. *Jesus: A Revolutionary Biography.* San Francisco: HarperSanFrancisco.

Daley, Brian. 1991. *The Hope of the Early Church. A Handbook of Patristic Eschatology.* Cambridge: Cambridge University Press.

Daly, Mary. 1973. *Beyond God the Father.* Boston: Beacon Press.

Danielou, Jean. 1953. *Essais sur le mystère de l' histoire.* Paris: Seuil.

Daube, David. 1973. *The New Testament and Rabbinic Judaism.* New York: Arno Press.

Davidson, Donald. 1984. What Metaphors Mean. In *Inquiries Into Truth and Interpretation.* Oxford: Clarendon Press.

Davis, J. J. 1967. Adultery in the Bible. In *New Catholic Encyclopaedia,* 1:151–152. New York: McGraw-Hill.

de Caussade, Jean Pierre. 1959. *Self-abandonment to Divine Providence.* London: Burns & Oates.

Delumeau, Jean. 1989. *Rassurer et Proteger: Le sentiment de securité dans l'Occident d'autrefois.* Paris: Fayard.

Derrett, John Duncan Martin. 1967. Law in the New Testament: The Parable of the Prodigal Son. *New Testament Studies,* 14:56–74.

Derrett, John Duncan Martin. 1970. *Law in the New Testament.* London: Darton, Longman & Todd.

Derrida, Jacques. 1977. *Of Grammatology.* Trans. Goyani Chakravorty Spivak. Baltimore: John Hopkins University Press.

Descartes, René. [1701]1931. The Search After Truth by the Light of Nature. In *The Philosophical Works of Descartes,* 1:305–327. Trans. Elizabeth S. Haldane and G. R. T. Ross. Cambridge: Cambridge University Press.

Dihle, Albrecht. 1962. *Die Goldene Regel.* Goettingen: Vandenhoeck & Ruprecht.

Dodd, C. H. 1935. *Parables of the Kingdom.* London: Nisbet.

Dodd, C. H. 1965. *The Parables of the Kingdom.* Revised ed. New York: Scribner.

Donahue, John R. 1988. *The Gospel in Parable: Metaphor, Narrative, and Theology in the Synoptic Gospels.* Philadelphia: Fortress Press.

Downing, F. Gerald. 1988. *Christ and the Cynics.* Sheffield: JSOT.

Dunn, James D. G. 1991. *The Parting of the Ways Between Christianity and Judaism and Their Significance for the Character of Christianity.* London: SCM Press.

Dupont, Jacques. 1967–1968. Les paraboles du Trésor et de la Perle. *New Testament Studies,* 14:408–418.

Dupont, Jacques. 1969–1973. *Les Béatitudes,* 3 vols. I. Le Problème Littéraire (1969); II. La Bonne Nouvelle (1969); III. Les Évangélistes (1973). Paris: J. Gabalda.

Eichholz, Georg. 1984. *Gleichnisse der Evangelien.* Neukirchen-Vluyn: Neukirchener Verlag.

Entrevernes Group. 1978. *Signs and Parables: Semiotics and Gospel Texts* (with a study by Jacques Geninasca). Trans. Gary Phillips. Pittsburgh: Pickwick Press.

Epictetus. 1995. *The Discourses of Epictetus.* London: J. M. Dent.

Evangelii Nuntiandi. 1989. *Apostolic Exhortation of Paul VI.* Homebush, NSW: St. Paul's Publications.

Expositor's Bible Commentary. 1984. *Vol. 8. Matthew, Mark, Luke.* Frank E. Gaebelein, ed. Grand Rapids, Mich.: Zondervan.

Fee, G. D. 1993. *New Testament Exegesis: A Handbook for Students and Pastors.* Louisville, Ky.: Westminster/John Knox.

Feldman, Asher. [1927]1975. *The Parables and Similes of the Rabbis, Agricultural and Pastoral.* Folcroft, Penn.: Folcroft Library Editions.

Feyerabend, Paul. 1995. Anything Goes. In Walter Truett Anderson, ed. *The Truth About the Truth,* pp. 199–203. New York: Putnam.

Filson, Floyd Vivian. 1960. *A Commentary on the Gospel According to St. Matthew,* 2nd ed. London: A. & C. Black.

Finnis, John. 1980. *Natural Law and Natural Rights.* Oxford: Clarendon Press.

Fitzmyer, J. A. 1976. The Matthean Divorce Texts and Some New Palestinian Evidence. *Theological Studies,* 37:197–226; reprinted in J. A. Fitzmyer, *To Advance the Gospel: New Testment Studies* (New York: Crossroad, 1981), pp. 79–111.

Fitzmyer, J. A. 1981. *The Anchor Bible. Vol. 28. The Gospel According to Luke 1–IX.* New York: Doubleday.

Fitzmyer, J. A. 1985a. Abba and Jesus' relation to God. In *À Cause de l'Évangile: Études sur les synoptiques et les Actes offertes au P. Jacques Dupont,* pp. 15–38. Paris: Cerf.

Fitzmyer, J. A. 1985b. *The Anchor Bible. Vol. 28A. The Gospel According to Luke X–XXIV.* New York: Doubleday.

Fitzmyer, J. A. 1994. *Scripture: The Soul of Theology.* New York: Paulist Press.

Flusser, David. 1981. *Die rabbinischen Gleichnisse und der Gleichniserzaehler Jesus.* Bern: Peter Lang.

Flusser, David. 1989. Aesop's Miser and the Parable of the Talents. In Clemens Thoma and Michael Wyschograd, eds. *Parable and Story in Judaism and Christianity,* pp. 9–25. New York: Paulist Press.

Flusser, David. 1991. Jesus, His ancestry, and the Commandment of Love. In James Charlesworth, ed. *Jesus' Jewishness: Exploring the Place of Jesus Within Early Judaism,* pp. 153–176. New York: Crossroad.

Foucault, Michel. 1995. *Strategies of Power.* In Walter Truett Anderson, ed. *The Truth About the Truth,* pp. 40–45. New York: Putnam.

Fox, Emmet. 1938. *The Sermon on the Mount: A General Introduction to Scientific Christianity in the Form of a Spiritual Key to Matthew V, VI and VII*. New York: Harper & Brothers.

Frost, Robert. 1949. *The Complete Poems of Robert Frost*. New York: H. Holt.

Frymer-Kensky, Tikva, David Nova, Peter Ochs, David Sandmel, and Michael Signer. 2000. *Christianity in Jewish Terms*. Boulder, Colo.: Westview Press.

Funk, Robert W. 1982. *Parables and Presence: Forms of the New Testament Tradition*. Philadelphia: Fortress Press.

Funk, Robert W. 1996. *Honest to Jesus: Jesus for a New Millennium*. San Francisco: HarperSanFrancisco.

Funk, Robert W., and the Jesus Seminar. 1998. *The Acts of Jesus: The Search for the Authentic Deeds of Jesus*. San Francisco: Harper.

Funk, Robert W., Roy Hoover, and the Jesus Seminar. 1993. *The Five Gospels: What Did Jesus Really Say?* New York: Macmillan.

Funk, Robert W., Bernard Brandon Scott, and James Butts. 1988. *The Parables of Jesus*. Sonoma, Calif.: Polebridge.

Gallo, Maria. 1984. Introduzione. In Isacco di Niniveh, *Discorsi Ascetici*, pp. 5–38. Roma: Città Nuova Editrice.

"Gaudium et Spes." 1966. (Pastoral constitution on the church in the modern world. Second Vatican Council.) Torino-Leumann: Elle di Ci.

Gelin, Albert. 1964. *The Poor of Yahweh*. Trans. Mother Mathryn Sullivan. Collegeville, Minn.: Liturgical Press.

Gesenius' Hebrew and Chaldean Lexicon to the Old Testament Scriptures. [1857]1979. Trans. Samuel Prideaux Tregelles. Grand Rapids, Mich.: Baker Book House.

Goddard, Cliff. 1998. *Semantic Analysis: A Practical Introduction*. Oxford: Oxford University Press.

Goddard, Cliff, and Anna Wierzbicka, eds. 1994. *Semantic and Lexical Universals*. Amsterdam: John Benjamins.

Goldin, Judah. 1974. *The Fathers According to Rabbi Nathan*. New Haven, Conn.: Yale University Press.

The Gospel According to St. Matthew. 1975. Intro. and Commentary H. Benedict Green. Oxford: Oxford University Press.

The Gospel of Thomas: The Hidden Sayings of Jesus. 1992. Interpreted Harold Bloom. Trans. Marvin Meyer. San Francisco: Harper.

Gourgues, Michel. 1995. *Foi, Bonheur, et Sens de la Vie*. Montréal: Médiaspaul.

Gourgues, Michel. 1997. *Les Paraboles de Luc*. Paris: Médiaspaul.

Greeley, Andrew, and Jacob Neusner. 1991. *The Bible and Us: A Priest and a Rabbi Read Scripture Together*. New York: Warner Books.

Green, J. B., ed. 1995. *Hearing the New Testament: Strategies for Interpretation*. Grand Rapids, Mich.: Eerdmans.

Gregor von Nyssa. 1971. *Die grosse katechetische Rede*. Stuttgart: Anton Hiersemann.

Gressmann, Hugo. 1929. *Der Messias*. Göttingen: Vandenhoeck & Ruprecht.

Griffin, David, and Huston Smith. 1989. *Primordial Truth and Postmodern Theology*. Albany: State University of New York Press.

Guelich, Robert. 1982. *The Sermon on the Mount: A Foundation for Understanding*. Dallas: Word Publishing.

Gundry, Robert H. 1982. *Matthew: A Commentary on His Literary and Theological Art*. Grand Rapids, Mich.: Eerdmans.

Gunkel, Hermann. [1927–1932]1969. The Israelite Prophecy from the Time of Amos.

In J. Pelikan, ed. *Twentieth Century Theology in the Making*, 1.1:48-75. New York: Harper & Row.

Haacker, Klaus. 1977. Der Rechtssatz Jesu zum Thema Ehebruch (Mt. 5, 28). *Biblische Zeitschrift*, 21:113-116.

Hahn, Ferdinand. 1969. *The Titles of Jesus in Christology: Their History in Early Christianity*. London: Lutterworth.

Hall, F. W. 1925. Adultery (Greek and Roman) In James Hastings, ed. *Encyclopaedia of Religion and Ethics*, 1:127-128, 134-135. Edinburgh: T. & T. Clark.

Hamerton-Kelly, Robert. 1981. God the Father in the Bible and the Experience of Jesus. In Johannes-Baptist Metz and Edward Schillebeeckx, eds. *Concilium: Religion in the Eighties. God as Father*, pp. 95-102. Edinburgh: T. & T. Clark.

Harnack, Adolf von. 1912. Ich bin gekommen. Die ausdrücklichen Selbstzeugnisse Jesu über den Zweck seiner Sendung und seines Kommens. *Zeitschrift für Theologie und Kirche* [ZThK], 22:1-30.

Harnisch, Wolfgang. 1985. *Die Gleichniserzählungen Jesu*. Göttingen: Vandenhoeck & Ruprecht.

Harrington, S. J. 1991. *The Gospel of Matthew*. Collegeville, Minn.: Liturgical Press.

Hayes, John. 1973. The History of the Form-critical Study of Prophecy. In George Macroe, ed. *SBL Seminar Papers*, 1:60-99. Cambridge, Mass: Society of Biblical Literature.

Hedrick, Charles W. 1994. *Parables as Poetic Fictions*. Peabody, Mass.: Hendrickson Publishers.

Hefley, James and Marti Hefley. 1988. *By Their Blood: Christian Martyrs of the 20th Century*. Grand Rapids, Mich.: Baker Book House.

Hendrickx, Herman. 1986. *The Parables of Jesus*. London: Geoffrey Chapman.

Heschel, Abraham. 1959. *Between God and Man: An Interpretation of Judaism. From the Writings of Abraham J. Heschel*. New York: Harper.

Heschel, Abraham. 1962. *The Prophets*. New York: Jewish Publication Society of America.

Hick, John. 1993. *The Metaphor of God Incarnate: Christology in a Pluralistic Age*. Louisville, Ky.: Westminster/John Knox Press.

Hirsch, E. D. 1967. *Validity in Interpretation*. New Haven, Conn.: Yale University Press.

The Holy Bible. New King James Version. 1990. Canberra: Bible Society.

Hryniewicz, Wacław. 1990. *Nadzieja zbawienia dla wszystkich*. Warszawa: Verbinum.

Hryniewicz, Wacław. 1996. *Dramat nadziei zbawienia. Medytacje Eschatologiczne*. Warszawa: Verbinum.

Hübner, Hans. 1973. *Das Gesetz in der synoptischen Tradition*. Witten: Luther Verlag.

Hunter, A. M. 1953. *Design for Life*. London: SCM Press.

Huntington, Samuel. 1996. *The Clash of Civilizations and the Remaking of World Order*. New York: Simon & Schuster.

Huxley, Aldous. [1947]1961. *The Perennial Philosophy*. London: Chatto & Windus.

Huxley, Thomas Aldous. 1984. *Evolution and Ethics and Other Essays*. London: Macmillan.

Imbach, J. 1987. *Himmel-Glaube und Höllen-Angst. Was wissen wir vom Leben nach dem Tod?* München: Keösel.

Imbach, Josef. 1995. *Und lehrte sie in Bildern: Die Gleichnisse Jesu–Geschichten für heute*. Würzburg: Echter.

Isaac of Niniveh (Isaac le Syrien). 1981. *Oeuvres Spirituelles*. n.p.: Desclée de Brouwer.

Iser, Wolfgang. 1978. *The Act of Reading: A Theory of Aesthetic Response*. Baltimore: John Hopkins University Press.

Jeremias, Joachim. 1954. *The Parables of Jesus*. New York: Scribner.

Jeremias, Joachim. 1961. *The Sermon on the Mount*. London: University of London Press.

Jeremias, Joachim. 1966a. ABBA *Studien zur Neutestamentlichen Theologie und Zeitgeschichte.* Göttingen: Vanhoeck & Ruprecht.
Jeremias, Joachim. 1966b. *Rediscovering the Parables.* London: SCM Press.
Jeremias, Joachim. 1967. *The Prayers of Jesus.* London: SCM Press.
Jeremias, Joachim. 1971. *New Testament Theology.* Trans. J. Bowden. London: SCM Press.
Jeremias, Joachim. 1972. *The Parables of Jesus,* 3d rev. ed. New York: Scribner.
Jeremias, Joachim. [1965]1988. *Die Gleichnisse Jesu.* Göttingen: Vandenhoeck & Ruprecht.
John Paul II. 1993. Encyclical Letter 'Veritatis splendor'. Australian ed. Homebush NSW: St. Pauls Publications.
John Paul II. 1994. *Crossing the Threshold of Hope.* New York: Knopf.
Johnson, Luke Timothy. 1989. The New Testament's Anti-Jewish Slander and the Conventions of Ancient Polemic. *Journal of Biblical Literature,* 108(3):419–441.
Johnson, Luke Timothy. 1991. *The Gospel of Luke. Sacra Pagina Series,* vol. 3. Collegeville, Minn.: Liturgical Press.
Johnson, Luke Timothy. 1996. *The Real Jesus.* San Francisco: Harper.
Johnson, Luke Timothy. 1999. *Living Truth.* San Francisco: HarperSanFrancisco
Jones, Geraint Vaughan. 1964. *The Art and Truth of the Parables.* London: SPCK.
Jülicher, Adolf. [1888]1963. *Die Gleichnisreden Jesu.* Darmstadt: Wissenschaftliche Buchgesellschaft.
Kane, Richard. 1994. *Through the Moral Maze: Searching for Absolute Values in a Pluralistic World.* New York: Paragon House.
Käsemann, Ernst. 1964. *Essays on New Testament Themes.* Trans. W. J. Montague. London: SCM Press.
Keating, Thomas. 1997. *The Kingdom of God Is Like. . . .* New York: Crossroad.
Kiley, Mark. 1994. The Lord's Prayer and Matthean Theology. In James H. Charlesworth, Mark Harding, and Mark Kiley, eds. *The Lord's Prayer and Other Texts from the Greco-Roman Era,* pp. 15–27. Valley Forge, Penn.: Trinity Press International.
Kimel, Alvin. 1990. *A New Language for God: A Critique of Supplemental Liturgical Texts. Prayer Book Studies 30.* Shaker Heights, Ohio: United Episcopalians.
King, Martin Luther, Jr. 1963. *Strength to Love.* New York: Harper & Row.
Kistemaker, Simon J. 1980. *The Parables of Jesus.* Grand Rapids, Mich.: Baker Book House.
Klassen, William. 1984. *Love of Enemies.* Philadelphia: Fortress Press.
Klausner, Joseph. [1925] 1949. *Jesus of Nazareth: His Life, Times and Teaching.* New York: Macmillan.
Koch, K. 1969. *The Growth of the Biblical Tradition.* London: A. & C. Black.
Küng, Hans. 1980. *Does God Exist?* Trans. Edward Quinn. New York: Doubleday.
Küng, Hans. 1993. *Credo. The Apostles' Creed Explained for Today.* Trans. John Bowden. London: SCM Press.
Kushner, Harold S. 1981. *When Bad Things Happen to Good People.* London: Pan Books.
Lachs, Samuel Tobias. 1987. *A Rabbinic Commentary on the New Testament.* Hoboken, N.J.: KTAV Publishing House.
Lambrecht, Jan. 1976. *Tandis qu'Il nous parlait: Introduction aux Paraboles.* Paris: P. Lethielleux.
Lambrecht, Jan. 1981. *Once More Astonished.* New York: Crossroad.
Lambrecht, Jan. 1985. *The Sermon on the Mount: Proclamation and Exhortation.* Wilmington, Del.: Michael Glazier.
Lambrecht, Jan. 1991. *Out of the Treasure.* Peeters Press Louvain: Eerdmans.
Lane, W. L. 1974. *The Gospel According to Mark, with English Text* (with Introduction, Exposition, and Notes). Grand Rapids, Mich.: Eerdmans.

Lapide, Pinchas. 1985. A Jewish Perspective. In Pinchas Lapide and Ulrich Luz. *Jesus in Two Perspectives: A Jewish-Christian Dialogue*, pp. 9–119. Trans. Lawrence Denef. Minneapolis: Augsburg.

Lapide, Pinchas. 1986. *The Sermon on the Mount: Utopia or Program in Action?* Maryknoll, N.Y.: Orbis Books.

Lapide, Pinchas, and Ulrich Luz. 1985. *Jesus in Two Perspectives. A Jewish-Christian Dialogue*. Trans. Lawrence Denef. Minneapolis: Augsburg.

La Potterie, Ignace de. 1977. *La Verité dans Saint Jean*. Rome: Biblical Institute.

Lawson, Hilary, and Lisa Appignanesi, eds. 1989. *Dismantling the Truth: Reality in the Post-modern World*. London: Weidenfeld & Nicolson.

Lecky, W. E. H. 1880. *History of European Morals from Augustus to Charlemagne*. London: Longmans, Green.

Leibniz, Gottfried Wilhelm. 1903. *Opuscules et fragments inédits de Leibniz*. Louis Couturat, ed. Paris: Presses universitaires de France; reprinted 1961, Hildesheim: Georg Olms.

Limbeck, Meinrad. 1995. *Matthäeus-Evangelium*. Stuttgart: Katholisches Bibelwerk.

Limbeck, Meinrad, Annelise Bausch, Günter Hegele, Peter Neumann, and Wolfgang Schöpping. 1987. *Die bessere Gerechtigkeit: Matthöusevangelium*. Stuttgart: Katolisches Bibelwerk.

Linnemann, Eta. 1966. *Parables of Jesus*. London: SPCK.

Lockyer, Herbert. 1963. *All the Parables of the Bible*. Grand Rapids, Mich.: Zondervan.

Loewenich, Walther Von. 1954. *Luther als Ausleger der Synoptiker*. Munich: Kaiser.

Loughlin, Gerard. 1997. The basis and authority of doctrine. In Colin E. Gunton, ed. *The Cambridge Companion to Christian Doctrine*, pp. 41–64. Cambridge: Cambridge University Press.

Loughlin, Gerard. 1999. *Telling God's Story: Bible, Church and Narrative Theology*. Cambridge: Cambridge University Press.

Lubich, Chiara. 1995. *Scrivere il Vangelo con la vita*. Roma: Citta Nuova Editrice.

Luther, Martin. 1931. *The Bondage of the Will*. Trans. Henry Cole. Grand Rapids, Mich.: Eerdmans.

Luz, Ulrich. 1985. A Christian Perspective. In Pinchas Lapide and Ulrich Luz. *Jesus in Two Perspectives: A Jewish-Christian Dialogue*, pp. 123–166. Trans. Lawrence Denef. Minneapolis: Augsburg.

Luz, Ulrich. 1989. *Matthew 1–7*. Minneapolis: Fortress Press.

Mack, B. L. 1988. *A Myth of Innocence. Mark and Christian Origins*. Philadelphia: Fortress Press.

Maillot, Alphonse. 1993. *Les paraboles de Jésus*. Paris: Cerf.

Mann, C. S. 1986. *The Anchor Bible. Mark: A New Translation with Introduction and Commentary*. Garden City, N.Y.: Doubleday.

Manson, T. W. [1937]1961. *The Sayings of Jesus as Recorded in the Gospels Aaccording to St. Matthew and St. Luke*. London: SCM Press.

Marmorstein, Arthur. [1920]1968. *The Doctrine of Merits in Old Rabbinical Literature; And the Old Rabbinic Doctrine of God*. New York: KTAV Publishing House.

Matisoff, James. 1979. *Blessings, Curses, Hopes, and Fears: Psycho-ostensive Expressions in Yiddish*. Philadelphia: Institute for the Study of Human Issues.

Maude, Aylmer. 1930. *The Life of Tolstoy: Later Years*, vol. 11. London: Oxford University Press.

McArthur, Harvey K. 1961. *Understanding the Sermon on the Mount*. London: Epworth Press.

McKenna, Megan. 1994. *Parables: The Arrows of God*. Maryknoll, N.Y.: Orbis Books.

McKenzie, S. L., and S. R. Haynes, eds. 1993. *To Each Its Own Meaning. An Introduc-

tion to Biblical Criticisms and Their Application. Louisville, Ky.: Westminster/John Knox.

Meier, John P. 1980. *Matthew*. Dublin: Veritas Press.

Meier, John P. 1991–1994. *A Marginal Jew: Rethinking the Historical Jesus*, 3 vols. New York: Doubleday.

Merton, Thomas. [1963]1996. *Life and Holiness*. New York: Doubleday.

Michaels, J. Ramsey. 1981. *Servant and Son: Jesus in Parable and Gospel*. Atlanta: J. Knox.

Moloney, Francis. 1988. *The Gospel of John*. Collegeville, Minn.: Liturgical Press.

Moloney, Francis. 1993. *Belief in the Word*. Minneapolis: Fortress Press.

Moltmann, Jürgen. 1967. *Theology of Hope*. London: Leitch.

Moltmann, Jürgen. 1981. *The Trinity and the Kingdom: The Doctrine of God*. Trans. Margaret Kohl. San Francisco: Harper & Row.

Moltmann, Jürgen. 1996. *The Coming of God: Christian Eschatology*. Trans. Margaret Kohl. Minneapolis: Fortress Press.

Moltmann, Jürgen. 1997. *Source–the Holy Spirit and the Theology of Life*. Minneapolis: Fortress Press.

Montefiore. C. G. [1927]1968. *The Synoptic Gospels*, 2 vols. New York: KTAV Publishing House.

Montefiore, C. G. [1930]1970. *Rabbinic Literature and Gospel Teachings*. New York: KTAV Publishing House.

Moore, Stephen E. 1989. *Literary Criticism and the Gospels: The Theoretical Challenge*. New Haven, Conn.: Yale University Press.

Morgan, G. Campbell. 1960. *The Parables of the Kingdom*. London: Hodder & Stoughton.

Morwood, Michael. 1998. *Tomorrow's Catholic*. Melbourne: Spectrum.

Müller, Paul-Gerhard. 1995. *Lukas-Evangelium*. Stuttgart: Katolisches Bibelwerk.

Neusner, Jacob. 1993. *Telling Tales: The Urgency and Basis for Judeo-Christian Dialogue*. Louisville, Kentucky: Westminster/John Knox Press.

Newbigin, Lesslie. 1986. *Foolishness to the Greeks: The Gospel and Western Culture*. London: SPCK.

Newbigin, Lesslie. 1989. *The Gospel in a Pluralist Society*. Grand Rapids, Mich.: Eerdmans.

The New Jerusalem Bible. 1990. London: Darton, Longman & Todd.

Newman, Barclay M., Jr. 1971. *A Concise Greek-English Dictionary of the New Testament*. London: United Bible Societies.

Nida, Eugene. 1994. The Sociolinguistics of Translating Canonical Religious Texts. In *Traduction, Terminologie, Rédaction: Études sur le texte et ses transformations*, pp. 191–217. Montréal: Concordia University.

Nocke, Franz-Joseph. 1995. *Eschatologie*. Düsseldorf: Patmos.

O'Farrell, F. P. 1967. Truth. In *New Catholic Encyclopaedia*, 14:327–328. New York: McGraw-Hill.

The Old Testment Pseudepigrapha. Vol. 1. Apocalyptic Literature and Testaments. 1983. James H. Charlesworth, ed. Garden City, N.Y.: Doubleday.

The Old Testament Pseudepigrapha. vol. 2. Expansions of the Old Testament, and Legends, Wisdom and Philosophical Literature, Prayers, Psalms, and Odes, Fragments of Lost Judeo-Hellenistic Works. 1985. James H. Charlesworth, ed. Garden City, N.Y.: Doubleday.

Oxford English Dictionary, 2nd ed. 1992. CD ROM.

Pascal, Blaise. [1667]1954. De l'esprit géométrique et de l'art de persuader. In J. Chevalier, ed. *Oevres Complètes*, pp. 575–604. Paris: Gallimard.

Percy, E. 1953. *Die Botschaft Jesu: Eine Traditions-kritische und exegetische Untersuchung*. Lund: C. W. K. Gleerup.

Perkins, p. 1981. *Hearing the Parables of Jesus*. New York/Ramsey, N.J.: Paulist Press.

Perrin, Norman. 1966. *The Kingdom of God in the Teaching of Jesus.* Norwich: Fletcher & Son.

Perrin, Norman. 1976. *Jesus and the Language of the Kingdom.* Philadelphia: Fortress Press.

Petzoldt, Martin. 1984. *Gleichnisse Jesu und christliche Dogmatik.* Göttingen: Vandenhoeck & Ruprecht.

Piper, John. 1979. *Love Your Enemies.* Cambridge: Cambridge University Press.

Pirot, Louis. 1935. *Évangile selon S. Marc.* Paris.

Plummer, Alfred. 1928. *A Critical and Exegetical Commentary on the Gospel According to St Luke* (International critical commentary on the Holy Scriptures of the Old and New Testament, v. 28.) Edinburgh: T. & T. Clark.

Porpora, Douglas. In press. *Landscapes of the Soul: American Views on the Meaning of Life at the Turn of the Millennium.* New York: Oxford University Press.

Powell, Mark Allan. 1998. *Jesus as a Figure in History.* Louisville, Ky.: Westminster/John Knox Press.

Pregeant, R. 1995. *Engaging the New Testament: An Interdiscipinary Introduction.* Minneapolis: Augsburg/Fortress.

Price, Reynolds. 1997. *Three Gospels.* New York: Simon & Schuster.

Ragaz, Leonhard. 1945. *Die Bergpredigt Jesu.* Bern: Verlag Herbert Lang.

Rahner, Karl. 1980. Die bleibende Bedeutung des II vatikanischen Konzils. In *Schriften zur Theologie. (Band XIV: In Sorge um die Kirche).* Zürich, Einsiedeln, Köln: Benziger.

Rahner, Karl, and Pinchas Lapide. 1987. *Encountering Jesus–Encountering Judaism: A Dialogue.* New York: Crossroad.

Revised Standard Version. 1962. (The Holy Bible: Revised standard version containing the Old and New Testaments.) New York: Oxford University Press.

Ricoeur, Paul. 1974. Fatherhood: From Phantasm to Symbol. In *The Conflict of Interpretations: Essays in Hermeneutics.* Evanston, Ill.: Northwestern University Press.

Ricoeur, Paul. 1975. *Essays on Biblical Interpretation.* Philadelphia: Fortress Press.

Ricoeur, Paul. 1990. The Golden Rule: Exegetical and Theological Perplexities. *New Testament Studies,* 36:392–397.

Riesenfeld, H. 1952. Die Perikope von der Ehebrecherin in der fruehkirchlichen Tradition. *Svensk Exegetisk Arsbok,* 17:106–111.

Robinson, John A. T. 1950. *In the End, God.* London: James Clarke.

Robinson, John A. T. 1984. *Twelve More New Testament Studies.* London : SCM Press.

Room, Adrian. 1991. *NTC's Dictionary of Changes in Meaning.* Lincolnwood, Ill.: National Textbook Company.

Rorty, Richard. 1989. *Contingency, Irony and Solidarity.* New York: Cambridge University Press.

Rost, H. T. D. 1986. *The Golden Rule: A Universal Ethic.* Oxford: George Ronald.

Ruether, Rosemary Radford. 1981. The Female Nature of God. In Johannes-Baptist Metz and Edward Schillebeeckx, eds. *Concilium: Religion in the Eighties, God as Father,* pp. 61–68. Edinburgh: T. & T. Clark.

Ryken, Leland. 1984. *The New Testament in Literary Criticism.* New York: Ungar.

Saldarini, Anthony J. 1975. *The Fathers According to Rabbi Nathan (Abot de Rabbi Nathan) Version B: A Translation and Commentary.* Leiden: Brill.

Salinger, J. D. 1962. *Franny and Zooey.* London: Heinemann.

Sanders, E. P. 1977. *Paul and Palestinian Judaism: Aion.* London: SCM Press.

Sanders, E. P. 1985. *Jesus and Judaism.* Philadelphia: Fortress Press.

Sanders, E. P. 1993. *The Historical Figure of Jesus.* London: Penguin.

Sanders, James A. 1987. Isaiah in Luke. In James Luther Mays and Paul J. Achtemeier, eds. *Interpreting the Prophets,* pp. 75–89. Philadelphia: Fortress Press.

Schechter, S. [1909]1961. *Aspects of Rabbinic Theology.* New York: Schocken.

Schlatter, A. 1933. *Der Evangelist Matthäus.* Stuttgart: Calver.

Schlosser, Jacques. 1980. *Le Règne de Dieu dans les Dits de Jésus.* Paris: Gabalda.

Schnackenburg, Rudolf. 1963. *God's Rule and Kingdom.* Trans. John Murray. New York: Herder & Herder.

Schnackenburg, Rudolf. 1987. *Neue Echter Bibel.* II. Würzburg: Echter.

Schneiders, Sandra. 1991. *The Revelatory Text: Interpreting the New Testament as Sacred Scripture.* San Francisco: HarperSanFrancisco.

Schottroff, Luise. 1975. Gewaltverzicht und Feindesliebe in der urchristlichen Jesustradition: Mt. 5, 38-48; Lk. 6, 27-36. In Georg Strecker, ed. *Jesus Christus in Historie und Theologie* (Festschrift in honor of Hans Conzelmann), pp. 197-221. Tübingen: Mohr.

Schottroff, Luise. 1978. Non-violence and the Love of One's Enemies. In Luise Schottroff, Reginald Fuller, Christoph Burchard, and M. Jack Suggs. *Essays on the Love Commandment,* pp. 9-40. Trans. Reginald H. and Ilse Fuller. Philadelphia: Fortress Press.

Schottroff, Luise. 1987. Das Gleichnis vom großen Gastmahl in der Logienquelle. *Evangelische Theologie,* 47:192-211.

Schüssler-Fiorenza, Elisabeth, ed. 1994. *Searching the Scriptures. Vol. 11: A Feminist Commentary.* New York: Crossroad.

Schweizer, Eduard. 1975. *The Good News According to Matthew.* Trans. David E. Green. London: SPCK.

Scott, Bernard Brandon. 1981. *Jesus, Symbol-maker for the Kingdom.* Philadelphia: Fortress Press.

Scott, Bernard Brandon. 1989. *Hear Then the Parable.* Minneapolis: Fortress Press.

Seneca. 1917. *Ad Lucilium Epistulae Morales,* vol. 1. Trans. Richard M. Gummere. London: Heinemann.

Sevin, Marc. 1997. *Les Paroles provocantes de Jésus.* Paris: Cerf.

Shorter, Aylward. 1997. *Toward a Theory of Inculturation.* Maryknoll, N.Y.: Orbis Books.

Shorto, Russell. 1997. *Gospel Truth: The New Picture of Jesus Emerging from Science and History and Why It Matters.* London: Hodder & Stoughton.

Sifre. 1986. *A Tannaitic Commentary on the Book of Deuteronomy.* Trans. Reuven Hammer. New Haven, Conn.: Yale University Press.

Smith, B. T. D. 1937. *The Parables of the Synoptic Gospels: A Critical Study.* Cambridge: Cambridge University Press.

Smith, Huston. [1958]1965. *The Religions of Man.* New York: Perennial Library.

Smith, Huston. 1992. *Forgotten Truth: The Common Vision of the World's Religions.* San Francisco: Harper.

Smith, Huston. 1995. Postmodernism and the World's Religions. In Walter Truett Anderson, ed. *The Truth About the Truth,* pp. 204-214. New York: Putnam.

Sölle, Dorothee. 1981. Paternalistic Religion as Experienced by Women. In Johannes-Baptist Metz and Edward Schillebeeckx, eds. *Concilium: Religion in the Eighties, God as Father,* pp. 69-74. Edinburgh: T. & T. Clark.

Solov'ev, Vladimir. [1883]1966. Velikij spor i xrist'janskaja politika. *Sobranie Sočinenij,* pp. 3-116. S. Petersburg: Prosveščenie; photo-reprinted, Bruxelles: Foyer Oriental Chrétien.

Sommer, F. 1948. *The World's Greatest Short Story: A Study of Present-day Significance of the Family Pattern of Life.* Oswega, Kans.: Carpenter Press.

Spaemann, Heinrich. 1973. *Wer ist Jesus von Nazareth—Für mich?: 100 Zeit-genössische Zeugnisse.* München: Kösel.

Spooner, W. A. 1937. Golden Rule. In James Hastings, ed. *Encyclopedia of Religion and Ethics*, 6:310-312.

Sproul, R. C. 1992. *Essential Truth of the Christian Faith: 100 Key Doctrines in Plain Language*. London: SCM Press.

St. Augustine. 1948. *The Lord's Sermon on the Mount*. Johannes Quasten and Joseph Plumpe, eds. New York: Newman Press.

St Augustine. 1984. *City of God*. London: Penguin Books.

Stenger, W. 1993. *Introduction to New Testament Exegesis*. Grand Rapids, Mich.: Eerdmans.

St. Gregory of Nyssa. 1917. *The Catechetical Oration of St. Gregory of Nyssa*. London: SPCK.

St. Gregory of Nyssa. 1954. *The Lord's Prayer; The Beatitudes*. New York: Newman Press.

St. Gregory of Nyssa. 1993. *The Soul and the Resurrection*. Trans. and intro. Catherine P. Roth. Crestwood, N.Y.: St. Vladimir's Seminary Press.

St. Isaac of Niniveh (Isaac le Syrian). 1981. *Oeuvres Spirituelles*. n.p.: Desclée de Brouwer.

St. Isaac of Nineveh. 1984. *Ascetical Homilies of St. Isaac of Niniveh*. Trans. D. Biller. Boston: Holy Transfiguration Monastery.

St. Isaac of Nineveh. 1995. *The Second Part*, chaps. IV-XLI. Lovanii: Peeters Press.

Stott, John R. W. [1978]1992. *The Message of the Sermon on the Mount: Christian Counterculture*. Leicester: Inter-Varsity Press.

Strack, Hermann Leberecht, and Paul Billerbeck. [1922-1928]1965. *Kommentar zum Neuen Testament aus Talmud und Midrasch*, 4 vols. Munchen: C. H. Beck.

Strecker, Georg. 1988. *The Sermon on the Mount*. Nashville, Tenn.: Abingdon.

St. Thomas Aquinas. 1964. *Summa Theologiae*. London: Blackfriars.

Tannehill, Robert C. 1975. *The Sword of His Mouth*. Philadelphia: Fortress Press.

Tannen, Deborah. 1992. *That's Not What I Meant*. London: Virago Press.

Taylor, C. [1897]1963. *Sayings of the Jewish Fathers*. Cambridge: Cambridge University Press.

Taylor, V. 1959. *The Gospel According to St. Mark: The Greek Text with Introduction, Notes and Indexes*. London and New York: Macmillan and St. Martins.

Te Selle, Sallie. 1975. *Speaking in Parables: A Study in Metaphor and Theology*. Philadelphia: Fortress Press.

Theissen, G., and A. Merz. 1998. *The Historical Jesus: A Comprehensive Guide*. Minneapolis: Fortress Press.

Thiselton, A. C. 1992. *New Horizons in Hermeneutics. The Theory and Practice of Transforming Biblical Reading*. Grand Rapids, Mich.: Zondervan.

Tillich, Paul. 1964. *The New Being*. London: SCM Press.

Todorov, Tsvetan. 1998. (untitled). In Simon Wiesenthal, *The Sunflower. On the Possibilities and the Limits of Forgiveness* (with a symposium), pp. 265-266. H. J. Cargas and B. Fetterman, eds. New York: Schocken Books.

Tolstoy, Leo. [1884]1958. What I Believe. In *A Confession, The Gospel in Brief, and What I Believe*, pp. 303-539. Trans. Aylmer Maude. London: Oxford University Press.

Torjesen, Karen Jo. 1998. "You are the Christ": Five Portraits of Jesus from the Early Church. In Marcus Borg, ed. *Jesus at 2000*, pp. 73-88. Boulder, Col.: Westview Press.

Torrey, Charles. 1936. *Our Translated Gospels*. New York: Harper.

Tucker, Gene M. 1987. Prophetic Speech. In James Luther Mays and Paul J. Achtemeier, eds. *Interpreting the Prophets*, pp. 27-40. Philadelphia: Fortress Press.

Turner, Nigel. 1980. *Christian Words*. Edinburgh: T. & T. Clark.

Unamuno, Miguel. [1912]1972. *The Tragic Sense of Life in Men and Nations*. London: Routledge.

Van Bragt, Jan. 1992. Inculturation in Japan. In Catherine Cornille and Veleer Neckebrouch, eds. *A Universal Faith? Peoples, Cultures, Religions, and the Christ*, pp. 49–72. Louvain: Peeters Press.

Vermes, G. 1973. *Jesus the Jew: A Historian's Reading of the Gospels*. London: Collins.

Vermes, G. 1993. *The Religion of Jesus the Jew*. London: SCM Press.

Via, D. O. 1974. *The Parables: Their Literary and Existential Dimension*. Philadelphia: Fortress Press.

Viviano, Benedict. 1990. The Gospel According to Matthew. In Raymond E. Brown, Joseph A. Fitzmeyer, and Roland E. Murphy, eds. *The New Jerome Biblical Commentary*, pp. 630–674. Upper Saddle River, N.J.: Prentice Hall.

Vögtle, Anton. 1996. *Gott und seine Gäste. Das Schicksal des Gleichnisses Jesu vom großen Gastmahl*. Neukirchen-Vluyn: Neukirchener Verlag.

Vorländer, H. 1975. Forgiveness. In Colin Brown, ed. *The New International Dictionary of New Testament Theology*, pp. 697–103. Grand Rapids, Mich.: Zondervan.

Wattles, Jeffrey. 1996. *The Golden Rule*. New York: Oxford University Press.

Weder, Hans. 1978. *Die Gleichnisse Jesu als Metaphern*. Göttingen: Vandenhoeck & Ruprecht.

Weeden, T. J., Sr. 1979. Rediscovering the parabolic intent of the parable of the sower. *Journal of the American Academy of Religion*, 47:97–120.

Weil, Simone. [1951]1973. *Waiting on God*. Trans. Emma Crauford. New York: Harper & Row.

Weiss, Johannes. 1901. *Die Evangelien des Markus und Lukas*, 9th ed. (MeyerK 1/2). Göttingen: Vandenhoeck & Ruprecht.

Wierzbicka Anna. 1985. *Lexicography and Conceptual Analysis*. Ann Arbor, Mich.: Karoma.

Wierzbicka, Anna. 1991. *Cross-cultural Pragmatics: The Semantics of Human Interaction*. Berlin: Mouton de Gruyter.

Wierzbicka, Anna. 1992. *Semantics, Culture and Cognition: Human Concepts in Culture-specific Configurations*. New York: Oxford University Press.

Wierzbicka, Anna. 1993. What Is Prayer? In Search of a Definition. In L. B. Brown, ed. *The Human Side of Prayer: The Psychology of Praying*, pp. 25–46. Birmingham, Ala.: Religious Education Press.

Wierzbicka, Anna. 1995. The iconicity of part-of-speech membership. In M. Landsberg, ed. *Syntactic Iconicity and Linguistic Freezes*, pp. 223–245. Berlin: Walter de Gruyter.

Wierzbicka, Anna. 1996. *Semantics: Primes and Universals*. Oxford: Oxford University Press.

Wierzbicka, Anna. 1997. *Understanding Cultures Through Their Key Words: English, Russian, Polish, German, Japanese*. New York: Oxford University Press.

Wierzbicka, Anna. 1998. The meaning of Jesus' Parables: A Semantic Approach to the Gospels. In Benjamin Biebuyck, René Dirven, and John Ries, eds. *Faith and Fiction: Interdisciplinary Studies on the Interplay Between Metaphor And Religion*, pp. 17–54. Frankfurt: Peter Lang Verlag.

Wierzbicka, Anna. 1999a. *Emotions Across Languages and Cultures. Diversity and Universals*. Cambridge: Cambridge University Press.

Wierzbicka, Anna. 1999b. What Did Jesus Mean? The Lord's Prayer Translated Into Universal Human Concepts. In Ralph Bisschops and James Francis, eds. *Metaphor, Canon and Community: Jewish, Christian and Islamic approaches*, pp. 180–216. Canterbury: Peter Lang.

Wilder, Amos N. 1982. *Jesus' Parables and the War of Myths*. Philadelphia: Fortress Press.

Willis, Wendell, ed. 1987. *The Kingdom of God in 20th-Century Interpretation*. Peabody, Mass.: Hendrickson Publishers.

Windisch, H. 1950. *The Meaning of the Sermon on the Mount: A Contribution to the Historical Understanding of the Gospels and to the Problem of Their True Exegesis*. Trans. S. MacLean Gilmour. Phildadelphia: Westminster.

Witherington, Ben, III. 1990. *The Christology of Jesus*. Minneapolis: Fortress Press.

Witherington, Ben, III. 1992. *Jesus, Paul and the End of the World: A Comparative Study in New Testament Eschatology*. Downers Grove, Ill.: InterVarsity Press.

Witherington, Ben, III. 1994. *Jesus the Sage: The Pilgrimage of Wisdom*. Minneapolis: Fortress Press.

Witherington. Ben, III. 1995. *The Jesus Quest: The Third Search for the Jew of Nazareth*. Downers Grove, Ill.: InterVarsity Press.

Witherington, Ben, III. 1998a. *The Many faces of the Christ: The Christologies of the New Testament and Beyond*. New York: Crossroad.

Witheringon, Ben, III. 1998b. Resurrection Redux. In Paul Copan, ed. *Will the Real Jesus Please Stand Up?* pp. 129–146. Grand Rapids, Mich.: Baker Books.

Wittgenstein, Ludwig. [1922]1974. *Tractatus Logico-Philosophicus* (with an introduction by Bertrand Russell). London : Kegan Paul, Trench, Trubner.

Wolff, Hans Walter. 1987. *Studien zur Prophetie: Probleme und Erträge Mit einer Werkbibliographie*. München: Kaiser.

Wright, N. T. 1992. *Who Was Jesus?* London: SPCK.

Wright, N. T. 1996. *Jesus and the Victory of God*. Minneapolis: Fortress Press.

Wright, Tom. 1996. *The Lord and His Prayer*. London: Triangle (SPCK).

Young, Brad. 1989. *Jesus and His Jewish Parables: Rediscovering the Roots of Jesus' Teaching*. New York: Paulist Press.

Index

abba, 147–148, 227–232, 234, 236–237, 333, 471
Abrahams, I., 78, 192, 197, 199–200, 202, 251
absolute truths, 167
achievement motif, 124
achievement, religion of, 124
Achtemeier, E., 82–83
adulteress, 182–183, 185
adultery, 71–89, 120, 467
  in the heart, 76, 81, 83, 86–87, 467
  word, 84, 86
agape, 116
Albright, W. F., 90, 126, 128, 211, 471
allegorizing interpretation, 129, 316, 475
allegory, 260, 262, 276, 301, 316, 342, 412, 415, 473
Ambrose, 367, 393
amen, 227
analogy, 115, 195, 235, 446
anawim, 36–40, 45, 466
Anderson, W. T., 100, 167
anger, 61–70, 82, 441–442
Anglo culture, 32, 100, 321, 457
anthropology, 168–169

anthropomorphism, 52
anxiety, 175–176
apatheia, 70
apocalyptic images, 23, 92, 343, 350, 358–359, 369, 393, 464
apocalyptic literature, 157
Apostles' Creed, 18, 453
Appignanesi, L., 99
Aramaic, 9, 16, 31–32, 35, 41, 93, 165, 227, 229–231, 395, 471
Arapesh, 13–14
Aristeas, Letter of, 202
Aristotle, 51
Arndt, W. F., 301
Ascension, 450
Augustine, 70, 181, 182, 200, 250, 352, 368, 464, 467, 480
Auschwitz, 50
authenticity, 5, 22, 23, 47, 58, 61, 80–81, 89, 92, 94, 102, 111–112, 122,126, 132, 140, 144, 149–150, 155–157, 175, 179–180, 183, 186, 192–194, 202, 218, 220, 257,275, 311–312, 316, 321, 332, 342, 346, 351, 357–360, 372, 381, 415, 465
authorial intention, 3–4

bad deeds, 207, 210-212, 248, 329-330
bad people, 365, 367, 378-379, 418-419, 432-433, 469
bad thoughts, 82
Bailey, K. E., 301, 304-306, 376-377, 390, 394-395, 415, 417, 433
Bakhtin, M. M., 137, 210
Ballantine, W., 455
Balthasar, H. U. von, 281, 350, 367, 369
Banks, R. J., 64, 93-94, 96, 114
Barbel, J., 353
Barclay, W., 32-33, 42, 80, 91, 154, 172, 215, 221, 238, 424, 453, 477
Barr, J., 227, 230-231
Basil of Caesarea, 367
Bauman, C., 130, 186
Beatitudes, 27-56, 92, 357, 381-383, 430-431, 433, 466
Bella, E., 457
Ben Avuyah, Elisha, 469-470
Ben Sirach, 88, 394, 442
Berdyaev, N., 287-288, 340, 353-354, 359, 362-363, 472, 476
Bettiolo, P., 284, 318, 353
Betz, H. D., 57, 61, 66, 67, 74, 81, 83-84, 87, 88, 97, 132, 136, 140, 142-143, 149, 151-155, 157-158, 166, 170-172, 176-178, 180-182, 190-191, 193, 203-206, 209, 213, 215, 227, 467
biblical hermeneutics, 11
Billerbeck, P., 64, 115, 192, 210
Bischoff, E., 199
blessed, 47-55
blindness, 163-164, 184
Blomberg, C., 260, 273, 286-287, 323, 364, 377, 382, 415
Blount, B. K., 6
Blumhardt, C., 290
Bockmuehl, M., 16
Bonhoeffer, A., 119
Bonhoeffer, D., 141-143, 188
Borg, M. J., 6, 235, 451-453
Bornkam, G., 243
Borsch, F. H., 258, 284, 293, 296, 410-411
Boucher, M., 257-260, 262, 264, 270, 285-286, 315, 374-375, 383, 395
Braun, H., 144
bread, 244-246. *See also* metaphor of bread

bread of life, 244, 246
Breech, J., 234-235, 253, 301, 376-377, 474, 478
broad-mindedness, 185
Broer, I., 36
brother, 63-64
Brown, C., 37
Brown, R. E., 3, 5, 6, 10, 17, 61, 182-183, 229-230, 240, 241, 277, 437, 473
Bruce, F. F., 72, 87, 108
Brunner, E., 87
Buber, M., 190, 424, 459
Buddhism, 201, 441-442
Bulgakov, S., 289, 350, 367, 473
Bull, N. J., 194, 196
Bultmann, R., 138-140, 198-199, 205, 221, 227, 305
Butts, J., 265
Butwin, F., 457, 461

Cadoux, A. T., 259, 455, 473
Caird, G. B., 235, 459, 479
Capon, R. F., 258, 270, 277, 279, 288, 291, 293, 328, 330
Carlston, C. E., 259, 261, 473
Carmignac, J., 472
Carson, D. A., 85, 89, 149-150
Casey, M., 14
Catechism of the Catholic Church, 28, 34, 233, 237, 244, 245, 251-252, 364, 468
Cathars, 95
Catholicism, 23
celibacy, 74
Chalcedon, Council of, 446
charitable deeds, 131-140, 143, 362
Charlesworth, J. H., 14, 226-231
Chen Chun, 199
Chesterton, G. K., 455
child-like attitude, 39-40
children, 38-40, 334. *See also* image of child
Chilton, B., 14, 61, 472
Chinese, 48-49
chosen people, 58
cleansing of the temple, 69
Clement of Alexandria, 46, 141-143, 232, 290, 352, 457
closeness to God, 53-54, 152-155
coherence, 5, 23, 95
communion of saints, 18

comparative religion, 168–169

compassion, 133, 137–138, 143, 362, 371, 376–379, 441

compliance, 107–108, 110

Compton, J. E., 301

conceptual primes, 6, 7, 8

Confucianism, 441–442

Confucius, 198–199

conscience, 165–166

consumerism, 178

Cope, L., 476

Cost. *See* metaphor of cost

covenant, 58

creation story, 73

criminal justice, 108

criterion of coherence, 162–163

criterion of depth, 162–163

Crosby, M., 48

Crossan, J. D., 6, 16, 119, 121, 259, 264–265, 266, 273, 276, 281, 296–297, 321, 339, 375–376, 379, 386, 398, 399–400, 426, 434–435, 442, 473

Cynics, 16, 70, 104, 119–121, 442

daily bread, 244–247

Daley, B., 370

Daly, M., 233

darkness, 166–167

darkness. *See* metaphor of light and darkness

Daube, D., 75

Davidson, D., 302

Davis, J. J., 78

day. *See* metaphor of day

De Caussade, J. P., 399, 403, 477

Decalogue, 64, 83, 199

deeds, 135, 141, 183, 207, 211–212, 225, 262–263, 407. *See also* bad deeds; good deeds

degrading look, 86–88

Delumeau, J., 463–464, 480

Demosthenes, 80

demythologization, 15

Derrett, J. D. M., 270, 273, 305

Derrida, J., 100

Descartes, R., 445

Desert Fathers, 91

detachment, 159

Deuteronomy, 84

dialogical function, 192, 197

dialogical use, 64

Dihle, A., 192–194, 200

discipleship, 127

dishonest steward. *See* parable of the dishonest steward

dissimilarity, criterion of, 5

distance and separation. *See* metaphor of distance and separation

distinctiveness, 157

divorce, 59, 71–81, 104, 467

Dodd, C. H., 6, 259, 260, 262, 271–272, 277, 282–284, 342, 405–406, 416, 473

Donahue, J. R., 6, 269, 284, 315, 321, 324–325, 328–329, 346, 357, 376, 392, 415, 418, 427, 476

doorkeeper. *See* metaphor of doorkeeper; parable of the doorkeeper

Downing, F. G., 70, 94, 104, 115, 120, 192, 199

Drohrede, 127, 205, 316, 350, 367, 411, 457, 459, 461–463, 474, 477, 479

dualism, 365–367

Dunn, J. D. G., 122, 134, 442, 456, 467, 474, 479

Dupont, J., 29–32, 34–41, 46–47, 51, 54, 207, 210–211, 267, 293–294, 347–348, 430, 433

early church, 29, 89, 91, 94, 149, 154, 183

Eastern Christian tradition, 23, 242, 289, 352–353

ecumenism, 23

Efrem, 442

Eichholz, G., 267–268, 304–305, 307, 343, 345–346

either-or, 92–93, 156, 171, 173

embarrassment, 5

enemies, 7, 105, 111–122, 124

enemy, concept of, 114

English, 64, 82, 141, 247, 447, 452, 478

Enoch, 62, 195–196

Entrevernes Group, 374–375

Epictetus, 70, 94, 104, 119–121

eschatological reward, 143

eschatology, 17–19, 238–239, 242–245, 253, 359, 368, 371, 392, 395, 400, 410, 456, 460, 472, 473, 480

Essenes, 62, 74, 114, 474

eternal life, 323, 451

ethic, new, 193
ethical achievement, 70-71
ethical advice, 64
ethical literature, 69
ethical radicalism, 93
ethical teaching, 197, 441-443, 454
ethics, 15, 16, 17, 18, 239, 242-243,
    253, 395, 442-444, 473, 480
European cultural tradition, 11
European languages, 11, 478
Evangelii Nuntiandi, 13
evangelization, 13
evil, 169, 469
evil eye, 162
exegesis, 6, 13
Exodus, 19, 63, 65, 84
eye and the light, 161-169
eye for an eye, 196
Ezekiel, 238, 288, 391

fairness, 321
faith versus works, 218
fasting, 149-155
father, God as a, 188-189, 217. *See also*
    metaphor of father
Fathers of the Church, 50, 290, 367,
    457
Fee, G. D., 6
Feldman, A., 470
feminine-maternal, 12, 233
Feyerabend, P., 99-100
fig tree. *See* parable of the barren fig tree
figurative language, 150, 349
Filson, F.V., 38
Finnis, J., 169, 469
fire, 91
Fitzmyer, J. A., 5, 6, 17, 74, 115, 128,
    150, 172, 175, 190, 204-205, 215,
    227-228, 230, 238, 253, 280, 283-
    284, 298, 305, 311, 338, 342, 344-
    346, 381, 393, 395, 406, 423, 427,
    477
Flusser, D., 405, 470, 478
Focolari movement, 476
forgiveness, 247-251, 313, 315-318,
    451, 457-458
Foucault, M., 100
Fourth Gospel, 22, 69, 78, 97-98, 120,
    130-131, 164, 182, 204, 213-214,
    443
Fox, E., 130
free will, 297, 353-354

French, 231-232
friend at midnight, *See* parable of the
    unjust judge and the friend at
    midnight
Frost, R., 110-111
fruit, 206-214, 261-263. *See also*
    metaphor of fruit
Frymer-Kensky, T., 14
Funk, R. W., 4, 5, 22, 31, 38, 46, 53,
    72, 80-81, 85, 89, 92, 93, 102,
    111, 114, 127, 128, 130, 132, 140,
    150, 155-157, 172, 175, 180, 183,
    186, 190, 192-193, 207, 212, 220,
    241, 265, 273-275, 311-314, 318,
    321, 332, 339, 342, 346, 351, 357-
    358, 375, 379, 381, 386, 398, 415-
    417, 423, 428, 437, 456, 467, 470,
    474
future, 177, 179

Gallo, M., 442
Gaudium et Spes, 164-165
Gehenna, 369
Gelin, A., 36
generosity, 162
Genesis, 59, 73, 75-77
Gentiles, 9, 72, 164, 467
German, 10, 64, 81-82, 141, 447, 471,
    475
gift to God, 152
glory, own, 154
God as light, 98
God, concept of, 7, 20-21, 233
Goddard, C., 7, 447
God's grace, 323-326, 328, 468
God's justice, 328-329
God's love, 216-219, 282, 284, 293-
    294, 303, 305, 316-318, 322, 327-
    328, 334, 336, 338, 349, 363, 366,
    369, 382, 457-461, 472
God's mercy, 316-318, 369, 371, 375,
    378, 430, 460, 475
God's plan, 449
God's will, 59, 70, 105, 112, 136, 143,
    148, 158, 161, 174, 215-219, 221,
    243, 334-336, 363, 371, 399-400,
    402, 426, 469
golden rule. *See* rule, golden
good deeds, 134-138, 141, 142-143,
    158, 207, 210-212, 214, 240, 322,
    327, 329-330, 362, 375, 470. *See
    also* good works; right deeds

good people, 365, 367, 378, 418–419, 432–433, 469

good Samaritan. *See* parable of the good Samaritan

good works, 130, 133, 136, 158, 240, 322, 339–340, 362. *See also* good deeds; right deeds

Gourgues, M., 31, 37, 45, 56, 214, 375, 381, 383, 415, 418, 434–435

grace, 124, 323–326, 328. *See also* God's grace

great feast. *See* parable of the great feast

Greek, 16, 31–32, 35, 40, 42–46, 63–64, 72, 80, 82–84, 93, 122, 132, 208, 227, 229–231, 240, 247, 252, 311, 376, 389, 395, 466, 471, 479

Greek literature, 157

Greek philosophy, 248

Greeley, A., 14

Green, J. B., 6

Gregory of Nyssa, 245, 282, 288–289, 350–353, 367–368, 457, 472, 473–474

Gressmann, H., 457

Griffin, D., 166, 168–169

Guelich, R., 35–37, 40, 82, 84, 93

Gulag archipelago, 49, 168

Gundry, R. H., 236

Gunkel, H., 457

Haacker, K., 83–84

Hall, F. W., 80

Hamerton-Kelly, R., 227

happiness, 158

Harnack, A. von, 57

Harnisch, W., 354

Harrington, D. J., 227

harvest. *See* image of harvest

hatred, 63, 65, 67, 70, 82, 113–114

Hayes, J., 457

Haynes, S. R., 6

hearing versus doing, 218, 220

heart, 211–212, 407, 468. *See also* people's hearts

heaven, 158

Hebrew, 31–32, 36–41, 80, 230, 395, 479

Hebrew Bible, 20, 58

Hedrick, C. W., 259, 270, 273, 473

Hefley, J., 188

Hefley, M., 188

hell, 295, 353–354, 360, 368–369, 463–464, 473, 477, 479–480

Hendrickx, H., 279–280, 285, 293–294, 381, 386, 420

Heschel, A., 20, 51–52, 134, 140, 459, 461

heteroglossia, 125, 137, 210, 434, 468, 480

Hick, J., 445

hidden treasure. *See* parable of the hidden treasure and the pearl of great price

hiddenness, 267–268, 275, 284–285

Hillel the Elder, 64, 112, 118, 192–194, 196–199

Hinduism, 201, 441

Hirsch, E. D., 4

historical Jesus, 29, 81, 93, 103, 130, 149–150, 193, 207, 211, 215, 218, 226, 332, 339, 360, 398, 475

Holocaust, 49, 168

holy Spirit, 190, 450

Hoover, R., 4

Hryniewicz, W., 281–283, 351, 359, 366, 457, 479

Hübner, H., 103

human values, 169

humility, 38

hungry, the, 34–36, 466

Hunter, A. M., 221, 245, 250

Huntington, S., 478

Huxley, A., 168

Huxley, T. H., 200

hyperbole, 16, 72, 99, 132, 134, 150, 172, 177, 181, 235, 286, 294, 317, 338, 345, 355, 437, 456–457, 459, 461, 474

hypocrisy, 132–133, 136, 141, 144, 146, 149, 153, 204, 441

illocutionary force, 382

image, 18, 90, 99, 120, 222, 233, 247, 254, 264, 267–268, 294, 302, 354, 366, 457, 477. *See also* apocalyptic images; metaphor

of child, 334

the gate or the door, 204

God as a rock, 224–225

harvest, 259, 261

last judgment, 18, 34, 51, 135, 181, 218, 222, 224, 315–316, 378, 393, 450

leaven, 278, 287–289, 312. *See also* metaphor of leaven

image (*continued*)
  the light of the world, 126–131
  lost coin, 289, 293
  lost sheep, 289, 293, 297
  master's return, 401
  narrow road, 204
  plank and speck, 181, 184
  rock, 224–225
  the salt of the earth, 126–131
  seed, 261
  self-mutilation, 91–92
  servant, 334–335
  sheep and goats, 363, 370
  shepherd, 296
  storms, floods and winds, 222, 224
  turning the other cheek, 102–111
  two foundations, 220
  two houses, 220
  two roads, 203, 216
Imbach, 52–53, 205, 284–285, 315,
  354, 366, 427–428, 457
imperative constructions, 8
impure motive. *See* motive, impure
incarnation, 449
inculturation, 11, 12, 13
injustice, 108
innate light, 166–167
inner conflict, 90
inner light, 167–169
intentional fallacy, 4
investment. *See* metaphor of investment
invincibility, 120
invitation, God's, 342–345, 347–348,
  363
ipsissima verba, 5, 58, 93, 129, 218,
  465
ipsissima vox, 94, 228, 465
iron rule, *See* rule, iron
irony, 137, 144, 164
Isaac of Niniveh (Isaac the Syrian), 23,
  282, 284, 317–318, 345, 349,
  353, 368–370, 473, 475, 477
Isaiah, 33, 37, 42–44, 50–51, 56, 69,
  296, 367, 458–461, 463, 480
Iser, W., 265
Islam, 201
Israel, 17, 58–60
Israelite law, 84
Italian, 232
I-Thou relationship, 147–148, 190, 235,
  424
ius talionis, 103–104, 106, 193

Jainism, 201
Jeremiah, 69, 457–459
Jeremias, J., 6, 41, 96–97, 130, 135–
  137, 139–140, 143–144, 147, 192–
  193, 197–199, 220–222, 225, 227–
  232, 241, 259, 261, 264, 270, 275,
  305, 315–316, 322, 324–325, 333–
  334, 357–358, 360, 405–407, 410,
  416, 427–428, 430, 432, 471, 473,
  475
Jesus' ethics, 7
Jesus' life, death and resurrection, 449–
  450
Jesus Seminar, 4, 5, 22, 23, 38, 85, 89,
  92, 93, 102, 111–112, 114, 127–
  128, 132, 150, 155–156, 171, 180,
  183, 186, 192–193, 207, 241, 274–
  275, 312, 321, 346, 351, 357–359,
  381, 398, 415, 423, 427
Jesus' teaching about God, 20
Jewish context, 9, 11, 14, 233, 375, 456,
  462–463
Jewish culture, 32
Jewish literature, 157
Jewish Messiah, 11
Jewish religion, 170
Jewish wisdom, 157
Job, 34, 88
John of the Cross, 364, 369–370
John the Baptist, 42–44, 149, 164, 207–
  208, 343, 471
John, Gospel of, 17, 69, 216
Johnson, L. T., 5, 16, 238, 251, 415,
  465, 479
Jones, G. V., 259, 473
Judaism, 51, 157, 202, 441, 442, 470
judging, 179–186, 208
judgment, 390–392
judgmental, 184–185, 197
Julian the Apostate, 415
Jülicher, A., 260–261, 276, 416, 430
justice, 52
  divine, *See* God's justice
  human, 185–186, 329

Kaddish, 239
Kane, R., 100
karma, 441
Käsemann, E., 61
Keating, T., 326–327, 329–330, 424
Kiley, M., 238
Kimel, A., 445

kindness, 441–442
King Jr., Martin Luther, 70
king, 217. *See also* metaphor of king
kingdom of God, 17–19, 53–54, 70, 92,
116, 123, 137–138, 161, 175, 177,
179, 204, 213, 215–217, 221, 235,
239, 241–244, 261–262, 264, 266–
268, 272–273, 276, 278, 280, 282,
285–286, 289, 296, 312, 314, 323–
328, 334, 343–347, 351, 353–354,
368, 375, 399–400, 402, 411, 471,
473, 480. *See also* living with God
Kistemaker, S. J., 280, 283, 286, 294, 315,
323, 326, 334, 338, 374, 402, 406
Klassen, W., 113
Klausner, J., 14
Koch, K., 457
Küng, H., 21, 233, 442, 447
Kushner, H. S., 210

La Potterie, I. de, 98
laborers in the vineyard. *See* parable of
the laborers in the vineyard
Lachs, S. T., 63, 112, 114, 117, 162,
165, 192, 210, 213, 470
lamb, 42–44
Lambrecht, J., 6, 65, 68, 72, 77, 96,
161, 162, 203–204, 206–208, 217,
266, 278, 281, 287, 302, 311–312,
321, 326, 330, 342, 347, 354, 357–
358, 360, 405–406, 411–412
Lane, W. L., 473
language of Jesus, 455–464
Lao-Tse, 201
Lapide, P., 14, 85, 87, 106, 109–110,
118, 123, 463
last judgment. *See* image of last
judgment; parable of the last
judgment
Latin, 63, 82, 140–141, 194–195
Law, 57–61, 62, 64, 193, 430
Lawson, H., 99
Lazarus. *See* parable of the rich man and
Lazarus
leaven. *See* image of leaven; metaphor of
leaven; parable of the leaven and
the mustard seed
Lecky, W. E. H., 80
left hand, 140–144
Leibniz, G. W., 6, 445
Leviticus, 63–66, 112–114, 475
lex talionis, 103–104, 106

lies, 100
life, 19, 91
light of the world. *See* image of the light
of the world
light, 98, 161–169
lilies of the field, 174–179
Limbeck, M., 77, 96, 143, 218, 222–
223
linguistic semantics, 5, 6, 11
Linnemann, E., 6, 259, 263, 267, 270,
272, 294, 430, 473
live, 466
living with God, 170, 174, 205, 213–
214, 217–219, 224–225, 241–243,
249, 264, 271–272, 276, 278–279,
287, 303, 327, 344, 364, 395, 400,
411, 436, 443, 472, 473. *See also*
kingdom of God
Lockyer, H., 128, 162, 258, 261, 391,
393
Loewenich, W. von, 212
Lord's Prayer, 29, 188–189, 226–254,
428, 471, 473
lost coin. *See* image of lost coin; parable
of the lost sheep and the lost coin;
lost sheep. *See* image of lost sheep;
parable of the lost sheep and the
lost coin
Loughlin, G., 451, 466
love, 7, 68, 105–107, 111–122,124, 160,
241, 244, 375, 378–379, 411, 476.
See also God's love
acts of, 135, 363
of God, 358, 360, 362–363, 374
of one's neighbor, 112–113, 118,
192–193, 197, 202, 246, 358, 360,
362–363, 374, 376, 378, 411, 434–
435, 467
universal, 105, 118, 124
love commandment, 113, 117–118, 197–
198
Lubich, C., 476
lust, 80, 81–89
Luther, M., 10, 11, 63, 212
Luz, U., 14, 60, 62, 67, 93–96, 132,
140–141, 145–147, 151, 162, 208,
212, 224, 229, 232, 238, 245, 253,
469

Mack, B. L., 16
Mahabharata, 200
Mahnrede, 205

Maillot, A., 267–268, 278, 280, 282, 295, 297, 305, 321, 326, 330, 384
mammon, 169–174, 176, 178, 393
Mann, C. S., 90, 126, 128, 211, 471, 473
Manson, T. W., 103, 162, 283, 305, 323, 325, 344, 358, 383, 398, 416
Marcion, 11, 208
marital intercourse, 77
Marmorstein, A., 470
marriage, 71–81, 87
marriage rituals, 75
Martha, 84
Mary Magdalene, 84
masculine-paternal, 12, 233
master's return. *See* image of master's return
materialism, 178
Matisoff, J., 457, 462
Maude, A., 467
McArthur, H. K., 124
McKenna, M., 270, 424, 433
McKenzie, S. L., 6
meaning 4, 5, 6, 7, 8, 9, 15, 23, 57
meek, the, 40–46
Meier, J. P., 5, 34, 48, 65, 81, 84, 113, 141, 149–150, 162, 209, 217–218, 220, 227, 232, 238–239, 242, 286, 311, 315–317, 358, 360–364, 371, 398–399, 402, 471, 472
mercy, acts of, 360–361, 363, 477. *See also* God's mercy
merits, 135
Merton, T, 115
Merz, A., 20, 217, 228, 379, 460
message, 267–268, 273, 382
metanoia, 208, 212, 315
metaphor, 90, 110, 116, 127, 144, 157–158, 171, 176, 178, 181, 203–204, 233, 235–236, 241–242, 244, 253–254, 267, 302, 359, 366, 445, 447–448, 451–452, 456–457, 461, 467. *See also* image
of bread, 244–247, 254, 445
closeness to God, 152–153
cost, 270
culture-specific, 12, 19, 241, 254, 451–452
day, 246–247
distance and separation, 249
the doorkeeper, 400
father, 12, 115, 227–228, 232–236, 241, 254, 432–433, 445, 471

fruit (fruitlessness and fruitfulness), 207, 213, 407
investment, 270
king, 228, 235, 360, 471
the kingdom of God, 241–244, 254, 273, 445
leaven, 286, 474
the left hand, 141
light and darkness, 167
light for truth, 98, 163–164
the mustard Seed, 286
name, 237, 241
reversal, 48–55, 381–382, 384, 435–436
reward, 134, 143–144
servant, 338, 399, 407
sheep and goats, 365, 367
spatial, 53–54, 235
temporal, 53–54, 351–352
treasures in heaven, 158–159
turning the other cheek, 110
two roads, 203
universal, 19, 152
Michaels, J. R., 259–260, 265, 427, 473
minatory sayings, 205, 345–346
mitsvah, 224–225
Modestinus, 80
Moloney, F., 6, 182
Moltmann, J., 28, 29, 50–51, 56, 242, 277, 281, 290, 355, 368, 370, 403, 466, 471, 472, 476
monitory sayings, 205
monogamy, 71–81
Montefiore, C. G., 62, 100, 112, 118, 138, 147, 150, 192, 199, 210–211, 239, 251, 253, 301, 358, 360, 369, 374–375, 382, 386, 405, 416, 434, 470, 471
Moore, S. E., 473
moral greatness, 119–120
moral law, 164
moral nihilism, 167
moral norms, 167
moral relativism, 167
moral values, 169
Morgan, G. C., 128
Morwood, M., 240, 247–248, 444
Mosaic Law, 73–74, 77–79
Moses, 59–61, 64, 74, 318
motive, 134, 138, 144, 146, 151–152, 361–362
impure, 136, 140
pious, 146, 153

profit, 136
pure, 136, 137, 152, 362, 409
self-interested, 146
selfish, 134
Muhammed, 201
Müller, P., 335
multiple attestation 5
murder, 63, 65–67, 70
in the heart, 82
mustard seed. *See* metaphor of the
mustard seed; parable of the leaven
and the mustard seed
mystery, 14

name. *See* metaphor of name
narrow gate, 202–206. *See also* image of
the gate or the door
narrow road. *See* image of narrow road
natural law, 165, 169
Natural Semantic Metalanguage, 466, 469
neighbor, 34, 64, 103, 112–117, 119–120
concept of, 375, 379
word, 115
Neusner, J., 14, 61
New Testament, language of, 19, 166
New Testament theology, 19
Newbigin, 185, 468
Newman, B. M., 42
Nicaea, Council of, 446
Nicene Creed, 60, 446, 451–454
Nida, E., 14, 237
nirvana, 441
Nocke, F., 338–339, 359, 457
nonresistance, 110, 455
nonretaliation, 104, 108, 120, 441
nonviolence, 70, 107, 110, 441–442
Nova, D., 14

oaths, 93–102
obedience, 10, 11, 145, 148, 152, 215–
216, 221, 469
Ochs, P., 14
O'Farrell, F. P., 467
Old Testament, 11, 63, 67, 84–87, 94,
103, 112–113, 116, 119, 133, 157,
162, 227, 296, 329, 374, 436, 457
openness, 100
Origen, 50, 208, 214, 282, 287, 367–
368, 457, 473
ostentation, 10, 153–154, 468
outculturation, 12, 13
overstatement, 72

Palestinian Judaism, 36, 134, 227
parable, of the
barren fig tree, 209
dishonest steward, 313, 316, 414–
421
doorkeeper, 339, 397–403
good Samaritan, 143–144, 197, 357,
362, 371, 373–379, 418
great feast, 282, 287, 341–355
hidden treasure and the pearl of great
price, 18, 137, 266–273, 316, 411,
426
laborers in the vineyard, 320–331,
343, 345–346, 417–418
last judgment, 356–372, 385, 398–
399, 407
leaven and the mustard seed, 268, 272,
274–291, 348, 354, 360, 417, 419
lost sheep and the lost coin, 280–281,
291–299. 302, 305, 321, 333, 344–
346, 360, 417, 419
Pharisee and the tax collector, 118,
123–124, 138, 142–143, 158, 181–
182, 306, 321–322, 407, 417–418,
429–437
prodigal son, 118, 181–182, 247, 278,
282, 297–298, 300–309, 316–317,
321, 323, 326, 343–346, 360, 366–
367, 376, 417, 432
rich fool, 388–396, 401
rich man and Lazarus, 35, 49, 52–53,
380–387, 393, 407
servant's reward, 332–340, 407, 409
sower, 257–265
talents, 316, 339, 404–413, 417, 419
two builders, 215, 219–225
two sons, 216, 218
unforgiving servant, 310–319, 372,
417, 419
unjust judge and the friend at
midnight, 191, 312–313, 316, 420,
422–428
paradox, 99
parallels, 156–157, 166, 192, 200–203,
239, 253, 360, 381, 441, 467, 475
Parousia, 398, 403
pater, 229–232
Paul, 73–74, 89–90, 96, 98, 106, 164,
407, 442, 467, 468, 474, 475
pearl of great price. *See* parable of the
hidden treasure and the pearl of
great price

people's hearts, 66–67, 122–123, 135, 287–288
Percy, E., 103
perfection, 115
perfectionism, 122–123
Perkins, P., 259, 473
Perrin, N., 6, 16, 17, 288–290, 348, 354, 472
persecuted, the, 46–47
persistence, 424–425, 427–428
Peter, 470
Petzoldt, M., 354
Pharisaic Judaism, 134, 434
Pharisee and the tax collector. *See* parable of the Pharisee and the tax collector
Pharisees, 60, 73, 78, 95–96, 122–125, 134, 138, 149, 185, 212, 405–406, 471
Philo, 94, 192, 213
picture-language, 41
pious motive. *See* motive, pious
Piper, J., 66–67, 103, 105–106, 111, 114–116, 119, 195
Pirot, L., 38
plank and speck. *See* image of plank and speck
platinum rule. *See* rule, platinum
Plummer, A., 338
Polish, 232
polygamy, 74–76
poor, the, 35, 36–40, 466
Pope John Paul II, 87, 163, 165–166, 473, 475, 476
Pope Paul VI, 13
Porpora, D., 185, 194, 197–198, 200
possessions, 155, 170–174, 176
postmodernism, 100, 102, 167–168
poverty, 29, 173, 178, 385–386
Powell, M. A., 23, 472
prayer, 144–149, 151. 186–191, 423–428
    efficacy of, 188
    private, 147–148
predestination, 441–442
Prejeant, R., 6
Price, R., 17, 441, 443, 461
primordial truths, 166
priorities, 346
prodigal son. *See* parable of the prodigal son
profit motive. *See* motive, profit

prophetic tradition 457–463
Prophets, 58–61
Protestantism, 23
Proverbia Aesopi, 207
providential care, 178
prudence, 180–181
public discourse, 22
pure motive. *See* motive, pure
purgatory, 441–442

Quakers, 95
Quelle, 30, 40, 80, 127, 156–157, 175, 186, 207, 211, 474
Qumran, 41, 114, 225, 475
quotation marks, 135, 137–138, 145, 339, 402, 434, 480

rabbinic Judaism, 63, 67, 115, 117, 133
rabbinic literature, 100–101, 114, 210, 224, 470
rabbinic sayings, 118, 162, 433
rabbinic teaching, 62–64, 136, 150, 210, 220, 479
radicalism of Jesus, 67, 72, 83, 87, 92–94, 156–157, 385, 416, 433, 474
radicalization, 65–66, 68, 76
Ragaz, L., 130
Rahner, K., 123, 368
reciprocity, 195–196, 202
recompense, 49–55, 137, 384
religious metaphors, 5
remarriage, 76
respect, 185
resurrection of the dead, 451
retaliation, 103–111
retribution, 103
retribution, law of, 193–194
Revelation, 19, 29, 56
revenge, 103–111, 117
reversal. *See* metaphor of reversal
reward, 134–140, 141, 143–145, 159, 322, 324–327, 335–336, 339–340, 362–363, 402, 480
    doctrine of, 140
rich fool. *See* parable of the rich fool
rich man and Lazarus. *See* parable of the rich man and Lazarus
Ricoeur, P., 6, 194, 198, 227
right deeds, 224–225. *See also* good deeds; good works
righteous, the, 34, 294, 322, 342, 365, 379, 430, 433–434, 478, 480

righteousness, 122–125, 225, 480
  acts of, 135
  greater, 68
rigorous ethics, 122–123
ritual, 150–152
Robinson, J. A. T., 69, 284, 473
Rock. *See* image of rock
Roger of Taizé, 424
Roman, 80
Room, A., 477
Rorty, R., 99, 467
Rost, H. T. D., 168, 192. 200–202
Ruether, R. R., 233
rule
  golden, 191–202
  iron, 196
  platinum, 252
  silver, 194–196, 198, 200, 202
  tinsel, 196
Russian, 232, 362
Ryken, L., 261, 263, 456

Saldarini, A. J., 64, 115
Salinger, J. D., 159
salt of the earth. *See* image of the salt of
  the earth
salvation, 92, 242–243, 279–282, 287,
  295, 328, 340, 344, 354–355, 363,
  369–370, 376
Samaritans, 115
Sanders, E. P., 14, 122–123, 134, 136,
  158, 225, 241, 460, 472
Sandmel, D., 14
Schechter, S., 135, 470
Schlatter, A., 96
Schlosser, J., 241, 472
Schnackenburg, R., 312
Schneiders, S., 3, 4, 6, 9
Schottroff, L., 70, 106–107, 342
Schüssler-Fiorenza, E., 6, 443
Schweizer, E., 82, 87, 227, 239, 243,
  245, 311
Scott, B. B., 259, 265, 273, 295, 430,
  473
second coming, 398, 401, 403, 450
seed, *See* image of seed
self-castration, 16
self-control, 70
self-defense, 108–110
self-fulfilment, 197
self-interest, 160. *See also* self-interested
  motive

selfishness, 160–161. *See also* selfish
  motive
self-mutilation. *See* image of self-
  mutilation
self-righteousness, 142, 144
semantic analysis, 199
semantic exegesis, 6, 254
Seneca, 115, 119–121, 199, 393–394
Septuagint, 45, 389, 395
Servant of the Lord, 42–44
Servant. *See* image of servant; metaphor
  of servant
servant's reward. *See* parable of the
  servant's reward
Sevin, M., 7
sexual intercourse, 80
Shaw. G. B., 195
sheep and goats. *See* image of sheep and
  goats; metaphor of sheep and goats
shepherd. *See* image of shepherd
Shorter, A., 12, 233
Shorto, R., 119
Sifre, 224, 470
Signer, M., 14
silver rule, *See* rule, silver
simple concepts, 7, 106
sin, 32–33, 69, 79, 88–93, 247–249
sinners, 69, 118, 208, 225, 249, 293–
  298, 303–305, 322, 342, 347,
  365, 379, 419, 430– 431,
  433–434, 436–437, 478,
  480
skopcy, 16
skopos, 146, 151, 468
Smith, B. T. D., 259–261, 383, 394,
  405–406, 416–417, 433, 473
Smith, H., 100, 166–169
smugness, 142–143
Sokołowska, Z., 161
Sölle, D., 233
Solov'ev, V., 362, 476, 478
Sommer, F., 301
Son of God, 451
sower. *See* parable of the sower
Spaemann, H., 267
spatial metaphors. *See* metaphors, spatial
Speyr, Adrienne von, 367
Spooner, W. A., 194–195
Sproul, R. C., 445–446, 452, 479–
  480
Stenger, W., 6
Stoics, 70, 104, 115, 119, 121

Stott, J. R. W., 75, 88, 91–92, 158,
    170, 172, 178, 187–188, 203–
    204, 468
Strack, H. L., 64, 192, 210
Strecker, G., 33, 62, 66, 85–86, 89, 91,
    93–94, 107, 136, 142–144,146–
    148, 150, 152, 162, 171, 173, 181,
    205, 222
submission, 107–108, 110
suffering, 28–56
swearing, 93–102
symbolic actions, 38

tabernacle of God, 19
talent, 477
talents. *See* parable of the talents
Talmud, 470
Tannehill, R. C., 132, 150
Tannen, D., 431
tax collector. *See* parable of the Pharisee
    and the tax collector
Taylor, V., 473
Te Selle, S., 267, 301–302, 308
temporal metaphors. *See* metaphors,
    temporal
temptation, 92, 251–254
Ten Commandments, 59, 83, 85
Testaments of the Twelve Patriarchs,
    152
Theissen, G., 20, 217, 228, 379, 460
theodicy, 29
theology, 15
theopathy, 50
theory versus practice, 218–219
Thérèse of Lisieux, 468
Thiselton, A. C., 6
Thomas Aquinas, 467, 469
Thomas, Gospel of, 46, 176, 211–212,
    257, 269, 342
Tillich, P., 196, 289, 314, 350, 359, 365
Time magazine, 17
tinsel rule. *See* rule, tinsel
Tobit, book of, 192
Todorov, T., 469
tolerance, 185, 441–442
Tolstoy, L., 95, 101, 162, 185–186, 290,
    467
tomorrow, 177
topos, 146
Torah, 61–62, 67, 76, 85, 192, 197,
    220, 470
Torjesen, K. J., 443

Torrey, C. C., 415
totalitarian movements, 102
transformation, 275, 278, 282, 286–288,
    350
treasure, 155–161, 176, 216. *See also*
    parable of the hidden treasure and
    the pearl of great price
treasures in heaven, 155–161, 173, 178
trees, 206–214
Trent, Council of, 468
Trinity, 445–447
tropos, 146, 151, 468
trust in God, 39, 175, 178, 190–191,
    237, 412, 425, 427
truth, 96–102, 163–164, 435, 467
    dismantling, 99–100
    and God, 98, 100, 467
truthfulness, 96–102
Turner, N., 38, 466
turning the other cheek. *See* image of
    turning the other cheek
two builders. *See* parable of the two
    builders
two foundations. *See* image of two
    foundations
two houses. *See* image of two houses
two roads. *See* image of two roads; *and*
    metaphor of two roads
two sons. *See* parable of the two sons

ultimate reality, 21
Unamuno, M., 50–51
unforgiving servant. *See* parable of the
    unforgiving servant
uniqueness, 94
universal constants, 168
universal human concepts, 6, 7, 8, 9, 13,
    15, 16, 21, 106, 116, 313, 441–
    443, 445–447, 451, 454, 463, 465,
    469, 480
universal love. *See* love, universal
universal message, 9, 10, 11, 13, 14, 34,
    233, 254, 272, 302, 342, 364, 405–
    406, 463
universal metaphor, 19
universal moral law, 167–168
universal moral truths, 167
universal relevance, 260, 371, 372
universal salvation, 18, 279–282, 285,
    287, 295, 354–355, 369–370, 474.
    See also salvation
universal words, 8,9, 106, 168, 313

universalism, 112, 218, 364, 378, 476
universalist commandment, 64
unjust judge. *See* parable of the unjust
    judge and the friend at midnight
unjust steward. *See* parable of the
    dishonest steward

values, 48
Van Bragt, Jan, 371
Veritatis Splendor, 163, 165
Vermes, G., 14
Via, D. O., 6, 323, 325, 400–401, 409
violence, 70
Viviano, B., 86. 172, 175
Vögtle, A., 342
Vorländer, H., 249
Vulgate, 63, 82, 195

watchfulness, 398, 400–403
Wattles, J., 192, 195–196, 200
Weder, H., 354
Weeden, T. J., 264
weeping ones, the, 32–34, 466
Weil, Simone, 143–144, 240, 361–363,
    376–377
Weiss, J., 416
well-wishing rule, 200–201
Western Christian tradition, 242

Western culture, 91, 321, 333
widow's two mites, 132
Wierzbicka, A., 7, 8, 21, 69, 90, 146,
    244, 362, 447, 471
Wilder, A. N., 259, 473
Willis, W., 472
Wisdom of Solomon, 442
wisdom sayings, 4
Witherington III, B., 5, 14, 16, 61, 125,
    277, 443, 446, 452–453
Wittgenstein, L., 446
woes, 30
Wolff, H. W., 457, 459
women, 74, 84
    attitudes towards, 87
    dignity of, 84
    Jesus' attitude to, 82–84, 88
    rights of, 82–83
    as sex objects, 85, 87
Wright, N. T., 4, 6, 7, 14, 15, 16, 22,
    277, 472
Wright, T., 240, 250

Yiddish, 457, 462
Young, B., 470

Zachariah, 44–5
Zwingli, 67